D1578659

THE GOSPEL
OF THE
FOUR

A Unique Conflation of the Four Gospels
into a Single Continuous Narrative,
Explicated by the Author's Commentary

Peter Boaz Jones

AuthorHouse™ UK
1663 Liberty Drive
Bloomington, IN 47403 USA
www.authorhouse.co.uk
Phone: UK TFN: 0800 0148641 (Toll Free inside the UK)
*   UK Local: (02) 0369 56322 (+44 20 3695 6322 from outside the UK)*

© 2020 Peter Boaz Jones. All rights reserved.

No part of this book may be reproduced, stored in a retrieval system, or transmitted by any means without the written permission of the author.

Published by AuthorHouse 10/28/2023

ISBN: 978-1-4343-9359-3 (sc)
ISBN: 978-1-7283-9941-6 (e)

Print information available on the last page.

Any people depicted in stock imagery provided by Getty Images are models, and such images are being used for illustrative purposes only. Certain stock imagery © Getty Images.

This book is printed on acid-free paper.

Because of the dynamic nature of the Internet, any web addresses or links contained in this book may have changed since publication and may no longer be valid. The views expressed in this work are solely those of the author and do not necessarily reflect the views of the publisher, and the publisher hereby disclaims any responsibility for them.

This book is Dedicated
to all
Seeking Truth

Though some feel they already have the truth, actually, it is a continuing process with untruth being sifted out, and new truth being added. Initially, of course, one has to have an inkling of truth, for it to be added to.

The evening before the crucifixion, when Jesus prayed to His Father about the disciples, and, those believers yet to come (John 17:20), He confirmed, "*Your word is truth*" (v. 17).

The next morning, at the trial of Jesus, Pilate, who was not interested in the whole truth, in ignorance rhetorically quipped, "*What is truth?*" (18:38).

> "The secret things belongs to the Lord our God: but those things which are revealed belong to us and our children forever..." (Deuteronomy 29:29).

> "It is the glory of God to conceal a thing: but the honor of kings is to search out a matter" (Proverbs 25:2).

> "And many other signs [attesting miracles] truly did Jesus in the presence of His disciples, which are not written in this book: but these are written, that you might believe that Jesus is the Messiah, the Son of God; and that believing you might have life through His Name" (John 20:30-31).

Unless otherwise noted, all of the Scriptural text in this book is based on the King James Version [KJV], or Authorized Version [AV], as it is also known.

Acknowledgements

Firstly, special, and loving thanks to my darling wife, Katy (RIP 01/12/2015), especially over the last thirty-three years, whose support and great patience has enabled me to write this book. She witnessed myself spend countless days and hours with my head in various books writing, and typing during the early years, and, subsequently later on, in front an Amstrad Word Processor, and eventually on the more modern PC.

Also, while they were at home, the same acknowledgments go to our splendid children, Petra, Mark and Helen, for their unwavering acceptance of 'dad's thing', as they all used to say. Petra ardent in her enthusiasm for my venture, even used to bring me various books from her RE classes to try and help me!

An appreciated thanks to my parents, to my step dad, the late Harry Jones (RIP 03/21/2008), who left us on a Good Friday, who also was a keen Bible scholar himself, for his interest in my endeavor through the years, who no doubt gave me part of the inclination for writing this book, and to my mother, llse Jones, for her special concern throughout.

Although he has also passed away, mention must be made of my dear friend, E G M Wallis (my Solicitor), who was at the inception of my idea for this book, paramount in giving me the inspiration and confidence in continuing with such a task. When first perusing the initial manuscript, he gave me much reassurance. God bless him!

I am also greatly indebted to Dr Margaret Brearley, who was Senior Research Fellow at the Centre for the Study of Judaism and Jewish/Christian Relations, at Selly Oak Colleges, Birmingham, for her help, advice, and encouragement in my wrestling's with this book, and, for putting me in touch with Dr Philip Seddon Professor of New Testament Studies at Selly Oak Colleges, who was invaluable in his critical advice on my original manuscript. Thanks, too, to Rabbi Dr Norman Solomon (who was Director of the Centre for the Study of Judaism and Jewish/ Christian Relations), who on several occasions allowed me to 'pick his brains', when I was 'stuck' over verifying certain information.

Thanks to Bryan Everett and Tony Chamberlain, for their advice, and for their help in the secular and monetary sense, and also, in enabling me to spend the time I needed while working for them in the completion of the first issue of this book. Further special thanks to Bryan Everett (RIP), my best friend, and his keen brain, and for the philosophical input to the many hours of discussions on the meaning to life, and the practicalities of my quest to get this book published.

Thanks to Rupert Sowe, who also has been a good friend to lean on at various times over the years and his concern for my aspirations.

Mention must also be made of Derek Jones, who gave me a particular insight to part of this book.

Credit to the original publishing team, with special thanks to Tom Deagan, and especially to Mike McGrath for his great patience and perseverance, to David Jesson-Dibley, Chris Gray, and Mr and Mrs Singh. Though no credit can be given to Pablo Sat-Bhambra, even though he was involved in the making the first issue of this book.

Also Ernie Martin whose advice has been invaluable in regards to this second edition.

And thanks to all at Author House who originally wished to take over the publication of this second edition in 2008, and thus made it a reality.

AUTHOR'S NOTE

One of the main purposes of this book is to demonstrate that really, there are no major contradictions throughout the texts of the Gospels. If it has appeared so to many before, then it is because, either, there is a lack of basic knowledge about the events themselves, or because, the more learned reader has overlooked certain factors. It has neither been the purpose of this book to take away any credit, or credence from the four individual authors of the Gospels, or any benefit in reading the Gospels separately: naturally, one can still do that. But, in the course of researching and writing this book, one Gospel has emerged. Thus, allowing the reader, if so choosing, to ignore the author's words, and to experience a Gospel that has all the accounts in consecutive order [as was one of Luke's (1:1-3) reasons for writing his], which, also, combines all the details of the parallel texts together, and dovetails the rest of the narratives in their correct sequential positions.

The Scriptural text for this book is based on the King James Version [KJV], or the Authorized Version [AV], as it is also known. However, we have chosen to use the abbreviation, 'AV', when referring to that particular version. Although any preferential translation can be used rather than the AV, when considering our specific findings.

When correlating the four texts together, great care has been taken so as not to leave out any English word as translated from the original Greek [Gr.] texts, other than, when the Greek is translated into English in referring to the connecting word 'and', where it is excessively repeated in combing the parallel accounts.

The Old English, 'thou', 'thee' and 'ye', have been changed to 'you', 'thine' to 'yours', and 'thy' to 'you'. We have also used 'author's license', in sometimes preferring the use of certain words, in place of some of the other archaic or Old English words used many times throughout the AV. Though, many translations have used the same words as we have, when having translated into more Modern English.

However, sometimes the author has used his own discretion, when preferring the use of some words, which other translations do not have. This should stretch the reader's imagination into checking the meaning of the individual words that they may not be that familiar with, by looking them up in a relevant Dictionary, or, in considering the variety of words contained in a Thesaurus, as certain words have similar meanings the options are sometimes manifold. Where different words have been used, other than those in the AV, it has been done to give the novice better understanding, as many are not familiar with the archaic or Old English words.

The first letters of personal pronouns have been capitalized when referring to Jesus, and where 'heaven', or 'kingdom', is referring to a divine characteristic. Additionally, other words, such as when relating to 'Holy Days', and a person's 'office' or a particular Institution, have had their first letter capitalized.

In the AV, every letter that begins a verse is always in capitals. We have changed these capitals to the modem usage of the lower case when following a comma, semicolon, or colon. We have also used quotation marks, where direct speech is indicated, and when the Old Testament [OT] is directly quoted, supplied the Scriptural reference too.

When reading of the author's text, unless there is a specific change of a Scriptural reference indicated, it follows, that the last particular reference given, i.e., Matthew = Mat. 1:1, or as with brackets (1:1) is still referring to the last particular Gospel previously indicated, or actually mentioned. Also, when the abbreviations, v. [verse] 2, or, vv. [verses] 3 - 4 are given, they also relate to the previous chapter, or verses indicated throughout the author's text. The same applies to chapter abbreviations i.e., ch. [chapter] 2, or any other chapter. In all cases the references apply to the Gospel previously mentioned, or lastly indicated, as in the previous Scriptural references above applying to Matthew, through the abbreviations or the actual wording in the author's text. In other words all references follow on successively in referring to the previous context, unless otherwise indicated.

TABLE OF CONTENTS

INTRODUCTION

Why This Book Was Formulated

Thirty-eight years ago I delved into a personal study of how the order of events surrounding the miracles and parables associated within the texts of the four Gospels specifically and successively related to each other. This study also included verifying the actual length of Jesus' ministry. After completing the initial framework of these findings, I realized others would be interested too. This I completed by the end of 1985, and entitled the original manuscript, *The Forty-Two Miracles of Jesus Christ*.

From the first instance, I embarked on the task in a tremendous mood of enthusiasm and excitement, and as I saw a pattern and plan developing in the way everything in the four Gospels related to each other, became even more excited. With the initial thrill of these original findings, I rushed to get them onto paper. In so doing, I did not take time to consider some of the critical arguments relating to certain prevalent factors in modern scholarship up to that date. Though subsequently this did not alter any of the main original findings and initial exegesis.

However, while trying to get the manuscript published in its existing form, I was led to send it to an expert in New Testament Studies, Dr. Philip Seddon, of Selly Oak Colleges in Birmingham, who found it - as written in his reply, *"interesting, fascinating and thought-provoking"*. He suggested if I could not get it published as it stood, I should consider enlarging on it and take into consideration relevant critical scholarship. In so doing, he also put me in touch with a John Wenham (a respected scholar of the harmonistic critical approach) of Wycliffe Hall, at Oxford University, and some of his books relating to the subject.

Taking his advice, I consequently decided to include and examine the entire texts of the four Gospels (instead of just from the beginning of Jesus' ministry and up to the crucifixion). Realizing what was needed was as it were - a 'Gospel' of the four Gospels. In other words, one complete Gospel, with the combined texts of the events of the four systematically placed in the successive order (as I had come to see), to which they were naturally relating to, so that the reader could clearly peruse the whole and complete scenario of the dialogue unfolding as it had subsequently occurred, and without any of the so-called contradictions associated with the explanations regarding the critical arguments of the text that certain scholars hold in question.

While I was completing the first draft of the book I had not heard of the *Diatessaron* (c. AD150-160), which is the earliest of the Gospel harmonies. Tatian, an early Christian combined Matthew, Mark, Luke, and John into a single narrative, though he omits the important genealogies of Matthew and Luke, and significant duplicated text which was reference to Jesus repeating some of the same teachings to other disciples than the twelve, and is paramount in establishing where Luke's Central Section takes place. Though, since I have checked his work, it does not follow the exact harmony discovered in *The Gospel of the Four*, or the precise order of the miracles, which are keys to understanding the specific order of all the events.

Of course over the centuries of time, various works on the happenings of the Gospels have found their way onto the shelves of our libraries and into the homes of those particularly interested in the subject. Also there are a plethora of books on the harmony of the Gospels. Moreover, certain aspects of it have become intrinsically enshrined within our religious circles, including various factors inherent to our culture. For instance, one such factor was the establishment of our calendar, relating to the calculation of the year we find ourselves in, which consequently became known as AD, and 2000 years since Jesus' birth. Other instances of this influence can even be found in numerous expressions associated within the very idiom of our language. Furthermore, if we pause and consider for a moment, especially the older generation, could no doubt point to several straightaway. Even though, this influence has been profound throughout our history, most of the time we are not aware of these factors, when busy with life's other preoccupations.

Over the centuries then, this profound influence came initially through word of mouth, after which the important aspects of it were written down by hand, and later subsequently even portrayed through art, architecture, and, eventually the printed word. In this recent age of electronic gadgets and wizardry, aspects of the Gospels and its teachings are still promulgated, though now through the reproduction of sound recordings, including the invention of the moving picture, and the Internet.

But in spite of the, various arguments cognizant to the aspects relating to this sometimes puzzling and controversial subject - nevertheless, it is basically and generally accepted by many of our people, and especially the older, and became part of our very Establishment. However, as far as the younger generation goes, many take little interest in the subject, and are certainly as a whole bemused by the historical and technical side of it.

Consequently, one of the main reasons for this is, generally speaking it has not been made particularly interesting or significantly easy to understand, and thus, is without any specific relevance to those born in the later years of this modern age. Additionally, many of our critical scholars believe there are blatant contradictions in the records of the Gospels, and when it comes to the problem of the miraculous aspect, cannot accept such things anyhow. Subsequently, this has resulted in the proper explanation of the subject being rationalized away, through certain books and TV documentaries, which in turn gave rise to an attitude of complete skepticism regarding any authenticity relating to the subject amongst those who would reflect on the concepts associated within its pages. Especially those surrounding the consideration, of whether the birth of our universe and the subsequent other happenings since, associated with life itself, were just a blind occurrence of chance, or whether it was set in motion by special design, as depicted in the beginning verses of the fourth and concluding Gospel.

Because of this nebulous spirit associated with much of the scenario regarding the works on the four Gospels - which feed the ideas relating to our aspirations on the subject - it should not be thought strange if many our young people then view the whole content (and even its aesthetical teachings) with some skepticism, when it comes to identifying any notion of a God and the concept of any benefit from reading the four books of the Gospels. Ironically, many of the very scholars whose word on the subject we can only take as 'gospel' so to speak are not in agreement or any closer now than they were a hundred years ago. Thus the importance attached to its teachings is placed at a low level.

This naturally results in a feed-back to the rest of the clergy, who predominantly represent the subject to our peoples (and especially to the young) as a somewhat ambiguous concept, which they are not able to market more successfully in getting across any worthwhile and wholesome ideas associated with its aesthetic values and historical basics in answer to questions that naturally come up with the subject.

Interestingly enough, this is highlighted through the words of John Wenham in his book, *Redating Matthew, Mark, & Luke* (Hodder & Stoughton), where this dilemma is addressed in his Introduction, *"In 1979 I found myself in the Synoptic Problem Seminar of the Society for New Testament Studies, whose members were in disagreement over every aspect of the subject. When this international group disbanded in 1982 they had sadly to confess that after twelve years' work they had not reached a common mind on a single issue"* (p. xxi).

He further mentions this dilemma in his book the *Easter Enigma* (Paternoster Press), saying, *"Forced harmonizing is worthless. The tendency today, however, is the opposite - to force the New Testament writings into disharmony, in order to emphasize their individuality. The current analytical approach to the Gospels often has the effect of making scholars more and more uncertain at more points, till eventually their view of Jesus and his teaching is lost in a haze. The harmonistic approach, on the other hand, enables one to ponder long and conscientiously over every detail of the narrative and to see how one account illuminate, and modifies another. Gradually (without fudging) people and events take shape and grow in solidity and the scenes come to life in one's mind. Such study is beautifully constructive and helps vindicate the presuppositions on which it is based. It is sad and strange when immense learning leads to little knowledge of the person studied"* (p. 128).

So, when it comes to these basic events in the Gospels, scholars are still in much confusion, leaving question marks, arguments, statements of contradictions, when comparing the books available on the subject. John Wenham's works are based on a better approach, which has the basis of a proper rationalized harmonistic foundation, it is with this harmonistic approach that I also proceeded, even though at the time of my first manuscript I was not aware of John Wenham and his works.

Hence, this, particular formulation of the four Gospels into one complete whole, with the given explanations of the text in question, including a complete *Scripture*

Graph, is an attempt to give the answer to the age-old problem of the natural synchronization of the successive events in the four Gospels, without any of the so-called contradictions. Thus, producing an entirely new work - for those who are seeking answers to some of the seemingly perplex anomalous questions that people interested in this field have halted at. Consequently, and hopefully, therefore, it will give the subject the proper credence it had from its original conception, when these miraculous events were first written down. Moreover, it will create one natural flowing Gospel, in combing the four, but, at the same time, not take anything away from the importance of the individuality of each of the authors and their separate books.

I had not realized when first starting to write the manuscript, any special significance to the numbering of the rest of the miracles, when finding there were 42 miracles up to the Resurrection. Nevertheless, afterwards, in 1986, in realizing I must combine the other manuscript I was preparing on the events surrounding the Resurrection, and concluding with the Ascension, amazingly and surprisingly I found that altogether - in all - there were 50 miracles when combining the 42 with the other miracles that follow, prior to the Ascension.

It became clear that indeed there was much significance relating to these findings, and predominantly, specific new meaning to the way the four texts are basically and intrinsically connected together. This also gave rise to the integral quintessence of the importance affiliated to how many of these miracles were chosen by the Gospel writers to be included within their narratives of the ministry of Jesus. Since many more miracles occurred than those chosen to be recorded.

These findings also concur that the events contained in the four Gospels were written in a manner, which adhered to a well-informed style in its overall format, specifically and precisely following the successive order in which they had originally transpired, except for five major dislocations which relate primarily to Matthew, and his reason for placing them otherwise:

1] the coming of the Baptist's disciples to Jesus the second time at the eighteenth, nineteenth, twentieth, and twenty first miracle (9:14-34), along with the conclusion of the final tour of Galilee (vv. 35-38).

2] the ordination of the twelve (10:1-42).

3] the narrative from the Sabbath question, *The Twelfth Miracle*, along with the first counsel of Pharisees, and Jesus healing great crowds, to His fulfilling of prophecy (12:1-21).

4] the fifteenth miracle and Jesus' dialogue with the Pharisees (vv. 22-45).

5] and the anointing of Jesus at Simon the Leper's (26:7-16).

Mark (14:3-11) also aligns and follows Matthew with the scenario at Simon the Leper's house, this being the only time he does not systematically follow on in successive order.

Luke, as his prime reason for writing was to make clear and add further detail to the knowledge of the events known at that particular time, compiled his unique input of findings to give additional credence to the successive order in which the accounts subsequently took place (1:1-3). Though in two instances he does not follow his normal orderly chronological style, to which he alluded to at the very beginning of his Gospel, but, reverses the lineage of Jesus and interjects it in between Jesus' baptism and return from the wilderness after forty days (3:23-38).

He also positions the imprisonment of the Baptist (vv. 19-20) directly before he was imprisoned, presupposing the reader would naturally be aware of that particular factor.

John, however [contrary to the opinion of some], adheres to a strict chronological style, organizing the whole of his narrative around specific days and the Holy Day seasons. Thus, we have a three dimensional perspective of the events through the witness of the Synoptics, with a prolific account by John of much more of Jesus' words surrounding His ministry, including an intensity of a more deeper understanding and enlightened spiritual aspect to his narrative.

So primarily, the purpose of the contents within this book predominantly concerns itself with explaining how every part in the four Gospels, intrinsically parallel, and dovetail together and how the text does not contradict itself, as many believe. Consequently, in the process of compiling this book, many aspects that were not originally clear became clearer as I painstakingly progressed through every chapter and verse.

Furthermore, because this book contains integral reference to various numbers in association to the miracles and certain days, several suggestions as to the significance of the numerical findings have been given briefly when appropriate [such as the criteria associated with the numbers 42, 43, 45, 50, and 51]. Nevertheless, I was amazed during the completion of the Introduction to this manuscript, while reading the book, *THE TRUTH BEHIND THE BIBLE CODE*, by Dr. Jeffrey Satinover, printed by Sidgwick & Jackson, to find the fascinating significance to the number 42, as associated with the Hebrew letters of the Forty-Two Lettered Divine Name (pp. 76, also 68-69, 81-83, 91, 95, 100, 269-272 and 275), and embodied within the first sentence of the Bible - '*In the beginning God created the heavens and the earth*'. Amazingly, here is encoded reference to the factor of God's activity before the physical creation and also afterwards.

So, as the beginning of this book begins with John 1:1-2 indicating a time before the physical creation of the universe, we see that the Word, who existed before the creation and the calculation of known time, was also of the One Godhead who came to the earth (vv. 9-11). Moreover, He was the One who did many miracles - 42, up to the greatest miracle of life itself - the Resurrection. Hence, the significance of the numbers 42, 43, 45, 50 and 51, are first considered at the subsequent sections, *The Returning From the Wilderness*, *The Next Day*, *The First Disciples*, *John Imprisoned*, *They Leave For Galilee*, and *The First Miracle* with the criteria surrounding the number 50 being further examined at each chapter dealing with the season Pentecost is found in. Additionally, the 7 miracles 44-50 in between the resurrection and the Ascension are also covered in their appropriate settings, with the number 51 in *The Conclusion* of this book (p.440).

However, the main purpose of this book was to facilitate and reveal how the four books of the Gospels specifically relate to each other in successive order. Hence, it is up to others to find any other significance to the numerology suggested therein. For those who are interested in exploring this aspect further, I also recommend E W Bullinger's book, *Number In Scripture*, printed by Kregel Publications.

Below, in successive order, are the unique major findings advanced by this book. Though the reader will no doubt find others, which are relevant to each particular individual's knowledge of the events. Some of these suggestions become apparent through the aspects surrounding the subsequent seasons intrinsically connected to the Holy Days that are mentioned in the requisite texts associated with this issue. These specific findings are further highlighted and made clearer, by referring to the *Scripture Graphs*, as well as to the relevant texts in question, when considering and coming to any of these fundamental conclusions.

1) While it is becoming increasingly known that Jesus could not have been born in December, it has not generally been considered that nonetheless, He no doubt was conceived at that particular time - at the darkest time of the year - even on the very day of Christmas itself. Thus, if this concept becomes generally accepted, it would herald a new and truer meaning to the Festival - and what further significance it would bring to the following years during the New Millennium.

2) That Matthew and Luke's account surrounding the events associated with the birth of Jesus, do not contradict each other.

3) That Jesus no doubt was baptized on the Day of Pentecost [Gr. *fiftieth*] in the summertime. This is clearly alluded to when studying the *Scripture Graphs* (pp. 449-466) where we see that in between each springtime in which Passover occurred, and each autumn wherein Tabernacles took place: naturally there would have been summer seasons in which Pentecost also fell. This is further suggested by virtue of the fact there would have been four autumn Festivals of Tabernacles during Jesus' 3½ or 42-month ministry. Furthermore, the summer seasons in which Pentecost would be found, is touched upon throughout this book in the prescribed successive places of the main text, which deals with each subsequent year relating to that particular time of year. This is first seen with the summer just prior to the start of Jesus' ministry, and lastly by the conclusion of His ministry on earth in the Ascension ten days before Pentecost through the beginnings of the NT Church in the book of Acts.

Consequently, altogether, there are five summer seasons in which we comment on the association of Pentecost with the Holy Spirit, which also combines the summer period preceding Jesus' ministry and the conclusion of His ministry. Moreover, when specifically considering all the consecutive places throughout this book dealing with the Day of Pentecost, and its sublime symbolism, we should see that Jesus' ministry would have begun in the autumn, and that subsequently He would have been baptized several months earlier, and in that case in the summer, and no doubt on the very Day of Pentecost itself - having been baptized not only by water, but through the Holy Spirit too.

Additionally, the whole period of Jesus' ministry, and following, would have also included four winters, after which would follow spring and Passover. However, though each subsequent Passover is specifically mentioned only three times throughout the Biblical text, surrounding Jesus' ministry, nonetheless, through careful deduction, we can see there would have been four inherent to this whole period.

4) How Matthew and Luke parallel and dovetail together precisely and explicitly over the account of Christ's trial in the wilderness, with John's Gospel actually dovetailing before and after.

5) That within the text of the Gospel of John's first two chapters, there are several days mentioned, which relate to Jesus' return after His baptism and trial in the wilderness, the calling of the first disciples, and additionally prefigures to fifty days, that leads us to Jesus' first miracle.

6) How John continues dovetailing directly after *The Temptation,* including when the Baptist is taken prisoner the first time.

7) How *The First Miracle* leads us into Jesus' ministry and thus sets the precedent for numbering the rest.

8) That Jesus subsequently toured the towns of Galilee four separate times.

9) That Jesus consequently purged the Temple six months after the start of His ministry and again six months before the end of His ministry.

10) That *The Sermon Up The Mount*, of Matthew 5 - 7 took place on the Mount of Olives overlooking Jerusalem, and should not be confused with *The Sermon Down The Mount* near Capernaum of (Luke 6:17-49).

11) That there are basically five miracles which appear to be the same, but in fact, on closer examination are all completely different instances, and take place in separate localities, and at differing times. As with the *Feeding Of The 5000*, and the 4000, although alike to some degree, one takes place near Bethsaida, and the other in the Decapolis at a later time.

Not counting these two obvious distinct miracles, of the *Feeding of the 5000* and the 4000, the five miracles which appear superficially to be the same, are firstly, *The Third Miracle* of the healing of *Simon The Leper* in Jerusalem, which should not be confused with *The Ninth Miracle* of the leper of Gergesa: the following ones are *The Centurion's Servant*, which are both, though separate incidents, The fifth and the thirteenth miracles; the storms on the Sea of Galilee, being both the eighth and sixteenth miracle; *The Tenth Miracle - The Two Demoniacs*, and the seventeenth miracle, the single man with the legion of devils; and lastly the blind men of Jericho [who actually were four individual blind men], subsequently becoming the thirty-seventh, the thirty-eighth, and the thirty-ninth miracle.

12) That John must have been released from prison the first time as he is baptizing again in Aenon near Salim in Samaria while Jesus baptizes adjacent in Judea before he is imprisoned finally, thus, consequently, resulting in his eventual death.

13) That Jesus preached three separate times to towns in Judea.

14) Why the narrative preceding Mat. 9:9-13 refers to only eleven disciples having been called at that particular junction.

15) That much of the Gospel's text is reiteration to *The Seventy Disciples*.

16) The reason why the following text of vv. 9:14-35, where the Baptists' disciples came to Jesus the second time, also includes the narration of the eighteenth, nineteenth, twentieth, and twenty-first miracles, yet, is dislocated, and does not follow in strict successive order.

17) That '*the Festival*' in John 5:1, refers to '*the Festival*' of Tabernacles.

18) Why both Matthew (17.1) and Mark (9:2), leading up to T*he Transfiguration*, witness '*after six days*', whereas Luke (9:28) phrases it '*about eight days*'.

19) That Jesus did not travel to Perea.

20) Where Luke's Central Section (9:51-17:10) actually takes place.

21) How Luke and John parallel and dovetail regarding *The Thirty-Fourth Miracle - Man With Oedema*, and that altogether John only mentions twelve miracles throughout his text, with five being specifically unique to his Gospel.

22) How the Synoptics and the Gospel of John relate to each other when Jesus leaves to heal Lazarus.

23) That Jesus rode into Jerusalem twice. Firstly, just prior to the last Tabernacles of His ministry, and finally six months later, five days before the ultimate Passover.

24) How from the particular start of the junction of the parallel texts of Mat. 21:23, Mark 11:27 and Luke 20:1, they relate to the Lamb presenting Himself to the Priests at the Temple, and dovetail with John 11:44-50 referring to the same concurrent time of four days prior to the last Passover. Thus, also, prefiguring and reflecting the original OT requirement of each household acquiring a lamb four days before the Passover (Ex. 12:3-6).

25) How all the combined periods of the narration preceding and including the Passover and the subsequent trial of Jesus, along with the following resurrection accounts do not contradict in any way at all. But, although they are individual narrations, notwithstanding, they nonetheless adhere rather to a subtle circumscribed manner of fourfold composition, which consistently, though sometimes through a characteristic intermittent manner, nevertheless do parallel and dovetail throughout all the requisite texts, further exemplifying and entirely verifying the conclusion, that the Gospels are the truly the Word of God. Through these inherent and sublime factors subsequently, we see that Caiaphas actually interrogated Jesus twice.

26) That Jesus ultimately died mercifully from the stroke of the Centurion's spear, as normally those crucified died much later, as the Romans devised this form of death to last as long as possible.

27) That Jesus presented Himself directly to the Father after first appearing to Mary early Sunday morning.

28) And that He reappeared after that, to Peter first, hours afterwards, though later in the afternoon of the same day, before He appeared to the rest of the women next, who were on their way to inform the rest of the disciples [not the apostles] of the good news that He had been resurrected.

29) That *The Fifth Appearance* was specifically *To The Ten* apostles.

30) That subsequently *The Sixth Appearance* was *To The Eleven* or twelve apostles, as Matthias was there but not ordained as an apostle yet.

31) That Jesus held two specific meetings with the apostles after returning from Galilee to Jerusalem, the final one resulting in His Ascension.

1   *THE BEGINNING OF THE GOSPEL*

THE BEGINNINGS

John 1

1 In the beginning was the Word [Gr. *logos*], and the Word was with God, and the Word was God.

2 The same was in the beginning with God.

The actual beginning of the Bible starts with the physical creation of Gen. 1:1. But, even before that time, we have another '*beginning*', which, the last of the Gospels writers, John, brings to our attention. It is the 'real beginning', before the universe and any matter came into existence.

All physical matter can be estimated, and, since 'God' cannot [or else there could not be God], conversely, therefore we have this '*beginning*' before the physical creation.

John 1

3 All things were made by Him; and without Him was not anything made that was made.

We now align with Gen. 1:1. This miracle of matter coming out of nothing as it were - of the universe, and our earth being brought into existence, becomes the greatest in scope, and panoramic magnitude of all miracles relating to inanimate nature, with the creation of living nature, afterwards coming out of it.

However, the crowning pinnacle of creation was the creating of man, and woman out of man - together, to be in the image of God, and thereafter - man - out of woman, equaling humankind.

John 1

4 In Him was life; and the life was the Light of humankind.

5 And the Light shines in darkness; and the darkness comprehended it not.

Our next beginning is the enlightenment of the mind. God created man and woman, and spoke to them, teaching - enlightening their minds through educating the pinnacle of His creation, in an ongoing process.

Note: we have relocated the three verses of John 1:6-8, referring to the much later scenario of John the Baptist's commission of teaching in the wilderness, and placed them in their correct sequence, according to their successive occurrence, as '*the True Light*' in v. 9, continues in subject-matter from v. 5.

John 1

9 That was the True Light, who enlightens everyone who comes into the world.

10 He was in the world, and He made the world, and the world didn't recognize Him.

11 He came to His own, and His own didn't receive Him.

12 But as many as received Him, to them gave He Power to become the Children of God, even to those who believe on His Name:

13 who were born, not of blood, nor of the will of the flesh, neither by the will of humans, but of God.

Mark 1

1 The beginning of the gospel of Jesus the Messiah, the Son of God.

The second Gospel that correlates to our next successive beginning, is Mark (1:1), who connects with John's last verses above with his start prefiguring before that of Matthew and Luke, becoming as it were a title for the Synoptics, as John had phrased his Gospel to precede the material realm.

Next, in successive order, Luke, progresses from the events leading up to John the Baptist's birth. Though later, he places the genealogy of Jesus directly after Jesus' baptism. We address this factor when we arrive at that particular junction.

However, '*The beginning of the gospel of Jesus the Messiah*' also relates to the enlightenment of the mind, not only in the sense to that which started with Jesus' human ministry on earth, but, the enlightenment which occurred at the creation of the first humans (John 1:9), as God spoke to both Adam and Eve, and subsequently to other individuals throughout the OT. John confirmed with his first verses, that it was the Word who spoke from the beginning, since no one had seen the Father (v. 18), or even heard His voice (5:37).

Conversely we could have placed Mark 1:1 before John 1:4-13, in the sense of the 'gospel' also applying to the beginning of the creation of the first humans, when they were a son and daughter to God, and that their progeny were intended to become sons and daughters of God, too, in the comprehension that the Word typified as the Sacrificial Lamb from that beginning, as well as when He came as a human being 4000 years later (Rev. 13:8). Thus, in actuality salvation was open to all - even from the very beginning of humanity.

Nevertheless, since this book is primarily about the Gospels, and Jesus and His life as a Human, therefore it confines itself basically to the 'gospel' being taught in the sense it was from when Mark first introduces the Word, and in his proceeding verses, where John the Baptist is preparing the way prior to Jesus' ministry (1:2-3). Thus, Mark's first verse must be placed so, and his subsequent verses in the appropriate successive settings to which they relate.

When we consider the Biblical text, which introduces the section, *The Voice in the Wilderness* (p. 23), we see it is the Gospel of John (1:6) who begins again, with Mark (1:2) directly following, once more.

Luke 1

1 Inasmuch as many have taken in hand to set out in order a declaration of those things that are most surely believed amongst us,

2 even as they delivered them to us, who from the beginning were eyewitnesses, and ministers of the Word;

3 it seemed good to me also, having had perfect understanding of all things from the very first, to write to you in order, most excellent Theophilus,

4 that you might know the certainty of those things, wherein you have been instructed.

Luke also tells us that many had set out declarations of those things in order, stating that he wanted to add certainty to the facts of those records.

Though he keeps to the objectivity of his first four verses, and continues in successive order directly afterwards, with the information surrounding the birth of both the Baptist and Jesus, with the two eventually having grown into men, immediately after Jesus' baptism he digresses (3:21-23), with a list of the genealogy from Joseph, Mary's husband, that goes back in time, though, nonetheless, its names in order.

However, Matthew introduces his Gospel with a part of Jesus' genealogy with a list progressing forward in time, from Abraham. Because the fundamental purpose of this book is to position the texts in the sequence of consecutive events as they occurred, we have Luke's genealogical verses below, in their natural successive order.

Luke 3

38 God created Adam, and Seth became his son, and Enos became his son,

37 and Cainan became his son, and Maleleel became his son, and Jared became his son, and Enoch became his son, and Methuselah became his son,

36 and Lamech became his son, and Noah became his son, and Shem became his became his son, and Arphaxad became his son, and Cainan became his son,

35 and Sala became his son, and Heber became his son, and Phalec became his son, and Ragau became his son, and Saruch became his son,

34a and Nachor became his son, and Thara became his son, and Abraham became his son.

Matthew 1

1 The book of the generation of Jesus the Messiah, the son of David, the son of Abraham.

Matthew the first of the Gospels actually comes last in succession of events. It should be noticed that his beginning starts from tracing the lineage of Jesus from Abraham, through to David, and does not include a genealogy before Abraham.

Also we come now to the first text where Matthew and Luke coincide with their subject.

Matthew 1:2 Luke 3:34b-33a

Abraham fathered Isaac, who became his son; and Isaac fathered Jacob, who became his son; and Jacob fathered Judah and his brothers, who became his sons;

Matthew 1:3 Luke 3:33b

and Judah fathered Phares and Zara of Thamar, who became his sons; and Phares fathered Esrom, who became his son; and Esrom fathered Aram, who became his son;

Matthew 1:4 Luke 3:33c-32a

and Aram fathered Aminadab, who became his son; and Aminadab fathered Naasson, who became his son; Naasson fathered Salmon, who became his son;

Matthew 1:5 Luke 3:32b

and Salmon fathered Boaz of Rahab, who became their son; and Boaz fathered Obed of Ruth, who became their son; and Obed fathered Jesse, who became his son;

Matthew 1:6 Luke 3:31a

and Jesse fathered David the King; and David fathered Nathan, whom became his son; and David the King fathered Solomon of her who had been the wife of Uriah;

In Luke 3:31a, above, Nathan was born before Solomon, and is placed accordingly.

It is at this conjunction that Matthew and Luke diverse into two different genealogies. Matthew's the Royal line, and Luke's the ordinary line.

Matthew 1	Luke 3
7 and Solomon fathered Rehoboam; and Rehoboam fathered Abijah; and Abijah fathered Asa;	31b and Nathan fathered Mattatha, and Menan became his son, and Melea became his son,

4

Matthew 1	Luke 3
8 and Asa fathered Jehoshaphat; and Jehoshaphat fathered Jehoram;	30 and Eliakim became his son, and Jonan became his son, and Joseph became his son, and Juda became his son, and Simeon became his son,
and Jehoram fathered Uzziah;	29 and Levi became his son,

It should also be noted that at Mat. 1:8, we left a gap, as he omits three notorious kings. We have left this space so as to keep in sequence with the general period of time relating to the longevity of the people in the list. Thus aligning with Luke's three names.

The missing Kings are: [1] Ahaziah, 2 Kings 8:25. [2] Joash, 2 Kings 11:1-2. [3] Amaziah, 2 Kings 14:1.

In continuing we leave further gaps as to align approximately with the same number of names as Luke.

Finally the genealogies diverge again at Zerubbabel.

9 and Uzziah fathered Joatham; and Joatham fathered Ahaz; and Ahaz fathered Hezekiah; 10 and Hezekiah fathered Manasseh: and Manasseh fathered Amon; and Amon fathered Josiah;	and Matthat became his son, and Jorim became his son, and Eliezer became his son, and Joses became his son, 28 and Er became his son, and Elmodam became his son, and Cosam became his son,

At this point, in between Josiah above, and Jechoniah on the next page, Matthew omits Jehoiakim, another notorious King in the lineage (2 Kings 23:34). Josiah was grandfather to Jechoniah.

11 And Josiah fathered Jechoniah and his brothers, about the time they were carried to Babylon.	and Melchi became his son, 27a and Neri became his son.

It is at this juncture that the two genealogies meet again, now through Salathiel and Zerubbabel in Babylon.

Matthew 1:12 Luke 3:27b
And after that they were brought to Babylon, Jechoniah fathered Salathiel.
Later Salathiel became the legal son of Neri; and Salathiel legally fathered
Zerubbabel, and Zerubbabel became his son;

We should notice that though Jechoniah was Salathiel's physical father, evidently
later, Salathiel became Neri's son-in-law, and, so Neri became father-in-law to
Salathiel.

Zerubbabel's physical father was Pedaiah (1 Chron. 3:19). Later Salathiel
became Zerubbabel's legal father.

Matthew 1	Luke 3
13and Zerubbabel fathered	27c and Zerubbabel fathered
Abiud; and Abiud fathered	Rhesa, who became his son,
Eliakim; and Eliakim fathered	and Joanna became his son,
Azor;	26 and Juda became his son,
14 and Azor fathered Sadoc;	and Joseph became his son,
and	and Semei became his son,
Sadoc	and Mattathias became his son,
fathered	and Maath became his son,
Achim;	25 and Nagge became his son,
and	and Esli became his son,
fathered	and Naum became his son,
Eliud;	and Amos became his son,
15 and	and Mattathies became his son,
Eliud	24 and Joseph became his son,
fathered	and Melchi became his son,
15a Eleazar;	and Levi became his son,
and Eleazar fathered Matthan;	and Matthat became his son,
and Matthan fathered Jacob.	23a Heli became his son.

The two genealogies now converge in concluding their purpose:
[1] That Jesus was born Human, of woman - thus the Son of Humanity.
[2] That Jesus was from the tribe of Judah and born to be King.

While Jesus, therefore, was the real of Mary, He could be reckoned as the
legal son of Joseph, and was descended from King David's first-born, Nathan,
through to Heli, as well as from his son, Solomon, through to Jacob.

Thus in Mary's marriage to Joseph, Heli, Mary's father, became Joseph's father-
in-law.

Because Luke in the concluding lists above has nine more names than Matthew's ten, we have placed Matthew's names in such a way so as to coincide with their conclusion - '*Joseph the husband of Mary*' (Mat. 1:16; Luke 3:23b).

Matthew, who we saw left various names out according to their notoriety, again in the previous section, did the same. Moreover he has three divisions to his list linking them to fourteen generations each from Abraham (1:17). Three times fourteen equals forty-two! Nevertheless, if we add up the three divisions, they actually come to a total of forty-one generations, when ending with Jesus' earthly descent. However, since Jesus was with God prior to His physical coming (John 1:1), it should become clear that Matthew in addition, was pointing to Jesus being with God again through His resurrection, and alluding to the concluding and ultimate regeneration - everlasting life. It should be noted that the findings of this book concur that there are forty-two miracles up to the resurrection of Jesus. Hence, Matthew's record also designates Abraham as being the father of the faithful, and of salvation (Gen. 12:3; Gal. 3:7-9, 29), and to the veracity of Jesus' Divinity, too, and His final Ascent. Nonetheless, Luke has more names in his list when comparing Matthew's last two generations, but the same as Matthew in the first section of Matthew's list. If we divide the number of Luke's nineteen names in the last section of his list, from the date of the completion of the Babylonian captivity of Judah [585BC], we find that the average factor of the number for the age of the names comes to '*about thirty*'.

Luke had started his genealogy with an ascending list from when '*Jesus began to be about thirty years of age*' (3:23c).

Matthew 1:16 Luke 2:23b
and Jacob fathered Joseph the husband of Mary (whom became the son-in-law of Heli), of whom was born Jesus, being (as was supposed) the son of Joseph, who is called the Messiah.
Matthew
17 So all the generations from Abraham to David are fourteen generations; and from David until the carrying away into Babylon are fourteen generations; and from the carrying away into Babylon to the Messiah are fourteen generations.

Keeping to the order of events, in which they successively happen, before we come to Mat. 1:18, Luke fills in with the details surrounding the birth of John the Baptist and Jesus, who was born six months after his cousin John (1:36), as Matthew (1:18-25) had recorded the detail from where Mary was already pregnant.

THE CONCEPTION OF JOHN

Luke 1

5 There was in the days [4BC] of Herod [74-4BC], the king of Judea [37-4BC], a certain Priest named Zacharias, of the Course of Abijah: and his wife was of the daughters of Aaron, and her name was Elisabeth.

6 And they were both righteous before God, walking in all the commandments and ordinances of the Lord blameless.

7 And they had no child, because that Elisabeth was barren and they both were now well advanced in years.

8 And it came to pass, that while he executed the Priest's Office before God in the order of his course [June],

9 according to the custom of the Priest's Office, his lot was to burn incense when he went into the Temple of the Lord.

10 And all the congregation of the people were praying outside at the time of incense.

11 And there appeared to him an angel of the Lord standing on the rightside of the altar of incense.

12 And when Zacharias saw him, he was troubled, and fear took a hold of him.

13 But the angel said to him,

"Don't be afraid, Zacharias: for your prayer is heard; and your wife Elisabeth shall bear you a son, and you shall call his name John.

14 And you shall have joy and gladness; and many shall rejoice at his birth.

15 For he shall be great in the sight of the Lord, and shall drink neither wine nor strong drink; and he shall be filled with the Holy Spirit, even from his mother's womb.

16 And many of the Children of Israel shall he turn to the Lord their God.

17 And he shall go before Him in the spirit and power of Elijah, TO TURN THE HEARTS OF THE FATHERS TO THE CHILDREN (Mal. 4:6), and the disobedient to the wisdom of the just; to make ready a people for the Lord."

18 And Zacharia said to the angel, "Whereby shall I know this? For I am an old man, and my wife is well advanced in years."

19 And the angel answering said to him,

"I am Gabriel, who stands in the presence of God; and am sent to speak to you, and to tell you this good news.

20 And, understand, you shall be dumb, and not able to speak, until the day that these things shall be performed, because you didn't believe my words, which shall be fulfilled in their season [March]."

Luke 1
21 And the people waited for Zacharias, and marveled that he stayed so long in the Temple.

22 And when he came out, he could not speak to them: and they perceived that he had seen a vision in the Temple: for he beckoned to them, and remained speechless.

23 And it came to pass, that, as soon as the days of his ministration were accomplished, he departed to his own house.

24 And after those days his wife Elisabeth conceived, and hid herself five months [November], saying,
25 "Thus has the Lord dealt with me in the days wherein He looked on me, to take away my reproach among humans."

Luke had known in which week and month '*the Course of Abijah*' fell (1:5, 8-9), according to the Temple duties (1 Chron. 24.10), and had purposely recorded this detail for us. These duties had been divided into twenty-four divisions, which lasted for a week, every six months (1 Chron. 24:19). When, taking all the factors of time Luke recorded in regards to the conception of John the Baptist, and his cousin Jesus, we see that Luke intended that we know in what month they were both conceived and born.

Luke further knew that Elisabeth for five months after knowing she would become pregnant, kept away from the normal daily routine that she was involved in previous to her pregnancy (1:24).

He also knew that one month later, in the sixth month of the pregnancy, that the angel Gabriel announced Mary's forthcoming pregnancy (v. 26). Luke highlighted this information for a very good reason. Had he not wanted to show this aspect, he could have omitted the reference to '*the Course of Abijah*', and not recorded any further months relating to the two pregnancies. But, let us not forget why he wrote in the first place - to relate the events in order (v. 3). Thus, Luke left us with detail revealing that John the Baptist was conceived six months before Jesus.

THE CONCEPTION OF JESUS

It is becoming increasingly known through the weight of opinion that Jesus could not have been born in the month of December, as the majority encyclopedias or authorities indicate. Nonetheless, though it may seem stranger than fiction, it is not considered or even accepted, moreover, that the time we celebrate as Christmas was the time of His conception. Since most authorities are now in agreement that Jesus was born in early autumn. In calculating back to the start of Mary's pregnancy, accepting the natural duration of nine months, from September, would bring us to December in winter anyhow - to the time of Mary's conception.

One of the main additional factors that Jesus could not have been born in December is that there were sheep out in the fields when He was born. It is Luke who exclusively once again gives us this poignant piece of information, as relating to this particular time (2:8).

This could not have normally taken place in the month of December, or the winter season, which lasted from late November to February, as, with the first rains starting in late autumn in October, "*It was an ancient custom among Jews of those days to... bring them* [their sheep] *home commencement of the first rain,*" says the *Adam Clarke Commentary* (Vol. 5, p. 370), New York ed.

Furthermore, the same authority states, "*During the time they were out, the shepherds watched them night and day. As... the first rain began early in the month Marchesvan, which answers to part of our October and November, we find that the sheep were kept out in the open country during the whole summer. And, as these shepherds had not yet brought home their flocks, it is a presumptive argument that October had not yet commenced, and that, consequently, our Lord was not born the 25th December, when no flocks were out in the fields; nor could He have been born later than September as the flocks were still in the field by night. The feeding of the flocks by night in the fields is a chronological fact. See the quotation from the Talmudists in Lightfoot.*"

Moreover, the eminent scholar, Bullinger, in his *Companion Bible* asserts, that the 25th December was the day most likely that Jesus was conceived in Mary. Hence, this one and only special conception, in the darkest phase of the week of the year, subsequently at the winter solstice, exactly when it actually starts to get fractionally lighter, '*the True Light, who enlightens*' (John 1:9), was conceived by Mary. Additionally, '*In Him was life; and the Life was the Light of humankind*' (v. 4).

Thus, as '*the True Light*' was conceived inside Mary, to be born nine months later, at the time, not only when the firstfruit of Mary's womb would be ready for birth, but, when the fruit of nature's final harvest was ready too, in the autumn, at the season of the last Festival, the Festival of Tabernacles, or the Festival of Ingathering as it is also called (Ex. 23:16).

In his Gospel, John further reveals, when referring to when Jesus was born, '*and dwelt* [Gr. *skenoo*] *amongst us*' (1:14), by choosing the Greek word he used, meaning '*to tent*', or '*to tabernacle*' amongst us. It relates, moreover, to the season wherein the tents, or tabernacles, were constructed for the Festival of Tabernacles, which falls in the Jewish month Tishri [September-October].

When we comprehend and understand the real significance of how, the conception, relates especially to Christmas, rather than the birth - though the conception naturally points to the birth, we can reflect on the Festival with a newer and completer understanding, deeper in insight than before, in awe, joy, and a subjectiveness based on the real beginnings of the only '*True Light*', in the apprehension that '*the light shines in darkness; and the darkness comprehended it not*' (v. 5).

Furthermore, since the conception of necessity took place in what is the darkest time of the year, and that comprehension can only come out of '*light*' - enlightenment, it was moreover the most fecundate and accordant time for the conception, which God had decided to place on record at that particular time.

Luke 1

26 And in the sixth month the angel Gabriel was sent from God to a city of Galilee, named Nazareth,

27 to a virgin engaged to a man whose name was Joseph, of the House of David; and the virgin's name was Mary.

28 And the angel came in to her, and said,

"Ave, you who are highly favored, the Lord is with you: blessed are you among women."

29 And when she saw him, she was troubled at his saying, and cast in her mind what manner of greeting this should be.

30 And the angel said to her,

"Don't be afraid, Mary: for you have found favor with God.

31 And, understand, you shall conceive in your womb, and bear a Son, and you shall call His name JESUS.

32 He shall be great, and shall be called the Son of the Highest: and the Lord God shall give to Him the Throne of His father David:

33 and He shall reign over the House of Jacob forever; and of His Kingdom there shall be no end."

34 Then said Mary to the angel,

"How shall this thing be, seeing I haven't known a man?"

35 And the angel answered and said to her,

"The Holy Spirit shall come upon you, and the Power of the Highest shall overshadow you: therefore also that Holy Thing which shall be born of you shall be called the Son of God.

36 And, understand, your cousin Elisabeth, she has also conceived a son in her advanced age: and this is the sixth month with her, who was called barren.

37 For with God nothing shall be impossible."

38 And Mary said,

"Consider me, the servant of the Lord; be it to me according to your word." And the angel departed from her.

It must be noted now that after the angel's pronouncement, Mary would from that point shortly conceive. It is now at that particular moment that Matthew fills in with the rest of the story.

Consider that neither of these Gospel writers goes over the same details at this time, but both continue complementing each other. As one leaves off from a point, the other one fills in where the other left off. This is a characteristic all the way through the Gospels.

Matthew 1
18 Now the birth of Jesus the Messiah was as follows.

When as His mother Mary was engaged to Joseph, before they came together, she was found pregnant through the Holy Spirit.
19 Then Joseph her husband, being a just man, and not willing to make her a public example, was minded to put her away privately.

20 But while he thought on these things, understand, the angel of the Lord appeared to him in a dream, saying,
"Joseph, you son of David, don't be afraid to take to yourself Mary your wife: for that which is conceived in her is through the Holy Spirit.
21 And she shall bear a Son, and you shall call His name JESUS: for He shall save His people from their sins."

22 Now this was done, that it might be fulfilled which was spoken of the Lord by the prophet (Isaiah 7:14), saying,
23 "CONSIDER, A VIRGIN SHALL BE WITH CHILD, AND SHALL BEAR A SON, AND THEY SHALL CALL HIS NAME EMMANUEL", which being translated is, "GOD WITH US."

24 Then Joseph being raised from sleep did as the angel of the Lord had directed him, and took to him his wife:

Luke (1:39) returns now with his narration. See how the Gospels amazingly continue relating to each other, though with different details of the same event, nonetheless, resume to both complement one another.

Luke 1
39 And Mary came up in those days, and went into the hill country with urgency, into a city of Judah;
40 and entered into the house of Zacharias, and greeted Elisabeth.
41 And it came to pass, that, when Elisabeth heard the good news from Mary,

the babe leaped in her womb; and Elisabeth was filled with the Holy Spirit:

42 and she spoke out with a loud voice, and said,

"Blessed are you among women, and blessed is the fruit of your womb.

43 And how is this to me that the mother of my Lord should come to me?

44 For, consider, as soon as the voice of your good news was in my ears, the babe leaped in my womb for joy.

45 And blessed is she who believes: for there shall be a performance of those things which were told her from the Lord."

46 And Mary said,

"My soul magnifies the Lord,

47 and my spirit rejoices in God my Saviour.

48 For He has regarded the low estate of His servant: for, understand, from now on all generations shall call me blessed.

49 For He who is Mighty has done to me great things; and Holy is His Name.

50 AND HIS MERCY IS ON THOSE WHO REVERE HIM FROM GENERATION TO GENERATION (Ps. 103:17).

51 He has shown strength with His arm; He has scattered the arrogant in the imagination of their hearts.

52 He has put down the mighty from their seats, and exalted them of low degree.

53 HE HAS FILLED THE HUNGRY WITH GOOD THINGS (Ps. 107:9); and the rich He has sent away empty.

54 He has helped His servant Israel, in remembrance of His mercy;

55 as He spoke to our fathers, to Abraham, and to his seed forever."

56 And Mary stayed with her about three months, and returned to her own house.

John the Baptist was born six months before Jesus (Luke 1:36, 56-57). If we accept that Jesus was conceived on the 25th December, that would place Elisabeth's conception of John, in June, directly after Zacharias had completed the Temple duty of '*the course of Abijah*', with the birth nine months later in March. Thus, this further confirms Jesus would have been born six months later in September.

John's Birth

Luke 1

56 And Mary stayed with her [Elisabeth] about three months, and rerterned to her own house.

57 Now Elisabeth's full time came that she should be delivered; and she gave birth to a son.
58 And her neighbors and her cousins heard how the Lord had shown great mercy towards her; and they rejoiced with her.

59 And it came to pass, that on the eighth day they came to circumcise the child; and they called him Zacharias, after the name his father.
60 And his mother answered and said, "Not so; but he shall be called John."

61 And they said to her, "There is none of your family who is called by this name."

62 And they made signs to his father, how he would have him called.
63 And he asked for a writing-tablet, and wrote, saying, "His name is John." And they all marveled
64 And his mouth was opened immediately, and his tongue loosed, and he spoke, and praised God.

65 And fear came on all who dwelt round about them; and all these sayings were noised abroad throughout all the hill country of Judea.
66 And all those who heard them laid them up in their hearts, saying, "What manner of child shall this be!"

And the hand of the Lord was with him.

At this juncture, we must consider the placing of Zacharias' prophecy about his son John, which directly follows after v. 66 above, but does not actually transpire until we are in the section, *The Prophecy of Zacharias* (p. 22). Vv. 65 and 66, include the event of the news spreading about John's birth.

Though the news would have spread virtually straightaway in the immediate neighborhood, nevertheless, it would have taken some time for it to reach the environs '*throughout all the hill country of Judea*'. Therefore, '*the hand of the Lord was with him*', implies further time in John's growth.

Also, if we notice v. 76, the language continues to address John, and is reminiscent of the child Samuel's teaching from Eli. Of course, John would have received instruction relating to all the detail of the prophecy from Zacharias, at any rate, as he was growing up.

Thus, we have relocated vv. 67-80, in the section covering *The Prophecy of Zacharias* (p. 22), where they would naturally transpire. Hence we come to these verses a little later on, when John has grown into a child.

In the sixth month of Elisabeth's pregnancy, the angel Gabriel announced to Mary, that she also would become pregnant (Luke 1:35-36). After hearing the news of Elisabeth's pregnancy, Mary leaves for Elisabeth's home in Judea (v. 39), where she stays three months until Elisabeth's ninth month [March], and then returns back to Nazareth (v. 56).

Six months later Joseph and Mary arrive at Bethlehem (2:4), where we continue with the next successive occurrence, the birth of John's cousin Jesus (v. 7).

It is clear that Luke supplied the details of what Matthew's account left out, as Matthew relates primarily to the consideration of Mary being already pregnant (1:18), and to Jesus already being born (vv. 24-25; 2:1).

JESUS' BIRTH

Luke 2

1 And it came to pass in those days [4BC], that there went out a decree from Caesar Augustus, that the entire land should be taxed.
2 This first taxation was made when Quirinius [45BC-AD21], was Quaestor [BC4-AD10] of Syria [Propraetor by AD11].
3 And all went to be taxed, every one into their own city.
4 And Joseph went up from Galilee, out of the city of Nazareth, into the city of David, which is called Bethlehem; (because he was of the House and Lineage of David:)
5 to be taxed with Mary his engaged wife, being great with child.
6 And so it was, that, while they were there, the days were accomplished that she should be delivered.

At this point, recalling in the section, *The Beginnings* (p. 2), we left the Gospel of John at ch. 1:13.

Now John relates the first part of his following v. 14(a), which occurs here in the story of Jesus' birth. However, the rest of v. 14(b) is not fulfilled until much later at Jesus' first miracle.

Luke 2:7 John 1:14a
And she gave birth to her first-born Son (the Word was made flesh, and dwelt among us), and wrapped Him in swaddling-clothes, and laid Him in a manger; because there was no room for them in the inn.

Luke 2

8 And there were in the same country shepherds staying in the fields, keeping watch over their flock by night.

9 And, suddenly, the angel of the Lord came upon them, and the glory of the Lord shone round about them: and they were extremely afraid.
10 And the angel said to them,
"Don't be afraid: understand, I bring you good news of great joy, which shall be to all people.
11 For to you is born this day in the city of David a Saviour, who is the Messiah the Lord.
12 And this shall be a sign to you;
'You shall find the Babe wrapped in swaddling-clothes, lying in a manger.'"

13 And suddenly there was with the angel a crowd of the Heavenly host praising God, and saying,
14 "Glory to God in the Highest, on earth peace, and good will toward all."

15 And it came to pass, as the angels were gone away from them into Heaven, the shepherds said one to another,
"Let us now go even to Bethlehem, and see this thing that is come to pass, which the Lord has made known to us."

16 And they came with urgency, and found Mary, and Joseph, and the Babe lying in a manger.

17 And when they had seen this, they made known abroad the saying which was told them concerning this Child.
18 And all those who heard it wondered at those things that were told them by the shepherds.
19 But Mary kept all these things, and pondered them in her heart.

20 And the shepherds returned, glorifying and praising God for all the things that they had heard and seen, as it was told to them.
21 And when eight days were accomplished for the circumcising of the Child, His name was called JESUS, which was so named of the angel before He was conceived in the womb.

HEROD AND THE MAGI

We will notice that Jesus had already been born when the Magi enquired in Jerusalem to where the Messiah should be found (Mat. 2:1-2). Herod, who had received this information from the Chief Priests and Scribes, then told the Magi to go to Bethlehem (vv. 4-8). Before that, the Magi were enquiring about

Jesus in Jerusalem, of the place where Jesus would be found. This would have taken some time, as when Herod heard about the Magi's enquiries, he sent privately for them (vv. 3, 7).

With Jesus being circumcised on the eighth day after His birth (Luke 2:21), and with the traveling of the Magi from Jerusalem to Bethlehem, we can only place Mat. 2:1-12, at this juncture.

Moreover, this is the seventh time we have seen how Luke and Matthew complement one another.

Matthew 2
1 Now when Jesus was born in Bethlehem of Judea in the days [4BC] of Herod the king [73BC-4BC], consider, Magi came from the East to Jerusalem,
2 saying,
"Where is He who is born King of the Jews? For we have seen His Star in the East, and are come to worship Him."

3 When Herod the king had heard these things, he was troubled, and all Jerusalem with him.

4 And when he had gathered all the Chief Priests and Scribes of the People together, he demanded of them where the Messiah should be born.
5 And they said to him, "In Bethlehem of Judea: for thus it is written by the prophet (Micah 5:2),
6 'AND YOU BETHLEHEM, IN THE LAND OF JUDAH, ARE IN NO WAY THE LEAST AMONG THE LEADERS OF JUDAH: FOR OUT OF YOU SHALL COME A RULER, WHO SHALL SHEPERD MY PEOPLE ISRAEL.'"

7 Then Herod, when he had privately called the Magi, inquired of them diligently what time the Star appeared.
8 And he sent them to Bethlehem, and said,
"Go and search diligently for the young Child; and when you have found Him, bring me word again, that I may come and worship Him also."

9 When they had listened to the king, they departed; and, suddenly, the Star, who they saw in the East, went before them, until it came and stood over where the young Child was.

10 When they saw the Star, they rejoiced exceedingly with great joy.

11And when they were come into the house, they saw the young Child with Mary His mother, and dropped down, and worshiped Him: and when they had opened their treasures, they presented to Him gifts; gold, and frankincense, and myrrh.

Matthew 2

12 And being warned of God in a dream that they should not return to Herod, they departed into their own country another way.

THEY LEAVE

Now we come to the eighth time that Matthew and Luke complement each other, with Luke (2:22) following on after Matthew (2:12).

We also saw previously that Luke had mentioned the eighth day that Jesus was circumcised (2:21), after which point we are brought forward to a month later (v. 22), where Mary, according to the Laws of Purification, had waited thirty-three days for to present herself and Jesus, at the Temple (Lev. 12:2-4, 6-7).

Luke 2

22 And when the days of her purification according to the Law of were accomplished, they brought Him to Jerusalem, to present Him to the Lord;
23 (as it written in the Law of the Lord (Ex. 13:2),
"EVERY FIRSTBORN WHO OPENS THE WOMB SHALL BE CALLED HOLY TO THE LORD");
24 and to offer a sacrifice according to that which is said in the Law of the Lord (Lev. 12:8), "A PAIR OF TURTLEDOVES, OR TWO YOUNG PIGEONS."

25 And, consider, there was a man in Jerusalem, whose name was Simeon; and the same man was just and devout, waiting for the consolation of Israel: and the Holy Spirit was upon him.
26 And it was revealed to him by the Holy Spirit, that he should not see death, before he had seen the Lord's Messiah.

27 And he came by the Spirit into the Temple: and when the parents brought in the Child Jesus, to do for Him after the custom of the Law,
28 then he took Him up in his arms, and blessed God, and said,
29 "Lord, now let Your servant depart in peace, according to Your word:
30 for my eyes have seen Your salvation,
31 which You have prepared before the face of all Your people Israel;
32 A LIGHT TO ENLIGHTEN THE NATIONS (Is. 42:6; 49:6), and the glory of Your people Israel."

33 And Joseph and His mother marveled at those things that were spoken of Him.
34 And Simeon blessed them, and said to Mary His mother, "Understand, this Child is set for the fall and rising again of many in Israel; and for a sign which shall be spoken against;
35 (yes, a sword shall pierce through your own soul also,) that the thoughts of many hearts may be revealed."

Luke 2

36 And there was one Anna, a prophetess, the daughter of Phanuel, of the Tribe of Asher: she was of a great age, and had lived with a husband seven years from her virginity;

37 and she was a widow of about eighty and four years, who didn't depart from the Temple, but served God with fastings and prayers night and day.

38 And she coming in that instant gave thanks likewise to the Lord, and spoke of Him to all those who looked for redemption in Jerusalem.

Next, our ninth correlating part, is read by some that Joseph, Mary and Jesus went straight to Egypt at Matthew's record (2:13), and confuse the issue with them returning to Nazareth first, as Luke (2:39) had made a point of mentioning.

Luke had revealed that after Mary and Jesus had been presented at the Temple (v. 22), it was directly afterwards they returned to Nazareth (v. 39).

Matthew had not mentioned that they went to Jerusalem before they returned to Nazareth, only that they left Bethlehem, and were to hide in Egypt (2:14-15), until the furor at Herod's Palace would abate (v. 16). Because of this the Magi had been warned in a dream not to return to Herod (v. 12).

There are two basic factors involved here. We have already established the successive order of the last events, covering these in the last explanations. Since that brings us to the point now under discussion, we will see the problem solved, when we consider further the two issues:

[1] It is clear that both Matthew (2:1) and Luke (2:4-7) establish that Jesus was born in Bethlehem. Also, that Luke stressed '*they returned to Nazareth*', after having '*performed all things according to the Law*' at the Temple (v. 39), which obviously would have been after leaving Bethlehem.

[2] The answer becomes clearer when in Mat. 2:12, we consider that the Magi had already left Bethlehem, and that Matthew's next v. 13, is not a repetition of that aspect, but antithesis to Joseph, Mary and Jesus, having also left and returned, too - '*were departed*', with Luke showing it to be Nazareth, from where they had originally come from over a month previously. Furthermore the Greek in v. 13, conveys '*having departed*', as it could have been translated.

[3] Also in the Greek text where v. 13 has '*de auton*' - it could alternatively have been translated - '*but they*'. Thus, the '*they*', should be emphasized in reading, meaning - they - Joseph, Mary and Jesus, '*were departed*', as the Greek allows.

Matthew 2:13 Luke 2:39

And when they had performed all things according to the Law of the Lord (Luke 2:22-24), when they were departed, they returned into Galilee, to their own city Nazareth; presently, the angel of the Lord appeared to Joseph in a dream, saying, "Rise, and take the young Child and His mother, and flee into Egypt, and stay there until I tell you: for Herod will seek the young Child to destroy Him."

Matthew 2
14 When he rose, he took the young Child and his mother by night, and departed into Egypt:
15 and was there during the death of Herod [November 4BC]: that it might be fulfilled which was spoken of the Lord by the prophet (Hosea 11:1), saying, "OUT OF EGYPT I HAVE CALLED MY SON."

16 Then Herod, when he saw that he was mocked of the Magi, was extremely furious, and sent out, and slew all the children who were in Bethlehem, and in the all environs thereof, from two years old and under, according to the time which he had diligently inquired off the Magi.
17 Then was fulfilled that which was spoken by Jeremiah (31:15) the prophet, saying,
18 "A VOICE HEARD WAS IN RAMAH, LAMENTATION, AND WEEPING, AND GREAT MOURNING, RACHEL WEEPING FOR HER CHILDREN, AND SHE WOULD NOT BE COMFORTED, BECAUSE THEY WERE NO MORE."

4   THE TWO GROWING BOYS

They Return

Herod had died in late 4BC.

Joseph, Mary and Jesus were now in Egypt. Archelaus, the elder son of Herod was now Ethnarch over Judea, Idumea and Samaria in AD1.

This brings us now to the part where Joseph, Mary and Jesus having escaped to Egypt, return to Galilee. Though, it seems from v. 22, they had considered traveling to Judea, no doubt to see Zacharias, Elisabeth and John.

We are not told how John the Baptist was spared Herod's slaughter of the children, only, that *'the Lord was with him'* (Luke 1:65).

Matthew 2
19 But when Herod was dead, presently, an angel of the Lord appeared in a dream to Joseph in Egypt,
20 saying,
"Rise, and take the young Child and His mother, and go into the land of Israel: for they are dead who sought the young Child's life."
21 And he rose, and took the young Child and His mother, and came into the land of Israel.

22 But when he heard that Archelaus [23BC-18AD] did reign in Judea [4BC-AD6] in the room of his father Herod, he was afraid to go there: notwithstanding, being warned of God in a dream, he turned aside into the parts of Galilee:
23 and they came and dwelt in a city called Nazareth [as overlooking theValley of Jezreel and Armageddon]: that it might be fulfilled which was spoken by the prophets, *"He shall be called a Nazarene."*

Jesus and His family returned to Nazareth from Egypt. John, who was six months older than his cousin Jesus, would now be somewhat older, too.

So allowing for the child John being able to start comprehending more fully the reason for his special upbringing as a Nazarite, and his mission, the next part of our successive text follows at this point.

Although we initially covered Luke 1:66 in its original setting, nevertheless, it also applies to the context of John being a lot older and thus, it is printed again to give sense to v. 67.

Jesus was able to understand His mission at twelve years old (Luke 2:42, 46-49). John would have also started to realize his, too, having been taught by his father. As John's comprehension grew, we can appreciate better Zacharias' prophecy of his son, and his cousin Jesus, below, as they were both growing, and that both of their families must have discussed these issues many times.

THE PROPHECY OF ZACHARIAS

Luke 1

66 And all those who heard them [the events surrounding John's birth] laid them up in their hearts, saying, "What manner of child shall this be!" And the hand of the Lord was with him.

67 And his father Zacharias was filled with the Holy Spirit, and prophesied, saying,
68 "Blessed be the Lord God of Israel; for He has visited and redeemed His people,
69 and has raised up a horn of salvation for us in the House of His servant David;
70 as He spoke by the mouth of His holy prophets, who have been since the world began:
71 that we should be saved 'FROM OUR ENEMIES AND FROM THE HAND OF ALL WHO HATE US (Ps. 106:10);'
72 to perform the mercy promised to our fathers, and to remember His Holy Covenant;
73 the oath which He swore to our father Abraham,
74 that He would grant to us, that we being delivered out of the hand of our hand of our enemies might serve Him without fear,
75 in holiness and righteousness before Him, all the days of our life.
76 And you, child, shall be called the prophet of the Highest: for you shall go 'BEFORE THE FACE OF THE LORD TO PREPARE HIS WAYS (Mal.3:1);'
77 to give knowledge of salvation to His people by the remission of their sins,
78 through the tender mercy of our God; whereby the Sunrise from on High has visited us,
79 'TO GIVE LIGHT TO THOSE WHO SIT IN DARKNESS AND IN THE SHADOW OF DEATH (Is.9:1),' to guide our feet into the way of peace."

80 And the child grew, and matured strong in spirit, and was in the wilderness until the day of his showing to Israel.

Notice the first part of Luke's last verse, above (v. 80), in connection to John, and the first verse after the next intersection, about Jesus' development (2:40). The two sentences are similar in wording, relating to the parallel childhoods of John and Jesus, and as we explained in our last intersection, in terms of growth as children conjunctional.

Luke 2

40 And the Child [Jesus] grew, and matured strong in spirit, filled with wisdom: and the grace of God was upon Him.

Luke 2

41 Now His parents went to Jerusalem every year at the Festival of the Passover.

42 And when He was twelve years old, they went up to Jerusalem after the custom of the Festival.

43 And when they had fulfilled the days, as they were returning, the Child Jesus stayed behind in Jerusalem.
44 But they, supposing Him to be in the caravan went a day's journey; and they looked for Him among their relatives and acquaintances.

45 And when they didn't find Him, they turned back again to Jerusalem, seeking Him.

46 And it came to pass, that after three days they found Him in the Temple, sitting in the midst of the Doctors, both hearing them, and asking them questions.
47 And all who heard Him were astonished at His understanding and answers.

48 And when they saw Him, they were amazed; and His mother said to Him, "Son, why have You so dealt with us? Look, Your father and I have sought You sorrowing."
49 And He said to them, "How is it you sought Me? Don't you know that I must be about My Father's business?"
50 And they didn't understand the saying that He spoke to them.

51 And He went down with them, and came to Nazareth, and was subject to them: but His mother kept all these sayings in her heart.
52 And Jesus increased in wisdom and stature, and in favor with God and the people.

It is now at the next strategic junction, that all the Gospel writers converge and dovetail, for the first time.

Though their individual sentences are separate, they dovetail, and are unique in their wording. They all tell us about the start of John the Baptist's mission.

Also they follow each other in succession of meaning, and moreover, we further see the reason for the beauty and purpose of the compilation of this version of the Gospels.

THE VOICE IN THE WILDERNESS

John 1

6 There was a man sent from God, whose name was John.

Mark 1

2 As it is written in the Prophets,

"UNDERSTAND, I SEND MY MESSENGER BEFORE YOUR FACE, WHO SHALL PREPARE YOUR WAY BEFORE YOU (Mal. 3:1)."

John 1

7 The same came for a witness of the Light, so all people through Him might believe.

8 He was not the Light, but was sent to bear witness of the Light.

Luke 3

1 Now in the fifteenth year [AD24] of the reign of Tiberius Caesar [42BC-AD37], Pontius Pilate [c.46BC-AD41] being Procurator of Judea [26BC-AD36], and Herod [21BC-AD39], being Tetrarch of Galilee [4BC-37AD], and his brother Philip [c.24BCAD34] Tetrarch of Ituraea and of the region Trachonitis [4BC-AD34], and Lysanias the Tetrarch of Abilene [AD14-34],

2 Annas [55BC-c.AD32] and Caiaphas [c.35BC-AD37] being the High Priests, the word of God came to John the son of Zacharias in the wilderness.

3 And he came into all the country about Jordan, preaching the baptism of repentance for the remission of sins.

Matthew 3

1 In those days came John the Baptist, preaching in the wilderness of Judea [AD27],

2 and saying, "Repent: for the Kingdom of Heaven is at hand."

Matthew 3:3a Luke 3:4a

For this is he who was spoken of, as it is written in the book of the words by the prophet Isaiah (40:3-5), saying,

Matthew 3:3b Mark 1:3 Luke 3:4b

"THE VOICE OF ONE CRYING IN THE WILDERNESS, 'PREPARE THE WAY OF THE LORD, MAKE HIS PATHS STRAIGHT.

Luke 3

5 EVERY VALLEY SHALL BE FILLED, AND EVERY MOUNTAIN AND HILL SHALL BE MADE LOW; AND THE CROOKED SHALL BE MADE STRAIGHT, AND THE ROUGH WAYS SHALL BE MADE SMOOTH;

6 AND ALL FLESH SHALL SEE THE SALVATION OF GOD.'"

Mark 1

4 John did baptize in the wilderness, and preach the baptism of repentance for the remission of sins.

This is the first place that all the Synoptics parallel together (Mat. 3:3; Mark 1:3; Luke 3:4). Notice, though the Synoptics correlate at this point, it is only Luke that continues with an extra two verses of the Old Testament prophecy (3:5-6).

Though Matthew and Mark go on to complement each other, at this our next intersection, and that much of their wording is similar, however they do not have the same order regarding their details of the crowds that came to John the Baptist, his clothing, and diet.

Matthew mentions John the Baptist's attire and diet (3:4), before that of Mark, and the crowds afterwards (vv. 5-6). Whereas Mark mentions the crowds first (1:5), and then John's attire, and diet (v. 6).

Of course this does not contradict the actual individual reporting of the details of these same events, but reveals only a different way in structuring the wording of the sentences. We have indicated when this happens throughout this book.

Matthew 3:5-6 Mark 1:5
And then there went out to him all the land of Judea, and they of Jerusalem, and all the region round about Jordan, and were all baptized of him in the river Jordan, confessing their sins.
Matthew 3:4 Mark 1:6
And the same John had his clothing of camel's hair, and a leather girdle of skin about his loins; and the food he ate was locusts and wild honey.

Matthew 3:7 Luke 3:7
But then he said to the crowds who came forward to be baptized of him, when he saw many of the Pharisees and Sadducees come to his baptism, he addressed them, "Oh generation of vipers, who has warned you to flee from the wrath to come?
Matthew 3:8-9 Luke 3:8
Therefore bear fruits worthy of repentance, and don't begin to think and say within yourselves, 'We have Abraham as our father:' for I say to you, that God is able of these stones to raise up children to Abraham.
Matthew 3:10 Luke 3:9
And now also the axe is laid to the root of the trees: therefore every tree which doesn't bear good fruit is cut down, and cast into the fire."

Because Mark's narration of the event had followed directly after Luke's unique dialogue (3:5-6), we chose to continue with Mark's order in his sentence structure, so as not to unnecessarily break the flow of his last sentence (1:4), with the mentioning above of the crowds first (v. 5).

Luke 3
10 And the people asked him, "What shall we do then?"
11 He answered and said to them, "Those who have two coats, let them give to

those who have none; and they who have food, let them do likewise."

12 Then came also the tax collectors to be baptized, and said to him, "Master, what shall we do?"
13 And he said to them, "Exact no more than that which is appointed you."

14 And the soldiers likewise demanded of him, saying, "And what shall we do?" And he said to them, "Extort from no one by violence, neither, neither accuse anyone wrongfully; and be content with your wages."

15 And as the people were in expectation, and everyone mused in their hearts of John, whether he were the Messiah, or not;
Matthew 3:11 Mark 1:7-8 Luke 3:16
John answered and preached, saying to them all,
"I indeed baptize you with water to repentance: but He who comes after me is mightier than I, the lace of whose sandals I am not worthy to stoop down and unloose, whose sandals I am not worthy to carry: indeed I have baptized you with water: but He shall baptize you with the Holy Spirit, and with fire:
Matthew 3:12 Luke 3:17
whose fan is in His hand, and He will thoroughly purge His floor, and will gather His wheat into His garner; but the chaff He will burn up with fire unquenchable."

A characteristic of Matthew's style of writing, is that of different phraseology, which is firstly seen in the dialogue where John the Baptist describes Jesus' preeminence, and the role of Jesus' part in baptism (Mat. 3:11; Mark 1:7-8; Luke 3:16).

In Mat. 3:11, the meaning of the Greek original is that of '*carrying*' sandals, not of '*unloosening*' them, as Mark (1:7) and Luke (3:16) portray. Matthew chose to recall the single idea of carrying, whereas the other two related solely to the undoing. Thus, we have the correlated emphasis of the two expressions, when they are read together, of what the Baptist was trying to get across to his audience - '*the Light*' (John 1:7) who '*was before me*' (v. 15).

Mark and Luke are two witnesses, both whom are united in their source of phraseology regarding the '*unloosening*' of the sandals. The Gospel of John refers to that aspect too (1:27). Thus, because of this dominant factor in the reference to '*unloose*' the sandals, we have placed the '*unloosening*' first, before that of '*carrying*'. Moreover, the act of '*unloosening*' would naturally precede that of carrying, and grammatically it makes better sense. However, the reference in John, as we shall see, is relating to a different incident later, when Jesus had already been baptized, and is after the forty days and nights in the wilderness. Shortly we will see this characteristic of different phraseology in

26

Matthew again, with the '*voice from Heaven*'.

John was the messenger who was preparing the way ahead of Jesus, and technically, if he wasn't worthy even to bend down to unloosen the laces of Jesus' sandals, let alone carry them, what should be the attitude of others.

John 1

15 John bore witness of Him, and cried, saying,

"This was He of whom I spoke (Mat. 3:11; Mark 1:7; Luke 3:16), '*He who comes after me is preferred before Me: for He was before me.*'

16 And of His fullness we have all received, even grace upon grace.

17 The Law was given through Moses, and grace and truth came through Jesus the Messiah.

18 No one has seen God at any time; the only begotten Son, who is in the heart of the Father, He has declared Him."

Luke 3

18 And many other things in his exhortation he preached to the people.

Notice at this point how the Gospel of John, with his style of writing in the beginning of his first chapter, begins with the Word, and enlightenment (vv. 1-5). He then shifts to the Baptist bearing witness of that factor (vv. 6-8), along with the second time, pointing back to the Light - the Messiah (vv. 9-14). Then, lastly at this our intersection, again to the Baptist, but now quotes him actually teaching the Messiah, at his baptisms (vv. 15-18).

The Baptist taught at his exhortations, and testified, teaching the subject matter just as explicitly as the Gospel of John had outlined in its first chapter, including teaching that Jesus was before him (v. 15).

The Synoptics had recorded that the Baptist had spoken on the pre-eminence of Jesus (Mat. 3:11; Mark 1:7; Luke 3:16), before that where John 1:15 mentions it. Thus, revealing that where the Baptist had said, '*This was He of whom I spoke*', meant that the Baptist had taught aspects of the first chapter of John previously. Hence, the positioning of the texts.

Since the Gospel of John quotes the Baptist actually in speech from and including John 1:15, we have favored the style of combining the three following verses of John (vv. 16-18) in quotation marks, as part of what the Baptist would have taught about the Messiah. Moreover, there is no indication of a change in the dialogue until v. 19, which we shall see was six weeks later, after Jesus' baptism, and the forty days and nights in the wilderness. Consider how fittingly Luke concludes the discourse on the subject (3:18).

Though Luke mentions in his following verses (19-20), about the Baptist's reproval of Herod Antipas Tetrarch of Galilee, and his subsequent imprisonment, his imprisonment does not occur at this intersection. Luke is bringing our attention to how John's preaching reached the hierarchy in the land, at the very start of his mission, and should be better placed in brackets.

Additionally he is showing us that John was at least imprisoned twice, as the second time caused his death. We cover this later on, in its proper setting to which it relates to. Moreover, it is clear from the context of the Synoptics relating to the following event of Jesus' baptism, after this intersection, where John baptizes Jesus, that he was not in prison yet (Mat. 3:13; Mark 1:9; Luke 3:21).

With the next event of Jesus' baptism, when studying in the main *Scripture Graph*, we see that between each spring time in which Passover occurred, and each autumn wherein Tabernacles took place, naturally there would have been summers seasons in which Pentecost also fell. This is further alluded to by virtue that there would have been four autumn Festivals of Tabernacles in Jesus' 3½ year or 42 month ministry. Additionally this whole period would also have included four winters, after which would follow spring and one more Passover. However, though the Passover is specifically mentioned only three times in the text surrounding Jesus' ministry, nonetheless, through deduction, we can see there would have been four inherent, in the whole period of His ministry.

Hence when considering all the consecutive places throughout this book dealing with the Day of Pentecost and its sublime symbolism, we should see that Jesus' ministry would have begun in the autumn, and that consequently He would have been baptized several months previous to that, in that case in summer, no doubt on the very Day of Pentecost itself - having been baptized not only by water, but in the Holy Spirit too. The summer seasons that Pentecost is found in is touched upon throughout this book in the prescribed successive places of the main text that deals with that particular time of year. Including firstly, prior to the start of Jesus' ministry in the first summer, and in the conclusion of His ministry in the last summer, ten days after the Ascension, with the beginning of the New Testament Church, in the book of Acts. Within that period altogether, there are five summer seasons in which we comment on the association of this day with the Holy Spirit combining the whole period preceding Jesus' ministry and the conclusion of His ministry.

5   *JESUS PREPARES FOR HIS MISSION*

Jesus' Baptism

Matthew 3:13 Mark 1:9a Luke 3:21a
And now it came to pass in those days, when all the people were baptized, Jesus also came from Nazareth of Galilee, to Jordon to John, to be baptized of him.
Matthew 3
14 But John forbade Him, saying,
"I have need to be baptized of You, and You come to me?"
15 And Jesus answering said to him,
"Allow it now to be so: for in this way it is also right for us to fulfill all righteousness."
He then allowed Him.
Matthew 3:16 Mark 1:9b-10 Luke 3:21b-22a
And Jesus, when He was being baptized of John in Jordan prayed, and immediately went up directly out of the water: and praying, suddenly, He saw the heavens were opened to Him, and saw the Holy Spirit of God descending in a bodily shape, like a dove, alighting upon Him.

The following main text is the second place where Matthew, in the style we mentioned back at our third intersection from this one, uses different phraseology again when quoting the '*voice from Heaven*' (3:17), than that of Mark (1:11) and Luke (3:22b). We have placed the two renderings accordingly, as they would have made sense to Jesus, the audience, and of course especially to us.

Luke chose the event of Jesus' baptism to indicate that Jesus was beginning to approach thirty years of age (3:23c). We had considered in the section, *The Annunciations* (pp. 8-13) that Jesus would have been born in autumn.

Thus, moreover, Luke had also in the beginning of his genealogy linked Jesus' age in the same sentence as indicating Joseph as the son of Heli (v. 23a). Furthermore, Luke recorded that Jesus was the supposed son of Joseph (v. 23b). Hence, because of Luke's ascending genealogy, and because we have reverted it into correlation with Matthew's shorter descending genealogical list, it was necessary to place a, b, and c, at the three distinct successive antecedents relating to Luke's sentence.

Matthew 3:17a Mark 1:11 Luke 3:22b
And, suddenly, there came a voice from Heaven, saying, "You are My beloved Son, in You I am well-pleased,"
Matthew 3
17b which, then said, "This is My beloved Son, in whom I am well-pleased."
Luke 3
23c And Jesus Himself began to be about thirty years of age.

THE TEMPTATION

Matthew 4:1 Mark 1:12 Luke 4:1
And Jesus being full of the Holy Spirit returned from Jordan, and then immediately the Spirit, which led up Jesus, drove Him into the wilderness, to be tempted of the Devil.
Matthew 4:2 Mark 1:13a Luke 4:2
And He was there in the wilderness forty days, tempted of Satan the Devil; and was with the wild animals; and in those days He did eat nothing: and when He had fasted forty days and nights, when they were ended, afterwards He was hungry.

When some compare the texts of Matthew and Luke regarding the Temptation, they seem to see a glaring contradiction in the order of the phraseology. If one reads the texts separately, it would seem superficially that this is the case. However, when understanding the characteristic way Matthew writes, the problem dissolves, when placing the verses together in their natural order of successive sense, and meaning. It becomes self-evident, as to what was said when, and to what transpired first.

Once more we see in correlating the texts, there is no contradiction as the meaning unfolds, only an emphasizing of expression, accentuation, and recall, as touched upon previously in regards to Matthew's particular style of phraseology.

Matthew 4:3 Luke 4:3
And when the Devil, the Tempter came to Him, he said to Him,
"If You be the Son of God, command that these stones - this stone, that it be made bread."
Matthew 4:4 Luke 4:4
But Jesus answered him, and said,
"It is written (Deut. 8:3), 'THAT ONE SHALL NOT LIVE BY BREAD ALONE, BUT BY EVERY WORD THAT PROCEEDS OUT OF THE MOUTH OF GOD.'"

Luke 4
5 And the Devil, taking Him up onto a high mountain, shows to Him all the kingdoms of the world in a moment of time.
6 And the Devil said to Him,
"All this power will I give You, and the glory of them: for that is delivered to me; and to whoever I will give it.
7 If You therefore will worship me, all this shall be Yours."
8 And Jesus answered and said to him,
"You get behind Me, Satan: for it is written (Deut. 6:13),
'YOU SHALL WORSHIP THE LORD YOUR GOD, AND HIM ONLY SHALL YOU SERVE.'"

Matthew 4:5-6a Luke 4:9
And then the Devil takes Him up to the Holy city, Jerusalem, and sets Him on a pinnacle of the Temple, and says to Him,
"If You be the Son of God, cast Yourself down from here:
Matthew 4:6b Luke 4:10
for it is written (Ps. 91:11-12), 'HE SHALL GIVE HIS ANGELS CHARGE CONCERNING YOU, TO KEEP YOU:
Matthew 4:6c Luke 4:11
AND IN THEIR HANDS THEY SHALL BEAR YOU UP, LEST AT ANY TIME YOU DASH YOUR FOOT AGAINST A STONE .'"
Matthew 4:7 Luke 4:12
And Jesus answering said to him,
"Again it is written, and said (Deut. 6:16), 'YOU SHALL NOT TEMPT THE LORD YOUR GOD'"
Matthew 4
8 Again, the Devil takes Him up onto an extremely high mountain, and shows Him all the kingdoms of the world, and the glory of them;
9 and says to Him, "All these things will I give You, if You will fall down and worship me."

Notice how Matthew mentions in v. 8, after his last conjunction with Luke, '*again, the Devil takes Him up*', but this time, '*onto an extremely high mountain*'. Jesus had just previously, experienced the first scenario up '*a high mountain*' (Luke 4:5), directly after the Devil's suggestion over the bread (Mat. 4:3-4; Luke 4:3-4).

Note the verbal differences between the two accounts of the high mountain - they are not the same. The second scenario on the high mountain, is further accentuated by the added word, '*extremely*', as being higher than the previous one, and as indicative to increased pressure, but now, in a different '*heightened*' scenario. Several times we have referred to this characteristic style of Matthew's phraseology.

Real testing through temptation is not much of one, if it only occurs once. If different pressures on a similar and then the crux issue are tried again and again, we can then say it was a complete trial.

As Satan knew he could not tempt Jesus over the first part of the trial, which related to the simplest most natural tendency, after being without food for '*forty days and nights*', he knew then he must turn to the key issue of governance, the reason for Jesus being on earth.

Thus the pressure and craftiness being applied by Satan subtlety, over the question of Jesus' rulership, had to be one that He was tested the most on.

Through the first test on the mountain, Jesus is shown all the kingdoms '*in a moment of time*' (Luke 4:5-6). Satan knew that if this didn't work, he could put heightened pressure on Jesus by further illustrating and re-emphasizing '*the glory of them*' (Mat. 4:8), rather than in the first scene, which was pictured as taking '*a moment of time*'.

Furthermore, in the first mountain scenario of Luke (4:5-8), Jesus said, '*You get behind Me, Satan*' - indicating Jesus' resolve, and superiority over Satan, and also that the trial was yet to continue, synchronizing further with Matthew over the scenario at the Temple in Jerusalem (Mat. 4:5-6; Luke 4:9-11).

Hence Luke (4:12) curtailed his version of the trial, in correlating with Matthew (4:7), with Jesus' third quote from Deuteronomy (6:16). Whereas, in the final part of the test, in Matthew, Jesus says, '*Get away*' (4:10), and reemphasizes again the same Scripture (Deut. 6:13). He had previously spoken at Luke's first scenario of the high mountain, thus closing and concluding the trial, knowing He had overcome this psychophysical battle with Satan.

Matthew 4

10 Then Jesus says to him,

"Get away, Satan; for it is written (Deut.6;13), 'YOU SHALL WORSHIP THE LORD YOUR GOD, AND HIM ONLY SHALL YOU SERVE.'"

Matthew 4:11 Mark 1:13b Luke 4:13

And when the Devil had completed every temptation, then the Devil leaving departed from Him for a season, and, suddenly, the angels came and ministered to Him.

Notice, how after the combined dialogue of Matthew and Luke on the Temptation, Mark has only one verse on the subject (1:13), simply mentioning the forty days in the wilderness (v. 13a), and the conclusion of the Temptation (v. 13b). However, all the Synoptics correlate together in the conclusion after the detail of Jesus' baptism and trial in the wilderness.

One could argue, that Mark's shorter version of the event refers to the angels at the beginning of Jesus' trial? Of course. But if we realize that the angels are always pictured as being close at hand anyway, then it becomes clear, it was intended by both the dialogue of Matthew (4:11) and Mark (1:13b), to correlate the narratives of the angels at the end of the trial, in showing us Jesus needed the ministering of the angels at that precise moment, in relation to His overcoming of Satan, and His need for food and drink, after the forty days and nights. Luke does not mention the angels (4:13).

Mark, at some places in his Gospel, has the characteristic style of curtailed references to some of the events, but, nevertheless focuses in on them with a few key words, as shown in the above mentioned example. We have indicated when that occurs throughout this book.

The next following event is after Jesus has overcome Satan, and has returned from the wilderness, where He proceeds with the calling of His first disciples, and His mission of spreading the gospel.

It is the Gospel of John that continues with these details, though he did not record Jesus' baptism. Nevertheless, he fills in with the event of Jesus arriving back after the *'forty days and forty nights'* in the Judean wilderness.

We shall discover, in actual fact, one of John's other reasons in writing, was to leave a record that did not conflict with the Synoptics, with his characteristic style of writing, having as it were, a different intensity of understanding regarding certain detail than the others.

Additionally, he was the disciple who gave us the real start of events, before the universe and our earth was brought into existence (1:1-2), and the only disciple who stated the actual point at which Jesus' miracles began (2:11).

Furthermore, he had had revealed to himself the most mysterious and intriguing of all books of the Bible - the book of Revelation - the concluding book of the Bible. Thus, he became the beginner and the finisher of the gospel, and in that sense an organizer of various detail that was in between, as he mentions certain days more than any of the Synoptics, and the hours of the day in relationship to certain pivotal events.

He was also the disciple who made sure he recorded for us three Passover Festivals (2:13; 6:4; 13:1), one Festival of Tabernacles (7:2), another Festival (5:1), which we shall see was also a Festival of Tabernacles - making two, and mentions the Festival of Rededication of the Temple (10:22). All which align with the three Synoptics, so as to keep the record in successive order.

John prolifically recorded for us much of the personal dialogue of Jesus, especially regarding the detailed conversations that took place in the evening of the last Passover.

John was also the apostle who outlived all the other original apostles, and was *'the disciple whom Jesus loved'* (21:20), in a special relationship, different in a way to the others. Also many believe he was the disciple personally known by the High Priest (18:15-16).

Throughout his Gospel though he does not mention himself by name, but either alludes he was one of *'the sons of Zebedee'* (21:2), or *'the disciple whom Jesus loved'*.

We continue now, with the narrative of the Gospel of John, and his record of various days within his text at this time, after Jesus had returned to Bethabara, having being baptized there over "*forty days and nights*" previously.

While Jesus had returned from the Judean wilderness after His baptism and trial, the Baptist is still baptizing at Bethabara (1:28). Jesus is there amongst the audience of people (v. 26), which included Priests and Levite Pharisees from Jerusalem (vv. 19, 24), having no doubt returned after forty-two days in all, when allowing for His traveling to and from the Judean wilderness.

We shall see that with forty-two [42 months] figuring in Jesus' 3½ year ministry up to His resurrection, that also there would be forty-two miracles up to His resurrection. Moreover, there would transpire forty-two days with Jesus' return from the wilderness, after which He would begin calling the first disciples.

Furthermore, as this book reveals, there are fifty miracles associated with Jesus' whole ministry prior to the Ascension. We shall also see there are fifty days revealed at the point, which Jesus' first miracle occurred, prior to the start of His ministry (pp. 46-48).

However, returning to the day that Jesus came back from the wilderness, we see that great pressure was now building up in regards to the Baptist from the authorities. Directly after Jesus left for Galilee, Herod would imprison John. As Jesus' mission was about to begin, so the Baptist's would subsequently wane.

THE NEXT DAY

John 1

19 And this is the record of John, when the Jews sent Priests and Levites from Jerusalem to ask him, "Who are you?"
20 And he confessed, and didn't deny; but confessed, "I am not the Messiah."

21 And they asked him, "What then? Are you Elijah?"
And he says, "I am not."
"Are you the Prophet?"
And he answered, "No."

22 Then they said to him, "Who are you, so that we may give an answer to those who sent us? What do you say of yourself?"
23 He said, "I am THE VOICE OF ONE CRYING IN THE WILDERNESS, 'MAKE STRAIGHT THE WAY OF THE LORD,' as the prophet Isaiah said (40:3)."

24 And they whom were sent were of the Pharisees.
25 And they asked him, and said to him, "Why baptize then, if you are not the Messiah, nor Elijah, neither the Prophet?"
26 John answered them, saying,
"I baptize with water: but there stands One among you, whom you don't know;
27 He it is, who coming after me is preferred before me, whose sandal lace I am not worthy to unloose."

28 These things were done in Bethabara beyond Jordan, where John was baptizing.

Notice John the Baptist's repeating again of the unloosening of sandal lace (v. 27), which we covered at pp. 26-27, and the next day after the first day of Jesus' return, the Baptist declares that he had seen the Spirit descending on Him previously, which would have been six weeks, as we shall see, and two days earlier (vv. 32-33).

Since the above dialogue is in the context of one day (vv. 19-28), relating to Jesus' returning from the wilderness, after the '*forty days and nights*', allowing a day for Jesus' returning, and another when He departed after His baptism, therefore at least forty-two days must have transpired.

Furthermore it is mentioned that Jesus was staying somewhere near to Bethabara (vv. 38-39), so, allowing for His return from the wilderness, and His composure in recovering from the trial, the dialogue where Jesus had already returned (vv. 19-28) and was standing amongst the Pharisees (v. 26) would be the day after Jesus refreshed Himself, renewed in vigor for the beginning phase of His mission, which also prefigures to the resurrection, the forty-third miracle. We can then count this first day as the forty-third.

We shall see the significance of John's recording of these days, when coming to Jesus' first miracle in the next chapter.

Meanwhile, following the '*next day*' that John was keen to point out would have been the forty-fourth (v. 29).

At v. 35, John indicates yet another day. Thus, this would have been the forty-fifth day.

John 1

29 The next day John sees Jesus coming to him, and says,
"Look the Lamb of God, who takes away the sin of the world."
30 This is He of whom I said (vv. 15, 27),
'*After me comes a Man who is preferred before me: for He was before me*'.
31 And I didn't recognize Him: but that He should be made manifest to Israel, therefore am I come baptizing with water."

32 And John bore record, saying,
"I saw the Spirit descending from the heavens like a dove, and it alighted upon Him (Mat. 3:16; Mark 1:10; Luke 3:22).
33 And I didn't recognize Him: but He who sent me to baptize with water, the same said to me, '*Upon whom you shall see the Spirit descending, and remaining on Him, the same is He whom baptizes with the Holy Spirit* (Mat. 3:11; Mark 1:8; Luke 3:16).'
34 And I saw and bore record that this is the Son of God."

6 JESUS BEGINS TO CALL HIS DISCIPLES

THE FIRST DISCIPLES

John had made a special point of recording various days throughout his text, with four days suggested, by the way he had laid out the detail in the first chapter. We had suggested Jesus had returned to Bethabara on the forty-third day from being in the wilderness, in allowing for travel and recuperation at the place where He was lodging (1:38-39). We had also suggested that the forty-third miracle of Jesus' resurrection, typified and related to the returning from the wilderness, in the sense that both events had to do with returning to life, and new beginnings.

The last day mentioned in the text of John's first chapter (v. 43), actually would be the fourth since Jesus' return to Bethabara, and in returning back to Galilee, the forty-sixth since Jesus' baptism. The day preceding the forty-sixth, below (v. 35), obviously would be the forty-fifth, and the third day since Jesus' return to Bethabara.

On this third day, with the first three disciples finding the Messiah (vv. 40-41), there is another significant factor, as it is Simon that Jesus names *Cephas* [Stone], or Peter (v. 42), at this point in concluding that day (v. 39), which would be the forty-fifth since Jesus' baptism. When considering the findings of this book where Jesus appeared to Peter after the resurrection, we see that the factor of forty-five is evident again in regards to Peter, as it would have been the forty-fifth miracle.

John 1

35 Again the next day after, John stood, and two of his disciples;

36 and looking upon Jesus as He walked, he says, "Look the Lamb of God!"

37 And the two disciples heard him speak, and they followed Jesus.

38 Then Jesus turned, and saw them following, and says to them,
"What are you looking for?"
They said to Him, "Rabbi, (which is to say, being translated, Master,) where are You staying?"
39 He says to them, "Come and see.

They came and saw where He lodged, and stayed with Him that that day; for it was about 4 p.m.
40 One of the two, who heard John speak, and followed Him, was Andrew, Simon Peter's brother.

41 He first finds his own brother Simon, and says to him,
"We have found the Messiah" (which translated is the Anointed One).

John 1

42 And He brought him to Jesus. And when Jesus looked at him, He said, "You are Simon the son of Jonas: you shall be called Cephas" (which translatd is Stone).

As we mentioned in the section, *The Returning From the Wilderness* (p. 33), John had not referred to himself throughout his Gospel directly by name. But, as is generally understood, indicated it subtly, as in the first instance, in the beginning of his Gospel, when he relates to himself with Andrew, Simon's brother, as, '*one of the two*' disciples of the Baptist (vv. 37, 40). Moreover, in closing his Gospel he reveals himself as '*the disciple whom Jesus loved... who also leaned on His chest at Supper*' (21:20), and testified that he was the same disciple who wrote the Gospel of John (v. 24).

Also, in the section, *All the Women Tell the Apostles* (pp. 406-410), we see how John [along with Peter] was one of the first apostles who had believed when he saw the empty tomb at the resurrection (20:8-9).

Similarly, he was also the first disciple who believed Jesus was the Messiah, when he, and Andrew, first saw '*the Lamb of God*', as pointed out by the Baptist (1:36). Though, John in recording the event gave the credit to Andrew in relating Andrew's words, '*We have found the Messiah*' (vv. 40-41).

Hence, John purposely wrote, averring to himself (v. 37), indicating that Andrew (v. 40), Simon (v. 41), Philip and Nathanael (v. 45), including himself, were five Galilean disciples of the Baptist in the first chapter, before that where Matthew and Mark depict the disciples later on. John deliberately placed the order of these disciples, as being away from the Galilee area. Whereas Matthew (4:12-22) and Mark (1:14-20) only relate to four disciples, Peter, Andrew, including James, and in that instance with John [the Gospel writer], at Galilee.

Simon had already been '*called Peter*', when the five returned to Galilee (Mat. 4:18), from Bethabara! Luke does not mention the five disciples being first called at Bethabara, or later when the four disciples left their fishing business to go with Jesus, but writes presupposing we should know that fact (4:14).

Likewise with John referring to these four days, and five disciples, in a way, he was assuming that we would know what these disciples, other than being with the Baptist, were doing away from Galilee, and at the same time away from their homes, and in Bethabara. Of course they followed the Baptist when time allowed. But, nevertheless, they had their ordinary livelihoods to contend with, as it was not until they actually started traveling with Jesus that they obviously followed the the Baptist whenever they could.

But if we consider that the disciples were Jew, and were interested in the prophecies regarding the Messiah (John 1:41), then it would not be strange if they came down from Galilee with the other pilgrims for certain days in the Jewish Calendar commemorative of days contemporary with Jewish history.

However, we can deduce, if we count backwards, what time of year it may have been, when these five disciples were with the Baptist. Since the Gospel of John gives us the Passover as being the first Festival that he specially mentions in his second chapter (v. 13), anything before that factor would obviously refer to the preceding spring. The findings of this book indicate, when we come to the sections dealing with the particular references before John 2:13, that Jesus would have begun His gospel mission in the autumn, in the season associated with the Festival of Tabernacles.

Also since the findings of this book indicate that Jesus' public ministry lasted three and a half years up until the last Passover, and in that case counting back, would bring us, when we consider that three and a half years also equals forty-two months, to the first Festival of Tabernacles. Moreover, the Gospel of John reveals, as touched upon previously in the last chapter (p. 33), three separate Passovers, during which time the events would cover a period of three years.

Furthermore, as also already referred to back in the last section (p. 33) the Gospel of John alludes to two Tabernacles within its text, and mentions a Festival of Rededication, as we shall eventually see for the specific reason of helping to indicate order to the successive events, and the narration in his Gospel.

Since we shall see that anything preceding John 2:13 covers a winter and an autumn and that any time before the autumn obviously must be summer, we can consider what Jewish commemorative days would fall at that time.

Now, we covered the forty days and nights in the wilderness, directly after Jesus' baptism, and the four days that were recorded in the text of John's first chapter, proceeding with Jesus, return to Bethabara, and suggested a further two days allowing for the completion of the two journeys to and from Bethabara. Also, we saw the factor of forty-two becoming predominate, when considering the forty-two miracles up to the resurrection, and the forty-two months [3½ years] of Jesus' public ministry. Thus, the forty-two days before Jesus returned to Bethabara would be six weeks, and relates to the time of year we are considering.

However, the Gospel of John had specifically revealed five disciples, including Jesus, all from Galilee staying in the region of Bethabara, which was the most appropriate place near to Jerusalem where there was sufficient water for the Baptist's mission at that particular time

Though the AV has Bethabara in its text, meaning *'place of passage, or ford'*, which description reflects the name of the area when the children of Israel originally came across with Joshua, nevertheless most translations have Bethany, which is an alternate name for the same place. However, where Bethabara was situated was known in Origen's day (c.AD250), and other ancient manuscripts also used that name.

Geographers, in *The Times Concise Atlas Of The Bible* [1991] p. 116, now establish Bethabara on Israel's side of the Jordan, without any question mark placed behind it, as had been the case in various atlases previously. In considering the word *'beyond'*

[Gr. *peran*], where translations have '*Bethany*' or '*Bethabara beyond Jordan*' (John 1:28), when we come to the section of this book, *They Leave For Samaria* (pp. 206 -207), we see that the word '*beyond*' also means over the west side of Jordan, on Israel's side. However, the same geographers also place a Bethany east of Jordan albeit with a question mark, associating it with Aenon, where the Baptist also baptized. Nevertheless, we shall see that Aenon was near to Bethshean or Scythopolis in the section of this book entitled, *Escape to Aeon Near Salim* (pp. 260-265).

In Jesus being baptized at Bethabara, or Bethany, in the area where the children of Israel came across, there is further significance in that Jesus went into the Judean wilderness from there and conquered the wiles of Satan, after having considered the kingdoms of this world. Also Joshua with the Israelites that came across progressed further into the Promised Land from there, after having taken account of the people living in that land. Moreover, Jesus gave Peter another name, having called the first disciples there. Thus, initiating the gospel from that particular point, in beginning to organize and teach His disciples, progressing further with the gospel throughout that land, and subsequently to the rest of the world.

Now, in understanding that these disciples had found Jesus, as they were seeking the Messiah, and consequently became His disciples from that point, Jesus even giving Simon [Peter] another name, and that they were to return to Galilee (1:43), before Jesus set up His base at Capernaum, from where they would shortly circuit Galilee with the first phase of the gospel in autumn, and that the months preceding autumn contained certain Jewish days in which certain historical events had transpired, it would not be strange if the disciples had come from Galilee at this time, with the Baptist baptizing in the area too.

Jesus also had come from Galilee, though He was baptized, over six weeks and had returned to Bethabara, and met the Baptist's disciples, who became His disciples. disciples. Now, the Jewish months of Tammuz [June-July] and Av [July-August] in the summer reveal this a time in which certain disasters occurred.

In the days of the First Temple, the walls of Jerusalem were finally breached on the 9th Tammuz (2 Kings 25:3-4), by the armies of the Babylonian king Nebuchadnezzar. Also, four other disasters are recorded to have occurred on the 17th Tammuz: Moses after receiving the Decalogue on the Day of Pentecost [as Jewish tradition avers], returned after forty days and nights, and broke them: the continual burnt offerings ceased during the siege of Jerusalem: and Apostomos, a Syrian officer, burnt the scrolls of the Torah and set up an idol in the Sanctuary [*Mishnah Taanith* iv, 6]: and lastly, though Jews in that time and the disciples would not yet be aware of the final disaster, tragically once again the walls of Jerusalem would be breached, and on this occasion on the 17thTammuz in AD70.

Three weeks after the 17th Tammuz on the 9th Av, the First Temple was destroyed by Nebuchadnezzar [586BC]. In addition, on this particular day the *Mishnah* reveals God sentencing the older generation of Israelites so that they would not enter the Promised Land (Num. 14:29). Also, at this time when the first disciples were called, and forty-three years later on, in this same day in AD70, Titus destroyed the Second Temple. However, before that, the days surrounding the destruction of the First Temple would nevertheless be poignant in the minds of any Jews, including the disciples, who were concerned with the Messiah, and the further possibility of any negative or positive fulfillment in the light of prophetical happenings associated within the Old Testament.

John began his Gospel with the Word, predating any physical history, and then went on to relate straight to Jesus and the message of the Baptist, focusing us into the first day to the scenario where Jesus had returned from His baptism, after the forty days and in the mountainous Judean wilderness. This was reminiscent and similar to Moses, where he had also spent the same amount of time in the wilderness. However, Moses in the first instance broke the Commandments and was afterwards pardoned and thus obtained grace, after which he had to return up the mountain for yet another forty days and nights, subsequently receiving further revelations, and returning again with the Commandments, but, now in a positive light.

Before Moses went up the mountain for the second forty days and nights, he prays to God regarding grace for himself, and the people. Five times the word grace [Heb. *chen*] is used by Moses (Ex. 33:12-15, 16-17).

Furthermore, John, in his Gospel, refers to Jesus as the one who is responsible for grace, and also the only one who could completely declare anything relating to the Father (1:17-18).

The Gospel of John, in revealing what the Baptist taught at his baptisms, also referred to "*grace upon grace*" (1:16), and relates to the same particular theme of grace after Moses had delivered the Law.

It is significant to reflect here on the number five which is also the number of grace, and as outlined by the the eminent scholar EW Bullinger in his book, *NUMBER IN SCRIPTURE* on pp. 135-149, and consider that John deliberately leads us into the first five disciples being present when John the Baptist was baptizing.

Moreover, with these themes John brings us up to the record of the first day where Jesus had returned from the wilderness, after His forty-day and night stay (1:19, 26).

Thus, the similarities between Moses and Jesus, the characteristic of grace, the factor of also five disciples, the same time of year associated with these incidents, with Jesus having overcome any temptation in not allowing Himself to become negative in returning to the people after His baptism at Bethabara, and the forty nights, is profoundly and symbolically entwined in the first chapter of John.

Hence, Jesus for the forty days and nights would have spent the time in communion with God, with reflection on the next phase of His work - the calling of His first disciples, who would make up the New Temple, which the Gospel of John was pointing out in the beginning chapter, as Moses had also during the first forty days and nights received instruction on the construction of the Tabernacle-'Temple', and the details surrounding it.

So at this time when the events associated with the original Tabernacle, or 'Tent-Temple', including the First Temple that Solomon built, which subsequently had been destroyed at the same time of year we are considering, and now reflecting on the Second Temple, which was still standing at this particular point, naturally the disciples and the people, would be considering factors relating to the Messiah too. Therefore, John the Baptist consequently highlighted the change of attitude that was required at his baptisms, including the same message at Bethabara at this specific instance, in receiving grace, along with the grace of God being needed at this particular time, in allowing the Temple to remain standing.

Thus, the people, the Pharisees (1:19-20) and the Baptist's disciples were seeking subsequent knowledge about the Messiah (v. 41), in relationship to any prophecies that might be forthcoming, which of necessity would relate to the Temple too. Consequently the prophet Zechariah, had mentioned this time, and prophesied that *'the fast of the fourth month* [17th Tammuz], *and the fast of the fifth month'* [9th Av], would be turned into Festivals of *'joy and gladness, and cheerful Festivals'* (Zech. 8:19), rather than times of solemn sadness.

At this time, Jesus had started calling the first five disciples, who would make up the new phase of the Spiritual Temple, and thus with the new excitement over them having found the Messiah, they started on their return journey to Galilee (John 1:43). Furthermore, in the next following chapter of John, at the first Passover of Jesus' ministry, which Festival is symbolic of freedom from sin, and purity, John shows Jesus purging the Temple (2:13-16), and then relating to the aspect that the body was the foremost Temple (vv. 19-21).

Earlier, we had considered that on their return journey to Galilee, it would have been the forty-sixth day, after Jesus' baptism, or four days after His return to Bethabara, after the forty days and nights in the wilderness, when allowing two days for traveling, from Bethabara and in returning. Interestingly enough in v. 20, there is mention relating to the building of the Second Temple and, of the factor of forty-six.

We should bear in mind at this particular point, as Jesus is about to return to Galilee with His new disciples, and when also taking all the factors given in the following sections, including, *The Baptist Released* (pp. 68-71) and *John's Death* (pp. 156-157), along with the next successive section, *John Imprisoned* (p. 43), it was at this specific juncture that the Baptist would be first taken prisoner, as his preaching was beginning to upset certain in the hierarchy, as well as irritating Herod more. This first imprisonment was four days after a delegation from Jerusalem had questioned him, when Jesus was inconspicuous that first day amongst the crowds, from His return to John at Bethabara (1:19, 26).

It is clear from Mark that though Herod was perturbed over the Baptist, nevertheless, he '*feared him*', and had a kind of respect for him, and actually '*saved him*' according to the margins of some earlier translations, and '*protected him*' as many modern translation now render Mark 6:20. No doubt Herod only wanted to dampen the Baptist's zeal by alleviating the fears of those at the very top of the religious hierarchy in Jerusalem. As we shall see, in arresting John the first time, it did not quell or temper his message. Similar to Jesus, those few at the very top of the hierarchy preferred John dead, but did not mind if he was punished and stifled in prison. Although, conveniently coupled to this situation, was the fact that Herodias, actually wanted him dead. Herod, consequently, only put the Baptist in prison because of Herodias' continual requests (vv. 17, 19), and because of his unabated preaching, which would result in his final incarceration and subsequent death months later.

Hence, John the Baptist's mission was about to wane, and afterwards subsequently start decreasing, as Jesus was preparing for His to begin.

7   THE RETURNING TO GALILEE

JOHN IMPRISONED

We now return to the place where we left off in the Gospel of John in the previous section where Jesus and the five disciples were preparing to leave for their return journey to Galilee (1:43), after John, Andrew, and Peter had stayed with Jesus in Bethabara (vv. 39-42). We saw that it would now be the fourth day since Jesus' return from the wilderness, and the forty-sixth including the forty days and nights in allowing two other days for traveling.

Moreover, Jesus having given Simon a new name wishes to embark on the journey back to Galilee, with the five new disciples, who had been in the area of Bethabara witnessing the baptism of John.

Matthew (4:12) and Mark (1:14) having both acknowledged though briefly, that Jesus after the trial in the wilderness returned back to Galilee, did not mention the name of the place where Jesus and the disciples were staying, nevertheless, they indicated that it was at this moment that the Baptist was taken prisoner.

John, since he wrote his Gospel last, would have known of the details that Matthew and Mark had not recorded, and that Jesus had left for Galilee, after the Baptist was arrested as both of their Gospels indicate. Moreover, he would have also known, that Jesus having seen the Baptist on the forty-fifth day (1:35-36), presupposes we would understand, that where he mentions '*the day following*' (v. 43), where Jesus left for Galilee, that Jesus had already heard that John had been arrested and was no longer baptizing: he was paralleling and indicating with Matthew and Mark, that it was time for Jesus to start His mission as the Baptist's would eventually, as Jesus stepped up His, decrease.

Similarly Luke, like John, also presupposes we should understand that factor, and interjects with the information of the Baptist's imprisonment. Though these verses should be in brackets in their normal setting as mentioned previously at Luke 3:18. They should also include the two times the Baptist was imprisoned, as in the next verse (v. 21), the Baptist was baptizing Jesus before He left for the wilderness.

Luke 3
19 But Herod the Tetrarch, being reproved by him for Herodias his brother Philip's wife, and for all the evils which Herod had done,
20 added yet this above all, that he shut up John in prison.

THEY LEAVE FOR GALILEE

The Evangelist John, though much later, also has the Baptist baptizing again (3:23-24), obviously indicating that he was later let out of prison. However we shall see, when the Baptist was baptizing the last time, was in the next year, after the first Passover (2:23), and after Jesus' discourse with Nicodemus (3:1-22).

Some look at the one verse of John 3:24, wherein it states that the Baptist was not in prison at that particular point, as proof that the Gospel of John cannot be synchronized with the Synoptics. They do not grasp that this Scripture is referring to the scenario of that year, after the first Passover, where '*John was not yet* [finally] *cast into prison*' not meaning that he had never been imprisoned before.

Now the Synoptics graphically cover the actual execution of John much later in their texts (Mat. 14:1-12; Mark 6:14-29), though Luke (9:7-9) has a curtailed version, while the Gospel of John (5:35-36), again presupposes we should know that fact, only briefly averring to it.

Thus, where we saw that '*the day following*' (John 1:43), and in the parallel text below, wherein Jesus and the disciples hear of the Baptist's imprisonment and then return to Galilee, would be the forty-sixth, since Jesus' baptism.

We will further see, when the Gospel of John specifically points out **The First Miracle** (2:11), the complete reason for his characteristic style of writing in accentuating these days, and the beginning of Jesus' miracles, when we come to that section. As he had similarly pinpointed various considerations associated with beginnings in the subsequent first verses of his first chapter.

Matthew 4:12 Mark 1:14a John 1:43
Now when Jesus had heard, the day following, after that John was arrested and put into prison, He purposed to depart into Galilee, and finds Philip, and says to him, "Follow Me."
John 1
44 Now Philip was of Bethsaida, the city of Andrew and Peter.
45 Philip finds Nathanael, and says to him,
"We have found Him, of whom Moses in the Law, and the Prophets, did write, Jesus of Nazareth, the son of Joseph."
46 And Nathanael said to him,
"Can there any good thing come out of Nazareth?"
Philip says to him, "Come and see."

47 Jesus saw Nathanael coming to Him, and says of him,
"See an Israelite indeed, in whom is no deceit!"
48 Nathanael says to Him, "How do you know me?"
Jesus answered and said to him,
"Before Philip called you, when you were under the fig-tree, I saw you."

John 1

49 Nathanael answered and says to Him,
"Rabbi, You are the Son of God; You are the King of Israel."

50 Jesus answered and said to him, "Because I said to you, '*I saw you under the fig-tree*' (v. 48), you believe? You shall see greater things than these."
51 And He says to him, "Indeed, truthfully, I say to you, afterwards you shall SEE HEAVEN open, AND THE ANGELS OF GOD ASCENDING AND DESCENDING via the Son ofHumanity (Gen. 28:12)."

THE FIRST MIRCALE - WATER INTO WINE

Jesus and the five new disciples were now on their way to Galilee. But, before Jesus moved from Nazareth, His hometown, and set up base in Capernaum, from where He would start teaching from, He was to go to Cana, where He, His mother, and the disciples were to attend an important marriage ceremony. It was there that Jesus miraculously changed the water into wine, marking His first miracle, which John the Evangelist makes a point of recording (2:11).

Both Mark 1:14b and Luke 4:14a parallel at the traveling back to Galilee in one part of their verses. Whereas Mark's other part of his verse (1:14c), covers the actual point when Jesus came preaching the gospel. Luke 4:14b, stresses the fame that spread abroad in the concluding part of his verse. Matthew confirmed that Jesus left Nazareth and preached from Capernaum (4:13, 17).

Before that, the Gospel of John specifically pointed out that in returning to Galilee they were to attend a wedding in Cana (2:1), before Jesus made Capernaum His base from where He would continue with His mission (v. 12).

We include the rest of the verses, with Luke 4:14b and Mark 1:14c, in the place of their specific fulfillment, when Jesus actually reached Capernaum and starts on His mission from there a little later in the next section.

Now we return to Jesus and the new disciples journeying to Cana in Galilee to attend the wedding there, where the Gospel of John brings our attention to the factor that Jesus is about to embark on His mission by highlighting the first miracle (2:11).

Mark 1:14b Luke 4:14a

And Jesus returned in the Power of the Spirit, coming into Galilee.

John 2

1 And the third day there was a marriage in Cana of Galilee; and Jesus' mother was there:

John 2

2 and both Jesus was invited, and His disciples, to the marriage.

3 And when they needed wine, Jesus' mother says to Him, "They have no wine."
4 Jesus says to her, "Dearest woman, how this has to do with Me, as My time until now had not yet arrived."

5 His mother says to the servants, "Whatever He says to you do it."

6 And there were set there six water pots of stone, after the manner of the purifying of the Jews, containing twenty or thirty gallons apiece.
7 Jesus says to them, "Fill the water pots with water."
And they filled them up to the brim.
8 And He says to them, "Draw out now, and take to the host of the reception."
And they took it.

9 When the host of the reception had tasted the water that was made wine, and didn't know where it came from: (but the servants who drew the water knew); the host of the reception called the bridegroom,
10 and says to him, "Everyone at the beginning does set out good wine; and when they have drunk freely, then that which is lesser in quality: but you have kept the good wine until now!"

11 This beginning of miracles did Jesus in Cana of Galilee, and manifested effectively His glory; and His disciples believed on Him.
John 1
14b And we witnessed His glory, the glory as of the only begotten of the Father, full of grace and truth.

Directly above, John 1:14b has the second part of its verse, transposed to its first place of fulfillment, as the first part of verse (14a), was fulfilled when Jesus was born.

We saw that John had made a special point in recording various days throughout his narrative, and as Jesus and the five new disciples traveled back to Galilee, we see when looking at a map, that Nazareth comes before Cana, and thus it would be natural to make for Nazareth first, as also Jesus' mother was to attend the wedding in Cana. John had indicated a further three from Nazareth to Cana, specifically mentioning '*the third day*' they attended this wedding (2:1). Thus, the time in allowing for travel was pinpointed further by

John.

When considering that they left Bethabara on the forty-sixth day since Jesus' arrival after His baptism, and the stay in the wilderness, we find that we are brought to a total of forty-nine days.

Now, because the disciples and Jesus were Jews, they counted their days, as starting in the evenings. Thus, the next subsequent day would be the fiftieth.

We had considered the significance of the factor forty-two, forty-three, forty-five and forty-six earlier, and now as we come to the first miracle, we can see further relevance in the factor of fifty.

The last miracle of this book, prior to the Ascension, we should see is the fiftieth. John, the beginner of the gospel story, also pointed out the first miracle. This miracle, becomes more relevant when understanding that these weddings, went on into the evenings, and, thus when the water was changed into wine, would no doubt have been in the evening, as the guests had already drunken wine earlier. The wine that Jesus had made was of such good quality that the bridegroom was complimented in presenting the wine at that particular moment in time, which was towards the last part of the celebrations (vv. 9-10). Moreover, we can better understand v. 4, where Jesus addressed his mother about the time being right, as indicative to waiting for the appropriate moment.

Thus, we have witnessed how the factor fifty was significant in concluding Jesus' earthly ministry, and at the same time, important in its initiation.

Because the Holy Spirit is the Power whereby miracles occurred, it will be worthwhile to reflect on this aspect at this juncture. Besides, when we arrive at the beginning of the next summer, and the subsequent ones in Jesus' ministry, as we look at the meaning of Pentecost [Gr. *fiftieth*] mentioned at various points in the intersections throughout this book, we will reflect further on its association with the Holy Spirit, and new beginnings throughout the Gospels in regards to the ordinations of the twelve and the seventy.

Furthermore, in projecting forward, after the forty days Jesus had appeared after His resurrection (Acts 1:3), and having ascended to Heaven (v. 9), ten days later the Holy Spirit would empower the disciples in the new phase of the gospel on the Day of Pentecost (2:1). Thus, after seven weeks [forty-nine days], from the resurrection, we are brought to the fiftieth day, being Pentecost, which is symbolic of receiving the Holy Spirit.

Reverting back again, and including a day's travel from Bethabara, after Jesus' baptism, and the forty days Jesus spent in the wilderness, and a further day allowing for travel from the wilderness back to Bethabara [forty-two altogether], the forty-third being the day Jesus actually reappeared from His recuperation in the wilderness, we see that when counting all the subsequent days, separate from the forty days and nights, there are ten again, in bringing us to the first miracle, and the start of Jesus commission.

After the wedding at Cana, Jesus, His mother and disciples would naturally have returned home to Nazareth first, before we come to Jesus leaving His home town (Mat. 4:13). Afterwards Jesus would shortly leave and set up base at Capernaum, with His mother, brothers, and disciples coming along, too, though staying but for a few days (John 2:12).

Thus, we have now embarked into the start of Jesus' mission, of preaching about the Kingdom of God.

THE FIRST GALILEAN MINISTRY

Matthew 4:13 John 2:12
And after this, leaving Nazareth He came, and His mother, and His brother, and His disciples, and went down to, and dwelt in Capernaum which is up the sea coast, in the borders of Zebulon and Naphtali: and they continued there not many days:
Matthew 4
14 that it might be fulfilled which was spoken by Isaiah (9:1-2) the prophet, saying,
15 "THE LAND OF ZEBULON AND THE LAND OF NAPHTALI, BY THE WAY OF THE SEA, BEYOND JORDAN, GALILEE OF THE GENTILES.
16 THE PEOPLE WHO SAT IN DARKNESS SAW A GREAT LIGHT; AND TO THOSE WHO SAT IN THE REGION AND SHADOW OF DEATH UPON THEM A LIGHT HAS DAWNED."

Below we have the fourth time that Matthew and Mark dovetail together, which gives us the confirmation of the point at which Jesus actually starts to preach the gospel of the Kingdom of God from Capernaum.

We should realize that although Jesus had already begun choosing His disciples back at John 1:37-51, just prior to the first miracle, it would not be until He was about to publicly preach, that they would finally leave their fishing business. Though, no doubt, hired servants replaced them, obviously their business was left in the cable hands of Zebedee, the, father of James and John while they were away (Mark 1:19-20).

However, even before and after Jesus was resurrected, in a short break, escaping from the rigors associated with spreading the good news of the gospel with Jesus, they went back to try their hand at fishing again (Luke 5:1-2, 10-11; John 21:1-3).

Matthew 4:17 Mark 1:14c-15
From that time Jesus began preaching the good news of the Kingdom of God, and

to say, "Repent: the time is fulfilled, and the Kingdom of God, from Heaven is at hand: repent, and believe this good news."

Matthew 4:18
And Jesus, walking by the sea of Galilee, saw two brothers, Simon called Peter, and Andrew his brother, casting a net into the sea: for they were fishers.
Matthew 4:19 Mark 1:17
And Jesus, He says to them, "Follow Me, and I will help you to become fishers of people."
Matthew 4:20 Mark 1:18
And they immediately left their nets, and followed Him.

Matthew 4:21 Mark 1:19-20a
And when He had gone on a little further, from there, He saw two other brothers, James the son of Zebedee, and John his brother, who were also in the boat with Zebedee their father, mending their nets; and immediately He called them.
Matthew 4:22 Mark 1:20b
And immediately they left the boat, and their father Zebedee in the boat with the hired servants, and went and followed after Him.

Luke 4
14b And there went out fame of Him through the entire region round about.
15 And He taught in their synagogues, being glorified of all.

The other half of Luke's verse (14b), is now fulfilled with the statement above that His fame was now beginning to spread after *The First Miracle*, and in continuing with His first Galilean ministry, when Jesus returns again to Nazareth (v. 16). It is clear that Jesus did many more miracles than those recorded (v. 23). But, as John the last Gospel writer tells us those, which were recorded, were '*written, that you might believe*' (20:30-31).

Luke 4
16 And He came to Nazareth, where He had been brought up: and, as His custom was, He went into the synagogue on the Sabbath Day, and stood up
17 And there was delivered to Him the scroll of the prophet Isaiah. And when He had opened the scroll, He found the place where it was written (61:1-2),
18 "THE SPIRIT OF THE LORD IS UPON ME, BECAUSE HE HAS ANOINTED ME TO PREACH THE GOSPEL TO THE POOR; HE HAS SENT ME TO HEAL THE BROKENHEARTED, TO PREACH DELIVERANCE TO THE CAPTIVES, AND RECOVERING OF SIGHT TO THE BLIND, TO SET AT LIBERTY THOSE WHO ARE BRUISED,
19 TO PREACH THE ACCEPTABLE YEAR OF THE LORD."

20 And He closed the Scroll, and He gave it to the Minister, and paused. And the eyes of all those who were in the synagogue were fastened on Him.

21 And He began to say to them, "This day is this Scripture fulfilled in your ears."
22 And all bore Him witness, and wondered at the gracious words that proceeded out of His mouth. And they said, "Is not this Joseph's son?"
23 And He said to them,
"You will surely say to Me this proverb, 'Physician, heal yourself: whatever we have heard done in Capernaum, do also here in your country.'"
24 And He said,
"Certainly I say to you, no prophet is accepted in his own country.
25 But I tell you a truth, many widows were in Israel in the days of Elijah, when the heavens was shut up three years and six months, when great famine was throughout all the land;
26 but to none of them was Elijah sent, save to Zarephath, a city of Sidon, to a woman who was a widow.
27 And many lepers were in Israel in the time of Elisha the prophet; and none of them was cleansed, saving Naaman the Syrian."

28 And all they in the synagogue, when they had heard these things, were filled with rage,
29 and rose up, and thrust Him out of the city, and led Him to the brow of the hill on which their city was built, that they might cast Him down headlong.
30 But He passing through the midst of them went His way.

8   *FROM GALILEE TO JERUSALEM*

THE SECOND DEMONIAC

After escaping from Nazareth, Jesus returns to Capernaum with the disciples (Mark 1:21), at which point at this amazing conjunction, with *The Second Miracle* recorded by Mark (vv. 23-26) and Luke (4:33-35), they parallel together again for the second time, without either of the other two Gospels.

The first time they had aligned together over the same details was when Jesus had returned earlier to Galilee to begin *The First Galilean Ministry*, in the previous section (Mark 1:14b; Luke 4:14a).

We should now see how the miracles and the surrounding details of the events are used as marker reference points to the accounts of the Gospels, and will see this even more clearly as we progress further.

Mark 1:21 Luke 4:31
And they came down to and went into Capernaum, a city of Galilee, and immediately on the Sabbath Day He entered into the synagogue, and taught them on the Sabbath Days.
Mark 1:22 Luke 4:32
And they were astonished at His teaching: for He taught them as one who had authority, and not as the Scribes - His word was with power.

Mark 1:23 Luke 4:33
And in their synagogue there was a man, who had an unclean spirit of a devil, and he cried out with a loud voice,
Mark 1:24 Luke 4:34
saying, "Let us alone; what have we to do with You, You Jesus of Nazareth? Are You come to destroy us? I know You, who You are - the Holy One of God."
Mark 1:25-26 Luke 4:35
And Jesus rebuked him, saying, "Hold your peace, and come out of him."
And when the unclean spirit of the devil had convulsed him, and thrown him in the midst, crying with a loud voice, he came out of him, not harming him.
Mark 1:27 Luke 4:36
And they were all amazed, insomuch that they questioned and spoke among themselves, saying, "What words these are! What refreshing communication this is! For with authority and power He even commands the unclean spirits, and they come out and do obey Him."

Mark 1:28 Luke 4:37
And immediately the fame of Him went out and spread abroad throughout the entire region, and into every place of the country round about Galilee.

THE FIRST GALILEAN MINISTRY ENDS

We saw after the first miracle in Cana that Jesus left Nazareth and made Capernaum His base for the start of His first Galilean ministry. Subsequently returning to Nazareth, from where He had to escape from being thrown headlong from the brow of a hill. Clearly He had already done more miracles than those that are recorded (Luke 4:23). Hence, with His fame increasing, it became a continuing development throughout His ministry.

Mark (1:28) and Luke (4:37) revealed in their verses above, that after the *second miracle*, which transpired back at Capernaum, His fame was now spreading throughout all of Galilee and the surrounding areas.

As Jesus continued on circuit throughout Galilee, His fame spread even further still, eventually to Syria, the Decapolis, Jerusalem, Judea, and Perea, with people converging to Galilee to see Him. We had left the Gospel of Matthew (4:22) at the point where the disciples left their fishing business to go with Jesus on the first Galilean ministry. Matthew returns at this juncture, to witness to that factor with the following verses, 23-25.

It is also Matthew that now closes Jesus' first ministry to Galilee. Because of the time element in healing the people throughout Galilee, and many thus following Jesus from there, from Syria, the Decapolis, Jerusalem, Judea, and Perea, this would have included the autumn and up to spring of the next year, when Jesus is about to travel to Jerusalem for the first Passover of His ministry.

Matthew 4
23 And Jesus went about all Galilee, teaching in their synagogues, and preaching the gospel of the Kingdom, and healing all manner of sickness and all manner of disease among the people.

24 And His fame went throughout all Syria; and they brought to Him all who were ill who were afflicted with different diseases and torments, those who were possessed with devils, those who were lunatic, and those who were paralytics; and He healed them.

25 And there followed Him great crowds of people from Galilee, and from the Decapolis, and from Jerusalem, and from Judea, and from beyond Jordan.

THE FIRST PASSOVER

Matthew, having closed the first Galilean ministry, which would have covered autumn and winter, we now arrive at the first Passover in the Gospels, and the first one mentioned by John. Only the last Passover is referred to by name in the Synoptic Gospels though. However, remember John's characteristic style - he records for us three Passovers, so as to keep the accounts straight.

Now in our next section, we connect back to where we left off at John 2:12, and the start of v. 13, now being Passover time. There is a gap of six months, whereby Jesus, having completed His first Galilean ministry, travels up to Jerusalem.

Here we see how John's style also plays a crucial role in keeping things in the correct sequence. Notice that the '*Passover was at hand*' (v. 13), meaning just before. As we come to v. 23, we have the next day in succession during the Passover week - the first Sabbath, the 15th Nissan, of that eight day period, whilst including the 14th. When Jesus overturned the moneychangers' tables, directly before the Passover began, it also pictured the cleansing of sin, symbolic of leaven (1 Cor. 5:7-8), which should have been removed before the Passover proper.

John 2

13 And the Jews' Passover [14th Nissan] was at hand, and Jesus went up to Jerusalem,
14 and found in the Temple those who sold oxen and sheep and doves, and the moneychangers sitting:

15 and when He had made a scourge of small cords, He drove them all out of the Temple, and the sheep, and the oxen; and poured out the changers' money, and overthrew the tables;
16 and said to them who sold doves, "Take these things away; don't make My Father's House a house of merchandise."

17 And His disciples remembered that it was written (Ps. 69:9),
"THE ZEAL OF YOUR HOUSE HAS EATEN Me UP."

18 Then answered the Jews and said to Him,
"What sign do You show to us, seeing that You do these things?"
19 And Jesus answered and said to them,
"Destroy this Temple, and in three days I will raise it up."

20 Then said the Jews, "Forty-six years [19BC-28AD] was this Temple in building, and You will rear it up in three days?"
21 But He spoke of the Temple of His body.

22 When therefore He was risen from the dead, His disciples remembered that He had said this to them; and they believed the Scripture, and the word which Jesus had said.

23 Now when He was in Jerusalem at the Passover, in the Festival Day [15th Nissan], many believed in His Name, when they saw the miracles that He did.

24 But Jesus did not commit Himself to them, because He knew them all,
25 and didn't need that anyone should elucidate on people: for He knew what was in people's minds.

Now following, with ch. 3:1-2, we have Nicodemus coming to Jesus by night - indicating yet another day [the third], as the days in Judaism start in the evening. Thus, when the dialogue of Nicodemus and Jesus was complete at v. 21 in our next intersection, as we shall see, the subsequent scenario would take place during the rest of the Days of Unleavened Bread, namely the rest of the Passover period.

John 3
1 There was a man of the Pharisees, named Nicodemus, a ruler of the Jews:
2 the same came to Jesus by night, and said to Him,
"Rabbi, we know that You are a Teacher come from God: for no one can do these miracles that You do, except God be with Him."
3 Jesus answered and said to him "Assuredly, indeed, I say to you, except on be born-again, they cannot see the Kingdom of God."

4 Nicodemus says to Him,
"How can one be born when they're old? Can they enter the second time into their mother's womb, and be born?"
5 Jesus answered,
"Sincerely, truthfully, I say to you, except one be born of water and of the Spirit, they cannot enter the Kingdom of God.
6 That which is born of the flesh is flesh; and that which is born of the Spirit is spirit.
7 Don't marvel that I said to you, you must be born-again.
8 The wind blows where it wishes, and you hear the sound thereof, but cannot tell where it comes from, and where it goes: so is everyone who is born of the Spirit."

9 Nicodemus answered and said to Him, "How can these things be?"
10 Jesus answered and said to him,
"Are you a Master of Israel, and you don't know these things?
11 Absolutely, categorically, I say to you, We speak what We do know, and testify what We have seen; and you don't receive Our witness.
12 If I have told you earthly things, and you don't believe, how shall you believe if I tell you Heavenly things?

John 3

13 And no one has ascended up to Heaven, but He who came down from Heaven, even the Son of Humanity who was in Heaven.

14 And as Moses lifted up the serpent in the wilderness, even so must the Son of Humanity be lifted up (Num. 21:9):

15 that whoever believes in Him should not perish, but have eternal life.

16 For God so loved the world that He gave His only begotten Son, that whoever believes in Him should not perish, but have everlasting life.

17 For God didn't send His Son into the world to condemn the world; but that the world through Him might be saved.

18 Those who believe on Him are not condemned: but they who don't believe are condemned already, because they have not believed in the Name of the only begotten Son of God.

19 And this is the condemnation, that Light is come into the world, and they loved darkness rather than Light, because their deeds were evil.

20 For everyone who does evil hates the Light, neither comes to the Light, lest their deeds should be reproved.

21 But they who practice truth come to the Light that their deeds may be made manifest, that they are done through God."

It is considered by some, that where we left off in Mat. 4:25 earlier, at the last verse of that chapter, when following through to his next chapter, the scenario must be in Galilee.

We saw at the beginning of the last section, after John 2:12, which covered the whole of Jesus' first Galilean ministry, that, when we read through to the next verse, in between these two verses we have a period of at least six months, allowing for Jesus' circuiting of Galilee, as v. 13 is in Jerusalem. Correspondingly, we shall see it is the same for Matthew. However, the reason for placing Matthew 5, 6 and 7 (*The Sermon Up The Mount*), in Galilee, is because later on, Luke 6 seems to have a record of a similar event there. But, we shall come to see, when adhering to all the guide factors of this book, that they are completely separate incidents.

There are also several other accounts, which seem to be similar, but are when looked at closer, actually very different, and at any rate are several months apart, and in some cases even a year later. Nonetheless, there is a chapel maintained by Franciscan Sisters, at the place in Galilee, believed to be where Jesus delivered the Sermon of Beatitudes, and other teachings. Though, we shall come to see, that this place is correct for the siting of the sermon in Luke, which sermon transpired when Jesus and the disciples had come down from the mount (6:17). Whereas, in Matthew 5, 6 and 7, the dialogue of the sermon to the disciples, is up the mount (5:1-2), with them coming down after that sermon; moreover, when the teachings were concluded (8:1).

Some of the related wording of these two events as scholars know, is somewhat similar, but there are also great differences. Matthew's account ranges to three chapters, with a hundred and eleven verses, whereas, Luke has only thirty-three verses.

Furthermore, Jesus was not teaching all of the twelve disciples in Matthew's account, as Matthew had not been called at this point, and he makes sure we know this, later on (9:9). Moreover, the relationship between the corresponding parallel accounts in the Synoptics, several months after the account of *The Sermon Up The Mount*, and the following incidents afterwards, further verifies that Matthew had not yet been called (Mat. 9:9-13; Mark 2:14-22; Luke 5:27-39). Hence, in the account of *The Sermon Down The Mount* in Luke, Jesus was teaching the twelve freshly ordained apostles (6:13-16), and other disciples who would eventually make up the seventy (v. 17).

In all the Gospels we have cases of abrupt changes between verses, and sometimes inside one verse itself, of suddenly changing from one area to a different place, or time, without actually the individual Gospel in question informing us of that aspect. And, thus, we have to consider another Gospel to know of any change in the scenario.

An example of this is first seen in Mark 1:28, which refers to Jesus' first circuit of Galilee, which we covered earlier, and his next verses, which we have not yet come to, as this event is the sixth recorded miracle (vv. 29-31), which took place in the following year months later, after (v. 28). On that incident the Synoptics all agree and align.

Thus, sometimes we have to search ahead, or go to another Gospel to give us the information of any change when we are considering certain criteria regarding the time of year in which the event occurs. For when we relate to all the relevant factors in the Gospels accounts, where they parallel together, or dovetail together, in journeying through the succession of events, the answers become clear.

The difference between the two versions of the Beatitudes is considerable. In Mat. 5:1, it is evident by the text that Jesus '*seeing the crowds, He went up onto the mount: and when He was set, His disciples came to Him*'. Whereas in Luke's account He comes down with them to the plain (6:17), and to the crowds, after having ordained them apostles (vv. 13-16), which was many weeks after Matthew's account, and in a different location. Furthermore, Matthew later on, in his version of the ordination of the twelve (10:1-4), synchronizes with Mark (3:13-19) and Luke (6:13-16) in total phraseological alignment.

THE SERMON UP THE MOUNT

Matthew 5

1 And seeing the crowds, He went up onto the mount: and when He was set, His disciples came to Him:

2 and He opened His mouth, and taught them, saying,

3 "Blessed are the needy in spirit: for theirs is the Kingdom of Heaven.

4 Blessed are they who mourn: for they shall be comforted.

5 Blessed are the humble: for they shall inherit the earth.

6 Blessed are they who hunger and thirst after righteousness: for they shall be filled.

7 Blessed are the merciful: for they shall obtain mercy.

8 Blessed are the pure in heart: for they shall see God.

9 Blessed are the peacemakers: for they shall be called the Children of God.

10 Blessed are they who are persecuted for righteousness' sake: for theirs is the Kingdom of Heaven.

11 Blessed are you, when you're insulted, and persecuted, and all manner of evil is spoken against you falsely, for My sake.

12 Rejoice, and be exceedingly glad: for great is your reward in Heaven: for so persecuted they the prophets who were before you."

When we come to Luke 6, seventy other disciples were also being taught over the months, and when Jesus addresses the crowds in Luke's account, he is also talking to the twelve, and *'the company of His* [seventy] *disciples'* (v. 17). Naturally, later on in Luke, Jesus would go over some of the same teaching as mentioned in Matthew's first account, many weeks before, as Luke was pointing out that this was the first opportunity of *The Seventy Disciples* to hear these teachings. Thus, the differences between the various details of the scenario of the two accounts of the relating of the Sermons are plain to see, when comparing the two together.

Matthew 5-8:1-3 - The Sermon Up The Mount

[1] Jesus wanted to get away from the crowds.

[2] He went up the mount.

[3] The eleven disciples came to Him.

[4] Jesus declares nine Beatitudes (vv. 2-12) with central teachings to the end of ch. 7.

[5] They come down after the Sermon Up The Mount (8:1).

[6] Jesus directly goes on to heal a leper, on coming down the (vv. 2-3).

Luke 6:17-7:1 - The Sermon Down The Mount

[1] Jesus wanted to teach the crowds.

[2] He came down the mount.

[3] The twelve disciples were now ordained apostles (vv. 13-16), who came down the mount with Jesus.

[4] Jesus relates only four Beatitudes, similar to those spoken up the mount, but rephrases them (vv. 20-23). Also He restates, though curtailing the same central teachings with variant differences, rephrasing those given up the mount (vv. 24-49).

[5] It is also clear that the twelve, '*stood in the plain*', and then after healing '*the whole crowd*' (vv. 18-19), Jesus began to teach, directing His gaze at the disciples, with '*the company of His* (seventy) *disciples, and a great crowd*', also present (v. 17).

[6] He returns to Capernaum (7:1).

The Seventy Disciples are mentioned in Luke (10:1), and before that, alluded to in ch. 7:11, when they, '*many of His disciples*' journey to Nain. However, other translations do not aver to that detail in v. 11. Readers will notice before we arrive at that particular section in Luke, when afterwards Jesus entered into Capernaum, the incident of the sending of the Elders (vv. 2-5), and the friends of the Centurion, to heal his servant (vv. 6-10), and wish to relate it with Matthew (8:5-13), where the Centurion came directly up to Jesus alone. But, as we can only cover properly one event at a time, we shall see, when we come to the first healing of *The Centurion's Servant*, that indeed, amazingly, they are once again two separate incidents.

9 ON THE MOUNT

THE FIRST PARABLES AND TEACHINGS

We had indicated in the start of the section, *The First Passover* (p. 52), that Matthew had closed his account with *The First Galilean Ministry* (4:23-25), which would have at least included up to the spring of the previous year, as the Gospel of John revealed that after *The First Galilean Ministry* Jesus traveled to Jerusalem (2:12, 13). Thus, the crowds mentioned in Matthew's following ch. 5:1, would have been indicative with the gathering at Passover time. These crowds would have been great in and around Jerusalem, as we should further come to see.

However, Jesus chose to teach the eleven disciples, in a respite from the crowds, as He did on numerous other occasions at one of His favorite spots, which the Mt. Olives in Jerusalem would have provided. Moreover, this first recording of collectively teaching these new disciples, the Beatitudes, the crux of Christian behavior and thought, transpires successively after the first Galilean ministry, at this significant time of Passover, and no doubt on the Mt. Olives.

Consequently, Jerusalem would be the focus of this first Passover, and the last one too, as the other two Passovers between the first and the last were subsequently in two different locations. Furthermore, the Mt. Olives was also the place where Jesus would relate His last words before ascending to Heaven: and as there were eleven disciples indicated by the texts of the Synoptics at this juncture, also there would be eleven who had Jesus' last words spoken directly to them before His Ascension, as the twelfth had not been specifically chosen (Acts 1:26). Significantly, the Mt. Olives is referred to eleven times in the Gospels!

The mentioning of '*the city set on the hill*' (Mat. 5:14) is an apt description of the city of peace - Jerusalem. Again there is another indication of '*Jerusalem: for it is THE OF THE GREAT KING*' (v. 35; Ps. 48:2).

Moreover, Jesus' discourse on the attitude to the Law, and in bringing offerings to the altar (Mat. 5:17-24), is further highlighted, as, from the Mt. Olives, one could see Jerusalem where the Supreme Court was, and the Temple.

Furthermore, directly after the Beatitudes, Jesus uses the analogy of '*salt*' in teaching this collective group of eleven disciples (v. 13).

Interestingly it is also the first record of Jesus teaching the disciples altogether, through analogies. Thus, as no offerings were to be given without salt (Lev. 2:13), the importance of the analogy in its setting overlooking the Temple, and the second analogy of '*light*' in regards to '*the city set on the hill*' (Mat. 5:14-16), with the disciples being the recipients whom the two analogies were to reflect, is amazingly entwined in the scene overlooking Jerusalem and the Temple.

Thus, this setting would have been a poignant focus point for Jesus at this time, as He was teaching how the correct attitude, and ultimate purpose of the Law should be illuminated and radiated from our hearts.

This ideal of the Law was echoed in the prophecy of Micah 4:2, '*And He will teach us of His ways, and we will walk in His paths: for the Law shall go out of Zion, and the Word of the Lord from Jerusalem.*'

Here was the first place in Jesus' mission, where He started teaching His disciples by parabolic analogy, though He had first spoken individually to Nicodemus in the same manner a few days before, about being born-again. On this first occasion where He is addressing the majority of new disciples, we have the beginning of many parabolic type analogies that would be characteristic throughout Jesus' mission when teaching the disciples and others

The complete scenario and narration of Matthew 5, 6, and 7, is exclusive to this time and does not parallel with any of the other Gospels at this point, though parts, and some of these teachings are used again later and at other times.

Matthew 5

13 "You are the salt of the earth: but if the salt has lost its savor, how shall it be salted? It is now good for nothing, but to be cast out, and to be trodden underfoot by anyone.

14 You are the light of the world. A city that is set on a hill cannot be hid.
15 Neither do people light a candle, and put it under a cover, but on a candlestick; so it gives light to all who are in the house.
16 Let your light so shine before all, that they may see your good works, and glorify your Father who is in Heaven.

17 Don't think that I am come to destroy the Law, or the Prophets: I didn't come to destroy, but to fulfill.
18 For truly I say to you, until the heavens and earth pass away, not even one smallest letter or one tiny pen stroke shall in no way pass away from the Law, until all things are accomplished.
19 Whoever therefore shall break one of these least commandments, and shall teach others so, they shall be called the least in the Kingdom of Heaven: but whoever shall do and teach them, the same shall be called great in the Kingdom of Heaven.
20 For I say to you, that except your righteousness shall exceed the righteousness of the Scribes and Pharisees, you shall in no case enter the Kingdom of Heaven.

21 You have heard that it was said originally, 'YOU SHALL NOT MURDER (Ex.20:13);' and 'Whoever shall murder shall be in danger of judgment (Deut. 16:18):'

Matthew 5

22 but I say to you, that whoever is angry with their brother or sister without a cause shall be in danger of the judgment: and whoever shall say to their brother or sister, '*Raca* [good-for-nothing],' shall be in danger of the Court: but whoever shall say, '*You moron*,' shall be in danger of hell-fire.

23 Therefore if you bring your gift to the altar, and remember that your brother or sister has something against you;
24 leave your gift there before the altar and go your way; first be reconciled to your brother or sister, and then come and offer your gift.

25 Agree with your opponent quickly, while you're on the way with them; lest your opponent deliver you to the Judge, and the Judge deliver you to the officer, and you be cast into prison.
26 Certainly I say to you, you shall by no means come out of there, till you have paid the last penny.

27 You have heard that it was said originally, 'YOU SHALL NOT COMMIT ADULTERY (Ex. 20:14):'
28 but I say to you, that whoever looks on a woman to crave after her has committed adultery with her already in their heart.

29 And if your right eye offends you, pluck it out, and cast it from you: for it is profitable for you that one of your members should perish, and not that your whole body should be cast into hell.
30 And if your right hand offend you, cut it off, and cast it from you: for it is profitable for you that one of your members should perish, and not that your whole body should be cast into hell.

31 It has been said, 'WHOEVER SHALL PUT AWAY HIS WIFE, LET HIM GIVE HER A DIVORCE CERTIFICATE (Deut. 24:1):'
32 but I say to you, that whoever shall put away his wife, saving for the cause of sexual immorality, causes her to commit adultery: and whoever shall marry her that is divorced commits adultery.

33 Again, you have heard that it was said originally,
'YOU SHALL NOT SWEAR FALSELY, BUT SHALL PERFORM YOUR OATHS TO THE LORD (Num. 30:2):'
34 but I say to you, don't swear at all; neither by Heaven; for it is God's Throne:
35 nor by the earth; for it is His footstool: neither by Jerusalem; for it is THE CITY OF THE GREAT KING (Psa. 48:2).
36 Neither shall you swear by your head, because you cannot make one hair white or black
37 But let your 'Yes' mean 'yes' and your 'No', 'No:' for whatever is beyond these evil can follow.

38 You have heard that it was said, 'AN EYE FOR AN EYE, AND A TOOTH FOR A
TOOTH (Ex. 21:24):'
39 but I say to you, that you oppose not evil: but whoever shall strike you on
your right cheek, turn to them the other also.

40 And if anyone will sue you at law, and take your shirt, let them have your
jacket also.
41 And whoever shall compel you to go a mile, go with them two.
42 Give to those who ask, and don't turn away those who would borrow from
you.

43 You have heard that it was said, 'YOU SHALL LOVE YOU NEIGHBOR (Lev. 19:18),
and hate your enemy (Deut. 23:6).'
44 But I say to you, love your enemies, bless those who curse you, do good to
those who hate you, and pray for those who maliciously use you, and
persecute you;
45 that you may be the children of your Father who is in Heaven: for He
makes His sun to rise on the evil and on the good, and sends rain on the just
and the unjust.

46 For if you love those, who love you, what reward do you have? Don't the
tax collectors do the same?
47 And if you greet your friends only, what more do you do than others?
Don't even the tax collectors do the same?
48 Therefore you shall be perfect, even as your Father who is in Heaven is
perfect.

Matthew 6
1 Take heed that you don't do your charitable giving before others, to be seen
of them: otherwise you have no reward of your Father who is in Heaven.
2 Therefore when you give charitably, don't sound a trumpet before you, as
the hypocrites do in the synagogues and in the streets, that they may have
glory off others. Certainly I say to you, they have their reward.
3 But when you give charity, don't let your left hand know what your right hand
does:
4 so your compassion may be in secret: and your Father who sees in secret
Himself shall reward you openly.

5 And when you pray, you shall not be as the hypocrites are: for they love to
pray standing in the synagogues and on the corners of the streets, that everyone
may see them. Actually I say to you, they have their reward.
6 But you, when you pray, ENTER INTO YOUR ROOM AND WHEN YOU HAVE SHUT
YOUR DOOR (Is. 26:20), pray to your Father which is in secret, and your Father who

sees in secret will reward you openly.

7 But when you pray, don't use vain repetitions, as the heathen do: for they think that they shall be heard for their much speaking.

8 Therefore do not be like them: for your Father knows what things you have need of, before you ask Him.

9 After this manner therefore pray:
'Our Father who is in Heaven, hallowed be Your Name.

10 Your Kingdom come. Your will be done in earth, as it is in Heaven.

11 Grant us daily our needful bread.

12 And forgive us our debts, as we forgive our debtors.

13 And lead us not into temptation, but deliver us from evil: for Yours is the Kingdom, and the Power, and the glory, forever. Amen.'

14 For if you forgive others their trespasses, your Heavenly Father will also forgive you:

15 but if you don't forgive others of their trespasses, neither will your Father forgive your trespasses.

16 Moreover when you fast, don't be, as the hypocrites, of a sad countenance: for they disfigure their faces that they may appear to all to fast.
Truly I say to you, they have their reward.

17 But you, when you fast, anoint your head, and wash your face;

18 so you are not seen by others to be fasting, but to your Father which is in secret: and your Father, who sees in secret, shall reward you openly.

19 Don't lay up for yourselves treasures upon earth, where moth and rust spoils, and where thieves break through and steal:

20 but lay up for yourselves treasures in Heaven, where neither moth nor rust spoils, and where thieves do not break through nor steal:

21 for where your treasure is, there will your heart be also.

22 The light of the body is through the eye: if therefore your outlook is positive, your whole body shall be full of light.

23But if your outlook is evil, your whole body shall be full of darkness.
If therefore the light that is in you is darkness, how great is that darkness!

24 No one can serve two masters: for either they will hate the one, and love the other; or else they will hold to one, and despise the other. You cannot serve God and wealth.

25 Therefore I say to you, take no thought for your life, what you shall eat, or or what you shall drink; nor yet for your body, what shall you put on. Isn't life

more than food, and the body than clothes?

26 Consider the fowls of the air: for they don't sow, neither do they reap, nor gather into barns; yet your Heavenly Father feeds them. nor gather into barns; yet your Heavenly Father feeds them.

Aren't you much better than they? Aren't you much better than they?

27 Which of you by taking thought can add any amount to their age?

28And why take thought of clothes? Consider the lilies of the field, how they grow; they don't toil, neither do they spin:they grow; they don't toil, neither do they spin:

29 and yet I say to you, that even Solomon in all his glory was not arrayed like one of these.

30 Wherefore, if God so clothe the flora of the field, which today is, and tomorrow is cast into the oven, shall He not much more clothe you, oh you of little faith?

31 Therefore take no thought, saying, 'What shall we eat?' or, 'What shall we drink?' or, 'Wherewithal shall we be clothed?'

32 (For after all these things do the Gentiles seek:) for your Heavenly Father knows that you have need of all these things.

33 But seek first the Kingdom of God, and His righteousness: and all these things shall be added to you.

34 Therefore take no thought for tomorrow: for tomorrow shall take thought for things itself. Each day's own evil is sufficient.

Matthew 7

1 Don't judge, in order that you are not judged.

2 For with what judgment you judge, you shall be judged: and with what measure you apportion, it shall be measured to you again.

3 And why consider the speck that is in your brother or sister's eye, but perceive not the beam that is in your own eye?

4 Or how will you say to your brother or sister, 'Let me pull out the speck in your eye:' and, see, a beam is in your own eye?

5 You hypocrite, first cast out the beam out of your own eye; and then shall you see clearly to cast out the speck out of your brother or sister's eye.

6 Don't give that which is holy to the dogs, neither cast your pearls before swine, lest they trample them under their feet, and turn and attack you.

7 Ask, and it shall be given you; seek, and you shall find; knock, and it shall be opened to you:

8 for everyone who asks, receives: and they who seek, find; and to those who

knock it shall be opened.

9 Or which one of you is there, who if your child asks for bread, will give them a stone?
10 Or if they ask for fish, will give them a serpent?
11 If you then, being inferior, know how to give good gifts to your children, how much more shall your Father who is in Heaven give good things to those who ask Him?
12 Therefore all things whatever you would that others should do to you, do also even so to them: for this is the Law and the Prophets.

13 Enter in at the narrow gate: for wide is the gate, and broad is the way, that leads to destruction, and many there be who go in that way:
14 because narrow is the gate, and narrow is the way, which leads to life, so there are few who find it.

15 Beware of false prophets, who come to you in sheep's clothing, but inwardly they are ravening wolves.
16 You shall know them by their fruits.
Does one gather grapes from thorn bushes, or figs from thistles?
17 Even so every good tree bears good fruit; but a corrupt tree bears bad fruit.
18 A good tree cannot bear bad fruit; neither can a corrupt tree bear good fruit.
19 Every tree that doesn't bear good fruit is cut down, and thrown into the fire.
20 Wherefore by their fruits you shall know them.

21 Not everyone who says to Me, 'Lord, Lord,' shall enter into the Kingdom of Heaven; but those who do the will of My Father who is in Heaven.
22 Many will say to Me in that day, 'Lord, Lord, haven't we prophesied in Your Name, and in Your Name cast out devils, and in Your Name done many wonderful works?'
23 And then will I profess to them, 'I never knew you: DEPART FROM ME, YOU WHO WORK LAWLESSNESS (Ps. 6:8)'.

24 Therefore whoever hears these sayings of Mine, and does them, I will liken them to a wise person, who built their house upon rock:
25 And the rain descended, and the floods came, and the winds blew, and beat upon that house; and it didn't fall: for it was founded upon a rock.
26 And everyone who hears these sayings of Mine, and doesn't do them, shall be likened to a foolish person, who built their house upon sand:
27 and the rain descended, and the floods came, and the winds blew, and beat upon that house; and it fell: and great was the fall of it."

SIMON THE LEPER – THE THIRD MIRACLE

Matthew 7
28 And it came to pass, when Jesus had ended these sayings, the crowd were astonished at His doctrine:
29 for He taught them as one having authority, and not as the Scribes.

Having completed the three chapters of Jesus' dialogue to the disciples, we come to where they were now preparing to leave the mount.

It is clear that Jesus' intent before the start of *The Sermon Up The Mount* was to get away from the crowds. He thus made a point of setting Himself on the *'mount, and when He was set, the disciples came to Him: and He opened His mouth and taught them'* (Mat. 5:1-2). Whether others or other disciples arrived while He was teaching is not stated, and is not paramount to our findings.

However most translators have translated the Greek word, *'ochlos'*, meaning *'crowd'*, in the verse of the text above (v. 28), as *'people'*, or *'multitudes'*, but, the word can also apply to *'the crowd'* of disciples, as shown in (Luke 6:17), where *'ochlos'* is translated 'company', and refers to the disciples.

Where the same Greek word is used in Mat. 8:1, it has the adjective *'great'* - *'polus'* next to *'ochlos'*, indicating, that *'when He was come down from the mount, great crowds followed Him'*, as being separate from the small crowd of disciples, who had already come down with Jesus, and that they had descended before any greater number was added to them.

Matthew wanted to point out that this sermon and teachings were directed to the disciples, and could have indicated precisely otherwise, if anything else had been intended. Correspondingly, at the close of Jesus' ministry again on the Mt. Olives with the section on p. 325 at the start of *The Olivet Prophecy* (Mat. 24), Matthew points out once more that *'the disciples came to Him privately'* (v. 3), where also the last parables addressed to the disciples (ch. 25) preceding the last Passover, were given (26:1-2).

Matthew 8
1 When He was come down from the mount, great crowds followed Him.

2 And, now, there came a leper and worshiped Him, saying,
"Lord, if You wish, You can make me clean."
3 And Jesus put out His hand, and touched him, saying, "I will; be clean."
And immediately his leprosy was cleansed.

Matthew 8

4 And Jesus says to him, "See you tell no one; but go your way, SHOW YOURSELF TO THE PRIEST (Lev. 13:39;14:2), and offer the sacrifice that Moses commanded, for the evidence of it."

This is the third miracle of our findings. Also it is the first leper that we come to. The miraculous healing of this leper is distinct from another leper mentioned in Mark 1:40-45, which aligns with Luke 5:12-15, and is in a different location weeks later, being the ninth miracle, and the second leper.

At this third miracle, Jesus and the disciples were down the mount, when the great crowds arrived. Whereas with *The Ninth Miracle*, He is already '*in a certain city*' (Luke 5:12) when the leper arrived, with the great crowds appearing later, after the leper had spread the knowledge of the healing around that certain city (Mark 1:45; Luke 5:15). Both Mark and Luke correlate and parallel at the events surrounding this other leper, which took place at Gergesa, in Gaulanitis, opposite Galilee, and weeks later when considering the geographical difference of that miracle in its natural order of succession. A study of the events before and after, and when looking at *Scripture Graph III-IV*, further proves this to be the case.

It is worth noting here that there are five miracles which appear on a superficial evaluation to be the same, but in fact all differ in their surrounding individual circumstances: they are, the leper, *The Centurion's Servant*, *The Tempest*, the demoniacs, and the blind men of Jericho. These we cover, as and when we come to them.

This mentioning of the first leper is significant, being indigenous to Matthew's Gospel, even more so, as Matthew and Mark both record '*the house of Simon the Leper*' at Bethany (Mat. 26:6; Mark 14:3), which was near to Jerusalem, on the east slope of the Mt. Olives. In this house, the incident of the anointing of Jesus took place. John, too, mentions the same event (12:1-9), but as he would have been familiar that it was '*the house of Simon the Leper*', does not repeat that this Simon used to be a leper (v. 4), as it would have been common knowledge that he had been, and whose home it was in Bethany anyhow.

However, John added further information that the others had not recorded, by referring to him as the father of Judas Iscariot (6:71, 12:4, 13:2, 26). Moreover, it was also the home of Martha (Luke 10:38), who was sister to Mary (v. 39), and Lazarus (John 11:1-3).

At the event of the Lord's anointing, six days before the last Passover, it would not be strange if Martha would be serving again (12:2), as she did previously (Luke 10:40), and Mary, who '*sat at Jesus' feet*' (v. 39), would ultimately anoint His feet (John 12:3), at '*Bethany, in the house of Simon the Leper*', though he had been healed years before, thus being nicknamed.

Recapping, we saw as Jesus and the disciples came down the mount, Simon the

Leper, who had come from Bethany, was now healed and had become a friend to Jesus. Jesus, by now, had already befriended Judas Iscariot and, also no doubt Martha, Mary and Lazarus at this first mission in Jerusalem, as afterwards when returning to Jerusalem He was to stay at their house on various occasions.

It is at this point that the Gospel of John interjects, and returns to the next successive events, after Jesus spent *The First Passover* in Jerusalem (2:13-15; 3:1-21), which included Matthew's indigenous record of The *Sermon Up The Mount* (ch. 5, 6, 7), and now the third miracle of Simon the Leper (8:1-4), who was from Bethany near Jerusalem.

THE BAPTIST RELEASED

John 3

22 After these things came Jesus and His disciples into the land of Judea; and there He stayed with them, and baptized.

23 And John also was baptizing in Aenon near to Salim, because there was much water there: and they came and were baptized.
24 For John was not yet [finally] cast into prison.

John refers to the fact that the Baptist '*was not yet cast into prison*' to highlight the factor that he was shortly to be arrested again, for the final time. It is obvious that John was bringing our attention to this, as if the Baptist was baptizing once more - then he was no longer in prison, and consequently John would have had no need to mention the Baptist's impending incarceration again.

We covered previously the references relating to this earlier imprisonment of the Baptist. Both Matthew (4:12) and Mark (1:14) establish that the Baptist originally went to prison when Jesus returned to Galilee, shortly after the Temptation. This further agrees and aligns with John 1:43, where he too points out that Jesus left at this time, subsequently coming to dwell in Capernaum (Mat. 4:13), after the first miracle when embarking upon His ministry (John 2:11-13). Because the Baptist was originally taken to prison, his mission waned for a short while and began to decrease, while Jesus' began to increase.

At some time afterwards the Baptist was released, as a human cry must have reached Herod as the common people respected him, as '*when he would have put him to death, he feared the people, because they counted him as a prophet*' (Mat. 14:5). This quotation refers though, to the final time of John being imprisoned too.

As mentioned earlier, in Mark 6:20 we have a reference to this aspect. Herod feared John, and moreover, in the margin of the AV the same verse has the Greek alternative that he, '*saved him*' including the more modern translations. Though Herodias had an inward grudge against him and would have killed him, because of the above factors, she could not exert enough pressure on Herod (v. 19) until months later at the time of Herod's birthday (v. 21).

With the Baptist now continuing with his message, and Jesus having concentrated His throughout Galilee the season before (Mat. 4:23-25), Jesus had already started His first Judean mission in coming to Jerusalem at springtime (John 2:13).

So the Baptist, no doubt having been warned and released, these two witnesses were now both baptizing side by side. Jesus and His disciples in Judea (3:22), and the Baptist in Aeon near Salim (v. 23), which we will see from (pp. 260-263), in the section *Escape To Aenon Near Salim*, was at the north-east border of Samaria.

The release of John, now with Jesus also baptizing, as it were side by side, though in separate adjacent areas, increased Herod's impetuousness with the predicament in having released John previously, and then having to imprison him again shortly, as John had not toned down his preaching. By then, Jesus and His disciples were to supersede the Baptist and his disciples (v. 30), when Herod would finally succumb to actually agreeing to John's death, which would transpire several months later, only with the increasing pressure from Herodias, due to her daughter, as we shall see in our journeying through the successive order of events.

John 3

25 Then there arose a question between John's disciples and the Jews about purification.

26 And they came to John, and said to him,

"Rabbi, He who was with you beyond Jordan, to whom you bore witness, understand, the same baptizes, and all come to Him."

27 John answered and said,

"No one can receive anything, except it be given them from Heaven.

28 You yourselves bear me witness that I said, '*I am not the Messiah, but that I am sent before Him* (1:20, 27, 30).'

29 The one has the bride is the Bridegroom: but the friend of the Bridegroom, who stands and hears Him, rejoices greatly because of the Bridegroom's voice: therefore, this my joy is fulfilled.

30 He must increase, but I must decrease.

31 He who comes from Above is above all: they who are of the earth are earthly, and speak of the earth: He who comes from Heaven is above all.

32 And what He has seen and heard, that He testifies; and no one receives His testimony.

33 He who receives His testimony has attested that God is true.

34 For He whom God has sent speaks the words of God: for God gives not the

Spirit by measure to Him.

35 For the Father loves the Son, and has given all things into His hand.

36 They who believe in the Son have everlasting life: and they who disobey the Son won't see life; but God's anger remains on them."

John 4

1 When therefore the Lord knew how the Pharisees had heard that He, Jesus baptized and made more disciples than John,

2 (though Jesus Himself didn't baptize, but His disciples).

3 He left Judea, and departed again into Galilee.

4 And He needed to pass through Samaria.

For several weeks Jesus and the Baptist baptized side by side, though in separate adjacent areas. And, as the Pharisees had done just before Jesus was to embark on His first mission to Galilee, the previous year (1:19), they would have sent again a delegation of their contemporaries to espy the situation of the Baptist's preaching; this time, though, because of the pressure, of the heightened scenario of the combined preaching of Jesus and the Baptist, which was now annoying those at the top once more (3:25-28; 4:1). Notice what they had originally been told by the Baptist when he was baptizing in Bethabara (1:28), regarding Jesus whom they did not recognize amongst them (v. 26), he had now twice affirmed to them, '*I am not the Messiah*' (1:20; 3:28).

Moreover, because of what the Pharisees had heard said about the Baptist in respect of the people accepting his words, as they themselves rejected his baptism (Luke 7:29-30), the situation had culminated in the people also talking about a Jesus, who had done amazing miracles in healing many people. Consequently, Jesus and His disciples had actually baptized more disciples than the Baptist. This resulted in the decision of Jesus and the disciples leaving Judea at that very point (John 4:1),with their stay in Samaria for a couple days (vv. 4, 40), as well as the aim of returning again to Galilee (vv. 3, 43).

Of course, this excitement of the crowds would have reached the ears of Herod too, on whom these wily Pharisees would have also put further persuasion over the situation of these two witnesses, being influential in baptizing more and more people. Thus, Herod, now at this time of this double exposure, decided to imprison the Baptist once again after his last warning, as Jesus leaves Judea for His second ministry to Galilee.

Jesus had awaited until the situation had warranted Him and His disciples moving on again, as they had planned anyway to return to Galilee. And no doubt when He finally had heard how the Pharisees would react, they made their way through Samaria. The same thing occurred when Jesus left for Galilee at the beginning of His ministry, after His baptism at Bethabara, and the forty days in the wilderness with the original calling of *The First Disciples* (1:43).

At this juncture, where John had been baptizing earlier in Samaria, and Jesus in Judea, his mission would now wane and finally cease as Jesus was stepping up His. Moreover, Jesus would presently be coming to the area where John had been. Furthermore, at this very point, there is a reference to the Baptist having completed his labors, when Jesus addresses the disciples in Samaria, with the *Parable of the Sower and the Reaper* (4:35-37). Jesus continues, '*I sent you to reap for which you exerted no labor: other men labored* [the Baptist and his disciples], *and you are entered into their labor*' (v. 38).

This would now be the second time that Jesus embarked again on a journey back to Galilee, subsequently culminating into His second Galilean ministry. The Gospel of John further highlights this event and correlates it with the second miracle at Cana (4:46, 54). Obviously it is reminiscent of the first miracle and the start of Jesus' ministry in Galilee.

JESUS IN SAMARIA

John 4

5 Then He comes to a city of Samaria, which is called Sychar, near to the parcel of ground that Jacob gave to his son Joseph (Gen. 33:18-19;48:21-22; Jos. 24:32).
6 Now Jacob's well was there. Jesus therefore, being wearied with His journey, sat thus on the well: and it was about noon.

7 Then comes a woman of Samaria to draw water: Jesus says to her, "Give Me a drink."
8 (For His disciples were gone away to the city to buy food.)
9 Then the woman of Samaria says to Him, "How is it that You being a Jew asks drink of me, who am a woman of Samaria?"
For the Jews have no dealings with the Samaritans.
10 Jesus answered and said to her,
"If you knew the gift of God, and who it is who says to you, '*Give Me a drink*;' you would have asked of Him, and He would have given you living water."

11 The woman says to Him,
"Sir, you have nothing to draw it with, and the well is deep, from where then have you the water?
12 Are You greater than our ancestor Jacob, who gave us the well, and drank from it himself, and his children, and his cattle?"
13 Jesus answered and said to her,
"Whoever drinks of this water shall thirst again:
14 but whoever drinks of the water that I shall give them shall never thirst; but the water that I shall give them shall be in them a well of water springing up into everlasting life."

15 The woman says to Him,
"Sir, give me this water, so I don't get thirsty, nor come here to draw."

16 Jesus says to her, "Go, call your husband, and return."
17 The woman answered and said, "I have no husband."
Jesus said to her, "You said well, 'I have no husband':
18 for you have had five husbands; and he whom you now have is not your husband: this you have said truly."

19 The woman says to Him, "Sir, I perceive that You are a Prophet.
20 Our fathers worshiped on this Mount [Gerizim]; and you say that in Jerusalem is the place where one ought to worship."
21 Jesus says to her,
"Woman, believe Me, the hour comes, when you shall neither on this Mount [Gerizim], nor yet in Jerusalem, worship the Father.
22 You worship that which you don't know: we know what we worship: for salvation is of the Jews.
23 But the hour comes, and now is, when the true worshipers shall worship the Father in spirit and in truth: for the Father seeks such to worship Him.
24 God is Spirit: and they who worship Him must worship Him in spirit and in truth."
25 The woman says to Him,
"I know that the Anointed comes, who called the Messiah: when He is come, He will tell us all things."
26 Jesus says to her, "I am He, the One who speaks to you."

27 And upon this came His disciples, and marveled that He talked with the woman: yet no one said, "What do You want?" or, "Why do You talk with her?"

28 The woman then left her water pot, and went her way into the city, and says to the men,
29 "Come, see a Man, who told me all about what I've done: is not this the Messiah?"
30 Then they went out of the city, and came to Him.

31 In the meanwhile His disciples prayed Him, saying, "Master, eat."
32 But He said to them, "I have food to eat that you don't know about."
33 Therefore said His disciples one to another,
"Has anyone brought Him anything to eat?"
34 Jesus says to them,
"My food is to do the will of Him who sent Me, and to finish His work.
35 Don't you say, 'There are yet four months, and then comes harvest?'
Look, I say to you, lift up your eyes, and look on the fields; for they are white already to harvest.
36 And they who reap receive a wage, and gather fruit to life eternal: that both they who sow and they who reap may rejoice together.

John 4

37 And in this saying it is true, 'One sows, and another reaps.'
38 I sent you to reap for which you exerted no labor: others labored, and you are entered into their labor."

39 And many of the Samaritans of that city believed on Him because of the words of the woman, who testified, 'He told me all about what I have done'.

40 So when the Samaritans were come to Him, they begged Him that He would stay with them: and He remained there two days.
41 And many more believed because of His own words;
42 and said to the woman,
"Now we believe, not because of your words: for we have heard Him ourselves, and know that this is indeed the Messiah, the Saviour of the world."

43 Now after two days He departed from there, and went into Galilee.
44 For Jesus Himself testified, that a prophet has no honor in their own local area [Nazareth].

BACK IN CANA AGAIN

Jesus and the disciples having spent two days in Sychar, in Samaria, get ready to continue their journey into Galilee.

To find out what time of the year it was, after having spent Passover in Jerusalem, and then having baptized side by side with the Baptist in Samaria, and Jesus in Judea, there is further proof in the text of the last section that it was shortly after the Passover season.

There were two harvests in Israel, firstly during April-May, the grain [barley in the uplands of Samaria, including the wheat in the lower areas also during April-May], and secondly, the general harvest of the other fruits during September-October.

In John 4:35, it is indicated, when realizing, *'there are yet four months, and then comes* [the general] h*arvest? Look, I say to you, lift up your eyes, and look on the fields* [grain harvest]; *for they are white already to harvest.'* Here we have a reference to two seasons: the general harvest would be four months after the grain harvest, indicating that the above events in Samaria took place several weeks after Passover.

Jesus had testified before about the negative aspect of *'a prophet in their own local area'* (v. 44), in the beginning of His ministry at Nazareth (Luke 4:24). John in his Gospel was now pointing out the positive factor, that when Jesus returned to Galilee this time, He was welcomed in complete antithesis. The people then had witnessed all the things He had done at the Passover, this time (John 4:45), whereas, in His home town Nazareth, in the previous year at the beginning of His mission some had wanted to throw Him off the edge of a hill (Luke 4:29), having only heard about the miracles at Capernaum they did not believe (v. 23).

Thus, after the first ministry in Galilee and Judea, and stopping off in Samaria, Jesus and His disciples now arrive in Galilee, progressing into the second Galilean mission.

John 4
45 Then when He was come into Galilee, the Galileans received Him, having seen all the things that He did at the Festival: for they also went to the Festival.

Remember, at the embarking of the start of the *First Galilean Ministry, The First Miracle* occurred at Cana (2:11).

Now, at the start of the second Galilean ministry, again, in Cana, John (4:46) uses the **fourth miracle** to focus us into the next order of successive events, and states in v. 54, *'This is again the second miracle that Jesus did, when He was come* *out of Judea into Galilee.*' Thus, it is the second miracle in the Gospel of John, which pinpoints that it was the second time again that Jesus came from Judea, progressing into the second Galilean mission, from Judea to Cana.

Though the second miracle recorded in Cana, it is, nevertheless, the fourth recorded since the first at Cana. Hence, it leads us into the start of *The Second Galilean Ministry*, as at the previous Passover season Jesus had worked other miracles at Jerusalem in Judea (2:23).

Interestingly, John purposely mentions only nine miracles up to Jesus' resurrection, along with his recording of the Festivals; he uses these factors to keep the events in harmony.

John 4
46 So Jesus came again into Cana of Galilee, where He made the water wine.
And there was a certain Nobleman, whose son was sick at Capernaum.

47 When he heard that Jesus was come out of Judea into Galilee, he went to Him, and implored Him that He would come down, and heal his son: for he was at the point of death.
48 Then said Jesus to him, "Except you see signs and wonders, you will not believe."
49 The nobleman says to Him, "Sir, come down before my child dies."
50 Jesus says to Him, "Go your way; your son lives."
And the man believed the word that Jesus had spoken to him, and he went his way.

51 And as he was now going down, his servants met him, and told him, saying, "Your son lives."
52 Then he inquired of them the hour when he began to amend. And they said to him, "Yesterday at 1 p.m. the fever left him."
53 So the father knew that it was at the same hour, in which Jesus to him, 'Your son lives:'and himself believed, and his whole house.
54 This is again the second miracle that Jesus did, when He was come out of Judea into Galilee.

We see, when keeping in mind the break between v. 54, the last verse of chapter 4 above, and John's next chapter 5 that, there is another Festival mentioned in his first verse.

As indicated previously, sometimes there are gaps between some verses of considerable time lapses. When looking at the *Scripture Graph VI* at John 5, we see that this chapter relates to *The Second Judean Ministry*, after *The Second*

Galilean Ministry, in the autumn at the Festival of Tabernacles, being months after the spring of *The First Passover*. Moreover, both Josephus and Philo indicate that the Feast of Tabernacles '*the most holiest and greatest Feast*', was known among the Jews as '*the Feast*' pre-eminently [see pp. 188-190 also].

Referring again to the gaps that sometimes are found in between certain verses, a similar characteristic gap transpired, as we considered earlier, between the end of Jesus' first ministry in Galilee ending with Mat. 4:23-25, and the start of Matthew's next chapter 5, being in Jerusalem, at *The First Passover*.

Since it would have been common knowledge among the disciples as to where major events took place, Matthew did not feel the need to record the exact naming of the season, as he had concluded the first Galilean mission by indicating other details: that Jesus went about all Galilee, and of the people coming to Galilee from outlying areas, which would have taken several months to complete.

However, in averring to the length of time *The First Galilean Ministry* would have taken, it would have naturally brought us up to the next season, with Jesus' next mission being in a different location. Nonetheless, Matthew did indicate the place, as alluded to in the beginning part of his dialogue where in Matthew ch. 5, as also mentioned previously in that section (pp. 59-60.)

The parallel Scriptures before Mat. 5 included Mat. 4:23-25, Mark 1:28, and Luke 4:37. If we look at the *Scripture Graph II-III* of that time, below, we see the significance of the sign of miracle one and two, in relationship to the Scriptures before and after.

Event	Matthew	Mark	Luke	John
John is Taken Prisoner			3:19-20	
Jesus Hears John is in Prison	4:12	1:14		
They Leave For Galilee				1:43-51
They Arrive		1:14	4:14	
1st Miracle Water into Wine				2:1-11
Jesus Leaves Nazareth	4:13			2:12
Fulfills Prophecy	4:14-16			
Disciples Join Him		1:14-15		
His Fame Disperses	4:17- 22	1:16-20	4:14-15	
Returns to Nazareth			4:16	
Fulfills Prophecy			4:17-28	
They Try to Kill Him			4:29-30	
2nd Miracle The Demoniac		1:21-27	4:31-36	
1st Circuit of Galilee	*4:23-25*	*1:28*	*4:37*	
Passover/Money-Changers				2:13-17
Three Days New Temple				2:18-22
Festival Day and Miracles				2:23-25
Nicodemus - Born Again				3:1-9
Answer to Nicodemus				3:10-21
The Beatitudes/11Disciples	5:1-12			
Salt, Light, Attitude to Law	5:13-48			
Charity and Lord's Prayer	6:1-15			
Fasting/True Treasure	6:16-21			
Illumination/What One Serves	6:22-24			
Attitude to God's Provision	6:25-34			

Event	Matthew	Mark	Luke	John
Judging Others/Giving	7:1-6			
Asking, Seeking, Knocking	7:7-12			
The Golden Rule/Two Ways	7:13-14			
False Prophets and The Doer	7:15-23			

THE FIFTH MIRACLE -THE CENTURION COMES

In the following graph, once again we have a time gap in between Mat. 8:4 at Jerusalem, and the fifth miracle, in Capernaum.

The fourth, fifth, sixth, and seventh miracle all occur in Galilee. Thus the grouping of the scriptures in the section of this graph, from the Synoptics, dovetail at this point, parallel, and flow into, and out of each other, when relating to the events surrounding Jesus' return '*into Capernaum*' (Mat. 8:5), after leaving Judea, as did the Scriptures that correspond to the events before that.

Event	Matthew	Mark	Luke	John
Two Foundations & Ends Sayings	7:24-28			
3rd Miracle *Simon the Leper*	*8:1-4*			
Jesus and Disciples Baptize				3:22
John Out of Prison Baptizing				3:23-26
Jesus and Disciples Leave Judea				4:1-5
The Woman of Samaria				4:6-34
Two Harvests				4:35-38
Two Days Later Leaves				4:39-45
4th Miracle *Nobleman's Son and Second in Cana*				4:46-54
5th Miracle *Centurion Comes*	*8:5-13*			
6th Miracle *Mother-in-Law*	*8:14-15*	*1:29-31*	*4:38-39*	
The City Gathers to be Healed	*8:16*	*1:32-34*	*4:40-41*	
Fulfills Prophecy	*8:17*			
Jesus Goes to a Solitary Place		1:35		
Disciples Follow		1:36		
Disciples & People Find Him		1:37	4:42	
Leaves for Second Circuit		1:38-39	4:43-44	
7th Miracle Catch of Fishes			5:1-11	
Discipleship/Sails to Gergesa	8:18-23			

Considering Mat. 8:13, in the graph above, which ends the dialogue of the fifth miracle of the Centurion's servant, we see that Luke and Mark directly afterwards both parallel with Matthew at this point, with miracle six, the healing of Peter's mother-in-law, being the synchronizing factor and sign.

The Greek word for '*miracle*' - '*semeion*', also means '*a sign*'. Jesus did numerous miracles, the most not even recorded in the Gospels. Thus we can conclude, that the ones that are mentioned, along with the preceding and proceeding incidents, were consequently also recorded for signs, or markers, which, moreover, could be used as a device to keep us in the correct order to the successive events throughout the Gospels.

Matthew 8

5 And when Jesus was entered into Capernaum, there came to Him a Centurion, imploring Him,

6 and saying, "Lord, my servant lies at home paralyzed, grievously tormented."

7 And Jesus says to him, "I will come and heal him."

8 And the Centurion answered and said,

"Lord, I am not worthy that You should come under my roof: but speak the word only, and my servant shall be healed.

9 For I am a man under authority, having soldiers under me: and I say to this man, 'Go,' and he goes; and to another, 'Come,' and he comes; and to my servant, 'Do this,' and he does it."

10 When Jesus heard it, He marveled, and said to those whom followed,

"Truly I say to you, I have not found such great faith, no, not in Israel.

11 And I say to you, that many shall come from the East and West, and shall sit down with Abraham, and Isaac, and Jacob, in the Kingdom of Heaven.

12 But the children of the Kingdom shall be cast out into darkness: there shall be weeping and gnashing of teeth."

13 And Jesus said to the Centurion,

"Go your way; and as you have believed, so be it done to you."

And his servant was healed the selfsame hour.

The fifth miracle above is distinct from miracle thirteen of Luke 7:1-10, in several aspects. Though both relate to *The Centurion*'s *Servant*, they are weeks apart, and are two separate incidents.

Matthew's detail of the account after the fifth miracle (8:16-17), parallels and dovetails with *The Sixth Miracle* (vv. 14-15), which synchronizes along with the same details covered also by Mark (1:29-31) and Luke (4:38-39). Subsequently, further, it gives us the correct time setting.

Luke, who referred to when *The Centurion's Servant* was ill again - later, knew that Matthew had recorded the first event. Luke's purpose was also to add certainty to declarations that were going around, and to various details that had been left out, keeping any debatable issue of the events in order, so they would not become confused. He had made this clear by the first verses in his opening chapter (1:1-3).

The differences of the two accounts are:

Matthew 8:1-13 - The Fifth Miracle - The Centurion Comes

[1] The Centurion came personally and directly to Jesus (v. 5).

[2] The servant was not dying of the illness, though it was grievous (v. 6).

[3] Jesus did not go to heal him (v. 8).

[4] The servant was healed from where Jesus spoke, telling the Centurion, '*Go your way*' (v. 13).

Luke 7:1-10 - The Thirteenth Miracle - The Centurion Sends a Delegate
[1] The Centurion sent Elders of the Jews this time (v. 2).
[2] The servant's illness was now concluding to his near death (v. 2).
[3] At this instant Jesus went with the Elders (v. 6).
[4] The Centurion states in a message, that he was not worthy, this time, as he had approached Jesus previously, to even come now to Jesus, and consequently has second thoughts about having sent the Elders, and actually sends friends to intercept them (vv. 6-7).

Though some of the wording in the above accounts of miracle five and thirteen, regarding the narration of the conversation are similar, this is not strange, as when talking or dealing with a situation or topic, it warrants the same reasoning. Nonetheless, Matthew's text has some different words (8:11-12), which are also used again later, but at another completely different event over a year later in Judea (Luke 13:28-29).

This characteristic is common throughout the Gospels, when reiterating to various individuals, groups, or to the disciples, or the seventy, who had the same teachings taught them, as did the disciples. We see this somewhat with *The Sermon Up The Mount* and *The Sermon Down The Mount*.

In any case, subsequently, and directly after the thirteenth miracle, Luke tells us *The Fourteenth Miracle* occurred next (7:11-14), with the Baptist's disciples informing the Baptist, who was still in prison (vv. 18-35), of the rumor which had evolved regarding the fourteenth miracle, '*that God had visited His people*' (Luke 7:15-17). Matthew (11:2-19) also parallels with this incident, too, adding to the criteria for the correct positioning of the successive ordering of events by Luke.

THE SIXTH MIRACLE - PETER'S MOTHER-IN-LAW

Matthew 8:14 Mark 1:29-30 Luke 4:38
And He rose, and immediately, when they were come out of the synagogue, as soon as they and Jesus arrived they entered into the house of Simon Peter and Andrew, with James and John.
Now Simon's wife's mother was taken sick with a severe fever; and He saw his wife's mother lying, and they now tell Him of her, and appealed to Him for her.
Matthew 8:15 Mark 1:31 Luke 4:39
And He came and stood over her, and He touched her hand, and rebuked the fever; and it immediately left her: and He took her by the hand, and lifted her up; and instantly she rose, and she ministered to them.

Matthew 8:16 Mark 1:32-34a Luke 4:40

And now when the sun was setting, as soon as the evening was come, after the sun did set, all those who had any sick with various diseases, brought them all to Him; and many who were possessed with devils: and all the city was gathered together at the door.

And He laid His hands on every one of them, and many, and healed all those who were sick of different diseases,

Mark 1:34b Luke 4:41

and cast out many devils also, who came out of many, crying out, and saying, "You are the Messiah the Son of God."

And He rebuking the spirits with His word didn't allow them to speak: because they knew that He was the Messiah.

Matthew 8

17 That it might be fulfilled which was spoken by Isaiah (53:4 the prophet, saying, 'HE TOOK ON OUR INFIRMITIES, AND BORE OUR SICKNESSES.'

Mark 1

35 And in the morning, rising up a great while before day, He went out, and departed into a solitary place, and there prayed.

36 And Simon and those who were with Him followed after Him.

Mark 1:37 Luke 4:42

And when it was day, He departed and went into a deserted place: and when they had found Him, they said to Him, "Everyone is looking for You."

And the people sought Him, and came to Him, and delayed Him, so that He wouldn't depart from them.

Mark 1:38 Luke 4:43

And He said to them, "I must preach the Kingdom of God to other cities also: let us go into the next towns that I may preach there too: for therefore I came forth and therefore am I sent."

THE SECOND GALILEAN TOUR

Mark 1:39 Luke 4:44

And He preached in their synagogues throughout all of Galilee, and cast out devils.

Some manuscripts in their translation of Luke 4:44, refer to the area of Judea. When understanding that indeed the '*synagogues of Judea*' or the '*land of Judea*' relates specifically to all the synagogues in the vicinity of Galilee belonging to the jurisdiction and authority of Judea, since the Headquarters of the Pharisees was in Jerusalem, the vicinity of Galilee belonging to the jurisdiction and authority of Galilee belonging to the jurisdiction and authority of Judea, since the Headquarters of the Pharisees was in Jerusalem, the meaning of the manuscripts which refer to this difference, is obviously averring to the synagogues in Galilee being '*of Judea*' in the sense that they belonged to Judea, or Jewry, not that Mark (1:39) was contradicting Luke (4:44). Moreover, the Pharisees came to visit the adjacent areas from Judea every now and then, as is clearly shown by the many references to that fact. Mark, in the last verse above, indicates how the emphasis should be inflected, when using the manuscript in question.

Notice Mark 1:39, indicates, '*their synagogues*', meaning - '*the synagogues of Jewry*', being in localities other than Judea. The Greek word '*Ioydaia*', which is sometimes used to refer to '*Judea*', depending on the context, can also refer to anything belonging to '*Jewry*'.

As Mark covers the same account of the previous events, it is he, if we are using the other manuscripts in question, who gives us the idiom of translation in that case, as at any rate, the scenario before and after is taking place in the Galilee area.

Nevertheless, as we are using the AV as our main basis, and that it has '*Galilee*' in the Greek, in either case, we have the correct location when progressing with our findings.

Thus, at our next intersection, it is clear that the dialogue from Luke 4:44 through to Luke 5, is still referring to the same area, as our next miracle, the seventh, would naturally take place in Bethsaida, Galilee, where Luke along with Matthew and Mark had earlier synchronized and paralleled together with the sixth miracle. This was in the home of Simon Peter and Andrew his brother.

Continuing, now at the seventh miracle, which occurred when they were fishing not far from the shore where they lived (Luke 5:1-11). To keep these records in order we should remember why Luke wrote in the first instance.

12   *THE NEXT EXCURSION*

The Seventh Miracle - The Catch Of Fishes

The incident of the seventh miracle is reminiscent of the seventh miracle after the resurrection (John 21:1-14). At both incidents the disciples had returned to try their hand at fishing, in a break from the events associated with the gospel. At the point where we are now in Luke, the disciples had taken a break from the rigor of traveling with Jesus throughout Galilee.

Though disciples were being called as Jesus went along announcing the good news, including the seventy, Matthew had not yet been called at this juncture, as Matthew (9:9-13), Mark (2:14-22), and Luke (5:27-39), witness to that fact. Matthew's calling occurred weeks after, from where we are at the moment.

Furthermore, the twelve would become ordained apostles many weeks later, after Matthew's calling (Mat. 10:1-42, Mark 3:14-19, Luke 6:13-16). Now, the eleven were disciples who were still being taught and influenced. Thus, at the last intersection, while Jesus and the disciples had traveled throughout Galilee again (Mark 1:38-39; Luke 4:43-44), in now the second Galilean tour, they had returned to the area where they lived, and decided to try their hand again at fishing, while awaiting the next phase of the tour.

Similarly, this had occurred previously after Jesus had first called the five at Bethabara, before embarking on their first Galilean tour [pp. 48-50].

Through the Scriptures, before this intersection, we can see that Matthew (8:14-17), Mark (1:29-39), including Luke (4:38-44) covered the same events surrounding the start of Luke's indigenous seventh miracle.

Luke 5
1 And it came to pass, that as the people pressed upon Him to hear the word of God, He stood by the Lake of Gennesaret,
2 and saw two boats standing by the lake: but the fishermen were gone out of them, and were washing their nets.
3 And He entered into one of the boats, which was Simon's, and prayed him that he would thrust out a little from the land.
And He sat down, and taught the people out of the boat.

4 Now when he had left speaking, He said to Simon,
"Launch out into the deep, and let down your nets for a catch."
5 And Simon answering said to Him,
"Master, we have toiled all the night, and have taken nothing: nevertheless at Your word I will let down the net."

Luke 5

6 And when they had done this, they enclosed a great number of fishes: and their net broke.

7 And they beckoned to their partners, who were in the other boat, that they should come and help them.

And they came and filled both the boats, so that they began to sink.

8 When Simon Peter saw it, he fell down at Jesus' knees, saying, "Depart from me; for I am a sinful man, oh Lord."

9 For he was astonished, and all who were with him, at the catch of the fishe s which they had taken:

10 and so also were James, and John, the sons of Zebedee, who were partners with Simon.

And Jesus said to Simon, "Fear not; from now on you shall catch people."

11 And when they had brought their boats to land, they forsook all, and followed Him.

The disciples at this point were now again psyched up, after witnessing the seventh miracle following Jesus' advice on fishing, for the next phase of their journeying in accompanying Jesus, in becoming fishers of people (v. 11). Of course, they would not be fully instrumental in actually '*catching people*', until they were ordained apostles, which while Jesus was teaching them, would be weeks later from where we are, and months, before they were actually sent out without Jesus. Additionally, they would receive extra Spirit at Pentecost, after the Ascension, which would enable them to promote that task even further.

Remember the seventh miracle is indigenous to Luke, with Matthew having recorded the next following event of the eighth miracle, surrounding that same time. It occurred after the seventh miracle, as they were ready once again to leave their hometown and follow Jesus.

Recalling that the town was Bethsaida, where the sixth and seventh miracle had occurred. the eighth miracle, as they were about to set sail from the shore of Bethsaida, was to transpire somewhere on their journey across the Sea of Galilee.

However, no doubt after having rested the following night, as Jesus had '*taught the people*' in the day (v. 3), and as they had previously '*toiled all the night*' (v. 5), now, in the next morning, before setting off, great crowds having arrived again, '*He gave commandment to depart to the other side*' (Mat. 8:18). Luke indicated it was to the next '*certain town*' (5:12).

Matthew had also revealed, they were traveling '*to the country of the Gergesenes*' (8:28). The nearest subsequent city would have been Gergesa, which was several miles below Bethsaida. Correspondingly, '*the country of the Gergesenes*' was named after the city of Gergesa.

Matthew 8

18 Now when Jesus saw great crowds about Him, He gave instructions to depart to the other side.

19 And a certain Scribe came, and said to Him, "Master, I will follow You wherever You go.
20 And Jesus says to him, "The foxes have holes, and the birds of the air have nests; but the Son of Humanity has nowhere to lay His head."

21 And another of His disciples said to Him, "Lord, allow me first to go and bury my father."
22 But Jesus said to him, "Follow Me; and let the dead bury their dead."

Some of the same words about discipleship [see section *At the Borders of Samaria/ Judea*], are used again, but at a different location more than a year later (Luke 9:57-62). As mentioned previously, this is common throughout the Gospels, and is indicative of Jesus using the same teachings, when calling others who needed that particular maxim, too.

Jesus was still calling other disciples. Even Matthew at this juncture had not become one of the twelve. Others who would eventually make up the seventy were also being called. The seventy, as we shall see, were no doubt

THE EIGHTH MIRACLE - THE TEMPEST

Matthew 8

23 And when He had entered into a boat, His disciples followed Him.
24 And, presently, there arose a great tempest in the sea, insomuch that the boat was covered with waves: but He was asleep.

25 And His disciples came to Him, and awoke Him, saying,
"Lord, save us: we will die."
26 And He says to them, "Why are you fearful, oh you of little faith?"

Then He rose, and rebuked the winds and the sea; and there was a great calm.
27 But the men marveled, saying,
"What manner of Man is this, that even the winds and the sea obey Him!"

The eighth miracle of the '*tempest*', Gr. '*seismos*', is similar, but is a completely different incident to the sixteenth miracle of the '*storm*', Gr. '*lailaps*', even though both relate to the Sea of Galilee. Recalling there are five miracles that appear to be the same, we are now at the third one.

The differences between the eighth and the sixteenth miracle are:

Matthew 8:23-27 - The Eighth Miracle - The Tempest
[1] Remember, the disciples had *'toiled all the night'* (Luke 5:5), after which the seventh miracle took place (v. 6). Thus, naturally they would have rested that particular day, sailing at the next opportunity (v. 11). During this time great crowds were already awaiting Jesus, precipitating their leaving (Mat. 8:18).
[2] They were to set sail from Bethsaida (v. 23), the home town of Peter and Andrew, where previously Peter's mother-in-law had been healed (vv. 14-15), and subsequently, where also many other people were healed (vv. 16-17), sailing *'to the country of the Gergesenes'* (v. 28).
[3] Both Mark (1:40-45) and Luke (5:12-15) agree that when they arrived *The Ninth Miracle - The Second Leper* occurred.

Mark 4:35-41, 5:1 Luke 8:22-27 - The Sixteenth Miracle - *The Storm*
[1] Mark tells us at this juncture it was evening (4:35), and thus, when this storm arose, they were making their way to the opposite side of the coast; by then it would have been night-time.
2] Here they traveled from Capernaum. From the dialogue we can establish where they came from, as the whole of Mark's narration from ch. 2 to the end of ch. 4 takes place at Capernaum, indicating, moreover, where the same events in Matthew and Luke transpired [see *Scripture Graph IV-V*]. Hence, when coming to Mark 5:1, and Luke 8:26, they are sailing *'to the country of the Gadarenes'*.
[3] The Synoptics all agree that they sailed the same day, after the *Parable of the Sower* and additional parables had been given (Mat. 13:53; Mark 4:34-35; Luke 8:21-22).

GERGESA

Some manuscripts have *'Gadarenes'*, in Matthew's account, and some *'Gergesenes'* in Luke's. Some even have *'Gerasenes'*, in either. Nonetheless, these are references to three distinct towns.

Gadara and Gerasa were within the region known as the Decapolis. Gergesa, a town on the coast of the Sea of Galilee, was just over the border of the Decapolis, in Gaulanitis, and the next town when traveling down from Bethsaida.

Gadara and Gerasa were also free, important city-states, thus giving name to their vicinities, as well as being cities of the Decapolis. Gadara was about five miles SE from the border of the Decapolis, whereas Gerasa was thirty-five miles SE.

Nevertheless, Gergesa, a town on the coast of the Sea of Galilee, is the one that fits the description of all our findings for the ninth, the next miracle, of the second leper, and the facts surrounding the seventh and eighth miracle.

The Sea of Galilee (Mat. 4:18) was also known as the Sea of Tiberias (John 21:1), and the Lake of Gennesaret (Luke 5:1); thus being named after three localities, like the towns above.

Gadara, the city of the area relating to the sixteenth miracle - *The Storm*, and the seventeenth miracle, of the single demoniac, was about five miles from the coast, and explicitly fits in with the topography surrounding the narratives in that instance, and of that particular town being further from the coast.

When we study the part of *Scripture Graph IV*, covering the beginning of our following text after Mat. 8.28, Luke 5:12, and Mark 1:40, we should understand that in Mark's version of the events, he had indicated before the healing of *The Ninth Miracle* of *The Second Leper*, that it was Jesus' intention to travel to the next towns (vv. 38-39).

Obviously Mark or the other Evangelists could have recorded other miracles and events, since Jesus did many more than these. But, the only ones that were, are those specifically recorded. Thus, when following the pattern of preaching to the next towns Gergesa, would have been the nearest in any case.

THE NINTH MIRACLE - THE SECOND LEPER

Event	Matthew	Mark	Luke	John
Leaves For Second Circuit		1:38-39	4:43-44	
7th Miracle Draught of Fishes			5:1-11	
Discipleship/Sails To Gergesa	8:18-23			
8th Miracle The Tempest	8:24-27			
They Arrive at Gergesa	8:28			
9th Miracle Second Leper		*1:40-45*	*5:12-15*	
Jesus Withdraws to Wilderness			5:16	
10th Miracle Two Demoniacs	8:28-34			
11th Miracle The Paralytic Man	9:1-8	2:1-12	5:17-26	

Though Matthew covers *The Tenth Miracle*, he chooses not to recall the event of this particular leper in that '*certain town*', when he states Jesus '*was coming to the other side into the country of the Gergesenes*'.

The record of the two demoniacs occurred directly away from the city, in the countryside or seaside area of Gergesa, as '*the whole city came out to meet Jesus, and when they saw Him they implored Him that He would depart out of their coasts*' (Mat. 8:34). After which Jesus and the disciples return to Capernaum.

Because, we have placed the beginning part of v. 28a in its appropriate position, the rest of the v. 28b follows in its natural place, after Luke 5:16.

Matthew 8:28a Mark 1:40 Luke 5:12

And when He was come to the other side into the country of the Gergesenes, it came to pass, when He was in a certain town, suddenly there came a leprous man, full of leprosy toward Him: who seeing Jesus fell on his face imploring Him, and kneeling down begged Him, saying to Him,
"Lord, if You wish, You can make me clean."

Mark 1:41-42 Luke 5:13
And Jesus, moved with compassion, put out His hand, and touched him, and says to him, "I will: be clean."
And as soon as He had spoken, immediately the leprosy departed from him and he was cleansed.
Mark 1:43-44 Luke 5:14
And He strictly advised him to tell no one: and immediately in sending him away, says to him, "See you say nothing to anyone: but go your way, and SHOW YOURSELF TO THE PRIEST (Lev. 13:39; 14:2), and offer for your cleansing, those things according to which Moses commanded, for evidence of it."

Mark 1:45 Luke 5:15
But he went out, and began to publish it much, and to blaze the matter abroad, insomuch Jesus could no more openly enter into the town, but was withdrawn in the deserted places.

But so much more went there abroad fame of Him: and they came to Him from every quarter, great crowds coming together to hear, and to be healed by Him of their sicknesses.

We already covered the major differences between the third, and ninth miracles, regarding the lepers, under the heading of *Simon the Leper - The Third Miracle* [p. 66].

Recapping, we saw at *The Eighth Miracle* of *The Tempest*, which would have taken place in the day time, when arriving at that '*certain town*' of Gergesa, directly on the coast, in '*the country of the Gergesenes*', the ninth miracle occurred within that '*certain town*'.

THE TENTH MIRACLE – THE TWO DEMONIACS

Jesus had told the leper not to tell anyone. But he blazes the matter abroad, resulting in Jesus having to withdraw from the town. It was at that point, Jesus came face to face with two demoniacs, as they had come out of the tombs, which would have been outside of the town. Moreover, the keepers of the pigs went to the town to tell of the event (Mat. 8:33).

Subsequently, the townspeople persuaded Jesus and the disciples to leave, as they were not too happy over their herd drowning in the sea (v. 34).

Luke 5
16 And He withdrew Himself into a deserted area, and prayed.

Matthew 8

28b And there met Him two possessed with devils, coming out of the tombs, extremely fierce, so that no one might pass that way.

29 And, suddenly, they cried out, saying,

"What have we to do with You, Jesus, You Son of God? Are You come here to torment us before the time?"

30 And there was a good way off from them a herd of swine feeding.

31 So the devils begged Him, saying,

"If you cast us out, allow us to go away into the herd of swine."

32 And He said to them, "Go."

And when they were come out, they went into the herd of swine: and, suddenly, the whole herd of swine ran furiously down a steep place into the sea, and perished in the waters.

33 And they who kept them fled, and went their ways into the town, and told everything, including what had happened to the possessed with devils.

34 And, shortly, the whole town came out to meet Jesus: and when they saw Him, they implored Him that He would depart out of their coasts.

Matthew 9:1 Mark 2:1a

And He entered into a boat, and passed over, and again He entered coming into His own city, Capernaum, after some days.

Because some do not see the differences between the demoniacs of the tenth, and the demoniac of the seventeenth miracle we will address them next:

Matthew 8:28-34 - The Tenth Miracle - The Two Demoniacs

[1] Occurred near to the '*certain town*' (Luke 5:12), being Gergesa by the sea (Mat. 8:28).

[2] Jesus had withdrawn from the town (Mark 1:45; Luke 5:16), thus, the demoniacs appeared afterwards.

[3] There were two, who were extremely fierce in attitude (Mat. 8:28).

[4] The whole town comes out to Jesus, and asks Him to leave (v. 34).

[5] They leave for Capernaum (Mat. 9:1; Mark 2:1), after originally having sailed from Bethsaida (Luke 5:11), to Gergesa.

Mark 5:1-20 Luke 8:26-39 - The Seventeenth Miracle - The Demoniac

[1] Occurred '*in the Decapolis*' (Mark 5:20), in '*the country of the Gadarenes*'

(Mark 5:1). The city of Gadara being about five miles away from the coast, and a city-state of the Decapolis.

[2] The demoniac met Jesus immediately as soon as He came ashore (Mark 5:2; Luke 8:27).

[3] There was only one (Mark 5:2; Luke 8:27), who worshiped Jesus (Mark 5:6), and wanted to travel with Him (Mark 5:18; Luke 8:38).

[4] Subsequently, '*the whole multitude of the country of the Gadarenes round about*' asks Him to leave (Luke 8:37).

5] They *return to* Capernaum from where they had sailed from (Mark 5:21; Luke 8:40).

In the next section we will see further how the Synoptics all relate to each other in their own particular unique way, as Jesus and the disciples arrive at Capernaum, after The Tenth Miracle at Gergesa (Mat. 9:1; Mark 2:1; Luke 5:17).

13   BACK TO CAPERNAUM

THE ELEVENTH MIRACLE – THE PARALYTIC MAN

Jesus and the disciples had sailed from Gergesa to Capernaum, which closed the last section after *The Tenth Miracle*, and included the last two references of Mat. 9:1 and Mark 2:la, where Matthew informs us they set sail for '*His own city*'. Though Mark does not record the detail of actually sailing, but nevertheless he mentioned Capernaum by name and Jesus arriving there.

With these references, we have another example of how the Synoptics all relate to the same particular event in their own special way. Luke (5:17a) and Mark (2:lb) below, align together on the various details of Jesus now being back at Capernaum. However, it was Matthew who exclusively recorded the region of the town Gergesa, to where they had originally set sail to (8:28a), when leaving Bethsaida after the seventh miracle.

Mark 2:1b Luke 5:17a
And it came to pass on a certain day that it was noised that He was at home.
Mark 2:2 Luke 5:17b
And straightaway many were gathered together, insomuch that there was no room to receive them, no, not so much as about the door: and as He was teaching - preaching the word to them, there were Pharisees and Doctors of the Law sitting by, who were come out of every town of Galilee and Judea, and Jerusalem: and the power of the Lord was present to heal.
Matthew 9:2 Mark 2:3 Luke 5:18
And, consequently, men were coming to Him bringing a man lying on a stretcher, who was motionless, a paralytic, being carried by four: and they tried to bring him in, to lay him before Him.
Mark 2:4 Luke 5:19
And when they could not find by what way they might bring him in, and come near to Him - because of the crowd, they went upon the housetop, uncovering the roof where He was: and when they had broken it up, they let down the stretcher bed in which the paralytic lay, through the tiling with his stretcher into the midst before Jesus.
Mark 2:5 Luke 5:20
And when Jesus saw their faith, He said to the paralytic,
"Son of humanity, be of good cheer, your sins are forgiven you."
Mark 2:6 Luke 5:21a
6 But there were certain of the Scribes and Pharisees sitting there, and began reasoning in their hearts, saying,
Mark 2:7 Luke 5:21b
And who this who speaks blasphemies? Who alone can forgive sins but God only?

Matthew 9:4 Mark 2:8 Luke 5:22

And immediately, when Jesus perceived, knowing in His spirit their thoughts that they so reasoned within themselves He answering said to them, "Wherefore think and reason these evil things in your hearts?

Matthew 9:5 Mark 2:9 Luke 5:23

For whether is it easier, to say to the paralytic, 'Your sins be forgiven you;' or to say, 'Rise, and take up your stretcher bed, and walk?'

Matthew 9:6 Mark 2:10-11 Luke 5:24

But that you may know that the Son of Humanity has Power upon earth to forgive sins," (then He said to the motionless paralytic, "I say to you, rise, and take up your stretcher bed, and go your way into your house."

Matthew 9:7-8 Mark 2:12 Luke 5:25-26

And immediately he rose, took up the stretcher, on which he lay, and went out before them all, departing to his own house, glorifying God.

But when the crowd saw it, they marveled insomuch that they were amazed, and they glorified God, who had given such power to humans, and were filled with fear, saying, "We never saw it in this fashion. We have seen strange things today."

Mark 2:13 Luke 5:27a

And after these things He went out again by the seaside; and the entire crowd came to Him and He taught them.

MATTHEW'S CALLING

After *The Eleventh Miracle*, of the healing of *The Paralytic*, at Capernaum, Matthew had still not been called to follow and make up the number of the twelve apostles. Thus, there were still eleven at this point. Hence, we can see on the following page that the Synoptics align together with the calling of Matthew.

   Mark (2:1, 13) having indicated it was after Jesus had taught at Capernaum by the seaside.

Matthew 9:9 Mark 2:14 Luke 5:27b-28

And as Jesus passed on from there, going by He saw a tax man, named Matthew Levi, the son of Alpheus, sitting at the Receipt of Custom: and He said to Him, "Follow Me."

And he rose up, left all, and followed Him.

Matthew 9:10 Mark 2:15 Luke 5:29

And Levi made Him a grand banquet in his own house: and it came to pass, that, as Jesus sat at dinner in his house, consider, there were a great company of tax collectors and other sinners who also came together, who sat down with them and Jesus and His disciples: for there were many, and they followed Him.

Matthew 9:11 Mark 2:16 Luke 5:30
And when their Scribes and Pharisees saw Him eating with tax collectors and sinners, they said murmuring against His disciples, "How is it that you, and He - Your Master, eat and drink with tax collectors and sinners?"

Matthew 9:12 Mark 2:17 Luke 5:31
But when Jesus heard that, Jesus answering said to them,
"They who are whole have no need of a physician, but those who are sick.
Luke 5
32 I came not to call the righteous, but sinners to repentance."

Mark 2:18 Luke 5:33
(Now the disciples of John and of the Pharisees used to fast:) and they came closer and said to Him, "Why do the disciples of John fast often, and make prayers, and likewise the disciples of the Pharisees fast, but Your disciples fast not, Yours eat and drink?"
Mark 2:19 Luke 5:34
And Jesus said to them,
"Can you make the children of the bride chamber fast, while the bridegroom is with them? As long as they have the bridegroom with them, they cannot fast.
Mark 2:20 Luke 5:35
But the days will come, when the bridegroom shall be taken away from them, and then they shall fast in those days."

Mark 2:21 Luke 5:36
And He spoke also a parable to them;
"No one sows a piece of new garment cloth upon an old garment: else if otherwise, the new piece that covers the tear, rips away from the old, making the tear worse, and also the piece from the new will not match the old.

Mark 2:22 Luke 5:37-38
And no one puts new wine into old wineskins: else the new wine burst the wineskins, and the wine leaks, and the skins become marred and ruin: but new wine must be put into new wineskins and both are preserved.
Luke 5
39 No one also having drunk old wine immediately desires new: for they say, 'The old is better.'
Matthew 9
13 But you go and learn what this means, 'I WILL HAVE MERCY, AND NOT SACRIFICE' (Hos. 6:6): *for I am not come to call the righteous, but sinners to repentance*" (Luke 5:32).

When studying the text surrounding the event of the grand banquet held for Jesus in Matthew's own house, because of the three analogies of the *Parable of the Children of the Bride Chamber*, the *Parable of the New Cloth on an Old Garment*, and the *Parable of the New Wine in Old Wineskins*, which Jesus uses again at a completely different time, though Matthew's (9:14-17) text has the Baptist's disciples arriving following the banquet scenario, confusion has arisen as to the exact synchronization of these incidents.

We will cover this so-called difficulty, in more detail after we have dealt with the previous main text. However, considering this initially in studying the next graph, with the details relating to John's disciples coming the first time, we see that the two witnesses of Matthew (11:2-6) and Luke (7:19-23) both agree when they first came.

Event	Matthew	Mark	Luke	John
11th Miracle Paralytic Healed	9-:1-8	2:1-12	5:17-26	
Jesus Teaches by Seaside		2:13		
Matthew Levi Called	9:9	2:14	5:27-28	
Jesus Dines at Matthew's With Sinners/Question on Company	*9:10-12*	*2:15-17*	*5:29-32*	
They Question on Fasting too		2:18-20	5:33-35	
New Cloth on an Old Garment		2:21	5:36	
New Wine in Old Wineskins		2:22	5:37-39	
Jesus Finally Reiterates	*9:13*			
Sabbath Questions	12:1-8	2:13- 28	6:1-5	
12th Miracle Withered Hand	12:9-13	3:1-5	6:6-11	
Pharisees Take Counsel	12:14	3:6		
Jesus Heals by the Seaside In Boat	12:15	3:7		
Fulfills Prophecy	12:16-21	3:8-12		
Goes up Mount to Pray		3:13	6:12	
Ordination of Twelve	10:1-42	3:14-19	6:13-16	
Starts to Teach and Heal	11:1		6:17-19	
Sermon Down the Mount			6:20-38	
Blind Leading Blind Commingled with Teaching of Sermon Up Mt.			6:39 6:40-49	
Jesus and Disciples Leave Plain		3:19-21	7:1	
13th Miracle Centurion's Servant Elders Sent Now			7:2- 10	
14th Miracle Man in Coffin			*7:11-17*	
John's Disciples Tell John			7:18	
John's Disciples Come To Jesus	*11:2-6*		*7:19-23*	
John The Baptist Extolled	11:7-15		7:24-30	
Jesus Compares Generation	11:16-19		7:31-35	

Returning to the main text of the last intersection, in the Synoptic accounts, Jesus answers the first question at the banquet, relating to the company He and the disciples kept, which aligns Matthew 9:12, Mark 2:17, and Luke 5:31-32.

Luke records that John's disciples were not present at that particular time, as it is he, who specifically reveals that "*they*" who asked Jesus the first question (Luke 5:33), were the '*Scribes and the Pharisees*' (v. 30), which synchronizes with the same "*they*" in Mark 2:18. Furthermore, there is no actual mentioning of John's disciples arriving in Luke's or Mark's account, or asking the question as in Matthew's (9:14) different account, where the Baptist's disciples are the ones who do the asking.

The specific statement of *'the disciples of John and the Pharisees used to fast'* (Mark 2:18), is found exclusively in Mark, and would be better placed in brackets, as we have indicated in the last main text.

The second question covers the query on fasting and praying, which both Mark (2:18) and Luke (5:33) correlate together on, when following our findings. The how, when, and why the *'Scribes and the Pharisees'* asked this question on fasting, further endorses our findings, in examining two words in the Greek text.

Having already retranslated *'come'* in Mark 2:18, and *'to'* in Luke 5:33, in the previous main text, into what is believed to be the intended idiom, taking into consideration the details of the whole setting of the scenario, we see that Mark uses the Greek word *'erchomai'*, meaning *'to come'*, or *'came'*. Whereas, Luke uses *'pros'*, meaning *'toward'*, *'closer'*, or *'nearer'*, as it may be translated.

Thus, when considering the whole context of the event at Matthew's *'own house'*, that *'there were a great company of tax collectors and other sinners'*, and, *'their Scribes and Pharisees'* who were dinning with Jesus and the disciples at the banquet, subsequently, having asked the first question addressed at the disciples (Mat. 9:11; Mark 2:l; Luke 5:30), no doubt they, the Scribes and Pharisees being nearer to the disciples, and Jesus having overheard them (Mat. 9:12; Mark 2:17; Luke 5:31), they consequently came closer to Jesus, to put the final question, which was on fasting, to Him (Mark 2:18; Luke 5:33).

Hence, the parables on fasting, and the *Children of the Bride Chamber*, the *New Cloth on an Old Garment*, and the *New Wine in Old Wineskins*, were used by Jesus to answer the only other question, which was on fasting.

Luke records Jesus' answer, in the conclusion of the first question with, *'I came not to call the righteous, but sinners to repentance'* (5:32). Matthew (9:12) and Mark (2:17) do not have this verse after the first question. Hence, we see from the previous graph, and the main text, that this concluded the first answer.

Jesus repeats, *'I came not to call the righteous, but sinners to repentance'* (Mat. 9:13), which concludes the event of the banquet at Matthew's house, yet it is Matthew who pointed out, through, the grouping of these two events at the banquet together (vv. 9-13), and the disciples of the Baptist coming the second time to Jesus (vv. 14-17)), to show the antithesis between the Baptist's disciples attitude in asking Jesus the same question on fasting, and that of the Pharisees. Moreover, Matthew uses this style of grouping events together, which are actually separate in successive order, several other times for the same reason of emphasizing a particular point. We will cover these and the reason why, when coming to each particular dislocation.

Therefore, the dining at Matthew's is concluded by the final, and second answer after the parables, as Jesus reiterates His previous statement (Luke 5:32), now with extra words, amplified and re-emphasized, beginning this time (Mat. 9:13), *"But you go and learn what this means, 'I WILL HAVE MERCY, AND NOT SACRIFICE'* (Hos. 6:6)"*.

Furthermore, proceeding after the banquet with Mat. 9:14, is the first place in his Gospel where he does not follow on systematically in successive order, and is reminiscent of when we consider in our minds a thought, which in turn leads to another one. So, he uses the two separate events, to emphasize the difference between the attitude of the Pharisees, and the Baptist's disciples, who, were seeking further enlightenment. These Pharisees in question, considered themselves righteous already, and did not realize they needed to repent, and show mercy in their psyche to others. Also, with grouping the two events together, Matthew would then not have to repeat the three analogies again.

The event of the second time John's disciples come to Jesus, which we see in the structure of the next graph, where the Synoptics align again, dovetail, and parallel together at the eighteenth and nineteenth miracle, further indicates that Matthew was clear - it was at the eighteenth and nineteenth miracle, when John's disciples came to Jesus, the second time because, *'While He spoke these things to them'* (9:18), that Jairus the President of the synagogue, and the woman with the issue of blood came to Jesus. The Synoptics all relate and parallel together over these same incidents.

Besides, Matthew was clear as to the first time, that the Baptist's disciples came, which we see was after the *Fourteenth Miracle* of the resurrection of the man in the coffin, as the news, which had spread around, even went to the Baptist in prison (Luke 7:17-18), resulting in John sending two of his disciples to Jesus (Mat. 11:2-6; Luke 7:19-23).

Now, as we have mentioned previously, the same question warrants the same answer. Because Jesus was not addressing the Scribes and Pharisees, at this later event in Matthew 9:14-17, when it was the second time whereby John's disciples came to Jesus, He certainly would not have replied, *'I came not to call the righteous, but sinners'* (v. 13), if addressing the Baptist's disciples, as they were sympathetic to Jesus' mission. Thus, Jesus relates the three analogies about the question on fasting, again, to the Baptist's disciples that he had originally addressed to the Pharisees.

The first word of v. 14 is *'then'*. It has been translated from the Greek word *'tote'*, which can also mean *'at that time'*, or, *'at this time'*. We have witnessed previously, that sometimes between a verse, and verses there is a considerable time lag. So it was in between of these two separate events.

Event	Matthew	Mark	Luke	John
Growth of Light and Hearing		4:26-29		
Wheat and Tares/Mustard Seed	13:24-32	4:30-32		
Leaven/Finishes Teaching	13:33-35	4:33-34		
They Leave for Gadara	13:35	4:35-36	8:22	

Event	Matthew	Mark	Luke	John
16th Miracle The Storm		4:37-41	8:23-25	
17th Miracle Legion of Devils		5:1-20	8:26-39	
Back again in Capernaum		5:21		
John's Disciples Come Again	*9:14-17*			
18th Miracle *Woman's Issue*	*9:18-22*	*5:22-34*	*8:41-48*	
19th Miracle *Jairus Daughter*	*9:23-26*	*5:35-43*	*8:49-56*	
20th Miracle Two Blind Men	9:31-34			
21st Miracle Dumb Man	9:27-31			
They Leave Capernaum Jesus	9:35, 13:54	6:1		
Marvels at the Unbelief	13:55-58	6:2-6		

Without confusing the second time John's disciples came to Jesus (Mat. 9:14-17), and considering the first time two of his disciples came, too (Mat. 11:2-15; Luke 7:18-30), in a section from the main *Scripture Graph IV*, below, where the events had already occurred previous to the graph, we see the twelfth miracle transpired directly following the question over the Sabbath, on which the three Evangelists all agree, which followed shortly after the grand banquet held for Jesus at Matthew's.

Event	Matthew	Mark	Luke	John
New Wine In Old Wineskins		2:22	5:37-39	
Jesus Finally Reiterates	*9:13*			
Sabbath Question	*12:1-8*	*2:23-28*	*6:1-5*	
12th Miracle *Withered Hand*	*12:9-13*	*3:1-5*	*6:6-11*	
Pharisees Take Counsel	12:14	3:6		
Jesus Heals by Seaside	12:15	3:7		
In Boat/Fulfills Prophecy	12:16-21	3:8-12		
Goes Up Mountain to Pray		3:13	6:12	
Ordination of Twelve	*10:1-42*	*3:14-19*	*6:13-16*	
Starts to Teach and Heal			6:17-19	
Sermon Down the Mount			6:20-38	
Matthew's Calling			6:39	
Blind Leading Blind Commingled			6:40-49	
with Teaching Of Sermon Up Mt.				
Jesus and Disciples Leave Plain		3:19-21	7:1	
13th Miracle Centurion's Servant			7:2-10	
[Elders Sent Then]				
14th Miracle *Man in Coffin*			*7:11-17*	
John's Disciples Tell John			*7:18*	
John's Disciples Come To Jesus	*11:2-6*		*7:19-23*	
John the Baptist Extolled	*11:7-15*		*7:24-30*	
Jesus Compares That Generation	11:16-19		*7:31-35*	

Mark and Luke continue directly with the Sabbath Question, testifying to the order of those events following on, and bring us back into synchronization again with Matthew at the questioning over the Sabbath.

We now have covered the first time Matthew does not follow on systematically in successive order. The next time this happens is at *The Ordination Of The Twelve*

(10:1-42). Thus, when following the Scriptures on through, we come to the first account of John's disciples coming to Jesus, which both Matthew and Luke cover, dovetailing and paralleling with the successive events surrounding each other (Mat. 11:2-19; Luke 7:19-35), indicating which events follow on from there.

Thus, the event of John's disciples coming the second time, where Jesus reiterates the three analogies again, cannot be the first time, as depicted by following Matthew chronologically at that point. Furthermore, this second arrival of John's disciples leads up to the twentieth and twenty-first miracle, which ushers in the leaving of Capernaum, with a stop-off at Nazareth, before Jesus and the disciples embark on *The Second Judean Ministry*, after which John's disciples come to Jesus the third and final time, at John's death (Mat. 14:12, Mark 6:29). This will be covered in further detail when we arrive at the main text relating to John's death.

14   COUNTING PENTECOST

'The Second Sabbath After The First'

We return to the main text below, with the Pharisees questioning about their Sabbath regulations and the next miracle - the twelfth, the *man with the withered hand*. Both events took place after Matthew's banquet for Jesus, considering also that Matthew was the twelfth disciple and, as it were, the last of the twelve until Judas' replacement.

We had in the last section seen how Matthew had concluded the banquet at his house with Jesus' answer to the Pharisees with the last question, beginning (Mat. 9:13), "*But you go and learn what this means, 'I* WILL HAVE MERCY, AND NOT SACRIFICE' (Hos. 6:6): *for I am not come to call the righteous, but sinners to repentance*" (Luke 5:32).

Matthew, amazingly, with the next following event, was no doubt pointing out that the same Pharisees at Capernaum, who had been present at the banquet [though his narration does not follow on in successive order after that event], are now questioning Jesus and His disciples once again; this time over plucking corn on the next Sabbath. Here Matthew exclusively uses the same quote from Hos. 6:6, once more, which is seen in the verse where Jesus answers the Pharisees, that they '*would not have condemned the guiltless*' (12:7), had they at the close of the banquet gone and learnt, as Jesus had suggested, the meaning of, '*I* WILL HAVE MERCY.'

Matthew 12:1 Mark 2:23 Luke 6:1
And it came to pass on the second Sabbath Day, after the first, at that time
Jesus went through the grain fields; and His disciples were hungry, and began,
as they went, to pluck the ears of grain, and did eat, rubbing them in their hands.

Matthew 12:2 Mark 2:24 Luke 6:2
But when certain of the Pharisees saw it, they said to Him and them, "Look,
why do You and Your disciples do that which is not lawful upon the Sabbath
Days?"
Matthew 12:3 Mark 2:25 Luke 6:3
And Jesus answering said to them,
"Have you never read (1 Sam. 21:4-5) the very thing, which David did, when
he had need, and was hungry, he, and those who were with him?
Matthew 12:4 Mark 2:26 Luke 6:4
How he entered into the House of God, in the days of Abiathar the High Priest,
and did take and ate the Showbread, and gave also to those who were with
him; which was, and is not lawful for him to eat, neither for those who were
with him, but only for the Priests alone?

Matthew 12

5 Or have you not read in the Law (Num. 28:9-10), how that on the Sabbath Days the Priests in the Temple profane the Sabbath, and are blameless?
6 But I say to you, that in this place is One greater than the Temple.
7 But if you had known what this means (9:13), 'I WILL HAVE MERCY, AND NOT SACRIFICE (Hos. 6:6)', *you would not have condemned the guiltless."*

Mark 2

27 And He said to them, "The Sabbath was made for humanity (Ex.23:12; Deut. 5:14), and not humanity for the Sabbath."
Matthew 12:8 Mark 2:28 Luke 6:5
And He said to them further, "For therefore, even, the Son of Humanity is Lord also of the Sabbath."

The mentioning of *'the second Sabbath Day after the first'*, at the start of the previous main text, is rather curious. Some conclude that it was Luke's way of showing us it was the second Sabbath, of the seven Sabbaths that are counted from the Sabbath in the Days of Unleavened Bread, to calculate the Festival of Weeks, or Pentecost.

This would correspond with the knowledge of the area as being near Capernaum, which was in a low-lying vicinity, where the wheat fields matured earlier [April-May], than in the highlands [May-June]. Thus the description of the wheat being ready allows for there being five Sabbaths before Pentecost. Surprisingly, there are five Sabbaths mentioned in both Matthew and Mark's texts, relating solely to the incident of plucking the corn.

From Luke's text at ch. 4:38, seen clearly in the *Scripture Graph II-III*, which begins the scenario of the healing of Peter's mother-in-law, and is in the next year after v. 37, the dialogue is referring directly to after the first Passover. Following through to ch. 6, the only reference in Luke's text actually specifically referring to any Sabbaths in word, are exclusively mentioned and found in the text of the whole of his ch. 6. Which includes both the texts of plucking the corn, and *The Twelfth Miracle* of the healing of the man with the withered hand.

These Sabbaths are in vv. 1, 2, 5, 6, 7, and 9. When including *'the first'* as also averring to a Sabbath, there are seven.

Moreover, in Matthew and Mark's separate, parallel individual accounts of these two incidents, there are actually seven Sabbaths recorded specifically in word in each.

Another, amazing factor relating to the number seven at this point, is that there are also seven miracles from the parallel junction of the healing of *Peter's Mother-in-Law* (Mat. 8:14; Mark 1:29; Luke 4:38), which was *The Sixth Miracle*. Hence,

Peter's wife's mother [1], *The Catch Of Fishes* [2], *The Tempest* [3], *Simon the Leper* [4], *The Two Demoniacs* [5], *The Paralytic Man* [6], and the *Man With Withered Hand* [7], which is the next one, *The Twelfth Miracle*, which we cover after this intersection.

Furthermore, when adding up all the Sabbaths, mentioned exclusively in the previous combined main texts, referring only to the event regarding the plucking of the corn, there are also seven.

Respectively the reference we mentioned, '*I WILL HAVE MERCY, AND NOT SACRIFICE*' (Mat. 12:7), in the previous main text including when Jesus at the incident of replying to the Scribes and Pharisees in Matthew's house, also used the same quote in concluding the second answer, when they were told to '*go and learn what that means*' (Mat. 9:13). No doubt this occurred shortly before '*the second Sabbath after the first*' (Luke 6:1), and could easily have been a week before, with Luke alluding to that being the case. Matthew would then have been called on '*the first*' Sabbath, before '*the second*', and the grand banquet held on the day after Matthew's calling. So, the reiterating of '*I WILL HAVE MERCY, AND NOT SACRIFICE*', subsequently, added further irony to Jesus having at Matthew's house previously told them, '*you go and learn what that means*', when they still, only the next week later, were condemning the guiltless, having not grasped what Jesus had said about their judgmental attitudes, is amazingly juxtaposed at this junction.

The following main text below, taking the factor of the second Sabbath into consideration, would now be the third Sabbath.

THE TWELFTH MIRACLE - MAN WITH WITHERED HAND

Matthew 12:9-10a Mark 3:1 Luke 6:6
And it came to pass also on another Sabbath, that when He was departed from there, He went and entered again into their synagogue and taught: and consider, there was a man there whose right hand was withered.
Matthew 12:10b Mark 3:2 Luke 6:7
And the Scribes and Pharisees watched Him, whether He would heal him on the Sabbath Day; that they might find an accusation against Him.

And they asked Him, saying, "Is it lawful to heal on the Sabbath Days?" that they might accuse Him.
Matthew 12
11 And He said to them,
"What individual shall there be among you, who shall leave one sheep, and if it fall into a pit on the Sabbath Day, will they not lay hold on it, and lift it out?
12a How much then is a human being better than a sheep?"
Mark 3:3 Luke 6:8
But He knew their thoughts, and He says to the man with the withered hand, "Rise up, and come forward and stand in the middle."

And he rose, came forward and stood.
Mark 3:4 Luke 6:9
And then He said to them,
"I will ask you one thing; is it lawful to do good on the Sabbath Days, or to do
 evil, to save life, or to destroy and kill?"

But they held their peace.
Matthew 12
12b "Therefore it is lawful to do well on the Sabbath Days."

Matthew 12:13 Mark 3:5 Luke 6:10
And when He had looked round about upon them all with anger, being grieved
for the hardness of their hearts, He then says to the man,
"Stretch out your hand."

And he stretched it out; and his hand was restored whole, like as the other.
Luke 6
11 And they were filled with madness; and communed one with another what
they might do to Jesus.

Now, when counting each Sabbath, in the individual separate accounts of the
Synoptics, regarding just the text of the twelfth miracle, and adding them together,
once again there are also seven, though there are six in the previous combined texts
of this book relating solely to the twelfth miracle.

Notice at the previous last verse, Luke is the one who ends the account of the
twelfth miracle (v. 11). Whereas, in the next following section it is Matthew
(12:14-21) and Mark (3:6-12) who fill in the details of the next events, at which
point, Luke (6:12) returns with Mark (3:13), synchronizing the detail of Jesus
praying on the mountain, before aligning with Matthew again, at *The Ordination
Of The Twelve* disciples (Mat. 10:1-42; Mark 3:14-19; Luke 6:13-16).

We should remember, that it is not the chapters and verses that give order to the
events, but the incidents themselves.

Thus, we saw previously that after Mat. 9:13, his dialogue does not follow on in
successive order. Moreover, another example of how Matthew sometimes places
his text to get a point across, is in Jesus' invitation to shoulder His easy yoke
(11:28-30), which he assigns directly ahead of the confrontation over plucking the
ears of corn on the Sabbath (12:1-8), highlighting that Jesus proclaimed Himself
'*Lord of the Sabbath*'.

We see from *Scripture Graph v* that the invitation to shoulder His easy yoke
(11:28-30), occurred directly after the third circuit of Galilee (vv. 20-24), and was
spoken specially to disciples (vv. 25-27).

However, returning to our next successive following event, which actually dovetails with the Sabbath questioning and the twelfth miracle, as the Synoptics reveal. It continues with the first reference to the Pharisees taking counsel with the Herodians (Mat. 12:14; Mark 3:6), on how to destroy Jesus after witnessing the twelfth in the synagogue, after being admonished again over their attitude to the Sabbath (Luke 6:11).

'MY BELOVED SON, IN WHOM I AM WELL-PLEASED'

Matthew 12:14 Mark 3:6
And then the Pharisees went out, and straightaway took counsel with the Herodians against Him, how they might destroy Him.

Matthew 12:15a Mark 3:7
But when Jesus knew it, He withdrew Himself from there with His disciples to the sea: and great crowds from Galilee followed Him, and from Judea,
Matthew 12:15b Mark 3:8
and from Jerusalem, and from Idumea, and from beyond Jordan; and they about Tyre and Sidon, a great crowd, when they heard what great things He did, came to Him, and He healed them all.

Mark 3
9 And He spoke to His disciples, that a small boat should wait on Him because of the crowd, lest they should throng Him.
10 For He had healed many; insomuch that they pressed upon Him for to touch Him, as many had plagues.
11 Those with unclean spirits, when they saw Him, fell down before Him, and cried, saying, "You are the Son of God."
Matthew 12:16 Mark 3:12
And He strictly cautioned them that they should not make Him known.
Matthew 12
17 That it might be fulfilled which was spoken by Isaiah the prophet (42:1-4), saying,
18 "UNDERSTAND MY SERVANT, WHOM I HAVE CHOSEN; MY BELOVED, IN WHOM MY SOUL IS WELL-PLEASED: I WILL PUT MY SPIRIT ON HIM, AND HE SHALL SHOW JUDGMENT TO THE NATIONS.
19 HE WILL NOT STRIVE, NOR CRY; NEITHER SHALL ANYONE HEAR HIS VOICE IN THE STREETS.
20 HE WON'T BREAK A BRUISED REED. HE WON'T QUENCH SMOKING FLAX, UNTIL HE BRINGS JUSTICE TO VICTORY.
21 AND IN HIS NAME SHALL THE NATIONS TRUST."

Mark 3:13a Luke 6:12
And it came to pass in those days, that He went out, and proceeded to the mount to pray, and continued all night in prayer to God.

Luke did not find and need to mention the specific details that Matthew and Mark had recorded in the previous main text, about Jesus firstly withdrawing Himself from the Pharisees, when He knew Luke did not find any need to mention the specific details that they were planning to destroy Him, and of the healing of the great crowds, but returns after the narrative of Matthew (12:14-21) and Mark (3:6-12) on Jesus retreating to the mount (Luke 6:12)

Moreover, Mark 3:7-8, complemented Mat. 12:15, with the added information, of naming the areas the crowds had come from. Matthew, noting that '*He healed them all*' at that point.

Also, Mark (3:9-11) exclusively related the detail of the boat standing by, because of the thronging of the great crowds, and mentions those who had '*unclean spirits*'. Furthermore, Mark acknowledged Matthew's recalling earlier, that '*He healed them all*' (12:15), states, '*For He had healed many*' (3:10). Thus, Mark dovetailed with Matthew over the above incidents.

Then, at Mark 3:12, he synchronizes together virtually word for word with Mat. 12:16. Matthew's following vv. 17-21, alone recalling the prophecy from Is. 42:1-4, by which Luke 6:12, returns to the dialogue paralleling with Mark 3:13.

Luke (6:12), exclusively, indicated that Jesus prayed through the night, whereas Mark (3:13), also agreed with Luke, that it was on the mount, before the ordaining of the disciples as apostles took place.

The part of the quote from the prophecy of Is. 42:1, in Mat. 12:18, '*My Beloved, in whom My soul is well-pleased*', is redolent of the time it actually occurred, when the Spirit descended from Heaven on Jesus at His baptism, with similar words spoken from Heaven, '*My Beloved Son, in whom I am well-pleased*' (Mat. 3:17; Mark 1:11).

Besides, the only other time these words were spoken from Heaven was at *The Transfiguration* (Mat. 17:5; Mark 9:7; Luke 9:35), which was in the following year from where we are at the moment, at that time the seventy were being trained, as the twelve had been in the previous year. However, before the seventy were ordained, the twelve were to be ordained first. See *Scripture Graphs IV-VII* for the difference in time and parallel relationships. The mentioning in Matthew of the prophecy, '*I WILL PUT MY SPIRIT ON HIM*' (12:17-21), in successive order, actually transpired just before the point where the twelve were to be ordained (Mat. 10:1; Mark 3:14; Luke 6:13).

Though Matthew does not follow on in successive order with these preceding events, is significant at this juncture, as we consider the ordination of the twelve firstfruits, which is our next following incident.

Event	Matthew	Mark	Luke	John
11th Miracle Paralytic Healed	9:1-8	2:1-12	5:17-26	
Jesus Teaches by Seaside		2:13		
Matthew Levi Called	9:9	2:14	5:27-28	
Jesus Dines at Matthew's With	9:10-12	2:15-17	5:29-32	
Sinners/Question On Company				
They Question on Fasting Too		2:18-20	5:33-35	
New Cloth on An Old Garment		2:21	5:36	
New Wine in Old Wineskins		2:22	5:37-39	
Finally Reiterates	9:13			
Sabbath Questions	12:1-8	2:23-28	6:1-5	
12th Miracle Withered Hand	12:9-13	3:1-5	6:6-11	
1st Counsel Of Pharisees	12:14	3:6		
Jesus Heals by the Seaside	12:15- 16	3:7-12		
Fulfills Prophecy	*12:17-21*			
Goes Up Mount to Pray		*3:13*	*6:12*	
The Ordination of Twelve	*10:1-42*	*3:14-19*	*6:13-16*	
Starts to Teach and Heal	11:1		6:17-19	
Sermon Down the Mount			6:20-38	
Blind Leading Blind Commingled			6:39	
With Teachings Of Sermon Up Mt.			6:40-49	
Jesus and Disciples Leave Mount		3:19-21	7:1	
13th Miracle Centurion's Servant			7:2-10	
Elders Sent Now				
14th Miracle Man in Coffin			7:11-17	

Now as we recalled earlier, Matthew on several occasions did not follow on in succession with the recording of certain sections in his Gospel, but rather, places the narration so as to emphasize a particular principle.

Thus, with his placing of *The Ordination Of The Twelve* (10:1), directly after, the reference to the harvesting of the souls (9:36-39), he positioned it to relate it to the principle - that more disciples were needed, even though the ordination actually occurred weeks before, that particular reference.

However, the reference to the harvest of the souls, along with the preceding incident of John the Baptist's disciples coming to Jesus the second time (vv. 14-17), including the eighteenth (vv. 18-22), the nineteenth (vv. 23-26), the twentieth (vv. 27-31), and the twenty-first miracle (vv. 32-34), all follow on successively, and lead up to the reference of the harvests of souls. Nonetheless, all these five successive incidents took place weeks after the ordination of the twelve. See following graph:

Event	Matthew	Mark	Luke	John
They Leave for Gadara	13:53	4:35-36	8:22	
16th Miracle The Storm		4:37-41	8:23-25	
17th Miracle Legion of Devils		5:1-20	8:26-39	

Event	Matthew	Mark	Luke	John
Back at Capernaum Again		5:21	8:40	
John's Disciple Come again	*9:14-17*			
18th Miracle *Woman's Issue*	*9:18-22*			
19th Miracle *Jairus' Daughter*	*9:23-26*			
20th Miracle *Two Blind Men*	*9:27-31*	*5:22-34*	*8:41-48*	
21st Miracle *Dumb Man*	*9-32-34*	*5:35-43*	*8:49-56*	
They Leave Capernaum	9:35, 13:54	6:1		
Jesus Marvels at the Unbelief	13:55-58	6:2-6		
Fourth and Final Tour/*Harvest*	*9:35-38*	6:6		

Consequently, Matthew (12:18) referred to the prophecy of Is. 42:1, mentioning the '*Spirit*', which is the '*Power*' that is received by all disciples so they can function effectively in the spreading of the good news of the gospel (Mat. 10:1).Though originally, the prophecy prefigured Jesus being the Forerunner, and Firstfruit who received this Spirit, in which it descended from Heaven at Jesus' baptism (Mat. 3:16), and subsequently on the hundred and twenty, on '*the Day of Firstfruits*' (Num. 28:26), as Pentecost is also called.

Deliberately, Matthew placed these distinct separate incidents, so as to relate particular aspects.

The text which includes the prophecy of the Spirit (12:14-21), quoting Is. 42:1-4, pointed to how the gospel would eventually change the attitude of all nations, and was the next actual successive event which proceeded to *The Ordination Of The Twelve* (10:1). Matthew placed the following dislocated text of the *Fifteenth Miracle of the Blind Dumb Man* (12:22-23), including the Pharisees' resentment of Jesus healing him (v. 24), and His answer to them (vv. 25-37), directly after the prophecy of the positive influence of the spirit (12:17-21), to juxtaposition antithesis to the completely separate incidents, surrounding this miracle, though these events actually occurred weeks after the ordination (10:1).

Event	Matthew	Mark	Luke	John
John's Disciples Inform John			7:18	
John's Disciples Come To Jesus	**11:2-6**		**7:19-23**	
John the Baptist Extolled	11:7-15		7:24-30	
Jesus Compares Generations	11:16-19		7:31-35	
Woman Anoints/The Two Debtors			7:36-50	
Third Tour			**8:1-3**	
The Unrepentant Cities	11:20-30			
15th Miracle *Blind Dumb Man*	**12:22-24**	3:22		
Parable - Satan Cast Out Satan?	*12:25-30*	*3:23-27*		
Blasphemy of the Holy Spirit	*12:31-32*	*3:28-30*		
Jesus Rebukes Pharisees	*12:33-37*			
Jonah and the Resurrection	*12:38-42*			
Unclean Spirits	*12:43-45*			
Jesus' Mother Siblings Come	12:45-50	3:31-35		
Jesus Leaves House For Shore	13:1		8:4	
Parable Of The Sower	13:2-9	4:1-9	8:4-8	

Event	Matthew	Mark	Luke	John
Explains Parable To Disciples	13:10-23	4:10-20	8:9-15	
Reason for Light and Hearing		4:21-25	8:16-18	
Crowds Return/Jesus' Mother			8:19-21	
and Siblings Try To Get Nearer				
The Growing Seed		4:26-29		
Wheat and Tares Mustard Seed	13:24-32	4:30-32		
Leaven Finishes Teaching	13:33-35	4:33-34		
Jesus Explains To Disciples	13:36-52			

With Matthew placing his text so, it prefigured in contrasting between the attitude of these Pharisees who were still blind and dumb, with that of the man who was just healed. In Jesus' discourse to the Pharisees, it included reference the nature of a negative attitude, which can lead to the blaspheming of the Spirit. Matthew further emphasized the contrast between these two attitudes associated with the scenario of this miracle, with the continuing dialogue where the Scribes and Pharisees, who now, ironically ask for a sign [Gr. *attesting miracle*]: Jesus then relates to them the sign of the prophet Jonah (Mat. 12:38-42). In conclusion, that aspect of this negative element of the mind in not accepting the true Spirit is again mentioned (vv. 43-45).

The text of the harvesting of the souls (9:35-38), which Matthew placed before the ordination (10:1), corresponds to the point being made by Matthew - that more laborers were needed for the spreading of the gospel. Thus he linked it directly before *The Ordination Of The Twelve* firstfruits, rather than the actual order in which the events transpired. Hence, obviously the twelve firstfruit disciples prefigured at this juxtaposition of his text, owing to the fact that more disciples would be called through their prayers, when in a years time, a further seventy had been ordained. When at that juncture, the prayers for still more laborers for the harvesting of the souls now applied to the seventy (Luke 10:1-2).

Curiously, as Matthew positioned the text of the incident relating to the prophecy of the Spirit, which prefigured to the ordaining of the twelve apostles, nevertheless, it specifically follows, and actually occurs, directly after *The Twelfth Miracle*, of the healing of the man with the *Withered Hand*, in the synagogue on the Sabbath (Mat. 12:9-13), in which the hand is always symbolic of work! This incident led to the Pharisees first attempt to figure out how they might destroy the Pharisees first attempt to figure out how they might destroy the work of Jesus (v. 14).

Now, *'the Day of Pentecost'* in Acts 2:1, is synonymous with the outpouring of the Holy Spirit, and we can consider the individual occurrence on Jesus at His baptism, prior to the calling of the twelve apostles, and later the hundred and twenty disciples, where at both incidents the Holy Spirit descended from Heaven. This happened just before the beginning of Jesus' mission, and the calling of His disciples, and after the conclusion of His mission, having ordained many more disciples.

At the beginning of Jesus' mission, only twelve disciples were being called. Nevertheless, other disciples were being added, the seventy, and the hundred and twenty, mentioned in the first place in the NT where *'Pentecost'* is actually referred to by name (Acts 2:1). These extra *'laborers of the harvest'*, also having grown to five hundred (1 Cor. 15:6), answered the prayer that Jesus had asked originally the twelve (Mat. 9:37-38), and seventy to pray for precisely a year later (Luke 10:1-2).

We indicated earlier, that Luke had recorded *'the second Sabbath after the first'* (6:1), as indicative to showing that the events were building up towards the Festival of Weeks, as also Pentecost is known (Ex. 34:22). Of course with Luke mentioning *'another Sabbath'* [the third] at *The Twelfth Miracle* (6:6), the incidents afterwards, and leading up to the ordination of the twelve, would at any rate place us near Pentecost.

Moreover, when we consider that Jesus' ministry lasted for 3½ years [42 months], up to His resurrection, and when counting back from the last Passover [see *Scripture Graph I-XVIII*], it would indicate that His ministry started in the autumn. Furthermore, His baptism was several months before that, and no doubt, could have been on the actual Day of Pentecost.

Conceivably, because the Day of Pentecost is associated with the Holy Spirit, and is the only Holy Day period that is not mentioned in the Gospels, although one can see the works, the results, or the fruit of the Spirit, the Spirit in essence is invisible. Correspondingly, the Day of Pentecost is not seen in the Gospels. Though, the description of the descending of the Spirit from Heaven at Jesus' baptism and on the hundred and twenty, at Pentecost, was nevertheless recorded for our consideration.

Thus, when deducing the time Jesus spent in the other seasons, we can see successively each year, where He would have been in the summer seasons in which Pentecost fell [see *Scripture Graph I-XVIII*].

Tabernacles was in autumn, which was the season Jesus started His preaching ministry to the environs of Galilee. Subsequently, all the other three Tabernacle seasons were pictured successively in and around Jerusalem.

The next following season, being winter, Jesus remained firstly in Galilee, with the subsequent winters at Jerusalem, Jerusalem and Aenon Salim, and lastly Ephraim.

After winter, the first Passover season, was at Jerusalem, then Galilee, Aenon Salim, and once more finally concluding in Jerusalem.

Because Pentecost falls between Passover and Tabernacles, we can derive where Jesus would have spent the summer seasons. Interestingly, the summer season, in which Pentecost fell, is the only season that Jesus spent in a different location each time. Beginning with His baptism in Judea, the following year was in Galilee, which we are now discussing, Iturea in the second year, and Aenon Salim in the third year.

15   THE PURPOSE OF THE SPIRIT

THE ORDINATION OF THE TWELVE

The three categorizations of the twelve, the seventy, and the hundred and twenty, all had to do with the formation of criteria in organizing the early Church and the spreading of the gospel, in which they would have received some measure of '*Power*' - Holy Spirit. Although, it was not until ten days after Jesus had ascended to Heaven that they were baptized with the increased Power of the Holy Spirit, leading to the dynamic start and initiation of the new phase of the gospel.

Nevertheless, the early Church was originally Jewish, and grew out of '*the Church in the wilderness*' (Acts 7:38), with Christianity being born, as it were, through Judaism. Thus we can reflect as Jewish tradition relates, that the Ten Commandments were received by Moses up a mountain, and were actually given at Pentecost, after which they were magnified into fifty civil, moral, and religious precepts (Ex. 21-23). As Moses taught them to the twelve leaders of the tribes, and also to seventy (Ex. 24:1), and so on to the rest, we can see the similarity to Jesus teaching the twelve, and the others. Moses also prophesied of that ultimate Prophet - Jesus (Deut. 18:15), whom the people would eventually hear (Acts 7:37).

The similarities relating to these events at Pentecost [Gr. *fiftieth*], and the Festival of Firstfruits, as it is also called, and the firstfruit twelve disciples at this point, is significant and worth noting:-

As the number fifty is associated with Pentecost, we had considered in the section of *The First Miracle*, pp. 45-48, various details relating to Jesus' baptism, and the calling of *The First Disciples*, and the fifty miracles. It may prove useful to reread the details again at this point, as we recount the significance of what time of the year we have come to, along with the number factor too.

The factor of twelve is also seen in *The Twelfth Miracle*. Matthew had directly afterwards mentioned the words, from the prophecy, '*MY BELOVED, IN WHOM MY SOUL IS WELL-PLEASED: I WILL PUT MY SPIRIT ON HIM*' (12:18), with these combined texts of the incidents leading to the ordination of the twelve.

The number, seven, was seen in the text of *The Twelfth Miracle*, as relating to the Sabbath. Furthermore, Luke had shown the twelfth occurred on the third Sabbath, which led to the text surrounding the prophecy of the Spirit, and the ordination of the twelve!

Also there were seven miracles preceding the twelfth, which when reverting back to the sixth one, is the first time the Synoptics paralleled together with a miracle. The factor of seven is also seen in the Sabbath representing three weeks, or twenty-one days [3 x7].

Additionally Matthew's text on the harvest of the souls follows directly after the twenty-first miracle, which he positions before the ordination of the twelve!

We mentioned in the previous page, how the Ten Commandments prefigured in the magnification into fifty precepts on Pentecost [Gr. *fiftieth*]. There were ten days alluded to in the Gospel of John, preceding *The First Miracle*, after the forty days and nights of Jesus' stay in the wilderness, from His baptism, which, no doubt, was on Pentecost. Ten again is related to, through the ten days following the Ascension, after the forty days from the Resurrection, which leads us up to Pentecost again, on which the Spirit descended upon the hundred and twenty. The number of fifty is reflected also, in being the number of miracles up to the Ascension.

Now, as already mentioned, the factor of three is also related to, in the events of Pentecost, as indicated by the three categorizations of the disciples, the twelve, the seventy, and hundred and twenty. The day falls '*in the third month*' (Ex. 19:1), called Sivan, in the Jewish calendar, figuring to May-June, in which the receiving of the Law occurred. Moreover, the people had to be clean '*the third day*' when it arrived (vv. 10-11). Luke specifically recorded three Sabbaths at this time preceding the Festival of Weeks (Luke 6:1, 6), as we mentioned earlier. Furthermore, mountains were involved three times in the Gospels at this particular time: firstly, directly after Jesus' baptism, secondly, at the ordination of the twelve, and thirdly, as we suggested, at *The Transfiguration*.

Quoting from E. W. Bullinger's amazing monumental work, *Numbers In Scripture* [Kregel], p. 107, under the heading on '*Three*':

"Seven denotes spiritual perfection;

Ten denotes ordinal perfection; and

Twelve denotes governmental perfection."

Mark 3:13b Luke 6:13
And when it was day, He called to Him His disciples: and of them whom He would choose twelve, also whom He named apostles and they came to Him;
Matthew 10:1 Mark 3:14-15
and having called to Him His twelve disciples, He ordained the twelve, that they should be with Him, and that He might send them out to preach, and to heal sickness, and to cast out devils: He giving them Power against unclean spirits, to cast them out, and to heal all manner of sickness and all manner of disease.
Matthew 10
2a Now the names of the apostles are these;

Matthew 10:2b Mark 3:16-18a Luke 6:14a
the first Simon, whom He surnamed Peter, who is also called Peter,
and Andrew his brother,
and James the son of Zebedee,
and John the brother of James; and He surnamed them Boanerges, who are,
the "Sons of Thunder",
Matthew 10:3 Mark 3:18b Luke 6:14b-16a
and Philip,
and Bartholomew,
and Thomas,
and Matthew the tax collector,
and James the son of Alpheus,
and Lebbeus Judas the brother of James, whose surname was Thaddeus,
Matthew 10:4 Mark 3:18c-19a Luke 6:16b
and Simon called Zelotes, the Canaanite,
and Judas Iscariot, who also was the traitor who also betrayed Him.

Because of certain predominant aspects associated with Matthew's list, we have used his order for the successive sequence of disciples. Additionally, he grammatically begins his list before Mark and Luke with an exclusive heading, commencing, *'Now the names of the apostles are these; the first...'* Moreover, he was the last disciple to be called, hence, the use of the adage, *'the last shall be first'* is further fulfilled in the choice of using the order of his list.

Nonetheless, we have noted, following, any differences between the order of the other two lists, as one can still refer to them in their individual settings for exegesis if need be.

Mark places Andrew, after James and John, and not alongside Peter.

Both Mark and Luke place Matthew before that of Thomas.

Luke positions Simon Zelotes after James the son of Alpheus.

Luke also lists Lebbeus Thaddeus, who was also known by the name Judas, and was brother to James the son of Alpheus, placing him before that of Judas Iscariot.

Mark, after his list, adds the exclusive information, that *'they went into a house'* (3:19b), or *'home'* as the margin has it in some Bibles. Better still, as we have translated it, *'the house'*, and have placed it in its natural position where it actually occurs, which is after the ordination on the mount (Mark 3:13-14), and the instruction on how to preach the gospel (Mat. 10:5-49). However, Mark and Luke do not mention any instruction on the mount.

Additionally, since none of the Synoptics have indicated a change of area from Capernaum (Mat. 9:1; Mark 2:1; Luke 5:17), with the events proceeding after *The Eleventh Miracle* up until *The Twelfth Miracle* and now, is indicative of the whole scenario still being in the same locality. Mark indicated, that the eleventh miracle '*was in the house*', at Capernaum. Of course Jesus set up this home base, as it were, in Capernaum after leaving Nazareth at the beginning of His mission.

It should be clear that as Jesus after having spent all night on the mount alone in prayer (Luke 6:12), had arranged for the disciples to come to Him when it was day (v. 13). Afterwards He came down with the disciples (v. 17), after the ordination (Mat. 10:1-4) and instruction on spreading the gospel (vv. 5-42-11:1). It could not have been until they had come down from the mount that Jesus spoke to the crowds below, to the new apostles and the [seventy] disciples, repeating some of the Beatitudes and teachings He taught previously (Luke 6:17-49), to the eleven in the previous year. It was after this, that they returned '*to the house*', or Jesus' temporary '*home*' (Mark 3:19b; Luke 7:1), before embarking on their next phase of the gospel from Capernaum (Mat. 11:1).

Furthermore, Mark (3:20-21) exclusively fills in on other detail with his following verses, to indicate that though he did not include the narration of the instructions, on how they were to approach teaching the gospel on their travels, at that particular junction, he nevertheless, wanted to add, that '*they went into the house*', after they had come down from the mount, with Jesus having finished healing and teaching the crowds, in front of the disciples. As it was at that point when, in returning from the mount near Capernaum, they could not even arrange for something to eat, as the crowds had converged to the house.

The crowds came '*to the house*', before the **thirteenth miracle** (Luke 7:2-10), and the next event of traveling to Nain, where '*many of His disciples* [the seventy] *went with Him, and numerous people*' (v. 11).

Interestingly, Mark, now remains silent until the scenario surrounding the fifteenth miracle.

Matthew 10
5 These twelve Jesus sent out, and instructed them, saying,
"Don't go throughout the roads of the Gentiles, and into any city of the Samaritans enter not:
6 but go rather to the lost sheep of the House of Israel.
7 And as you go, preach, saying, 'The Kingdom of Heaven is at hand.'
8 Heal the sick, cleanse the lepers, raise the dead, and cast out devils: freely you have received, freely give.

9 Provide neither gold, nor silver, nor brass in your money-belts,
10 or a travel-bag for your journey, neither two coats, neither sandals, nor yet staves: for the worker is worthy of their meals.

11 And into whatever city or town you shall enter, inquire who in it is worthy; and stay there until you're ready to depart, and stay there until you're ready to depart.

12 And when you come to a house, greet it.

13 And if the house is worthy, let your peace remain with it: but if it be not worthy, let your peace return to you.

14 And whoever doesn't receive you, nor hear your words, when you depart out of that house or city, shake off the dust from your feet.

15 Truly I say to you, it shall be more tolerable for the land of Sodom and Gomorrah in the Day of Judgment, than for that city.

16 Understand, I send you out as sheep in the midst of wolves: therefore be as wise serpents, and as harmless as doves.

17 But beware of certain people: for they will deliver you up to the councils, and they will scourge you in their synagogues;

18 and you shall be brought before governors and kings for My sake, for a witness against them and the Gentiles.

19 But when they deliver you up, take no thought how or what you shall say: for it shall be given you in that same hour what you will say.

20 For it is not you who speaks, but the Spirit of your Father who speaks in you.

21 And the brother shall deliver up the brother to death, and the father his children: and the children shall rise up against their parents, and cause them to be put to death.

22 And you shall be hated by everyone for My Name's sake: but they who endure to the end shall be saved.

23 But when they persecute you in this city, flee to another: for surely I say to you, you shall not have gone over the cities of Israel, before the Son of Humanity appears.

24 The disciple is not above their master, nor the servant above their lord.

25 It is enough for the disciple that they be as their master, and the servant as their lord. If they have called the Master of the House Beelzebub, how much more shall they call them of His Household?

26 Therefore don't be afraid of them: for there is nothing covered, that shall not be revealed; and hid, that shall not be known.

27 What I tell you in darkness, expound in the light: and what you hear inwardly, preach that over the rooftops.

28 And don't be afraid of those who kill the body, but are not able to kill the soul: but rather fear Him who is able to destroy both soul and body in hell.

29 Aren't two sparrows sold for a penny: and not one of them shall fall on the

ground, outside the control of your Father.

30 But the very hairs of your head are all numbered.

31 Therefore don't be afraid, you are of more value than many sparrows.

32 Whoever therefore shall confess Me before anyone, these I will confess also before My Father who is in Heaven.

33 But whoever shall deny Me before anyone, I will also deny them before My Father who is in Heaven.

34 Don't think that I came to send peace on the earth. I didn't come to send peace, but a sword.

35 For I am come to SET A MAN AT VARIANCE AGAINST HIS FATHER, AND THE DAUGHTER AGAINST HER MOTHER, AND THE DAUGHTER-IN-LAW AGAINST HER MOTHER - IN-LAW.

36 And ONE'S ENEMIES SHALL BE THE MEMBERS OF ONE'S OWN HOUSEHOLD (Mic. 7:6).

37 They who love their father or mother more than Me are not worthy of Me: and those who love son or daughter more than Me are not worthy of Me.

38 And they who don't bear their burden, and follow after Me, are not worthy of Me.

39 Those who find their lives shall lose them: and they who lose their lives for My sake shall find them.

40 Those who receive you receives Me, and they who receive Me receives Him who sent Me.

41 Those who receive a prophet in the name of a prophet shall receive a prophet's reward; and they who receive a righteous person in the name of a righteous person shall receive a righteous person's reward.

42 And whoever shall give to one of these little ones just a cup of cold water to drink in the name of a disciple, truly I say to you, they shall in no way lose their reward."

After Jesus had ordained the twelve disciples - apostles Gr. *'ones sent out'*, up the mount, and now having instructed them on how to preach the gospel of the Kingdom of God, we come to the point where they come down from the mount, where the crowds are awaiting Jesus. Here we must also consider other factors.

The emphasis in Mat. 11:1 should be that they were now ready, rather than they went immediately, with knowledge of the first instruction on how to preach the gospel in the next phase of Jesus' mission. Before they were to leave, they had to come down the mount, where the crowds were awaiting, *'and the company of His disciples'*, also indicated that the seventy (Luke 10:1) were being prepared for their mission. Though they would not leave until a year later [see *Scripture Graph IV-VII*].

Moreover, the twelve did not actually leave for their first mission [see next sections in pp. 151-155 dealing with these references and *Scripture Graph VI*], without Jesus, until several months after coming down the mount, at *The Second Judean Ministry* (Mark 6:7-13; Luke 9:1-6), when John the Baptist was beheaded (Mat.14:12; Mark 6:29-30; Luke 9:10). This was after the fourth circuit of Galilee with Jesus' teachings, given in Mat. 5 to 7, at *The Sermon Up The Mount*, mingled with new attributes of edification and some completely different precepts, to the crowds, and the company of His disciples [the seventy], who obviously had not yet heard them before. Though, He would go on also to repeat some of these teachings again later.

The various differences between *The Sermon Up The Mount*, at Jerusalem, in Matthew to the eleven, and the sermon down the Mount near Capernaum, in Luke, after the ordination of the twelve, and why Luke included the detail that he mentions should now be clearer.

Besides, we saw why Mark, after the ordination, added his brief piece of information contained in that '*they went into the house*' (Mark 3:19b), relating it to and complementing Matthew (10:5-42-11:1) and Luke (7:1), informing us it was when, '*He had ended all His sayings in the audience of the people*'. Hence, they left the plain to return back into Capernaum, to Jesus' house, where the crowds converged (Mark 3:20-22), and where directly afterwards the Elders came, having been sent by the Centurion, before they set out again as newly ordained apostles.

THE SERMON DOWN THE MOUNT

Matthew 11

1 And it came to pass, when Jesus had made an end of instructing His twelve disciples, He departed therefore to teach and to preach in their cities.

Luke 6

17 And He came down with them, and stood in the plain, and the company of His disciples, and a great crowd of people out of all Judea and Jerusalem, and from the sea coast of Tyre and Sidon, who came to hear Him, and to be healed of their diseases;

18 and those who were troubled with unclean spirits: and they were healed.

19 And the whole crowd sought to touch Him: for there went virtue out of Him, and healed them all.

20 And He lifted up His eyes on His disciples, and said,

  "Blessed are you poor: for yours is the Kingdom of God.

21 Blessed are you who hunger now: for you shall be filled.

  Blessed are you who weep now: for you shall laugh.

Luke 6

22 Blessed are you, when people shall hate you, and when they shall separate
you from their company, and shall criticize you, and banter around your name
as evil, for the Son of Humanity's sake.
23 Rejoice in that day, and leap for joy: for, understand, your reward is great in
Heaven: for in the same manner did their father's to the prophets."

While we have considered in this section the particular mount near Capernaum,
where the twelve were ordained, and, where the seventy heard the sermon
down the Mount, it will prove interesting at this point to consider the end of
the Gospel story, in the section where *The Five Hundred* disciples met with
Jesus [pp. 431-434], no doubt on the same mount in Galilee, where Jesus had
informed the apostles to meet (Mat. 28:16; 1 Cor. 15:6). Jesus had also appeared
to the women to instruct them to they tell '*my brothers*' [*The Five Hundred*],
that they would see Him in Galilee too (Mat. 28:10).

In the meantime, we return to the continuing narrative after four Beatitudes,
with four woes.

Luke 6

24 "But woe to you who are rich! For you have received your comfort.
25 Woe to you who are full! For you shall hunger.
 Woe to you who laugh now! For you shall mourn and weep.
26 Woe to you, when everyone shall speak well of you! For so did their
father's to the false prophets.

27 But I say to you who hear, love your enemies, do good to those who hate
you,
28 bless those who curse you, and pray for them who abusively use you.
29 And to those who hit you on the one cheek offer also the other; and to
those who take away your overcoat forbid them not to take your jacket also.

30 Give to everyone who asks of you; and those who take away your goods
ask for them not again.

31 And as you would that people should do to you, do you also to them
likewise.

32 For if you love them who love you, what thanks have you? For sinners
also love those who love them.
33 And if you do good to them who do good to you, what thanks have you?

For sinners also do even the same.

34 And if you lend to them of whom you hope to receive, what thanks
have you? For sinners also lend to sinners, to receive as much again.
35 But love your enemies, and do good, and lend, hoping for nothing
again; and your reward shall be great, and you shall be the children of the
Highest: for He is kind to the unthankful and to the evil.

36 Be therefore merciful, as your Father also is merciful.
37 Don't judge, and you won't be judged: don't condemn and you won't
be condemned: forgive and you shall be forgiven:
38 give, and it shall be given to you; good measure, pressed down, and
shaken together, and running over, shall people give into your pockets.
For with the same measure that you evaluate the same it shall be
measured to you again."

39 And He spoke a parable to them,
"Can the blind lead the blind? Shall they not both fall into the ditch?
40 The disciple is not above their teacher: but everyone who is perfectly
trained shall be as their teacher.
41 And why consider the speck that is in your brother or sister's eye, but
don't perceive the beam that is in your own eye?
42 Either how can you say to your brother or sister, 'Brother or sister, let
me remove the speck that is in your eye', when you yourself don't
consider the beam that's in your own eye?
You hypocrite, cast out first the beam out of your own eye, and then you
shall see clearly to remove the speck that is in your brother or sister's
eye.

43 For a good tree doesn't produce or bear corrupt fruit; neither does a
corrupt tree produce or bear good fruit.
44 For every tree is known by its own fruit. For from thorns people do
not gather figs, nor from a bramble bush gather grapes.
45 A good person out of the good treasure of their heart brings forward
that which is good; and an evil person out of the evil treasure of their
heart brings forward that which is evil: for out of the abundance of the
heart their mouth speaks.

46 And why call you Me, 'Lord, Lord,' and do not the things, which I say?
47 Whoever comes to Me, and hears My sayings, and does them, I will
show you to whom they are like:
48 they are like someone who built a house, and dug deep, and laid the
foundation on a rock: and when the flood arose, the stream beat vehemently

upon that house, and could not shake it: for it was founded upon a rock.
49 But those who hear, and do not, are like someone who without a foundation built a house upon earth; against which the stream did beat vehemently, and immediately it fell; and the ruin of that house was great."

Mark 3:19b Luke 7:1
Now when He had ended all His sayings in the audience of the people, He entered into Capernaum, and they went into the house.

Mark 3
20 And the crowds came together again, so as they could not so much as eat bread.
21 And when His friends heard it, they went out to lay hold of Him: for they said, "He is besides Himself."

THE RE-HEALING OF THE CENTURION'S SERVANT

Jesus' healing of the people down on the plain gave the setting to *The Sermon Down The Mount* (Luke 6:17-19). This evoked a stupendous atmosphere to the scenario of the giving of the Beatitudes and the other teachings, with Mark uniquely (3:19-21), drawing to a close this episode by showing the jealous annoyance of some of Jesus' acquaintances, or *'friends'* [margin, and some translations *'kinsmen'*] in Capernaum. They were aggravated over *'the crowd'* (v. 20), who now were converging into the town to Jesus' house. This in turn, brings us to *The Re-healing Of The Centurion's Servant*, the thirteenth miracle, and *'the Elders of the Jews'* (Luke 7:3), which no doubt is a reference to Jesus' *'friends'*, *'kinsmen'* or acquaintances - *'His own'* people, of Capernaum, as Mat. 9:1 at *The Eleventh Miracle* weeks previously had indicated [p. 90], in the sense of Capernaum being *'His own city'*.

These Elders of the Jews, of the synagogue (Luke 7:5), whom Jesus would have known, no doubt of the same Synagogue, where the man with the withered hand had been healed, would also have been instrumental in instigating the attempt *'to lay hold of Him'* (Mark 3:21), as after *The Twelfth Miracle*, they were still looking for the right opportunity to destroy Jesus.

Mark, however, deliberately mentions that the Scribes which would come down from Jerusalem (v. 22), though it actually occurred weeks after the above incidents, who came down no doubt to discuss the issue of destroying Jesus and His reputation, with their contemporaries at Capernaum, and subsequently branding Jesus' works from the Devil. Though, they did not come down until after hearing about the fifteenth miracle, as we shall see. Nevertheless, Mark relates v. 22 to the circumstances surrounding Jesus' so-called *'friends'*, trying to spread it around that *'He is besides Himself'* (v. 21), at the first place in the Synoptics, where the Pharisees start to try and discredit Jesus' work by labeling Jesus of the Devil.

Now, with this excited crowd converging to *'the house'*, these Elders sought *'to lay hold'* on Jesus, no doubt through the Roman authorities, in the pretense that a riot would develop. The Centurion was responsible for controlling any potential riot, but because he loved the Jewish nation, even having been involved in the building of their synagogue, and being familiar with Jesus too, since having come previously and directly to Jesus himself, over the healing of his servant months before [see *The Fifth Miracle*, pp. 77-79]. Obviously, he would influence the outcome, of whether a riot was actually in the making. Thus at this point, where the crowds came into the city, the Centurion also having heard Jesus was home again, requested these Elders idea of laying hold of Jesus at this point, as they were now obliged personally to go to Him, craftily reversing their stance, requesting, *'That he was worthy for whom He should do this'* (Luke 7:4). After Jesus had gone with them, the Centurion now sends his '*friends*' to intercept Jesus and these crafty Elders (v. 6), to save Him coming this time. No doubt the Centurion realized the situation, and thus Luke highlighted the antithesis between the two types of '*friends*'.

Luke 7

2 And a certain Centurion's servant, who was dear to him, was sick, and ready to die.

3 And when he heard of Jesus, he sent to Him the Elders of the Jews, asking Him that He would come and heal his servant.

4 And when they came to Jesus, they implored Him earnestly, saying, "That he was worthy for whom He should do this:

5 for he loves our nation, and he has built us a Synagogue."

6 Then Jesus went with them.
And when He was now not far from the house, the Centurion sent friends to Him, saying to Him,
"Lord, trouble not Yourself: for I am not worthy that You should enter under my roof:

7 wherefore neither thought I myself worthy to come to You: but say in a word, and my servant shall be healed.

8 For I also am a man set under authority, having under me soldiers, and I say to one, 'Go,' and he goes; and to another, 'Come,' and he comes; and to my servant, 'Do this,' and he does it.'"

9 When Jesus heard these things, He marveled at him, and turned Him about, and said to the people that followed Him,
"I say to you, I have not found so great faith, no, not in Israel."

10 And they who were sent, returning to the house, found the servant whole that had been sick.

FOURTEENTH MIRACLE – YOUNG MAN IN COFFIN

Now, the re-healing of *The Centurion's Servant*, being the thirteenth miracle, leads us to Luke's next indigenous miracle, the fourteenth (v. 11). Luke uniquely remembers and places it in its successive order, occurring directly after the thirteenth miracle of the re-healing of the Centurion's servant. He mentions '*many of His disciples went with Him*', as being further reference to the the seventy (6:17), as the twelve would have been already traveling with Jesus full time, anyhow.

Luke 7

11 And it came to pass the day after, that He went into a city called Nain; and many of His disciples went with Him, and many people.

12 Now when He came near to the gate of the town, consider, there was a dead man carried out, the only son of his mother, and she was a widower: and many people of the town was with her.

13 And when the Lord saw her, He had compassion on her, and said to her, "Don't cry."

14 And He came and touched the coffin: and those who carried him stood still. And He said, "Young man, I say to you, rise."

15 And he who was dead sat up, and began to speak. And He delivered him to his mother.

16 And there came a fear on all: and they glorified God, saying, "That a great Prophet is risen up amongst us;" and, "That God has visited His people."

17 And this rumor of Him went abroad throughout all Judea, and throughout the entire region round about.

After the people had witnessed the resurrection of the young man in the town of Nain, in the first place in the Gospels in which a person is brought back to life, once again a stupendously exciting atmosphere arose in the outlying are as (vv. 17-18), which resulted in the disciples of the Baptist being sent to Jesus the first time (Mat. 11:2-3; Luke 7:19-20).

Afterwards they returned to inform the Baptist of the miraculous events that were transpiring (Mat. 11:4-5; Luke 7:21-22).

We already dealt with the two times John's disciples came to Jesus in the section dealing with *Matthew's Calling* [pp. 91-97].

Back at Mat. 11:1, where Jesus had been ready with the twelve apostles to embark on the next phase of His ministry, but still remained in the area for a while, we now see that significant incidents had transpired between v. 1, and before v. 2, and that Luke was our guide to the order of those events.

FIRST TIME JOHN'S DISCIPLES COME

Moreover, Luke (7:18-35) was clear as to the successive order of the last incidents since the ordination of the twelve, in that he parallels with Matthew (11:2-19). He also knew, after the dialogue on who to compare that generation to, in mentioning the difference between John the Baptist's role, and that of Jesus', one of the Pharisees, known as Simon, invited Jesus to dine at his house (Luke 7:36).

After the *fourteenth miracle* at Nain, Jesus would have returned to Capernaum, as he disciples of John the Baptist knew He was most likely to be found there, because looking for Him in any other place would have been a hit-or-miss situation. Additionally, Matthew did not indicate a change of area after the instruction to the twelve. Neither did Mark in his text, as their next events continued to take place at Capernaum, as we shall shortly see.

Luke 7
18 And the disciples of John told him about all these things.

Matthew 11:2-3 Luke 7:19
And now when John had heard in the prison the works of the Messiah, summoning two of his disciples, he sent the two disciples to Jesus, to ask Him, saying, "Are you He who should come? Or do we look for another?'"

Luke 7
20 When the men were come to Him, they said to Him,
"John Baptist has sent us to You, saying, '*Are You He who should come? Or do we look for another?*'"

21 And in that same hour He cured many of their infirmities and plagues, and of evil spirits; and to many who were blind He gave sight.

Matthew 11:4-5 Luke 7:22
Then Jesus answered and said to them, "Go your way, and tell John again those things what you have seen and heard: how that the blind receive their sight, and the lame walk, the lepers are cleansed, and the deaf hear, the dead are raised up, and the poor have the gospel preached to them.
Matthew 11:6 Luke 7:23
And they are blessed, whoever shall not be offended in Me."

Matthew 11:7 Luke 7:24
And as the messengers of John were departing, Jesus began to say to the crowds concerning John,
"What did you go out into the wilderness to see? A reed shaken with the wind?
Matthew 11:8 Luke 7:25
But what did you go out to see? A man clothed in fine clothing?
Consider, they who are gorgeously appareled, who wear fine clothing, and live luxuriously, are in kings' courts and houses.
Matthew 11:9 Luke 7:26
But what did you go out to see? A prophet? Yes, I say to you, and much more than a prophet.
Matthew 11:10 Luke 7:27
For this is he, of whom it is written (Mal. 3:1, 'UNDERSTAND, I SEND MY

Messenger before Your face, who shall prepare Your Way before You.'
Matthew 11:11 Luke 7:28
For truly I say to you, among those who are born of women there has not risen a greater prophet than John the Baptist: but, notwithstanding those who are least in the Kingdom of God, from Heaven, are as great as he.
Matthew 11
12 And from the days of John the Baptist until now the Kingdom of Heaven requires effort, and the passionate obtain it through spirit [see Luke 16:16].
13 For all the Prophets and the Law prophesied even to John.
14 And if you will receive it, he is Elijah, who was to come.
15 Those who have ears to hear let them hear."

Luke 7
29 And all the people who understood, and the tax collectors, acknowledged God, having been baptized with the baptism of John.
30 But the Pharisees and lawyers rejected the counsel of God against themselves, being not baptized by him.

Matthew 11:16a Luke 7:31
And the Lord said,
"But whereto then shall I liken the people of this generation? And what are they like?
Matthew 11:16b-17 Luke 7:32
It is that they are like children sitting in the marketplace, in the markets, calling one to another, to their fellows, and saying, '*We have piped to you, and you didn't dance; we mourned for you, and you didn't weep or mourn.*'
Matthew 11:18 Luke 7:33
For John the Baptist came neither eating bread nor drinking wine; and you and they say, '*He has a devil.*'
Matthew 11:19 Luke 7:34
The Son of Humanity came eating and drinking; and you and they say, '*Look a gluttonous man, and a drunkard, a friend of tax collectors and sinners*!'
Luke 7
35 So wisdom is proved right by the manner of her children."

JESUS DINES AT SIMON THE PHARISEE'S

36 And one of the Pharisees invited Him to eat with him. And He went into the the Pharisee's house, and sat down to eat.
37 And, consider, a woman in the city, who was a sinner, when she knew that Jesus reclined in the Pharisee's house, brought an alabaster box of ointment,
38 and stood at His feet behind Him weeping, and began to wash His feet with her tears, and did wipe them with the hairs of her head, and kissed His feet, and anointed them with the ointment.

Luke 7

39 Now when the Pharisee who had invited Him saw it, he spoke within himself, saying, "This Man, if He were a prophet, would have known who and what manner of woman this is who touches Him: for she is a sinner."
40 And Jesus answering said to him, "Simon, I have somewhat to say to you."
And he says, "Master, say on."

41 "There was a certain creditor who had two debtors: the one owed five hundred pence, and the other fifty,
42 and when they had nothing to pay, the creditor frankly forgave them both. Tell me therefore, which of them will love the creditor most?"

43 Simon answered and said,
"I suppose that, the creditor who forgave most."
And He said to him, "You have rightly judged."

44 And He turned to the woman, and said to Simon,
"You see you this woman? I entered into your house, you gave Me no water for My feet: but she has washed My feet with her tears, and wiped them with the hairs of her head.
45 You gave Me no kiss: but this woman since the time I came in has not ceased to kiss My feet.
46 My head with oil you did not anoint: but this woman has anointed My feet with ointment.
47 Wherefore I say to you, her sins, which are many, are forgiven; for she loves much: but to whom little is forgiven, the same loves little."

48 And He said to her, "Your sins are forgiven

49 And those who reclined with Him began to say within themselves, "Who is this who also forgives sins?"
50 And He said to the woman, "Your faith has saved you; go in peace."

Directly afterwards, both Luke (8:1-3) and Matthew (11:20-30) dovetail together, correlating to the next subsequent event in leaving Capernaum again, for now the third tour of Galilee. Though the scenario returns after the tour, once more back to Capernaum. We cover this in detail in the following section.

17   *THE PHARISEES SCHEME*

THIRD TOUR OF GALILEE

Recalling that Jesus had ordained the twelve disciples - apostles, and had directly on coming down the mount near Capernaum, healed and preached to the crowds, and *The Seventy Disciples*. He then goes on to re-heal *The Centurion's Servant*, after returning to the house. Then the next day, He traveled to Nain with the disciples, resurrecting the young dead man, which created the rumor that spread *'throughout all Judea, and throughout the region round about'* (Luke 7:17), *'that God had visited His people'* (v. 16).

John's disciples had informed John in prison of the things Jesus had done. From there, John had sent them back to Jesus (Mat. 11:2; Luke 7:18-19), who would normally be found at Capernaum, unless it was known He was otherwise somewhere else. No doubt Jesus and the disciples had returned to Capernaum after the excursion to Nain, as John and his disciples would also have known that Jesus used a house in Capernaum there. Anyway, Jesus and the disciples at this instance were preparing for a third circuit of Galilee (Luke 8:1), as just recently newly ordained apostles, and it would be natural to set out from there.

Additionally, when Jesus *'had ended all His sayings'* (Luke 7:1), down the mount near Capernaum, Luke indicates in his continuing dialogue of the combined events, that after the arriving of John's disciples, Jesus dined with Simon the Pharisee *'in the city'* (v. 37). Subsequently, Simon, no doubt, would have been one of Jesus' *'friends'* referred to in Mark 3:21 of Capernaum.

Now Mat. 11:2-19 dealt with the first arrival of John's disciples, with which Luke synchronized and paralleled. Thus, Mat. 11:1 was telling us that after the ordination they were now prepared to preach the gospel, not that they had already left for the third tour yet.

Luke is the one who tells us when they went, by his ordering of the events and informing us, it was after the ordination *'He entered into Capernaum'* (7:1), re-healed *The Centurion's Servant* (vv. 2-10), resurrected the young man (vv. 2-10), resurrected the young man (vv. 11-17), of the first arrival of John's disciples (vv. 18-35), which aligned with Matthew's text (11:2-19), and the following, the dining at Simon the Pharisee's (Luke 7:36-50), which brings us up to where they are now ready for the third circuit of Galilee (8:1).

Jesus and the apostles were now ready for the third tour of Galilee, with Mat. 11:20-24 being the narrative, which concluded that particular tour, before they would return, back again to Capernaum once more. This led to Jesus comparing the attitude of those in the cities, who had witnessed His many miracles, with that of the disciples' attitude (vv. 25-27). Continuing afterwards, he exhorted them that His yoke was easy, and His burden light (vv. 28-30).

Consequently, where Mat. 11:20 begins, in the following main Scripture text, is near the conclusion of the preaching tour, revealing that after all the miracles, and this, the third time that Jesus had gone *'throughout every city and village'* of

Galilee (Luke 8:1), *'He began to rebuke the cities wherein most of his mighty works were done, because they didn't repent'* (Mat. 11:20).

Moreover, Capernaum has the most recorded number of miracles attributed to any city, and with Jesus mentioning Capernaum as the last of the cities (Mat. 11:23), alluded to them having now returned.

Luke 8

1 And it came to pass afterwards, that He went throughout every city and village, preaching and showing the glad news of God: and the twelve were with Him,

2 and certain women, who had been healed of evil spirits and illnesses - Mary called Magdalene, out of whom went seven devils,

3 and Joanna the wife of Chuza Herod's Steward, and Susanna, and many others, who ministered to Him of their substance.

Matthew 11

20 Then He began to rebuke the cities wherein most of His mighty works were done, because they didn't repent:

21 "Woe to you, Chorazin! Woe to you, Bethsaida! For if the mighty works, which were done in you, had been done in Tyre and Sidon, they would have repented long ago in black clothes and ashes.

22 But I say to you, it shall be more tolerable for Tyre and Sidon at the Day of Judgment, than for you.

23 And you Capernaum, who is exalted to Heaven, shall be BROUGHT DOWN TO HELL (Eze. 26:20; 31:14; 32:18): for if the mighty works, which have been done in you, had been done in Sodom, it would have remained until this day.

24 But I say to you, that it shall be more tolerable for the land of Sodom in the Day of Judgment, than for you."

25 At that time Jesus answered and said,

"I thank You, Oh Father, Lord of Heaven and earth, because You hid these things from the wise and prudent, and have revealed them to babes.

26 Even so, Father, for so it seemed good in Your sight.

27 All things are delivered to Me by My Father: and no one knows the Son, except the Father; neither does anyone know the Father, except the Son, and to whom the Son wishes to reveal Him.

28 Come to Me all you who labor and are heavy laden, and I will give you rest.

29 Take My yoke upon you, and learn of Me; for I am gentle and humble in heart: and YOU SHALL FIND REST FOR YOUR SOULS (Jer. 6:16).

30 My yoke is easy, and My burden light."

Having already mentioned why Mat. 12:1-21 follows in successive order after 9:13, at the intersections dealing with those references. It is clear from the references of Mark 2:23-28, 3:1-12 and Luke 6:1-11, which cover some of the same detail, of the specific synchronization of those events.

It is indicated that after *The Twelfth Miracle* in the synagogue, the Pharisees sought '*what they might do to Jesus*' (Luke 6:7, 11), which dovetails with Mat. 12:14 where he aligns and parallels with Mark 3:6. Both mention they held counsel on how to destroy Jesus, with Mark pointing out that it included the Herodians too.

Matthew placed his indigenous **fifteenth miracle** of the blind and dumb man (12:22-24), and the narrative surrounding the *Parable of Satan Casting Out Satan* (vv. 25-32), as we mentioned previously, to highlight the difference between the Holy Spirit of God and the spirit of Satan (vv. 33-37). He positioned it antithetically next to, though not in actual successive order, after the prophecy of the Spirit upon My Beloved Son (vv. 17-21), to show the stark contrast of the two attitudes.

Also, Mark's version of the text surrounding the *Parable of Satan Casting Out Satan* (3:23-30), which aligns and parallels with Matthew, uniquely indicated that the Scribes of Jerusalem (v. 22), came down to Capernaum. They came no doubt to counsel with their fellow Pharisees over what the people were saying about Jesus, as this third preaching tour of Galilee had caused the Pharisees ultimate annoyance, combined with the news of the resurrected young man having spread '*abroad throughout all Judea*' (Luke 7:17).

Matthew also used the fifteenth miracle, with the text surrounding the *Parable of Satan Casting Out Satan*, and the rest of his ch. 12, to highlight the next events of the Scribes and Pharisees having come down from Jerusalem to Capernaum. Jesus also called them to His house to discuss their false ideas about Him. It was Mark however, who pointed out the fact that Jesus called them to Him (3:23). Matthew's unique continuous dialogue, and his next chapter, indicating it all took place at the house (13:1).This parallels with Mark, too, though he does not mention the house at that point, but, nevertheless, covers the same incident (4:1), with his narration previous, having also been in the house (3:19-21). Both Matthew (12:46-50) and Mark (3:31-35) relate His mother and siblings arriving too, who had to wait outside, because the house was full. Hence, we can deduce, that both the texts of Mat. 12:25-50, and Mark 3:23-35, all took place in Jesus' house.

Furthermore, the fifteenth miracle preceded the *Parable of Satan Casting Out Satan*, which was addressed specifically at the Pharisees. The people having witnessed the fifteenth miracle, and others having witnessed the fifteenth miracle (Mat. 12:22-24), with others having heard too, marveled further, with the whole area having been astounded earlier at the news of the resurrection of the young man, the *Fourteenth Miracle* when they exclaimed, '*that God had visited His people*' (Luke 7:16). They now added, '*is not this the Son of David*' (Mat. 12:23), which also pointed to Jesus' Kingship! Thus, this was compounding the issue to the increased annoyance of the Pharisees, over which the Pharisees of Capernaum met with their contemporaries from Jerusalem, with Jesus calling them to His house.

Both Mat. 12:24 and Mark 3:22, relate to the Pharisees having afterwards heard about the **fifteenth miracle**, with it not having taken place with them present. Matthew's verses preceding relate to the people having witnessed that miracle, and that the people were attesting to Jesus' Kingship (12:22-23), where no Scribes or Pharisees are mentioned, as the tense in the following verse is relating to, '*when the Pharisees heard it*'.

Additionally, the context of Mat. 12:24 and Mark 3:22, also includes the conversation of the Pharisees among themselves, not that it was directed at Jesus, as we see in the next combined verses when, '*Jesus knew their thoughts, and He called them to Him*' (Mat. 12:25; Mark 3:23), over the issue of claiming He did miracles through the Devil.

Amazingly, as already mentioned, this no doubt took place in Jesus' house, as when we follow the dialogue of Jesus addressing the Scribes and Pharisees, which as suggested, includes Mat. 12:25-37 and Mark 3:23-30, we see further along the text, through Mat. 12:38-42, Jesus is still talking to them, but now, about the sign they wished to see, though Mark does not include this part of the scenario.

Then in Mat. 12:43-45, Jesus reverts back to the theme of the *Parable of Satan Casting out Satan*, in the context of unclean spirits, which related to the fact of the Pharisees accusing Him that He had the spirit of Beelzebub, after the healing of the fifteenth miracle. So, when we come to where His mother and siblings were standing outside (Mat. 12:46-50; Mark 3:31-35), we see that they could not get into the house and near Jesus, because it was full. Mat 13:1 indicates that it was in Jesus' house, where the conversation of the Scribes and Pharisees took place, and all in '*the same day*'.

Matthew 12

22 Then was brought to Him one possessed with a devil, blind and dumb: and He healed him, insomuch that the blind and dumb both spoke and saw.

23 And all the people were amazed, and said, "Is not this the Son of David?"

Matthew 12:24 Mark 3:22

But when the Pharisees heard it, and the Scribes who came down from Jerusalem, Jerusalem, they said, "He has Beelzebub, and this Fellow He does not cast out devils, but by Beelzebub the Prince of the Devils."

Matthew 12:25 Mark 3:23-25

And Jesus knew their thoughts, and He called them to Him, and said to them, in parables,"How can Satan Cast out Satan? And if every kingdom be divided against itself is brought to desolation, that kingdom cannot stand; and every city - or if a house be divided against itself, that house cannot stand:

Matthew 12:26 Mark 3:26

and if Satan rises up against himself, casting out Satan, and he is divided against himself, how shall his kingdom stand? He cannot stand, but has an end.

Matthew 12

27 And if I by Beelzebub cast out devils, by whom do your children cast them out? Therefore they shall be your judges.

28 But if I cast out devils by the Spirit of God, then the Kingdom of God is come to you.

Matthew 12:29 Mark 3:27

Or else how can one enter into a strong person's house? No one can enter into a strong person's house, and seize his goods, except they first bind the strong person, and then they can seize their house.

Matthew 12

30 They who are not with Me are against Me; and they who gather not with Me scatter abroad.

Matthew 12:31 Mark 3:28-29

Wherefore, truly I say to you, all manner of sins and blasphemy shall be forgiven the progeny of humans: and blasphemies by any extent which they shall blaspheme: but they who shall blaspheme, blasphemy against the Holy Spirit shall not be forgiven - having never forgiveness, but are in danger of eternal damnation.

32 And whoever speaks a word against the Son of Humanity, it shall be forgiven them: but whoever speaks against the Holy Spirit, it shall never be forgiven them, neither in this world, neither in the world to come."

Mark 3

30 Because they said, *"He has an unclean spirit* (Mat.12:24; Mark 3:22)."

Matthew 12

33 "Either make the tree good, and its fruit good; or else make the tree corrupt, and its fruit corrupt: for a tree is known by its fruit.

34 Oh generation of vipers, how can you, being evil, speak good things? For out of the abundance of the heart the mouth speaks.

35 A good person out of the good treasure of their heart brings forward good things: and an evil person out of evil treasure brings forward evil things.

Matthew 12

36 But I say to you, that every idle word that anyone shall peak, they shall give account thereof in the Day of Judgment.

37 For by your words you shall be justified, and by your words you shall be condemned."

38 Then certain of the Scribes and of the Pharisees answered, saying, "Master, we would see a sign from You."

39 But He answered and said to them,

"An evil and adulterous generation seeks after a sign; and there shall no sign be given to it, but the sign of the prophet Jonah:

40 for as JONAH WAS THREE DAYS AND NIGHTS IN THE GREAT FISH'S BELLY (Jon. 1:17); so shall the Son of Humanity be three days and three nights within the earth.

41 The people of Nineveh shall rise in judgment with this generation, and shall condemn it: because they repented at the preaching of Jonah; and, understand, a greater than Jonah is here.

42 The Queen of the South shall rise up in the judgment with this generation, and shall condemn it: for she came from a distant land to hear the Wisdom of Solomon; and, understand, a greater than Solomon is here.

43 When the unclean spirit is gone out of one, it walks through dry places, seeking rest, and finds none.

44 Then it says, '*I will return into my house from where I came out*;' and when it appears, it finds it empty, swept, and garnished.

45 Then it goes, and takes with itself seven other spirits more wicked than itself, and they enter in and dwell there: and the last state of that person is worse than the first. Even so shall it be also to this wicked generation."

JESUS' MOTHER AND SIBLINGS

We saw in the context of the last intersection, that when Jesus' mother and siblings came at this time, it was that He was talking to Scribes and Pharisees in His house.

Shortly, in the next section, still in the same day, we will see from Luke, that a similar event of Jesus' mother and siblings trying to come near to Him arose again. The difference between the two separate events should become self-evident, as the first arrival was at Jesus' house.

The incident in Luke was during the time Jesus was teaching several parables, after having given one parable from a boat, including other parables on the land. In this instance, His mother and siblings tried to get near to Him once again, but were hindered at this time particularly by the great number of crowds on the open shore and land, and not at His house.

Matthew 12:46 Mark 3:31-32a
While He yet talked to the people, consider, there came then His mother and
His siblings, who were standing outside, desiring to speak with Him, and they
sent to Him, calling Him.

As the crowd sat about Him,
Matthew 12:47 Mark 3:32b
then one and they said to Him, "Look Your mother and Your siblings stand
outside seeking for You, desiring to speak with You."
Matthew 12:48 Mark 3:33
But He answered and said to him, and they who told Him,
"Who is My mother and who are My siblings?"
Matthew 12:50 Mark 3:35
For whoever shall do the will of God My Father who is in Heaven, the same is
My brother, and sister, and mother."

Matthew 13:1 Mark 4:1a
The same day Jesus went out of the house, and sat by the seaside, and He began
again to teach.

Matthew 13:2 Mark 4:1b Luke 8:4a
And when many people were come to Him out of every city, great crowds were
gathered together, so that He went into a boat in the sea, and sat; and the whole
crowd was by the sea on the land, standing on the shore.

Jesus' calling of the Scribes and Pharisees to His house in Capernaum (Mark
3:22-23), when His mother and siblings arrive (Mat. 12:46-50; Mark 3:31-35),
including directly afterwards, when He goes out to the seashore from the house
(Mat. 13:1), sets the stage for next scene with the teaching of various parables
(Mat.13:2-52; Mark 4:1-34; Luke 8:4-21).

At the conclusion of all of these parables, it is Mark, who confirms and
correlates with Matthew (13:53), to the effect of agreeing that all these things
occurred in one particular memorable day (Mark 4:35).

18   BY SEASIDE NEAR JESUS' HOUSE

PARABLE OF THE SOWER

Matthew 13:3 Mark 4:2-3 Luke 8:4b-5a
And He spoke teaching many things to them in parables, and related to them in His didactic manner, saying,
"Listen; consider, there went out a Sower to sow His seed;
Matthew 13:4 Mark 4:4 Luke 8:5b
and it came to pass when they were sowing, some seeds fell by the wayside; and it was trodden down, and the fowls of the air came and devoured them up:

Matthew 13:5 Mark 4:5 Luke 8:6a
and some fell upon a rock, and stony ground, where they had not much earth: and soon, it immediately sprang up, because they had no depth of earth:
Matthew 13:6 Mark 4:6 Luke 8:6b
and when the sun was up, they were scorched; and because they had no root, they withered away through lack of moisture.

Matthew 13:7 Mark 4:7 Luke 8:7
And some fell among thorns; and the thorns sprang up, growing with them, and choked them: and yielded no fruit.

Matthew 13:8 Mark 4:8-9a Luke 8:8a
And still others fell into good ground, and did yield, and brought forth, bearing fruit that sprang up and increased: bringing forth, some a hundredfold, some sixtyfold, and some thirtyfold."

And when He had said these things, He cried, saying to them,
Matthew 13:9 Mark 4:9b Luke 8:8b
"Those who have ears to hear let them hear."

Mark has a reversed order to that of Matthew, at the ending of the parable above (v. 9a), and at the conclusion of the explanation of the parable, beginning with '*thirtyfold*' (v. 20). Luke, in the explanation of the parable, does not mention any reference to quantity (8:15).

Though it does not make any difference to the meaning of the parable, we have used Matthew's order for the quantity, as we followed his priority with the list of apostles, and because Luke relates exclusively to '*a hundredfold*' at the beginning of the parable.

In the next dialogue, we have a reference to two sets of disciples again, in the sense that when Jesus was alone and in a break away from the crowds, it is stated by Mark that the disciples came to Him, and '*those who were about Him with the twelve'* (v. 10), no doubt alluding to the seventy, since Jesus went on to give the meaning of the parable to these two sets of disciples.

Matthew 13:10 Mark 4:10 Luke 8:9
And when He was alone, the disciples came to Him, and those who were about Him with the twelve asked Him of the parable, and said to Him, "Why speak to them in parables?"
And His disciples asked Him, saying, "What might this parable be?"

Matthew 13:11 Mark 4:11a Luke 8:10a
And He answered and said to them,
"Because to you it is given to know the secret mysteries of the Kingdom of God from Heaven: but to the others who are not here, it is not given.
Matthew 13
12 For whoever has, to them shall be given, and they shall have more abundance; but whoever has not, from them shall be taken away even what they have.
Matthew 13:13 Mark 4:11b-12 Luke 8:10b
Therefore all these things are done in parables: moreover, I speak to them in parables, because that SEEING THEY MAY SEE, AND NOT PERCEIVE - that they might not see; AND HEARING THEY MAY HEAR, AND NOT UNDERSTAND - that they might not hear, neither comprehend; LEST AT ANY TIME THEY SHOULD BE CONVERTED, AND THEIR SINS SHOULD BE FORGIVEN THEM (Is. 6:9-10).
Matthew 13
14 And in them is fulfilled the prophecy of Isaiah (6:9-10), who says,
'BY HEARING YOU SHALL HEAR, AND SHALL NOT UNDERSTAND; AND SEEING YOU SHALL SEE, AND SHALL NOT PERCEIVE:
15 FOR THIS PEOPLE'S HEART IS WAXED GROSS, AND THEIR EARS ARE DULL OF HEARING, AND THEIR EYES THEY HAVE CLOSED; LEST AT ANY TIME THEY SHOULD SEE WITH THEIR EYES, AND HEAR WITH THEIR EARS, AND SHOULD UNDERSTAND WITH THEIR HEART, AND SHOULD BE CONVERTED, AND I SHOULD HEAL THEM.'
16 But blessed are your eyes, for they see: and your ears, for they hear.
17 For truly I say to you, that many prophets and righteous people have desired to see those things which you see, and have not seen them; and to hear those things which you hear, and have not heard them."
Mark 4
13 And He said to them, "You don't understand this parable? And then how will you understand all parables?

PARABLE OF THE SOWER AND LIGHT

Matthew 13

18 Therefore you, listen to the *Parable of the Sower*.

Luke 8

11 Now the parable is this: The seed is the word of God.

Mark 4

14 The Sower sows the word.

Matthew 13:19 Mark 4:15 Luke 8:12

And these are those by the wayside, where the word is sown. When anyone hears the word of the Kingdom, these are those who hear; but when they have heard, and don't understand it, then comes the wicked one, Satan the Devil, and immediately catches, and takes away the word out of their hearts (that which was sown in their hearts), lest they should believe and be saved. These are those who received seed by the wayside.

Matthew 13:20 Mark 4:16 Luke 8:13a

But he, and these, are they who are likewise sown, that received the seed on the rock, and into stony ground. The same is he, and they, who, when they hear the word, having heard it immediately they receive it, experience joy and gladness;

Matthew 13:21 Mark 4:17 Luke 8:13b

yet he has no root in himself, and neither these in their selves, who so enduring, but for a while, or a season, believe, and afterwards, in time of temptation, or when tribulation, affliction or persecution arises, because of the word's sake, immediately, he, and they are offended, and fall away.

Matthew 13:22a Mark 4:18 Luke 8:14a

And he and these are also those who are seeds sown - those who fell, being received among thorns; such are they who hear the word, who, when they have heard, go forward,

Matthew 13:22b Mark 4:19 Luke 8:14b

and are choked with the anxiety and cares of this world, and the deceitfulness of riches, the lusts of other things, and the pleasures of this life entering in, choke the word, and they become unfruitful, bringing no fruit to perfection.

Matthew 13:23 Mark 4:20 Luke 8:15

But he, and these are those whom are seeds sown, being received on good ground; such is he who hears the word, and receiving it, understand; these are they, who in a honest and good heart, having heard the word, keep it, who also bear fruit, bringing forward fruit with patience, some a hundredfold, some sixty, and some thirtyfold."

Mark 4:21 Luke 8:16

And He said to them,

"Is a candle brought to be put under a cover? No one, when they have lit a candle, covers it with a vessel, or puts it under a bed. But is it not to be set on a candlestick, that those who enter in may see the light?

Mark 4:22 Luke 8:17

For there is nothing hidden, neither anything secret, which shall not be made manifest and clear; neither was anything kept secret, that shall not be known, but that it should come abroad.

Mark 4

23 If anyone has ears to hear, let them hear."

Mark 4:24 Luke 8:18a

And He said to them,

"Take heed therefore how and what you hear: with what degree you measure, it shall be measured to you: and to you who hear, shall be given more.

Mark 4:25 Luke 8:18b

For whoever has, to them shall be given: and whoever doesn't have, from them shall be taken that which they think they have."

MOTHER AND SIBLINGS COME AGAIN

Previously in the same day, we saw that Jesus' mother and siblings came when He was in the house, when talking with the Scribes and Pharisees, before He left the house to give the *Parable of the Sower*.

Luke, who wrote to keep the events in their successive order, tells us at this juncture, Jesus' mother and siblings came again. This time, in a respite from the crowds, as Mark (4:10), informs us, He was alone before giving the interpretation of the *Parable of the Sower* to the twelve, with no doubt '*they who were about Him with the twelve*', being a reference to the seventy, as He went on to explain the parable to those who had remained behind (v. 11), rather than those who primarily came just to witness the miracles.

Moreover, at the point where the crowds dispersed in a break after the *Parable of the Sower*, Jesus would have left the boat, from where He had given the parable, and subsequently gave the interpretation, as the twelve and the other disciples now gathered around Him, and asked Him meaning of the parable. Consequently, He went on to specifically give to them the analogy of the reason for light and the consequences of how one hears.

As Jesus was talking to all these disciples, the crowds once again approached after their break. It was at this precise moment that His mother and siblings could not get near again, but, this time, because the crowds were returning and had converged on Jesus, '*could not come near to Him because of the crowd*' (Luke 8:19).

Furthermore, with the context of Jesus using the opportunity of His mother and siblings trying to get close to Him near the seashore, Luke now reveals that the crowds had converged again, and that Jesus used the analogy of those '*who hear the word of God*' (v. 21), as to also being, '*My mother and My siblings*'. Additionally, it is Mark (4:23) who dovetails with Luke's text in averring that Jesus had just finished relating the aspect of how we hear (vv. 24-25), which aligns and parallels with Luke (8:18). Luke exclusively mentions Jesus' mother and siblings coming again at this amazing point (vv. 19-20).

Besides, Luke concludes his input to the record for that day in ending his text with Jesus' mother and siblings trying to get close to Jesus this second time (v. 21), and does not return to Matthew and Mark's continuation of that day's events, until that day had ended, when the evening had arrived, with Jesus and the disciples now leaving Capernaum, with wishing to sail across the lake again (Mat. 13:53; Mark 4:35; Luke 8:22).

Before that, and returning to where we left off, Mark continues with the next subsequent *Parable of the Growing Seed* (4:26-29, being unique to his Gospel.

Matthew (13:24-30) continues after Mark also with his next indigenous *Parable of the Wheat and Tares*, and after dovetailing with Mark, parallels again with his Gospel over the *Parable of the Mustard Seed* (Mat. 13:31-32; Mark 4:30-32).

Luke 8

19 Then His mother and His siblings came to Him, but could not come near Him because of the crowd.

20 And it was told Him by certain who said,

"Your mother and siblings stand over there, desiring to see You."

21 And He answered and said to them,

"My mother and siblings are these who hear the word of God, and do it.

LAST PARABLES TO CROWDS

Mark 4

26 And He said,

"So is the Kingdom of God, as if one should cast seed into the ground;

27 and should sleep, and rise night and day, and the seed should spring up and grow up, how, they don't know.

28 For the earth brings forth fruit of herself; first the blade, then the ear, after that the full corn in the ear.

29 But when the fruit is brought forth, immediately they put in the sickle, because the harvest is come."

Matthew 13

24 Another parable He put before them, saying,

"The Kingdom of Heaven is comparable to a man who sowed good seed in his field:

Matthew 13

25 but while he slept, his enemy came and sowed tares among the wheat, and went their way.

26 But when the blade was sprung up, and produced fruit, then appeared the tares also.

27 So the servants of the landowner came and said to him,

'Sir, didn't you sow good seed in your field? From where then has it tares?'

28 He said to them, 'An enemy has done this.'

The servants said to him, 'Do you then wish that we go and gather them up?'

29 But he said, 'No; lest while you gather up the tares, you root up also the wheat with them.

30 Let both grow together until the harvest: and in the time of the harvest I will say to the reapers, 'You gather together first the tares, and bind them in bundles to burn them: but gather the wheat into my barn.'"

Matthew 13:31 Mark 4:30-31a

Another parable He put before them, and He said,

"To what shall we liken the Kingdom of God? Or with what comparison shall we compare it?

The Kingdom of Heaven it is comparable to a grain of mustard seed, which, someone took, and sowed in their field:

Matthew 13:32a Mark 4:31b

which indeed when it was sown in the earth, is one of the smallest of all the seeds that is in the earth:

Matthew 13:32b Mark 4:32

but when it is sown, it comes up, and having grown, it becomes one of the largest among all of the herbs, and shoots out extensive branches; and becomes a tree, so that THE BIRDS OF THE SKY MAY COME AND REST IN ITS BRANCHES (Ps. 104:12), AND UNDER ITS SHADE (Eze. 17:23; 31:6; Dan. 4:12)."

Matthew 13

33 Another parable He spoke to them;

"The Kingdom of Heaven is comparable to leaven, which a woman took, and hid in three measures of meal, till the whole was leavened."

34 All these things Jesus spoke to the crowds in parables;

Mark 4

33 and with many such parables He spoke the word to them, as they were able to receive it.

Matthew 13:34b Mark 4:34

And besides without a parable He didn't speak to them: and when they were

alone, He expounded all things to His disciples,
Matthew 13
35 that it might be fulfilled which was spoken by the prophet, saying (Ps. 78:2),
"I WILL OPEN MY MOUTH IN PARABLES; I WILL UTTER THINGS WHICH HAVE BEEN KEPT
SECRET FROM THE FOUNDATION OF THE WORLD."

After Jesus had given the last parables in that certain same day to the crowds
(Mark 4:35; Luke 8:22), He sent them away, and returned with the disciples back
to the house (Mat. 13:36), wherein He went on to explain the *Parable of the
Wheat and Tares*, also giving four more parables, before setting off that particular
night across the lake (Mat. 13:37-53).

IN THE HOUSE AGAIN

Matthew 13
36 Then Jesus sent the crowd away, and went into the house: and His disciples
came to Him, saying, "Declare to us the parable of the tares of the   field."
37 He answered and said to them, "He who sows the good seed is the Son of
Humanity;
38 the field is the world; the good seed are the children of the Kingdom; but the
tares are the children of the wicked;
39 the enemy who sowed them is the Devil; the harvest is the end of the world;
and the reapers are the angels.
40 As therefore the tares are gathered and burned in the fire; so shall it be in the
end of this world.
41 The Son of Humanity shall send out His angels, and they shall gather out of
His Kingdom all THINGS THAT OFFEND, AND THOSE WHO ARE LAWLESS (Zeph. 1:3);
42 and shall cast them into a furnace of fire: there shall be wailing and gnashing
of teeth.

43 Then shall THE RIGHTEOUS SHINE FORTH AS THE SUN (Dan. 12:3) in the Kingdom of
their Father, who has ears to hear, let them hear.

44 Again, the Kingdom of Heaven is comparable to treasure hidden in a field;
which when someone has found, they hide, and for the joy thereof goes and sell
s all that they have, and buys that field.

45 Again, the Kingdom of Heaven is comparable to a merchant, seeking fine
pearls:
46 who, when they had found one pearl of great price, went and bought it.

47 Again, the Kingdom of Heaven is comparable to a net that was cast into the

sea, and gathered of every kind:

48 which, when it was full, they drew to shore, and sat down, and gathered the good into vessels, but cast the bad away.

49 So shall it be at the end of the world: the angels shall come forth, and sever the wicked from the just,

50 and shall cast them into the furnace of fire: there shall be wailing and gnashing of teeth."

51 Jesus says to them, "Have you understood all these things'?" They say to Him, "Yes, Lord."

52 Then He said to them,

"Therefore every Scribe who is instructed in the Kingdom of Heaven is comparable to someone who is a householder, who brings forward out of their treasure things old and new."

Notice, that Luke returns back to the same events of that day, and parallels, after having given his last reference about Jesus' mother and siblings (8:21), specifically indicating all these incidents took place on that '*certain day*' (v. 22).

Mark, also parallels again, agreeing that it was '*the same day*' (4:35), which Matthew informed us they '*went into the house*' (13:36).

All this took place after that day's earlier event of the meeting in the house with the Scribes and Pharisees, which concluded with Jesus' mother and siblings arriving the first time, whereby Jesus leaves the house to go to the seashore, where He gives the *Parable of the Sower* from a boat.

Moreover, with the reference from Mark about '*there were also with Him other smaller boats*' (4:36), alluded again no doubt to the seventy being present.

THEY SAIL FOR COUNTRY OF THE GADARENES

Matthew 13:53 Mark 4:35 Luke 8:22a
And now it came to pass, on that certain same day, that when Jesus had finished these parables, when evening was come, He says to them, "Let us pass over to the other side."
He departing from there.

Mark 4:36 Luke 8:22b
And they having sent the crowd away, as He was leaving they His disciples took Him into a boat: and He said to them, "Let us go over to the other side of the lake."

And they launched out. And there were also with Him other smaller boats.

MIRACLE SIXTEEN - THE STORM

Having already dealt with the specific differences between *The Eighth Miracle* and the sixteenth, of the two storms, and the tenth and the seventeenth miracle, of *The Two Demoniacs* and the single demoniac, we see that the emphasis of Jesus' words this time, at the sixteenth miracle, is on asking the disciples where their faith was by now, and should be understood in the sense that they had already experienced one storm, and of course many miracles. Jesus was now asking, '*How is it that you* [still] *have no faith?*' (Mark 4:40), after all the miracles.

Mark 4:37-38a Luke 8:23
But as they sailed He fell asleep; and there emerged descending a great storm of wind on the lake; and the waves beat into the boat, and they were filled with water, so that it was now full and were in jeopardy. And He was in the hinder part of the boat, asleep on a pillow:
Mark 4:38b-39 Luke 8:24
and they came to Him, and arousing Him awoke Him, and exclaimed saying to Him, "Master, Master, we perish. Don't You care that we perish?"

And then He rose, and rebuked the wind and said to the raging of the water, "Sea, peace, be still."

And the wind ceased, and they subsided, and there was a great calm.
Mark 4:40-41 Luke 8:25
And He said to them, "Where is your faith? Why are you so fearful? How is it that you have no faith?"

And they being afraid, exceedingly feared, wondering, and exclaimed, saying one to another, "What manner of Man is this! That He even commands the wind and the water of the sea, and they obey Him?"

MIRACLE SEVENTEEN - LEGION OF DEVILS

Mark 5:1 Luke 8:26
And they came over to the other side of the sea, arriving at the country of the Gadarenes, which is over against Galilee.
Mark 5:2-3 Luke 8:27
And when He went forwards to land, coming out of the boat, immediately there met Him out of the city tombs a certain man with an unclean spirit, who had devils a long time, and wore no clothes, neither lived in any house, but he had his dwelling in among the tombs; and no man could bind him, no, not with chains.

Mark 5

4 Because that he had often been bound with fetters and chains, and the chains had been plucked asunder by him, and the fetters broken in pieces: neither could anyone tame him.

5 And always, night and day, he was in the hills, and in the tombs, crying out, and cutting himself with stones.

6 But when he saw Jesus far off, he ran and worshiped Him,

Mark 5:7 Luke 8:28

and he cried out with a loud voice, and said, "What have I to do with You, Jesus, Son of the Most High God? I adjure and beg You by God, that You don't torment me."

Mark 5:8 Luke 8:29

For He had commanded saying to him, "Come out of the man, you unclean spirit!"

For many times it had caught him: and he was kept bound with chains and in fetters; and he broke the bands, and was driven of the Devil into the wilderness.

Mark 5:9 Luke 8:30

And Jesus asked him saying, "What is your name?"

And he answered, saying, "My name is Legion: for we are many."

Because many devils were entered into him.

Mark 5

10 And he begged Him much that He would not send them away out of the country.

Luke 8

31 And they begged Him that He would not command them to go out into the deep.

Mark 5

11 Now there were near to the hillsides great herds of swine feeding.

Mark 5:12 Luke 8:32

And there was a herd of sufficient swine feeding on the hillside: and all they, the devils implored Him that He would allow them to enter into them, saying, "Send us into the swine, so we may enter into them."

And He allowed them.

Mark 5:13 Luke 8:33

And immediately Jesus gave them leave. And then went the devils, the unclean spirits out of the man, and entered into the swine: and the herd ran furiously down a steep bank into the deep of the water, they were about two thousand; and were choked in the sea.

Mark 5:14a Luke 8:34
And when they who fed the swine saw what was done, they fled, and went, and told it in the city, and in the country.

Mark 5:14b Luke 8:35a
And then they went out to see what it was that was done.
Mark 5:15 Luke 8:35b
And they came to Jesus, and searching, found the man, out of whom the devils departed, him who was possessed with the Devil, and who had the legion, sitting at the feet of Jesus, and clothed, and in his right mind: and they were afraid.
Mark 5:16 Luke 8:36
And they also who saw it told them how it occurred to him, and by what means he who was possessed with the devils was healed, and also concerning the swine.

Mark 5:17 Luke 8:37a
And then all the people of the country of Gadarenes round about called Him to one side, and they began desire and to pray Him to depart from them out of their coasts. For they were taken with great fear:
Mark 5:18 Luke 8:37b-38a
and when He was come, to return back again He went up into the boat.

Now the man out of whom the devils were departed, who had been possessed with the Devil, begged, and prayed Him that he might be with Him.
Mark 5:19 Luke 8:38b-39a
However Jesus didn't allow him, and Jesus sent him away, saying to him, "Return to your own house, and go to your friends, and tell them, and relate how great things the Lord God has done for you, having had compassion on you."

Mark 5:20 Luke 8:39b
And he went his way, and began to proclaim throughout the whole city, and throughout the Decapolis how great things Jesus had done to him: and everyone did marvel.

We see that directly after the sixteenth and seventeenth miracle, Jesus was to return again to Capernaum, at which point the people were eagerly awaiting His arrival (Mark 5:21; Luke 8:40). It is at this juncture, we must remember as we covered previously back at the text surrounding Mat. 9:13, regarding v. 14, as this verse follows in successive order after Mark 5:21 and Luke 8:40, now as Jesus returns to Capernaum.

See *Scripture Graph IV-V*, and our findings surrounding Mat. 9:13, and Mat. 11:2, where John's disciples came the first time, and the reasons for Matthew's dislocation of his text, if needed at this juncture, as Mat. 9:14-17 now dovetails, and leads into and parallels with the eighteenth and nineteenth miracle (Mat. 9:18-25; Mark 5:22-43; Luke 8:41-56).

JOHN'S DISCIPLES SECOND ARRIVAL

Remember, Matthew had positioned the Baptist's disciples coming this final time and second time to Capernaum (9:14-17), with the eighteenth to the twenty-first miracle (vv. 18-34), the last tour of Galilee (v. 35), and the prayer for the harvesting of the souls (vv. 36-38), before his chapter on the ordination (10:1). Though the preceding events of Mat. 9:14-38 actually occurred weeks after the ordination. Also it was while the apostles were on their first mission alone, that John the Baptist was beheaded (Mat. 14:1-2, 12-13; Mark 6:14, 30; Luke 9:7, 10).

Returning to where Jesus had arrived back at Capernaum, after the sixteenth and the seventeenth miracle, now, amongst the crowds were John's disciples, who at this second time of coming to Jesus (Mat. 9:14-17), were somewhat perplexed as their teacher was still in prison, and they could see Jesus' disciples enjoying the tremendous opportunity of traveling with Jesus, and witnessing the miraculous events, in observing the joy on people's faces and the whole invigorating atmosphere of being around Jesus.

We had indicated previously that Matthew (9:14-35) had placed his text surrounding John the Baptist's disciples arriving the final time at Capernaum, and the eighteenth miracle following through to the twenty-first miracle, with the prayer for the harvesting of the souls (9:36-38), to emphasize certain factors, rather than keeping to the successive order.

Moreover, as the Baptist would shortly be beheaded in prison, thereby concluding his mission, and the mission of his disciples, and Jesus having previously indicated that His work was to increase and the Baptist's decrease, Matthew also pointed out, correlating this last time the disciples of John are recorded as coming to Jesus at Capernaum, with the last tour of Galilee (9:35). Directly afterwards Jesus and the apostles would leave for Judea, with the twelve being sent on their first mission since their ordination without Jesus (Mark 6:7-13; Luke 9:1-6).

Conversely, the disciples of John, knowing that Jesus was to be found at Capernaum, and concerned over whether the Baptist would be freed again, could only talk to their mentor from prison (Mat. 11:2), and observing the joyful disposition of Jesus' disciples, asked despondently why they did not fast at this time, as they did (Mat. 9:14).

Though, now at this time, just before the eighteenth miracle, because of Jesus' concern for John's disciples, He would have given the *Parable of the Children of the Bride Chamber* in empathy, by emphasizing (Mat. 9:15), '*but the days will come, when the bridegroom* [Himself] *shall be taken from them*' [the apostles]. In retrospect John's disciples had already experienced the Baptist being taken from them, now that their teacher was in prison. However, when Jesus originally gave the same parable to the Scribes and Pharisees at Matthew's house at the banquet, in answer to their same question on fasting, when John's disciples were not present, the Baptist's disciples, now asking the same question, it required the same answer, albeit given with different expression as the Pharisees had a judgmental attitude in Matthew's house, and here the Baptist's disciples in the crowds had not.

Furthermore, while the disciples of John were listening to Jesus, it is Matthew (9:18) who points out that '*while He spoke these things to*' John's disciples, that Jairus came about the healing of his daughter, which was the nineteenth miracle (Mark 5:22; Luke 8:41).

Preceding the actual healing of Jairus' daughter, a woman was to touch the hem of Jesus' garment, and subsequently become healed. This now becoming the eighteenth miracle, before Jesus healed Jairus' daughter. Though Matthew only mentions '*a certain ruler* [Gr. *archon*]' arriving, it is both Mark and Luke who reveal more detail, using a different Greek word [*archisunagogos*] to further define his status, which can better be rendered as a '*director of the synagogue*'. Once again, we witness the correlating of the Gospels at this juncture. No doubt, Jairus, who was also likely one of Jesus' acquaintances would have been familiar with the incidents in surrounding the second, the twelfth, and thirteenth miracle, all associated with this synagogue!

Hence, the Synoptics agreeing to the successive order of the incidents of the eighteenth miracle and the nineteenth miracle, with the event of the final and second time of John's disciples coming to Capernaum. This related and synchronized with these two particular miracles, and is a classic example of the way Matthew places together some of his key dialogue, in bringing our attention to certain aspects.

Previously we considered the factor of twelve, in regards to Matthew being the twelfth disciple, after *The Eleventh Miracle*, with the next miracle after Matthew's calling, obviously being *The Twelfth Miracle*, and the surrounding text leading up to *The Ordination Of The Twelve*. Amazingly, we have in our next successive text following, which Matthew placed directly before *The Ordination Of The Twelve* (10:1), two more references to twelve again.

The first is with the age of Jairus' daughter, which Matthew curiously does not mention (Luke 8:42). And the second, the length of time the woman had the illness (Mat. 9:20; Mark 5:25; Luke 8:43).

Mark 5:21 Luke 8:40
And it came to pass, that, when Jesus was returning, passing over again
by boat to the other side, many people gathered to Him, and He was near to the
sea, the people gladly received Him: for they were waiting for Him.

Matthew 9
14 Then came to Him the disciples of John, saying,
"Why do we and the Pharisees fast often, but Your disciples don't fast?
15 And Jesus said to them,
"Can the children of the bride chamber mourn, as long as the bride groom is
with them?
But the days will come, when the bridegroom shall be taken from them, and
then they shall fast.

16 No one puts a piece of new cloth upon an old garment, for that which is put
on to fill it up takes from the garment, and the rip is made worse.

17 Neither do people put new wine into old wineskins: else the skins burst, and
the wine runs out, and the skins ruin: but they put new wine into new wineskins,
and both are preserved."

MIRACLES EIGHTEEN TO TWENTY-ONE

Matthew 9:18a Mark 5:22 Luke 8:41
And, while He spoke these things to them, consider, approaching, came a man
named Jairus, and he was a certain ruler, and one of the directors of the
synagogue; and when he saw Him he fell down at Jesus' feet and worshiped
Him, and implored Him that He would come into his house,
Matthew 9:18b Mark 5:23
and urging Him greatly, said, "My little daughter lies at the point of death - is
now even dead: I pray You but come and lay your hands upon her, that she may
be healed: and she shall live."

Matthew 9:19 Mark 5:24 Luke 8:42
For he had only one daughter, about twelve years of age, and she lay dying.
And Jesus rose, and followed, going with him, and so did His disciples.
But as He went and many people followed Him, the people thronged Him.

Matthew 9:20a Mark 5:25 Luke 8:43a
And, consider, a certain woman, was diseased with an issue of blood twelve
years,
Mark 5:26 Luke 8:43b
and suffered many things of many physicians, and who had spent all her living
that she had upon physicians, neither could be healed of any, and was nothing
advantaged, but rather grew worse,

Matthew 9:20b Mark 5:27 Luke 8:44

when she heard of Jesus, came in the press behind Him and touched the hem of His garment.

Matthew 9:21 Mark 5:28

For she said, within herself, "If I may but touch His garment, I shall be whole."

Mark 5:29 Luke 8:44

And at once the fountain of her issue of blood stopped, and immediately dried up; and she felt in her body that she was healed from her suffering.

Mark 5:30-31 Luke 8:45

And Jesus immediately knowing in Himself that virtue had gone out of Him, turned Him about in the crowd, and said, "Who touched My clothes?"

When all denied, Peter, His disciples, and those who were with Him, said to Him, "Master, You see the people thronging and crowding, and pressing, and You say, *'Who touched Me?'"*

Luke 8

46 And Jesus said, "Somebody has touched Me: for I perceive that virtue has gone out of Me."

Matthew 9:22a Mark 5:32

However Jesus turned Himself, looking round about to see, when He saw her who had done this thing.

Mark 5:33 Luke 8:47

But the woman fearing and trembling, knowing what was done in her, when seeing that she was not hid, she came and fell down before Him, and she declare to Him all the truth before all the people for what cause she had touched Him, and how she was healed immediately.

Matthew 9:22b Mark 5:34 Luke 8:48

And He said to her, "Daughter, be of good comfort: your faith has made you whole; go in peace, and be free of your suffering."

And the woman was made whole from that hour.

Mark 5:35 Luke 8:49

While He yet spoke, there came from the director of the synagogue's house certain representatives, one who said, declaring to him,

"Your daughter is dead; trouble not the Master. Why trouble the Master any further?"

Mark 5:36 Luke 8:50

But Jesus having listened, overheard the remark that was spoken, says to the director of the synagogue, answering him,

"Don't be afraid, don't fear: only believe and she shall be made whole."

Mark 5

37 And He allowed no one to follow Him, save Peter, and James, and John the brother of James.

Mark 5

38 And He came to the house of the director of the synagogue, and sees the tumult, and those who wept and wailed greatly.

Matthew 9:23 Mark 5:39 Luke 8:51a

And when Jesus was come into the ruler's house, and saw the funeral music and the people making a noise,
Matthew 9:24 Luke 8:51b

He said to them, "Give room."
He allowing no one to go in, save Peter, and James, and John, and the father and mother of the girl.
Mark 5:39 Luke 8:52

And all wept, and grieved for her: He says to them,
"Why make you this ado, and weep?"
And He said, "Don't weep; for the young girl is not dead, but sleeps."
Luke 8

53 And they laughed scornfully at Him, knowing that she was dead.

Matthew 9:25a Mark 5:40 Luke 8:54a

And He put them all out. But when He had put all the people out, He takes the father and the mother of the young girl, and those who were with Him, and entering in where the young girl was lying,
Matthew 9:25b Mark 5:41 Luke 8:54b

takes the young girl by the hand, and called, saying to her, "Talitha cumi."
Which is, being translated, "Young girl, I say to you, rise."
Matthew 9:25c Mark 5:42a Luke 8:55

And her spirit came again, and the young girl rose immediately and walked; and she was twelve years old: and He prescribed food to be given her.

Mark 5:42b Luke 8:56a

And her parents were amazed with great astonishment.
Mark 5:43 Luke 8:56b

But He exhorted them stressing that they should tell no one what was done, that no one should know it: still requesting that something should be given her to eat.

Matthew 9

26 And the fame thereof went abroad into all the land.

27 And when Jesus departed from there, two blind men followed Him, crying, and saying, "You Son of David, have mercy on us."

28 And when He was come into the house, the blind men came to Him: and Jesus says to them, "Do you believe that I am able to do this?"
They said to Him, "Yes, Lord."

Matthew 9

29 Then He touched their eyes, saying, "According to your faith be it to you."

30 And their eyes were opened; and Jesus strictly warned them, saying, "See that no one knows it."

31 But they, when they were departed, His fame spread abroad in all that country.

32 As they went out, consider, they brought to Him a dumb man possessed with a devil.

33 And when the devil was cast out, the dumb spoke: and the crowds marveled, saying, "So it was never seen in Israel."

34 But the Pharisees said, "He casts out devils through the Prince of Devils."

CONCLUSION OF SECOND GALILEAN MINISTRY

We saw in the previous section, how the last and second time that John's disciples came to Jesus at Capernaum (Mat. 9:14-17), was shortly before their teacher's death, and was directly connected to the nineteenth miracle the arrival of Jairus and his request for his daughter's healing (Mat. 9:23-26; Mark 5:35-43; Luke 8:49-56). This was interwoven with the event of the eighteenth miracle, of the woman with the issue of blood (Mat. 9:18-22; Mark 5:22-34 Luke 8:41-48), which further led intrinsically into the twentieth and twenty-first miracle (Mat. 9:27-34).

John's disciples had arrived at Capernaum just before the eighteenth and nineteenth miracle was to transpire. Jesus, after *Miracle Seventeen* in the country of the Gadarenes, had returned to Capernaum (Mark 5:21; Luke 8:40), wanting to get back to His house. But, the people were awaiting His return, and the subsequent incidents of the eighteenth and nineteenth miracle, did not allow Him that opportunity, until eventually He finally did '*come into the house*' at the twentieth miracle (Mat. 9:28).

Nonetheless, the twentieth miracle of the two blind men, who followed Jesus to His house (v. 27), from the healing of Jairus' daughter, and the twenty-first miracle of the dumb man being healed, directly after the two blind men had left, brings us to the fourth and final preaching circuit of Galilee (v. 35), before Jesus and the disciples embark into their second Judean ministry, when the apostles are sent on alone, ahead of Jesus (Mark 6:7,12; Luke 9:2, 6, 10).

Of course, Jesus was to return to Capernaum and Galilee again in the following year, with more miracles and preaching. However, after this first year of concentrated proclaiming of the gospel of the Kingdom of God, four times to the cities of Galilee, there is no record that He circulated that area again, only that He continued to visit certain individual towns in traveling through the areas in returning to Galilee, and while digressing further afield from there at each opportunity.

We should notice that Mark 5:43 closes his narration with the nineteenth miracle, and so goes on to Jesus and the disciples leaving Capernaum for Nazareth, just before the final phase of touring the area of Galilee again - this the fourth time, in this first year of His ministry. The final tour of Galilee mentioned at Mark 6:6, also correlates and parallels with Mat. 9:35, before the twelve were to leave for Judea the first time on their own. Though, the final tour of Galilee would occur prior to them leaving for Judea.

However, Matthew informed us that, before traveling to Nazareth and embarking on this last circuit of Galilee, two blind men had come to Jesus' house to be healed, at which point He also healed a dumb man (9:27-34). While, v. 35 is a reference to the circulating of Galilee, it actually includes the stopping off at Nazareth first, which, Matthew because of the dislocation of his text actually refers to at 13:54.

The influence, and the great effect of the last preaching tour of Galilee (Mat. 9:35; Mark 6:6), resulted in the prayer for the harvesting of the souls (Mat. 9:36-38), which Matthew included in his narration following the reference to the last tour.

Thus, Mark pointed out in what successive order these events transpired, since Matthew does not always follow in succession. This is borne out by the fact that Matthew mentions the arriving at Nazareth in descriptive detail (13:54-58), which parallels with the same event in Mark (6:1-5). Although Matthew did not actually mention in detail the journey across the lake from Capernaum to Gadara, but, nevertheless, he aligns with Mark and Luke in alluding to it (Mat. 13:53; Mark 4:34-36; Luke 8:22). The event all in one day, of the Pharisees in Jesus' house, where His mother and siblings arrive, the *Parable of the Sower*, with all the other parables, after which Jesus and the disciples leave for Gadara, covers Mat. 12:25-13:53, Mark 3:23-4:36 and Luke 8:4-22.

Mat. 13:53 related to the boat journey across the lake to Gadara, after having discussed several parables with the disciples in the house at Capernaum (vv. 36-52), and, the events of the sixteenth, and seventeenth miracle (Mark 4:37-40; 5:1-20; Luke 8:23-39): through which the incidents of John's disciples coming the second time (Mat. 9:14-17), together with the eighteenth (Mat. 9:18-22; Mark 5:21-34; Luke 8:40-48), the nineteenth (Mat. 9:23-26; Mark 5:35-43; Luke 8:49-56), the twentieth and twenty-first miracle (Mat. 9:27-34), come full circle, as it were, to return us to Mat. 13:54, and the arrival at Nazareth before the final circuit of Galilee, as Matthew's text previous to 9:35 is dislocated. See *Scripture Graph V-VI*, for further clarity.

Vv. 36-38 about the harvest of souls, and that there were not enough reapers, actually relates to the fourth circuit of Galilee having been completed, after Jesus and the disciples had proceeded from Nazareth into that last tour. Intentionally Matthew placed it next to the ordination of the twelve (10:1), as we discussed in the section relating to that event, so as to point out certain other factors, too.

The next preaching tour, after this last preaching tour of Galilee, with the twelve being sent on alone before Jesus this time (Mark 6:7, 12-13; Luke 9:1-2, 6, 10), culminates in the death the Baptist, and Herod afterwards wondering whether he had risen. Over this detail the Synoptics parallel again (Mat. 14:2; Mark 6:14; Luke 9:7). Matthew, however, does not include in his text the sending of twelve apostles on alone, before Jesus, and thus it fits in successive order after Mat. 9:38.

The reputation surrounding this first year of preaching, with more miracles having been done in that year and in the Galilee area than elsewhere, would now give the basis to the rest of Jesus' ministry, as three Passovers were yet to transpire!

Remember, Jesus had begun His mission, His first preaching tour in Galilee after His baptism, subsequently after autumn and winter in Galilee, He then came down to Jerusalem for the first Passover of His ministry (John 2:12-13). Thus, when

He returned, His second Galilean ministry began (4:45), wherein He toured Galilee three more times during that first summer.

After the fourth preaching circuit of Galilee, which was part of *The Second Galilean Ministry*, He was to travel to Jerusalem in the following season, wherein the next Festival of Tabernacles would fall (5:1), the second of His ministry, as the first Festival of Tabernacles would have been during His first Galilean ministry.

Jesus had said previously that His ministry would increase, whereas John's would decrease. As the second Judean ministry was about to begin, John was finally beheaded. Furthermore, the harvest of souls is mentioned again, when the twelve had increased, with Jesus ordaining seventy, and sending them on alone before Him in the following year (Luke 10:1-2).

Mark 6
1 And He went out from there, and came into His own hometown; and His disciples followed Him.

Matthew 13:54 Mark 6:2
And when He was come into His own hometown, when the Sabbath Day was come, He began to teach them in their synagogue: insomuch that the majority hearing Him were astonished, and said, exclaiming,
"From where has this Man these things and what wisdom is this which is given to Him, and that even such mighty works are performed by His hands?
Matthew 13:55 Mark 6:3a
Isn't this the artificer - the artificer's son, the son of Mary? Isn't His mother called Mary, and His brothers, James, and Jose, and Juda, and Simon?
Matthew 13:56 Mark 6:3b
And His sisters aren't they all here with us? From where then has this Man all these things?"

Matthew 13:57 Mark 6:3c-4
And they were offended in Him. But Jesus said to them,
"A prophet is not without honor, except in his own country, and among his own kin, and in his own house."
Matthew 13:58 Mark 6:5
And He did not do many mighty works there because of their unbelief, except that he laid His hands upon a few sick folk, and healed them.
Mark 6
6a And He marveled because of their unbelief.

Matthew 9:35 Mark 6:6b
And Jesus went round about all the cities and villages, teaching in their

synagogues, and preaching the gospel of the Kingdom, and healing every sickness and every disease among the people.

Matthew 9

36 But when He saw the crowds, He was moved with compassion on them, because they fainted, and were scattered abroad, as sheep having no shepherd.

37 Then says He to His disciples,
"The harvest truly is plenteous, but the laborers are few;
38 You pray therefore the Lord of the harvest, that He will send out laborers into His harvest."

THE SECOND JUDEAN MINISTRY

Matthew's dislocated text of 13:54-58, actually relates to and dovetails between where the Baptist's disciples come the last time to Capernaum, along with the eighteenth to the twenty-first miracle (9:14-34), as the death of John was inherently linked to Jesus' last circuit of Galilee and the second Judean ministry.

The tremendous atmosphere of Jesus' message with the healing of the people throughout Galilee, and subsequently Judea through the twelve (Mark 6:12-13; Luke 9:6), would shortly reach Herod (Mat. 14:1; Mark 6:14; Luke 9:7). Thus Mathew 13:54-58 leads to 14:1, where the Baptist's death is mentioned.

We had also previously shown that Matthew had closed *The First Galilean Ministry* of Jesus with ch. 4:23-25, which would have covered the months before the first Passover, namely autumn through to winter. Furthermore, Matthew again is the one who concludes the second Galilean ministry with ch. 9:35-38.

The second Galilean ministry was now over, and the apostles first preaching mission, wherein Jesus would send '*them two by two*' on ahead of Him was about to start.

At this first preaching mission on their own, with Jesus and the apostles having just completed the fourth circuit of Galilee (Mat. 9:35; Mark 6:6), and the fact that Jesus had remarked that they were to pray for more laborers to be added and sent to the harvest (Mat. 9:36-38), and that the seventy were also being trained ready for their '*two by two*' mission a year later (Luke 10:1), would indicate that the prayer for more laborers was a continuing one, and that it was being answered, as they now left the Galilean region.

Mark 6:7 Luke 9:1

He called to Him the twelve disciples together, and began to send them out two by two; and gave them power and authority over all the unclean spirits of devils; and to cure diseases.

Luke 9

2 And He sent them to preach the Kingdom of God, and to heal the sick.

Mark 6:8-9 Luke 9:3

And instructing them, He said to them,

"Take nothing for your journey, save a staff only, no travel-bag, neither bread, no money in your money-belts: wear a pair of sandals; and neither have two coats apiece."

Mark 6:10 Luke 9:4

And He said to them,

"And in what place wherever you enter, whether into a house, stay there until you are ready to depart.

Mark 6:11 Luke 9:5

And whoever doesn't receive you, nor hear you, when you depart from there, as you go out of that city, shake off the very dust from under your feet for a testimony against them. Truly I say to you, it shall be more tolerable for Sodom and Gomorrah in the Day of Judgment, than for that city."

Mark 6:12 Luke 9:6a

And they went out and departed, and went through the towns, preaching the gospel; and preached that everyone should repent.

Mark 6:13 Luke 9:6b

And they cast out many devils, and anointed many with oil who were sick, and healed them everywhere.

It is clear from Jesus' first instructions to the apostles on how to preach the gospel, that they were not yet to concentrate their efforts within the area of Samaria (Mat. 10:5), but were to go *rather to the lost sheep of the House of Israel*' (v. 6), referring then to the area of Judea, before they were to preach to the Samaritans. However, a year later, when a further seventy disciples had been called, in that mission, they did preach to Samaria (Luke 9:51-56), in journeying to Judea again (v. 57).

This then being the case, the apostles were now traveling to Judea ahead of Jesus, and were to meet up with Him after that mission. With hearing the news from the Baptist's disciples that John had been beheaded (Mat. 14:12-13, Mark 6:29-30), with Mark (6:30), and Luke (9:10) not using the word *'disciples'*, as they had previous to that, when the disciples met up with Jesus, both made sure they highlighted the issue by now using the word *'apostles'* [Gr. *'ones sent out'*].

The apostles after meeting up with Jesus, were to travel, as we shall see, months later following Tabernacles in Jerusalem, and winter, to the Sea of Tiberias, arriving there, and then sailing over to Bethsaida by boat (Mat. 14:13; Mark 6:32; Luke 9:10; John 6:1), before the second Passover of their ministry (John 6:4). All four Gospels converge in agreement as to those facts.

Remember, that within a verse, or in between a verse, sometimes there are considerable time gaps.

But before coming to this second Passover, we had previously stated that John in his Gospel mentioned in his actual text three Passovers, one Festival of Tabernacles, one Festival of Dedication, and '*a Festival*' (5:1). Though the one at which point we have now arrived, and are about to consider is not actually indicated by name.

Moreover, these Festivals were synonymous with the seasons. Passover in spring, Pentecost in summer, and Tabernacles in autumn, which together covered a half-year period, the rest of the months surrounding those Festivals would obviously cover autumn through to winter and the spring months, coming full circle to Passover again.

We will see that after the sending out of the newly ordained apostles, as the mission of the Baptist had ended, that both the Baptist's disciples (Mat. 14:12), and the apostles were to meet up with Jesus after the death of John (Mark 6:30; Luke 9:10). This aspect is intrinsically wound up with John 5 and 6, too, and the time for the next successive Festival of Tabernacles, in our progression throughout this first year, and with the following mentioned twenty-second miracle.

Since Jesus and the disciples had left Galilee, with the disciples going on ahead before Jesus through Judea, they would have prearranged a meeting place. Also, the Baptist's disciples knew where to find Jesus too, and no doubt were aware that Jesus would be attending the Festival of Tabernacles shortly, knowing also where to find Him in Jerusalem.

The narrative of John 5 is portrayed as being in Jerusalem, which transpired before his next ch. 6, which naturally referred to the period preceding that of ch. 6, which was back at Galilee and related to the springtime at the following Passover and after. Thus, when returning to ch. 5:1, where '*a Festival of the Jews*' is recorded, when following the Biblical Calendar it would refer to the previous successive event, Tabernacles, which was the last major Festival before Passover (Lev. 23:1-8, 33-44).

This reference to '*a Feast*' [Festival] is averred to in Isidore Fishman's book, *Introduction to Judaism* [Jewish Chronicle Publications 1978], p. 74, "*In the Bible and the Talmud, the Festival* [of Tabernacles] *is also known simply as* [in Hebrew] '*Chag*' - '*Feast*'", so as not to distinguish it with any other. Moreover, in the Greek of the NT there is no single equivalent for an '*a*', as in '*a Festival*', and could just as readily be translated '*the Festival*', as it was fondly known by Jews preeminently in that day, as is revealed by Josephus and Philo, as well as in the Talmud.

Nevertheless, autumn is the next season, which would naturally transpire, when following our journeying of Jesus and the disciples through the Gospels. Recalling, that Jesus' public preaching ministry began in Galilee and as we suggested in the autumn, at the time of the Feast Tabernacles. Three more would follow, with Jesus and the disciples being in Jerusalem at each subsequent season.

Also, the Festival of Tabernacles was known as the Festival of Ingathering, too (Ex. 23:16). The ingathering was synonymous with the ingathering of the last harvest, and thus symbolic, of the great harvest of souls (Mat. 9:36-38), as alluded to previously when the apostles and the seventy went out to preach (Luke 10:1-2). Of course, a resurrection is needed before the spiritual produce can be of any lasting value. Moreover, in the text of John 5 (vv. 21-29), which follows in our next section, there is reference to that particular resurrection time.

Additionally, the last two references of Matthew and Luke to the harvest of the souls, both are descriptive of the autumn season, referring to the greater harvest of the land, as well as relating to the events when they actually occurred. The final tour of Galilee being complete, it would be nearing autumn anyhow, and with the second reference of the harvest of souls in the following year, the seventy were also asked to pray for more laborers, which would have taken place in autumn.

JOHN'S DEATH

Recapping, Jesus had now sent off the twelve (Mark 6:7-13; Luke 9:1-6), after which the Synoptics aligned at the beheading of the Baptist (Mat. 14:1-11; Mark 6:14-28; Luke 9:7-9). Interestingly, John in his Gospel refers to the fact that those whom Jesus was addressing in this next Festival of Tabernacles, *'were willing for a season to rejoice in his* [the Baptist's] *light'*, and, that, *'he was a burning light'* (5:35). Furthermore he avers to the Baptist having been beheaded at that time, and additionally indicates Jesus having *'to finish, the same works'* (v. 36). Hence, the dovetailing of John 5:1, in its only natural position, and our reasons in placing it so.

John 5
1 After this there was a Festival of the Jews; and Jesus went up to Jerusalem.

Matthew 14:1-2 Mark 6:14 Luke 9:7
And now at that time king Herod the Tetrarch heard of the fame of all that was done by Jesus; for His name spread abroad: and he was perplexed, because that it was said of some, that John was risen from the dead; and he said to his servants, "This is that John the Baptist; he's risen from the dead, and therefore mighty works do manifest themselves through him."

Mark 6:15 Luke 9:8
And some of the others said, "That it is Elijah - that Elijah had appeared."

And still others said, "That he is a prophet, or like one of the prophets - that one of the old prophets was risen again."

Mark 6:16 Luke 9:9
But when Herod heard that, he further exclaimed,
"Is it John, whom I have beheaded: has he risen from the dead - but who then is this of whom I hear such things!?"
And he desired to see Him.
Matthew 14:3 Mark 6:17
For Herod himself had sent out and laid hold upon John, then bound him, and put him in prison for Herodias' sake, his brother Philip's wife: for he had married her.
Matthew 14:4 Mark 6:18
For John had said to Herod, "It is not lawful for you to have her - your brother's wife."
Mark 6
19 Therefore Herodias had a quarrel against him, and would have killed him; but she couldn't.

Mark 6

20 For Herod feared John, knowing that he was a just man and holy, and saved him; and when he heard him, he agreed to many things, and heard him gladly.

Matthew 14

5 And when he would have put him to death, he feared the people, because they counted him as a prophet.

Matthew 14:6a Mark 6:21

But however when a convenient day was come, when Herod's birthday was kept - Herod on his birthday made a supper to his Lord's, High Captains, and Chief of the Estates of Galilee.

Matthew 14:6b Mark 6:22

And when the daughter of Herodias came in, and danced before them, and pleased Herod and those who sat with him, the king said to the young woman, "Ask of me whatever you want, and I will give it to you."

Matthew 14:7 Mark 6:23

Whereupon he promised with an oath and swore to her, to give her whatever she would ask. "Whatever you shall ask of me, I will give it you, to the half of my Kingdom."

Mark 6

24 And she went forth, and said to her mother, "What shall I ask?"
And she said, "The head of John the Baptist."

Matthew 14:8 Mark 6:25

And she, being before instructed by her mother, came immediately with haste toward the king, and asked, saying, "I want you to give me right now, the head of John the Baptist on a platter."

Matthew 14:9a Mark 6:26

And the king was extremely sorry; yet nevertheless for the oath's sake, and for their sakes - those who sat with him at supper, he didn't wish to refuse her.

Matthew 14:9b Mark 6:27a

And immediately the king sent the executioner, and he commanded his head to be brought and given her:

Matthew 14:10 Mark 6:27b

and he having sent him, the executioner went, and beheaded John in the prison.

Matthew 14:11 Mark 6:28

And his head was brought on a platter, and was given to the young woman: and the young woman brought and gave it to her mother.

Matthew 14:12 Mark 6:29
And when his disciples heard of it, they came, and took up the corpse, and
laid it, burying it in a tomb, and went and told Jesus.

Matthew 14:13a Mark 6:30 Luke 9:10a
When Jesus heard of it, and the apostles when they were returned, gathered
themselves together to Jesus, and told Him all things, both what they had
done, and what they had taught.
Mark 6
31 And He said to them, "You go yourselves apart into a deserted place, and
rest a while."
For there were many coming and going, and they had no leisure so as to eat.

THE TWENTY-SECOND MIRACLE - CRIPPLED MAN

It is clear from the last verses above and the combined evidence we covered
in the last intersection, that the disciples of John told Jesus about the
Baptist's death at Jerusalem, where they knew they would find Him at this
time of the year. Jesus was to meet up with His disciples also there (Mark
6:30), and no doubt the reference, '*for there were many coming and going*',
alludes to the attendance at the Festival of Tabernacles (v. 31).

Subsequently, after '*the Festival*' and the winter season, Jesus and the
disciples were to return to Galilee, after the twenty-second miracle in John 5
and the events of that whole chapter, as John's following chapter dovetails
and parallels with the Synoptics at this first instance (Mat. 14:13; Mark 6:32;
Luke 9:10; John 6:1).

Luke 9:10 had two factors included in his reference, firstly [a], where the
disciples returned from Judea and met up with Jesus in Jerusalem at the Festival
of Tabernacles, and secondly [b], where the rest of the verse, months later at
spring and the next Festival at the Passover season, refers to when Jesus '*took
them, and went aside privately into a deserted place belonging to a city called
Bethsaida*'.

Correspondingly, in Mat. 14:13a, '*When Jesus heard*' the news of John's
death, includes the same two points as Luke 9:10a and b, because Jesus and the
disciples did not arrive at Bethsaida, in Galilee until shortly before the next
Passover, which would be in the following year.

John 5
2 Now there is at Jerusalem by the Sheep Market a pool, which is called in the
Hebrew tongue Bethesda, having five porches.
3 In these lay a great crowd of impotent folk, of blind, lame, withered, waiting
for the moving of the water.

John 5

4 For an angel went down at a certain season into the pool, and moved the water: whoever then first after the moving of the water stepped in was made whole of whatever disease he had.

5 And a certain man was there, who had an infirmity thirty-eight years.

6 When Jesus saw him lying, and knew that he had been now long time in that situation, He says to him, "Do you wish to be made whole?"
7 The impotent man answered Him,
"Sir, I have no one, when the water is moving, to put me into the pool: but while I am coming, another steps down before me."

8 Jesus says to him, "Rise, take up your stretcher, and walk."
9 And immediately the man was made whole, and took up his stretcher bed, and walked: and on the same day was a Sabbath.

10 The Jews therefore said to him who was cured,
"It is the Sabbath Day: it is not lawful for you to carry your stretcher."
11 He answered them, "He who made me whole, the same said to me,
'Take up your stretcher, and walk .'"

12 Then they asked Him,
"Who is the Man who said to you, *'Take up your stretcher and walk?'*"

13 And he who was healed knew not who it was: for Jesus had conveyed Himself away, a crowd being in that place.

14 Afterwards Jesus finds him in the Temple, and said to him,
"Look you are made whole: sin no more, lest a worse thing come to you."

15 The man departed, and told the Jews that it was Jesus, who had made him whole.
16 And therefore did the Jews persecute Jesus, and sought to kill Him, because He had done these things on the Sabbath Day.

17 But Jesus answered them, "My Father works even now, and I work."

18 Therefore the Jews sought all the more to kill Him, because He not only had broken the Sabbath, but said also that God was His Father, making Himself equal with God.

19 Then answered Jesus and said to them,

"Truly, truly, I say to you, the Son can do nothing of Himself, but what He sees the Father do: for whatever things He does, these the Son also does likewise.

20 For the Father loves the Son, and shows Him all things that He Himself does: and He will show Him greater works than these, so you may marvel.

THE RESURRECTION

21 For as the Father raises up the dead, and awakens them, even so the Son awakens whom He will.

22 For the Father judges no one, but has committed all judgment to the Son:

23 that all people should honor the Son, even as they honor the Father. They who do not honor the Son do not honor the Father who has sent Him.

24 Truly, truly, I say to you, they who hear My words, and believe on Him who sent Me, have everlasting life, and shall not come into condemnation; but are passed from death to life.

25 Truly, truly, I say to you, the hour is coming, and now is, when the dead shall hear the voice of the Son of God: and they who hear shall live.

26 For as the Father has life in Himself; so has He given to the Son to have life in Himself;

28 Marvel not at this: for the hour is coming, in which all who are in the graves shall hear His voice,

29 and shall come forth; they who have done good, to the resurrection of life; and they who have done evil, to the resurrection of damnation.

THE GREATER WITNESS

30 I can of My own self do nothing: as I hear, I judge: and My judgment is just; because I seek not My own will, but the will of the Father who sent Me.

31 If I bear witness of Myself, My witness is not true.

32 There is another who bears witness of Me; and I know that the witness, which He bears, is true.

33 You sent to John, and he bore witness to the truth.

34 But the verification, which I receive, is not from humans: however, I say these things so that you might be saved.

35 He was a burning and shining light: and you were willing for a season to rejoice in his light.

36 But I have a greater witness than that of John: for the works which the Father has given Me to finish, the same works that I do, bear witness of Me, that the Father has sent Me.

37 And the Father Himself, who has sent Me, has borne witness of Me. You have neither heard His voice at any time, nor seen His shape.

John 5

38 You don't have His word living in you: because you don't believe Him whom He has sent.

39 Search the Scriptures; for in them you think you have eternal life: and they are they that testify of Me.
40 Yet you will not come to Me, that you might have life.

41 I don't receive glory from humans.
42 But I know you, that you don't have the love of God in you.

43 I am come in My Father's Name, and you don't receive Me: if others shall come in their own name, those you will receive.
44 How can you believe, when you receive honor from one another, and don't seek the honor that comes from the only God?

45 Don't think that I will accuse you to the Father: there is one whom you trust.
46 For had you believed Moses, you would have believed Me: for he wrote of Me.
47 But if you don't believe his Writings [Genesis to Deuteronomy], how shall you believe My words?"

THEY RETURN TO GALILEE

We saw in the last two intersections that the Baptist's disciples would have come to Jesus in Jerusalem, at the time of the death of the Baptist (Mat. 14:12; Mark 6:29). Also, in this intersection Jesus' disciples were still in Jerusalem having preached '*two by two*' (Mark 6:7, 30). No doubt after spending the winter there, shortly, The Second Judean Ministry would conclude. The Gospel of John had filled in with what time of year it was (5:1), and part of what had occurred at the Festival (vv. 2-47). Due to the fact that they were to travel to Tiberias on the Sea of Galilee (6:1), and then on to Bethsaida (Luke 9:10), for the next Festival at Passover time (John 6:4), indicates that in returning to Galilee would initiate the third phase of His Galilean ministry. Though Jesus did not tour Galilee again, only traveling from there to other areas.

Moreover, when considering the AV translation of John 6:1 [not our particular text], we notice '*the sea*' is in italics, next to '*of Tiberias*', which indicates its absence in the original Greek. In understanding the direction of travel from Jerusalem, we see Jesus and the disciples journeyed to Tiberias, and took a boat to Bethsaida, from Tiberias. This is further seen in the reference several days later, when other boats also sailed '*from Tiberias*' to Bethsaida (v. 23).

Furthermore, this is the first place that all four Gospels parallel and align together, synchronizing in complete agreement over the **twenty-third miracle**, with Matthew, Mark, and John paralleling together with the twenty-fourth miracle, also in that Passover week. John, in his eminent way, now alludes to certain days again as he had previously in his text.

When they arrived at Bethsaida, some had seen them departing from Tiberias. For the others around the outlining area to have heard and then to have confirmed it, with some of these great crowds also running ahead of where Jesus and the disciples were making for, would have taken some time (Mat. 14:13c; Mark 6:33; Luke 9:11a). Because Jesus and the disciples had originally been heading for a reclusive spot, meant they must have finally achieved their aim where John 6:3-4 informs us that the Passover was near when they went up onto a mount.

Matthew 14:13b Mark 6:32 Luke 9:10b John 6:1

And after these things Jesus took them, and they departed from there, and went over the Sea of Galilee, which is the Sea of Tiberias, by boat privately, and went aside privately into a deserted place, apart, belonging to the city called Bethsaida.

Matthew 14:13c Mark 6:33 Luke 9:11a John 6:2

And the people saw them departing, and many knew Him.

And when the people had heard thereof, when they knew it, a great crowd followed Him and ran on afoot from out of all the cities and out went them, and came together to Him, because they saw His miracles, which He did, on those who were diseased.

Matthew 14:14 Mark 6:34 Luke 9:11b

And Jesus when He came forward, saw the great crowd, and was moved with compassion toward them, because they were as sheep not having a shepherd: and He received them, and began to teach them many things, and spoke to them of the Kingdom of God, and healed their sick who had need of healing.

John 6

3 And Jesus went up onto a mount, and there sat with His disciples.

4 And the Passover [14th Nissan], a Festival of the Jews, was near.

22   THE BREAD FROM HEAVEN

THE TWENTY-THIRD MIRACLE - FEEDING OF 5000

With the teaching of many things, and the healing of the sick, of those who had followed them after they came ashore at Bethsaida, as well as those who had emerged from the outlining areas, that particular day must now have been drawing to a close.

Following that day, all the Gospels parallel again the second time, with the Synoptics alluding to yet another day (Mat. 14:15; Mark 6:35; Luke 9:12; John 6:5). Because the days in Judaism are counted from the evening, as Gen. 1:5 portrays, '*the evening and the morning were the first day*', hence, we have the start of another day. Though, the day referred to is mentioned by the Synoptics, John now at this point does not mention it.

However, as the disciples were with Jesus on the mount at John 6:3, and moreover, when we get to v. 5, which synchronizes with the Synoptics at that particular part of the day, we see that the disciples now approached Jesus at the point where the great crowds also must have returned. The people must have returned at the transitional phase before the ending of one day and the beginning of the next, as the Synoptics all point out (Mat. 14:15; Mark 6:35; Luke 9:12a)

The twenty-third miracle, with the spectacular and miraculous scenario of the feeding of the five thousand and the clearing up afterwards (Mat. 14:16-21; Mark 6:36-44; Luke 9:12-17; John 6:5-14), would have taken some considerable time, and must have gone well on into that particular night. After that, the great crowds had wanted to make Jesus King! Jesus then insists that the disciples go down to where the boats were, while He sends the crowds away, wishing to be alone on the mount so He could pray (Mat. 14:22-23; Mark 6:45-47; John 6:15-16).

Nonetheless, the disciples did not go over the lake immediately, as they did not leave until the next evening. Obviously, Jesus had instructed them not to wait for Him, but make their own way across the lake when it was dark again, to Gennesaret, where eventually He would meet up with them, while He spent the rest of the time alone in prayer and in contemplation. Subsequently, in the following night He catches up with them through walking on the water (Mat. 14:24-33; Mark 6:48-52; John 6:17-21).

Matthew 14:15a Mark 6:35 Luke 9:12a John 6:5
And when the day [13th Nissan] began to wear away, being now far spent, and evening was coming, Jesus lifted up His eyes, and saw a great company come to Him, then His twelve disciples came to Him, and said to Him,
"This is a deserted place, and now the time is far past [14th Nissan]:

Matthew 14:15b Mark 6:36 Luke 9:12b
send the crowds away, that they may go into the towns and villages into the country round about, and lodge, and get provisions, and buy themselves bread: for they have nothing to eat: for we are in a deserted place."
Matthew 14
16 But Jesus said to them, "They needn't leave. You give them to eat."

John 6
5b He says to Philip, "Where shall we buy bread, that these may eat?"
6 And this He said to test him: for He Himself knew what He would do.
7 Philip answered Him, "Two hundred pennyworth of bread is not sufficient for them, that everyone of them may take a little."

Mark 6:37 Luke 9:13
But He answered and said to them, "You give them to eat."
And they say to Him, "Shall we go and buy two hundred pennyworth of bread, and give them to eat?"
Mark 6
38 He says to them, "How many loaves have you? Go and see."
John 6
8 One of His disciples, Andrew, Simon Peter's brother, says to Him,
Matthew 14:17 Mark 6:38 Luke 9:13 John 6:9
"There's a lad here, who has five barley loaves, and two small fishes: but what are they among so many?"
And when they knew, they said, exclaiming to Him,
"We have here no more than five loaves and two fishes; except we should go and buy food for all this people."
Matthew 14:18-19a Mark 6:39 Luke 9:14 John 6:10a
For they were about five thousand men. He said, "Bring them here to Me."

And Jesus requested, saying to His disciples,
"Make all the men of the crowds, to sit down in companies, fifties in a company, upon the green grass."
Now there was much grass in the place.

Mark 6:40 Luke 9:15 John 6:10b
And they did so, and made them all sit. The men sat down in ranks, by hundreds, and by fifties, in number about five thousand.
Matthew 14:19b Mark 6:41 Luke 9:16 John 6:11
And then Jesus when He had taken the five loaves and the two fishes, He looked up to the heavens; and when He had given thanks, He blessed them, and broke the loaves, and gave them, distributing the loaves to the disciples,

and the disciples to set before the people who were sat down; and likewise of the two fishes He divided as much as they would among them all.

Matthew 14:20a Mark 6:42 Luke 9:17a John 6:12
And they did all eat, and were all filled: when they were filled, He said to His disciples, "Gather up the fragments that remain, that nothing be lost."

Matthew 14:20b Mark 6:43 Luke 9:17b John 6:13
Therefore they took up gathering them together, and there were taken twelve baskets filled full of the fragments from the five barley loaves, and of the fishes, that which remained over and above of those who had eaten.
Matthew 14:21 Mark 6:44
And they who had eaten of the loaves were about five thousand men, besides women and children.
John 6
14 Then those people, when they had seen the miracle that Jesus did, said, "This is truly the Prophet who should come into the world."

We have seen by the combined text of the four Gospels, how each one remembers certain details crucial to the establishment of being able to fathom what part of the scenario follows on in successive order. Though Luke now, was content to finish his discourse with the filling of the twelve baskets with the fragments of bread (9:17). He does not mention along with Matthew, Mark and John, the twenty-fourth miracle but returns with his dialogue at the narration about the Messiahship of Jesus, some months later, at the third excursion away from Galilee, and the twenty-ninth miracle, *The Transfiguration,* in the region of Caesarea Philippi in Ituraea (Mat. 16:13-28-17:1-13; Mark 8:27-38-9:1-13; Luke 9:18-36).

Some translations are not in agreement as to where the disciples and Jesus were about to journey to, at the point of leaving the mount near Bethsaida. But, considering all of the facts, with the topography combined with the double evidence of Matthew (14:34) and Mark (6:53) categorically stating it was to the Land of Gennesaret, the emphasis in translation on the wording in question should be in that light. Some translators have considered this and translated accordingly.

We have followed the translators, which understand that from the mount Bethsaida their boat traveled over against Bethsaida and Capernaum, and at some point afterwards Jesus came to them walking on the sea, whereby, they were traveling in a direct line from Bethsaida passing Capernaum to the Land of Gennesaret.

Matthew 14:22 Mark 6:45 John 6:15a
And when Jesus therefore perceived that they would come and take Him by
force, to make Him a King, immediately Jesus constrained His disciples to
a boat, and go to the other side ahead Him over against Bethsaida, while He
sent the crowds away.

Matthew 14:23a Mark 6:46 John 6:15b
And when He had sent the crowds away, He departed again and went up
onto the mount Himself apart, alone to pray.

Matthew 14:23b Mark 6:47a John 6:16
And when the evening [15th Nissan] was now come, His disciples went down
to the sea (He being there alone),
Matthew 14:24a Mark 6:47b John 6:17
and entered into a boat and went over toward Capernaum. And it was now
dark. But the boat was now in the midst of the sea, and Jesus was alone on
the land and not come to them.

Matthew 14:24b John 6:18
And the sea rose tossing with waves by reason of a great wind that blew.
Matthew 14:25 Mark 6:48
And He saw them toiling in rowing; for the wind was contrary to them: and
at about the fourth watch [3 a.m.] of the night Jesus came toward them
walking on the sea, and would have passed them by.

Matthew 14:26 Mark 6:49 John 6:19
So when they had rowed about three to four miles, when the disciples saw
Jesus walking upon the sea, and drawing near to the boat, they were afraid,
and they cried out for fear, saying, "It is a spirit!"
Supposing it had been a spirit.
Matthew 14:27 Mark 6:50 John 6:20
For they all saw Him, and were troubled. And straightaway Jesus spoke with
them, and He says to them, "Cheer up! It is I! Don't be afraid."
Matthew 14
28 And Peter answered Him and said,
"Lord, if it be You, command me come to You on the water."
29 And He said, "Come."
And when Peter was come down out of the boat, he walked on the water to
go to Jesus.
30 But when he saw the wind boisterous, he was afraid; and beginning to
sink, he cried, saying, "Lord, save me!"
31 And immediately Jesus stretched out His hand, and caught him, and said

to him, "Oh you of little faith, why did you doubt?"

Matthew 14:32 Mark 6:51 John 6:21a
And when they were come into the boat, then they willingly received Him, and
He went up to them into the boat; and the wind ceased: and they were greatly
amazed in themselves beyond measure, and wondered.
Mark 6
52 For they considered not the miracle of the loaves: for their heart was
hardened.
Matthew 14
33 Then they who were in the boat, came and worshiped Him, saying,
"Truthfully You are the Son of God."

EXCURSION TO GENNESARET

Matthew 14:34 Mark 6:53 John 6:21b
And when they were gone over, they came into the Land of Gennesaret, and
immediately drew to the shore, the boat being at the land to which they went.
Matthew 14:35a Mark 6:54
And when they were come out of the boat, immediately the people of that
place had knowledge of Him, they sent out into all that countryside round
about,
Matthew 14:35b Mark 6:55
and ran through that whole region round about and began to carry on stretchers
   those who were sick, and brought to Him all who were diseased, where they
heard He was.
Matthew 14:36 Mark 6:56
And where He was likely to enter, into villages, or cities, or country, they laid
the sick in the streets, and implored Him that they might only touch if it were
but the hem of His garment: and as many as touched Him were made perfectly
whole.

We had considered the mentioning of days in the section, dealing with the twenty-
third, and **twenty-fourth miracle**, and found that there were various days lying
within the combined texts.

With the beginning of the following text we have another day, since this day,
is referring to '*the day following*' The Twenty-Third Miracle of the feeding of the
five thousand, near Bethsaida, including the twenty-fourth miracle, '*when the
people who stood on the other side of the sea*' from Bethsaida, having witnessed
the situation of the boats, and that the disciples and Jesus had left, they assumed that
they had gone to Capernaum instead of the Land of Gennesaret (John 6:22-24). We
see, nonetheless, that they found Jesus eventually, enquiring at what point He had
arrived in Capernaum anyhow (v. 25).

Now John was no doubt familiar with the story of what Matthew and Mark had recorded, as they revealed that the twenty-fourth miracle of Jesus walking on the water to catch up with the disciples transpired on the way to, '*the Land of Gennesaret*' (Mat. 14:34; Mark 7:53).

John (6:17), in his case did not refute this, but confirmed what direction they were sailing in from Bethsaida, as they were heading '*toward Capernaum*'. If one looks at a map, one will see that sailing in a direct line from Bethsaida to the Land of Gennesaret, one has to bypass Capernaum on the right, anyway, and that by the time Jesus had arrived, '*they had rowed about three to four miles*' (v. 19). This would thus precisely place their course as being opposite Capernaum at that particular point, and halfway to the Land of Gennesaret, in any case.

Obviously, when considering all the facts, the references to the various days, and with John (vv. 24-25) indicating the people found Jesus in Capernaum directly afterwards, we see they stayed only a short time in the area of Gennesaret.

The translation of Mark 6:56, as given in our text, gives emphasis to the idiom, as the Greek allows, that when the people knew He had arrived, they hoped He would stay a lot longer, and assumed He would enter all the villages and cities throughout that vicinity; though, actually He healed only those at this time who were fortunate enough to touch Him: and consequently, He stayed for a relatively short visit before returning to Capernaum. Matthew (14:34-36), however, in his verses on the same, does not record any reference to Him actually moving from the place whence they brought the sick.

BACK AT CAPERNAUM IN SYNAGOGUE

John 6

22 The day following [16th Nissan], when the people who stood on the other side of the sea saw there was no other boat there, save that one where into His disciples were entered, and that Jesus went not with His disciples into the boat, but that His disciples were gone away alone;

23 (nevertheless there came other boats from Tiberias near to the place where they did eat bread, after that the Lord had given thanks:)

24 when the people therefore saw that Jesus was not there, neither His disciples, they also took boats, and came to Capernaum, looking for Jesus.

25 And when they had found Him on the other side of the sea, they said to Him, "Rabbi, when did You arrive here?"

26 Jesus answered them and said,

"Surely, surely, I say to you, you seek Me, not because you saw the miracles, but because you did eat of the loaves, and were filled.

27 Don't work for the food which perishes, but for the food which endures to everlasting life, which the Son of Humanity shall give to you: for Him has God the Father approved.."

John 6

28 Then said they to Him,

"What shall we do, that we might work the works of God?"

29 Jesus answered and said to them,

"This is the work of God that you believe on Him whom He has sent."

30 They said therefore to Him,

"What sign then will You reveal, that we may see, and believe You - what work do You do?

31 Our fathers did eat manna in the desert; as it is written (Neh. 9:15), 'HE GAVE THEM BREAD FROM HEAVEN TO EAT.'"

THE BREAD OF LIFE

32 Then said Jesus to them,

"Truly, truly, I say to you, Moses did not give you that Bread from Heaven; but My father gives you the True Bread from Heaven.

33 For the Bread of God is He who comes down from Heaven, and gives life to the world."

34 Then said they to Him, "Lord, always give us this bread."

35 And Jesus said to them,

"I am the Bread of Life: they who come to Me shall shall never hunger; and they who believe on Me shall never thirst.

36 But I told you that you have seen Me, and yet you don't believe.

37 All who the Father gives Me shall come to Me; and they who come to Me I will in no way cast out.

38 For I came down from Heaven, not to do My own will, but the will of Him who sent Me.

39 And this is the Father's will who sent Me, that of all those He has given to Me I shall lose no one, but should raise them up again at the Last Day.

40 And this is the will of Him who sent Me, that everyone who sees the Son, and believes on Him, may have everlasting life: and I will raise them up at the Last Day."

41 The Jews then murmured at Him, because He said, '*I am the Bread of Life who came down from Heaven*'.

42 And they said,

"Is this not Jesus, the son of Joseph, whose father and mother we know? How is it then that He says, '*I came down from Heaven*?'".

43 Jesus therefore answered and said to them,

"Murmur not amongst your selves.

John 6

44 No one can come to Me, except the Father whom has sent Me draw them: and I will raise them up at the Last Day.

45 It is written in the Prophets (Is. 54:13), 'AND THEY SHALL ALL BE TAUGHT BY GOD.' Everyone therefore who has heard, and has learned of the Father, comes to Me.

46 Not that anyone has seen the Father, save He who is from God, He has seen the Father.

47 Truly, truly, I say to you, they who believe on Me have everlasting life.

48 I am that Bread of Life.

49 Your fathers did eat manna in the wilderness, and are dead.

50 This is the Bread, who comes down from Heaven so that one may eat thereof, and not die

51 I am the Living Bread who came down from Heaven: if anyone eats of this Bread, they shall live for ever: and the Bread that I will give is My flesh, which I will give for the life of the world."

52 The Jews therefore strove among themselves, saying, "How can this Man give us His flesh to eat?"

53 Then said Jesus to them, "Truly, truly, I say to you, except you eat the flesh of the Son of Humanity, and drink His blood, you have no life in you.

54 Whoever eats My flesh, and drinks My blood, has eternal life; and I will raise them up at the last day.

55 For My flesh is food indeed, and My blood is drink indeed.

56 They who eat My flesh, and drink My blood, dwell in Me, and I in them.

57 As the Living Father has sent Me, and I live because of the Father: so they who eat Me, even they shall live because of Me.

58 This is that Bread who came down from Heaven: not as your fathers did eat manna, and are dead: they who eat of this Bread shall live forever."

59 These things He said in the synagogue, as He taught in Capernaum.

60 Many therefore of His disciples, when they had beard this, said, "This is a hard saying; who can understand it?"

It is amazingly ironic to note, that some of the people who were familiar with the miraculous events surrounding the incidents associated with the synagogue at Capernaum, now, where Jesus proclaimed He was *The Bread of Life* from Heaven still did not accept Him. No doubt, some of them had even witnessed the healing of *The Second Miracle - The Demoniac,* and *The Twelfth Miracle - Man With Withered Hand* in this same synagogue! Including the circumstances surrounding the Centurion who had helped to build this synagogue - who also had his servant healed twice, and one of the directors of this synagogue, who had his daughter raised from the dead, must have been familiar knowledge that many of these people, not only of Capernaum, but also in the outlining areas had heard too. Certainly the members of the synagogue would have all been aware of these facts.

However, it also seems, that the disciples, and those who were making up the number of the seventy, many no doubt, had been drawn from this synagogue. Incredulously, in v. 66, many from this moment would no longer walk with Jesus.

23 *JESUS AVOIDS JEWRY*

JESUS REMAINS IN GALILEE

John tells us that the whole of the dialogue from 6:25-71 took place at the synagogue at Capernaum (v. 59), in which the congregation were also quite familiar with the aspects of Jesus earthly family (v. 42).

It is conceivable that as there were certain days referred to, with the subsequent facts of travel, this took place towards the end of the Days of Unleavened Bread.

In vv. 60-66, there is mention of some who would have become His disciples, and no doubt a reference to *The Seventy Disciples* being sifted out.

John 6

61 When Jesus knew in Himself that His disciples murmured at it [eating and drinking Him], He said to them, "Does this offend you?
62 What and if you shall see the Son of Humanity, ascend up to where He was before?
63 It is the Spirit that enlivens; the flesh profits nothing: the words that I speak to you, they are spirit, and they are life.
64 But there are some of you who don't believe."

For Jesus knew from the beginning whom they were who didn't believe, and who should betray Him.

65 And He said, "Therefore I said to you, that no one can come to Me, except it were given to them of My Father."

66 From that time many of His disciples went back, and walked no more with Him.
67 Then said Jesus to the twelve, "Will you also go away?"
68 Then Simon Peter answered Him, "Lord, to whom shall we go? You have the words of eternal life.
69 And we believe and are sure you are the Messiah, the Son of the Living God."

70 Jesus answered them, "Didn't I choose you twelve, and one of you is a devil?"
71 He spoke of Judas Iscariot the son of Simon: for it was he who would betray Him, being one of the twelve.
John 7
1 After these things Jesus walked in Galilee: for He wouldn't walk in Jewry, because the Jews sought to kill Him.

After the teaching in the synagogue in Capernaum, Jesus continued with His third mission in Galilee, because after the second Judean mission, the Jews there were still seeking ways to kill Him (7:1). From this time onwards Jesus was extra careful when venturing down into Judea, and especially Jerusalem. There were two more Tabernacles to be held there, before the closing of Jesus' mission at the last Passover.

Matthew and Mark now return to the narrative of the continuing story and fill in on the events after John 7:1, as v. 2, refers to six months later at the second Tabernacles at Jerusalem.

The Scribes and Pharisees, who were seeking ways to kill Jesus, now come from Jerusalem again to Jesus, who was still in Capernaum at this point, after returning from Gennesaret. They knew they were liable to find Him there, as they would have heard from their contemporaries of Capernaum of the past events around that region, and they were still considering a way to deal with Him.

DEFILEMENT

Matthew 15:1 Mark 7:1
Then came together to Jesus the Pharisees, and certain of the Scribes, who were come from Jerusalem.

Mark 7
2 And when they saw some of His disciples eat bread with defiled, that is to say, with unwashed hands, they found fault.
3 For the Pharisees, and all the Jews, except they wash their hands often, don't eat, holding the tradition of the Elders.
4 And when they come home from the market, except they wash, they don't eat. And many other such things there be, which they have received to hold, as the washing of cups, and pots, brazen vessels, and of tables.

Matthew 15:2 Mark 7:5
Then the Pharisees and Scribes asked Him, saying,
"Why don't Your disciples walk according to the tradition transgressing the tradition of the Elders? For they don't wash their hands when they eat bread - but eat bread with unwashed hands?"
Matthew 15:3 Mark 7:6
But He answered and said to them,
"But why do you transgress the Commandment of God through your tradition? Well has Isaiah (29:13) prophesied of you hypocrites, as it is written,
'THIS PEOPLE HONOURS ME WITH THEIR LIPS, BUT THEIR HEARTS ARE FAR FROM ME.
Mark 7
7 NEVERTHELESS IN VAIN DO THEY WORSHIP ME, TEACHING FOR DOCTRINES HUMAN COMMANDMENTS.'

Mark 7

8 For laying aside the Commandments of God, you hold the tradition of humans, as the washing of pots and cups: and many such other things you do."

9 And He said to them, "Full well you reject the Commandments of God, so that you may keep your own tradition.

Matthew 15:4 Mark 7:10

For God commanded Moses saying,

'HONOURYOUR FATHER AND MOTHER' (Ex. 20:12); and, 'WHOEVER CURSES FATHER OR MOTHER, LET THEM DIE THE DEATH' (21:17):

Matthew 15:5-6a Mark 7:11

but you say, if someone - whoever, shall say to their father or mother, 'Anything of mine which might be used for your benefit is Corban' (meaning, set apart for God), and honors not their father or their mother shall be free.

Mark 7

12 And allow them no more to do anything for their father or their mother; Matthew 15:6b Mark 7:13

thus invalidating the word, you have made the Commandments of God none effective through your tradition, which you have delivered: and you do many things such as that.

Matthew 15

7 You hypocrites, well did Isaiah (29:13) prophesy of you, saying,

8 'THIS PEOPLE DRAWS NEAR TO ME WITH THEIR MOUTH, AND HONOURS ME WITH THEIR LIPS; BUT THEIR HEARTS ARE FAR FROM ME.

9 BUT IN VAIN DO THEY WORSHIP ME, TEACHING FOR DOCTRINES HUMAN COMMANDMENTS.'"

Matthew 15:10 Mark 7:14

And when He had called all the people to Him, He said to them,

"Listen to Me every one of you, hear, and understand:

Matthew 15:11 Mark 7:15

that which enters into the mouth doesn't defile the individual. There is nothing from outside a person that entering into them can defile them: but the things which come out of their mouth, these are they which defile the person.

Mark 7

16 If anyone has ears to hear, let them hear."

The answer Jesus gave to the Pharisees and Scribes, regarding defilement, is emphasized by His using the quote from Is. 29:13, twice, thus ending the dialogue spoken directly to them.

This is reminiscent of the first time this style of answering was recorded, in the way Jesus replied to Satan, when after the *'forty days and nights'*, He quoted the same Scripture twice in concluding the conversation, then, too. [See pp. 30-32 in the section on the text of Luke 4:8 and, following that of Mat. 4:10].

Matthew 15

12 Then came to Him His disciples, and said to Him,

"You know that the Pharisees were offended, after they heard this saying?"

13 But He answered and said,

"Every plant, which My Heavenly Father didn't plant, shall be rooted up.

14 Let them alone: they are blind leaders of the blind. And if the blind lead the blind, both shall fall in the ditch."

EXPLANATION OF DEFILEMENT

Matthew 15:15 Mark 7:17

And when He was entered into the house from the people, then responding, Peter and His disciples asked, saying to Him, "Concerning the parable, explain it to us".

Matthew 15:16-17a Mark 7:18

And Jesus said to them, "Are you yet so without understanding also? Don't you yet understand - and perceive, that whatever thing from outside enters in at the mouth, and into the stomach - into the person, it cannot defile them;

Matthew 15:17b Mark 7:19

because it doesn't enter into their heart, but goes into their stomach, and is cast out, going into the sewer, having depurated all the matter."

Matthew 15:18 Mark 7:20

And He said, "But those things which proceed out of the mouth, out of the individual, come out from the heart; and they defile the person.

Mark 7

21 For within, from out of the hearts of individuals, proceed evil thoughts, adulteries, sexual sins, murders,

Matthew 15:19 Mark 7:22

thefts, false witness, covetousness, wickedness, deceit, lasciviousness, an evil eye, blasphemies, pride, foolishness:

Matthew 15:20 Mark 7:23

all these things come from within, and these are the things, which defile the individual. But to eat with unwashed hands does not defile anyone."

Jesus, giving the explanation of the *Parable of Defilement* to the disciples, in the house once again at Capernaum, ends Matthew's and Mark's recording of the previous events.

The next incident is the excursion to Phoenicia, in the area of Tyre and Sidon, and the **twenty-fifth miracle**.

Jesus, not wishing to go back to Jerusalem at this time, as the Pharisees wanted to kill Him there (John 7:1), was to spend the next six months in and around Galilee, and the northern area, away from Judea, as He was planning eventually to go to the second Festival of Tabernacles of His ministry at Jerusalem, when it was nearer the time and more expedient (v. 10).

At the moment it was still near spring after the second Passover, when the Pharisees and Scribes having come up to Capernaum from Jerusalem, questioned Him over defilement. He subsequently upset them (Mat. 15:12), and then decided on the excursion '*into the borders, and coasts of Tyre and Sidon*' (Mat. 15:21; Mark 7:24).

Matthew 15:21 Mark 7:24
And then from there Jesus rose, and went into the borders and coasts of Tyre and Sidon, and entered into a house, and would have no one know it: but He could not be hid.

Matthew 15:22a Mark 7:25
And, consider, for a certain woman of Canaan, whose young daughter had an unclean spirit, heard of Him, came out of the same coasts, and fell at His feet:
Matthew 15:22b Mark 7:26
the woman was Greek a Syro-Phoenician by nation; and she implored Him that He would cast out the devil out of her daughter, and cried to Him, saying, "Have mercy on me, oh Lord, You Son of David; my daughter is grievously vexed with a devil."
Matthew 15
23 But He answered her not a word.

And His disciples came and urged Him, saying, "Send her away; for she cries after us."
24 But He answered and said, "I wasn't sent to anyone but the lost sheep of the House of Israel."

25 Then she came and worshiped Him, saying, "Lord, help me."

Matthew 15:26 Mark 7:27
But Jesus answered and said to her,
"Let the children first be filled: for it is not fitting to take the children's bread and cast it to puppies."
Matthew 15:27 Mark 7:28
And she answered and said to Him,
"Yes, true, Lord: yet the puppies under the table eat of the children's crumbs which fall from their masters' table."

Matthew 15
28a Then Jesus answered and said to her, "Oh woman, great is your faith: be it to you even as you wish."
Mark 7
29 And He said to her, "For this saying go your way; the devil is gone out of your daughter."
Matthew 15
28b And her daughter was made whole from that very hour.

Mark 7
30 And when she was come to her house, she found the devil gone out, and her daughter laid upon the bed.

EXCURSION INTO THE DECAPOLIS

In Jesus' second Galilean ministry, about a year previously, the people '*about Tyre and Sidon*' (Mark 3:8), had come to Capernaum just before Jesus ordained the twelve, and those '*from the sea coast of Tyre and Sidon*', were also still there after the ordination (Luke 6:17).

However, Jesus' excursion into the region of Tyre and Sidon in Phoenicia, and the healing of the Syro-Phoenician woman's daughter, the **twenty-fifth miracle**, closes this episode, with Jesus' next long excursion across to the other side of the Sea of Galilee to the middle of the coastline of the Decapolis.

Also previously, about a year before, in the second Galilean ministry, in an excursion away from Capernaum, Jesus and the disciples had arrived by boat in the country of the Gadarenes, on the middle of the coastline border of the Decapolis, too, after the second storm on the Sea of Galilee, where the seventeenth miracle of the man with the legion of devils occurred (Mark 5:13; Luke 8:33).

The people then had wanted Jesus to leave, no doubt because of the threat associated to their livelihoods (Mark 5:14, 17; Luke 8:34, 37), as their pig-farm farm businesses, which was administered on a hillside, which supplied that area, totaling two thousand pigs, was wiped out (Mark 5:13). But, now about a year later, with their worries forgotten, were more receptive, as they had heard of the other miracles Jesus had done, which outweighed the previous problem in their minds.

When looking at a map of this area, we see that traveling from the region of Tyre and Sidon, if coming directly '*to the Sea of Galilee up to the middle of the coasts of the Decapolis*' (Mark 7:31), would bring us to the same area. Here we have a record of three miracles: the seventeenth, the man with the legion of devils, the **twenty-sixth miracle**, the deaf mute, which we come to next, and the following one, the twenty-seventh, the feeding of the four thousand people, who were now very receptive to Jesus, having even been with Him for three days (Mat. 16:32; Mark 8:2).

Matthew (15:29) only mentions the leaving of the region of Tyre and Sidon, and that they '*came near to the Sea of Galilee; and went up onto a mount*'. It is Mark (7:31) who exclusively tells us that the setting of the hillside was, '*of the coasts of the Decapolis*', though he does not mention the mount by word. Some see Jesus traveling from Tyre and Sidon, through Gaulanitis, to the middle of the coasts of the Decapolis, and then to the Sea of Galilee.

However, Matthew and Mark mention the arrival at the Sea of Galilee, first, in its natural orientation of travel, when returning from Sidon, before that of coming into the coasts of the Decapolis, as Jesus and the disciples had originally left from Capernaum to travel to Tyre and Sidon earlier.

Looking closer at Mark 7:31, the Greek word '*ana*', was translated '*through*' in the AV and moreover '*in*', at Rev. 7:17. When considering all the previous facts, with the Greek proposition of '*ana*', tending to mean '*up*', would rather lead us to the conclusion in translation, in that case, meaning '*up to the middle of the coasts of the Decapolis*', as indicating the point at which Jesus and the disciples were going to sail to, after returning '*near to the Sea of Galilee*', from Sidon.

Of course in either case, Matthew and Mark both meant the Sea of Galilee on the other side as well, which is reflected by Matthew in stating Jesus '*came near to the Sea of Galilee*', first, before He '*went up* [Gr.'*anabaino*'] *onto a hillside*' (15:29), and in Mark's choice of word in using the word '*ana*' too.

Furthermore, the Greek word '*ana*' in both Mark 7:31, and Rev. 7:17, includes next to it the same Greek word '*mesos*', meaning '*middle*' or '*midst*', depending on the connotation of the scenario it is referring to. Thus, we felt that the words '*through to*', instead of '*in*' serves better the main text below, as keeping to the significance of the excursion as it has been alluded to by both Mat. 15:19 and Mark 7:31.

Thus, after the **twenty-seventh miracle** of the feeding of the four thousand at the hillside in the middle of the coastline of the Decapolis, they once more leave by boat, sailing through to the coasts of Magdala-Dalmanutha (Mat. 15:39; Mark 8:10).

Matthew 15:29 Mark 7:31
And again, Jesus departed from the coasts of Tyre and of Sidon, and He came near to the Sea of Galilee, through to the middle of the coasts of the Decapolis. And He went up onto a hillside, and sat down there.

Matthew 15
30 And great crowds came to Him, having with them those who were lame, blind, dumb, maimed, and many others, and deposited them down at Jesus' feet; and He healed them:

Mark 7
32 and they brought to Him one who was deaf, and had an impediment in his speech; and they begged Him to put His hand upon him.

33 And He took him aside from the crowd, and put his fingers into his ears both with spit, and touched his tongue;
34 and looking up to the heavens, He sighed, and He says to him, "Ephphatha:" that is, "Be opened."
35 And immediately his ears were opened, and the string of his tongue was loosed, and he spoke plainly.

36 And He instructed them that they should tell no one: but the more He told them, so much the more a great deal they proclaimed it;
37 and were astonished beyond measure, saying,
"He has done all things well: He makes both the deaf and the dumb to speak."
Matthew 15
31 Insomuch that the crowd wondered, when they saw the dumb speak, the maimed walk, and the blind see: and they glorified the God of Israel.

Matthew 15:32a Mark 8:1
In those days the crowd being very great, and having nothing to eat, Jesus then called His disciples to Him, and spoke to them, saying,
Matthew 15:32b Mark 8:2
"I have compassion for the people, because they have now been continuing with Me three days, and have nothing to eat:
Matthew 15:32c Mark 8:3
and if I send them away fasting to their own houses, they will faint by the way - I will not send them away, lest they faint: for some of them come from far."
Matthew 15:33 Mark 8:4
And His disciples answering says to Him,
"From where can anyone satisfy these people with bread here in this isolated place? Where should we have so much bread, as to fill so great a crowd?"

Matthew 15:34 Mark 8:5
And Jesus asked, saying to them, "How many loaves have you?"
And they said, "Seven, and a few little fishes."

Matthew 15:35-36 Mark 8:6-7
And He commanded the crowds to sit down on the ground: and He took the
seven loaves, also they had a few small fishes, and He blessed them, gave
thanks, and broke them, and commanded to set them before them, and gave
to His disciples and the disciples to the people; and they did set them before
the crowds.

Matthew 15:37 Mark 8:8
And so they did all eat, and were all filled: and they took up of the broken
food that was left seven baskets full.
Matthew 15:38 Mark 8:9a
And those who had eaten were four thousand men, besides women and
children.
Matthew 15:39 Mark 8:9b-10
And He sent away the crowds, and straightaway He took the boat and entered
into it with His disciples, and came into the coasts and parts of
Magdala-Dalmanutha.

It is interesting to note that after the feeding of the four thousand, the
twenty-seventh miracle, naturally the twenty-eighth miracle would follow,
and when multiplying the two single digits 7 x 4 in the account of the feeding
of the four thousand, and the seven full baskets, they figure to 28!

24   THE SIGN FROM HEAVEN

IN MAGDALA-DALMANUTHA

In Matthew's parallel account, after the feeding of the four thousand, when sailing away from '*the midst of the coasts of the Decapolis*' to the next place, he has '*Magdala*' and Mark '*Dalmanutha*'. Though other manuscripts have '*Magadan*', for either Gospel. It is because the three names for the same area came to be used interchangeably in those times and subsequently. Since, we are using the AV, we have thus related the double term Magdala-Dalmanutha, in the main text, as we have already twice used Matthew's style of phraseology for the placing of certain individual words in order.

Note the previous information on the names of '*Gergesa*', and the '*Sea of Galilee*' [pp. 85-86], with the interchangeability of those names. Of course Mary Magdalene has the same name derivative of the town '*Magdala*', to which area they had just sailed.

After the feeding of the four thousand, they went by boat to Magdala-Dalmanutha, where the Pharisees and Sadducees asked Jesus for '*a sign from Heaven*' (Mat. 16:1; Mark 8:11). The only sign Jesus gave was '*the sign of the prophet Jonah*' (Mat. 16:4), as they were blinded to all the attesting miracle signs that Jesus had worked.

Previously, about a year before in Jesus' house in Capernaum, He had given the same sign to the Scribes and Pharisees (Mat. 12:38-40), '*who came down from Jerusalem*' to see their contemporaries over their dilemma with Jesus (Mark 3:22).

However, at the point we are now covering, Mark's version does not mention the phrase '*the prophet Jonah*'. But, it is clear from Matthew that Jesus did mention that sign. When the two accounts are read together, it becomes obvious that Mark would have known that Jesus had given the sign, which Matthew had recorded. With this in mind, considering the original Greek of Mark 8:12b, the passage in any case, tends to relate to the meaning, '*if a sign shall be given to this generation*', rather than '*no sign*', at all. Thus, if using v. 12 alone, it would be better read as, '*Why does this generation seek after a sign? Truly I say to you, shall there be given a sign to this generation?*'

Had they been able to '*discern the signs of the times*', as Mark wanted to emphasize, the proposition of, '*shall there be given*'- to them - referring to the meaning of the '*sign*'- had their attitude been better, they no doubt would have been given the understanding, and obviously received the meaning of the sign of the prophet Jonah. Jesus had given the same sign previously, twice now, and uniquely revealed by Matthew on each separate occasion.

Nonetheless, if using both parallel accounts together, it is clear that, grammatically Jesus would have related the physical signs of nature first (Mat. 16:2-3), and then continued to give '*the sign of the prophet Jonah*' (v. 12b), as we have placed in the main text.

Clearly, when the two accounts are paralleled and dovetailed together, as in our text, then the so-called problem of any contradiction disappears.

Amazingly, also at this juncture, but now conversely, Mark mentions '*the leaven of Herod*' (8:15), whereas Matthew is silent! Thus a similar pattern can be seen again, with the structure of the sentences, when Mark exclusively mentions certain facts, in the way the verses fit together with Matthew's account, and viceversa. This is clearly shown also with both the texts of Matthew and Mark in our last intersection, and the beginning of our next intersection.

Of course, as already mentioned, in any case, '*the sign of the prophet Jonah*' had been given twice so far. It was yet to be given once more, the third time, several months later (Luke 11:29-32), but then, to the people of Jerusalem in the autumn, when Jesus was to leave Galilee until His resurrection for the second Festival of Tabernacles of His ministry there (John 7:2).

SIGN OF JONAH

Matthew 16:1 Mark 8:11

And the Pharisees also with the Sadducees came forward, and began to question Him, and tempting Him desired seeking of Him that He would show them a sign from Heaven.

Mark 8

12a And He sighed deeply in His spirit, and says, "Why does this generation seek after a sign?"

Matthew 16

2 He answered and said to them,

"When it is evening, you say, '*It will be fair weather: for the sky is red.*'

3 And in the morning, '*It will be foul weather today: for the sky is red and lowring.*' Oh you hypocrites, you can discern the face of the sky; but can you discern the signs of the times?

Matthew 16:4 Mark 8:12b-13

A wicked and adulterous generation seeks after a sign; and truly I say to you, there shall no sign be given to this generation, but the sign of the prophet Jonah."

And He left them, and entered into the boat again and departed to the other side [Capernaum].

LEAVEN OF HYPOCRISY

Matthew 16:5 Mark 8:14

And now when His disciples were come to the other side, they had forgotten to take bread, neither had they in the boat with them more than one loaf.

Mark 8:15

And then Jesus spoke to them, cautioning them, saying,

"Take heed and beware of the leaven of the Pharisees and of the Sadducees, and of the leaven of Herod."
Matthew 16:7 Mark 8:16
And they reasoned among themselves, saying. "It is because we have taken no bread."
Matthew 16:8-9a Mark 8:17
And when Jesus perceived it, He said speaking to them,
"Oh you of little faith, why reason you among yourselves, because you have brought no bread? Don't you perceive yet, neither understand? Is your heart still hardened?
Matthew 16:9b Mark 8:18
'HAVING EYES, DON'T YOU SEE? AND HAVING EARS, DON'T YOU HEAR' (Ezek.12:2)?
And don't you even remember,
Matthew 16:9c Mark 8:19
when I broke the five loaves among you, of the five thousand, and how many baskets full of fragments you took up [Mat. 14:17-21; Mark 6:38-44; Luke 9:13-17]?"

They say to Him, "Twelve."
Matthew 16:10 Mark 8:20
"And neither when the seven loaves were distributed to the four thousand, and how many baskets full of fragments you took up [Mat. 15:34-38; Mark 8:5-10]?"

And they said, "Seven."
Matthew 16:11 Mark 8:21
And He said to them, "How is it that you don't yet understand, that I did not speak to you concerning bread? But beware of the leaven of the Pharisees and of the Sadducees?"
Matthew 16
12 Then they understood how that He told them not beware of the leaven of bread, but of the teaching of the Pharisees and of the Sadducees.

MIRACLE TWENTY-EIGHT AND EXCURSION TO ITUREA

Mark 8
22 And He comes to Bethsaida; and they brought a blind man to Him, and implored Him to touch him.
23 And He took the blind man by the hand, and led him out of the town; and when He had wiped spit onto his eyes, having put His hands upon him, He asked him if he saw anything.
24 And he looked up, and said, "I see people as trees, walking."
25 After that He put His hands again upon his eyes, and made him look up:
26 And He sent him away to his house, saying, "Neither go into the town, nor tell it to any in the town."

After the journey from the coast of the Decapolis across to Magdala-Dalmanutha, and the request for a sign again by the Pharisees and the Sadducees, Jesus and the disciples sailed across '*to the other side*' (Mark 8:13). Both Matthew and Mark do not mention by name where '*the other side*' was upon mooring their boat. However, the omission would no doubt be indicative of '*the other side*' being Capernaum, as they had not been back to Capernaum for a considerable time, since their excursions to Phoenicia, Decapolis and Magdala-Dalmanutha. In either case when traveling from Magdala-Dalmanutha, in a direct line, Capernaum [along with Bethsaida] would be the only logical place to go, as they were about to prepare for their next excursion to Iturea. However, Mark mentions Bethsaida, with the healing of the blind man, after the scenario of mooring the boat, and the situation that they were ready for a meal.

Nevertheless, since Capernaum was Jesus' base, as it were, and Bethsaida was near to Capernaum, it would be natural for them to go to both places before leaving for their next excursion into Iturea. Both Peter and Andrew came from Bethsaida (John 1:44), and John had a business arrangement with Peter there (Luke 5:10), also John was brother to James. Hence, it would be naturally understood had a business arrangement with Peter there (Luke 5:10), also John was brother to James. Hence, it would be naturally understood had a business arrangement with Peter there (Luke 5:10), also John was brother to James. Hence, it would be naturally understood where they were sailing to, as they had now traveled from various coasts, over the other sides of the lake, three different times since being at Capernaum last.

Matthew omitted the incident at Bethsaida, and thus, in the setting of his particular dialogue, Jesus and the disciples were ready sometime after the narrative relating to not having any bread, for the excursion into Ituraea (16:13). It would be illogical to think that Matthew was not presupposing that we should realize in sailing '*to the other side*' would naturally be associated with Capernaum, in preparation for their next excursion into Iturea.

Furthermore, it was time for a meal when they left Magdala-Dalmanutha, in arriving at '*the other side*', as Mark exclusively mentioned, that they had only '*one loaf*' (8:14). Jesus then relates '*the leaven of the Pharisees*' to them, and as they were concerned over eating the next meal they did not grasp Jesus' analogy. Jesus then goes on to connect the feeding of the five thousand with the four thousand, in respect to the leftovers they had taken up, and their mistake over assuming '*the leaven of the Pharisees*' referred to them not having enough food for their next meal.

Having already '*come to the other side*' (Mat. 16:5), before coming to Bethsaida, where Mark tells us it was afterwards that Jesus restored the blind man's sight [the twenty-eighth miracle], '*the other side*', no doubt referring to Capernaum, where they stopped off, as after the twenty-eighth miracle, at Bethsaida (8:22-26), they were ready in preparation for the next excursion into Iturea (Mat. 16:13; Mark 8:27).

Moreover, the twenty-eighth miracle, being the second indigenous one in Mark, along with his first indigenous twenty-sixth, were both used by Mark also as signs in association when establishing where the disciples and Jesus were, and what had happened, after coming from another place. Mark has, including the twenty-sixth, the twenty-eighth, and the thirty-eighth, three indigenous miracles, which he uses for the purpose of pointing out certain factors surrounding locations.

Thus, they returned for a short stay to their hometown region of Capernaum and Bethsaida, as the disciples [and the seventy], await for their journey away from Galilee again.

After Luke's previous omission from his ch. 9:17, he returns to the narrative, and the Synoptics once more align with Luke (v. 18), until *The Seventy Disciples* are sent out (10:1). At that time Luke fills in where both Matthew and Mark leave out an even greater omission.

THE MESSIAH AND HIS PASSION

Matthew 16:13 Mark 8:27 Luke 9:18
And when Jesus went out, and His disciples, they came into the parts and towns of Caesarea Philippi: and it came to pass, near the road, as He was alone praying, His disciples being with Him, He asked His disciples, saying, to them, "Who do men and the people say that I the Son of Humanity am?"
Matthew 16:14 Mark 8:28 Luke 9:19
And they said, replying, "Some say You are John the Baptist: but some say Elijah; and others say, Jeremiah, or that one of the old prophets has risen again."

Matthew 16:15-16 Mark 8:29 Luke 9:20
And He says to them, "But whom do you say that I am?"
And Simon Peter answered, and declared saying to Him,
"You are the Messiah, the Son of the Living God."
Matthew 16
17And Jesus answered and said to him,
"Blessed you are, Simon son of Jonas: for flesh and blood has not revealed it to you, but My Father who is in Heaven.
18 And I say also to you, that you are Peter, and upon this Rock I will build My Church; and the gates of hell shall not prevail against it.
19 And I will give to you the keys of the Kingdom of Heaven: and whatever you shall bind on earth shall be bound in Heaven: and whatever you shall loose on earth shall be loosed in Heaven."

Matthew 16:20 Mark 8:30 Luke 9:21
And then He strictly warned His disciples, and instructed them to tell no one that thing of Him, that He was Jesus the Messiah.
Matthew 16:21 Mark 8:31 Luke 9:22
And from that time onward began Jesus to teach, showing to His disciples, how that He must go to Jerusalem, and declared that the Son of Humanity must suffer many things, and be rejected of the Elders, and of the Chief Priests, and Scribes, and be killed, and after three days rise again, to be resurrected the third day.
Matthew 16:22 Mark 8:32
And He spoke that saying openly.

And then Peter took Him, and began to rebuke Him, saying, "Far be it from You, Lord: this shall never be done to You."
Matthew 16:23 Mark 8:33
But when He had turned about and looked on His disciples, rebuking Peter He spoke, saying, "Get behind Me, Satan: you are an offence to Me: for you savor not the things that be of God, but the things that are human."

DISCIPLESHIP

Matthew 16:24 Mark 8:34 Luke 9:23
And when He had called the people to Him with His disciples also, then Jesus said to them, and all His disciples, "If anyone - whoever, will come after Me, let them deny themselves, and take up their cross daily, and follow Me.
Matthew 16:25 Mark 8:35 Luke 9:24
For whoever will save their life shall lose it; but whoever shall lose their life for My sake and the gospel's the same shall save it.
Matthew 16:26a Mark 8:36 Luke 9:25
For what is one advantaged - what shall it profit, if they shall gain the whole world, and lose themselves, or be cast away, and lose their own soul?
Matthew 16:26b Mark 8:37
Or what shall one give in exchange for their soul?

Matthew 16:27 Mark 8:38 Luke 9:26
For whoever therefore shall be ashamed of Me and of My words in this adulterous and sinful generation; of them also shall the Son of Humanity be ashamed.
For when the Son of Humanity shall come in His Own glory, and in the glory of His Father, and of the holy angels with His angels, THEN HE SHALL REWARD EVERYONE ACCORDING TO THEIR DEEDS" (Ps. 62:12; Prov. 24:12).

Matthew 16:28 Mark 9:1 Luke 9:27

And He said to them,

"But sincerely I speak to you truthfully, that there be some of those who stand here, who shall not taste of death, till they have seen the Son of Humanity coming in His Kingdom, the Kingdom of God come with Power."

25   THE SEASON OF THE SPIRIT

THE SEVENTY DISCIPLES

The completion in the previous section on *Discipleship* (p. 186), where Luke had returned to the narrative, with the Synoptics once again paralleling together, is somewhat, though only in a very concise sense, reminiscent of Matthew's broader outlining of discipleship, when Jesus had ordained the twelve (10:24-42). As *The Ordination Of The Twelve* a year previously, transpired between the first Passover season of spring and the second Festival of Tabernacles in autumn, no doubt, having taken place in the summer season in which Pentecost fell, we must now again consider in what season we find ourselves.

Recalling we had just covered the second Passover season, and when evaluating the incidents proceeding from there, we see they would have taken several months to transpire, which would once again bring us into the next summer season, in which Pentecost falls, about three months before the third Tabernacles season of Jesus' three and a half year ministry.

Moreover, as we are shortly coming to where the seventy disciples were also sent out, we must further take into consideration that though Luke at the instruction of the sending of the seventy (10:1-16), recorded similar but much briefer words than Matthew in his version of the ordination of the apostles (10:1-42), in Luke's version the sending of the seventy follows directly after the instruction to them (10:17).

Also, in the actual sending of the twelve, Luke further revealed that though they had been instructed at the ordination, as Matthew had recorded, nonetheless, they did not leave '*two by two*', without Jesus until several months later, as both Mark (6:7-13) and Luke (9:1-6) convey, and as we related back at those references. Furthermore, Mark and Luke both indicate that upon the actual leaving of the twelve, Jesus recapitulated some of the same instructions that He originally gave to them, as Matthew had indicated at their ordination several months before.

Thus, Luke as he included the recapitulation of Jesus' instruction with the actual leaving of the twelve '*two by two*', in a similar manner he did the same with the sending of the seventy, though with a greater summary than the brief given to the twelve. As had been the case with the twelve, the seventy were already prepared for their mission of shortly leaving '*two by two*' without Jesus. They too, had been instructed in the same manner as the twelve had; however when they were actually sent at the point in Luke, his text contained, moreover, a repeated exhortation before they directly left - not they were not familiar with the brief on how to preach the gospel before that juncture.

Furthermore, we saw in the section entitled *Conclusion of Second Galilean Ministry* [pp. 149-152], and the following section, *The Second Judean Ministry* [pp. 152-155], regarding the connection of the combined text of Mark (6:7-13) and Luke (9:1-6) in the sending out of the twelve, that it related and emphasized the phase of *The Second Judean Ministry*, and that the disciples had been ordained several months before they left on their own (Mat. 10:1; Mark 3:14; Luke 6:13). Likewise, Luke was indicating with his unique dialogue of where Jesus sent messengers ahead of Him to Samaria (9:51-56), that it was subsequently leading into the third Judean ministry, in which the seventy were sent 'two by two'.

Now in recapturing certain of the aspects of the ordination of the apostles, and the season it fell in, it would be worthwhile to reconsider and recapitulate at this point the section, '*My Beloved Son, in Whom I am Well-Pleased*' [pp. 102-107], which dealt with the Day of Pentecost at that time, and *The Ordination Of The Twelve*. We mentioned in that section, because Pentecost is synonymous with the Holy Spirit, and although one can see the aspects relating to its physical applications, the Spirit in essence is invisible. Correspondingly, the Day of Pentecost is the only Holyday period not mentioned nor seen in the Gospels. Hence, there is no specific direct quote in the texts of the Gospels relating to that season of time. Its first mentioning though is at the start of the Great Commission in Acts 2:1, where the disciples were to begin preaching to rest of the world from Jerusalem, Judea, and outwards, ten days after the Ascension.

We touched formerly on the '*other seventy*' disciples, at *The Ordination Of The Twelve*, a year before, where Luke mentions the twelve coming down the mount to that other '*company of His disciples*' (6:17). Additionally, as we shall be shortly arriving in Luke where the seventy were ordained (10:1), and that John in his Gospel, at the previous Passover, only several months back (6:4, 59), indicates that a sifting of these other disciples was still taking place (6:66-67), it is important that we continue to consider these other disciples at this particular time.

Thus, at this juncture, several months after the second Passover these seventy other disciples would by now be nearer to the point of being sifted out, having formulated into the number and grouping of the seventy, as Jesus would soon send '*them two by two*'. They also would have been trained, no doubt, as Jesus taught the twelve, traveling with Him and the twelve, after the twelve's ordination, a year before, as they specifically appear in the text after the ordination. This also explains the teachings of Jesus being repeated after the ordination, and at various other times, and furthermore an indication of these other disciples being present.

Moreover, Luke is foremost in referring to these disciples, and in repeating Jesus' teachings, which Matthew had recorded at earlier events. Though at this juncture where the seventy were no doubt ordained too, Matthew is silent in referring to these other disciples.

In addition, Mark (4:10), and as already mentioned in the case of John (6:66-67), both had previously referred to these other disciples. This indicates that they were familiar with the settings of the events in deciding when to punctuate with a reference to these other disciples. It is seen particularly when the texts dovetail and parallel, such as with John 6:4, in showing us what year they were being sifted and where (v. 59), along with the Synoptics also relating to this time (Mat. 14:15-16; Mark 6:35-56; Luke 9:12-17). Nonetheless, it is only Luke who specifically gives the number of these seventy. Of course, by the end of Jesus' ministry even more disciples had been added, numbering five hundred at that point (1 Cor. 15:6), as the last of all the apostles, Paul revealed (v. 8).

However, Luke also is the first Evangelist to mention these other disciples in his text (6:17), and again, the next place where there can be found any further hint of these disciples, is shortly after his first reference, wherein the AV avers to *'many of His disciples'* (7: 11).

Mark's reference, as already quoted, mentions the next successive reference, the third, to these disciples, when recounting the *Parable of the Sower*, informing us that it was when Jesus was alone, with the twelve, and these other disciples, in a respite from the crowds that He explained the meaning of the parable to the twelve, and to those who were becoming part of that additional group of other disciples (4:10-14).

It is John who records the fourth successive reference. He recalls these other disciples (6:66-67), after He had pointed them out at the second Passover (v. 4), six months before his next mentioning of them again, just before *The Third Festival Of Tabernacles* of Jesus' ministry (7:2-3).

Jesus was in Galilee in autumn, at the first Festival of Tabernacles of His ministry, and subsequently, altogether, in Jerusalem three times at Tabernacles.

Furthermore, John also indicates that Jesus was planning to go into Judea before arriving at Jerusalem for His second Festival of Tabernacles there, and moreover, that these other disciples, though no doubt they had witnessed some of the miracles previously (vv. 3-4), had not yet had the opportunity to go *'two by two'*, ahead of Jesus, as the twelve had. Hence, Jesus' brothers inference *'that Your disciples also may see Your works that You do'*, refers to the sending out of the seventy, not that they had not seen any of His miracles. This is further endorsed by Jesus' brothers' comment, *'Depart from here* [Galilee], *and go into Judea'*, as if they were aware of Jesus' next mission to Judea, and that these other disciples had not yet had the experience of being sent out without Jesus, as the twelve had.

The twelve had already experienced *'these works'* of the *'Power'* of the Holy Spirit (Mark 6:7; Luke 9:1), in preaching the gospel, a year before. The seventy would also soon experience the same works of the Spirit when returning to Jesus, after being instrumental in the third Judean ministry (Luke 10:17).

Now, when the seventy are recorded as actually leaving for their mission, relates to several months after the junction to which we have now arrived, in Caesarea Philippi, near the foot of Mt. Hermon and no doubt in the summer, at Pentecost time. Nonetheless, it would prove worthwhile at this junction to consider the translation of the word *'appointed'* in v. 1, after the last considerations, as the phrasing of the first part of that verse gives the impression Jesus *'appointed other seventy'*, at that particular point in question.

The Greek word used for *'appointed'*, *'anadeiknumi'*, which in essence means *'to show'*, or *'point out'*, is only used one other time in the NT where it is used in that basic sense, in the prayer for the replacement of Judas, where the apostles asked God to *'show'*, which of the two it would be (Acts 1:24).

When considering all the above factors, and the translation of the word *'appointed'*, we see that it was rather the purpose of Luke 10:1, to indicate that Jesus at that time of coming into autumn, now wanted *'to show'* these *'other seventy also'*. It was at that particular reference that they were to be sent out *'two and two before His face into every city and place, where He Himself would come'*. It was precisely the time for the third Judean ministry, after having already *'sent messengers before His face'* in Luke's previous chapter (9:52), when traveling through Samaria [as we shall see further when we come to that section]. Jesus specifically then sent the seventy through Judea, whereby they were all to end up afterwards at Jerusalem for the penultimate Festival of Tabernacles. Hence, we see the indubitable meaning in John 7:3, *'that Your disciples also may see the works that You do'*, fulfilled when the seventy were first sent.

Nonetheless, we have left the word *'appointed'*, as originally translated, rather than replacing it with *'to show'*, though, we can see that the time had come *'to show'* these disciples, and that it was the purpose and meaning of the Greek word used. Thus, when we come to the section where the text of Luke 10:1 is found, we have subsequently left the AV as it is, only indicating the past tense, by rendering the first part of the sentence, *'After these things the Lord* [had] *appointed other seventy'*, which suffices the intended meaning anyhow.

THE TRANSFIGURATION

Now we return to where we left off, where Jesus and the disciples were in Iturea, near the foot of Mt. Hermon, this mountainous range being the highest in the area, with the towns of Caesarea Philippi to which they had traveled, below. As Jesus and three of the disciples were about to ascend, we can only wonder, whether Jesus ordained the seventy other disciples on the Day of Pentecost, after He had returned with the Peter, James and John from the mountain, with the instructions now to *'hear Him'*. Certainly, the seventy were to hear Him, too.

These three disciples were privy to this special incident, having seen Jesus talk with Moses and Elijah, two renowned leaders of the OT Church at crucible times in its history, both leaders of *'the Church in the Wilderness'*: Moses throughout the time of escaping from Egypt [pictured as a type of sin], and in the physical wilderness (Acts 7:38), and Elijah the Prophet to the Church during a time of an unprecedented lapse into the into the wilderness of a spiritual and moral low state (1 Kings 16:30-33, 17:1).

With these two renowned leaders depicted talking with Jesus, the object and conversation at the Transfiguration was the relationship of Jesus' decease to the NT Church (Luke 9:31), of which the seventy also played a crucial part. Correspondingly, there is a similarity between Moses going up Mt. Sinai, with Aaron, Nadab, and Abihu and the seventy of those days worshiping afar off (Ex. 24:1), at the season of the giving of the Law, on the Day of Pentecost, and as traditional Judaism avers with Shavuot.

Now when Jesus embarks several months later on the third Judean ministry where the seventy are sent ahead, traveling through Samaria, Jesus rebukes James and John for not quite understanding the revelation having been given by Jesus over the role of the work of Elijah (Luke 9:54-55), at the Transfiguration, several months previously (Mat. 17:9-13; Mark 9:9-13).

Before that though, and directly after the Transfiguration, on their journey back through Galilee, there is reference to them having witnessed *'the mighty Power of God'*, which Luke (9:43) exclusively mentioned. He did not indicate this conversation took place in Galilee though, as Matthew (17:22) and Mark (9:31) had recorded, but, continued with his narrative after the Transfiguration, and *The Thirtieth Miracle*, as the disciples had witnessed many such like incidents.

Matthew (17:1) and Mark (9:2a) both mention that Jesus took Peter, James and John, with the purpose of leading them up to [as the Greek can mean] a high mountain, *'after six days'*, after having addressed the people on *Discipleship*, Mark (8:34) exclusively indicating, that He spoke to the people *'with His disciples'*. However, Luke (9:28) on the other hand, clearly states they *'went up on* [as the Greek can also mean] *the mountain to pray'*, *'about the eighth day after those sayings'*, adding and pointing out that they continued up the mountain after two days, and *'as He* [Jesus] *prayed'* it was then the Transfiguration took place.

Also, the reference to the *'high mountain'*, Peter's mentioning of the making of tabernacles, and the disciple's tiredness, indicates they were prepared to stay overnight. Luke (v. 37) exclusively recording that they came down *'on the next day'*, also relates with the other days, that they spent at least three days in the mountain.

Matthew 17:1 Mark 9:2a
And after six days Jesus takes with Him Peter, and James, and John his brother, and leads them up to a high mountain apart by themselves.

Luke 9

28 Now it came to pass about eight days after those sayings, He took Peter, John, and James, and went up on the mountain to pray.

Matthew 17:2 Mark 9:2b Luke 9:29

And as He prayed, the fashion of His countenance was altered, and He was transfigured before them, and His face did shine as the sun, and His clothing was white as light, becoming shiny, and glistened extraordinarily white as snow; so as no launderer on earth can whiten them.

Matthew 17:3 Mark 9:4 Luke 9:30

And, consider, there appeared to them, two men, who were talking with Jesus, and they were Moses together with Elijah:

Luke 9

31 who appeared in glory, and spoke of His decease which He should accomplish at Jerusalem.

32 But Peter and they who were with Him were heavy with sleep: and when they were awake, they saw His glory, and the two men who stood with Him.

Matthew 17:4 Mark 9:5 Luke 9:33

And it came to pass, as they departed from Him, then Peter answered and said to Jesus,"Lord, Master, it is good for us to be here: and if You wish, let us make here three tabernacles; one for You, and one for Moses, and one for Elijah:" not knowing what he said.

Mark 9

6 For he knew not what to say; for they were very afraid.

Matthew 17:5a Mark 9:7a Luke 9:34

And while he yet thus spoke, suddenly, there came a bright cloud, that overshadowed them and they feared as they entered into the cloud:

Matthew 17:5b Mark 9:7b Luke 9:35

and suddenly there came a voice out of the cloud, which said,

"This is My beloved Son, in whom I am well-pleased; hear Him!"

Matthew 17

6 And when the disciples heard it, they fell on their faces, and were extremely afraid.

Matthew 17:7 Mark 9:8a Luke 9:36a

And when the voice had ended, suddenly, when they had looked around, Jesus came and touched them, and said, "Rise, and do not be afraid."

Matthew 17:8 Mark 9:8b Luke 9:36b

And when they had lifted up their eyes, they saw no one, save Jesus only, being found alone with themselves.

The voice from Heaven, also spoke the same words as recorded at the Transfiguration as was spoken at Jesus' baptism, except this time, the phrase, '*This is My Beloved Son, in whom I am well-pleased*', had the extra words, '*hear Him*', added to it, as was related by all three Evangelists (Mat. 17:5b; Mark 9:7b; Luke 8:35). Though both Mark and Luke omit '*in whom I am well pleased*', this time, yet they included the phrase at Jesus' baptism. These two incidents, at Jesus' baptism, and at the Transfiguration, are the only times the voice from Heaven is recorded speaking these words.

Matthew 17:9 Mark 9:9
And as they came down from the mountain, Jesus instructed them, saying,
"That they should tell the vision, what things they had seen to no one,
except, when the Son of Humanity was risen from the dead."
Mark 9:10 Luke 9:36c
And they kept that saying close to themselves, questioning one with another what the rising from the dead should mean, and told no one in those days any of those things which they had seen.

Matthew 17:10a Mark 9:11
And His disciples asked Him, saying,
"Why then say the Scribes that Elijah must first come?"
Matthew 17:11 Mark 9:12
And Jesus answered and said informing them,
"Elijah truly shall come first, and restore all things; and how it is written of the Son of Humanity, that He must suffer many things, and be made of no importance.
Matthew 17:12 Mark 9:13
But I say to you, that Elijah is indeed come already, and they didn't recognize him, and they have done to him whatever they wanted, as it is written about him. Likewise shall also the Son of Humanity suffer of them."
Matthew 17
13 Then the disciples understood that He spoke to them of John the Baptist.

26 *THE GOSPEL FOR CHILDREN*

The Thirtieth Miracle - Deaf Mute Child

Luke had omitted five miracles after the feeding of the five thousand, and returned with his narrative about the disciple's understanding whether Jesus was the Messiah (9:18-22), including some aspects of *Discipleship* (vv. 23-27). He also covered unique detail of *The Transfiguration*, one being the indication of its conclusion the next day with the thirtieth miracle (vv. 37-42). He continued his narrative after the thirtieth miracle, with Jesus and the disciples returning to Galilee (vv. 43-50). After that, all the disciples were awaiting to leave again, according to Luke's exclusive recording of the journey through Samaria (vv. 51-62). Directly afterwards the seventy were sent '*two by two*', (10:1), which subsequently led to the third Judean ministry, upon which Luke reported his indigenous information, including the incidents surrounding these other disciples, for the next eight chapters.

The next day after *The Transfiguration*, Jesus, Peter, James and John, now return to all the rest of the disciples, who were surrounded by a great crowd, with the Scribes questioning them.

Luke (9:37a) is the only Gospel to specifically mention when they had returned transpired on yet another day, and had previously pointed out relating to time ['*the day after*', AV], where the thirteenth miracle led into the fourteenth (7:10-11). Here Luke had repeated this aspect, after *The Transfiguration*, which led into the thirtieth miracle. Obviously, he was familiar with this additional detail of the circumstances surrounding the time connected with the two events.

Mark 9:14 Luke 9:37a
And it came to pass, that on the next day, when they were come down from the mountain, and when He came toward His disciples, He saw a great crowd about them, and the Scribes questioning them.

Mark 9:15 Luke 9:37b
And straightaway all the people, when they saw Him, were greatly amazed, and many people who ran to meet Him greeted Him.
Matthew 17:14a Mark 9:16
And they [Jesus, Peter, James and John] having come to the crowd, He asked the Scribes, "What were you discussing with them?"

Matthew 17:14b-15 Mark 9:17 Luke 9:38
And, suddenly, there came to Him a certain man, one of the company who kneeling down to Him, cried out, and declared saying,
"Lord, Master, I implore You, I have brought to You my son, having a dumb

195

spirit; have mercy on my son: look upon my son: for he is a lunatic, my only child, and severely vexed: for often he falls into the fire, and often into the water.

Mark 9:18a Luke 9:39

And, look, wherever the spirit takes him, he suddenly cries out; and it convulses him that he foams again, and gnashes with his teeth, and pines away, and bruising him hardly departs from him.

Matthew 17:16 Mark 9:18b Luke 9:40

And I brought him to Your disciples, and speaking to Your disciples, I pleaded that they should cast it out; and they could not cure him."

Matthew 17:17 Mark 4:19 Luke 9:41

And then Jesus answered him, and spoke, saying,

"Oh faithless and perverse generation, how long shall I be with you? And how long shall I suffer you? Bring him - your son here to Me."

Mark 9:20 Luke 9:42a

And they brought him to Him: and as he was coming, when He saw him, immediately the devil threw him down, and convulsed him; and he fell on the ground, and wallowed foaming.

Mark 9

21 And He asked his father, "How long ago is it since this came to him?" And he said, "From childhood.

22 And often it has cast him into the fire, and into the water, to destroy him: but if You can do anything, have compassion on us, and help us."

23 Jesus said to him,

"If you can believe, all things are possible to those who believe."

24 And straightaway the father of the child cried out, and said with tears, "Lord, I believe; You help my unbelief."

Matthew 17:18a Mark 9:25 Luke 9:42b

When Jesus saw that the people came running together, Jesus rebuked the devil, the unclean foul spirit, saying to him,

"You dumb and deaf spirit, I demand you, come out of him, and enter no more into him."

Matthew 17:18b Mark 9:26

And the spirit cried, and convulsed him severely, and it came out of him: and he was as one dead; insomuch that many said, "He is dead."

Matthew 17:18c Mark 9:27 Luke 9:42c

But Jesus took him by the hand, and lifted him up, and healed the child, and he rose: and the child was cured from that very hour, and delivered again to his father.

Matthew 17:19 Mark 9:28
Then came the disciples to Jesus apart, and when He was come into the
house, His disciples asked Him privately, and said, "Why couldn't we cast it
out?"
Matthew 17:20 Mark 9:29a
And Jesus said to them,
"Because of your unbelief: for truly I say to you, if you have faith as a grain
of mustard seed, you shall say to this mountain, 'Remove from here to that
place,' and it shall move; and nothing shall be impossible for you. Matthew
17:21 Mark 9:29b
Nevertheless this kind cannot go out by nothing, but by prayer and fasting."

THE THIRTY-FIRST MIRACLE - PAYING TRIBUTE

The excursion and mission into Iturea being completed, on their way back
to Capernaum, they also stayed somewhere in Galilee, as Matthew exclusively
informs us (17:22a).

In arriving at Capernaum, Matthew (vv. 24-27) alone mentions the thirty-first
miracle; though both Matthew (v. 24) and Mark (9:33a), mention that they arrived
at Capernaum.

Matthew (17:25) uniquely revealed that Jesus questioned Peter over the
tribute money back in the house, with Mark (9:33b) adding that the next
events, of who should be the greatest, continued to take place in the same
house.

Mark 9
30 And they departed from there, and passed through Galilee; and He would
not that anyone should know it.

Matthew 17:22a Mark 9:31a Luke 9:43
And while they stayed in Galilee, they were all amazed at the mighty Power
of God. But while they wondered everyone at all the things that Jesus did, for
Jesus was teaching His disciples, Jesus said to His disciples,
Matthew 17:22b-23 Mark 9:31b Luke 9:44
"Let these sayings sink down into your ears: for the Son of Humanity shall be
delivered into the hands of men, and they shall kill Him; and after that He is
killed, He shall rise the third day, and be raised again."
And they were exceedingly sorry.

Mark 9:32 Luke 9:45
But they didn't understand this saying, and it was hid from them that they should not perceive it: and they were afraid, fearing to ask Him about this saying.

Matthew 17:24 Mark 9:33a
And when He and they arrived, having come to Capernaum, those who received tribute money came to Peter, and said, "Doesn't your Master pay tribute?"
Matthew 17
25 He says, "Yes."

And when he was come into the house Jesus anticipating him said,
"What do you think Simon? Of whom do the kings of the earth take custom or tribute, of their children, or strangers?"

26 Peter says to Him, "Of strangers."
Jesus says to him,
"Then are the children free.
27 Notwithstanding, lest we should offend them, you go to the sea, and cast a hook, and take up the first fish that comes up; and when you have opened its mouth, you shall find a piece of money: that take, and give to them for Me and you."

DEBATE ON RANK

The discussion of who should be the greatest, which the disciples argued about amongst themselves on the way back to Capernaum, and still reasoned about it in the house at Capernaum, is rather intriguing: having all experienced aspects surrounding *The Transfiguration*, though only three of the disciples were privileged to witness the miraculous scenario of Moses and Elijah, leaders of the OT Church, the episode indicates that they were now ashamed to admit their vanity (Mark 9:34). Luke exclusively records that all the disciples had witnessed some of '*the mighty Power of God*' in the transpired events of *The Transfiguration* (9:43).

Moreover, when we follow Mark's version of the event of the journey back to Galilee (9:30-32), and the returning to the house in Capernaum, we see that all the disciples were also in the house (v. 33). However, Mark goes on to elaborate further with a distinction between these disciples, in that Jesus went on to call the twelve disciples nearer to Him (vv. 34-35), when he could have just written '*called them*', if he had not wanted to indicate otherwise.

Matthew 18:1 Mark 9:33b Luke 9:46

At the same time came the disciples to Jesus: and being in the house, then there arose an argument among them, which of them should be the greatest, saying, "Who is the greatest in the Kingdom of Heaven?"

Mark 9:33c Luke 9:47a

And Jesus perceiving the thought of their hearts, He asked them,

"What was it that you disputed among yourselves on the way?"

Mark 9

34 But they held their peace: for on the way they had disputed among themselves, who should be the greatest.

35 And He sat down, and called the twelve, and said to them,

"If anyone desire to be first, the same shall be last of all, and servant of all."

Matthew 18:2-3 Mark 9:36a Luke 9:47b

And Jesus called and took a little child to Him, and set the child by Him in the midst of them: and when He had taken the child in His arms, said,

"Truly I say to you, except you be converted, and become as little children, you shall not enter into the Kingdom of Heaven.

Matthew 18

4 Whoever therefore shall humble themselves as this little child, they are the greatest in the Kingdom of Heaven."

Matthew 18:5 Mark 9:36b-37 Luke 9:48

And He said to them,

"And whoever shall receive this one such little child - one of such children in My Name, receives Me: and whoever shall receive Me, doesn't receive Me, but Him who sent Me: for those who are least among you all, the same shall be great."

Mark 9:38 Luke 9:49

And John answered Him and spoke saying,

"Master, we saw someone casting out devils in Your Name, and they wouldn't follow us: and we forbade them, because they wouldn't come along with us."

Mark 9:39 Luke 9:50a

But Jesus said to him,

"Don't forbid them: for there is no one who shall do a miracle in My Name, who can lightly speak of Me.

Mark 9:40 Luke 9:50b

For those who are not against us are for us and on our side.

Mark 9

41 For whoever shall give you a cup of water to drink in My Name, because you belong to the Messiah, truly I say to you, they shall not lose their reward."

OFFENDING CHILDREN

Matthew 18:6 Mark 9:42

"And whoever shall offend one of these little ones who believes in Me, it is better for them that a millstone were hung about their neck, and that they were cast to drown into the depths of the sea.

Matthew 18

7 Woe to the world because of offenses! For it must needs be that offenses come; but woe to that person by whom the offence comes!

Mark 9

43 And if your hand offends you, cut it off: it is better for you to enter into life maimed, than having two hands to go into hell, into the fire that shall never be quenched:

44 where THEIR MAGGOTS DON'T DIE, AND THE FIRE ISN'T QUENCHED (Is. 66:24).

Matthew 18:8 Mark 9:45

And therefore if your or foot or your hand offends you, cut them off, and cast them from you: it is better for you to enter into life lame or maimed, rather than having two hands or two feet to be cast into hell, into the everlasting fire that shall never be quenched:

Mark 6

46 where THEIR MAGGOTS DON'T DIE, AND THE FIRE ISN'T QUENCHED (Is. 66:24).

Matthew 18:9 Mark 9:47

And if your eye offends you, pluck it out and cast it from you: it is better for you to enter into life - the Kingdom of God with one eye, rather than having two eyes to be cast into hell-fire:

Mark 9

48 Where THEIR MAGGOTS DON'T DIE, AND THE FIRE ISN'T QUENCHED (Is. 66:24).

49 For everyone shall be salted with fire, AND EVERY SACRIFICE SHALL BE SALTED WITH SALT (Lev. 2:13).

50 Salt is good: but if the salt has lost its saltiness, with what will you season it? Have salt in yourselves, and have peace one with another.

Matthew 18

10 Take heed that you despise not one of these little ones; for I say to you, that in Heaven their angels do always see the face of My Father who is in Heaven.

11 For the Son of Humanity came to save those who are lost.

12 How do you think? If someone has a hundred sheep, and one of them goes

astray, do they not leave the ninety and nine, and go into the hills, and seek the one who is gone astray?

13 And if so be that they find them, truly I say to you, they rejoice more over that sheep, than of the ninety-nine who went astray.

14 Even so it is not the will of your Father, who is in Heaven that one of these little ones should perish.

FORGIVENESS

15 Moreover if your brother or sister shall trespass against you, go and tell them their fault between you and them alone: if they shall hear you, you have gained your brother or sister.

16 But if they will not hear you, then take with you one or two more, that IN THE MOUTH OF TWO OR THREE WITNESSES EVERY WORD SHALL BE ESTABLISHED (Deut. 19:15).

17 And if they shall neglect to hear them, tell it to the Church: but if they neglect to hear the Church, let them be to you as a heathen and a tax collector.

18 Truly I say to you, whatever you shall bind on earth shall be bound in Heaven: and whatever you shall loose on earth shall be loosed in Heaven.

19 Again I say to you, that if two of you shall agree on earth as touching anything that they shall ask, it shall be done for them of My Father who is in Heaven.

20 For where two or three are gathered together in My Name, there I am in the midst of them."

21 Then came Peter to Him, and said,
"Lord, how often shall my brother or sister sin against me, and I forgive them? Until seven times?

22 Jesus says to him,
"I say not to you, until seven times: but, until seventy times seven.

23 Therefore is the Kingdom of Heaven likened to a certain king, who would take account of his servants.

24 And when he had begun to reckon, one was brought to him, who owed him ten thousand talents.

25 But since he had not anything to pay, his lord commanded him to be sold, and his wife, and children, and all that he had, and payment to be made.

26 The servant therefore fell down, and worshiped him, saying, 'Lord, have patience with me, and I will pay you all.'

27 Then the lord of that servant was moved with compassion, freed him, and forgave him the debt.

28 But the same servant went out, and found one of his fellow servants, who

owed him a hundred pence: and he laid hands upon them, and took them by the throat, saying, 'Pay me what you owe.'

29 And his fellow servant fell down at his feet, and begged him, saying, 'Have patience with me, and I will pay you all.'

30 And he would not: but went and cast them into prison, till they should pay the debt.

31 So when his fellow servants saw what was done, they were sorry, and came and told their lord all that was done.

32 Then his lord, after that he had called him, said to him,

'Oh you wicked servant, I forgave you all that debt, because you desired me: 33 shouldn't you also have had compassion on your fellow servant, even as I had pity on you?'

34 And his lord was angry, and delivered him to the tormentors, till he should pay all that was due to him.

35 So likewise shall My Heavenly Father do also to you, if each of you from your heart does not forgive their brother or sister their trespasses."

Matthew (17:25) revealed earlier that at the same time Jesus questioned Peter over the tribute money, the dialogue of who should be the greatest, took place successively back at the house in Capernaum (18:1), over which Mark (9:33) paralleled with Matthew in agreement. Luke (9:46), however, also parallels and correlates at that specific point, though he did not indicate it was at the house, or that it took place at Capernaum.

THEY PREPARE TO LEAVE GALILEE

The indigenous *Parable of the Unmerciful Servant* in Matthew (18:23-35) brings to a close the episode in the house, and the stay in Capernaum, after their excursion to Iturea, as Jesus, the twelve, and the seventy, prepare for the next mission into Samaria and Judea. Matthew (19:1b) recalls after his previous unique *Parable of the Unmerciful Servant* that they were to leave for Galilee. Mark closed his narration earlier than Matthew, but also relates with Matthew about leaving Galilee (10:1a). We will see the translation of Matthew's *'beyond Jordan'* (19:1c), and Mark's *'farther side of Jordan'* (10:1c) meant the Judean side, when we arrive at those verses in the main text [p. 208]. At that junction we show the word *'beyond'* in Matthew, Greek *'peran'*, and Mark *'farther side'*, also *'peran'* again, refers to the west side of Jordan as firstly indicated in the prophecy referring to the start of Jesus' mission in Mat. 4:15 [p. 48].

Luke (9:50), nonetheless, having ended his narration before that of both Matthew and Mark, his next verse indicating the mission to Samaria and Judea with the ultimate purpose of ending up in Jerusalem (v. 51). Thus, Luke recorded the sending of these messengers ahead of Jesus when they leave Galilee traveling through Samaria (v. 52), with the aim of preaching through Judea, too (v. 53).

We had suggested that *The Transfiguration* fell between the Passover in spring and Tabernacles in autumn, and occurred in the summer season. With that season now turning to autumn and Jesus having prepared for His next mission with the seventy about to go on before Him, the Gospel of John returns now with his dialogue after a gap of six months, which had included Jesus' excursion into Iturea and the returning to Capernaum. Since John 6:4-71 and 7:1, took place in the previous Passover season, and after, in addition v. 2 indicated the six months was drawing to an end. Hence this was to be the third Tabernacles of Jesus' ministry, with one more Passover and Tabernacles before the final Passover after that.

We had also considered John 7:3-4 at *The Transfiguration* in regards to the seventy, in the sense that John was not referring to Jesus' disciples not having seen His miracles, but that the seventy had not experienced '*the works*' of the Power of healing in going '*two by two*' before Jesus (Luke 10:9, 17), and that Jesus' brothers were aware of this.

With Jesus, the twelve and the seventy, now preparing to leave Galilee once again for the next mission into Samaria and Judea, with the purpose of attending the penultimate Festival of Tabernacles at Jerusalem, the Gospel of John fills in with the next successive details.

John 7

2 Now the Jews' Festival of Tabernacles was at hand.

3 His brothers therefore said to Him,

"Depart from here, and go into Judea, that Your disciples also may see the works that You do.

4 For there's no one who does anything in secret, when they themselves seek to be known openly. If You do these things, show Yourself to the world."

5 For neither did His brothers believe on Him.

6 Then Jesus said to them, "My time is not yet come: but your time is always ready.

7 The world cannot hate you; but Me it hates, because I testify of it, that the works thereof are evil.

8 You go up to this Festival: I'm not going up yet to this Festival; for My time has not yet fully come."

Matthew 19:1a John 7:9

And it came to pass, that when Jesus had finished saying these words to them,

He remained still in Galilee.

The dialogue between Jesus and His brothers about these other seventy disciples experiencing '*the works*' of the Power of the Spirit, without Jesus being present (7:3-4), as the twelve had a year previously, and the aspect of how they, and Jesus' brothers, were all going up to the next Festival of Tabernacles, was decided by Jesus indicating that His intention was to go up separate from them (vv. 8-9), and, as it were, in secret (v. 10). The official festal caravan was received at Jerusalem by a public procession of Priests and Levites. Thus Jesus would remain discrete in avoiding being recognized by the authorities when deciding to appear at the Festival, as He knew they would be expecting Him (v. 11). Moreover, six months previously they had wanted to kill Him (v. 1).

John (v. 9) nevertheless blends in with Matthew (19:1a) at this point, with Matthew (18:23-35) indicating that it was after the discourse of the *Parable of the Unmerciful Servant* in the house at Capernaum that they were prepared for the next mission (19:1b). John gave further details to that time, by showing it was also after the additional conversation with Jesus' brothers of Nazareth (v. 10). No doubt Jesus and the disciples had chosen to stop-off at Nazareth again, after traveling from Capernaum, before embarking on their next mission to Samaria and Judea, to go up ultimately to Jerusalem, rather than joining the festal caravan, choosing then, not to leave with his brothers when they left from Nazareth.

Hence Matthew 19:1 includes three factors, with his version of the leaving of Galilee: a) when Jesus had finished these '*sayings*' [Gr. *logos*], which can relate to the '*logos*' in John 7:9, where it is translated '*words*' [thus we have phrased the two individual sentences of Matthew and John, in the main text, with these two words, so as to comply with the meaning of both the combined references]: and b) the departing from Galilee; along with c) the coming into Judea.

Now because factor b) did not transpire straightaway, as Jesus and the disciples remained in Galilee a short while, after the dialogue with Jesus' brothers, and c) occurred somewhat later after stopping-off in Samaria, we have placed b) and c) in their natural consecutive positions when they start their journey.

Mark (10:la on the other hand does not relate specifically to actually mentioning the conclusion of any dialogue, but only refers to the leaving of Galilee.

We have left the rendering in Luke 9:51, '*received up*' as it is in the main text, though various translators have thought this was a reference to the conclusion of Jesus' mission, after the last Passover.

However, when taking all the evidence of the findings of *The Gospel of the Four* into consideration, we see that at this particular juncture, there is yet still a penultimate Tabernacles and Passover to transpire before we come to the final Passover.

Thus, though the Greek word '*analepsis*' translated '*received up*' in the AV, in this case, is used only once throughout the NT, it does nonetheless, at this juncture correlate with the phraseology of combining v. 51, *'and it came to pass, when the time was come that He should be received up'*, with John 7:10, *'when His brothers were gone up'* to the Festival, as shown in our main text, as, after the mission into Samaria, Judea, and Jerusalem, Jesus did not return to Galilee, where He had preached the most, until after the resurrection!

Moreover, He was to be *'received up'*, to Jerusalem, as it were, after completing His mission in Galilee, in purpose, as *'He steadfastly* [or resolutely] *set His face to go to Jerusalem'* (Luke 9:51). This was in the sense of making it His predominate and ultimate focus point from that particular junction onwards, as He knew it would be increasingly dangerous for Him in that area from thereon. Furthermore, He also knew that He would be *'received up'* on the cross at Jerusalem, and after that be *'received up'* to Heaven again in the Ascension from the Mt. Olives at Jerusalem. Thus, He resolutely went at this time, careful not to jeopardize any premature timing.

Ironically, maybe there is also an inkling hint that with the festal caravan being officially received up in Jerusalem by the Priests and Levites, Jesus especially should have been *'received up'* by them. But, conversely, Jesus had to plan His coming into Jerusalem secretly so as not to compromise Himself in allowing Himself to be killed prior to the final Passover, as His witnessing was to escalate from now on, specifically to Jerusalem. However, as we shall see, Jesus, in another sense, was *'received up'* as a guest of honor, by *'One of the Chief Pharisees'* who was sympathetic towards Him, at the first Sabbath of the Festival of Tabernacles [see pp. 230-234], and contained in the sections *The Third Festival of Tabernacles* and *The First Evening of Tabernacles*!

THEY LEAVE FOR SAMARIA

Matthew 19:1b Mark 10:1a Luke 9:51 John 7:10

But when His brothers were gone up, and it came to pass when the time was come that He should be received up, He steadfastly set His face, and He rose from there, and then went He also up to go to the Festival at Jerusalem; and He departed from Galilee, not openly, but as it were in secret,

Luke 9

52 and sent messengers ahead of Him: and they went, and entered into a village of the Samaritans, to make ready for Him.

53 And they did not receive Him, because His demeanor was as though He would go to Jerusalem.
54 And when His disciples James and John saw this, they said,
"Lord, do You wish that we command fire to come down from Heaven, and consume them, even as Elijah did?"
55 But He turned, and rebuked them, and said,
"You don' understand of what kind of attitude you have.
56 For the Son of Humanity is not come to destroy people's lives, but to save them."

And they went to another village.

Jesus sent certain disciple messengers before Him. They having been instructed to look for a convenient village to lodge (9:52), as the campaign of traveling through Samaria, with the third Judean ministry in mind, commenced. But as Jesus' primary purpose was to go to Judea, and Jerusalem, the village people expecting Him to stay longer, took offence (v. 53), and thus they had to make arrangements to stay at '*another village*' (v. 56).

The attitude of the Samaritans of the first village contrasts with that of the people of Sychar over a year previously, in which they had asked Jesus to stay for two days. Jesus at that time obliged their request (John 4:40). Now at this juncture, they had to go on to another village wherein they would be accepted. This second village may well have been Sychar once again, where they had remembered Jesus from before, as it is near the borders of Samaria/Judea, from where the seventy no doubt were subsequently sent out. Remember, Luke informed us they were traveling through Samaria (9:52, 56), with the purpose of ending up in Jerusalem (v. 51).

Matthew (19:1c) however, tells us, though referring to the same time, that they were making their way up to '*the borders of Judea*', which borders also with Samaria.

As Luke (10:17) later records the seventy having returned, we must concur that the seventy returned from Judea (John 7:3), to where the seventy had been sent, as Jesus would also shortly come to the towns, to which they had been announcing His coming (Luke 10:1), before ending up at the Festival in Jerusalem.

Being in that particular area is further endorsed by the *Parable of the Good Samaritan* (Luke 10:30-37), as the seventy returned to the borders of Samaria/ Judea to Jesus before they were all to leave again. Besides, Luke in his following verse, directly after the *Parable of the Good Samaritan*, points out that later they had subsequently made their way to a house in Judea, the home of Mary and Martha (v. 38), who resided in Bethany (John 11:1).

Besides, the border of Samaria/Judea and the parable are significantly applicable to the divergent characters of the Samaritans and the Jews, in the sense of the indignant Samaritans of the first village Jesus had wanted to stop at, and the other good Samaritans of the second village. Conversely, there were many enlightened Jews, the disciples and Jesus being some, though the Priest and Levite, in the parable were not. Thus this incident was highlighted by the borderlines of the area, and by the borderline differences in the two attitudes, whether Samaritan or Jew, or vice versa.

At this point it should be mentioned that some have concluded that Jesus had a ministry in Perea. But the name Perea, the area adjacent to Samaria/ Judea, is not to be found in the Bible. Though the Greek word '*peran*', translated '*beyond*', does have a resemblance to Perea. However, Mat. 19:1c does not state at this juncture, Perea '*beyond Jordan*', but '*Judea beyond Jordan*'. Moreover, in Mark's version of the same time when they came into Judea, the word '*peran*' is in that instance translated '*farther side*' (10:1b)! But, once again, we have left the two expressions as they are, in combining them in the main text, as in any case it further emphasizes and enhances the description of the scenario of Jesus and all the disciples journeying. Thus, '*by the farther side of Jordan*' (v. 1b) would relate to the natural border of the Jordan River, including the borders of Samaria/Judea, whose furthest reach from the Mediterranean was the Jordan.

Additionally, we see the Greek word '*peran*', which is used at the commencement of Jesus' mission [p. 53], in the prophecy where it reads, '*beyond* [peran] *Jordan, Galilee*' (Mat. 4:15), actually refers to the west side of Jordan, '*the land of Zebulun and the land of Naphtali*', Israel's side, in any case.

Furthermore, it is common throughout the Gospels, and in fact with all writers, that if a writer mentions the name of a place or area, it is concluded that until the dialogue, or other information reveals a change otherwise, it is still referring in context to the same place. As Luke is the next writer who reports through the following nine chapters detail covering the subsequent events solely found in his Gospel, regarding the great omissions of Matthew and Mark, nonetheless, from this particular point, we shall see as we continue, he does nevertheless give clear signs as to where the following events actually transpired.

Matthew 19:1c Mark 10:1b Luke 9:57a
And it came to pass, that, as they journeyed on the way and came into the borders of Judea beyond Jordan, by the farther side of Jordan,
Matthew 19:2 Mark 10:1c Luke 9:57b
also great crowds followed Him; and the people resorted to Him again; and, as He was inclined, He taught them again, and there healing them, a certain man said to Him, "Lord, I will follow You wherever You go."
Luke 9
58 And Jesus says to him, "Foxes have holes, and birds of the air have nests; but the Son of Humanity has nowhere to lay His head."

59 And He said to another, "Follow Me."
But he said, "Lord, allow me first to go and bury my father."
60 Jesus said to him, "Let the dead bury their dead: but you go and preach the Kingdom of God."

61 And another also said, "Lord, I will follow You; but let me first go wish them farewell, who are at home at my house."
62 And Jesus said to Him, "No one, having put their hand to the plough, and looking back, is fit for the Kingdom of God."

The using of similar and at times, the same sayings, naturally becomes more frequent from this intersection, as Jesus was teaching the seventy the same as He had taught the twelve, and no doubt the five hundred. This pattern of teaching for these groups would be an ongoing thing throughout the rest of the Gospels with both original and new sayings being repeated by Jesus at various times.

We mentioned previously at the section, *The Seventh Miracle - The Catch of Fishes*, p. 105, regarding Luke's mentioning, now at this juncture, of a similar incident that took place in Matthew (8:19-22), when Jesus and the eleven were about to sail by boat across the Sea of Galilee (8:18, 23) over a year before. Matthew though, indicated in that particular case, it was '*a certain Scribe*' who asked the first question (v. 19), whereas Luke only mentions '*a certain man*' at this subsequent intersection. This included three different disciples who asked questions, to Matthew's two.

It should not be thought as incredulous, that once more one of these disciples had not wanted to follow Jesus at this particular time, but sought, to leave after hearing about his father's death. Since now, there were many more disciples, naturally would have had the same terms put to them. Significantly, Luke also infers, by adding the words, '*but you go and preach the Kingdom of God*' (9:60), just before the crucial point where the seventy are about to go on ahead of Jesus into Judea. Though the seventy had already been called, other disciples were naturally still being sifted out. We cannot know whether those three disciples, referred to by Luke, went on to follow Jesus later.

Furthermore, Luke by using the word '*another*' v. 59, and by way of this third person, obviously was pointing out the distinction between a new disciple, as being separate from the seventy, in asking for permission to wish those of his household farewell (v. 61), which is not mentioned in Matthew's earlier scenario. This adds to the differences between the two narratives further confirming they were separate incidents, besides Luke's unique analogy of putting ones '*hand to the plough, and looking back*' (v. 62). This concludes Luke's discourse, before the setting out of the seventy without Jesus.

Additionally, Matthew's (8:19-22) dialogue of discipleship, before sailing the across the lake, in that particular mission, '*great crowds*' had also arrived, with Jesus directly afterwards wanting to get away from them by boat (v. 18). This He subsequently did (v. 23)! But now, conversely, in reference to discipleship now at this time, as shown by the last dovetailed main text, healed these '*great crowds*' (19:2), before sending the seventy on without Him. Some of the '*great crowds*' would have been traveling through Judea to where Jesus was to send the seventy. Afterwards '*the seventy returned again*' back to Jesus from where they had earlier left (Luke 10:17).

At the point no doubt, where the seventy had already been called over a year ago [pp. 108-114], when the twelve had been ordained (Mat. 10:1; Mark 3:14; Luke 6:13), the twelve likewise had about a years' experience of being with Jesus [except Matthew's half of the time], before they were ordained, with several months transpiring before they were sent out without Jesus (Mark 6:7; Luke 9:1-2).

With Jesus and the seventy now arriving at the borders of Samaria/Judea, '*also great crowds followed*' (Mat. 19:2). No doubt these were some of the people of the festal caravan traveling down early so as to make arrangements at Jerusalem. The ones furthest away would have to arrive early so as to secure a place for their booths [tabernacles] in the crowds of people converging around the area of the city and the Temple.

Amazingly, Matthew had connected Jesus' words on praying for [the seventy] more laborers for the harvest (9:37-38), directly preceding *The Ordination Of The Twelve* (10:1-2), when, actually in successive order [see section *Conclusion Of Second Galilean Ministry*, [pp. 149-152], the narrative is referring to when the twelve left to go two by two'several months later, for the second Judean campaign, after the fourth and last Galilean circuit.

However, Luke also recalled from his source, that Jesus spoke the same words again, which Matthew had recorded earlier, to the twelve, about praying for even more laborers for the harvest, addressed now specifically to the seventy (10:2), including their instructions before they actually left '*two by two*' (vv. 3-16). Obviously the fact that Luke 10:1 is referring to the specific point when Jesus subsequently sent the seventy from the border of Samaria/ Judea, whereas the following verses, relate to the directive given preceding that mission. At the actual commencement of the mission of the seventy when they left Galilee with the sending of those messengers, they had originally begun their mission earlier in Samaria (v. 52). This is further indication that the directions on going '*two by two*' were given previously before actually leaving Galilee, and that Luke 10:2-16 is a recapitulation, just before the seventy left, as had also been the case before sending the twelve '*two by two*' (Mark 6:7-13; Luke 9:1-6).

As we come to ch. 10:1 in the main text we must remember that we covered in detail the various aspects of the ordination of the seventy in the section entitled, *The Seventy Disciples* [pp. 188-192]. We also related that the word '*appointed*' should be in the context of the past tense. In John 18:24, the translators placed the word '*had*' in the AV, as v. 13 indicates Jesus was led to Annas first.

Likewise we have done the same with Luke 10:1. Luke's unique Central Section (9:52-18:14), which started with the leaving of Galilee and the coming into Samaria (v. 51), with the mission of the seventy, and the subsequent events surrounding transpiring in Judea, no doubt was Luke's specialty, and thus distinguishes him as the writer of *The Acts Of The Apostles*, and the other disciples.

Luke 10

1 After these things the Lord [had] appointed other seventy also, and sent them two by two ahead of Him into every city and place, where He Himself would come.

2 Therefore He said to them,

"The harvest truly is great, but the laborers are few; you pray therefore the Lord of the harvest, that He would send out laborers into His harvest.

3 Go your ways: be aware, I send you out as lambs among wolves.

4 Carry neither purse, nor travel-bag, nor sandals: and entertain no one on the way.

5 And into whatever house you enter, first say, 'Peace be to this house.'

6 And if anyone of peace be there, your peace shall rest upon it: if not, it shall turn to you again.

7 And in the same house remain, eating and drinking such things as they give: for the laborer is worthy of his hire. Don't go from house to house.

8 And whatever city you enter, and they receive you, eat such things as are set before you:

9 and heal the sick that are therein, and say to them, 'The Kingdom of God is come near to you.'

Luke 10

10 But into whatever city you enter, and they don't receive, go your ways out into the streets of the same, and say,

11'Even the very dust of your city, which sticks to us, we do wipe off against you: notwithstanding be sure of this, that the Kingdom of God is come near to you.'

12 But I say to you, that it shall be more tolerable in that day for Sodom, than for that city.

13 Woe to you Chorazin! Woe to you Bethsaida! For if the mighty works had been done in Tyre and Sidon, which have been done in you, they had a great while ago repented, wearing black clothes and ash.

14 But it shall be more tolerable for Tyre and Sidon at the Judgment, than for you.

15 And you Capernaum, who are exalted to Heaven, shall be thrust down to hell.

16 Those who hear you hear Me; and they who despise you despise Me; and those who despise Me despises Him who sent Me."

Whenever the twelve (Mark 6:13); Luke 9:6) or the seventy were sent ahead of Jesus, there were able to heal (Luke 10:90). but, as soon as they were not involved in the mission of going ahead of Jesus, the Power of healing was not present (Mat. 17:16), that is, not until the day of Pentecost, ten days after the ascension (Acts 1:4-5; 2:1).

The seventy, having announced that Jesus was shortly coming through Judea, return to the borders of Samaria/Judea, from where they were sent out, and were amazed at having experienced firsthand *the Power of God* (Luke 10:17).

---

17 And the seventy returned again with joy, saying,
"Lord, even the devils are subject to us through Your Name."
18 And He said to them,
"I saw Satan as lightning descend from Heaven.
19 Consider, I give to you Power to tread on serpents and scorpions, and over all the power of the enemy: and nothing shall by any means hurt you.
20 Nevertheless, don't rejoice in this, that the spirits are subject to you; but rather rejoice, because your names are written in Heaven."

21 In that hour Jesus rejoiced in spirit, and said,
"I thank You, Oh Father, Lord of Heaven and earth, that You have hid these

things from the wise and prudent, and have revealed them to babes: even so, Father; for so it seemed good in Your sight.
22 All things are delivered to Me of My Father: and no one knows whom the Son is, but the Father; and who the Father is, but the Son, and to whom the Son will reveal Him."

23 And He turned Himself to His disciples, and said privately,
"Blessed are your eyes which see the things that you see:
24 for I tell you, that many prophets and kings have desired to see those things that you see, and have not seen them; and to hear those things which you hear, and have not heard them."

25 And, consider, a certain lawyer stood up, and tempted Him, saying,
"Master, what shall I do to inherit eternal life?"
26 He said to him, "What is written in the Law? How do you read?"

27 And he answering, said,
"YOU SHALL LOVE THE LORD YOUR GOD WITH ALL YOUR HEART, AND WITH ALL YOUR SOUL, AND WITH ALL YOUR STRENGTH, AND WITH ALL YOUR MIND (Deut. 6:5); AND YOUR NEIGHBOUR AS YOURSELF (Lev.19:18)."
28 And He said to him,
"You have answered right: THIS DO, AND YOU SHALL LIVE (Lev. 18:5)."
29 But he, willing to justify himself, said to Jesus, "And who is my neighbor?"

30 And Jesus answering said,
"A certain man went down from Jerusalem to Jericho, and fell among thieves, who stripped him of his clothing, and wounded him, and departed, leaving him half dead.
31 And by chance there came down a certain Priest that way: and when he saw him he passed by on the other side.

32 And likewise a Levite, when he was at the place, came and looked on him and passed by on the other side.

33 But a certain Samaritan, as he journeyed, came where he was: and when he saw him, he had compassion on him.
34 And went to him and bound up his wounds, pouring in oil and wine, and set him on his own animal, and brought him to an inn, and took care of him.

35 And on the crack of dawn when he departed, he took out two pence, and gave them to the host, and said to him 'Take care of him; and whatever you spend more, when I come again, I will repay you.'

Luke 10

36 Now which of these three, do you think, was neighbor to him who fell among thieves?"

37 And he said, "He who showed mercy to him."
Then said Jesus to him, "You go, and do likewise."

ARRIVAL AT BETHANY, JUDEA

If Luke had wanted to inform us otherwise that the disciples and Jesus had traveled to anywhere other than where he indicated in the last places in his text (9:51-53, 56-57), he could have easily done so. But no, Luke informs us by referring to the home of Mary and Martha (10:38), which was known as being in Bethany in Judea (John 11:1), thus confirming the logical direction of travel from the border of Samaria/Judea.

Luke 10
38 Now it came to pass, as they went that He entered into a certain village: and a certain woman named Martha received Him into her house.
39 And she had a sister called Mary, who also sat at Jesus' feet, and heard His word.
40 But Martha was cumbered about much serving, and came to Him, and said, "Lord, don't You care that my sister has left me alone? Tell her therefore to help me."
41 And Jesus answered and said to her,
"Martha, Martha, you are careful and troubled about many things:
42 but one thing is needful: and Mary has chosen that good part, which shall not be taken away from her."

Luke's mentioning of the house of Mary and Martha, and that it was known their home was in Bethany, only two miles from Jerusalem, is indicative that his following text also took place in the same area, as he does not inform us to the contrary.

Moreover, Luke had not shown, since his last points of reference, at the beginning of the seventy's mission where Jesus had '*set His face to go to Jerusalem*' (9:51), traveling through Samaria and Judea (vv. 52-53), any change to that effect. Having then arrived at Bethany, near Jerusalem, the next reference to '*a certain place*', though not actually named by Luke, is where '*one of His disciples*' asked Jesus, how to pray (11:1).

However, Luke specifically referred to this '*certain place*', in relationship to where Jesus was once again teaching the disciples to pray, as shown through the Lord's Prayer, in that he knew where it was, and that it would be understood where he was referring to without directly naming it. Furthermore, Jesus had originally taught the eleven how to pray through the Lord's Prayer on the Mt. Olives [p. 63], as we had suggested, at the first Passover season of His ministry.

Consequently, as Jesus had already presented the outline of praying as contained in the Lord's Prayer originally to the eleven (Mat. 6:9-14), '*one of His disciples*' at this juncture, as of course now there were many more other disciples as indicated by the seventy, obviously relates to those other than the apostles (Luke 11:1). In this similar setting, though here at this juncture with a much shorter dialogue, this scenario '*in a certain place*', and with many more disciples, is nowhere as long as Matthew's three chapters 5-7, where the original comprehensive narrative of the fundamental teachings, en bloc, of Christianity was given to the eleven. Nonetheless, it is certainly reminiscent of when the eleven went up the mount in that first instance (Mat. 5:1).

Subsequently, and uniquely, Luke is the only Gospel writer to specifically point out that the Mt. Olives was '*the certain place*' when Jesus was in the vicinity of Jerusalem, He usually and specially used to go (22:39).

Here once more, in that familiar spot, after leaving the home of Mary and Martha in Bethany, near the base of the east side of the Mt. Olives where their home was situated, Luke having also indicated later in his text the topography in conjunction to Bethany and the Mt. Olives (19:29), made sure we could understand that the next logical and nearest '*certain place*' wherein they would go in a short respite from the crowds, would naturally be the Mt. Olives, once again.

Furthermore, the narration which includes ch. 11:1-13, is directed exclusively at the disciples and does not contain any reference to the crowds being with Jesus and the disciples at that particular point, as does the proceeding narration, where a crowd had arrived with *The Thirty-Second Miracle* subsequently taking place (v. 14).

Luke 11

1 And it came to pass, that as He was praying in a certain place, when He ceased, one of His disciples said to Him, "Lord, teach us to pray, as John also taught His disciples."

2 And He said to them, "When you pray, say,

'Our Father who is in Heaven, hallowed be Your Name.

Your Kingdom come. Your will be done, as in Heaven, so in earth.

3 Give us day by day our daily bread.

4 And forgive us our sins; for we also forgive each one who is indebted to us. And lead us not into temptation; but deliver us from evil.'"

5 And He said to them,

"Which of you shall have a friend, and shall go to them at midnight, and say to them, 'Friend, lend me three loaves;

6 for a friend of mine on their journey has come to me, and I have nothing to

set before them?'

7 And they from within shall answer and say, 'Don't trouble me: the door is now shut, and my children are with me in bed; I cannot get up and give it you.'

8 I say to you, though they will not rise and oblige them, because they are friends, yet because of their persistence they will rise and give them as much as they need.

9 And I say to you, ask, and it shall be given you; seek, and you shall find; knock and it shall be opened to you.

10 For everyone who asks, receives; and those who seek, find; and to those who knock it shall be opened.

11 If a child shall ask for bread off any of you who is a father, will he give them a stone? Or if they ask for fish, will he give them a serpent?

12 Or if they shall ask for an egg, will he offer them a scorpion?

13 If you then, being sinners, know how to give good gifts to your children: how much more shall your Heavenly Father give the Holy Spirit to those who ask Him?"

THE THIRTY-SECOND MIRACLE - CASTS OUT DEVIL

Jesus directed the words contained in the complete dialogue of Luke 11:1-13 specifically at the disciples, and no doubt '*in a certain place*' near Bethany, alluding to the Mt. Olives. The scenario then changes relating to the thirty-second miracle (v. 14); thus informing us that now at this particular point, there were other people present, and that after the Lord's Prayer, and the complementary allegory on asking (vv. 5-13), indicated that these people had been gathering as soon as they had known He was there (vv. 15-16). Luke, further endorsed this, by indicating that the people were still gathering '*thick together*' just proceeding the previous point (v. 29).

After the thirty-second miracle (v. 14), the evil accusation that Jesus healed through the Devil continued to be promulgated by a certain '*some*' to the people again (v. 15).

At another event, though similar, they had accused Jesus of casting out devils through Beelzebub, over a year before at the fifteenth miracle (Mat. 12:22-24). Mark at that particular time added further detail to the same incident, with the Scribes having come down from Jerusalem (3:22), established that they had come to see their contemporaries of Capernaum (Mat. 12:24). We saw then in the section, *Satan Casting Out Satan?* [pp. 126-127], that the Scribes had specially arrived to counsel at Capernaum with their contemporaries, because of their resentfulness to the news of Jesus' continuing exploits. We also saw in the following section, *Satan Casting Out Satan? - In House* [pp. 128-129] that

Jesus even went on to call them to His house (Mark 3:23), to set the record straight through whom He did His miracles (Mat.12:27-28).

Thus, Luke alludes through his indigenous thirty-second miracle, and the subsequent details, taking place near Jerusalem, that no doubt some of these same Scribes and Pharisees had continued to spread the rumor around that Jesus was of the Devil. This then becoming an influencing factor in Jerusalem, in trying to persuade the people against Him (11:14-15). Hence, Jesus continues, when addressing these people near Jerusalem, to relate things He had spoken previously at Capernaum, when dealing with the same rationalizations.

Luke 11
14 And He was casting out a devil, and it was dumb. And it came to pass, when the devil was gone out, the dumb spoke; and the people wondered.
15 But some of them said,
"He casts out devils through Beelzebub the Chief of the Devils."

16 And others testing Him sought from Him a sign from Heaven.
17 But He, knowing their thoughts, said to them,
"Every kingdom divided against itself is brought to desolation: and a house divided against a house falls.
18 If Satan shall be divided against himself, how shall his kingdom stand? Yet you say that I cast out devils through Beelzebub.
19 And if I by Beelzebub cast out devils, by whom do your children cast them out? Therefore they shall be your judges.
20 But if I with the finger of God cast out devils, no doubt the Kingdom of God is come to you.

21 When a strong person armed keeps their palace, their goods are in peace:
22 but when a stronger than they shall come upon them, and overcome them, they take from them all their armor wherein they trusted, and divide their spoils.

23 Those who are not with Me are against Me: and they who gather not with Me, scatter.
24 When the unclean spirit is gone out of someone, it walks through dry places, seeking rest; and finding none, it says, 'I will return to the house which I came out.'
25 And when it comes, it finds it swept and garnished.
26 Then it goes, and takes seven other spirits more wicked than itself, and they enter in, and dwell there: and the last state of that person is worse than

the first."

27 And it came to pass, as He spoke these things, a certain woman of the company lifted up her voice, and said to Him,
"Blessed is the womb that bore you, and the breasts which nursed You!"
28 But He said,
"Yes rather, blessed are those who hear the word of God, and keep it."

SIGNS AND LIGHT

29 And when the people were gathered thick together, He began to say,
"This is an evil generation: they seek a sign; and there shall no sign be given it, but the sign of Jonah the prophet.
30 For as Jonah was a sign to the Ninevites, so shall also the Son of Humanity be to this generation.

31 The Queen of the South shall rise up in the judgment with the people of this generation, and condemn them: for she came from a distant land to hear the Wisdom of Solomon; and, understand, a greater than Solomon is here.

32 The people of Nineveh shall rise up in the judgment with this generation, and shall condemn it: for they repented at the preaching of Jonah; and, understand, a greater than Jonah is here.

33 No one, when they have lit a candle, puts it in a secret place, neither under a container but on a candlestick, that those who come in may see the light.
34 The light of the body is the eye: therefore when your eye is positive, your whole body also is full of light; but when your eye is evil, your body also is full of darkness.
35 Take heed therefore that the light, which is in you, be not darkness.
36 If your whole body therefore be full of light, having no part dark, it will be wholly full of light, as when the bright shining of a lamp gives you light."

Now, after the narrative which included vv. 14-36, Luke indicates in v. 37, a Pharisee amongst the crowds: this no doubt being indicative to many more also being present, and of the ones who had traveled to meet with their contemporaries in Capernaum, who also had been invited into Jesus' house, as we have indicated on the next page dealing with the same, Luke later in his text confirms the presence of Scribes too, in v. 44 and v. 53.

JESUS DINES WITH THE PHARISEES

Luke indicated as Jesus was addressing the crowds, which would have included Scribes and Pharisees, that one of the Pharisees asks Jesus to dine with him. We see by the context of the narrative, which covers the scenario of the actual dining, Jesus directed His admonition to them (v 39), which, moreover, also included lawyers (12:46). Hence, with Luke using this style of writing, of portraying details of the whole setting later, we have to read further ahead to find out the complete picture of the situation preceding.

We had suggested the events preceding took place at the Mt. Olives. The setting regarding the scenario of dining with the Pharisee no doubt was near to Jerusalem as the context of the account indicates prominent Scribes and lawyers present, who would in any case reside near Jerusalem. Thus, we must conclude that the convergence of the '*innumerable crowd*' later (12:1), transpired there too, as Luke had assumed we would naturally understand his style of writing, by this type of composition. Possibly, the '*innumerable crowd*' had proceeded to the Temple area, where Jesus, the disciples, and the Scribes and Pharisees, went after dining together.

Subsequently, just before Jesus' crucifixion, in the Temple area the Scribes and Pharisees received again a similar, but, a much longer and, moreover, the final admonition, as recorded by Matthew (ch. 23). However, Jesus was not dinning with them at that particular time.

Also, the other differences when comparing with Matthew's final admonition this scenario in Luke, is that there are six '*woes*', to Matthew's eight '*woes*', with varying degrees of differing terminology. Additionally, Matthew's greater thirty-nine verses, is twice as long as Luke's eighteen verses and at a completely different time and setting. Besides, at the final admonition, both Mark (12:38-40) and Luke (20:45-47) combine in paralleling with Matthew, though with a curtailed version, indicating their agreement to this other latter incident being at a different time.

Luke 11

37 And as He spoke, a certain Pharisee entreated Him to dine with him: and He went in, and sat at dinner.

38 And when the Pharisee saw it, he marveled that He had not first washed before dinner.

39 And the Lord said to him,

"Now you Pharisees make clean the outside of the cup and plate; but your inward part is full of ravening and wickedness.

40 You fools, didn't He who made that which is outside make that which is within also?

41 But rather give kindness with such things as you have; and, understand, all things are clean to you.

42 But woe to you, Pharisees! For you tithe mint and rue and all manner of herbs, and pass over judgment and the love of God: these ought you to have done, and not left the other undone.

43 Woe to you, Pharisees! For you love the upper most seats in the synagogues, and greetings in the markets.

44 Woe to you, Scribes and Pharisees, hypocrites! For you are as unseen graves, and the people who walk over them are not aware of them."

45 Then answered one of the lawyers, and said to Him,
"Master, in saying this you insult us also."
46 And He said,
"Woe to you also, you Lawyers! For you load people with burdens grievous to be carried, and you yourselves won't even lift one finger to help carry those burdens.
47 Woe to you! For you build monuments to the prophets, and your fathers killed them.
48 Truly you bear witness that you allow the deeds of your fathers: for they indeed killed them, and you build their monuments.
49 Therefore also said the Wisdom of God, 'I will send them prophets and apostles, and some of them they shall kill and persecute:
50 that the blood of all the prophets, which was shed from the foundation of the world, may be required of this generation;
51 from the blood of Abel to the blood of Zechariah, who perished between the altar and the Temple: surely I say to you, it shall be required of this generation.'
52 Woe to you, lawyers! For you have taken away the key of knowledge: you didn't enter in yourselves, and those who were entering in you hindered."

53 And as He said these things to them, the Scribes and the Pharisees began to urge Him vehemently, and to provoke Him to speak of many things:
54 laying wait for Him, and seeking to catch something out of His mouth, that they might accuse Him.

LEAVEN OF THE PHARISEES

The combined vv. 37-54, all took place at dinner with '*the Scribes and Pharisees*'. Concluding that event, the scene now changes again and depicts Jesus and the disciples once again outside, whereby the crowds had now increased further as compared to what they had been before Jesus' invitation to dine.

Thus, Luke revealed the buildup of people in three stages, firstly in vv. 14-16, secondly in v. 29, and thirdly the gathering where Luke recorded what the Leaven of the Pharisees actually meant, by quoting Jesus' words that were addressed directly at the disciples (12:1).

The Leaven of the Pharisees was also mentioned previously by Matthew (16:6-12), only a season before when they were still in Galilee, just prior to the Iturean excursion, and now the Judean campaign, which we are covering.

Luke 12

1 In the meantime, when there were gathered together an innumerable crowd of people, insomuch that they trod one upon another, He began to say to His disciples first of all,
"You beware of the leaven of the Pharisees, which is hypocrisy.
2 For there is nothing covered that shall not be revealed; neither hid, that shall not be known.
3 Therefore whatever you have spoken in darkness shall be heard in the light; and that which you have spoken in whispers behind closed doors shall be proclaimed upon the housetops.

4 And I tell you My friends, don't be afraid of those who kill the body, and after that have no more that they can do.
5 But I will forewarn you whom you shall fear: fear Him, who after He has killed has Power to cast into hell; yes, I say to you fear Him.

6 Are not five sparrows sold for two pennies, and not one of them is forgotten before God?
7 But even the very hairs of your head are all numbered. Don't be afraid therefore: you are of more value than many sparrows.

8 Also I say to you, whoever shall acknowledge Me before all, the Son of Humanity shall also acknowledge them before the angels of God:
9 but they who deny Me before all shall be denied before the angels of God.
10 And whoever shall speak a word against the Son of Humanity, it shall be forgiven them: but they who blaspheme against the Holy Spirit it shall not be forgiven.

11 And when they bring you to the synagogues, and to the magistrates, and powers, you take no thought how or what thing you shall answer, or what you shall say:
12 for the Holy Spirit shall teach you in the same hour what you ought to say."

After dining with the Pharisees, the dialogue, which included vv. 1-12, was directed specifically at the disciples with the grown number of the innumerable crowd of people, nonetheless also being present too.

The '*certain woman of the company*' who cried out just prior to Jesus dining with the Pharisees (11:27), who was from the first crowd, further adds to the scenario, along with the fact of '*one the company*' being from the next arrival of the third gathering (12:13). Which as we have seen would have included Scribes and Pharisees, with Jesus addressing the disciples once again, advising them to beware of their doctrine, sadly pervaded with hypocrisy (v. 1).

Moreover, Luke tells us in his following narrative, through antithesis, in distinguishing between the crowds, which included the Scribes and Pharisees, that Jesus, having directed His words to the disciples in the previous text (vv. 1-12), afterwards relates Luke's indigenous *Parable of the Rich Fool*, now addressed at '*one of the company*' of the grown crowd (vv. 13-21), goes on to relay, directing back again His next discourse to the disciples (vv. 22-34), including the *Parable of the Watchful Servants* (vv. 35-40).

Peter, directly afterwards, then wonders if the parable was applicable to the crowds, too (v. 41), with Jesus going on to indicate by the next *Parable of the Faithful Steward* (vv. 42-48), that there was no discrimination, and indeed it applied to anyone who was ready, or '*watching*', as the previous *Parable of the Watchful Servants* had alluded.

THE RICH FOOL

Luke 12

13 And one of the company said to Him,
"Master, speak to my brother, that he divide the inheritance with me."
14 And He said to him, "Man, who made Me a judge or divider over you?

15 And He said to them,
"Take heed, and beware of covetousness: for an individual's life doesn't consist of the abundance of the things which they possess."

16 And He spoke a parable to them, saying,
"The ground of a certain rich person was very productive:
17 and they thought within themselves, saying,
'What shall I do, because I have no room where to store my crops?'
18 And they said, 'This is what I'll do; I'll pull down my barns, and build greater; and there I'll store all my fruits and my goods.
19 And I'll say to my soul, "Soul, you have much goods laid up for many years; take your ease, eat, drink, and be merry."'
21 So are they who lay up treasure for themselves, and are not rich toward God."

Luke 12

22 And He said to His disciples,

"Therefore I say to you, take no thought for your life, what you shall eat; neither the body, what you shall put on.

23 Life is superior to food, and the body superior to clothing.

24 Consider the ravens: for they neither sow nor reap; who have neither storehouse nor barn; and God feeds them: how much more are you better than birds?

25 And which one of you with taking thought can add to his lifespan any amount?

26 If you then are not able to do that thing which is nominal, why take you thought for the rest?

27 Consider the lilies how they grow: they don't toil, they don't spin; and yet I say to you, that Solomon in all his glory was not arrayed like one of these.

28 If then God so clothe the flora, which is today in the field, and tomorrow is cast into the furnace; how much more will He clothe you, Oh you of little faith?

29 And don't seek what you shall eat, or what you shall drink, neither live in doubtful suspense.

30 For all these things do the nations of the world seek after: and your Father knows that you have need of these things.

31 But rather seek the Kingdom of God; and all these things shall be added to you.

32 Don't fear, little flock; for it is your Father's good pleasure to give you the Kingdom.

33 Sell what you have, and give kindness; provide yourselves money-bags which don't wear out, a treasure in the Heavens that fails not, where no thief approaches, neither moth spoils.

34 For where your treasure is, there your will heart be also.

THE WATCHFUL SERVANTS AND FAITHFUL STEWARD

35 Be dressed in readiness, with your lights lit;

36 and yourselves like to people who wait for their lord, when he returns from the wedding; that when he comes and knocks, they may open to him immediately.

37 Blessed are those servants, whom the lord when he comes shall find watching: truly I say to you, that he shall prepare himself, and make them sit down to eat, and will come forward and serve them.

38 And if he shall come in the second watch [9 p.m.], or come in the third

watch [midnight], and find them so, blessed are those servants.

39 And this know, that if the head of the house had known what the thief would come, he would have watched, and not have allowed his house to be broken through.
40 You therefore be found ready also: for the Son of Humanity comes at a hour when you don't think."

41 Then Peter said to Him,
"Lord, did You speak this parable to us, or even to all?"
42 And the Lord said,
"Who then is that faithful wise steward, whom his lord shall make ruler over his household, to give them their portion of provisions in due season?
43 Blessed is that servant, whom his lord when he comes shall find so doing.
44 Of a truth I say to you, that he will make them ruler over all he has.

45 But and if that servant say in his heart, 'My lord delays his coming,' and shall begin to beat the menservants and maidservants, and to eat and drink, and be drunk;
46 the lord of that servant will come in a day when they look not for him and at a hour when they are not aware, and will cut them off, and appoint them their portion with the unbelievers.

47 And that servant, who knew his lord's will, and prepared not themselves, neither did according to his will, shall be beaten with many strokes.
48 But they who didn't know, and did commit things worthy of blows, shall be beaten with few strokes. For to whomever much is given, of those shall be required much: and to themselves, neither did according to his will, shall be beaten with many strokes.
For to whomever much is given, of those shall be required much: and to whom much is committed, of those they will ask more.

DISCERNMENT AND ATTITUDE

49 I am come to send fire on the earth; and what will I, if it were already kindled?
50 But I have a baptism to be baptized with; and how constrained am I until it is accomplished.

51 You suppose that I am come to give peace on earth? I tell you, no; but rather division:
52 for from now on there shall be five in one house divided, three against two, and two against three.

Luke 12

53 FATHER WILL BE DIVIDED AGAINST SON, AND THE SON AGAINST FATHER;
MOTHER AGAINST DAUGHTER, AND THE DAUGHTER AGAINST HER MOTHER, AND THE
DAUGHTER-IN-LAW AGAINST HER MOTHER-IN-LAW (Mic. 7:6)."

Luke continues, indicating in vv. 54-59 through antithesis once more, in distinguishing between the disciples, and '*the people*', who now Jesus was specifically addressing, after He had directed His previous words to the disciples. After answering Peter's question on whether the *Parable of the Watchful Servants* applied to all (vv. 41-53), though the crowds were present, Jesus now reverts back once more to directing His words '*also to the people*' (v. 54), which, as we have seen, included the Scribes and Pharisees.

---

54 And He said also to the people, "When you see a cloud rise out of the west, immediately you say, '*A storm is coming*,' and so it does.

55 And when you see the south wind blow, you say, '*It will be hot*,' and so it occurs.

56 You hypocrites, you can discern the face of the sky and of the earth; but how is it that you do not discern this time?

57 Yes, and why even of yourselves don't you judge what is right?

58 When you go with your adversary to the Magistrate, as you are on the way, give diligence that you may be delivered from them; lest they drag you to the to the Judge, and the Judge deliver you to the officer, and the officer send you to prison.

59 I tell you, you shall not depart from there, till you have paid the very last mite."

Luke 13

1 There were present at that season some who told Him of the Galileans, whose blood Pilate had mingled with their sacrifices.

2 And Jesus answering said to them,
"You suppose that these Galileans were sinners above all the Galileans, because they suffered such things?

3 I tell you, no: but, except you repent, you shall all likewise perish.

4 Or those eighteen upon whom the Tower of Siloam fell, and killed them, do you think that they were sinners above any individual who dwelt in Jerusalem?

5 I tell you, no: but, except you repent, you shall all likewise perish."

6 He spoke also this parable;

"A certain man had a fig-tree planted in his vineyard; and he came and sought fruit on it, and found none.

7 Now he said to the dresser of his vineyard, 'Look, these three years I come seeking fruit on this fig-tree, and find none: cut it down; why does it cumber the ground?'

8 And he answering said to him, 'Lord, let it alone this year also, till I shall dig about it, and fertilize it:

9 and if it bear fruit, well: and if not, then after that you shall cut it down.'"

Luke refers to '*that season*' (13:1), which was now coming up to *The Third Festival of Tabernacles*. Moreover, with Jesus and the disciples, having come up from Galilee also to go to the Festival, and the people who came from that region, Jesus went on to relate, no doubt specifically to the Scribes and Pharisees of Jerusalem, who were amongst these '*innumerable crowd*' (12:1), about having a perspicacious attitude (v. 54-59), and directly following, the correct attitude to disasters that had occurred (13:1-5).

Luke, thus continued to show through antithesis, by contrasting the two factors of the areas, and the attitude of the disciples as compared to the Pharisees, through Jesus addressing the question of a tragedy which had taken place amongst the Galileans, who had come up to Jerusalem, by referring to a tragedy that had also occurred at Jerusalem.

Luke then, showed how Jesus proceeded to relate directly afterwards to the two tragedies, ironically, the following indigenous *Parable of the Barren Fig-Tree* (vv. 6-9), aimed at some of the hierarchy in the crowd, and those who had mentioned the tragedy of the Galileans. This brought the episode of that day to a close, as we shall see in the next section.

JESUS COMPLETES THE MISSION

Luke, through the next event, informs us Jesus was now in a synagogue, and introduces the **thirty-third miracle** of the healing of the crippled woman, which also took place on a Sabbath (13:10-17), where Jesus mentions the *Parable of the Mustard Seed* (vv. 18-19), and the *Parable of Leaven* both in relation to the Kingdom of God (vv. 20-21). Jesus had mentioned previously the *Parable of the Mustard Seed*, and the *Parable of Leaven*, at Capernaum the year before [p. 136]. Luke had written much of his last preceding incidents, in leaving the other detail of the complete scenario until later in his text, including the following event in the synagogue of the healing of the crippled woman, the thirty-third miracle, and now indicates a change of direction, but not the vicinity of Judea in traveling towards Jerusalem again at v. 22.

We see that after the discourses on the Mt. Olives, the dining with the Pharisees, and the subsequent narrative which no doubt took place at Jerusalem, the scene now shifts again with the reference to it being in the synagogue on the Sabbath Day (v. 10), and the healing of the crippled woman (vv. 11-13). Of course, when considering this whole event in its entire context, which includes vv. 10-21, we see that from v. 10, as shown by a new paragraph as indicated in many other translations, this event was separate and distinct from the preceding narrative, which was in a different setting and on an ordinary day. The detail of that referred to the great crowds outside, as we saw, with the Scribes and Pharisees in the audience. However, inappropriately older versions of the AV start the new paragraph with v. 11.

When we consider how Luke had written certain detail last, we see then that this was once again Luke's style in indicating that a change in the setting had taken place. But because Luke had not revealed a complete change in the actual general area, moreover, it was his way of confirming that this event was in any case, still in the same specific vicinity, knowing that Jerusalem was in the area of Judea.

It is not until the dialogue at the synagogue had concluded at v. 21, that Luke reveals that, at any rate Jesus had left Jerusalem, where He had been addressing the Scribes and Pharisees, before the thirty-third miracle in the synagogue, and was continuing with the mission of visiting some of '*the cities and villages, teaching, and journeying toward Jerusalem*' again (v. 22), as the seventy had earlier announced His coming (10:1).

Thus, once more we must conclude that this was Luke's way of indicating that the event of the thirty-third miracle was in one of those towns of Judea that he had referred to by his style of writing, in mentioning those details in the proceeding of his narration.

Also, we see moreover, that the factor of '*three*' is alluded to, at this time, in the sense that *The Third Festival of Tabernacles* was about to start. Including three being actually mentioned three times, in regards to the indigenous *Parable of the Barren Fig-Tree* (13:6-9), the *Parable of Leaven* again, this time in the synagogue (vv. 20-

21), and where Jesus enters Jerusalem at the start of the Festival, in referring *'today and tomorrow, and the third day'* (v. 32). Additionally, the number eighteen, the years in which the woman was crippled and made free from her infirmity on the Sabbath, can be divided by six, three times, symbolizing the *'six days in which we ought to work'* (v. 14), and the freedom by which we can be set loose from any bond in the completeness of the healing Power of the Holy Spirit, on the Sabbath and any day.

Elaborating even further, Jesus uses the same prophecy about Jerusalem (vv. 34-35), again, just before the final Passover (Mat. 23:37-39). But at this juncture, it alluded to *The Third Festival of Tabernacles*, in the sense that He must still yet finish His work *'today, and tomorrow, and the day following'* (Luke 13:33). Three sets of time, in which there was now, still the third Tabernacles, of that year [today] to be completed, the third Passover of the following year [tomorrow], with the fourth Tabernacles in the same year and then the concluding ultimate Passover in the next year [the day following].

Luke 13

10 And He was teaching in one of the synagogues on the Sabbath.

11 And, consider, there was a woman, who had a spirit of infirmity eighteen years, and was bowed together, and could in no way lift up herself.

12 And when Jesus saw her, He called her to Him, and said to her,
"Woman, you are loosed from your infirmity."

13 And He laid His hands on her: and immediately she was made straight, and glorified God.

14 And the president of the synagogue, answered with indignation, because that Jesus had healed on the Sabbath Day, and said to the people,
"There are six days in which we ought to work: in them therefore come and be healed, and not on the Sabbath Day."

15 The Lord then answered him,
"You hypocrite, doesn't each one of you on the Sabbath untie their ox or their ass from the stall, and lead them away to watering?

16 And ought not this woman, being a daughter of Abraham, whom Satan has bound, see, these eighteen years, be loosed from this bond on the Sabbath Day?"

17 And when He had said these things, all His adversaries were ashamed: and all all the people rejoiced for all the glorious things that were done by Him.

18 Then He said,
"To what is the Kingdom of God like? And to what shall I resemble it?

Luke 13
19 It is like a grain of mustard seed, which an individual took, and cast into their garden; and it grew, and became a tree; and THE BIRDS OF THE SKY SHELTERED IN ITS BRANCHES (Ps. 104:12; Eze. 17:23; 31:6; Dan. 4:12)."

20 And again He said, "To what shall I liken the Kingdom of God?
21 It is like leaven, which a woman took and hid in three measures of flour, till the whole was leavened."

We had seen when considering the sending of the seventy into Judea, that Jesus would be going through the towns and villages, to where they had originally been sent (10:1).

Luke had informed us of the consecutive order of their travels, because of the reason why he wrote in the first instance. He had shown that when Jesus and the seventy originally left Galilee and came through Samaria (9:51-57), that subsequently, after their mission without Jesus, '*it came to pass, as they went* [after meeting up again], *that He entered*' also the '*certain village*' of Bethany (10:38), which meant from the border of Samaria/Judea they came through Judea, to Bethany, near to Jerusalem.

Moreover, '*the teaching in one of the synagogues*' would have been the fulfillment of Jesus' arrival to where the seventy had been and announced His coming. Thus Luke indicated, by following his normal characteristic of recording when a change had occurred, that Jesus had gone through some of the towns, and left going through some of the others until nearer Tabernacles, in '*journeying toward Jerusalem*' again (13:22), timing His entry to coincide exactly when Tabernacles was about to begin, as we shall see, with its first Sabbath, which would begin when the sun had set, as the days are reckoned in Judaism. '*The same day*' (v. 31), or as some translations read, '*At*', or '*In that very hour*', poignantly describes the setting for this entry into Jerusalem.

The Gospel of John refers to this time by mentioning the aspect of the Pharisees, '*the Jews*' (7:13), as he describes them, who were expecting Jesus, and the difference between '*the people*' (v. 12), the common Jews. Thus, John shortly dovetails with Luke 13:31 with his references, by synchronizing along with Luke's record corresponding to the start of Tabernacles (7:11).

Furthermore, the mentioning again by Luke as his characteristic style had been before Pentecost, in the recording of Sabbaths in his text then, several months back [pp. 102-103], moreover, is significant, as now, he once more has Sabbaths, and now eight in his text of ch. 13:10-14:1-6, at this autumn season.

Amazingly, there are in fact in the Biblical Calendar, eight Annual Holy Day Convocations (Lev. 23), which concludes with the Last Great Sabbath at the end of the Festival of Tabernacles in that eighth day period to which point we have now also come at John 7:37.

Luke 13

22 And He went through the cities and villages, teaching and journeying toward Jerusalem.

23 Then someone said to Him, "Lord, are there few who are saved?"
And He said to them,
24 "Strive to enter in at the narrow gate: for many, I say to you, will seek to enter in, and shall not be able.

25 When once the Master of the house is risen up, and has shut the door, and you begin to stand outside, and to knock at the door, saying, 'Lord, Lord, open to us,' and He shall answer and say to you, 'I don't know where you are from.'
26 Then shall you begin to say, 'We have eaten and drunk in Your presence, and You have taught in our streets.
27 But He shall say, 'I tell you, I don't know where you are from; (Ps. 6:8) DEPART FROM ME, ALL YOU WORKERS OF INJUSTICES.'

28 There shall be weeping and gnashing of teeth, when you shall see Abraham, and Isaac, and Jacob, and all the prophets, in the Kingdom of God, and you yourselves thrust out.
29 And they shall come from the East, and from the West, and from the North, and from the South, and shall sit down in the Kingdom of God.
30 And, understand, there are some who are last who will be first, and there are some who are first who will be last."

THE THIRD FESTIVAL OF TABERNACLES

The point at which John dovetails with Luke's narrative must refer to the point where Jesus had completed His going into the towns and villages that the seventy had been, and included Jesus' original purpose, '*to go*' and '*be received up*', at '*Jerusalem*' (Luke 9:51).

With the discourse of Jesus having addressed the disciples, the Scribes Pharisees, and the great crowds now over, and in regards to the fact that He had left the Jerusalem area afterwards, to go to complete the mission to the rest of the towns and villages, resulted in the Pharisees and the people of Jerusalem wondering where He had gone (John 7:11). Additionally, as He had already been there earlier, the division amongst the people, whether He was a good Man or not (v. 12), was fueled by the Scribes and Pharisees persistent and nefarious claim that He worked through the Devil (Luke 11:15). Luke's narrative after completing the mission referred to Jesus' return, '*journeying toward Jerusalem*' again (13:22), and would in any case place the dialogue following near Jerusalem (vv. 23-30). Whereas, the next conversation with the Pharisees, again (vv. 31-33), the prophecy about Jerusalem (vv. 34-35), and the reference to '*the house of one of the Chief Pharisees*' (14:1), would be at the point where Jesus had now directly arrived in the city itself, as it was becoming dark, at the very hour when the first Sabbath of the Festival began. Jesus obviously having been '*invited*' to dine again (v. 12), but this time, at the first meal of the Festival, as we allude, by a Pharisee who was sympathetic to Him (v. 1).

John 7

11 Then the Jews sought Him at the Festival, and said, "Where is He?"
12 And there was much murmuring among the people concerning Him: for some said, "He is a good Man"; others said, "No; but He deceives the people."
13 Nevertheless no one spoke openly for fear of the Jews.

Luke 13

31 The same day there came certain Pharisees, saying to Him,
"You get out, and depart from here: for Herod will kill You."
32 And He said to them,
"You go, and tell that fox, 'Consider, I cast out devils, and I do cures today and tomorrow, and the third day I shall be perfected.
33 Nevertheless I must walk today, and tomorrow, and the day following: for it cannot be that a prophet perish out of Jerusalem.

34 Oh Jerusalem, Jerusalem, who kills the prophets, and stones them whom I sent to you; how often would I have gathered your children together, as a hen gathers her brood under her wings, and you refused!
35 Understand, your House is left desolate: and truly I say to you, you will not see Me, until the time comes when you shall say, (Ps. 118:26) 'BLESSED IS HE WHO COMES IN THE NAME OF THE LORD.'"

Luke 14

1 And it came to pass, as He went into the house of one of the Chief Pharisees to eat bread on the Sabbath Day [15th Tishri], that they watched Him.

2 And, consider, there was a certain man before Him who had oedema.
3 And Jesus, retorting, spoke to the Lawyers and Pharisees, saying,
"Is it lawful to heal on the Sabbath Day?"
4 And they held their peace.

And He took him, and healed him, and let him go;
5 and responding to them, said,
"Which of you shall have an ass or an ox fallen into a pit, and wouldn't immediately pull him out on the Sabbath Day?"

6 And they could not answer Him again regarding these things.

Jesus' quote in v. 35 on the previous page, taken from the Psalms, 'BLESSED IS HE WHO COMES IN THE NAME OF THE LORD', subsequently has a fulfillment, as we shall see, a year later just before the last Tabernacles (Mat. 21:9; Mark 11:9; Luke 19:38), and again just before the final Passover (John 12:1, 12-13). Jesus fulfilling this prophecy, ultimately, would ride into Jerusalem before the last Festival of Tabernacles, and culminate the prophecy by the final entry into Jerusalem before His Passion; thus, riding into Jerusalem twice, as we shall see.

The invitation, as we suggest, at the Festival at the house of one the of the Chief Pharisees, where the thirty-fourth miracle transpired, is rather intriguing at this point, as we now consider other factors.

Some of the Pharisees obviously were not sympathetic towards Jesus, and were extremely annoyed over His miracles and His teachings. Nevertheless, not all of the Pharisees, Scribes and Lawyers despised Him. Predominantly, it was some of those at the top, along with the influence of the Sadducees, who prevailed in causing His death. Moreover, this was the third time that Luke had recorded, exclusively, that a Pharisee had asked Jesus to dine (7:36; 11:37). Consequently, later in this Festival, even the officers of the Pharisees, were loath to arrest Jesus (John 7:45-48). Thus, confirming the general disagreement with those at the top.

With this understanding of these facts we must elucidate further at this juncture, on what actually took place. It is clear that Jesus had wanted to go up to this Festival (7:2-8), after He had sent the seventy ahead of Himself to Judea (Luke 10:1).

Having decided not to go with His brothers, '*not openly, but as it were in secret*' (John 7:10), and in that sense not with any of the festal caravan at that time, He thus left Galilee with the mission of the seventy separately. Also the impression at Jerusalem that He may not have attended this time, would have further developed through His leaving Jerusalem and completing the mission of the seventy before returning again (Luke 11:22).

Remember in the section, *They Prepare to Leave Galilee* [pp. 202-203], we concluded that His brothers in Galilee had heard that He and the seventy were planning the mission to Judea (John 7:3). However, Jesus had not wanted to include traveling with His brothers, along with the mission to Judea. Thus for a short while He stayed behind in Galilee, directly after they left (v. 9).

Some of the people would start arriving at Jerusalem two weeks before the first day and Sabbath of Tabernacles (Lev. 23:34-35), as the Day of Atonement, the most solemn day in the calendar, fell five days prior to the first day and first Sabbath of Tabernacles (v. 27), and Rosh Hashanah the Head of the year [or Festival of Trumpets] ten days earlier than Yom Kippur the Day of Atonement (v. 24). Additionally, the location of the booths [tabernacles] would have to be arranged before the first Sabbath of Tabernacles (vv. 40-42).

However, Jesus would thus appear at the Festival in Jerusalem when most were busy with the final arrangements, and hence be *'received up'* at the reception (Luke 14:13) of one of one of the Chief Pharisee's as near to the start of the festivities as possible. Therefore, it now being dark, and with dining in the evening at supper time (v. 12), as is also alluded to by the *Parable of the Great Banquet* (vv. 16, 24), with the dignitaries, and Lawyers, who were nevertheless somewhat interested, intrigued, and sympathetic towards Jesus, in being discreet in the situation, He would be safe. Of course, those at the top had to be devious and be sure of any workable arrest, as those sympathetic to Jesus and His following, could easily upset and thwart their plan.

THE FIRST EVENING OF TABERNACLES

Luke 14

7 And He put forward a parable to those who were invited, when He marked how they chose out the chief rooms; saying, to them,
8 "When you are invited by someone to a wedding, don't sit down in the highest rooms; lest someone more honorable than you be invited by them;
9 and they who invited you and them come and say to you,
'Give this person place', and you begin with shame to take the lowest room.
10 But when you are invited, go and sit down in the lowest room; that when they who invited you comes, they may say to you, 'Friend, go up higher': then shall you have honor in the presence of those who sit at dinner with you.
11 For whoever exalts themselves shall be abased; and they who humble themselves shall be exalted."

12 Then He said also to him that invited Him,
"When you make a dinner or a supper, call not your friends, nor your brother and sisters, neither your kinsfolk, nor your rich neighbors, lest they also invite you again, and a recompense be made you.
13 But when you hold a reception, call the poor, the maimed, the lame, the blind:
14 and you shall be blessed; for they cannot recompense you: for you shall be recompensed at the Resurrection of the Just."

Before the Festival of Tabernacles commenced, people had been busy with the circumstances surrounding the arrangements of where the booths or tabernacles would be positioned, and had been involved in purification, and some in caring for the offerings they had brought, as well as the joyful fellowship associated with this time. The day before the Festival, when Jesus had returned to Jerusalem, most of the pilgrims would now have arrived. The city and surroundings provided a unique picturesque appearance, with the booths or tabernacles located all over the city, by the roads, in the gardens, and all around Jerusalem, even on the roofs of the dwellings, in the courts of the houses and the Temple, and even in the public square as shown in Nehemiah's day (Neh. 8:1-2).

No doubt on this first Sabbath at the initiation of the Festival, after *The Thirty-Fourth Miracle* of the healing of the man with oedema (Luke 14:1-6), it is significant when Jesus '*marked how they chose out the chief rooms*' (v. 7), and that He directed the *Parable of the Places of Honor* at a wedding to those who were invited to this reception (vv. 8 -14).

It is recorded that Jesus spoke on three different occasions to the Pharisees over the choosing of so-called places of honor.

The first reference is preceding this coming Festival of Tabernacles, where it is mentioned that Jesus dined with them (11:43): secondly, at the point which we are now considering: and thirdly, again alluding to an evening meal, also taken at the opening of each Festival, with the scenario prior to the final Passover (Mat. 23:6; Mark 12:39; Luke 20:46).

The *Parable of the Places of Honor* at a wedding, captures the setting as translated in the NIV, as a guests suggest it would be a blessing to '*eat at the Feast in the Kingdom of God*' (Luke 14:15), which was typified by this Festival [or Feast] of Tabernacles.

Jesus then goes on to relate the *Parable of the Great Banquet*, which further alludes to the Kingdom of God, and the scenario and setting of that first supper meal of the Festival, and the prevalent attitude of some (vv. 16-24). Thus, the first evening meal of the Festival was about to a close with the next day's forthcoming events shortly to unfold.

Luke 14

15 And when one of them who sat at dinner with Him heard these things, he said to Him, "Blessed are they who shall eat bread in the Kingdom of God."
16 Then said Jesus to him,
"A certain person made a great supper, and invited many:
17 And sent his servant at suppertime to say to those who were invited,
'Come; for all things are now ready.'
18 And they all with one consent began to make excuses.

The first said to him, 'I have bought a piece of ground, and I must need go and see it: I pray you have me excused.'

19 And another said, 'I have bought five yoke of oxen, and I go to try them: I pray you have me excused.

20 And another said, 'I have married a wife, and therefore cannot come.'

Luke 14

21 So that servant came, and showed his lord these things
Then the master of the house being angry said to his servant,
'Go out quickly into the streets and lanes of the city, and bring in here the poor, and the maimed, and the cripples, and the blind.'

22 And the servant said, 'Lord, it is done as you have commanded, and yet there is room.'
23 And the lord said to the servant, 'Go out into the highways and hedges, and compel them to come in, that my house may be filled.
24 For I say to you, that none of those guests who were invited shall taste of my supper.'"

'ONE OF THE CHIEF PHARISEES'

Luke had mentioned the evening meal where Jesus dined, at '*the house of one of the Chief Pharisees*' (14:1). In collecting this unique information, which Matthew and Mark had not recorded, Luke would have known the name of this Chief Pharisee. However, Luke only chose to mention certain facts in his narrative, which were paramount to one of the reasons for compiling his Gospel, as he stated at the beginning, '*to write to you in order*,' (1:3). As we have now seen on numerous occasions, and as we shall see with this incident, sometimes, when one Gospel writer omits a certain piece of information, it is the case that another Gospel writer fills in with the particulars that the others left out.

We saw previously that the main reason '*the Jews sought Him* [Jesus] *at the Festival, and said,* "*Where is He?*"' (John 7:11), was because they had wanted to kill Him (v. 1), and that these '*Jews*' were those of the hierarchy, and did not refer to the ordinary common Jews - the people.

Now, because it was not the time for Jesus to accomplish His mission on the cross at Passover, He had to be careful in dealing with that situation, as there was a year and a half to go before the last Passover.

With the concluding of His mission in the vicinity of Judea, and His planning to be received up at Jerusalem just as the first Sabbath was about to begin, combined with the invitation to dine with '*one of the Chief Pharisees*', who was sympathetic and discreet along with the majority of his guests to Jesus, meant that it was extremely difficult for the antagonistic Pharisees to fulfill their wish to kill Him at this time, and in this situation.

Hostile Pharisees were waiting as Jesus came into Jerusalem, and sardonically warned Him that Herod would kill Him (Luke 13:31), as they knew He had been fortuitous in arriving at this most inconvenient time for them, in anticipating their wish to take Him and have Him killed. Nonetheless, Jesus goes on to inform them, He was about to '*do cures today*' (v. 32), through the miracle of the healing of the man with oedema, the thirty-fourth miracle, at '*the house of one of the Chief Pharisees*', and continues to inform them that He still had yet further work to accomplish before His decease at Jerusalem (v. 33).

After Jesus had related ironically, '*Jerusalem, Jerusalem, which kills the prophets*' (v. 34), and the prophecy relating to the fall of Jerusalem (v. 35), these Pharisees who wanted Jesus dead, would report back and inform their unsympathetic contemporaries that He had arrived. But, because of the crowds at the Festival, and that it was the first Sabbath of Tabernacles, the unreceptive Pharisees knowing there would likely be an uproar, Jesus was protected as He had been invited to the reception of the Festival as a guest at the first supper, and by the factor of many dignitaries being present, too.

This, '*one of the Chief Pharisees*', to whose house Jesus went, would have also been '*a Ruler of the Jews*', and would have been a member of the Sanhedrin, too.

And since the Gospel of John, is the only Gospel which relates to where we now are in Luke, and the next following events, and moreover, was the last Gospel to be completed, it is he who would give us the information who this particular Chief Pharisee may have been. Furthermore, amazingly John also includes reference to the thirty-fourth miracle, later in his dialogue (7:21-23), of which we will cover in more detail when we arrive at that subsequent point. The answer to whom this influential Pharisee may have been, is found in the same chapter of John, that refers to this Festival, and the **thirty-fourth miracle**!

As John is complementing Luke's account, by originally informing us directly through the particular time of year being the '*Festival of Tabernacles*' (v. 2), as we covered previously, he goes on further to mention '*the middle of the Festival*' (v. 14), and also, '*the Last Day, that Great Day of the Festival*' (v. 37), at which point the Pharisees were continuing to look for an opportunity, now as the Festival was concluding, to take Jesus (v. 45). They admonish the officers as to why they had not taken Jesus, and then go onto ask, '*Have any of the Rulers or the Pharisees believed on Him?*' (v. 48).

It was Nicodemus, '*a Pharisee... a Ruler of the Jews*' (3:1), who not only '*came to Jesus by night, being one of them*' (7:50), originally at *The First Passover* (2:23) and now no doubt at this Tabernacles, who spoke up for Jesus, admonishing that the Law does not condemn anyone until one has had the ability to speak up on any accusation (7:51). Thus John further revealed that Nicodemus had a genuine interest in Jesus, through the dialogue about being born-again that originally transpired between them (3:2-21). One and half years later he still had an interest.

Furthermore, Luke had recorded that the *Parable of the Places of Honor* at a wedding was especially addressed to, and elucidated on, to this friendly Pharisee who had invited Jesus (14:12-14). In the same manner Jesus explained the particular meaning of parables to disciples who did not fully grasp the intended meaning immediately, and as He had explained the meaning of being born-again, originally to Nicodemus.

Moreover, in this unique Central Section, Luke so far had indicated from the juncture where the seventy and Jesus came into Samaria and Judea (9:51), right up to the text we are about to consider (14:25), at least twenty-five changes, as relating to location, including describing when an incident changed in detail from one scenario to another setting, and whether it had changed to a different day, even to pointing out the differences between whom Jesus was addressing!

THE NEXT DAY AT THE FESTIVAL

Luke, now once more indicates a shift in setting, also, thus relating to a different time of day, from Jesus having dined at supper, no doubt in the first evening of the Festival, and at the residence of Nicodemus, to the next incident, where *'there went great crowds with Him'* (v. 25). Jesus would have left the scenario of dining with this Pharisee, as obviously in the light of the next daytime, these great crowds would have now followed Him.

Thus, in this next daylight, as Luke does not again, at this juncture, reveal any other time or scenario change, Jesus would teach the rest of the narrative, recorded in Luke's *Conclusion of the Central Section* (14:25-17:10), to the great crowds and the disciples. No doubt this took place in the Temple area, as the Gospel of John reveals in dovetailing with Luke, and in referring to yet another day subsequently, indicated by *'the middle of the Festival Jesus went up into the Temple and taught'* (7:14). It would be in the vicinity of this area, as Jesus taught, where the crowds would listen and afford Him protection and respite from being arrested by the Pharisees, during the next half of this eight day Festival.

John, having written various detail preceding, too, verified that these events took place at this Festival, and as to some of the aspects of its setting. Furthermore, he related to the middle of the eight day Festival, indicating that Jesus was also, in point of fact teaching in the vicinity of the Temple area. Thus, he further complements Luke, dovetailing precisely, and continues with his text (vv. 14-53), after *Luke's Conclusion of the Central Section* (17:10), proceeding after the day that Luke had alluded to, in teaching the *'great crowds'* who had followed Jesus since the reception supper with the Pharisee and dignitaries (14:25).

Thus, John fills in his narrative with the rest of the events at the Festival. Luke had, preceding this next day, where Jesus is teaching the great crowds, indicated numerous changes in the details of his text. Conversely, as there are no changes suggested in the narrative from Luke 14:25-17:10, we can conclude it was Luke's particular method of indicating that this concluding part of the *Conclusion of the Central Section* all transpired on this same particular day, as Jesus taught the great crowds, before yet again another day where John's dialogue dovetails with *'the middle of the Festival'*.

Luke 14
25 And there went great crowds with Him: and He turned and said to them,
26 "If anyone comes to Me, who doesn't love less their father, and mother, and wife, and children, and brothers, and sisters, yes, and their own life also, they cannot be My disciple.
27 And whoever does not bear their cross, and come after Me cannot be My disciple.

28 For which of you, tending to build a tower, sits down first, and counts the

cost, whether they have sufficient to finish it?

29 Otherwise, after they have laid the foundation, and are not able to finish it, all who observe it begin to mock them.

30 Saying, 'This person began to build, and was not able to finish.'

31 Or what king, going to make war against another king, will not sit down first, and consults whether he is able with ten thousand to meet him that comes against him with twenty thousand?

32 Or else, while the other is yet a great way off, he sends a delegation, and desires conditions of peace.

33 So likewise, whoever they are of you who doesn't renounce all that they have, they cannot be My disciple.

34 Salt is good: but if the salt has lost its savor, with what shall it be seasoned?

35 It is neither fit for the land, nor yet for fertilizer; but people throw it out. Those who have ears to hear, let them hear."

Jesus, teaching the great crowds that followed Him after the first supper of the Festival (v. 25), goes on to relate to them aspects of *Discipleship* (vv. 26-27), repeating part of what He had taught previously to the disciples [p. 113, at Mat. 10:37-38], as many were becoming increasingly interested to know more of what they had heard about Him.

However, at this juncture Jesus includes two synonymous analogies found only in Luke: about counting the cost of becoming a disciple, through the *Parable of Building a Tower* (14:28-30), and the *Parable of the Warring King* (vv. 30-33). Jesus concludes with the analogy, typified by the *Parable of Salt* (vv. 34-36), which He had mentioned twice previously to His disciples at separate incidents [p. 60, at Mat. 5:13, and p. 200 at Mark 9:50], before his next discourse the '*tax collectors and sinners*', who also came near to hear (Luke 15:1).

The Pharisees and Scribes also noticing this, but indignant at the situation (v. 2), Jesus thus repeats the P*arable of the Lost Sheep*, directed specifically '*to them*' (vv. 3-7), which He had related before at Mat. 18:12-14 [pp. 200-201], with Luke synonymously continuing, includes two further parables, indigenous to him - the *Parable of the Lost Coin* (15:8-10), and the *Parable of the Prodigal Son* (vv. 11-32).

Luke 15

1 Then drew near to Him all the tax collectors and sinners for to hear Him.

2 And the Pharisees and Scribes murmured, saying, "This Man receives sinners, and eats with them."

3 And He related these parables to them, saying,
4 "Which one of you, having a hundred sheep, if losing one of them, wouldn't leave the ninety and nine in the wilderness, and go after that which is lost, until they find it?
5 And when they have found it, they lay it on their shoulders, rejoicing.
6 And when they come home, they call together their friends and neighbors, saying to them, 'Rejoice with me; for I have found my sheep who was lost.'
7 I say to you, that likewise joy shall be in Heaven over one sinner who repents, more than over the ninety and nine just persons, who need no repentance.

8 Either what woman having ten silver coins, if she lose one coin, wouldn't light a lamp, and sweep the house, and seek diligently till she find it?
9 And when she has found it, calls her friends and her neighbors together, saying, 'Rejoice with me; for I have found the coin which I had lost.'

10 Likewise, I say to you, there is joy in the presence of the angels of God over one sinner who repents."

PARABLE OF THE PRODIGAL SON

11 And He said, "A certain man had two sons:
12 and the younger of them said to his father, 'Father, give me the portion of goods that falls to me.'
And he divided to them his living.

13 And not many days after the younger son gathered all together, and took his journey into a far country, and there wasted his substance with riotous living.
14 And when he had spent all of it, there arose a severe famine in that land; and he began to be in want.
15 And he went and joined himself to a citizen of that country; and he sent him into his fields to feed swine.
16 And he would gladly have filled his stomach with the husks that the swine did eat: and no one gave to him.

17 And when he came to himself, he said, 'How many hired servants of my father's have bread enough and to spare, and I perish with hunger!
18 I will rise and go to my father, and will say to him, 'Father, I have sinned against Heaven, and before you,

Luke 15

19 and am no more worthy to be called your son: make me as one of your hired servants.

20 And he rose up, and came to his father. But when he was yet a great way off, his father saw him, and had compassion, and ran, and fell on his neck, and kissed him.

21 And the son said to him, 'Father, I have sinned against Heaven, and in your sight, and am no more worthy to be called your son.

22 But the father said to his servants, 'Bring out the best robe, and put it on him; and put a ring on his hand, and shoes on his feet:

23 and bring the fatted calf, and kill it; and let us eat, and be merry:

24 for this my son was dead, and is alive again; he was lost, and is found.' And they began to be merry.

25 Now his elder son was in the field: and as he came and drew near to the house, he heard music and dancing.

26 And he called one of the servants, and asked what these things meant.

27 And he said to him, 'Your brother has come; and your father has killed the fatted calf, because he has received him safe and sound.'

28 And he was angry, and would not go in: therefore his father came out, and called him.

29 And answering said to his father, 'Look, these many years I have served you, neither did I neglect at any time your orders: and yet you never gave me a goat, that I might make merry with my friends:

30 but as soon as this your son was come, who has devoured your living with prostitutes, you have killed the fatted calf for him.'

31 And he said to him, 'Son, you are always with me, and all that I have is yours.

32 It was proper that we should make merry, and be glad: for this your brother was dead, and is alive again; and was lost, and is found.'"

PARABLE OF THE UNJUST MANAGER

With the great crowds, the tax collectors, sinners, Pharisees and Scribes still present, in the day after dining at the house of one of the Chief Pharisees, Jesus switches from speaking directly to them, '*also to His disciples*' (16:1), relating the Parable of the Unjust Manager, unique to Luke (vv. 1-8), and elucidates on it further to the disciples (vv. 9-13).

Luke confirms that the Pharisees were still present at that point, as continuing Jesus again returns to address them, in admonishing them in the following scenario of this day (vv. 14-15).

Luke 16

1 And He said also to His disciples,
"There was a certain rich man, who had a manager; and the same was
accused by him that they had wasted his goods.

2 And he called them, and said to them, 'How is it that I hear this of you?
Give an account of your management; for you may no longer be a manager.'

3 Then the manager said within himself, 'What shall I do? For my boss takes
the management away from me: I cannot dig; to beg I am ashamed.
4 I am resolved what to do, that, when I am removed from management, they
may receive me into their houses.'

5 So he called each one of his boss's debtors to him, and said to the first,
'How much do you owe my boss?'
6 And they said, 'A hundred measures of oil.'
And he said to him, 'Take your bill, and sit quickly, and write fifty.'

7 Then said he to another, 'And how much do you owe?'
And they said, 'A hundred measures of wheat.'
And he said to them, 'Take your bill, and write eighty.'

8 And the boss commended the unjust manager, because they had done
wisely: for the children of this world are in their generation wiser than the
children of light.

9 And I say to you, make to yourselves friends of the riches of
unrighteousness; that when you fail, they may receive you into everlasting
habitations.

10 They who are faithful in that which is least are faithful also in much: and
they who are unjust in the least are unjust also in much.

11 If therefore you have not been faithful with unrighteous riches, who will
commit to your trust the true riches?
12 And if you have not been faithful in that which is another's who shall give
you that which is your own?

13 No servant can serve two masters: for either they will hate the one, and
love the other; or else they will hold to the one, and despise the other.
You cannot serve God and riches."

After the Pharisees had '*heard all these things*' too (v. 14), and Jesus had admonished them (vv. 15-18), He proceeds to relate the *Parable of the Rich Man and Lazarus*, indigenous to Luke to them (vv. 19-31).

Luke 16

14 And the Pharisees, who were covetous, heard all these things: and they ridiculed Him.

15 And He said to them,

"You are they who justify yourselves before humans; but God knows your hearts: for that which is highly esteemed among humans is abomination in the sight of God.

16 The Law and the Prophets were even until John: because of that, then the Kingdom of God is preached, and everyone strives toward it.

17 And it is easier for the heavens and the earth to pass, than one stroke of a letter of the Law to fail.

18 Whoever puts away his wife, and marries another commits adultery: and whoever marries her who is put away from her husband commits adultery.

PARABLE OF THE RICH MAN AND LAZURUS

19 There was a certain rich man, who was clothed in purple and fine linen, and fared sumptuously every day:

20 and there was a certain beggar named Lazarus, who was laid at his gate, full of sores,

21 and desiring to be fed with the crumbs that fell from the rich man's table: moreover even dogs came and licked his sores.

22 And it came to pass, that the beggar died, and was carried by the angels to Abraham's side: the rich man also died, and was buried;

23 and in hell he lifted up his eyes, being in torments, and sees Abraham afar off, and Lazarus by his side.

24 And he cried and said, 'Father Abraham, have mercy on me, and send Lazarus, that he may dip the tip of his finger in water, and cool my tongue; for I am tormented in this flame.'

25 But Abraham said, 'Son, remember that you in your lifetime received your good things, and likewise Lazarus evil things: but now he is comforted, and you are tormented.

26 And beside all this, between you and us, there is a great gulf fixed: so that they who would pass from here to you cannot; neither can they pass to us, who would come from there.

Luke 16

27 Then he said, 'I pray you therefore, father, that you would send him to my father's house:

28 for I have five brothers; that he may testify to them, lest they also come to this place of torment.'

29 Abraham says to him, 'They have Moses and the Prophets; let them hear them.'

30 And he said, 'No, father Abraham: but if one went to them from the dead, they will repent.'

31 And he said to him, 'If they hear not Moses and the Prophets, neither will they be persuaded, though one rose from the dead.'"

CONCLUSION OF THE CENTRAL SECTION

Luke had concluded the last part of his Conclusion of the Central Section (17:1-10), with Jesus and the disciples in this particular same day of Tabernacles, after the great crowds (14:25), tax collectors, sinners (15:1), and Scribes (v. 2), had converged around them, with once again Jesus addressing the disciples, after admonishing the Pharisees (vv. 14-15), when He related the Parable of the Rich Man and Lazarus specifically to them (vv. 16-31).

This Conclusion of the Central Section, had included the sending of the seventy, and Jesus teaching them the same things He had the twelve. Luke, now through antithesis, once again, indicates the difference at this juncture between the scenario of the variant settings, by the two groups of disciples, with Jesus relating '*to the* [seventy] *disciples*' what He had previously taught the twelve (17:1-4), in now referring to the twelve as '*the apostles*'. At which point they ask Jesus to increase their faith (v. 5), after having heard once more what Jesus had just mentioned to the seventy.

It is significant in having discussed previously about the two groups of disciples, in association with the events surrounding *The Transfiguration* that Jesus now at this juncture, continues once again with the *Parable of Faith as a Grain of Mustard Seed*. Though having referred to it before after the healing of thirtieth miracle, when having returned down from the mountain after *The Transfiguration* (Mat. 17:20), here in Luke, Jesus is recorded replacing the word '*mountain*' with '*mulberry tree*' (17:6).

The *Parable of the Unprofitable Servants* (vv. 7-10) ends that day's notable events of the concluding part of Luke's narrative connected totally to the Central Section.

Luke 17

1 Then said He to the disciples,

"It is impossible but that offenses will come: but woe to those through whom they come!

2 It were better for them that a millstone were hung about their neck, and they were cast into the sea, than that they should offend one of these little ones.

3 Take heed to yourselves: if your brother or sister trespass against you, rebuke them; and if they repent, forgive them.

4 And if they trespass against you seven times in a day, and seven times in a day turn again to you, saying, 'I repent,' you shall forgive them."

5 And the apostles said to the Lord, "Increase our faith."

6 And the Lord said,

"If you had faith as a grain of mustard seed, you might say to this mulberry tree, 'Be plucked up by the root, and be planted in the sea'; and it should obey you.

7 But which of you, having a servant ploughing or feeding cattle, will say to them immediately, when they are come from the field, 'Go and sit down to eat?'

8 And will not rather say to them, 'Make ready whereupon I may eat, and prepare yourself, and serve me, till I have eaten and drunk; and afterwards you shall eat and drink?'

9 Do they thank that servant because they did the things that were commanded them? I think not.

10 So likewise you, when you shall have done all those things which are commanded you, say, 'We are unprofitable servants: we have done that which was our duty to do.'"

Concluding with the events of this day of the Festival, we return to the Gospel of John, whereby he fills in and continues with the information relating to the rest of the Festival. Jesus continued teaching in the Temple grounds, as we suggested when considering the combined text of Luke 14:25-36 including ch. 15-16, right through to ch. 17:10, at which point Luke concluded that day's teaching, and at which junction the Gospel of John returns, with Jesus teaching again this next day.

Thirty-Fourth Miracle - Man With Oedema

After the Scribes and Pharisees had listened to what Jesus had taught the great crowds, they proceeded to put the poison down, because of their jealousy over Jesus' insight particularly regarding where Jesus had received His education (John 7:15-18). John continued to relate further to the fact that they were still looking for ways to kill Him (vv. 19-20).

Referring to the only miracle, at that particular junction in John, as we should see, was the thirty-fourth, Jesus declared, '*I have done one work, and you all marvel*' (v. 21). Jesus then goes on to refer to the irony that they circumcised on the Sabbath Day (v. 22), and yet they were perturbed over a healing on that day.

Next, John continues, mentioning the healing of a man, which had taken place on a particular Sabbath (v. 23). But nowhere in his text, at this juncture, is there any description to what actually occurred previously. John only relates to this miracle in the past tense.

From 7:2, including vv. 3-13, all relate to aspects of going up to this specific Festival at Jerusalem from Galilee. Anything before then, and including reverting back to 6:1, all takes place previously, in the area of Galilee, and covers a period of six months back, relating to the last Passover there.

Retrospectively, reverting even further back still, to the whole of ch. 5, which includes yet another six months, and relates to the previous Festival of Tabernacles, before the one we are now considering. Thus, the narrative of ch. 5 takes place a complete year before that of ch. 7, with ch. 6, six months before ch. 7. However, of course in ch. 5, there is a reference to Jesus also healing a man on the Sabbath [*the twenty-second miracle*]. Nevertheless, the one in ch. 5, was a year previous, and cannot be the miracle John referred to a whole year later at 7:23.

Obviously, John must have known that Luke had recorded the detail regarding '*one of the Chief Pharisees*' (Luke 14:1), and as we suggested it was actually John who went on to actually name him (7:50). Thus, once more, in the same manner, John connects with Luke again, through the healing in '*the house of* [Nicodemus] *one of the Chief Pharisees*', and also relates to this first Sabbath of the Festival in which the thirty-fourth miracle took place. John further related to this particular incident, by referring to the thirty-fourth miracle only a couple of days later, in the respect of it being still fresh in the Pharisee's minds (vv. 21, 23). Moreover, v. 21 poignantly confirms that Jesus had not at that specific juncture done any other miracles since that first night of the Festival, and the middle of the eight-day Festival.

John 7

14 But when it was now the middle of the Festival [18th Tishri] Jesus went up into the Temple, and taught.

John 7

15 And the Jews marveled, saying,

"How knows this Man letters, having never learned?"

16 Jesus answered them, and said,

"My doctrine is not Mine, but His who sent Me.

17 If anyone will do His will, they shall know of the doctrine, whether it be of God, or whether I speak of Myself.

18 They who speak about themselves seek their own glory: but He who seeks the glory of Him who sent Him, the same is true, and no unrighteousness is in Him.

19 Did not Moses give you the Law, and yet none of you keep the Law? Why do you go about to kill Me?"

20 The people answered and said,

"You have a devil: who goes about to kill You?"

21 Jesus answered and said to them,

"I have done one work, and you all marvel.

22 Moses therefore gave to you (Lev. 12:3) circumcision; (not because it is of Moses, but of (Gen. 17:10-12) the Fathers;) and you on the Sabbath Day circumcise a boy.

23 If boys on the Sabbath Day receive circumcision, that the Law of Moses should not be broken; are you angry at Me, because I have made a man every whit whole on the Sabbath Day?

24 Don't judge according to appearance, but judge righteous judgment."

25 Then said some of them of Jerusalem, "Isn't this He, whom they seek to kill?

26 But, look, He speaks boldly, and they say nothing to Him. Do the Rulers know indeed that this is the very Messiah?

27 Nevertheless we know this Man where He is from: but when the Messiah comes, no one knows where He is from."

28 Then Jesus cried out in the Temple as He taught, saying,

"You both know Me, and you know where I am from: I am not come of Myself, but He who sent Me is true, whom you know not.

29 But I know Him: for I am from Him, and He has sent Me."

30 Then they sought to take Him: but no man laid hands on Him, because His hour was not yet come.

31 And many of the people believed on Him, and said, "When the Messiah comes, will He do more miracles than these which this Man has done?"

32 The Pharisees heard that the people murmured such things concerning Him; and the Pharisees and the Chief Priests sent officers to take Him.

33 Then said Jesus to them,
"Yet a little while I am with you, and then I go to Him who sent Me.
34 You shall seek Me, and shall not find Me: and where I am, you cannot come."

35 Then said the Jews among themselves,
"Where will He go, that we shall not find Him? Will He go to the Diaspora among the Gentiles, and teach the Gentiles?
36 What manner of saying is this that He said, '*You shall seek Me, and shall not find Me: and where I am, you cannot come*?'"

We have seen throughout Luke's *Conclusion of the Central Section* [and indeed throughout the four texts of the Gospels so far] that, as with all writers, one must assume the text each time is referring to the last place of reference, unless it is indicated otherwise.

With John concluding the events of the Festival with the Last Great Day (7:37-8:1), we saw that previously John had mentioned '*the middle of the Festival*', which included vv. 14-36.

THE LAST GREAT DAY

37 In that Last day, that Great Day of the Festival [22nd Tishri], Jesus stood and cried, saying, "If anyone thirsts, let them come to Me, and drink.
38 They who believe on Me, as the Scriptures (Isaiah 44:3; 55:1; 58:11) have said, 'Out of their inner being shall flow rivers of living water.'"

39 (But this He spoke of the Spirit, which they who believe on Him should receive: for the Holy Spirit was not yet given; because that Jesus was not yet glorified.)

40 Many of the people therefore, when they heard this saying, said,
"Of a truth this is the Prophet."
41 Others said, "This is the Messiah."
But some said, "Shall the Messiah come out of Galilee?
42 Hasn't the Scripture (Mic. 5:2) said, that the Messiah comes of the seed of David, and out of the town of Bethlehem, where David was?"

43 So there was a division among the people because of Him.
44 And some of them would have taken Him; but no one laid hands on Him.

John 7

45 Then came the officers to the Chief Priests and Pharisees; and they said to them, "Why have you not brought Him?"

46 The officers answered, "Never a man spoke like this Man."

47 Then, answered them the Pharisees, "Are you also deceived?

48 Have any of the Rulers or of the Pharisees believed on Him?

49 But this people who know the Law are cursed."

50 Nicodemus says to them, (he who came to Jesus by night, being one of them.)

51"Does our Law judge anyone, before it hears them, and knows what they have done?"

52 They answered and said to him, "Are you also of Galilee? Search, and look: for out of Galilee arises no prophet."

53 And everyone went to their own homes.

John 8

1 Jesus went to the Mount of Olives.

THE DAY AFTER THE LAST GREAT DAY

After the Last Great Day, John relates to yet another day, as he does throughout his Gospel by referring to '*the morning*' (8:2), with the case of the woman taken in adultery, which includes vv. 2-11.

However, some versions of the NT place 7:53-8:1-11 in brackets indicating it not being in some manuscripts, with others placing it in varying places.

---

2 And early in the morning [23rd Tishri], He came again into the Temple, and all the people came to Him; and He sat down, and taught them.

3 And the Scribes and Pharisees brought to Him a woman taken in adultery; and when they had set her in the midst,

4 they say to Him,

"Master, this woman was taken in adultery, in the very act.

5 Now Moses in the Law (Deut. 22:22) commanded us, that such should be stoned: but what do You say?"

6 This they said tempting Him, so as they could accuse Him. But Jesus stooped down, and with His finger wrote on the ground, as though He didn't hear them.

7 So when they continued asking Him, He lifted Himself up, and said to them, "He who is without sin among you, let him first cast a stone at her."

John 8

8 And again He stooped down, and wrote on the ground.

9 And they who heard it, being pricked by their own conscience, went out one by one, beginning at the eldest, even to the last: and Jesus was left alone, and the woman standing in the midst.

10 When Jesus had lifted Himself up, and saw none but the woman, He said to her, "Woman, where are those your accusers? Has no man condemned you?"

11 She said, "No man, Lord."
And Jesus said to her, "Neither do I condemn you: go and sin no more."

THE NEXT SABBATH

In this next section, following the woman taken in adultery (8:2-11), we shall see when combing through the text of the next subsequent scenario recorded in which the **thirty-fifth miracle** took place, with the details leading up to it, including the dialogue proceeding after it.

The Last Great Day was the concluding annual Sabbath of the Festival, and after '*everyone went to their own homes*' (7:53), as the booths or tabernacles were no longer necessary, emphasized the completion of that eight day period, with the last and seventh annual Sabbath now being over.

Hence, the next incident '*in the morning*' (8:2), would be in that case another day, on which the dialogue surrounding the woman taken in adultery by the Scribes and Pharisees, who had accused her, and subsequently left with their consciences pricked, included vv. 3-11. John goes on to point out, after the incident of the woman taken in adultery, that '*Jesus spoke again to them*' (v. 12-13), which as we shall see, was a completely different event, and on another particular Sabbath, on a day after the incident of the woman taken in adultery, with the Pharisees being addressed once again.

John further adds, that this next event was taking place in the Temple Treasury, and stated through antitheses, in highlighting the phrase, '*these words*' (8:20), as being separate from the last incident and those words, which related to the discourse of the woman taken in adultery.

Furthermore, John reveals that the whole of this next discourse, of 8:12-59, including ch. 9, right through to 10:21, related to that subsequent Sabbath, as in following through the dialogue of '*these words*', we see that this led the Pharisees wanting to take '*up stones to cast at Him: but Jesus hid Himself, and went out of the Temple, going through the midst of them, and so passed by*' (8:59). In passing by and leaving the Temple, Jesus proceeded directly from there, where the thirty-fifth miracle took place, with the healing of the blind man (9:1-7), which John indicated was still on the same Sabbath (v. 14), which also included the following dialogue relating to that particular Sabbath, and the thirty-fifth miracle (vv. 15-41).

John 8

12 Then spoke Jesus again to them, saying,
"I am the Light of the World: they who follow Me shall not walk in darkness, but shall have the Light of Life."

13 The Pharisees therefore said to Him,
"You bear record of Yourself; Your record is not true."
14 Jesus answered and said to them,
"Though I bear record of Myself, yet My record is true: for I know from where I came, and where I go; but you cannot tell from where I came, and where I go.
15 You judge after the flesh; I judge no one.
16 And yet if I judge, My judgment is true: for I am not alone, but I am with the Father who sent Me.
17 It is written in (Deut. 19:15) your Law that, 'THE TESTIMONY OF TWO PEOPLE IS TRUE.'
18 I am one who bears witness of Myself, and the Father who sent Me bears witness of Me."

19 Then said they to Him, "Where is Your Father?"
Jesus answered, "You neither know Me, nor My Father: if you had known Me, you would have known My Father also."

20 These words Jesus spoke in the Treasury, as He taught in the Temple: and no man laid hands on Him; for His hour was not yet come.

21 Then said Jesus again to them, "I go My way, and you shall seek Me, and shall die in your sins: where I go, you cannot come."

22 Then said the Jews, "Will He kill Himself? Because He said, '*Where I go, you cannot come.*'"
23 And He said to them,
"You are from beneath; I am from Above: you are of this world; I am not of this world.
24 I said therefore to you, that '*You shall die in your sins:*' for unless you believe that I AM He, you shall die in your sins."

25 Then said they to Him, "Who are You?"
And Jesus says to them, "Even the same who I told to you from the beginning.
26 I have many things to say and to judge concerning you: but He who sent Me is true; and I speak to the world those things which I have heard from Him."

27 They didn't understand that He spoke to them of the Father.

28 Then said Jesus to them, "When you have lifted up the Son of Humanity, then you shall know that I AM He, and that I do nothing of Myself; but as My Father has taught Me, I speak those things.

29 And He who sent Me is with Me: the Father hasn't left Me alone; for I always do those things that please Him."
30 And as He spoke these words, many believed on Him.

31 Then said Jesus to those Jews who believed on Him,
"If you continue in My word, then are you My disciples indeed;
32 and you shall know the truth, and the truth shall make you free."
33 They answered Him, "We be Abraham's seed, and were never in bondage to anyone: how can You say, '*You shall be made free?*'"

34 Jesus answered them, "Truly, truly, I say to you, whoever commits sin is the servant of sin.
35 And a servant doesn't remain in the house forever: but the Son remains forever.
36 If the Son therefore shall make you free, you shall be free indeed.
37 I know that you are Abraham's seed; but you seek to kill Me, because My word has no place in you.
38 I speak that which I have seen with My Father: and you do that which you have seen of your father."

39 They answered and said to Him, "Abraham is our father."
Jesus says to them,
"If you were Abraham's children, you would do the works of Abraham.
40 But now you seek to kill Me, a Man who has told you the truth, which I have heard from God: Abraham didn't do this.
41 You do the deeds of your father."

Then said they to Him,
"We weren't born through sexual immorality; we have one Father, even God."
42 Jesus said to them,
"If God were your Father, you would love Me for I proceeded forth and came from God; neither came I of Myself, but He sent Me.
43 Why don't you understand what I'm saying? Because you don't hear My words.
44 You are of your father the Devil, and the lusts of your father you will do. He was a murderer from the beginning, and doesn't stand in the truth, because

there is no truth in him. When he speaks a lie, he speaks of his own: for he is a liar, and the father of it.

45 And because I tell you the truth, you don't believe Me.

46 Which of you convicts Me of sin? And if I say the truth, why don't you believe Me?

47 Those who are of God hear God's words: you therefore can't hear them, because you're not of God."

48 Then answered the Jews, and said to Him,

"Don't we say well that you are a Samaritan, and have a devil?"

49 Jesus answered,

"I don't have a devil; but honor My Father, and you dishonor Me.

50 And I don't seek My glory: there is One who seeks and judges.

51 Truly, truly, I say to you, if a anyone keeps My sayings, they shall never see death."

52 Then said the Jews to Him,

"Now we know that You have a devil. Abraham is dead, and the prophets; and you say, '*If anyone keeps My sayings, they shall never taste of death.*'

53 Are You greater than our father Abraham, who is dead? And the prophets are dead: whom do You make Yourself?

54 Jesus answered,

"If I honor Myself, My honor is nothing: it is My Father who honors Me; of whom you say that, 'He is your God.'

55 Yet you have not known Him; but I know Him: and if I should say, I don't know Him, I shall be a liar like you: but I know Him, and keep His words.

56 Your father Abraham rejoiced to see My day: and he saw it, and was glad."

57 Then said the Jews to Him,

"You are not yet fifty years old, and You have seen Abraham?"

58 Jesus said to them,

"Truly, truly, I say to you, before Abraham was, I AM."

59 Therefore they wanted to take up stones to cast at Him: but Jesus hid Himself, and went out of the Temple, going through the midst of them, and so passed by.

THE THIRTY-FIFTH MIRACLE - THE BLIND MAN

We related in the previous section, that the whole discourse of '*these words*' (8:20), on this next day, continues with the subsequent text from v. 59-9:1, and proceeds to follow on, with the detail surrounding the thirty-fifth miracle on the same particular Sabbath (9:14).

John 9

1 And as Jesus passed by, He saw a man who was blind from his birth.

2 And His disciples asked Him, "Master, who sinned, this man or his parents, that he was born blind?"

3 Jesus answered, "Neither has this man sinned, nor his parents: but that the works of God be made manifest in him.

4 I must work the works of Him who sent Me, while it is day: the night comes, when no one can work.

5 As long as I am in the world, I am the Light of the World."

6 When He had thus spoken, He spat on the ground, and made clay of the spit, and He anointed the eyes of the blind man with the clay.

7 And He said to him, "Go, wash in the Pool of Siloam" (which is by translating, Sent).

He went his way therefore and washed, and came seeing.

8 The neighbors therefore, and they who before had seen him that he was blind, said, "Is not this he who sat and begged?"

9 Some said, "This is he," others said, "He's like him."

But he said, "I am he."

10 Therefore they said to him, "How were your eyes opened?"

11 He answered and said, "A Man who is called Jesus made clay, and anointed my eyes, yes, and said to me, 'Go to the pool of Siloam, and wash': and I went and washed, and I received sight."

12 Then they said to him, "Where is He?"

He said, "I don't know."

13 Then they brought to the Pharisees him who was formerly blind.

14 And it was the Sabbath Day when Jesus made the clay, and opened his eyes.

15 Then again the Pharisees also asked him how he had received his sight.

He said to them, "He put clay upon my eyes, and I washed, and do see."

16 Therefore some of the Pharisees said, "This Man is not of God, since He doesn't keep the Sabbath Day."

Others said, "How can a Man who is a sinner do such miracles?"

And there was a division among them.

17 They say to the blind man again,
"What do you say about Him, that He has opened your eyes?"
He said, "He is a Prophet."

18 But the Jews did not believe concerning him, that he had been blind, and received his sight, until they called the parents of him who had received his sight.

19 And they asked them, saying,
"Is this your son, who you say was born blind? How then does he now see?"
20 His parents answered them and said,
"We know that this is our son, and that he was born blind:
21 but by what means he now sees, we don't know; or who has opened his eyes, we don't know: he is of age; ask him: he can speak for himself."

22 These words spoke his parents, because they feared the Jews: for the Jews had agreed already, that if anyone did confess that He was the Messiah, they should be put out of the synagogue.
23 Therefore said his parents, "He is of age; ask him."

24 Then they again called the man who was blind, and said to him,
"Give God the praise: we know that this Man is a sinner."
25 He answered and said,
"Whether He is a sinner or not, I don't know: one thing I know, that, whereas I was blind, now I see."

26 Then said they to him again,
"What did He do to you? How did He open your eyes?"
27 He answered them,
"I have told you already, and you didn't hear: wherefore would you hear it again? Will you also be His disciples?"

28 Then they insulted him, and said,
"You are His disciple; but we are Moses' disciples.
29 We know that God spoke to Moses: as for this Fellow, we don't know where He is from."
30 The man answered and said to them,
"Why herein is an amazing thing, that you don't know where He is from, and yet He has opened my eyes.

John 9

31 Now we know that God doesn't hear sinners: but if anyone is a worshiper of God, and does His will, such He hears.

32 Since the world began was it not heard that anyone opened the eyes of one who was born blind.

33 If this Man were not from God, He could do nothing."

34 They answered and said to him,

"You were altogether born in sins, and you do teach us?"

And they put him out.

35 Jesus heard that they had put him out; and when He had found him, He said to him, "Do you believe in the Son of God?"

36 He answered and said,

"Who is He, Lord, that I might believe on Him?"

37 And Jesus said to him, "You have both seen Him, and it is He who talks with you."

38 And he said, "Lord, I believe."

And he worshiped Him.

39 And Jesus said, "For judgment I am come into this world, that they who can't see might see; and they who see might be made blind."

40 And some of the Pharisees who were with Him heard these words, and said to Him, "Are we also blind?"

THE DOOR AND THE GOOD SHEPHERD

It is obvious that the dialogue surrounding the thirty-fifth miracle, which related also to that particular Sabbath, continued after 8:59, and includes the whole of ch. 9, wherein vv. 39-41 refer to Jesus' indictment of the Pharisees' blindness, regarding the whole issue stemming from the blind man. They were still present at that juncture, which resulted in Jesus answering their question, over their blindness, relating to the *Parable of the Door* (10:1-10), and the *Parable of the Good Shepherd* (vv. 11-18).

John 10

1 "Truly, truly, I say to you, they who don't enter by the door into the sheepfold, but climb up some other way, the same is a thief and a robber.

2 But they who enter in by the door are the shepherds of the sheep.

3 To them the doorkeeper opens; and the sheep hears their voice: and they call their own sheep by name, and lead them out.

4 And when they put out their own sheep, they go before them, and the sheep

follows them: and they know their voice.
5 They will by no means follow a stranger, but will flee from them; for they don't know the voice of strangers."

6 This parable Jesus spoke to them, but they didn't understand what things they were which He spoke to them.
7 Then said Jesus to them again,
"Truly, truly, I say to you, I am the Door of the sheep.
8 All who ever came before Me are thieves and robbers: but the sheep did not hear them.
9 I am the Door: by Me if anyone enters in, they shall be saved, and shall go in and out, and find pasture.
10 The thief only comes to steal, and to kill, and to destroy: I am come that they might have life, and that they might have it more abundantly.

11 I am the Good Shepherd: the Good Shepherd gives His life for the sheep.
12 But those who are hired hands, and not shepherds, who aren't owners of the sheep, see the wolf coming, and leave the sheep, and flee: and the wolf catches them, and scatters the sheep.
13 The hired hand flees, because they are a hired, and doesn't care for the sheep.
14 I am the Good Shepherd, and know My sheep, and am known of Mine.
15 As the Father knows Me, even so I know the Father: and I lay down My life for the sheep.

16 And other sheep have I, who are not of this fold: them also must I bring, and they shall hear My voice; and there shall be one fold, and One Shepherd.
17 Therefore does My Father love Me, because I lay down My life, that I might take it again.
18 No one takes it from Me, but I lay it down by Myself. I have the Power to lay it down, and I have the Power to take it again. This authority have I accepted from My Father."

19 There was a division therefore again among the Jews for these sayings.
20 And many of them said, "He has a devil, and is mad; why do you hear Him?"
21 Others said, "These are not the words of one who has a devil. Can a devil open the eyes of the blind?"

John concludes the details of the scenario on that particular Sabbath, in again referring to the subject matter of the *Thirty-Fifth Miracle* in connection to the healing of the man's blindness (v. 21), and the fact that the same Pharisees who had been at the last setting surrounding The Blind Man, come to Jesus once again in the next section (vv. 24-26).

Moreover, Jesus had also proclaimed at the commencement of the dialogue surrounding that Sabbath, and the healing of the blind man, '*I am the Light of the World*' (8:12). Furthermore, since Tabernacles falls at the conclusion of summer, and ushers in as it were the autumn season, and that the days now were getting relatively darker, with the discourse on that Sabbath, and the miracle of the healing of *The Blind Man*, which took place after the preceding Tabernacles, the poignancy of Jesus' declaration that He was the *Light of the World*, and the reference throughout two chapters regarding blindness, leads into the next subsequent event, which would have followed shortly after, and was now even in darker days still, of the following winter (10:22).

THE FESTIVAL OF REDEDICATION

With the factor of Jesus being the True Light having been stressed from the very outset of the previous scenario, on the next subsequent Sabbath, of the healing of *The Blind Man*, significantly, John now again brings us into focus at a different setting, sometime shortly afterwards, at the next event in the Jewish Calendar, at the Festival of Lights, or Hanukkah, as the Festival of Rededication of the Temple is also known.

John 10

22 And it was at Jerusalem the Festival of Rededication [25th Kislev], and it was winter.

23 And Jesus walked in the Temple in Solomon's Porch.

24 Then came the Jews round about Him, and said to Him,
"How long do you make us to doubt? If you be the Messiah, tell us plainly.
25 Jesus answered them,
"I told you, and you don't believe: the works that I do in My Father's Name, they bear witness of Me.
26 But you don't believe, because you are not My sheep, as I said to you,
27 'My sheep hear My voice, and I know them, and they follow Me (vv. 3-4, 14)':
28 and I give to them eternal life; and they shall never perish; neither shall anyone pluck them out of My hand.
29 My Father, who gave them Me, is greater than all; and no one is able to pluck them out of My Father's hand.
30 I and the Father are One."

31 Therefore the Jews avowed to take up stones again to stone Him.

32 Jesus answered them,
"Many good deeds have I shown you from My Father; for which of those deeds do you stone Me?
33 The Jews answered Him, saying,
"We don't stone You for a good deed; but for blasphemy; and because that You, being a Man, make Yourself God.

34 Jesus answered them, "Isn't it written in your Torah (Ps. 82:6), 'I SAID, YOU ARE GODS'?
35 If He called them gods, to whom the word of God came (then the Scripture cannot be broken);
36 say you of Him, whom the Father has sanctified, and sent into the world,

'You blaspheme'; because I said, *'I am the Son of God'*?

37 If I don't do the deeds of My Father, don't believe Me.
38 But if I do, though you don't believe Me, believe the deeds: so that you may know, and believe, that the Father is in Me, and I in Him."

39 Therefore they sought again to take Him: but He escaped out of their hands.

ESCAPE TO AENON NEAR SALIM

In John's closing dialogue, of this separate event, on a day in the winter Festival of Rededication, once again at the Temple, Jesus, having spent the last several months in the subsequent area, the pressure from the Pharisees was becoming so great that He was now in danger of being killed (v. 31). With the indictment of the way these Pharisees looked at Scripture (vv. 34-35), and their lack of understanding as to the meaning of blasphemy (v. 36), He is about to leave the area of Jerusalem and Judea and escape to where John the Baptist had baptized previously (vv. 39-40).

Moreover, note, we now return to the particular point where Luke had concluded his Central Section (17:10), where Jesus was preparing to leave Jerusalem and Judea (v. 11). The Gospel of John thus parallels with Luke, complementing and agreeing to Jesus' retreat from Jerusalem at this junction.

We should also notice in this section, that Mark 10:1 is quoted once more, though now with the letter '*d*'. We have concluded this factor because Mark's verse can just as aptly apply to this particular time, with the paralleling again of the text, since the long gap where the seventy were originally sent to Judea. Though we had indicated in the appropriate section previously [pp. 206-208], that Mark 10:1a applied to Mat.19:1b with Luke 9:51 and John 7:10, where back at that junction, the seventy leave Galilee traveling through the area of Samaria.

Consequently, Mark 10:1b, related to Mat. 19:1c with Luke 9:57a, in traveling to Judea. Whereas, Mark 10:1c specified the crowds of people, along with Mat. 19:2, by which Luke 9:57b-58, ascribed to one of the people from the crowds, followed by two others (vv. 59-62).

Thus, so as to keep these two separate events distinct, and because, now Mark 10:1 corresponds also directly to his following v. 2, whereas previously it did not, we see with the aligning context of Mat. 19:3 and Mark 10:2, where the Pharisees are about to question Jesus over divorce, in remaining precisely clear when quoting Mark 10:1 in future, it is easier when applying it at this juncture, to refer to it as Mark 10:1d.

However, it would make no difference if we did not use Mark 10:1 twice, to the findings at this juncture, or the previous one, because Luke and John nonetheless complement each other at this particular point. But, since Matthew and Mark remain silent over any details within Luke's Central Section, and though Matthew related to the leaving of Galilee, with Mark, nevertheless, Matthew does not allow at this section, through his sentence structure, for any synchronization in the combined text below. Thus, Mark 10:1, because of its unique sentence structure, becomes as it were a reference to either event, with leaving Galilee, and when later, leaving Jerusalem.

Mark 10:1d Luke 17:11 John 10:40
And it came to pass, as He rose and went into Jerusalem, and went away again from there, coming into the boundary of Judea, that He passed through between Samaria and Galilee, beyond the farther side of Jordan to the place where John baptized earlier; and there He stayed.

Luke continued after his Central Section (17:11) with the narrative where Jesus had been in and around Jerusalem for the rest of the Festival, of which John had complemented, along with the events leading into winter. Nonetheless, Luke 17:11 had depicted Jesus still in the vicinity of Jerusalem, at that particular point, but now about to leave. On closer examination of v. 11, the Greek actually relates, as Jesus *"Went 'to'* [Gr. *'eis'*, also meaning *'into'*] *Jerusalem, that He passed through between Samaria and Galilee,"* obviously traveling through the northern part of Judea. Mark 10:1d also indicates this aspect of travel, in using his reference again.

Though Luke had not originally mentioned *'Judea'* by name [where Mat. 19:1c and Mark 10:1b had], but as we suggested, did so by inference, indicating that aspect, as in the reference when Jesus and the seventy had come from Galilee into Samaria, to the borders of Samaria/Judea, and through Judea, and up to Jerusalem (9:51-52). Hence, as we also suggested, Luke's following text from that particular junction would thus be taking place in those subsequent areas, and concluding at Jerusalem.

Now, the AV also relates John 10:40, as Jesus going *'away again beyond Jordan to the place that John first* [Gr. *'proton'*] *baptized; and there He stayed'*. Now, when we establish where John in His Gospel was referring to, it also collaborates further the intended meaning of the word *'beyond'* at this particular junction.

There are actually three different places mentioned where John baptized. Though Jesus originally started to preach the gospel of the Kingdom in Galilee, John before that would have also baptized there, which is clearly seen when comparing Luke 1:79 with Mat. 4:15-16, and the prophecy of Is. 9:1-2. Moreover, John was to prepare the way, before Jesus came preaching (Mark 1:2-3).

It is also recorded that John baptized not far from the spot where Jesus spent forty days and nights in the Judean Wilderness (Mark 1:5-12). However, this place does not fit the description at this junction of Jesus traveling from Jerusalem through Judea to '*midway of Samaria and Galilee*', as Luke 17:10 could have alternatively been translated.

The other place is in the Gospel of John, where the Baptist '*was baptizing in Aenon near to Salim*' (3:23), while Jesus was baptizing with His disciples in Judea (v. 22). Furthermore, this was the only other place, mentioned by John in his Gospel previous to his last reference, which we are now considering (10:40).

When placing all these various factors together, we see Aenon near Salim is the only place to which all the facts align and agree. And since the Greek word '*proton*' translated '*first*' in John 10:40 AV, can also mean '*earlier*', as translated in the CEV and NEB, we see, moreover, that John in his Gospel was relating to the previous place he had lastly referred to as '*the place where John baptized earlier*'.

Additionally, the precise description by Luke, in ch. 17:11, of the direction of travel, in which he was qualified, through having compiled the journeying of The Acts of the Apostles fits accurately the location of the geographic spot to where John, in ch. 10:40 was referring.

Quoting from John Wenham's book, Redating Matthew, Mark & Luke, p. 211, which discusses Luke 17:11, "... *nearly all atlases show a roughly triangular section of the Decapolis in the Valley of Jezreel to the west of Jordan which thrusts its apex between the two territories. Along this valley runs a road down which would proceed Galilean pilgrims...*". The RSV translation '*passing along between Samaria and Galilee*' *precisely fits this location.*" Though his quote from the RSV in his book (1991 ed.) is inversely printed in error.

The Moffatt Translation has, '*passed between Samaria and Galilee*', and the NAS, '*passing between Samaria and Galilee*', with an added comment in the margin, '*or, along the borderlands*' of Samaria and Galilee. The NEB has '*through the borderlands of Samaria and Galilee*', with the NCV, CEV, and the NIV all agreeing.

Eusebius, of the third and fourth century AD, refers to a place in the valley of Jordan, which is in the limits of Samaria, near Bethshean [Scythopolis]. Here, in this location, is Tell Ridgha, also called Tell Sheikh Selim, and nearby are several springs that fit the description of '*Aenon* [Gr. springs, (*natural*) *fountains*] *near Salim.*'

Hence, as Jesus left the Temple, with Luke's precise description so aptly relating to that event, '*as He went into Jerusalem, that He passed through between Samaria and Galilee*' (17:11), '*and there He stayed*' (John 10:40), brings us to the next stage of events. Also, we saw in the previous sections how John related to and synchronized with Luke, and again after Luke's *Conclusion Of The Central Section.*

So Jesus finally leaves Jerusalem after having been in the area several weeks before Tabernacles, and escapes directly in the winter during Hanukkah, arriving at the place that John the Baptist earlier had no doubt concluded his baptism. This was where the Baptist had foretold that his own mission was to decrease and Jesus' to increase (John 3:23, 30). This is also the place where Jesus now decided to stay until the final Tabernacles, where '*many believed on Him there*' (10:42), after having listened to the Baptist teachings, which had prepared them for Him (v. 41).

THE PHARISEES ARRIVE AGAIN

The people believing on Jesus there, and His arrangements to stay in that particular area, where Mark alone had specifically mentioned a house to which Jesus returned to after talking to the Pharisees (10:10), would have all taken some considerable time to transpire. Furthermore, these Pharisees had also come directly to Jesus, of which Matthew (19:3) and Mark (10:2) are in complete agreement, and align together at this subsequent junction. These Pharisees would have heard that many people of that area believed on Jesus. Thus, because it was difficult for the Pharisees in that jurisdiction to arrest Jesus, He was safer there, as this place was near to Scythopolis, the greatest city of the Decapolis, as described by Josephus.

In allowing for the subsequent time this would have all taken, including the Pharisees coming directly to Jesus certainly would place their arrival near the spring of the following year.

Mark 10:1e John 10:41
And many people resorted to Him again, and said,
"John did no miracles: but all things that John spoke of this Man was true;"
John 10
42 And many believed on Him there.

Matthew 19:3 Mark 10:2
And the Pharisees also came to Him, tempting Him, and asked saying to Him,
"Is it lawful for a man to put away his wife for every cause?"
Matthew 19
4 And He answered and said to them,
"Haven't you read, that He who made them at the beginning MADE THEM MALE AND FEMALE (Gen. 1:27),
5 and said, 'FOR THIS CAUSE SHALL A MAN LEAVE HIS FATHER AND MOTHER, AND SHALL STICK TO HIS WIFE: AND THEY TWO SHALL BE ONE FLESH (Gen. 2:24).'
6 Wherefore they are no more two, but one flesh. What therefore God has joined together, don't let anyone put asunder."

Mark 10

3 And He answered and said to them, "What did Moses command you?"

4 And they said, "Moses allowed A CERTIFICATE OF DIVORCE TO BE WRITTEN, AND TO DIVORCE HER (Deut. 24:1, 3)."

Matthew 19

7 They say to Him, "Why did Moses then command to GIVE HER A CERTIFICATE OF DIVORCE AND DIVORCE HER (Deut. 24:1, 3)?"

Matthew 19:8 Mark 10:5

And Jesus answered and He said to them,

"Moses because of the hardness of your heart allowed you to put away your wives, writing you this precept: but from the beginning it was not so."

Matthew 19

9 And I say to you, "Whoever divorces his wife, except it be for sexual immorality, and marries another, commits adultery: and whoever marries her who is put away commits adultery.

Mark 10

6 But from the beginning of creation, GOD MADE THEM MALE AND FEMALE (Gen. 1:27).

7 FOR THIS CAUSE SHALL A MAN LEAVE HIS FATHER AND MOTHER, AND STICK TO HIS WIFE;

8 AND THEY TWO SHALL BE ONE FLESH (Gen. 2:24): so then they are no more two, but one flesh

9 Who therefore God has joined together let no one put asunder."

IN THE HOUSE

10 And in the house His disciples asked Him again of the same matter.

11 And He says to them, "Whoever divorces his wife, and marries another, commits adultery against her.

12 And if a woman divorces her husband, and marries another, she commits adultery."

Matthew 19

10 His disciples say to Him,

"If the case of the man be so with his wife, it is not expedient to marry."

11 But He said to them,

"Not everyone can accept this saying, save they to whom it is given.

12 For there are some eunuchs, who were born so from their mother's womb: and there are some eunuchs, who were made eunuchs by others: and there be eunuchs, who have made themselves eunuchs for the Kingdom of Heaven's sake. Those who are able to accept it let them accept it."

We saw in the last intersection that Mark and John, had correlated, at the area of Aenon near Salim, where the Baptist had earlier baptized, and no doubt had concluded his mission there, in being taken prisoner for the final time. Then Matthew and Mark paralleled together once more, with the incident of the Pharisees arrival.

After Jesus had answered the Pharisees two questions on divorce and marriage, He and the disciples went back to the house, where the disciples asked for further clarification on the matter. No doubt this being in the village of Salim, as Aenon referred to the springs nearby.

THE TEN LEPERS

Following the discourse on divorce and marriage with the Pharisees, and the clarification at the house with the disciples, Luke returns to the setting, and once again, as he had done in many other cases, alludes to '*a certain village*' with his next verse (17:12), after mentioning Jesus traveling to '*between Samaria and Galilee*'. This subsequent area to which Jesus went, from where the certain village of Salim was situated, is endorsed further by the closing paragraph from where we quoted earlier in John Wenham's book, *Redating Matthew, Mark & Luke*, p. 211, "*At no place would it be more likely that Jesus would meet a mixed group of lepers, which included a Samaritan.*"

Luke's indigenous narration of the ten lepers (17:12-19) makes it the thirty-sixth miracle. After this, the Pharisees continue again to question Jesus (v. 20), after He was about to return again to the village, obviously having left earlier, where Jesus answers their next question relating to '*when the Kingdom of God should come*' (v. 21). He further revealed aspects of it, directing His conversation to the disciples (vv. 22-36).

Luke 17

12 And as He entered into a certain village, there met Him ten men who were lepers, who stood afar off:

13 and they lifted up their voices, and said, "Jesus, Master, have mercy on us."

14 And when He saw them, He said to them, "Go show yourselves to the Priests."

And it came to pass, that as they went, they were cleansed.

15 And one of them, when he saw that he was healed, turned back, and with a loud voice glorified God.

16 And fell down on his face at His feet, giving thanks: and he was a Samaritan.

17 And Jesus answering said,

"Weren't there ten cleansed? But where are the nine?

18 Were there none found who returned to give glory to God, save this stranger?"

19 And He said to him, "Rise go your way: your faith has made you whole."

It is interesting to consider while we are still in this area, of the borders of Samaria/Galilee, where the ten lepers were healed, some other people who once lived in the same territory. That was before they were deported in stages by the Assyrians, in 736BC in the northern parts, and subsequently in 721-718BC. These people, originally part of the twelve tribes of Israel, were the House of Jacob, and became known as the ten tribes after their split from the other two tribes. After their captivity and deportation, only the tribe of Judah [with Benjamin] remained, and became known as the House of Judah, and the Jews (2 Kings 15:29; 17:5-6, 18). These, 'lost tribes', as they eventually became known, ten in all, because of their relinquishment in honoring the One true God, when breaking away from the throne, which was situated in Jerusalem with the House of Judah (1 Kings 12:19-20), with their deportation from the land, became 'lost', so to speak, even to most historians and scholars, remaining an enigma to this very day.

The town of Samaria, became the capital of the region of Samaria, which belonged to the ten tribes, when they ostracized themselves from the other two tribes, which is specially endorsed by their individual relationship pictured in Ezek. 23:4, and that whole chapter. The territory of Samaria and Galilee was where most of these tribes resided, Manasseh and Ephraim being the most dominant. The remaining tribes were situated across the Jordan in what was known in Jesus' time as the Decapolis, and Perea. In Jesus' day they were still the 'lost tribes' to most historians and scholars, never as a whole returning again.

The ten lepers, were also physically 'lost', too, before they were healed, and had to remain 'outside of the camp', until they were healed and able to return. Thus, there is a comparison with the ten tribes, who had been in that particular area, and the ten lepers. These lepers were in precisely the same location where the triangular part of the Decapolis juts out. It belonged to the area of the Decapolis also over the other side of Jordan, where the rest of the tribes had lived, and protruded its apex into the Samaria/Galilee border, where the majority of tribes dwelt before their deportation.

There is further significance in relationship to where the ten lepers were healed, as in truth, there is neither Samaritan nor Jew who are ostracized from God. Though Jesus had prophesied to the hierarchy of the remnants of the tribe of Judah, that even *the Kingdom of God shall be taken from you, and given to a nation bringing forth fruits*, as had occurred with the ten tribes, if their attitude did not change (Mat. 21:43-45). Nonetheless, all the tribes were eventually to be healed in the unity of God (Rom. 11).

The other instances of various events which occurred in this particular area are; John the Baptist baptizing in Aenon near Salim: Jesus talking to the Samaritan woman at Jacob's Well: the that the fields were already white to harvest there: of these people of Samaria believing in Jesus being the Messiah, the Saviour of the World; in respect of the mission of the seventy, and with the seventy returning from Judea to Jesus; where subsequently in Samaria He related the *Parable of the Good Samaritan*: and now where Jesus had returned to the place where John had earlier baptized. All these instances profoundly add to the symbolism of not letting borders, and the mentality of selfish tribalism stand in the way of getting on with ones neighbors.

Moreover, still in the same place, a little later, Jesus addresses the disciples over further aspects in relation to the twelve tribes, and the Kingdom of God (Mat. 19:28)! In fact, while Jesus was in that area, most of the dialogue in the Synoptics covers detail relating to the Kingdom of God!

After healing the lepers, the Pharisees continue again to question Jesus, but at that point, on '*when the Kingdom of God should come*' when He was about to return again in entering the village, obviously having had no opportunity to enter with the healing of the lepers. Jesus further revealed aspects of the Kingdom, now directing His conversation to the disciples (Luke 17:22-36). Eleven of these verses, though with slight variations, are repeated again by Jesus at *The Olivet Prophecy* in Matthew's Gospel (ch. 24) two days before the final Passover.

With the returning also of both Matthew and Mark to the scenario again shortly, as shown in the next section, it is clear that Luke's indigenous part of the dialogue, dovetails as placed, as his following narration (18:15-30) parallels with Matthew (19:13-30) and Mark (10:13-31) once more.

ASPECTS OF THE KINGDOM

Luke 17

20 And when He was demanded of the Pharisees, when the Kingdom of God should come, He answered them and said,
"The Kingdom of God comes not with observation:
21 Neither shall they say, 'Look here!' nor, 'Look there!' For, understand, the Kingdom of God is within you."

22 And He said to the disciples,
"The days will come, when you shall desire to see one of the days of the Son of Humanity, and you shall not see it.
23 And they shall say to you, 'See here;' or, 'See there:' go not after them, nor follow them.
24 For as the lightning, that flashes from one part of the heavens, shines to the other part of the heavens; so shall also the Son of Humanity be in His day.
25 But first He must suffer many things, and be rejected of this generation.

26 And as it was in the days of Noah, so shall it be also in the days of the Son of Humanity
27 They did eat, they drank, they married wives, they were given in marriage, until the day that Noah entered into the ark, and the flood came, and destroyed them all.
28 Likewise also as it was in the days of Lot; they did eat, they drank, they bought, they sold, they planted, they built;
29 but the same day that Lot went out of Sodom it rained fire and brimstone from the heavens, and destroyed them all.

30 Even so shall it be in the day when the Son of Humanity is revealed.

Luke 17

31 In that day, those who shall be upon the housetop, when their stuff is in the house, let them not come down to take it away: and those who are in the field, let them likewise not return back.

32 Remember Lot's wife.

33 Whoever shall seek to save their life shall lose it; and whoever shall lose their life shall preserve it.

34 I tell you, in that night there shall be two in one bed; the one shall be taken, and the other shall be left.

35 Two shall be grinding grain together; the one shall be taken, and the other left.

36 Two shall be in the field; the one shall be taken, and the other left."

37 And they answered and said to Him, "Where, Lord?"
And He said to them, "Wherever the Body is, there will the eagles be gathered together.

After Jesus had spoken to the Pharisees and the disciples over aspects of the Kingdom of God, Jesus further relates the *Parable of the Persistent Widow*, which is unique to the Gospel of Luke (18:1-8).

Luke once again shows through antithesis, by the next indigenous *Parable of the Pharisee and the Tax Collector* (vv. 9-14), that it was directed '*to certain who trusted in themselves that they were righteous, and despised others*', and was indicative to the Pharisees being still present. Here both Matthew (19:13) and Mark (10:13) now return, after previously dovetailing and paralleling since both their records of the previous questioning on divorce and marriage (Mat. 19:3-12; Mark 10:2-12), again with the dialogue of Luke, regarding the little children being brought to Jesus (18:15). This indicated the correct sequence to the successive order of events, thus, dovetailing Luke's events surrounding the '*certain village*' (17:12-37), into its natural position.

LUKE RELATES TO MATTHEW WITH MARK

Luke 18

1 And He spoke a parable to them to this end, that everyone ought always to pray, and not faint;

2 saying,
"There was in a certain city a Judge, who didn't fear God, neither respected anyone:

3 and there was a widow in that city; and she came to him, saying,
'Vindicate me of my adversary.'

4 And he would not for a while: but afterwards he said within himself, 'Though I do not fear God, nor respect anyone;
5 yet because this widow troubles me, I will vindicate her, lest by her continual coming she weary me.'"

6 And the Lord said, consider what the unjust Judge says.
7 Won't God avenge His own elect, who cry day and night to Him, though He bear long with them?
8 I tell you that He will avenge them speedily. Nevertheless when the Son of Humanity comes, shall He find faith on the earth?"

9 And He spoke this parable to certain who trusted in themselves that they were righteous, and despised others:

10 "Two men went up into the Temple to pray; the one a Pharisee, and the other a Tax Collector.
11 The Pharisee stood and prayed thus within himself, 'God, I thank You, that I am not as other people, extortioners, unjust, adulterers, or even as this Tax Collector.
12 I fast twice in the week, I give tithes of all that I possess.'

13 And the publican, standing afar off, would not lift up so much as his eyes to the heavens, but beat upon his chest, saying, 'God be merciful to me a sinner.'
14 I tell you, this man went down to his house justified rather than the other: for everyone who exalts themselves shall be abased; and they who humble themselves shall be exalted."

Matthew 19:13 Mark 10:13 Luke 18:15
And then were there brought young children to Him, also babies, that He would touch them, to put His hands upon them, and pray: but when His disciples saw it, the disciples rebuked those who brought them.

Matthew 19:14 Mark 10:14 Luke 18:16
But when Jesus saw it, He was very displeased. But Jesus called them to Him. And notwithstanding Jesus said,
"Allow the little children to come to Me, and don't forbid them: for of such is the Kingdom of God from Heaven.
Mark 10:15 Luke 18:17
Truly I say to you, whoever shall not receive the Kingdom of God as a little child, they shall not in no way enter therein."

Matthew 19:15 Mark 10:16
And He took them up in His arms, and put His hands, laying them upon them, and blessed them, and departed from there.

THEY CONTINUE TO PROCEED AGAIN

In checking the whole discourse from when Jesus had already arrived at Aenon near Salim, and had been there some time, where He was about to go '*into a certain village*', and subsequently '*there met Him ten men who were lepers*' (Luke 17:12), we see that none of the writers indicate a change in setting, only that the Pharisees were still around, and listening to what Jesus was teaching His disciples (Luke 17:20-22; 18:9), and who were there from the healing of the lepers. With the closing of the dialogue, in which were brought to Him children, Matthew at this point reveal Jesus and the disciples having now actually '*departed from there*' (19:15).

Mark also, relates to the same departure after the scenario of the children, but gives additional detail, pointing out it was '*when He had proceeded to the road*' (10:17). No doubt a reference to the factor of having had no opportunity to actually continue directly into the village itself, though that was the original purpose, because the ten lepers had prevented it, and the subsequent questioning of the Pharisees. This indicated Jesus and the disciples were continuing with their original intention of returning back to the village where they no doubt were staying.

Now as they were advancing again, with fulfilling their original purpose of entering the village, it is Luke who exclusively reveals there was '*a certain ruler*', who stops Jesus and asks Him a question, who, as Mark alone specifically pointed out, '*came running, and knelt*'. Thus, Mark and Luke both synchronize and parallel with Matthew at this incident, with Matthew's unique piece of information, that he was moreover, a '*young man*' (19:20), too.

TRUSTING MATERIALISM

Matthew 19:16 Mark 10:17 Luke 18:18
And when He had proceeded to the road, suddenly, there came one running to Him, a certain ruler, who knelt before Him, and exclaiming, asked Him, saying, "Good Master, what good thing shall I do, that I may inherit and obtain eternal life?"
Matthew 19:17 Mark 10:18 Luke 18:19
And Jesus said to him,
"Why do you call Me good? There is none good, save but One, who is God: but if you will enter into life, keep the Commandments."
Matthew 19:18 Mark 10:19a Luke 18:20a
He said to Him, "Which?"
Jesus said, "You know the Commandments, 'YOU SHALL NOT MURDER, YOU SHALL NOT COMMIT ADULTERY, YOU SHALL NOT STEAL, YOU SHALL NOT BEAR FALSE WITNESS (Ex. 20:13-16), do not defraud,

Matthew 19:19 Mark 10:19b Luke 18:20b
HONOUR YOUR FATHER AND MOTHER (Ex. 20:12): and YOU SHALL LOVE YOUR
NEIGHBOUR AS YOURSELF (Lev. 19:18)'".

Matthew 19:20 Mark 10:20 Luke 18:21
And the young man answered and exclaimed saying,
"Master, all these things have I kept, observing them from my youth up: what
do I lack yet?"
Matthew 19:21 Mark 10:21 Luke 18:22
Now when Jesus heard these things, then Jesus beholding him loved him, and
He said to him,
"Yet you lack one thing: if you will be perfect, go your way, and sell all,
whatever you have, and distribute and give to the poor, and you shall have
treasure in Heaven: and come, take up the cross, and follow Me."

Matthew 19:22 Mark 10:22 Luke 18:23
But when the young man heard this, he was very sorrowful, saddened at that
saying, and he went away grieved: for he was very rich: for he had great
possessions.
Matthew 19:23 Mark 10:23 Luke 18:24
And Jesus looked round about, and when Jesus saw that he was very
sorrowful, then Jesus exclaimed saying to His disciples,
"Truly I say to you, that, how hardly shall a rich person, those who have
riches enter into the Kingdom of God from Heaven!"
Mark 10
24 And the disciples were astonished at His words.
But Jesus answered again, and says to them, "Children, how hard is it for
those who trust in riches to enter the Kingdom of God!

Matthew 19:24 Mark 10:25 Luke 18:25
And again I say to you, for it is easier for a camel to go through the eye of a
needle, than for a rich person to enter into the Kingdom of God."
Matthew 19:25 Mark 10:26 Luke 18:26
And His disciples who when they heard it, were exceedingly amazed, and
astonished out of measure, and exclaimed, saying among themselves,
"Who then can be saved?"

Matthew 19:26 Mark 10:27 Luke 18:27
But Jesus looking upon them, beheld them, and spoke saying to them,
"With humans this is impossible, but not with God: the things which are
impossible with humans are possible with God. For with God all things are
possible."

Matthew 19:27 Mark 10:28 Luke 18:28
Then Peter began to answer and say exclaiming to Him,
"Look, we have forsaken and left all, and have followed You; what shall we
have therefore?"
Matthew 19
28 And Jesus said to them,
"Truly I say to you, that you who have followed Me, in the regeneration when
the Son of Humanity shall sit on the Throne of His glory, you also shall sit up
on twelve thrones, judging the Twelve Tribes of Israel."

Matthew 19:29a Mark 10:29 Luke 18:29
And Jesus answered and said to them,
"Truly I say to you, there is no one who has left home (and everyone who has
forsaken), houses, or brothers, or sisters, or parents, father, or mother, or wife,
or children, or lands, for My Name's sake, and the gospel's - for the Kingdom
of God's sake,
Matthew 19:29b Mark 10:30 Luke 18:30
nevertheless they shall receive a hundredfold. Who shall not only receive
manifold more now in this present time, houses, brothers, and sisters, and
mothers, and children, and lands, with and persecutions; and in the world to
come shall inherit everlasting life.
Matthew 19:30 Mark 10:31
But many who are first shall be last; and the last first."

THE WORKERS IN THE VINEYARD

Matthew, with his indigenous *Parable of the Workers in the Vineyard*, continues with Jesus' unbroken dialogue, after the discourse of the certain young rich ruler (19:16-23), and the narration on materialism spoken to the disciples (vv. 24-30). Matthew's previous verse, relating to the first shall be last (19:30), is repeated at the end of this next parable too (20:16): thus, framing as it were, the whole of this unique parable, and dovetailing it into its natural consecutive position, in concluding the scenario at that particular point.

Matthew 20

1 "For the Kingdom of Heaven is like a man who is a landowner, who went out early in the morning to hire laborers into his vineyard.
2 And when he had agreed with the laborers for a penny a day, sent them into his vineyard.

3 And he went out about 9 a.m., and saw others standing idle in the market place,
4 and said to them; 'You go also into the vineyard, and whatever is right I will give you.'
And they went their way.

5 Again he went out about noon and 3 p.m., and did likewise.

6 And about 5 p.m. he went out, and found others standing idle, and says to them, 'Why do you stand here all the day idle?'
7 They say to the landowner, 'Because no one has hired us.'
The landowner says to them, 'You go also into the vineyard; and whatever is right, that you shall receive.'

8 So when evening was come, the owner of the vineyard says to his manager, 'Call the laborers, and give them their hire, beginning from the last to the first.'
9 And when they came who were hired about 5 p.m., they received everyone a penny.
10 But when the first came, they supposed that they should have received more; and they likewise received everyone a penny.
11 And when they had received it, they murmured against the landowner,
12 saying, 'These last have labored but one hour, and you have made them equal to us, who have borne the burden and heat of the day.'

13 But the landowner answered the certain one, and said, 'Friend, I do you no

wrong, did you not agree with me for a penny?

14 Take yours, and go your way: I will give to this last, even as to you.

15 Is it not lawful for me to do what I will with my own? Is your viewpoint envious, because I am good?'

16 So the last shall be first, and the first last: for many are called, but few chosen."

We saw how the Gospel of John (10:40-42), when Jesus left Jerusalem gave the name to the area where Jesus escaped to, by mentioning the last place the Baptist had baptized earlier (3:23). Luke (17:11) had related to the area, too, by indicating with the direction of travel. Mark (10:1-2) had alluded to that factor, but, moreover, aligned with Matthew (19:3), regarding the aspect of Jesus teaching the people there, with the Pharisees subsequently arriving, when they had heard where Jesus was sighted last.

We also considered earlier that this would all have taken considerable time, and that Jesus having left Jerusalem in winter, it would put the above text, including the dialogue surrounding the **thirty-sixth miracle** in the previous section, to where the Pharisees had originally arrived at about spring and namely around Passover time.

THE LAST SUMMER

Previously, we outlined that Jesus spent the first Passover in Jerusalem, in Judea, and the second near Bethsaida, in Galilee. Thus, the third Passover would have taken place in the area of Aenon near Salim, between Samaria and Galilee, with the final Passover concluding at Jerusalem. Hence, with the first Passover of Jesus' mission at Jerusalem, He would also conclude His physical ministry there, having divided and spent the Passover seasons between the three areas, Judea, Galilee, and Samaria.

Furthermore, we had also suggested, Pentecost in the summer season, which follows the Festival of Passover in the spring, must have uniquely been spent in a different location each time, as, moreover, it signified the spreading of the Holy Spirit through the gospel. Thus, in the summer, a year after Jesus' baptism and firstly in Galilee, we have the ordination of the twelve. Secondly, a year later, the disciples were in Caesarea Philippi at Mt. Hermon in the same season, with the now grown number of the seventy. Thirdly, and subsequently, another year later, now in this section, we will be coming into, summertime again, though, still in the vicinity of Aenon near Salim, with no doubt, an ever increasing number of disciples having been added, making up the five hundred, in which area Jesus and the disciples were still residing. Lastly, Pentecost culminates at Jerusalem, with the continued growing of the NT Church, eventually reaching further into the world.

The first Tabernacles after Pentecost would have been in Galilee, at the beginning of Jesus' ministry, with the following three all taking place at Jerusalem. We are about to consider, after Pentecost and covering the summer season in Aenon near Salim, at this junction, the final Tabernacles at Jerusalem.

We had established that Jesus had escaped and left Jerusalem after *The Third Festival of Tabernacles*, having spent the rest of autumn there, and part of winter with *The Festival of Rededication*. He would have thus arrived at Aenon near Salim still during the rest of the winter season, subsequently teaching the people there, where many believed on Him (John 10:42). Consequently, this would have taken some time, progressively bringing us into springtime and the third Passover season.

However, the Day of Pentecost is specifically mentioned in the following book proceeding the Gospels, with *The Acts of the Apostles*, with the inception of the recommissioning of the disciples to go progressively into the entire world, starting from Jerusalem. In that case it was unique, and a special manifestation of that new beginning.

Moreover, similarly, there was just one other eventful instance of the manifestation of the Holy Spirit, prior to Jesus' preaching mission, at His baptism, when the voice from Heaven said, '*My beloved Son in whom I am well-pleased.*'

Also a year later, and in its actual successive occurrence, directly before T*he Ordination Of The Twelve*, Matthew related to a prophecy referring to Jesus and the Spirit, reaffirming what the voice from Heaven had originally said at Jesus Baptism (12:18). Matthew, nonetheless, recorded this incident and placed it to prefigure and stress the prophecy of Is. 42:1-4, with the initiation of the mission of the twelve (Mat. 10:1-42; Mark 3:13-19; Luke 6:12-16). See the sections dealing with those Scriptures, and the reasons as to why Matthew does not follow in consecutive order with his text at that particular junction. Again, a year later, in the summer with *The Transfiguration*, once more, a voice spoke the same words from Heaven, but, now added, '*hear Him*', no doubt also prefiguring to the seventy's ordination and soon the start of their mission to go '*two by two*' without Jesus.

Returning back now to the scenario after the penultimate Passover season at spring, in the area of Aenon near Salim where Jesus escaped to from Jerusalem: we see there would be yet one more Tabernacles transpiring at Jerusalem following the summer season in which Pentecost fell, which was now drawing to a close, even though there is no mention of any specific details which occurred in that last summer.

Thus with all the various incidents which would have transpired in the previous summers, when we arrive at the last one in Jesus' earthly ministry, there is an exclusion of any details whatsoever. This omission, and the apparent growth of the number of disciples at this time, with one more year to follow before the first mentioning of the Day of Pentecost, and that moreover by Luke, in *The Acts of the Apostles*, who wrote more about the two different groups of disciples than any other Gospel writer, when considering all these aspects, through the absence of any details at this particular junction the lack of narrative also becomes conspicuous.

The conclusion of this summer season would have taken place in the same area, as the following indication of journeying again coming from the Synoptics relates to when Jesus and the twelve are about to finally leave the area of Aenon near Salim midway between Samaria and Galilee, and return to Jerusalem once again, via Jericho. Furthermore, the Gospel of John dovetails at this particular juncture, though preceding the Synoptics, and adds further amazing detail poignant to this time.

Jesus and the disciples would leave Aenon near Salim, traveling up to Jerusalem for the last Tabernacles, also for another reason, as will emerge. In the meantime, the following references of Mat. 20:17, Mark 10:32, Luke 18:31, and John 11:1, when compared to their previous ones which relate to springtime (Mat. 20:16; Mark 10:31 Luke 18:30; John 10:42), should all be noted as taking place near to the season of autumn prior to the next Tabernacles.

Luke, who had referred to the direction of travel, in indicating when Jesus and the disciples originally left Jerusalem to where they were heading (17:11), now mentions that it was while they were still in the same vicinity he had previously referred to, and as John had averred, Aenon near Salim, that Jesus informs the disciples He had now decided about going up to Jerusalem once more (Luke 18:31). This specific information correlates with John 11:7, where Jesus had waited two days in the area of Aenon near Salim, that Jesus informs the disciples He had now decided about going up to Jerusalem once more (Luke 18:31). This specific information correlates with John 11:7, where Jesus had waited two days in the area of Aenon near Salim, after receiving the message about Lazarus, and then deciding to return to Jerusalem. Additionally, Mark (10:32) shortly afterwards, converges and parallels once again with Matthew (20:17), when they are actually on their way going up to Jerusalem, before traversing through Jericho with the aim of ending up in Jerusalem.

Now before they actually leave, John (10:40-42), having already indicated where Jesus originally escaped to, now returns to the scenario, with the message from Mary and Martha, who knew where Jesus was, by asking Jesus to come up to Bethany, as Lazarus, their brother was ill (11:1-3). Jesus thus decides to use that particular request for His precise timing once again, in returning to Jerusalem where the last Festival of Tabernacles was also to take place.

John 11

1 Now a certain man was ill, named, Lazarus, of Bethany, the town of Mary and her sister Martha.

2 It was that Mary who anointed the Lord with ointment, and wiped His feet

with her hair (Mat. 26:6-13; Mark 14:3-9; John 12:1-8), whose brother was ill.
3 Therefore his sisters sent to Him, saying, "Lord, consider, he whom You love is ill."

4 When Jesus heard that, He said,
"This illness is not to death, but for the glory of God, that the Son of God might be glorified thereby."

5 Now Jesus loved Martha, and her sister, and Lazarus.
6 When He heard therefore that he was ill, He stayed two days still in the same place that He was.

7 Then after that He says to His disciples, "Let us go into Judea again."
8 His disciples say to Him,
"Master, the Jews of late sought to stone You; and You go there again?"
9 Jesus answered, "Aren't there twelve hours in the day? If anyone walks in the day, they don't stumble, because they see the light of this world.
10 But if they walk in the night, they stumble, because there is no light about them."

11 He said these things, and after that He says to them,
"Our friend Lazarus sleeps; but I go, that I may awake him out of sleep."
12 Then said His disciples, "Lord, if he sleeps, he shall do well."

13 Nevertheless Jesus spoke of his death: but they thought that He had spoken of taking of rest in sleep.

14 Then said Jesus to them plainly, "Lazarus is dead.
15 And I am glad for your sakes that I was not there, to the intent you may believe; nevertheless let us go to him."

16 Then said Thomas, who is called Didymus, to his fellow disciples,
"Let us also go, that we may die with Him."

After Jesus had received the message from Mary and Martha, He decided to stay two days still in the area of Aenon near Salim, and then afterwards return into the adjacent vicinity of Judea again (John 11:6-7), with the purpose of arriving at Bethany, and subsequently Jerusalem, where He and the disciples had originally left about nine months previously. John, as he did with dovetailing in Luke's Central Section, once more relates to the setting and timing of the scenario, and repeats the detail about the Pharisees wishing Jesus dead and that it would be unsafe to venture there again (v. 8), after the earlier escape.

Luke 18:31, however, follows in successive order after John 11:16, after Jesus had now informed an apprehensive group of disciples of His intention to leave. At this they wax somewhat bold, and Jesus then relates to them subsequent events surrounding His Passion that would ultimately unfold at Jerusalem. Though, He was referring to the Passover about six months away. Thomas' naive, brash, and rich statement to the disciples, of being prepared to die with Jesus, over the fact certain Pharisees had vowed to kill Him about nine months previous (John 11:8, 16), adds to the scene, and is typical in that they did not yet fully understand Jesus' accomplishment in the role of the Messiah, and would thus become further apprehensive again when leaving (Mark 10:32).

It is clear that Luke's next four verses are referring to still being in the area of *Aenon near Salim*, with the disciples not fully comprehending the prophecy of Jesus' Passion (18:31-34).

Matthew and Mark who parallel with each other, dovetail and follow on after Luke, distinctly mentioning that it was when they had started out, and were now '*on the way*', that Jesus repeated aspects surrounding the Passion. At that point it is Mark who exclusively confirms, '*they were amazed*', and that '*they were afraid*', before Jesus repeats further details about Himself regarding His Passion, which corresponds with John 11:8 a little earlier, in establishing their apprehension at this particular time.

THEY LEAVE FOR JUDEA

Luke 18
31 Then He took to Him the twelve, and said to them,
"Consider, we go up to Jerusalem, and all things that are written by the Prophets concerning the Son of Humanity shall be accomplished.
32 For He shall be delivered to the Gentiles, and shall be mocked, and spitefully treated, and spat on:
33 and they shall scourge Him, and put Him to death: and the third day He shall rise again."

34 And they understood none of these things which were spoken.
Matthew 20:17 Mark 10:32
And He and they were on the way going up to Jerusalem; and Jesus went before them: and they were amazed; and as they followed, they were afraid.

And again He took the twelve disciples apart on the way, and began to tell them what things should happen to Him, and said to them,
Matthew 20:18 Mark 10:33
"Understand, we go up to Jerusalem; and the Son of Humanity shall be betrayed, and be delivered to the Chief Priests and to the Scribes, and they shall condemn Him to death,
Matthew 20:19 Mark 10:34
and shall deliver Him to the Gentiles to mock, and they shall mock Him, for

scourging - and they shall scourge Him, and shall spit upon Him, and crucify Him, and they shall kill Him: and the third day He shall rise again."

We conclude this section with the subsequent arrival of the mother of James and John coming to Jesus, and directly after the second traumatic affirmation relating to Jesus' Passion, requesting places of honor in the Kingdom for her two sons (Mat. 20:20-21). It is significant at this particular time, since she was from Galilee, and the festal caravans from there, traveled via that route where they were all '*on the way*' going up to Jerusalem.

'ON THE WAY'

Matthew 20

20 And then came to Him the mother of Zebedee's children, with her sons, worshiping Him, and desiring a certain thing of Him.

21 And He said to her, "What do you want?"

She says to Him,

"Grant that these my two sons may sit, the one on Your right-hand, and the other on the left, in Your Kingdom."

Mark 10

35 And James and John, the sons of Zebedee, came to Him, saying,

"Master, we would that You should do for us whatever we shall desire."

36 And He said to them, "What do you wish that I should do for you?"

37 They said to Him,

"Grant to us that we may sit, one on Your right-hand, and the other on Your left side, in Your glory."

Matthew 20:22a Mark 10:38

But Jesus answered and said to them,

"You don't know what you're asking: are you able to drink of the cup that I drink, and be baptized with the baptism that I am baptized with?"

Matthew 20:22b Mark 10:39a

And they said to Him, "We can, we are able."

Matthew 20:23a Mark 10:39b

And Jesus said to them,

"You shall indeed drink of My cup that I drink of, and with the baptism that I am baptized with shall you be baptized:

Matthew 20:23b Mark 10:40

but to sit on My right-hand and on My left-hand is not Mine to give; but it shall be given to those for whom it is prepared through My Father."

Matthew 20:24 Mark 10:41

And when the ten heard it, they began to be very displeased, being moved with indignation against the two brothers, James and John.

Matthew 20:25 Mark 10:42

But Jesus called them to Him, and spoke saying to them,

"You know that the princes of the Gentiles, they who are accounted to rule over the Gentiles exercise lordship - dominion over them; and those who are their great ones exercise authority over them.

Matthew 20:26 Mark 10:43

But it shall not be so among you, but whoever will be great among you, you shall let them be your minister:

Matthew 20:27 Mark 10:44

and whoever of you will be the chief among you, you shall let them be your
servant to all.

Matthew 20:28 Mark 10:45

For even as the Son of Humanity came not to be ministered to, but to minister,
and to give His life a ransom for many."

With the arrival of the mother of James and John, directly after the second
affirmation relating to Jesus' Passion, requesting places of honor in the Kingdom
for her two sons, we see that Mark (10:35-37) follows dovetailing with Matthew
(20:20-21), and portrays, that her two sons also asked the same request for
themselves, obviously reaffirming their mother's original appeal. Thus, the
collusive request of both the mother of James and John, and her two sons, at this
particular junction, regarding places of honor, which Jesus had earlier referred to,
before leaving the area of Aenon near Salim, in respect of the thrones of the
Twelve Tribes of Israel (Mat. 19:28), would thus still be prominent in their minds
at this subsequent Tabernacles.

Furthermore, because of the Jewish expectation of the Messiah's Kingdom
being established during the season in which Tabernacles fell, and Jesus' referral
to the scrolls of The Prophets, in relationship to Himself and His resurrection
(Luke 18:31-33), of which the disciples still did not fully understand the
accomplishment of (v. 34), added to their confused anticipation, along with many
of the people, of the expectation of the Messiah taking over rulership from the
Romans at this time of year.

Now, John in his Gospel does not mention in name this last Tabernacles!
However, with the way he outlined his record, he nevertheless indicates it. When
Jesus had eluded the Pharisees of Jerusalem in the previous winter, to *Escape To
Aenon Near Salim* (10:39-40), John goes on to reveal again, after the ultimate
Passover (v. 55). This means all the text preceding the finale Passover, next
forthcoming events at Jerusalem, which we are now covering, that Jesus had to
leave and escape once more (11:53-54), before He returns for related to the
season before that, which, when counting backwards, would include another
winter, a Tabernacles in autumn, at which point we are now coming to, and the
summer of which we have just considered, right back to the penultimate
Passover.

THEY HEAD FOR JERICHO

Now with the disciples and Jesus journeying again towards Bethany and
Jerusalem, after subsequently having been '*on the way*' to arriving at Jericho, the
tremendous excitement of the people, the cries of the blind men, all allude to

Jesus' Kingship. This predominant factor, of this same fervent atmosphere extended even to the entry of riding into Jerusalem the following day, as will become apparent, and further contributes to these events having taken place in autumn at the season of Tabernacles. Moreover, Jesus went on to relate the *Parable of the Ten Pounds* [or Minas] to dispel anyone thinking '*the Kingdom of God should immediately appear*', there and then, at that particular time (Luke 19:11).

John had earlier recorded that He knew where Jesus had originally escaped to, and obviously did not have to repeat it. Even Mary and Martha knew the place where Jesus was staying at, when they sent their message regarding Lazarus.

From Aenon near Salim on the border of Samaria, Jesus and the disciples took a further two days to arrive at Bethany, by then, Lazarus had been dead four days (John 11:17). This resurrection of Lazarus at the time was the ultimate miracle to annoy the Pharisees (11:47-48, 12:10), which actually in successive order transpired six months before the final, and thus Jesus' second entry in riding into Jerusalem preceding the concluding Passover (12:12-14).

Hence, Jesus was also to ride into to Jerusalem at this particular juncture, as well as before the following Passover. But now at this final Tabernacles, after the healing of Lazarus, Jesus sent two disciples from the junction of the road near Bethpage and Bethany, at which point the Synoptics all parallel and agree, correlating together on the first entry into Jerusalem (Mat. 21:1; Mark 11:1; Luke 19:29).

Furthermore, John is the one who exclusively recorded the final time Jesus rode into Jerusalem just before the concluding Passover (12:11-15). He also specifically indicated that after this last Tabernacles Jesus escaped again, this next time '*into a city called Ephraim*' (11:54), where Jesus awaits the final Passover before returning to Jerusalem once again. John mentioned this scenario prior to Jesus returning (vv. 55-57), and reveals He returned '*six days before Passover came*' (12:1).

The Synoptics do not mention the final entry into Jerusalem only that Jesus was already there, again at the Temple. They converge accordingly after the events of this last Tabernacles, their references all paralleling together, relating to just prior to the final Passover (Mat. 21:23; Mark 11:27; Luke 20:1), with all the verses preceding, applying to this particular Tabernacles (Mat. 21:22; Mark 11:26; Luke 19:48).

John (11:55-57), however, corresponds and fills in, dovetailing with the details of the scenario a few days before the Synoptics references, to Jesus being at the Temple at the concluding Passover.

But prior to that, and moreover six months, after having traveled from Aenon near Salim, Jesus and the disciples are now about to arrive at Jericho, where we shall see, they stopped-off for the night, ready for the next day's journey to Bethany, and the first entry into Jerusalem.

Luke 18

35 And it came to pass, that as He was come near to Jericho, a certain blind man sat by the wayside begging:

36 and hearing the crowd pass by, he asked what it meant.

37 And they told him, that Jesus of Nazareth passes by.

38 And he cried out, saying, "Jesus, You Son of David, have mercy on me."

39 And they, who went ahead, rebuked him, that he should be quiet: but he cried out all the more, "You Son of David, have mercy on me."

40 And Jesus stood, and ordered him to be brought to Him: and when he was come near, He asked him,

41 saying, "What do you want Me to do?"

And he said, "Lord, that I may receive my sight."

42 And Jesus said to him "Receive your sight: your faith has saved you."

43 And immediately he received his sight and followed Him, glorifying God: and all the people, when they saw it, gave praise to God.

When following the dialogues of the texts of Matthew and Mark through successively since Luke 18:34, Luke now returns and dovetails, giving the exact order and details to the next subsequent event. They had now arrived 'near to Jericho' (v. 35), where Jesus went on directly to heal a blind man (v. 43), the thirty-seventh miracle. Just before they were about to actually enter the city, of which Luke is quite clear about, he confirmed that they did not enter until, after the healing of the first blind man (19:1).

Luke (19:1) goes onto synchronize with Mark (10:46) at that particular point, with Mark's next healing of blind Bartimeus, thus becoming the **thirty-eighth miracle**. This miracle in Mark is distinct from the first blind man of Luke. Mark was clear that the healing of his blind man, of whom he was familiar with, was called '*Bartimeus, the son of Timeus*', and transpired not as they were near Jericho, as Luke was quite sure of with his record (18:35). Mark's event actually occurred, after, '*they came to Jericho*' (10:46), having subsequently '*entered and passed through*' the city as Luke (19:1) informed us. This is further corroborated with Luke linking with Mark's text, in that Bartimeus was healed after Jesus '*went out*' of the city (10:46).

Moreover, Luke's purpose was in specifically revealing that Zaccheus' house was in the suburbs of the city, and thus returns with the dialogue of the events that surrounded Jesus staying at his house (19:2-10) after the thirty-eighth miracle of Mark (10:46-52). Thus, Mark's v. 46, where '*they came to Jericho*', is better translated '*into*', as the Gr. '*eis*' is often rendered, and is more appropriate with Luke's additional information.

Mark further relates, solely in his Gospel, that Bartimeus, left his garment when approaching Jesus (10:50), and moreover, when healed, continued with Jesus '*on the way*'. Subsequently, this would have been '*on the way*' out of the city, to the suburbs where Zaccheus' house was situated.

BARTIMEUS AND ZACCHEUS OUTSIDE JERICHO

Mark 10:46 Luke 19:1
And they and Jesus came into Jericho, entering and passing through.
As He went out of Jericho with His disciples and a great number of people, blind Bartimeus, the son of Timeus, sat by the wayside begging.

Mark 10
47 And when he heard that it was Jesus of Nazareth, he began to cry out, and say, "Jesus, You Son of David, have mercy on me."

48 And many rebuked him that he should be quiet: but he cried out much more, "You Son of David, have mercy on me."

49 And Jesus stood still, and said, "Call him."
And they called the blind man, saying to him, "Cheer up! Get up. He is calling you."

50 And he casting away his cloak, sprang up, and came to Jesus.
51 And Jesus answered and said to him,
"What do you wish that you I should do for you?"
The blind man said to Him, "Lord, that I might receive my sight."

52 And Jesus said to him, "Go your way; your faith has made you whole."
And immediately he received his sight, and followed Jesus along the way.

Luke 19
2 And, consider, there was a man named Zaccheus, who was a chief of the tax collectors, and he was rich.
3 And he wanted to see who Jesus was; and couldn't because of the crowd, because he was short.
4 And he ran on ahead, and climbed up into a sycamore tree to see Him: for He was to pass that way.

5 And when Jesus came to the place, He looked up, and saw him, and said to him, "Zaccheus, hurry, and come down; for today I must stay at your house."
6 And he hurried, and came down, and received Him joyfully.

7 And when they saw it, they all murmured, saying,
"That He was gone to be guest with a man who is a sinner."

8 And Zaccheus stood, and said to the Lord;
"Look, Lord, the half of my goods I give to the poor; and if I have taken
anything from anyone by false accusation, I restore them fourfold."
9 And Jesus said to him,
"This day is salvation come to this house, since he also is a son of Abraham.
10 For the Son of Humanity is come to seek and to save that which was lost."

We saw in previous sections how John outlined his Gospel, interspersed with
time indicators to the various settings, in designating the context of the text
through the seasons. Moreover, this also related to the Synoptics, adding further
order and placing the many incidents into a framework of these periods.
Furthermore, John also highlighted certain days to verify aspects surrounding the
traveling factor, as is now shown once more through the days associated with
Lazarus' death.

JESUS STAYS AT ZACCHEUS'

The disciples and Jesus having traveled, after staying two days still in Aenon
near Salim, when first hearing of Lazarus' illness (John 11:3, 6), had now
arrived at Jericho, where Jesus indicated to Zaccheus that He wished to stay
at his house (Luke 19:5), before continuing again with their journey, to
Bethany, and ultimately Jerusalem.

Jesus indicated that Lazarus had died sometime after the message from
Mary and Martha (John 11:14). By the time Jesus had arrived in Bethany,
John reveals that Lazarus '*had lain four days in the grave already*' (v. 17).
Thus, allowing for the traveling to Jericho, and no doubt an overnight stop-
off at Zaccheus', the next day they would carry on with their journey, to
Bethany first, as Lazarus lay dead, and then Jerusalem.

At Zaccheus' (Luke 19:5-6) Jesus went on to give the *Parable of the Ten
Pieces of Money* (vv. 12-27), to try and dispel the notion that He was going
to take over the government from the Romans at that time (v. 11). Jesus,
moreover, also used the analogy of money in this parable, as Zaccheus was a
tax collector and rich. Zaccheus had addressed Jesus, trying to console the
notions of some of the people that he was a profiteer, and greedy (vv. 7-8).
And Jesus wanted to also show, that not all rich people are like that (v. 9).

Jesus also used the outline of this parable once more, just before the last
Passover, where, after the *The Olivet Prophecy*, when He was talking exclusively
to the disciples, He replaces the '*pound*' [Gr. '*mina*'] with the greater '*talent*' [Gr.
'*talanton*'] and varies other detail slightly (Mat. 25:14-30). Thus, in that sense,
though very similar, the two parables are unique to either Gospel writer.

Luke 19

11 And as they heard these things, He added and spoke a parable, because He was near to Jerusalem, and because they thought that the Kingdom of God should immediately appear.

12 He said therefore,

"A certain Nobleman went into a far country to receive for himself a kingdom, and to return.

13 And he called his ten servants, and delivered them ten pounds, and said to them, 'Occupy till I come.'

14 But his citizens hated him, and sent a message after him, saying, 'We will not have this man reign over us.'

15 And it came to pass, that when he had returned, having received the kingdom, then he commanded his servants to be called to him, to whom he had given the money, that he might know how much everyone had gained by trading.

16 Then came the first, saying, 'Lord, your pound has gained ten pounds.'

17 And he said to them, 'Well done, you good servant: because you have been faithful with very little, you have authority over ten cities.'

18 And the second came, saying, 'Lord, your pound has gained five pounds.'

19 And he said likewise to them, 'You be over five cities.'

20 And another came, saying, 'Lord, see, here is your pound, which I have kept laid up in a napkin:

21 for I feared you, because you are an austere man, you take up what you didn't lay down, and reap what you didn't sow.'

23 'Wherefore then didn't give you my money into the bank, that at my coming I might have required my own with interest?'

24 And he said to the others, who stood by,

'Take from them the pound, and give it to the one who has ten pounds.'

25 And they said to him, 'Lord, that servant has ten pounds.'

26 I tell you, that to everyone who has shall be given; and from those who don't have, even what they have shall be taken away from them.

27 But those my enemies, who would not that I should reign over them, bring here, and slay them before me."

Matthew 20:29 Luke 19:28

And when He had thus spoken, as they departed from Jericho, He went on ahead, and a great crowd followed Him ascending up to Jerusalem.

We saw that Jesus stayed at Zaccheus', as the forty-mile journey from Aenon near Salim to Jericho would have required. Luke further indicates after Jesus had related the parable, and had been cordially received, after being refreshed, no doubt with an overnight stay, the next day, Jesus goes in front of the disciples, leading them, as they leave Zaccheus', with the crowds following (19:28).

Thus, Luke this time links with Matthew, paralleling as they continue their journey. Matthew further revealing that the **thirty-ninth miracle** occurred, '*as they departed from Jericho*', and the vicinity of the suburbs of the city (20:29). The next day being light again, they would continue their journey. The people following Jesus and the disciples, still jubilant with the atmosphere of hoping the establishment of the Kingdom was about be fulfilled with this Tabernacles, and that Jesus would become King. This stirring emotional scene even continued right up to the time they subsequently reached Jerusalem. With the shouts ascribing Jesus as King also being exclaimed by the now grown number of disciples, as Luke again indicated by referring to '*the whole crowd of the disciples*' (19:37-38), with his specialty of relating to these increased number of disciples, which by now would have included the five hundred, as we suggested in the section *The Last Summer* [pp. 275-277]. Paul was the one who went on to specifically mention the number of these disciples, in relation to having witnessed the resurrected Messiah (1 Cor. 15:6).

THEY LEAVE THE SUBURBS

After the first blind man of Luke, the thirty-seventh miracle, Mark's Bartimeus, the thirty-eighth, Jesus having stayed at Zaccheus' house, the great number of people, no doubt part of the festal caravan, in the light of the next day prepare to converge on Jerusalem for the forthcoming Festival of Tabernacles. With Jesus and all disciples at the front of the procession (Luke 19:28), the jubilant atmosphere coupled with the miraculous incidents of Jesus healing the blind men, and the wish in Jesus becoming King over their country, leads into the next amazing event of Matthew's two blind men (20:30-34)!

It becomes obvious that Matthew's two blind men were healed the next day, '*as they departed from Jericho*' (v. 29), in continuing their journey to Bethany and Jerusalem, as the other blind men had subsequently been healed when they had first arrived at Jericho.

Interestingly, Matthew, altogether, exclusively recorded three miracles [the tenth, twentieth, and the **thirty-ninth miracle**], of which each had two people healed simultaneously. Each of these particular miracles, when looking at the main *Scripture Graph x*, we see, is a connecting factor to the detail surrounding the next incidents. Each one dovetails with the subsequent parallel events of all the three Synoptics.

Thus, Matthew's two blind men in being unique to his Gospel, with both Mark's and Luke's single blind men to theirs, each of the Synoptics had specifically recorded individual detail paramount to linking and dovetailing the whole story together. Moreover, all, nonetheless, echo the fervent atmosphere of the crowds, relating to all the four blind men, as depicted in the shouting of, "*You Son of David*", with the hope of Jesus becoming King at that time. The atmosphere is further highlighted with the cries of Kingship by the disciples and the people, in the scenario when Jesus shortly rides into Jerusalem (Mat. 21:7-9; Mark 11:7-10; Luke 19:35-39), with even the children shouting the same in the Temple, the next day (Mat. 21:15)!

Now, the Synoptics could have mentioned any other detail in the incidents that occurred surrounding this particular time at Zaccheus', as no doubt Jesus had said other things, and healed others, as is reflected in the statement when they are about to enter Jerusalem, '*for all the mighty works that they had seen*' (Luke 19:37), rather than exclusively just recording the healing of these four blind men. All the Synoptics mention that when they arrive at the Mt. Olives, Jesus sent '*two disciples*' (Mat. 21:1; Mark 11:1; Luke 19:29) with not one of them just referring to 'disciples' or 'disciple'. Thus, they were explicit in the recording of the detail they had wanted to include surrounding this particular time.

TWO BLIND MEN LEAVING JERICHO

Furthermore, had each one, with the miracles of the blind men, been referring to the same miracle, then in the same manner they would have written '*two*', with no difference occurring in the stages of the arriving near Jericho and going through. It would have been plain, as with the scenario of the sending of the two disciples.

But, amazingly, we have just before this last Tabernacles, the record of these four blind men being healed, connected with the traveling, and the purpose of resurrecting Lazarus, who by the time they had arrived at Bethany, had been dead four days.

All this culminates together with a reference by John, in the dialogue covering Lazarus' resurrection, of the fact that John knew of this astonishing conglomeration of factors, with the significance of the healing of these four blind men, of which also some people at the grave of Lazarus were aware of, too (11:37). No doubt these four blind men, as alluded to in the narration of their healing, all went on to follow Jesus along with the festal caravan, and right up to the final approach of Jesus riding into Jerusalem.

Matthew 20

30 And, suddenly, two blind men sitting by the wayside, when they heard that Jesus passed by, cried out, saying, "Have mercy on us, oh Lord, You Son of David."

31 And the crowd rebuked them, so they should be quite: but they cried the more, saying, "Have mercy on us, oh Lord, You Son of David."

32 And Jesus stood still, and called them, and said, "What do you wish that I should do for you?"

33 They said to Him, "Lord, that our eyes may be opened."

34 So Jesus had compassion on them, and touched their eyes: and immediately their eyes received sight, and they followed Him.

DOUBLE ENTENTE!

Both Mark (11:1-2) and Luke (19:29-30) now return to the scenario, and linkup and parallel with Matthew once more (21:1-2), as they come near to Bethpage and Bethany, at which point Jesus sends two disciples to a village opposite them. No doubt the village was Bethpage, and not Bethany, since it was highlighted by Matthew naming it, and that, they were also to stop-off at Bethany with the healing of Lazarus, before Jesus was to ride into Jerusalem.

Matthew 21:1 Mark 11:1 Luke 19:29

And it came to pass, when He and they came drawing near to Jerusalem, and were come near to Bethpage and Bethany, towards the mount called the Mount

of Olives, then Jesus sent off two of His disciples,
Matthew 21:2 Mark 11:2 Luke 19:30
and spoke to them, saving, "Go you your way into the village over against
you: and in which entering - as soon as you are entering into it, immediately
you shall find an ass tied, and a colt tied with her, where on no one yet sat;
loose them, and bring them to Me.
Matthew 21:3 Mark 11:3 Luke 19:31
And if anyone asks anything saying to you, 'Why do you do this untying?'
Thus you shall say to them, 'Because that the Lord has need of them;' and
immediately they will send them here."

Matthew 21
4 All this was done, that it might be fulfilled which was spoken by the prophet
(Zechariah 9.9), saying,
5 "TELL THE DAUGHTER OF SION, 'CONSIDER, YOUR KING COMES TO YOU GENTLE,
AND SITTING UPON AN ASS, EVEN A COLT THE FOAL OF THE ASS.'"

Matthew 21:6 Mark 11:4a Luke 19:32a
And the disciples who were sent went their way, and did as Jesus instructed
them.

Both Mark and Luke refer only to the colt of the she-ass in the same parallel
scenario of the fetching of the two animals, as Matthew also relates. Undoubtedly
Mark and Luke were pointing to the factor that Jesus actually rode the colt
itself, the young but grown foal of the she-ass. We have witnessed many times
the way the Gospel writers have left out certain detail that the other has
supplied in referring specifically to parallel or successive incidents. Both Mat.
21:1 and Mark 11:1 relate only to '*they*', coming near to Bethpage, as the two
disciples were sent, whereas, Luke 19:29 has, '*He*' came near to Bethpage.
This did not mean that either category were not there, but rather that both were.
So it was with the two categories of animals.

Moreover, the prophecy of Zechariah 9:9 should be read in emphasizing the
fact that the colt was the progeny of the ass, and thus in that sense, the colt
was also part ass, though, in its fulfillment at that particular time there were
two animals. Reading it as applying to one animal is also seen in the second
fulfillment six months later, when Jesus once more comes riding into Jerusalem
before the final Passover, this time there is no mention of a second animal in
the text. *The Gospel According to John*, which refers to this, relates to the
same prophecy, and reads, 'DON'T BE AFRAID, DAUGHTER OF SION: LOOK, YOUR
KING COMES, SITTING ON AN ASS'S COLT' (12:15).

However, back to just before the first time Jesus was about to ride into Jerusalem.

While the two disciples had gone to fetch the two animals, Jesus having no doubt told them where to meet up again, He continues with His journey to Bethany to heal Lazarus, before this entry into Jerusalem.

Both Mark 11:4b-6 and Luke 19:32b-34 cover the specific setting of the finding of the animals, which transpires while the scenario surrounding Lazarus takes place (John 11:17-46). Matthew is silent regarding the narration dealing with the actual finding of the animals. Whereas, both Mark 11:7 and Luke 19:35 parallel again and synchronize with Mat. 21:7, in the bringing of the animals, while Jesus deals with the healing of Lazarus.

THE FORTIETH MIRACLE - LAZARUS

John fills in with the details surrounding this event of the fortieth-miracle, of the resurrection of Lazarus, the most remarkable miracle so far of all Jesus' miracles: in the sense that Lazarus had been dead four days, and, moreover, that the blind men mentioned in the Synoptics, are no doubt alluded to in ch. 11:37, as they came to Jerusalem with the festal caravan. This set of combined circumstances (v. 47), with especially the healing of Lazarus, coupled with the children at the Temple, thus, was the main factor which went on to annoy the Pharisees so much, and which led to the prevailing situation of crucifying Jesus at the next following Passover (12:10-11).

Hence, Jesus could no longer walk openly among the Jews, after the protection from the great crowds at this Tabernacles had bated, and once again He has to escape and withdraw to Ephraim to await the final Passover (11:53-54).

John 11

17 Then when Jesus came, He found that he [Lazarus] had lain in the grave four days already.

18 Now Bethany was near to Jerusalem, about two miles off:

19 and many of the Jews came to Martha and Mary, to comfort them concerning their brother.

20 Then Martha, as soon as she heard that Jesus was coming, went and met Him: but Mary sat still in the house.

21 Then said Martha to Jesus,

"Lord, if You had been here, my brother had not died.

22 But I know, that even now, whatever You will ask of God, God will give it You."

23 Jesus says to her, "Your brother shall rise again."

24 Martha said to Him,

"I know that he shall rise again in the resurrection at the last day

John 11

25 Jesus said to her,

"I am the Resurrection, and the Life: they who believe in Me, though they were dead, yet shall they live:

26 and whoever lives and believes in Me shall never die. You believe this?"

27 She says to Him,

"Yes, Lord: I believe that You are the Messiah, the Son of God, who should come into the world."

28 And when she had said this, she went her way, and called Mary her sister secretly, saying, "The Master is come, and calls for you."

29 As soon as she heard that, she rose quickly, and came to Him.

30 Now Jesus was not yet in the town, but was in the place where Martha met Him.

31 The Jews then who were with her in the house, and comforted her, when they saw Mary, that she rose up hastily and went out, followed her, saying, "She goes to the grave to weep there."

32 Then when Mary was come where Jesus was, and saw Him, she fell down at His feet, saying to Him," Lord, if You had been here, my brother had not died."

33 When Jesus therefore saw her weeping, and the Jews also weeping who came with her, He groaned in the spirit, and was troubled,

34 and said, "Where have you laid him?"

"They said to Him, "Lord, come and see."

35 Jesus wept.

36 Then said the Jews, "See how He loved him!"

37 And some of them said, "Could not this Man, who opened the eyes of the blind, have caused that even this man should not have died?"

38 Jesus therefore again groaning in Himself comes to the grave. It was a cave, and a stone lay upon it.

39 Jesus said, "Take away the stone."

Martha, the sister of him who was dead, says to Him,

"Lord, by this time he smells: for he has been dead four days."

40 Jesus says to her, "Didn't I say to you, that, if you would believe, you should see the glory of God?"

41 Then they took away the stone from the place where the dead was laid. And Jesus lifted up His eyes, and said, "Father, I thank You that You have heard Me.

42 And I knew that You hear Me always: but because of the people who stand by I said it, that they may believe that You have sent Me."

43 And when He thus had spoken, He cried with a loud voice, "Lazarus, come forth!"
44 And he who was dead came out, bound hand and foot with grave clothes: and his face was bound about with a napkin.
Jesus says to them, "Loose him, and let him go."

45 Then many of the Jews who came to Mary, and had seen the things that Jesus did, believed on Him.
46 But some of them went their ways to the Pharisees, and told them what things Jesus had done.

THE END OF THAT DAY

It is now at this intersection that both Mark 11:4b-6 and Luke 19:32b-34, dovetail between John 11:46 and Mat. 21:7, with the finding of the two animals, while Lazarus was healed.

Both Mark 11:7, and Luke 19:35, now parallel and synchronize with Mat. 21:7, while the animals are being brought. With Mark exclusively revealing it occurred in the village '*where the two ways met*' (11:4b), no doubt referring to Bethpage.

Mark 11:4b Luke 19:32b
And finding even as He had said to them, the colt tied by the door outside in a place where two ways met [Mat. 21:2; Mark. 11:2; Luke 19:30].
Mark 11:4c-5 Luke 19:33
And as they were loosing the colt, certain of the owners thereof who stood there said to them, "What are you doing, why are you loosing the colt?"
Mark 11:6 Luke 19:34
And they said to them even as Jesus had instructed [Mat. 21:3; Mark 11:3; Luke 19:31], "The Lord has need of him:" and they let them go.

Matthew 21:7 Mark 11:7 Luke 19:35
And they brought the ass, and the colt, to Jesus, and they threw their coats, positioning them over them, mounting Jesus on [the colt], and He settled upon him.
Matthew 21:8 Mark 11:8 Luke 19:36
And as He went, a very great crowd spread their clothes on the road: and others cut down branches from off the trees, and strewed them on the road.

Matthew 21:9 Mark 11:9
And the crowds who went ahead, and those who followed, cried, saying (Ps. 118:26), "Hosanna; to the Son of David: BLESSED IS HE WHO COMES IN THE NAME OF THE LORD: HOSANNA in the Highest!
Mark 11
10 Blessed be the Kingdom of our ancestor David; HOSANNA in the Highest!"

It is here with the tumultuous scenario of the excited crowds that Luke uniquely informs us, '*even now at the descent of the Mount Olives*', that '*the whole crowd of the disciples*' also joined in with the cries relating to Jesus' Kingship (19:37-38). As mentioned previously, this no doubt is a reference to the seventy, and the many others that had increased the number of disciples to five hundred, of which Paul indicated, by the time of Jesus' resurrection (1 Cor. 15:6).

Luke 19
37 And when He was come near, even now at the descent of the Mount of Olives, the whole crowd of the disciples began to rejoice and praise God with a loud voice for all the mighty works that they had seen;
38 saying (Ps. 118:26), "BLESSED BE THE KING WHO COMES IN THE NAME OF THE LORD: peace in is Heaven, and glory in the Highest."

39 And some of the Pharisees from among the crowds said to Him, "Master, rebuke Your disciples."
40 And He answered and said to them, "I tell you that, if these should hold their peace, the stones would immediately cry out."

41 And when He was come near, He beheld the city, and wept over it,
42 saying, "If you had known, even you, at least in this your day, the things which belong to your peace! But now they are hid from your eyes.
43 For the days shall come upon you, that your enemies shall cast a trench about you, and compass you round, and keep you in on every side.
44 And shall lay you even with the ground, and your children within you; and they shall not leave in you one stone upon another; because you knew not the time of your visitation."

Matthew 21:10 Mark 11:11a
And when Jesus was entered into Jerusalem, and into the Temple, all the city was moved, saying, "Who is this?"
Matthew 21:11 Mark 11:11b
And the crowds said, "This is Jesus the Prophet of Nazareth of Galilee."

And when He had looked about on all things, and now the evening [15th Tishri] was come, He went out to Bethany with the twelve.

This day of leaving Jericho now drew to a close as, highlighted by Mark 11:11.

But before we consider the texts surrounding the next miracle, the **forty-first miracle** of the barren fig-tree, it is interesting to note that the children of Israel wandered in the wilderness for forty years (Josh. 5:6), before they saw the Promised Land. Though, thirty-eight years was actually spent in wandering, before there was any indication they were now to head towards Israel. Subsequently, the other two years related to their journeying towards the Promised Land, with the final instruction by Moses in the thirty-ninth year, before they went across Jordan. Israel was to come across the Jordan, to where no doubt Jesus was baptized [Bethabara], and continue, after its first Passover in the Promised Land (Josh. 7:10), towards Jericho. Which like Jerusalem, in the previous main text, was to be compassed with armies in having its walls removed, because it did not understand the time of its visitation (Luke 19:44).

Moreover, after the fortieth miracle of the resurrection of Lazarus, who had lain dead four days, there are two more miracles recorded in the Gospels, revealing forty-two altogether, preceding the greatest miracle of all - the resurrection of Jesus into eternal spirit and everlasting life after three days. Furthermore, there were forty-two recorded stop-off places mentioned in the wanderings of the children of Israel (Num. 33:1-49), before they were to see the reality of life in the Promised Land.

We must also consider, in relating to the texts surrounding the forty-first miracle of the barren fig-tree, in its fertile context it was a symbol of the prophecy referring to a time of growing peace (Mic. 4:3-4), and additionally a symbol of Israel. This is further borne out by the *Parable of the Barren Fig-Tree*, where the tree was given the chance to produce fruit in the fourth year, after being fruitless for three (Luke 13:7-9). Thus we must reflect on Jesus having these last three years, done many more miracles than the forty we have now covered, and consider the symbolism, as we continue into the next six months up to the concluding Passover, realizing that the ones specifically recorded were indeed for signs (John 20:29-30).

THE NEXT DAY

Both Matthew (21:10-11) and Mark (11:11) had correlated and paralleled together, after dovetailing with Luke (19:44), with Jesus having now entered Jerusalem and the Temple, and having surveyed the situation, He returns back to Bethany, where Lazarus had been resurrected only hours before. Moreover, another day had concluded, as highlighted specifically by Mark 11:11.

This triumphant day, that all the Gospel writers had recorded various pieces of information on, had started with Jesus leaving Jericho, with the healing the two blind men, and subsequently arriving near Bethany, where two disciples fetched the animals for the journey into Jerusalem, after the healing of Lazarus. Before, and on the way to Jerusalem, the great crowds had shouted praises about Jesus' Kingship, and now along with the whole company of disciples continued their cries, which led to the descent into Jerusalem, down the Mount of Olives, overlooking the Temple, to Jesus beholding the city, and weeping over the cities ignorance as to what brings peace. Jesus then prophesied over the city, and finally arrived in Jerusalem and the Temple. Thus, Mark exclusively pointed out that this day had now ended (11:11).

Moreover, for the next successive order of the days that follow on, it is Mark alone who highlights these days, as Matthew had placed his next dialogue in actual reverse order to their successive occurrences. Matthew, as he did on several other occasions, now at this junction, does not follow on systematically with the details in his text, but places the scenario of Jesus purging the Temple the final time (21:12-17), preceding the cursing of the fig-tree. No doubt Matthew, as he had done previously, in several other places in his text, now positions the detail to ally the importance he was trying to emphasize, rather than the order, with the reason for the cursing of the fig-tree (21:18-22).

In Judaism as mentioned previously, the days end, and begin again with the evening. Now the commencement of Tabernacles starts with an annual Sabbath. Undoubtedly, Jesus once more wanted to arrive in Jerusalem as the Festival was about to begin [as similar to the previous Tabernacles], subsequently entering the city as the evening was shortly advancing, with the first Sabbath of the Festival. Having prophesied over the city, and having entered the city and surveyed the scene at the Temple, He returns to Bethany that evening and in the morning of this next day again reappears. This is highlighted, through the importance of both incidents, of the cursing of the fig-tree and the final cleansing of the Temple, taking place simultaneously, in the day of the first Sabbath of the Festival.

Mark (11:12), however, parallels and correlates together with Matthew (21:18) at that particular point, in affirming that it was the next day that they returned in the morning. Moreover, it is obvious by the topography, and the direction in returning to Jerusalem from Bethany that the fig-tree was cursed in first coming back to the city.

Furthermore, Jesus had purged the Temple also at the very beginning of *The First Passover* of His ministry [p. 52], and thus, at this last Tabernacles, as a final and complete admonition before His Passion, which would include the Ultimate Sacrifice of all time, as the administrative practices of some of the Temple sacrifices and procedure had not improved since the first Passover, He went on to purge the Temple once more, also at the very beginning of that Festival.

Hence, the purpose of the **forty-first miracle** of the cursing of the fig-tree, as a symbolic gesture, becomes apparent with the scenario relating to the prophecy over the city, the previous evening.

A further indicator, as to this having occurred at the season of Tabernacles, is that the fruit of the fig-tree should be ripe at this particular time of the year of the general harvest. Hence, Jesus' natural expectation of hoping there would be fruit on this single tree, before entering the city again. Elsewhere, in subsequent isolated places, in not having been harvested, these trees would be full of fruit at this time.

The phrase, in the AV, *'for the time of figs was not'* has the *'yet'* (Mark 11:13) in italics, indicating it not being in the original Greek. Thus, we have omitted it, as it is surplus to the intended meaning. The phrase *'for its time of was not'*, referred solely to this single tree Jesus had pointed out, and that it was not the time of figs for that particular individual tree. Its process, or time of producing fruit did not transpire, as it should have done. Hence, which Jesus chose to use at that relevant time, was correct in every aspect. Moreover, Jerusalem in prophecy was likened to the fruit of the fig-tree in Jer. 24:1-10. Consequently, Jesus the previous evening had pronounced a similar prophecy over the events to develop in Jerusalem forty years later on.

Though the two incidents, the prophetic cursing of the fig-tree, and the cleansing of the Temple directly afterwards, as Mark clearly pointed out with chronological precision, all took place in the daytime that followed the riding into Jerusalem. Uniquely, He further indicates yet another day, a second one, in the returning to Bethany again the second time, as that day came to an end in which the fig-tree was cursed (11:19).

In this day, in which the fig-tree was cursed, Luke (19:45) returns once more, paralleling and correlating with Matthew (21:12) and Mark (11:15) in the final purging of the Temple.

Matthew 21:18 Mark 11:12
And now in the morning [15th Tishri], when they were come from Bethany, as He returned to the city, He was hungry:
Matthew 21:19a Mark 11:13
and seeing beside the road a fig-tree afar off having leaves, He comes, if

perhaps He might find anything upon it: and when He came to it, however He found nothing upon it, but leaves only; for its time of figs was not.
Matthew 21:19b Mark 11:14
And Jesus answered and said to it, "Let no one eat fruit from you, and let no fruit grow on you hereafter forever."
And His disciples heard it.

And presently the fig-tree withered away.

Matthew 21:12 Mark 11:15 Luke 19:45
And they came into Jerusalem: and Jesus went into the Temple of God, and began to throw out all them who sold therein, and those who bought in the Temple courtyards, and overthrew the tables of the money-changers, and the seats of those who sold doves;
Mark 11
16 and would not allow anyone to carry anything through the Temple courtyards.
Matthew 21:13 Mark 11:17 Luke 19:46
And He taught, and exclaimed, saying to them,
"Is it not written (Is. 56:7), 'MY HOUSE IS THE HOUSE OF PRAYER AND SHALL BE CALLED OF ALL NATIONS THE HOUSE OF PRAYER'? But you have made it a den of thieves."
Mark 11
18 And the Scribes and the Chief Priests heard it, and sought how they might destroy Him, because all the people were astonished at His teachings.

Matthew 21
14 And the blind and the lame came to Him in the Temple; and He healed them.

15 And when the Chief Priests and Scribes saw the wonderful things that He did, and the children crying out in the Temple, and saying, "Hosanna to the Son of David;" they were very displeased,
16 and said to Him, "You hear what these say?"
And Jesus says to them,
"Yes; have you never read (Ps. 8:2), 'OUT OF THE MOUTHS OF CHILDREN AND BABES YOU HAVE PERFECTED PRAISE'?"

Matthew 21:17 Mark 11:19
And He left them, and when the evening was come He went out of the city into Bethany; and lodged there.

THE NEXT DAY AGAIN

As mentioned, it was Mark who exclusively pointed out the next day, wherein the fig-tree was cursed, before the purging of the Temple took place. Once again it is Mark who uniquely indicates it was on the following day after, that the curse on the fig-tree had subsequently taken its effect (11:20). This, no doubt, would be the second day of the Festival, in which the **forty-first miracle** had now been completed. Matthew did not mention any days, though he relates with Mark that the fig-tree had now died.

This is the last recorded miracle before the healing of Malchus' ear.

Matthew 21:20 Mark 11:20
And in the morning, as they passed by, when the disciples saw the fig-tree dried up from the roots, they marveled, saying, "How soon is the fig-tree withered away!"
Mark 11
21 And Peter calling to remembrance [Mat. 21:19; Mark 11:13-14] says to Him, "Master, look, the fig-tree which You cursed is withered away."

Matthew 21:21a Mark 11:22
And Jesus answered and spoke saying to them,
"Have faith in God.
Matthew 21:21b Mark 11:23
For truly I say to you, if you have faith, and doubt not, you shall not only do what was done to the fig-tree, but also that if you whoever, shall say to this mount, 'Be removed, and be cast into the sea'; and shall not doubt in their heart, but shall believe those things which they say shall come to pass; they shall have whatever they say - it will happen.

Matthew 21:22 Mark 11:24
And all things, therefore I say to you whatever you shall desire when you ask in prayer, believe that you will receive them, and you shall receive them.

Mark 11
25 And whenever you stand fast praying, forgive, if you have anything against any: that your Father also who is in Heaven may forgive you your trespasses.
26 But if you do not forgive, neither will your Father who is in Heaven forgive your trespasses."

THE MIDDLE AND LAST DAY

Luke remained silent over the fig-tree, and returns to the scene, with the information that Jesus '*taught daily in the Temple*', no doubt referring to the rest of this Tabernacles, and concludes with the fact of the Head of the Sanhedrin and some of the other members wanting to destroy Jesus (19:47-48).

John also returns to this particular setting, which follows on directly, no doubt indicating and correlating with Luke's reference on the following page to the Sanhedrin, that it was after the Festival that the Council met to discuss the situation of Jesus and His disciples influence on the people.

No doubt, after the Last Great Day of the Festival, as alluded to in the phrase, '*from that day on*' (John 11:53), Jesus again could no longer walk openly among the Jews, and retired to Ephraim for six months (v. 54) before returning for His Passion (12:1).

Luke 19

47 And He taught daily in the Temple. But the Chief Priests and the Scribes and the Chief of the People sought to destroy Him,
48 and they couldn't find what they might do: for all the people were very attentive to hear Him.

John 11

47 Then gathered the Chief Priests and the Pharisees a Council, and said, "What shall we do? For this Man does many miracles.
48 If we let Him thus alone, everyone will believe on Him: and the Romans shall come and take away both our place and nation."

49 And one of them, named Caiaphas, being the High Priest that same year, said to them, "You know nothing at all,
50 nor consider that it is expedient for us, that one Man should die for the people, and that the whole nation perish not."

51 And this he spoke not of himself: but being High Priest that year, he prophesied that Jesus should die for that nation;
52 and not for that nation only, but that also He should gather together in one the children of God who were scattered abroad.

53 Then from that day [22nd Tishri] on they took counsel together for to put Him to death.

54 Jesus therefore walked no more openly among the Jews; but went from there to a country near to the wilderness, into a city called Ephraim and there continued with His disciples.

THE ULTIMATE PASSOVER

It is John who continues with his narrative, of the next events just prior to the last Passover, with the festal caravan, and the expectation of the people whether Jesus would come to this particular Festival (11:55-57).

We saw there had been a six month omission of any detail, from the penultimate

Passover, up until the events of this last Tabernacles, likewise there would be another six months gap from this last Tabernacles to the final Passover.

John 11

55 And the Jews Passover was near at hand: and many went out of the country up to Jerusalem before the Passover, to purify themselves.

56 Then they sought for Jesus, and spoke among themselves, as they stood in the Temple, "What do you think, that He won't come to the Festival?"

57 Now both the Chief Priests and the Pharisees had given an order, that if anyone knew where He was, he should show it, that they take Him.

John continues with his narrative, with the next successive events, indicating it was six days before the Passover that Jesus returned to Bethany again (12:1). This would be the 8th Nissan in the Jewish calendar. Jesus and the disciples ate the New Testament Passover in the evening of the start of the 14th Nissan, before His crucifixion in the same day, since they had wanted to crucify Him before the first annual High Sabbath of the Passover week, which fell in the beginning part of the evening the 15th Nissan. Remember, the Jewish Calendar ends its days and starts them again in the evenings.

Six days prior to the disciples eating the Passover Supper with Jesus, John, who also knew certain details about the particular meal where Jesus was anointed, which, no doubt, was at the home of Mary and Martha, and Simon the Leper, as Matthew and Mark had both recorded, added additional information that he recalled was important in addressing these subsequent events. John had uniquely revealed, while Matthew and Mark had shown that Jesus' head was anointed, that Jesus' feet were, too. John also exclusively relates this particular aspect. However, both Matthew (26:12) and Mark (14:8) allude, moreover, that even Jesus' body could have been anointed as well.

Now Matthew (21:22) and Mark (11:26) do not follow on after their last successive incidents six months previously, as they placed the next following event of the anointing of Jesus (Mat. 26:6-16; Mar. 14:3-11), between the last two days which led to the disciples and Jesus eating their Passover Supper (Mat. 26:1-5; Mar. 14:1-2).

No doubt Matthew had placed his text as he had on various other occasions. Though this is the only time Mark does not follow in successive order, both wanted to highlight the importance of Judas deciding from that instance to betray Jesus, along with the final ratification of Judas' betrayal, which occurred two days before their Passover meal. John accurately chronologized these events, mentioning again certain days, as he had done many times before, pointing out that the anointing occurred in the 8th Nissan, six days prior to the first evening of the 14th Nissan, when Jesus and the twelve ate their Passover Supper.

JUDAS BETRAYS JESUS

John 12

1 Then Jesus six days before the Passover came to Bethany, where Lazarus was, who had been dead, whom He raised from the dead.
Matthew 26:6 Mark 14:3a John 12:2
And now when Jesus was in Bethany in the house of Simon the Leper, there they made Him a supper; and Martha served: but Lazarus was one of them who sat at the table with Him, as He sat at supper.

Matthew 26:7 Mark 14:3b John 12:3
Then there came to Him Mary having taken an alabaster box of a pound of ointment of genuine spikenard very costly; and she broke the box and poured it on His head, and anointed the feet of Jesus, and wiped His feet with her hair: and the house was filled with the odor of the ointment.
Matthew 26:8 Mark 14:4
But when His disciples saw it, there were some - those who had indignation within themselves, exclaimed saying, "Why, and to what purpose was this waste of the ointment made?
Matthew 26:9 Mark 14:5
For this ointment, it might have been sold for much - more than three hundred pence, and given to the poor."
And they murmured against Him.

John 12
4 Then says one of His disciples, Judas Iscariot, Simon's son, who would betray Him,
5 "Why wasn't this ointment sold for three hundred pence, and given to the poor?"

6 He said this not that he cared for the poor; but because he was a thief, and had the bag, and bore what was therein.
Matthew 26:10 Mark 14:6 John 12:7
And when Jesus understood it, Jesus then said to them,
"Leave her alone; why do you trouble her? For she has done a good work upon Me: against the day of My burying has she kept this.
Matthew 26:11 Mark 14:7 John 12:8
For you have the poor with you always, and whenever you wish you may do them good: but you don't always have Me.

Mark 14

8 She has done what she could: she is come beforehand to anoint My body for the burial.

Matthew 26

12 For in that she has poured this ointment on My body, she did it for My burial.

Matthew 26:13 Mark 14:9

Truly I say to you, wherever this gospel shall be preached in the whole world, this also what she has done shall be spoken of her for a memorial to her."

John 12

9 Many people of the Jews therefore knew that He was there: and they came, not for Jesus' sake only, but rather that they might see Lazarus also, whom He had raised from the dead.

10 But the Chief Priests consulted that they might put Lazarus also to death; 11 because that by reason of him many of the Jews went away, and believed on Jesus.

Matthew 26:14 Mark 14:10

And then one of the twelve, called Judas Iscariot went to the Chief Priests, to betray Him to them.

Matthew 26:15 Mark 14:11a

And said to them, "What will you give me, and I will deliver Him to you?" And when they heard it, they were glad, and promised to give him money. And they covenanted with him for thirty pieces of silver.

Matthew 26:16 Mark 14:11b

And from that time he sought opportunity how he might conveniently betray Him.

Matthew exclusively and specifically states it was '*from that time*' (26:16), of that particular evening meal, with the anointing of Jesus, that Judas decided to betray Jesus, with Mark paralleling and correlating with him (Mark 14:11b). Thus, Judas decided to betray Jesus after the meal at which he became annoyed over the expense of the anointing, seeking initially when it would subsequently be an opportune time for this.

John had not included Judas betraying Jesus after the meal, nevertheless, he presupposed we would understand that aspect, as he added the unique dialogue surrounding Judas' uncaring attitude towards the poor, in that he was a thief (12:4-6), and the exclusive information that '*the Chief Priests consulted that they might put Lazarus also to death*' (v. 10), inserting this sentence at the appropriate time after the narrative of the anointing. Additionally, John knew that the Chief Priests would still be consulting on how they might put Jesus to death (11:53), and that at this juncture Jesus would have been prominent on their list before Lazarus. Thus, he alluded to those aspects, with the recording of his select details relating to Judas regarding that particular evening. Judas now provided the Chief Priests an easier and opportune way of ratifying their plans.

However, Luke did not include this incident of the evening meal at Bethany, even though he had solely revealed that Jesus had been served at the home of Martha and Mary her sister a year previously (10:38-40). We shall see, whereas Matthew, Mark and John, related to the details of when, and what caused Judas' betrayal, whereas Luke relates to the actual ratification of Judas betraying Jesus '*to the Chief Priests and captains*', two days preceding Jesus and the disciples eating their Passover Supper (22:1-6).

Matthew and Mark had positioned their texts on the meal and anointing to also highlight, that it was two days before Jesus and the disciples ate their Passover meal, and that further ratification had been agreed as per Luke's reference, when Judas went again to the Chief priests to ratify how they were going to entrap Jesus.

'THE NEXT DAY'

John continues with the next following event after the evening meal and the anointing of Jesus, which led to Judas betraying Jesus, from that particular time.

'The next day' as John (12:12) relates, would now make this the fifth day before the Passover, the 9th Nissan, as he in his usual manner had again indicated the time factor.

John 12

12 On the next day many people who were come to the Festival, when they heard that Jesus was coming to Jerusalem,

13 took branches of palm trees, and went out to meet Him, and cried, "Hosanna: BLESSED IS HE the King of Israel WHO COMES IN THE NAME OF THE LORD (Ps. 118:26)."

14 And Jesus, when He had found a yearling, sat on it; as it is written (Zech. (9:9),

15 'DON'T BE AFRAID, DAUGHTER OF SION: LOOK, YOUR KING COMES, SITTING ON AN ASS'S COLT.'

16 His disciples didn't understand these things at first: but when Jesus was glorified, then remembered they that these things were written of Him, and they who had done these things to Him.

17 The people therefore who were with Him when He called Lazarus out of his grave, and raised him from the dead, bore record.

18 For this cause the people also met Him, for that they heard He had done this miracle.

19 The Pharisees therefore said among themselves, "You perceive how we prevail nothing? Look, the whole world is gone after Him."

20 And there were certain Greeks among them who came to worship at the Festival:

21 the same came therefore to Philip, who was of Bethsaida of Galilee, and desired him, saying, "Sir, we would see Jesus."

22 Philip comes and tells Andrew: and again Andrew and Philip tell Jesus.

23 And Jesus answered them, saying, "The hour is come, that the Son of Humanity should be glorified.

24 Truly, truly, I say to you, except a corn of wheat fall into the ground and die, it remains alone: but if it die, it brings forth much fruit.

25 They who love their life shall lose it; and they who hate their life in this world shall keep it to life eternal.

John 12

26 If anyone serves Me, let them follow Me; and where I am, there also shall My servant be: if anyone serves Me, Him will My Father honor.

27 Now is My soul troubled; and what shall I say?
Father, save Me from this hour: but for this cause came I to this hour.
28 Father, glorify Your Name."
Then came there a voice from the heavens, saying,
"I have both glorified it, and I will glorify it again."

29 The people therefore, that stood by, and heard it, said that it thundered: others said, "An angel spoke to Him."
30 Jesus answered and said, "This voice hasn't come for My sake, but for your sakes.
31 Now is the judgment of this world: now shall the Prince of this world be sent away elsewhere.
32 And I, if I be lifted up from the earth, will draw all people to Me."
33 This He said, signifying what death He should die.

34 The people answered Him,
"We have heard out of the Torah that the Messiah remains forever (Ps. 110:4; Is. 9:6-7; Dan. 7:14): and how do You say, 'The Son of Humanity must be lifted up (John 3:14)?' Who is this Son of Humanity?"
35 Then said Jesus to them,
"Yet a little while the Light is with you. Walk while you have the Light lest darkness come upon you: for they who walk in darkness don't know where they are going.
36 While you have the Light, believe in the Light, that you may be the children of the Light."

These things spoke Jesus, and departed, and did hide Himself from them.
37 But though He had done so many miracles before them, yet they didn't believe in Him:
38 that the saying of Isaiah (53:1) the prophet might be fulfilled, which he spoke, "LORD, WHO HAS BELIEVED OUR MESSAGE? AND TO WHOM HAS THE ARM OF THE LORD BEEN REVEALED?"
39 Therefore they couldn't believe, because that Isaiah (6:10) said again,
40 "HE HAS BLINDED THEIR EYES, AND HARDENED THEIR HEART; THAT THEY SHOULD NOT SEE WITH THEIR EYES, NOR UNDERSTAND WITH THEIR HEART, AND BE CONVERTED, SO I SHOULD HEAL THEM."
41 These things said Isaiah, when he saw His glory, and spoke of Him.

42 Nevertheless among the Chief Rulers also many believed on Him; but because of the Pharisees they did not confess Him, lest they should be put out of the synagogue:

43 for they loved the praise of humans more than the praise of God.

The combined text from vv. 12-43 relates to the events of *'the next day'*, the 9th Nissan, as Jesus rode the final time into Jerusalem (vv. 12-16).

Verses 17-18, continue with the people having also followed Jesus, because they had witnessed the resurrection of Lazarus, six months earlier, and that the Pharisees were increasingly perturbed as the news of Jesus had subsequently over the years even spread to Greece and the surrounding vicinities and, no doubt, the other countries (vv. 19-20).

At that point, Philip asks Jesus about the Greeks wishing to see Him (vv. 21-22), at which Jesus answers in showing the reason for losing one's life (vv. 23-26), and asks the Father to glorify His Name (vv. 27-28).

Directly after the voice from Heaven spoke, it confirmed that the Father would continue to glorify His Name (vv. 29-31), with Jesus referring to His death (vv. 32-33). The people whom Jesus was addressing enquired further of His death, as they thought that the Messiah did not have to die (v. 34), whereby Jesus answered stating that, they could only begin to see, if they could comprehend the True Light (vv. 35-36). With John using that particular fitting statement about darkness and light to conclude this specific day's events, Jesus, the True Light, hides Himself from the Pharisees (v. 36), as the evening and darkness now loomed.

John elaborates further on the events of this day, relating that Jesus had carried out many miracles up to this particular junction, and in retrospect and conclusion typifies two prophecies from Isaiah also explaining the disbelief of the Pharisees (vv. 37-41). With this conclusion, John also mentions in keeping the record straight, the fact that it was only a small nucleus of the Sanhedrin, who wanted Jesus dead (vv. 42-43).

Furthermore, John, in pointing out the *'six days before the Passover'*, the 8th Nissan, and *'the next day'*, the 9th Nissan, which text we have just covered, once again draws our attention to another amazing fact that the Lamb presents Himself.

THE LAMB PRESENTS HIMSELF

It was on the 10th Nissan that the original Passover Lamb was chosen (Ex. 12:3), and kept up until the 14th Nissan, wherein it was subsequently slain and eaten (v. 6).

With the 9th Nissan having drawn to a close, and Jesus hiding Himself, no doubt that night (John 12:36), and the following dialogue of John having related to aspects of the conclusion of that particular day (vv. 37-43), it should be clear that John's next verse (v. 44) would be referring to the following day on the 10th Nissan wherein Jesus had subsequently returned to the Temple, for the final witness to the Pharisees and Sadducees before the Passover.

Thus, John, in referring to Jesus' short prayer before He hid Himself, in asking the Father to save Him from that hour, though it was the reason Jesus had come to that specific hour, further alluded, now as the 9th Nissan was drawing to an end, and the 10th was about to begin, that this day was the day the voice from Heaven affirmed that the Father would continue to glorify His Name through His Son. It confirmed that Jesus was the ultimate Sacrificial Passover Lamb (12:27-28), and subsequently, in three days again, through the events of the Passover Day, and the culmination of incidents surrounding the Resurrection. Hence, as we shall see, all the Gospel writers converge and parallel together on this next day's memorable discourse - on the 10th Nissan, symbolic of the original choosing of the lamb for the Passover.

John then, through indicating these days before the Passover, was directing us to this factor. He supplemented the details surrounding these days, adding them to what was already known, as he also would have been familiar with the scenario as depicted by Luke, in uniquely mentioning, '*on one of those days*' (20:1). At that particular juncture the context explicitly synchronizes and parallels with Matthew and Mark, with the ensuing scenario where the Pharisees question Jesus on His authority (Mat. 21:23; Mark 11:27-28; Luke 20:2). As we shall see, this leads subsequently into the last admonition that Jesus was to give them before the Passover.

But preceding that, we had just concluded that Judas in the 8th Nissan had ratified the agreement to betray Jesus, with the episode the following day of the final riding into Jerusalem, and the Pharisees concern of those from the whole region around wishing to see Jesus, including those from the Greek world [which the Romans had taken over], consequently all having taken place on the fifth day before the Passover, the 9th Nissan. No doubt, as this day had come to an end, Jesus hid until the morning light of the next day, the 10th Nissan, with the great crowds in the Temple affording Him protection, as the Pharisees were becoming more efficacious in their efforts to kill Him.

Thus, the next '*one of those days*' as Luke had exclusively written (20:1), and whose subsequent narrative parallels with the other Synoptics, would be the fourth day before the 14th Nissan - the 10th Nissan. This, the day that was associated with the taking of the original Passover lamb for each household to keep ready until the evening of the 14th (Ex. 12:3-6). Hence, Jesus who was symbolic of the ultimate Passover Lamb without any blemish, would present Himself to the Temple, firstly to the Chief Priests (Mat. 21:23; Mark 11:27; Luke 20:1, and moreover, for the last witness to both the Pharisees and Sadducees.

Consequently, the inclusive dialogue from where the Synoptics depict firstly the

Chief Priests, Scribes and Elders asking Jesus about His authority, all takes place on this one particular day, and is the last conversation that Jesus has with these Pharisees and Sadducees, as the Mt. Olivet Prophecy, spoken specifically to the disciples, follows on directly after the final discourse of that day with them, and leads us into the scenario of just prior to the Passover. Jesus does not converse again with them until His arrest.

Furthermore, when examining the text of John, from 12:44-50, which dovetails with the Synoptics (Mat. 21:23a; Mark 11:27a; Luke 20:1a), we see that though all the Gospels synchronize and correlate together over the narration which would have taken place on the 10th Nissan, once again, it is John who leads us into the opening dialogue of that new day, in the morning no doubt, at the outset of this next day, in which Jesus had returned again to the Temple, where the people at Festival times converged. Consequently, the Pharisees question Jesus on His authority (Mat. 21:23; Mark 11:27-28; Luke 20:2). As we shall see, this leads subsequently into the last admonition that Jesus was to give them before the Passover. Chief Priests, Scribes and Elders to come over, and after undoubtedly having listened to what Jesus had said, decided to question Him over His authority, in saying and doing the things He did.

The dialogue surrounding the prophecy from Isaiah (John 12:37-43), had related to the day Jesus hid (v. 36). The next opportunity, in the following day, Jesus returned again for His final discourse with the Pharisees and Sadducees. Moreover, Jesus presented Himself at the Temple, as *The Ultimate Passover* Lamb on the 10th Nissan, where the Synoptics relate as Jesus taught, a delegation of the Chief Priests, Scribes and some of the Elders of the People [Sanhedrin], approached to question Him (Mat. 21:23b; Mark 11:27b; Luke 20:1b).

Matthew 21:23a Mark 11:27a Luke 20:la
And it came to pass, that on one of those days, they came again to
Jerusalem: and when He was come into the Temple, as He was walking in
the Temple, subsequently teaching the people in the Temple, and preaching
the gospel,
John 12
44 Jesus cried out and said,
"They who believe in Me believe not in Me, but in Him who sent Me.
45 And they who see Me see Him who sent Me.
46 I am come, as the Light into the world that whoever believes in Me
should not stay in darkness.
47 And if anyone hears My words, and doesn't believe, I don't judge them:
for I came not to judge the world, but to save the world.

John 12

48 Those who reject Me, and don't receive My sayings, have this to judge them: the words that I have spoken, the same shall judge them in the Last Day.

49 For I have not spoken of Myself; but the Father who sent Me, He gave Me the authority, of what I should say, and what I should speak.
50 And I know that His directive is life everlasting: whatever I speak therefore, even as the Father said to Me, so I speak."

Matthew 21:23b Mark 11:27b Luke 20:1b
The Chief Priests and the Scribes with the Elders of the People approached, and moved toward Him as He was teaching, and came near,
Matthew 21:23e Mark 11:28 Luke 20:2
and spoke exclaiming to Him, saying,
"Tell us, by what authority You do these things? And who is he who gave You this authority to do these things?"
Matthew 21:24 Mark 11:29 Luke 20:3
And Jesus answered and said to them,
"I will also ask you one thing; which if you tell Me, and answer Me, likewise I will tell you by what authority I do these things.
Matthew 21:25a Mark 11:30 Luke 20:4
The baptism of John, from where was it? Was it from Heaven, or of the people? Answer Me."

Matthew 21:25b Mark 11:31 Luke 20:5
And they reasoned with themselves, saying,
"If we shall say, 'From Heaven;' He will say to us, 'Why then didn't you believe him?'
Matthew 21:26 Mark 11:32 Luke 20:6
But if we shall say, 'Of the people;' we fear all the people will stone us; for they all being persuaded, count John that he was as a prophet indeed."
Matthew 21:27a Mark 11:33 Luke 20:7
And they answered, and said to Jesus, "We cannot tell from where it was."

Matthew 21:27b Mark 11:33 Luke 20:8
And Jesus answering said to them, "Neither do I tell you by what authority I do these things."

LAST PARABLES TO PHARISEES

We have seen how the Synoptics with the questioning over Jesus' authority correlated and paralleled together, with John dovetailing and highlighting through the time of year, and the very day.

Jesus on this notable day in the Temple, in which He presented Himself to the

Chief Priests, Scribes, and Elders of the People, directly after the discourse on His authority, now begins to speak to them in parables. Note John 12:49, where the AV has '*a commandment*', in Greek '*entole*', which also relates to '*an authoritative prescription*'. We have translated our text accordingly.

Though, John led us into the dialogue on this day in the Temple, he does not return to the narrative until the 14th Nissan at the Supper, four days from this day (13:1-2).

As Jesus concluded the conversation over His authority, He then continued teaching, by giving the last three parables spoken to the Pharisees and Sadducees. Matthew related that He gave the first *Parable of the Two Sons* (21:28-32), indigenous to His Gospel.

Mark, agreeing that it was at that particular juncture, dovetails, setting the scene to Matthew in stating, '*He began to speak to them in parables*' (12:1a), though Mark only refers to the single *Parable of the Wicked Tenants*, at which point Luke also returns to the text: both now paralleling together and aligning with Matthew too, through the same parable (Mat. 21:33; Mark 12:lb; Luke 20:9). This being both Mark and Luke's last, and only parable in which, they recorded Jesus addressing the Pharisees at this juncture.

Matthew concludes with the third *Parable of the Wedding Banquet*, his second indigenous one, and thus, is the last one spoken to the Pharisees (22:2-14).

Mark 12:la

And He began to speak to them in parables.

Matthew 21

28 "But what do you think? A certain man had two sons; and he came to the first, and said, 'Son, go work today in my vineyard.'

29 And he answered and said, 'I will not:' but afterwards he repented, and went.

30 And he came to the second, and said likewise. And he answered and said, 'I'll go, sir:' and didn't go.

31 Which of them two did the will of his father?"

They say to Him, "The first."

Jesus says to them, "Truly I say to you, that the tax collectors and the prostitutes go into the Kingdom of God before you.

32 For John came to you in the way of righteousness, and you didn't believe him: but the tax collectors and the prostitutes believed him: and you, when you had seen it, didn't repent afterwards, so you might believe him.

Matthew 21:33 Mark 12:lb Luke 20:9

Hear another parable:"

Then He began to speak to the people this parable;

"There was a certain man a landowner who PLANTED A VINEYARD (Ps. 80:8; Is. 5:1-2), AND

SET A HEDGE, HEDGING IT ROUND ABOUT, AND DUG A WINEPRESS IN IT, FOR THE JUICE, AND BUILT A TOWER, and let it out to farmers, and went into a far country for a longtime:

Matthew 21:34 Mark 12:2 Luke 20:10a
and at the season, when the time of the fruit drew near, he sent his servant, with servants to the farmers, that they should give him the fruits, that they might receive from the farmers the fruits of the vineyard:
Matthew 21:35 Mark 12:3 Luke 20:10b
and they caught him, and the farmers beat him, and sent him away empty, and took his servants, and beat one, and killed another, and stoned another.

Matthew 21:36 Mark 12:4 Luke 20:11
And again, he sent to them another servant, and other servants more than the first: and at him they cast stones, and wounded him in the head, and they beat him also, and treated him shamefully, and sent him away empty, shamefully handled, and they did likewise to the others.
Mark 12:5 Luke 20:12
And again he sent another; a third: and they wounded him too, and they cast him out, and killed him, and many others; beating some, and killing some.

Matthew 21:37 Mark 12:6 Luke 20:13
But last of all then said the lord of the vineyard, 'What shall we do?'
Having yet therefore one son, his well-beloved: 'I will send my beloved son:'
Thus, He sent his son also to them, saying, 'It may be they will reverence my son, when they see him.'

Matthew 21:38 Mark 12:7 Luke 20:14
But when the farmers saw the son, those farmers, they reasoned speaking among themselves, saying, 'This is the heir: come, let us kill him, and let us seize on his inheritance, that the inheritance may be ours.'
Matthew 21:39 Mark 12:8 Luke 20:15a
And they caught him, and so they took him, and threw him out of the vineyard, and killed him.

Matthew 21:40 Mark 12:9a Luke 20:15b
When the lord therefore of the vineyard comes, what therefore will the lord of the vineyard do to them, those farmers?"
Matthew 21:41 Mark 12:9b Luke 20:16
He continued, "He will come and he will miserably destroy those wicked farmers, and will let out, and shall give the vineyard to other farmers, who shall render him the fruits in their seasons."

And when they heard it, they said, "God forbid."

Matthew 21:42a Mark 12:10 Luke 20:17
And He beheld them, and Jesus spoke saying to them,
"Did you never read in the Scriptures? What then is this that is written (Ps. 118:22-23), 'THE STONE WHICH THE BUILDERS REJECTED, THE SAME WAS MADE TO BECOME THE CAPSTONE;
Matthew 21:42b Mark 12:11
THIS WAS THE LORD'S DOING, AND IT IS MARVELLOUS IN OUR EYES?'
Matthew 21
43 Therefore I say to you, the Kingdom of God shall be taken from from you, and given to a nation bearing the fruits thereof.
Matthew 21:44 Luke 20:18
And whoever shall fall upon that Stone - this Stone, shall be broken: but on whomever it shall fall, it will grind them to powder."

After the *Parable of the Wicked Tenants* Jesus further related a prophecy. Both Matthew (21:45-46) and Mark (12:12a) confirm that the same group of Chief Priests, Scribes and Elders of the People, who were there earlier in that day, were still present. However, angry over the realization that the two parables and the prophecy applied to them, they now wished to seize Him, but because they feared the response of the crowds, could not.

Jesus then goes on to relate Matthew's indigenous last *Parable of the Wedding Banquet* (22:2-14), which was specifically directed at this annoyed delegation.

Matthew 21
45 And when the Chief Priests and Pharisees had heard His parables, they perceived that He spoke of them.
Matthew 21:46 Mark 12:12a
And they sought to lay hands on Him, but they feared the people because they took Him for a Prophet: for they knew that He had spoken the parable against them.
Matthew 22
1 And Jesus answered and spoke to them again by parable, and said,
2 "The Kingdom of Heaven is like to a certain king, who made a marriage for his son,
3 and sent out his servants to call those who were invited to the wedding: and they would not come.

4 Again, he sent out other servants, saying, 'Tell them who are invited, consider, I have prepared my dinner: my oxen and my fatlings are killed, and all things are

ready: come to the marriage.'
5 But they made light of it, and went their ways, one to their farm, another to their merchandise:
6 and the remnant took his servants, and treated them spitefully, and and killed them.
7 But when the king heard thereof, he was angry: and he sent out his armies, and destroyed those murderers, and burned up their city.

8 Then says he to his servants, 'The wedding is ready, but those who were invited were not worthy.
9 Go you therefore into the highways, and as many as you shall find, invite to the marriage.'

10 So those servants went out into the highways, and gathered together all as many as they found, both good and bad: and the wedding was furnished with quests.

11 And when the king came in to see the guests, he saw there someone who didn't have on a wedding garment:
12 and he says to them, 'Friend, how came you in here not wearing a wedding garment?'
And they were speechless.

13 Then said the king to the servants, 'Bind this person hand and foot, and take them away, and cast them into outer darkness; there shall be weeping and gnashing of teeth.'
14 For many are called, but few are chosen."

Matthew 22:15 Mark 12:12b Luke 20:19
And the Chief Priests and the Scribes the same hour sought to lay hands on Him; and they feared the people: for they perceived that He had spoken this parable against them.

Then went the Pharisees and they left Him, and went their way, and took counsel how they might entrap Him by His words.

PAYING TAXES TO CAESAR

As mentioned, Mark and Luke did not record the *Parable of the Wedding Banquet*. Nevertheless, they both parallel with Matthew (22:15) at the point when the delegation left after the last parable (Mark 12:12b; Luke 20:19). Moreover, Luke confirms it was '*the same hour*', they continued in their effort of trying to figure a way of seizing Him. Though they left briefly to counsel together on how to stop Jesus' influence. This resulted in certain spies being sent, disciples of the Pharisees, and Herodians, to now try and find a way through which they could twist Jesus' words, and thus arrest Him for not honoring Rome (Mat. 22:16; Mark 12:13; Luke 20:20). Subsequently, certain of the Sadducees arrived, too, who then question Jesus over their beliefs (Mark 12:18; Luke 20:27). Matthew further collaborates that these things were still taking place in 'the same day' (22:23) that Jesus had first come to the Temple (21:23).

Matthew 22:16a Mark 12:13 Luke 20:20
And they watched Him, and they sent out to Him their disciples, spies, certain of the Pharisees and of the Herodians, to catch Him in His words, who should feign themselves just men, that they might take hold of His words, so that they might deliver Him to the power and authority of the Governor.

Matthew 22:16b Mark 12:14a Luke 20:21
And when they were come, they addressed Him asking,
"Master, we know that You speak and teach rightly, and are true, and are swayed by no one: for You do not regard, neither accept You the guise of any, but nevertheless teach the way of God truly, in truth:
Matthew 22:17 Mark 12:14b Luke 20:22
tell us therefore, what do You think? Is it lawful for us to give tribute to Caesar, or not?
Matthew 22:18 Mark 12:15a Luke 20:23
Shall we give, or shall we not give?"

But Jesus knowing their hypocrisy perceived their crafty wickedness, and said to them, "Why do you tempt Me you hypocrites?
Matthew 22:19a Mark 12:15b Luke 20:24a
Bring Me, and show Me the penny tribute money, that I may see it."

Matthew 22:19b Mark 12:16a
And they brought to Him a penny.
Matthew 22:20 Mark 12:16b Luke 20:24b
And He says to them, "Whose is this image, and whose superscription has it?"

Matthew 22:21a Mark 12:16c Luke 20:24c
And they answered and said to Him, "Caesar's."
Matthew 22:21b Mark 12:17 Luke 20:25
And then Jesus says answering, declared to them,
"Give therefore to Caesar the things which are Caesar's, and to God the things
which are God's."

And they marveled at Him.
Matthew 22:22 Luke 20:26
And when they heard these words, they could not take hold of His words
before the people: and they marveled at His answer, and held their peace, and
left Him, and went their way.

So as to confirm this was all still taking place in this one notable day, when the
ultimate Passover Lamb presented Himself to the Temple, Matthew, who has the
greater dialogue of the Synoptics regarding this day, highlights this day, by stating
that the Sadducees, who were in cahoots with the Pharisees over trapping Jesus
through His words, came towards Him, in '*the same day*' (22:23), as the preceding
group of Pharisees and Herodians left (v. 22).

SADDUCEES QUESTION JESUS

Matthew 22:23 Mark 12:18a Luke 20:27
Then the same day came toward Him the Sadducees, those who deny, saying
that there is not any resurrection and they asked Him,
Matthew 22:24 Mark 12:18b-19 Luke 20:28
saying, "Master, Moses wrote saying to us (Deut. 25:5), 'IF A MAN'S BROTHER DIE,
HAVING A WIFE, AND LEAVE HIS WIFE BEHIND HIM, AND HE DIE WITHOUT HAVING
CHILDREN, LEAVING NONE, THAT HIS BROTHER SHOULD TAKE IN MARRIAGE HIS WIFE,
AND RAISE UP OFFSPRING INSTEAD OF HIS BROTHER.'
Matthew 22:25 Mark 12:20 Luke 20:29
Now there were therefore with us seven brothers: and the first having married
a wife, dying, died childless, having left no offspring, left his wife to his
brother.
Matthew 22:26a Mark 12:21a Luke 20:30
And likewise the second also took her to wife, neither left he any offspring
and he died childless.
Matthew 22:26b Mark 12:21b-22a Luke 20:31
And the third took her, and likewise to the seventh, and they all left no
children, and died.

Matthew 22:27 Mark 12:22b Luke 20:32
And last of all the women also died.

Matthew 22:28 Mark 12:23 Luke 20:33
Therefore in the resurrection when they shall rise, whose wife shall she be of the seven? For the seven they all had her as a wife."

Matthew 22:29 Mark 12:24 Luke 20:34
And Jesus answered and said to them,
"In this you are mistaken because you don't understand the Scriptures, nor either the Power of God. The children of this world marry, and are given in marriage:
Matthew 22:30a Mark 12:25a Luke 20:35
but those who shall be accounted worthy to obtain that world, and the resurrection, for when they shall rise from the dead, in the resurrection they neither marry, nor are given in marriage:
Matthew 22:30b Mark 12:25b Luke 20:36
neither can they die anymore: but are as the angels of God, for they are equal to the angels of God who are in Heaven; and are the children of God, being the children of the resurrection.
Matthew 22:31-32a Mark 12:26 Luke 20:37
And nevertheless, that as touching the resurrection of the dead, that they are raised: have you not read that which was spoken in the book of Moses (Ex. 3:6) to you by God, how even Moses revealed at the bush, when he calls the Lord THE GOD OF ABRAHAM, AND THE GOD OF ISAAC, AND THE GOD OF JACOB, and as God spoke to him, saying, 'I AM THE GOD OF ABRAHAM, AND THE GOD OF ISAAC, AND THE GOD OF JACOB'?
Matthew 22:32b Mark 12:27 Luke 20:38
For God is not a God of the dead, but the God of the living: for all live to Him: you therefore do greatly err."

Luke 20
39 Then certain of the Scribes answering said, "Master, well said."
Matthew 22
33 And when the company heard this, they were astonished at His teachings.
Luke 20
40 And after that they dared not ask Him any question at all [regarding the resurrection].

THE GREATEST COMMMANDMENTS

It should be clear that though Luke (20:40) who was referring to '*any question*' relating to the resurrection, the next subsequent dialogue refers to the questioning of Jesus on the Law, which both Matthew (22:35-40) and Mark (12:28-34) had recorded, though Luke had not. Thus, Matthew and Mark parallel and align together at the particular juncture regarding the next question on the Law, and dovetail with Law. Here, Luke (20:41-44) returns to the scenario, paralleling once more with Matthew (22:41-45) and Mark (12:35-41), where Jesus turns the tables on those asking the questions, by now questioning them about whose Son the Messiah was.

Mark, also, before the question on whose Son the Messiah was, similarly stated, *'no one after that dared ask Him any question'* (12:34), which obviously was referring to the subsequent question on the Law. This similar phrase compared to what Luke had said earlier, in relation to the Sadducees first question over the resurrection, nevertheless, is uniquely captured by Mark, in that it refers solely to the question on the Law.

The phrase *'question at all'*, in Luke (20:40), and *'any question'*, in Mark (12:34), are in italics in the AV, indicating these words were added. They should have been translated with regards to the two separate questionings on the two individual subjects. This is clear by Matthew (22:46) also using the similar phrase, still a little later; though, Matthew elaborates further on his sentence, by indicating that now the questionings had all concluded, after the paralleling together of the three Synoptics over Jesus questioning the Pharisees and Sadducees on whose Son the Messiah was.

Matthew 22
34 But when the Pharisees had heard that He had put the Sadducees to silence, they were gathered together.
Matthew 22:35 Mark 12:28a
And then one of them a Scribe came, who was a lawyer, and having heard them reasoning together, and perceiving that He had answered them well, asked Him a question, tempting Him, and said,
Matthew 22:36 Mark 12:28b
"Master, which is the first and greatest Commandment of all in the Law?"

Matthew 22:37a Mark 12:29
And Jesus answered saying to him,
"The first of all the commandments is, 'HEAR, OH ISRAEL; THE LORD OUR GOD IS ONE LORD:
Matthew 22:37b-38 Mark 12:30
AND YOU SHALL LOVE THE LORD YOUR GOD WITH ALL YOUR HEART, AND WITH ALL YOUR SOUL, AND WITH YOUR ENTIRE MIND, AND WITH ALL YOUR STRENGTH (Deut. 6:4-5):'
this is the first and greatest Commandment.

Matthew 22:39 Mark 12:31

And the second is like to it, namely this, 'YOU SHALL LOVE YOUR NEIGHBOUR AS YOURSELF (Lev. 19:18).' There are no other Commandments greater than these.

Matthew 22

40 On these two Commandments hangs all the Law and the Prophets."

Mark 12

32 And the Scribe said to Him,

"Well, Master, You have said the truth: for THERE IS ONE GOD; AND THERE IS NONE OTHER BUT HE (Deut. 4:35):

33 AND TO LOVE HIM WITH ALL YOUR HEART, AND WITH ALL YOUR UNDERSTANDING, AND WITH ALL YOUR SOUL, AND WITH ALL YOUR STRENGTH (Deut. 6:5), AND TO LOVE YOUR NEIGHBOUR AS ONESELF (Lev. 19:18), is more than all whole burnt offerings and sacrifices."

34 And when Jesus saw that he answered discreetly, He said to him, "You are not far from the Kingdom of God."

And no one after that dared ask Him any question [relating to the Law].

The previous two questions both took place in this day, the original delegation of Chief Priests, Scribes and Elders had sent spies, disciple Pharisees, with the Herodians, who now had just been put to silence earlier on in this the same day, over their question on paying taxes to Caesar too.

The Sadducees also tried to confound Jesus with their question about the resurrection, however, they too, were put to silence, after which, gathering with the Pharisees, they conferred together (Mat. 22:34).

The outcome of this discussion, was for one of their top Lawyers (Mat. 22:35), who was also a Scribe (Mark 12:28), to approach Jesus in asking what he thought would be a hard question, which related to which commandment was the most important. This questioning by these certain groups, led Jesus, now while He was still teaching, as the ordinary people heard Him gladly (Mark 12:37) to turn the tables, and put a question to the Pharisees, who were still gathered together (Mat. 22:41).

WHOSE SON THE MESSIAH?

Matthew 22:41 Mark 12:35a

And Jesus answered and said asking them, while He taught in the Temple, while the Pharisees were gathered together,

Matthew 22

42 saying, "What do you think of the Messiah? Whose Son is He?" They say to Him, "The Son of David."

Mark 12:35b Luke 20:41
And He said to them,
"How say the Scribes that the Messiah is the Son of David - David's Son?"
Matthew 22:43 Mark 12:36a Luke 20:42a
And He says to them,
"How then does David in spirit call Him '*Lord,*' for David himself said by the
Holy Spirit, in the book of Psalms (110:1), saying,
Matthew 22:44a Mark 12:36b Like 20:42b
'THE LORD SAID TO MY LORD, "SIT AT MY RIGHTHAND,
Matthew 22:44b Mark 12:36c Luke 20:43
UNTIL I MAKE YOUR ENEMIES YOUR FOOTSTOOL?"'
Matthew 22:45 Mark 12:37 Luke 20:44
If David therefore himself then calls Him 'Lord', from where and how is He
then his Son?"

And the common people heard Him gladly.
Matthew 22
46 And no one was able to answer Him a word, neither dared anyone from that
day on ask Him any more questions.

It is Matthew who closes the episode of this subsequent questioning, highlighting
once more that it was continuing to take place in this same day (22:46). And,
moreover, at this particular juncture, Mark also, further indicates that the setting
surrounding the events of this day were still taking place in the Temple (12:35),
at which point this day's scenario had originally begun (11:27).

The next section follows with the last admonition of the Pharisees, still in this
same day, directly after Mat. 22:46, where Jesus in the company of His disciples
continues speaking to the crowds, who gladly heard Him with the silenced
Pharisees listening in quiet indignation.

LAST ADMONITION OF PHARISEES

With the Pharisees not being able to give a proper answer to whose Son was the Messiah (Mat. 22:41-46; Mark 12:35-37; Luke 20:41-44). Jesus continues with the last admonition of the Pharisees in front of the crowds and disciples still on this same day.

Matthew, later in his narrative, when compared to Mark and Luke, has a reversed order in his phraseology with two of his verses, as he has with other phrases in his text at several places. He places 'the uppermost rooms at the Festivals' before 'the chief seats in the synagogues' (23:6), with the 'greetings in the market places, and to be called by everyone, 'Rabbi, Rabbi' (v. 7), following. Whereas, though both Mark (12:38-40) and Luke (20:45-47) recorded a curtailed version of the last admonition, nevertheless, because they are two witnesses, we adhere to their identical order of phraseology at that junction.

However, Mark (12:40) and Luke (20:47) in their concluding verse on the admonition, follow Matthew's order of phraseology (23:14).

Matthew 23:1 Mark 12:38a Luke 20:45
Also then spoke Jesus to the crowd, and said to His disciples in the audience of all the people as He taught,
Matthew 23
2 declaring, "The Scribes and the Pharisees sit in Moses' place:
3 all therefore whatever they command you observe, that observe and do; but not according to their works: for they say, and don't do.
4 For they bind heavy burdens and grievous to be borne, and lay them on people's shoulders; but they themselves will not lift a finger to help them.
5 But all their works they do for to be seen: they make broad their phylacteries, and enlarge the borders of their garments.

Matthew 23:7a Mark 12:38b Luke 20:46a
Beware of the Scribes, who desire and love to go walking in long robes, and love greetings in the market places,
Matthew 23:6 Mark 12:39 Luke 20:46b
and the highest chief seats in the synagogues, and love the chief uppermost rooms at Festivals;
Matthew 23
7b and to be called by everyone, 'Rabbi, Rabbi'.
8 Now don't you be called Rabbi: for One is your Master, even the Messiah; and you are all brothers and sisters.
9 And call no man on earth your father: for One is your Father, who is in Heaven.

Matthew 23

10 Neither be called masters: for One is your Master, even the Messiah.

11 But they who are the greatest among you shall be your servants.

12 And whoever shall exalt themselves shall be abased; and they who shall humble themselves shall be exalted.

13 But woe to you, Scribes and Pharisees, hypocrites! For you shut up the Kingdom of Heaven against everyone: for you neither go in yourselves, neither do you allow those who are entering in to enter.

Matthew 23:14 Mark 12:40 Luke 20:47

Woe to you, Scribes and Pharisees, hypocrites! Because you devour widows' houses, and for a show and pretense make long prayers: therefore you and such shall receive the greater damnation.

Matthew 23

15 Woe to you, Scribes and Pharisees, hypocrites! For you compass sea and land to make one proselyte, and when they are made, you make them twofold more the child of hell than yourselves.

16 Woe to you, you blind guides, who say, 'Whoever shall swear by the Temple, it is nothing; but whoever shall swear by the gold of the Temple, they are a debtor!'

17 You fools and blind: for whether is greater, the gold, or the Temple that sanctifies the gold?

18 And, 'Whoever shall swear by the altar, it is nothing; but whoever swears by the gift that is upon it, they are guilty.'

19 You fools and blind: for whether is greater, the gift, or the altar that sanctifies the gift?

20 Whoever therefore shall swear by the altar, swears by it, and all things upon it.

21 And whoever shall swear by the Temple, swears by it, and by Him who dwells therein.

22 And they who shall swear by Heaven, swear by the Throne of God, and by Him who sits on it.

23 Woe to you, Scribes and Pharisees, hypocrites! For you pay tithe of mint and anise and cumin, and have omitted the weightier matters of the Torah, judgment, mercy, and faith: these ought you to have done, and not leave the other undone.

24 You blind guides, who strain at a gnat, and swallow a camel.

25 Woe to you, Scribes and Pharisees, hypocrites! For you make clean the outside of the cup and the dish, but within they are full of extortion and excess 26 You blind Pharisee, cleanse first that which is within the cup and dish that the outside of them may be clean also.

27 Woe to you, Scribes and Pharisees, hypocrites! For you are like whitened tombs who indeed appear beautiful outward, but within are full of dead people's bones, and of all uncleanness.
28 Even so you also outwardly appear righteous to everyone, but within you are full of hypocrisy and iniquity.

29 Woe to you Scribes and Pharisees, hypocrites! Because you build the tombs of the prophets, and garnish the sepulchers of the righteous,
30 and say, 'If we had been in the days of our fathers, we would not have been partakers with them in the blood of the prophets.'

31 Wherefore you be witnesses to yourselves, that you are the children of them who killed the prophets.
32 You verify completely therefore the evaluation of your fathers.
33 You serpents, you generation of vipers, how can you escape the damnation of hell?

34 Wherefore, consider, I send to you prophets, and wise ones, and Scribes: and some of them you shall kill and crucify; and some of them shall you scourge in your synagogues, and persecute them from city to city:
35 that upon you may come all the righteous blood shed upon the earth, from the blood of righteous Abel to the blood of Zechariah son of Berechiah, whom you killed between the Temple and the altar.
36 Truly I say to you, all these things shall come upon this generation.

37 Oh Jerusalem, Jerusalem, you that kills the prophets, and stones those who are sent to you, how often I would have gathered your children together, even as a hen gathers her chickens under her wings, and you refused!
38 Understand, your House is left to you desolate.
39 For I say to you, you shall not see Me from now on, till you shall say, 'BLESSED IS HE WHO COMES IN THE NAME OF THE LORD (Ps. 118:26).'"

After the last admonition of the Pharisees, Jesus moved nearer to the Treasury, calling His disciples closer to Him (Mark 12:43), as He beheld the people throw their money into the Treasury.

Afterwards, the disciples and Jesus start to leave the Temple area, and as they did so, some of them speak of the array of buildings and the adornment of workmanship that went into the Temple (Mat. 24:1; Mark 13:1; Luke 21:5).

Mark 12:41 Luke 21:1
And Jesus sat over against the Treasury, and He looked up and beheld how the people cast money into the Treasury, and saw the rich people casting their gifts into the Treasury: and many who were rich cast in much.
Mark 12:42 Luke 21:2
And He saw also approaching a certain poor widow, and she threw casting in there two mites, which make a farthing.

Mark 12:43 Luke 21:3
And He called to Him His disciples, and He says declaring to them,
"In reality I surely tell you, that this poor widow has cast more in, than all those who have cast into the Treasury:
Mark 12:44 Luke 21:4
for all these have of their abundance put in gifts for God: but she in her penurious want has cast in even all the living that she had."

THE OLIVET PROPHECY

Matthew 24:1 Mark 13:1 Luke 21:5a
And as Jesus went out of the Temple, and departed from the Temple, His disciples came to Him for to show Him the buildings of the Temple: and as some spoke of the Temple, how it was adorned with beautiful stones and gifts, one of His disciples says to Him,
"Master, see what manner of stones and buildings are here!"
Matthew 24:2 Mark 13:2 Luke 21:5b-6
And Jesus answering said to him, and them,
"Don't you see these great buildings, all these things which you consider?
Truly I say to you, the days will come, in which there shall not be left here one stone upon another, that shall not be thrown down."

After Jesus and the disciples had finally left the Temple grounds, they made their way to the Mt. Olives, Jesus arriving before them, where they asked Him two questions relating to the impending destruction of the Temple, and two other questions.

Mark uniquely and specifically points out that it was one of the disciples who addressed Jesus about the adornment of the Temple buildings (13:1). Though, Jesus as the other two Synoptics reveal, directs His prophecy about what the disciples had been considering, and some of them discussing, to all of them (Mat. 24:1; Luke 21:5).

Also Mark once again exclusively and unambiguously, reveals Peter, James, John and Andrew, who were obviously grouped together, asking Jesus the two questions relating to when, and what sign there would be indicating the destruction of Temple (13:3-4).

However, while all the disciples had come to Jesus privately (Mat. 24:3), nonetheless, they all were involved in the previous discussion relating to the Temple. Because of this, and that it was the group of four disciples, Peter, James, John, and Andrew, that Mark uniquely and purposely pointed out who asked Jesus the two questions relating to the destruction of the Temple, nevertheless, these questions were poignant to the others and were directed at them too. Luke (21:7) parallels with Mark over the same two questions relating to the destruction of the Temple, though Luke did not pen the names of those who asked any of the questions.

Matthew, exclusively points out that Jesus was asked a further two questions, one relating to what sign there would be of Jesus' return, and another, associated with what sign there would be revealed in indicating '*the end of the world*' or age. Though Matthew recorded three questions (24:3), and omitted the phraseology of the sign when the destruction of the Temple would come, nonetheless, there are four distinct questions within the parallel texts of the Synoptics.

Matthew 24:3a Mark 13:3
And as He sat upon the Mount of Olives over against the Temple, the disciples came to Him privately, and Peter, James, John, and Andrew asked Him privately,
Matthew 24:3b Mark 13:4 Luke 21:7
and they, asked Him, saying,
"Master, tell us, but when shall all these things be? And what shall be the sign when all these things shall come to pass and be fulfilled? And what shall be the sign of Your coming, and of the end of the world?"

Matthew 24:4 Mark 13:5 Luke 21:8a
And Jesus replying answered and began to speak saying to them,
"Take heed lest anyone deceive you - that you don't get led astray:
Matthew 24:5 Mark 13:6 Luke 21:8b
for many shall come in My Name, saying, 'I am the Messiah;' and shall deceive many: and the time draws near; don't you therefore go after them.

Matthew 24:6 Mark 13:7 Luke 21:9
But when you shall hear of wars and rumors of wars and commotions, see that you aren't troubled or terrified: for such things must needs be; for all these things must first come to pass; but the end is not directly yet."

Matthew 24:7a Mark 13:8a Luke 21:10
Then He said to them,
"For nation shall rise against nation, and kingdom against kingdom:

Matthew 24:7b Mark 13:8b Luke 21:11a
and there shall be great earthquakes in several places, and there shall be famines,
and pestilences and troubles:
Matthew 24:8 Mark 13:8c Luke 21:11b
all these are the beginning of sorrows; and fearful sights and great signs shall
there be in the heavens.

Though Matthew (24:7) has '*earthquakes*' after '*pestilences*', nevertheless, once
again, we follow Mark and Luke's order with their phraseology, with the earthquakes
preceding the famines. Moreover, Mark has '*troubles*' as the last of these '*beginning
of sorrows*', and does not have the same Greek word that Matthew and Luke has for
'*pestilences*'.

Furthermore, since earthquakes are not a natural result of wars, as famines are, as
they would intrinsically follow on after wars, with pestilences after famines, the
point of the Synoptics is that the earthquakes would be in the midst of the other
human-made curses, and transpire before or after any of them.

Mark 13:9a Luke 21:12
But before all these take heed to yourselves: for they shall lay their hands on you,
and persecute you, delivering you up to the synagogues, and in the synagogues
you shall be beaten: for they shall deliver you up to Councils, and into prisons,
and you shall be brought before Kings and Rulers for My Name's sake.
Mark 13:9b Luke 21:13
And it shall turn out as a testimony for you, against them.

Mark 13
10 And the gospel must first be published among all nations.

11 But when they shall lead you, and deliver you up, take no thought beforehand
what you shall say, neither premeditate: but whatever shall be given you in that
hour, express that: for it is not you who speaks, but the Holy Spirit.
Luke 21
14 Settle it therefore in your hearts, not to meditate beforehand what you shall
answer.
15 For I will give you the words and wisdom, which your adversaries shall not be
able to refute nor contradict.

Mark 13:12a Luke 21:16a
And both parents, and brothers and sisters shall betray you. Now brother shall betray
brother and sister to death, and fathers their children; and children shall rise up against
their parents. And relatives, and friends shall betray you:

Matthew 24:9a Mark 13:12b Luke 21:16b
and then shall they deliver some of you up to be afflicted, and they shall cause
them to be put to death - killing you.
Matthew 24:9b Mark 13:13a Luke 21:17
And you shall be hated of all nations for My Name's sake.
Matthew 24
10 And then shall many be offended, and shall betray one another, and shall
hate one another.

11 And many false prophets shall rise, and shall deceive many.
12 And because lawlessness shall abound, the love of many shall wax cold.

Matthew 24:13 Mark 13:13b
But those who shall endure to the end, the same shall be saved.
Luke 21
18 But there shall not a hair of your heads perish.
19 In your patience possess your souls.

Matthew 24
14 And this gospel of the Kingdom shall be preached in the whole world for
a witness to all nations; then shall the end come.

Luke 21
20 And when you shall see Jerusalem compassed with armies, then know that
the desolation is near.

Matthew 24:15 Mark 13:14a
But when you therefore shall see the ABOMINATION OF DESOLATION, spoken by
Daniel the prophet, stand in the Holy Place, standing where it ought not
(whoever reads [Dan. 9:27], let them understand:)
Matthew 24:16 Mark 13:14b Luke 21:21
then let those who are in Judea flee to the mountains: and let them who are in
the midst of her depart out; and let those who are in the country not enter into
that place.
Luke 21
22 For these are the days of vengeance, that all things which are written may
be fulfilled.
Matthew 24:17 Mark 13:15
And let those who are on housetops not come down into the house, neither
enter therein, to take anything out of their house:
Matthew 24:18 Mark 13:16
and neither let those who are in the field not return back again for to take their
clothes.

Matthew 24:19 Mark 13:17 Luke 21:23
And woe to those who are with child, and to them who nurse in those days!
For there shall be great distress in the land, and wrath upon this people.

Luke 21
24 And they shall fall by the edge of the sword, and shall be led away captive
into all nations: and Jerusalem shall be trodden down of the Gentiles, until the
times of the Gentiles be fulfilled.

Matthew 24:20 Mark 13:18
But you pray that your flight won't be in winter, neither on the Sabbath Day.

Matthew 24:21 Mark 13:19
For then in those days shall be great tribulation, such as there has not been the
like from since the beginning of the creation of the world, which God created
to this time, no, nor shall either ever be.
Matthew 24:22 Mark 13:20
And except those days should be shortened, and that the Lord had shortened
those days, there should no flesh be saved: but for the elect's sake, whom He
has chosen, those days shall be, as He has shortened the days.

Matthew 24:23 Mark 13:21
And then if anyone shall say to you, 'Look, here is the Messiah;' or, 'Look, He
is there;' don't believe them:
Matthew 24:24 Mark 13:22
for there shall arise false Christs and false prophets, and shall show great signs
and wonders, to seduce, insomuch that, if it were possible, to even deceive
the very elect.
Matthew 24
25 Understand, I have told you in advance.

26 Wherefore if they shall say to you, 'Consider, He is in the desert;' don't go
out: 'Consider, He is in the secret chambers;' don't believe it.
27 For as the lightning comes out of the east, and shines even to the west; so
shall also the coming of the Son of Humanity be.
28 For wherever the carcass is, there will the eagles be gathered together.

Mark 13
23 But you take heed: understand, I have foretold you all things.

Matthew 24:29a Mark 13:24 Luke 21:25a

And nevertheless in those days, immediately after the tribulation of those days there shall be signs in the sun, and in the moon, and in stars: THE SUN WILL BE DARKENED, AND THE MOON SHALL NOT GIVE IT'S LIGHT (Is. 13:10; 24:23; Eze. 32:7; Joel 2:10, 31; 3:15; Amos 5:20; 8:9; Zeph. 1:15),

Matthew 24:29b Mark 13:25 Luke 21:25b

AND THE STARS OF THE HEAVENS SHALL FALL from the heavens, and the POWERS THAT ARE OF THE HEAVENS and IN THE HEAVENS SHALL BE SHAKEN (Is. 34:4); and upon the earth distress of nations, with perplexity; the sea and the waves roaring.

Luke 21

26 And people's hearts failing them for fear, and for looking after these things that are coming on the earth.

Matthew 24:30 Mark 13:26 Luke 21:27

And then shall appear the sign of the Son of Humanity in the heavens: and then shall all the tribes mourn, AND THEN THEY SHALL SEE THE SON OF HUMANITY COMING IN A CLOUD - IN THE CLOUDS OF THE HEAVENS (Dan. 7:13) with great Power and great glory.

Matthew 24:31 Mark 13:27

And then shall He send His angels WITH A GREAT SOUND OF A TRUMPET, AND THEY SHALL GATHER TOGETHER (Is. 27:13) His elect FROM THE FOUR WINDS (Zech. 2:6), FROM one end of THE UTTERMOST PART THE HEAVENS TO THE OTHER (Deut. 30:4).

Luke 21

28 And when these things begin to come to pass, then look up, and lift up your heads; for your redemption draws near."

THE LAST PARABLES

Jesus in the previous section had given the concluding sign of His prophecy - '*the sign of the Son of Humanity in the heavens*', which was the seventh and last sign He gave, when counting the first sign as '*false Christs*', the second '*wars*', the third '*famines*', the fourth '*pestilences*', the fifth '*persecutions*', and the sixth, the sign '*in the sun, moon and stars*', as comparing them to the seven seals in the book of Revelation, ch. 6.

Moreover, directly after this Jesus continues addressing the disciples on the Mt. Olives with the seven last parables, which all relate to various aspects of the prophecy He had just given.

At that point all the Synoptics align once more and parallel together with the *Parable of the Fig-Tree* (Mat. 24:32-36; Mark 13:28-33; Luke 21:29-33), the first parable of the seven.

Subsequently, Mark exclusively recalled directly after the first *Parable of the Fig-Tree*, that Jesus mentioned the second *Parable of the Watching Household* (13:34-36). With this Mark concludes his composition of that days events, with the last sentence of his unique parable relating to watching (v. 37).

Following Mark's unique second *Parable of the Watching Household*, Luke dovetails directly afterwards, and concludes his narration (21:34-36), on the same subject as Mark's parable on watching.

Matthew 24:32a Mark 13:28a Luke 21:29

And He spoke to them a parable;

"Now learn a *Parable of the Fig-Tree*;

consider the fig-tree, and all trees; when its branch is yet tender,

Matthew 24:32b Mark 13:28b Luke 21:30

when they now shoot, and put out leaves, you see and know of your own selves that summer is near at hand.

Matthew 24:33 Mark 13:29 Luke 21:31

So in like manner, when you shall see all these things come to pass, you know that the Kingdom of God is near at hand, even at the doors.

Matthew 24:34 Mark 13:30 Luke 21:32

Truly I say to you, that this generation will not pass away, until all these things are fulfilled.

Matthew 24:35 Mark 13:31 Luke 21:33

The heavens and the earth shall pass away: but My words will not pass away.

Matthew 24:36 Mark 13:32

But of that day and that hour knows no one, no, not the angels who are of and in Heaven, neither the Son, but the Father only.

Mark 13

33 You take heed, watch and pray: for you don't know when the time is.

34 For the Son of Humanity is as a Man taking a long journey, who left his house, and gave authority to his servants, and to everyone their work, and commanded the porter to watch.
35 You watch therefore: for you know not when the master of the house comes, at evening, or at midnight, or at the cock crowing, or in the morning:
36 lest coming suddenly he find you sleeping.
37 And what I say to you I say to all, 'Watch.'

Luke 21

34 And take heed to yourselves, lest at any time your hearts be weighed down with overindulgence, and drunkenness, and the cares of this life, and so that day come upon you unawares.
35 For as a snare it shall come upon all those who dwell on the face of the whole earth.
36 You watch therefore, and pray always, that you may be accounted worthy to escape all these things that shall come to pass, and to stand before the Son of Humanity.

Matthew 24

37 But as the days of Noah were, so shall also the coming of the Son of Humanity be.
38 For as the days of Noah were before the flood they were eating and drinking, marrying and giving in marriage, until the day that NOAH ENTERED INTO THE ARK (Gen. 7:7).
39 And they didn't know until the flood came, and took them all away; so shall also the coming of the Son of Humanity be.

40 Then shall two be in the field; one shall be taken, and the other left.
41 Two women shall be grinding at the mill; the one shall be taken, and the other left.
42 Watch therefore: for you know not what hour your Lord comes.

Matthew's previous dialogue, had ended after the aligning and paralleling together of the *Parable of the Fig-Tree* (24:36), with Mark relating Jesus' words which subsequently followed, and was Mark's second *Parable of the Watching Household* (13:34-37). With that, Mark concluded his record of that day's events.

Luke, however, recalled another part of Jesus' words with the unique recording of his dialogue on the previous subject of watching (21:34-36). Still on the same theme, this naturally would have related to Mark's exclusive *Parable of the Watching Household* afterwards, and thus follows and elaborates further on Mark's second parable of Jesus' allegory on watching. Moreover, it also ends Luke's compilation of that particular day.

Consequently, Luke (21:34-36) dovetails with Mark (13:37) and Matthew (24:37) as Matthew further recalled additional words that Jesus also spoke at this particular in substance to the previous subject on watching.

Hence, Matthew, Mark and Luke, had all aligned and paralleled together with the *Parable of the Fig-Tree*, at which junction Mark had exclusively added the second parable (13:34-37), and concluded his narrative surrounding the fig-tree, with the first verse on watching, which related to the first parable (v. 33). Mark thus, continued with Jesus addressing the disciples after the first parable, with his second *Parable of the Watching Household*, whose theme Luke also continues with and relates to. With that, Luke ends his version of that day's events (21:34-36).

Matthew's narration on the same subject of the continuing subject on watching, thus follows Luke at that precise point, after which he mentions '*the days of Noah*', where he leads into the third parable [though his second] on watching, the *Parable of the Thief* (24:43-44). Matthew's following parable, the fourth [actually his third], the *Parable of the Faithful and Wise Servant*, elaborates further on the same perspective of watching (vv. 45-51).

However, Matthew continues directly after, with the next three parables, his exclusive *Parable of the Ten Virgins* (25:1-13), the *Parable of the Talents* (vv. 14-30), and his last unique one, the *Parable of the Sheep and Goats* (vv. 31-46).

Matthew 24

43 But know this, that if the head of the house had known in what watch the thief would come, they would have watched, and would not have suffered their house to be broken up.

44 You therefore be also ready: for in such an hour as you think not the Son of Humanity comes.

45 Who then is a faithful and wise servant, whom their lord has made ruler over their household, to give them food in due season?

46 Blessed is that servant, whom their lord when he comes shall find so doing.

47 Truly I say to you, that he shall make them ruler over all his goods.

48 But and if that evil servant shall say in his heart, 'My lord delays his coming;'

49 and shall begin to hit their fellow servants, and to eat and drink with drunks;

50 the lord of that servant shall come in a day when they don't look for him, and in an hour that they aren't aware of.

51 And shall cut them asunder, and appoint them their portion with the hypocrites: there shall be weeping and gnashing of teeth.

Matthew 25

1 Then shall the Kingdom of Heaven be likened to ten virgins, who took their lamps, and went out to meet the bridegroom.

2 And five of them were wise, and five were foolish.

3 Those who were foolish took their lamps, and took no oil with them:

4 but the wise took oil in their vessels with their lamps.

5 While the bridegroom delayed, they all slumbered and slept.

6 And at midnight there was a cry made, 'Look, the bridegroom comes; go out to meet him!'

7 Then all those virgins rose, and trimmed their lamps.

8 And the foolish said to the wise, 'Give us of your oil; for our lamps are gone out.'

9 But the wise answered, saying, 'Not so; lest there's not enough for you and us: but go rather to those who sell, and buy for yourselves.

10 And while they went to buy, the bridegroom came; and those who were ready went in with him to the marriage: and the door was shut.

11 Afterwards came also the other virgins, saying, 'Lord, Lord, open to us.'

12 But he answered and said, 'Truly I say to you, I don't know you'.

13 Watch therefore, for you know neither the day nor the hour wherein the Son of Humanity comes.

14 For the Kingdom of Heaven is as a man traveling into a far country, who called his own servants, and delivered to them his goods.

15 And to one he gave five talents, to another two, and to another one; to every one according to their several abilities; and immediately took his journey.

16 Then those who had received the five talents went and traded with the same, and made themselves other five talents.

17 And likewise those who received two, they also gained another two.

18 But those who received one went and dug in the earth, and hid their lord's money.

19 After a long time the lord of those servants comes, and reckons with them.

20 And so those who received five talents came and brought another five talents, saying, 'Lord, you delivered to me five talents: see, I have gained besides these five talents more.'

21 Their lord said to them, 'Well done, you good and faithful servant: you have been faithful over a few things. I will make you ruler over many things: enter into the joy of your lord.'

Matthew 25

22 They who also received two came and said, 'Lord, you delivered to me two talents: see, I have gained two other talents besides these.'
23 Their lord said to them, 'Well done, you good and faithful servant; you have been faithful over a few things. I will make you ruler over many things: enter into the joy of your lord.'

24 Then they who had received the one talent came and said, 'Lord, I knew you that you are a hard man, reaping where you did not sow, and gathering where you did not scatter.
25 and I was afraid, and went and hid your talent in the earth: look, here you have what is yours.'
26 Their lord answered and said to them, 'You wicked and slothful servant, you knew that I reap where I didn't sow, and gather where I didn't scatter:
27 you ought therefore to have put my money to the exchangers, and then at my coming I should have received my own with interest.
28 Take therefore the talent from them, and give it to the one who has ten talents.'

29 For to everyone who has shall be given, and they shall have abundance: but from those who have not shall be taken away even that which they have.
30 And cast you the unprofitable servant into outer darkness: there shall be weeping and gnashing of teeth.

31 When the Son of Humanity shall come in His glory, and all the holy angels with Him, then shall He sit upon the Throne of His glory:
32 and before Him shall be gathered all nations: and He shall separate them one from another, as a shepherd divides the sheep from the goats:
33 and He shall set the sheep on His right hand, but the goats on the left.
34 Then shall the King say to them on His right hand, 'Come, you blessed of My Father, inherit the Kingdom prepared for you from the foundation of the world:
35 for I was hungry, and you gave Me food: I was thirsty, and you gave Me drink: I was a stranger, and you took Me in:
36 naked, and you clothed Me: I was sick, and you visited Me: I was in prison, and you came to Me.'

37 Then shall the righteous answer Him, saying, 'Lord, when did we see You hungry, and fed You? Or thirsty, and gave You drink?
38 When did we see You as a stranger, and took You in? Or naked, and clothed You?
39 When did we see You sick, or in prison, and came to You?'

40 And the King shall answer and say to them, 'Truly I say to you, inasmuch as you have done it to one of the least of these My brothers and sisters, you have done it to Me.'

41 Then shall He say also to those on the left hand,
'Depart from Me, you cursed, into everlasting fire, prepared by the Devil and his angels.
42 for I was hungry, and you gave Me no food: I was thirsty, and you gave Me nothing to drink:
43 I was a stranger, and you didn't take Me in: naked, and you didn't clothe Me: sick, and in prison, and you didn't visit Me.'
44 Then shall they answer Him, saying, 'Lord, when did we see You hungry, or thirsty, or a stranger, or naked, or sick, or in prison, and did not minister to You?'
45 Then shall He answer them, saying, 'Truly I say to you, inasmuch as you didn't do it to one of the least of these, you didn't do it to Me.'
46 And these shall go away into everlasting punishment: but the righteous into life eternal."

THAT GREAT DAY ENDS

Matthew 26
1 And it came to pass, when Jesus had finished all these sayings, He said to His disciples,
2 "You know that after two days [13th Nissan] is the Festival of the Passover, and the Son of Humanity is betrayed to be crucified."

Luke 21
37 And in the daytime He was teaching in the Temple; and at night He went out, and stayed in the Mount that is called Olives.
38 And all the people came early in the [13th Nissan] morning in the Temple, for to hear Him.
Luke 22
1 Now the Festival of Unleavened Bread drew near, which is called the Passover.

In this particular day, that we saw related to the 10th Nissan, in which the people of the original Exodus, four days before 14th Nissan, were to arrange a lamb for each of their subsequent households (Ex. 12:3-6), we see it was further typified, as Jesus had presented Himself - as the ultimate Passover Lamb - to the Temple - the House of God, with the last admonition to the guardians of the Temple, through which scenario the Synoptics had paralleled together over, and dovetailed completely with John.

Matthew specifically indicated that it was, '*when Jesus had finished all these sayings*' (26:1), on this particular day wherein Jesus had presented Himself to the Pharisees at the Temple, relating to them the last parables, and directly afterwards, also the last parables to the disciples, '*that after two days is the Festival of the Passover*' (v. 2).

Matthew stated, '*that after two days is the Festival of the Passover*', which directly followed and was linked to his verse where the phrase,'*all these sayings*' related specifically to the last parables spoken to the disciples. Moreover, these two verses were also indicative of Matthew signifying it was now evening, as that day was over, and another had begun, as then, and as in Judaism to this day, the days were counted from the start of the evenings.

Hence, Matthew pointed out that '*when Jesus had finished all His sayings*', in concluding with the last parables to the disciples that day had now ended, and it had elapsed into the beginning part of the evening and thus, the 11th Nissan.

Luke (21:37) confirms this factor along with Matthew's indication and designation of these various days at this particular junction, in which Jesus had been teaching in the Temple by day on the 10th, and later through that same day now ending. After Jesus had finished teaching the disciples on the Mt. Olives, it would be the evening of the 11th as Jesus went out from the area of Jerusalem, stayed in Bethany on the other side of the Mt. Olives, and returned later in the morning (v. 38), which would still be the 11th, until the following evening.

Also in this day, the 11th Nissan, directly after the day Jesus had presented Himself to the Temple, all the Synoptics parallel once again, with '*the Chief Priests and the Scribes, and the Elders of the People*' assembling together for the final ratification of the plan in taking Jesus (Mat. 26:3-5; Mark 14:1-2; Luke 22:2). However, Luke's main objective at that junction was to establish when, the ratification of Judas communing with them over the details, occurred (22:3-6).

'AFTER TWO DAYS'

Now, where Matthew specifically recorded, '*you know that after two days is the Festival of the Passover*', he additionally indicated, following two days' time it would be the 13th, in which the disciples would prepare for their Passover Supper for the evening of the 14th as Jesus had instructed them (Mat. 26:17-19; Mark 14:12-16; Luke 22:7-13). That day would commence as the 13th ended, on the eve of the beginning of 14th Nissan (Mat. 26:20-21; Mark 14:17; Luke 22:14-16).

Matthew 26:3 Mark 14:1a Luke 22:2a
After [11th Nissan] two days was the Festival of the Passover, and of Unleavened Bread [13th–14th Nissan]: and then assembled together the Chief Priests and the Scribes, and the Elders of the People, to the Palace of the High Priest, who was called Caiaphas,

Matthew 26:4 Mark 14:1b Luke 22:2b

and consulting sought how that they might take Jesus by stealth, and put Him to death killing Him; for they feared the people.

Matthew 26:5 Mark 14:2

But they said, "Not on the Festival [Sabbath] Day [15th Nissan], lest there be an an uproar among the people."

Luke 22

3 Then entered Satan into Judas surnamed Iscariot, being of the number of the twelve.

4 And he went his way, and communed with the Chief Priests and captains, how he might betray Him to them.

5 And they were glad, and covenanted to him money.

6 And he promised, and sought opportunity to betray Him to them in the absence of the crowds.

We dealt with the fact that Judas had decided to betray Jesus, regarding the issue of the very expensive ointment used on Jesus' body on the sixth day before Passover (Mat. 26:16; Mark 14:11; John 12:4-5).

However, Luke had decided not to mention the details of that particular incident, but focused into the later time of the ratification of the arrangements of when and how the Chief Priests were planning to take Jesus (22:3-6). He indicated it was on the day after Jesus had presented Himself to the Temple. Though Luke (22:2) parallels with Matthew (26:3-4) and Mark (14:1), and dovetails afterwards (vv. 3-6), Mark nonetheless, further establishes that the ratification took place two days prior to Jesus and the twelve partaking of their Passover Supper. He pinpoints the day time part of the 11th, when *'the Chief Priests and Scribes sought how they might take Him'*, rather than where Matthew had specifically related his *'two days'*, to the beginning part of the 11th, after Jesus had given the last parables to the disciples, and the 10th had ended in that evening.

Furthermore, Luke had shown when he was referring to *'in the morning'* (21:38), which also related to the 11th, and where he continued with *'now the Festival of Unleavened Bread drew near'* (22:1), his intention was to correlate the ratification of Judas' betrayal with the Chief Priests, on this day, as specifically pointed out by Mark (14:1). Also, Luke uniquely reveals that this ratification was now confirmed with *'the captains'* (22:4), who would be instrumental in trying to organize the arrest of Jesus before the Festival Sabbath High Day of the 15th rather than when Judas had initially gone to the Chief Priest directly after the anointing of Jesus on the 8th Nissan, several days previously.

Moreover, Luke purposely indicates in his last verse on the subject, that Judas was now awaiting for the right moment, when Jesus would be away from the crowds (v. 6), and even better still if it could take place in darkness, too. Thus, the Chief Priests would have given their captains permission to no doubt arrange to spy on Jesus, and to await the signal from Judas when the best opportunity would arise to arrest Him.

Thus, now in these circumstances, with only two days to the start of the Passover week [14th-21st Nissan], the Pharisees had not much time left to take Jesus, as they did not want to take Him on the first Sabbath High Day of the Festival, the 15th Nissan, in which there could be a riot (Mat. 26:5; Mark 14:2). Hence, Luke's last verse on the subject further agrees, that Judas had promised to betray Jesus without the possibility of any tumult arising from the crowds at this particular time just directly before the first Festival Sabbath Passover (22:6).

'The First Day'

The next reference related to by all the Synoptics to the next day, is to '*the First Day of Unleavened Bread*' (Mat. 26:17; Mark 14:12; Luke 22:7). This phrase refers to the 13th, in the sense that the disciples had to get everything ready, including the bread for their Passover Supper, prior to the concluding eve of the 13th, and in the same eve before the 14th arrived. Thus, as the disciples and Jesus ate their Passover in the beginning part of the 14th, the 13th involved the last opportunity for the arrangements of their meal and the unleavened bread. Paul further highlights the symbolism of the unleavened bread and the importance of this at the beginning of the Passover (1 Cor. 5:7-8).

Hence, Jesus and the disciples had arranged for their Passover Supper to be ready in the upper room, for the eve of the 14th Nissan, having completed the arrangements by the afternoon of the 13th (Mat. 26:19; Mark 14:16; Luke 22:13).

Matthew 26:17 Mark 14:12 Luke 22:7

And then came the First Day of Unleavened Bread [13th Nissan], when the Passover must be killed [14th Nissan], and when they killed the Passover.

Now the disciples came to Jesus and said to Him, "Where do You wish that we go and prepare for You so You may eat the Passover?"

Mark 14:13a Luke 22:8

And He sends two of His disciples Peter and John, saying, "Go and prepare us the Passover that we may eat."

Luke 22

9 And they said to Him, "Where do You wish that we prepare it?"

Matthew 26:18a Mark 14:13b Luke 22:10a

And He explains saying to them,

"You go into the city, to a certain man, and look, when you have entered into the city, there shall a man meet you, carrying a pitcher of water; follow him.

Mark 14:14a Luke 22:10b

And wherever he shall go in follow him into the house in which he enters.

Matthew 26:18b Mark 14:14b Luke 22:11

And you shall say to the head of the house,

'The Master says to you, My time is at hand; I will keep the Passover at your house with My disciples. Where is the quest room, where I shall eat the Passover with My disciples?'

Mark 14:15 Luke 22:12

And he shall show you a large upper room furnished and prepared: there make it ready for us."

Matthew 26:19 Mark 14:16 Luke 22:13

And His disciples went off, and came into the city, and found as He had said to them: and the disciples did as Jesus had appointed them; and they made ready the Passover.

'THE PASSOVER'

Three specific references in the Synoptics relate to the ending of the 13th Nissan and the beginning of the 14th, pointing out the specific time when the 13th ended and the 14th began, when Jesus and the apostles are about *'to eat this Passover'* (Luke 22: 15).

Firstly, where Mark states *'in the evening'* (14:17), as they came to the upper room, as the one day was ending, and the other was about to begin: secondly, as they are about to partake of the meal, Matthew has *'now when the evening was come'* (26:20), whereas, thirdly, Luke refers to *'when the hour was come'* (22:14). Both Matthew and Luke indicate the fact that it was now the 14th, the eve of their Passover, when they actually sat down for the commencement of the Last Supper.

The original Passover was also eaten in the first evening of the 14th Nissan, in which the people ate it in their homes (Ex. 12:6-7, 13). However, later on when the Temple was built, and because of the great volume involved, the great volume involved, the Passover sacrifices were slaughtered from midday of the 14th until the afternoon, wherein they were roasted, before the arrival of 15th, the first Sabbath of the Festival. Moreover, Jesus was on the cross from early morning of the 14th, until the afternoon, at which point it even went dark at midday (Mat. 27:45; Mark 15:33; Luke 23:44), at the very time when the Temple sacrifices were being slain.

John had remained silent since he first led us into the 10th Nissan (12:44-50), when Jesus had presented Himself to the Pharisees, after they had been wondering if Jesus would dare show Himself at the Passover (11:56-57). Though, he now returns to the scenario at the eve of the Passover, before Jesus and the disciples are about to partake of the Supper (13:1-3).

Though John 13:2 in the AV has *'Supper being ended'*, even so, the word *'ended'* can give the impression that the Supper was over. Actually, the preparation for the Supper had *'ended'*, and now they could begin. The majority of translators have captured the essence of this aspect, and thus, we have translated it accordingly.

It is interesting to note that though John does not indicate at which point they sat down at the Supper, as both Matthew (26:20) and Luke (22:14) had, nonetheless, he states that Jesus rose from Supper to wash the disciples' feet (13:4-5), and thus confirms with both Matthew and Luke that obviously they initially sat down before the foot washing, and afterwards sat down again (v.12) preceding the start of the actual partaking of their Passover Supper.

Thus, from the combined information in the individual texts of the Gospels, we can see when reading all of the narratives that the foot washing occurred prior to the actual partaking of the Supper. Nevertheless, we have placed the accounts of the events in their natural successive order and integral sense, as they would have transpired, as in any case Judas left the upper room at the end of the Supper, as John alone had recorded.

John 13

1 Now before the Festival of the Passover [13th Nissan], when Jesus knew that His hour was come that He should depart out of this world to the Father, having loved His own who were in the world, He loved them to the end.

Mark 14

17 And in the evening He comes with the twelve.

Matthew 26:20 Luke 22:14

And now when the evening hour was come [14th Nissan], He sat down, and the twelve apostles with Him.

John 13

2 And Supper being ready, the Devil having now put into the heart of Judas Iscariot, Simon's son, to betray Him;

3 Jesus knowing that the Father had given all things into His hands, and that He was come from God, and was going to God;

Luke 22

15 moreover He says to them, "With desire I have desired to eat this Passover with you before I suffer:

16 for I say to you, I will not eat again thereof, until it be fulfilled in the Kingdom of God."

John 13

4 He rises from supper, and lays aside His robe; and takes a towel, and girds Himself.

5 After that He pours water into a basin, and begins to wash the disciples' feet, and to wipe them with a towel, that was wrapped around Him.

6 Then He comes to Simon Peter: and Peter says to Him,

"Lord, You do wash my feet?"

7 Jesus answered and said to him,

"What I'm now doing you won't understand; but you shall realize afterwards."

8 Peter says to Him, "You shall never wash my feet."

Jesus answered him, "If I don't wash you, you have no part with Me."

9 Simon Peter says to Him, "Lord, not my feet only, but also my hands and my head."

10 Jesus says to him,

"Someone who has bathed, only needs to wash their feet, but is completely clean: and you are clean, but not all."

11 For He knew who should betray Him; therefore He said, '*You are not all clean'*.

12 So after He had washed their feet, and picked up His robe, and was set down again, He said to them,
"You know what I have done to you?
13 You call Me Master and Lord: and well you say; for so I am.
14 If I then, your Lord and Master, have washed your feet; you also ought to wash one another's feet.
15 For I have given you an example that you should do as I have done to you.
16 Indeed, indeed, I say to you, the servant is not greater than their lord; neither they who are sent greater than the one who sent them.
17 If you know these things, happy are you if you do them.
18 I don't speak of you all: I know whom I have chosen: but that the Scripture (Ps. 41:9) may be fulfilled, 'HE WHO EATS BREAD WITH ME HAS LIFTED UP HIS HEEL AGAINST ME.'
19 Now I tell you before it come, that, when it is come to pass, you may believe that I AM He."

THE BETRAYER AND THE FIRST TOAST

Before Jesus and the disciples actually started partaking of the Last Supper, Jesus mentioned that someone was going to betray Him, which related to the analogy of not all being clean (John 13:10). He then goes on to mention the betrayer who was about to partake of their Passover (vv. 18-19). Hence, further still, they had not partaken of the meal before the washing.

Luke is the first one to mention the actual specific start of the meal, which begins naturally with a toast (22:17-18). Moreover, preceding the toast, Luke had also mentioned the first conversation of Jesus when originally sitting down at the meal (vv. 15-16), before He rose and proceeded to wash their feet, as John alone pointed out.

John exclusively recorded the foot washing (13:4-19), through which his next statement, about receiving Jesus and the Father (v. 20) dovetails in context, and moreover, after the first toast in Luke (22:17-18), also symbolizing the wine in the cup, that they were about to receive, dividing it amongst themselves. Furthermore, John's following verse synchronizes and parallels virtually word for word, when comparing the Greek with Matthew (26:21) and Mark (14:18) regarding the betrayer (13:21), except that John has the Greek word '*amen'* - '*indeed'*, twice, whereas both Matthew and Mark have it once. Matthew adds the specific aspect that they were now eating at that point, before the sentence on the betrayer, though Mark combines the phrase that they were also eating at the end of the same sentence.

Thus, the rest of the dialogue covering the twelve's concern, who the betrayer was, follows on systematically, bringing us right into the Eucharist (Mat. 26:22-25; Mark 14:19-22; John 13:22). Luke however, did not record any mention of the betrayer preceding the meal but refers to him after the Eucharist. However, John does not refer to the Eucharist.

Luke 22

17 And He took the cup, and gave thanks, and said,
"Take this, and divide it among yourselves:
18 for I say to you, I will not drink of this fruit of the vine, until the Kingdom of God comes.
John 13
20 Truly, truly, I say to you, they who receive whomever I send receives Me; and they who receive Me receives Him who sent Me."

Matthew 26:21 Mark 14:18 John 13:21

When He had thus said, and as they sat and did eat, He was troubled in spirit, and testified, and Jesus said, "Most assuredly, I say to you, that one of you, that one of you who eats with Me shall betray Me."
John 13
22 The disciples looked one on another, doubting of whom He spoke.
Matthew 26:22 Mark 14:19
And they began to be extremely sorrowful, and began every one of them to say to Him one by one, "Is it I?"
And another said, "Lord, is it I?"

Matthew 26:23 Mark 14:20

And He answered and said to them,
"It is one of the twelve, he who dips his hand with Me in the dish the same shall betray Me.
Matthew 26:24 Mark 14:21
The Son of Humanity indeed goes, as it is written of Him: but woe to the very one by whom the Son of Humanity is betrayed! Good it had been of that person if they had not ever been born."

Matthew 26

25 Then Judas, who betrayed Him, answered and said, "Master, is it I?"
He said to him, "You said it."

THE EUCHARIST

After the toast, Jesus had now spoken the second time regarding the betrayer, at which point the Eucharist follows.

Because of the Eucharist's great importance, with the apostle Paul referring to it in 1 Cor. 11:24, albeit using only one other different Greek word '*klaomia*', meaning '*broken*', when comparing all the Synoptics at that point with Paul's version (Mat. 26:26; Mark 14:22; Luke 22:19), we see, nevertheless, his verse reads, '*this is My body which is broken for you*', whereas the Synoptics read '*given for you*'. We have combined the two expressions to give the whole and complete meaning to the main text, in the sense that Jesus both freely gave Himself, and allowed His body to be broken, too.

The other reference of Paul in 1 Cor. 11:25 regarding the phraseology relating to the wine, reads: '*This cup is the new testament in My blood*', though Luke [in a slightly different order to Paul] has the same Greek words (22:20). Luke also has following, the phrase '*which is shed for many*', where Paul does not. Furthermore, Paul added, '*you do this, as often as you drink it, in remembrance of Me*'. However, though Matthew (26:27) and Mark (14:23) parallel with Luke with the context of his verse at that particular point, nonetheless, they stress the fact of the next subsequent action, of actually taking and drinking from the cup at the precise moment, after having partaken of the bread. Thus, we have combined the texts to indicate those elements.

Directly afterwards, both Matthew (26:28) and Mark (14:24) continue to parallel together in closer verbal similarity with their next reference, '*For this is My blood of the new testament, which is shed for many*', though Matthew included and recalled at that specific instant that Jesus had also said '*for the remission of sins*'.

Hence, Jesus at that point had obviously continued to repeat the symbolism of the wine, which He had just previously mentioned, and concluded the Eucharist, through which the references of both Matthew (26:29) and Mark (14:25) once again resume their parallel accounts, in recording that Jesus indicated He would not partake of the Eucharist until He was in the Kingdom of His Father.

Matthew 26:26 Mark 14:22 Luke 22:19 1 Corinthians 11:24
And as they were eating Jesus took the bread, and gave thanks, and when He had given thanks, and blessed it, He broke it, and gave it to the disciples, and declared saying, "Take, eat; this is My body which is given, broken for you: do this in remembrance of Me."
Matthew 26:27 Mark 14:23 Luke 22:20 1 Corinthians 11:25
And likewise also He took the cup after eating, and gave thanks, and when He had given thanks, He gave it to them, saying, "This cup is the new testament in My blood, which is shed for you. You do this, as often as you drink it, in remembrance of Me. Drink all of it."

And they each and every one drank of it.
Matthew 26:28 Mark 14:24
And He said to them,
"For this is My blood of the new testament, which is shed for many for the remission of sins.
Matthew 26:29 Mark 14:25
But truly I say to you, I will from now on not drink again this fruit of the vine, until that day when I drink it anew with you in the Kingdom of God, My Father.
Luke 22
21 But, consider, the hand of him who betrays Me is with Me on the table.
22 And truly the Son of Humanity goes, as it is determined: but woe to that person by whom He is betrayed!"

THE BETRAYER IS REVEALED

With Matthew (26:28-29) and Mark (14:24-25) having both ended their dialogue relating to the Eucharist, at that point, Luke returns to the text with more detail regarding the betrayer, though now, Luke indicated specifically that the hand of the betrayer was on the table (22:21). Although the account of the Eucharist had concluded, nevertheless, they were still at the table, and moreover, John also returns to the particular part of the scenario, where, after remaining silent regarding the Eucharist, he describes the additional detail that they were still eating, and further confirmed who the betrayer was (13:23-26).

At the point where Luke relates to Jesus speaking about the tribulation the betrayer would naturally go through (22:22), directly afterwards, the twelve *'began to inquire among themselves'*, this time, who the betrayer was (v. 23), rather than just preceding the Eucharist, where *'every one'* of the disciples had firstly asked Jesus (Mat. 26:22), *'one by one'* (Mark 14:19). When reading Luke alone we see that he mentions next *'there was strife among them'* regarding *'which of them should be accounted the greatest'* (22:24), and the subsequent narration afterwards where Jesus corrects their attitude (vv. 25-30). However, we shall see these words are the penultimate words of Jesus, and apply and dovetail next to His last words (John 13:33-36) before they leave the upper room together.

As John had not recorded the details of the Eucharist, His last verse in the main text, about the when disciples *'looked one on another, doubting about whom He spoke'* (13:22), would naturally refer to the setting earlier, directly before the Eucharist, where each of the disciples had originally asked Jesus personally, and moreover, at the very point where John (v. 21) had paralleled both with Matthew (26:21) and Mark (14:18).

Also, because of the basic context of the complete scenario, preceding and proceeding, where Luke had revealed *'they began to inquire among themselves'* who it was that would betray Jesus (22:23), the only natural and appropriate place where John's account of himself leaning on Jesus (13:23-26), would actually be applicable to, and precisely dovetail with, is next to Luke's account, where now the twelve were questioning amongst each other who the betrayer could be. Thus, John's descriptive detail, of where he is laying his head on Jesus' chest, highlights the particular scene, which Luke first led us into. Not until Jesus had eventually indicated to John [and no doubt John to Peter], directly before Judas decides to leave (John 13:27-30), do the disciples abate their query on who the betrayer was.

Hence, Luke's entire narrative of when '*there was also strife among them*' (22:24-30) can only dovetail after John relates Jesus' glorification in the Father, after Judas had left the upper room and the subsequent events which were to follow (13:31-32). It thus belongs next to the last words of Jesus in the upper room, of which John had recorded regarding the disciples having love toward one another (vv. 33-35), before they leave for the Mt. Olives.

We shall further see this is the case as we progress into the next section, where they leave the upper room, as John's proceeding verses dovetail and parallel in context (vv. 36-38), with each one of the Synoptics regarding Peter's denial of Jesus.

Luke 22
23 And they began to inquire among themselves, which of them it was who should do this thing.
John 13
23 Now there was lying against Jesus' chest one of His disciples, whom Jesus loved.
24 Simon Peter therefore beckoned to him, that he should ask who it should be of whom He spoke.
25 He then leaning forwards, from Jesus' body, asked Him, "Lord, who is it?"
26 Jesus answered, "It is he, to whom I shall give the bread, when I have dipped it."

And when He had dipped the bread, He gave it to Judas Iscariot, the son of Simon.
27 And after the bread Satan entered into him.
Then said Jesus to him, "What you do, do quickly."

28 No man at the table knew for what intent He spoke this to him.
29 For some of them thought, because Judas had the bag, that Jesus had said to him, 'Buy those things that we have need of for the Festival [Sabbath, 15th Nissan];' or, that he should give something to the poor.
30 He then having received the bread immediately went out: and it was night.

John 13

31 Therefore, when he was gone out, Jesus said,
"Now is the Son of Humanity glorified, and God is glorified in Him.
32 If God is glorified in Him, God shall glorify Him in Himself, and shall glorify Him shortly."

LAST WORDS IN UPPER ROOM

With Jesus having revealed to John who the betrayer was, Judas subsequently leaves the upper room (John 13:27-30), at which point Jesus mentions being glorified (vv. 31-32). This included being glorified through the next stage of the following events.

No doubt the mentioning of His glorification, after Judas had left, led to a misunderstanding, with their egos filling up again, as had happened nearly one and half years previously at Capernaum, when at that time Jesus had referred to His Passion and His Resurrection (Mark 9:30-34). This resulted in the disciples *'reasoning among them, which of them should be the greatest'* (Luke 9:46). It is Luke who now, at this junction, after Jesus had once again alluded to His coming glorification, who returns to the dialogue indicating and connecting that aspect once more (22:24-30), thereby dovetailing again with John. Though Luke had at this instant indicated poignantly that there was now *'strife among them'*, he continues dovetailing and paralleling again with John's text a little later, after they have left the upper room, with the foretelling of Peter's denial (vv. 31-34).

However, now, John continues directly afterwards, albeit in antithesis to fill in where Luke had left off, with the desired attribute of character (John 13:33-35), rather than the attitude of self-elevation, which Luke had just referred to.

Luke 22
24 And there was also a strife among them, which of them should be accounted the greatest.
25 And He said to them,
"The kings of the Gentiles lord it over them; and they who exercise authority over them are so-called friends of the people.
26 But not so with you: therefore they, who are greatest among you, let them be as the younger; and they who are chief, as they who do serve.
27 For whether is greater, they who sit at a meal, or they who serve? Are not they who sit at a meal? But I am among you as He who serves.

28 You are they who have continued with Me in My trials.
29 And I appoint to you a Kingdom, as My Father has appointed to Me;
30 that you may eat and drink at My table in My Kingdom, and sit on thrones judging the Twelve Tribes of Israel.

John 13
33 Little children, yet a little while I am with you. You shall seek Me: and as I said to the Jews, *'Where I go, you cannot come (7:34);'* so now I say to you:
34 a new commandment I give to you, that you love one another; as I have

loved you, so that you also love one another.

35 By this shall everyone know that you are My disciples, if you have love one to another."

36 Simon Peter says to Him, "Lord, where're You going?"
Jesus answered him, "Where I go, you cannot follow Me now; but you shall follow Me afterwards."
Matthew 26:30 Mark 14:26
And when they had sung a psalm, they went out to the Mount of Olives.

ON THE MT. OLIVES

After Jesus had eased the strife that they had amongst themselves over who should be the greatest, Peter asks Jesus where He was about to go, whereby Jesus assures him, he would follow Him afterwards (John 13:36). Subsequently, in this positive atmosphere before leaving the upper room, they conclude in singing a psalm together before venturing out to the Mt. of Olives (Mat. 26:30; Mark 14:26). With both Matthew and Mark, once again paralleling together, and, word for word, moreover, at the particular juncture of leaving the upper room, we see, that though they obviously did not record the detail that Luke and John had after the conclusion of *The Eucharist*, nevertheless, they both recorded the very point where the rest of any narration, following their ending of the Eucharist, would naturally have taken place. This was on the Mt. of Olives.

Having left the upper room, they now make their way to the Mt. of Olives. At that specific junction, both Matthew (26:31-33) and Mark (14:27-29), relate Jesus informing the disciples of shortly being offended through the prophecy of the Striking of the Shepherd. At which particular point, Peter continues with his question regarding why he could not follow Jesus; this time, not being content in the assurance of following Jesus later, he stresses the query of why he cannot follow Jesus now, and insists he would lay down his life for Jesus' sake (John 13:37). Answering Peter, Jesus poses the question, '*Will you lay down your life for My sake?*' (v. 38a), before John continues with the dialogue leading into the foretelling of Peter's denial. It is here John (v. 38b) directly parallels with the Synoptics (Mat. 26:34; Mark 14:30; Luke 22:34). Also, through the aspect of John (13:37-38a) dovetailing once again with Luke (22:31-33), we further know that John (13:33-36) had naturally dovetailed and followed Luke (22:30) with the conclusion of the narration relating to the strife among the disciples.

PETER'S DENIAL

Matthew 26:31 Mark 14:27
And then Jesus says to them, "All you shall be offended because of Me this night: for it is written (Zech. 13:7), 'I WILL STRIKE THE SHEPHERD, AND THE SHEEP OF THE FLOCK SHALL BE SCATTERED ABROAD.'

Matthew 26:32 Mark 14:28
But after that I am risen again, I will go before you into Galilee."

Matthew 26:33 Mark 14:29
And Peter answered and said to Him, "Although all shall be offended, because of You, yet I will not ever be offended."

John 13
37 Peter says to Him, "Lord, why can't I follow You now? I will lay down my life for Your sake."

38a Jesus answered him, "Will you lay down your life for My sake?"
Luke 22
31 And the Lord said, "Simon, Simon, understand Satan has desired to have you, that he may sift you as wheat:
32 but I have prayed for you, that your faith wouldn't fail: and when you are converted, strengthen your brothers and sisters."

33 And he said to Him,
"Lord, I am ready to go with You, both into prison, and to death."
Matthew 26:34 Mark 14:30 Luke 22:34 John 13:38b
And Jesus declared saying to him,
"I tell you Peter, truly, truly, I say to you, that this day, even this night, before the rooster crows twice - the rooster won't crow, until you deny that you know Me three times."

Matthew 26:35 Mark 14:31
But Peter spoke saying to Him the more vehemently,
"Though if I should die with You, I will not deny You in any way."

Likewise also said all the disciples.
Luke 22
35 And He said to them, "When I sent you without purse, and bag, and shoes, did you lack anything?"
And they said, "Nothing."

36 Then He said to them,
"But now, he who has a purse, let him take it, and likewise his bag: and he who has no sword, let him sell his garment, and buy one.
37 For I say to you, that this that is written (Is. 53:12) must yet be accomplished in Me, 'AND HE WAS RECKONED AMONG THE TRANSGRESSORS': for the things concerning Me have an end."

Luke 22

38 And they said, "Lord, look, here are two swords."

And He said to them, "It is enough."

JESUS COMFORTS THEM

Luke concludes with his exclusive dialogue regarding the two swords (22:35-38), after which John (14:1-30) returns dovetailing once again with Luke's dialogue, indicating at the end of his narrative, that they had all moved to another spot (v. 31).

Moreover, all the Gospel writers had synchronized and paralleled together over Peter's Denial (Mat. 26:31-35; Mark 14:27-31; Luke 22:31-38; John 13:37-38). Also, they further dovetailed with each other regarding the subsequent conversations that they as individual writers, decided to record preceding and proceeding *Peter's Denial*. However, both Matthew and Mark revealed that the setting of *Peter's Denial* took place after leaving the upper room, with their walk to the Mt. Olives (Mat. 26:30; Mark 14:26). John thus continued with the dialogue after the narrative on the two swords (14:1-30), until he indicates in the last verse of his chapter, that they now had moved from their original spot on the Mt. Olives (v. 31), and, as we shall see subsequently, with the view of eventually reaching Gethsemane.

John 14

1 "Don't let your heart be troubled: you believe in God, believe also in Me.

2 In My Father's House are many mansions: if it weren't so, I would have told you. I go to prepare a place for you.

3 And if I go and prepare a place for you, I will come again, and receive you to Myself; that where I am, there you may also be.

4 And where I go you know, and the way you know."

5 Thomas says to Him,

"Lord, we don't know where You are going; and how can we know the way?"

6 Jesus says to him,

"I am the Way, the Truth, and the Life: no one comes to the Father, but by Me.

7 If you had known Me, you should have known My Father also: and from now on you know Him, and have seen Him."

8 Philip says to Him, "Lord, show us the Father, and it suffices us."

9 Jesus says to him, "Have I been so long a time with you, and yet you do not know Me, Philip? They who have seen Me have seen the Father; and how then do you say, 'Show us the Father?

10 Don't you believe that I am in the Father, and the Father in Me? The

words that I tell you, I speak not from Myself: but the Father who dwells in Me does His works.

11 Believe Me that I am in the Father, and the Father in Me: or else believe Me for the very works sake.

12 Truly, truly, I say to you, those who believe on Me, the deeds that I do shall they do also; and greater deeds than these shall they do; because I go to My Father.

13 And whatever you shall ask in My Name, that will I do, that the Father may be glorified in the Son.

14 If you shall ask anything in My Name, I will do it.

15 If you love Me, keep My Commandments.

16 And I will pray the Father, and He shall give you another Comforter, that it may stay with you forever;

17 even the Spirit of Truth; whom the world cannot receive, because it does not consider it, neither understands it: though it and it be in you.

18 I will not leave you comfortless: I will come to you.

19 Yet a little while, and the world sees Me no more; but you see Me: because I live, you shall live also.

20 In that day you shall know that I am in My Father, and you in Me, and I in you.

21 Those who have My Commandments, and keep them, are the ones who love Me: and they who love Me shall be loved of My Father, and I will love them, and will manifest Myself to them."

22 Judas says to Him, not Iscariot,
"Lord, how is it that You will manifest Yourself to us, and not to the world?"

23 Jesus answered and said to him,
"If someone loves Me, they will keep My words: and My Father will love them, and We will come to them, and make Our dwelling with them.

24 Those who don't love Me don't keep My sayings: and the word which you hear is not Mine, but the Father's who sent Me.

25 These things have I spoken to you, being yet present with you.

26 But the Comforter, which is the Holy Spirit, which the Father will send in My Name, it shall teach you all things, and bring all things to your remembrance, whatever I have said to you.

27 Peace I leave with you, My peace I give to you: not as the world gives, do I give to you. Don't let your heart be troubled, neither let it be afraid.

John 14

28 You have heard how I said to you (vv. 2-4), '*I go away, and come again to you* (vv. 3, 18).' If you loved Me, you would rejoice, because I said, '*I go to the Father* (v. 12):' for My Father is greater than I.

29 And now I have told you before it come to pass, that, when it is come to pass, you might believe.

30 Afterwards I won't speak with you much: for the Prince of this world comes, and has no power against Me.

31 But that the world may know that I love the Father; and as the Father gave Me instructions, even so I do.

Rise, let us go from here."

ANOTHER SPOT ON MT. OLIVES

John was clear that after the dialogue of where Jesus had naturally, and just explicitly, comforted the disciples (14:1-30), which directly followed Jesus having first related to them the perturbing prophecy of the sheep being scattered through the Striking of the Shepherd, and the disturbing statement by Jesus, of Peter's subsequent denial, along with the stirring factor of having two swords. Jesus, in concluding His comforting exhortation, suggests they now move from the spot on the Mt. Olives (v. 31), where they had originally settled after leaving the upper room (Mat. 26:30; Mark 14:26).

Thus, they move again nearer to the prime objective of subsequently arriving at Gethsemane. All the Gospels parallel together at that particular setting, and further indicate what transpired after first arriving at the mount and before moving once more (Mat. 26:36; Mark 14.32; Luke 22:40; John 18:1).

We had established that both Matthew and Mark were clear as to the point where Jesus and the disciples left the upper room, with Luke (22:31-34) and John (13:37-38) having aligned together, through *Peter's Denial*, where they also dovetailed and paralleled with Matthew and Mark over the narration surrounding *Peter's Denial*.

Luke, who was actually aware of where the setting of *Peter's Denial* occurred, in that he alone indicated the incident of the two swords taking place directly after *Peter's Denial* (22:35-38), where subsequently with his following verse (v. 39), later dovetails with John again, and substantiates the information that John had also pointed out at the particular junction where he shows Jesus and the disciples rising to move to another spot (14:31), deciding to converge closer to the Garden of Gethsemane. Nevertheless Luke's next verse is where they have moved from this second spot and arrive at Gethsemane (22:40).

Most translators have used words sympathetic in translating the Greek words in Luke 22:39 to give the impression that they thought they left the upper room at this verse, considering where Matthew and Mark had indicated that fact much earlier. However, in the original Greek, it can read with the alternative English words that might be used, '*Kai* [And] *exerchomai* [having gone: going forward:

came: went] *poreuomai* [He departed: to go: to pass on: made way: proceeded: went] *kata* [according to: after] *ethos* [custom: manner: disposition: be wont] *eis* [to]...'.

Of course, Luke was aware that Jesus often went to the Garden of Gethsemane in the vicinity of the Mt. Olives, and thus, the Greek text in its wording actually shows that aspect too.

Hence, following text has been retranslated taking into consideration all these characteristics and findings. Though we have rather chosen the word '*accordingly*', as its meaning, '*in an appropriate manner*' or, '*as suggested or required by* (stated) *circumstances*' satisfies the combined sense of the two Greek words '*kata ethos*' [according to custom].

Furthermore, after John had indicated the precise point at which they were to move nearer to Gethsemane (14:31), his following and considerable narrative, infers they stopped this last time, to sit and listen again to the last discourse from Jesus (ch. 15-16). Afterwards, Jesus prayed on the mount (17:1-26), before they actually arrived at Gethsemane (18:1).

Luke 22
39 And He went forward, proceeding accordingly to the Mount of Olives; and His disciples followed Him.

THE VINE AND THE BRANCHES

John 15
1 "I am the True Vine, and My Father is the Vine-Dresser
2 Every branch in Me that doesn't bear fruit He takes away: and every branch that bears fruit He purges it, so that it may bring forth more fruit.
3 Now you are clean through the word that I have spoken to you.

4 Dwell in Me, and I in you. As the branch cannot bear fruit by itself, except it stays in the vine; no more can you, except you dwell in Me.
5 I am the Vine, you are the branches: they who dwell in Me, and I in them, the same brings forth much fruit: for without Me you can do nothing.
6 If anyone does not dwell in Me, they will be struck off as a branch, and become withered; so as people gather them, and cast them into the fire, and they are burned.

7 If you dwell in Me, and My words dwell in you, you shall ask what you will, and it shall be done to you.
8 Herein is My Father glorified, that you bear much fruit; so shall you be My disciples.
9 As the Father has loved Me, so have I loved you; continue in My love.

10 If you keep My Commandments, you will continue through My love; even as I have kept My Father's Commandments, and continue with His love.
11 These things have I spoken to you, that My joy might remain in you, and that your joy might be full.

12 This is My commandment, that you love one another, as I have loved you.
13 Greater love has no one than this that they lay down their life for their friends.
14 You are My friends, if you do whatever I command you.

15 No longer do I call you servants; for the servant doesn't know what their lord does: but I have called you friends; for all things that I have heard of My Father I have made known to you.
16 You have not chosen Me, but I have chosen you, and ordained you, that you should go and bring forth fruit, and that your fruit should remain: that whatever you shall ask of the Father in My Name, He may give it to you.
17 These things I command you, that you love one another.

WORLDLY HATE

18 If the world hate you, you know that it hated Me before it hated you.
19 If you were of the world, the world would love its own: but because you are not of the world, but I have chosen you out of the world, therefore the world hates you.
20 Remember the word that I said to you, '*The servant is not greater than their lord* (13:15).' If they have persecuted Me, they will also persecute you; if they have kept My saying, they will keep yours also.

21 But all these things will they do to you for My Name's sake, because they don't know Him who sent Me.
22 If I had not come and spoken to them, they would not be sinning: but now they have no excuse for their sin.

23 They who hate Me also hate My Father.
24 If I hadn't done the works, which no other person did, they wouldn't be sinning: but now they have both seen and hated both Me and the Father.
25 But this comes to mind, that the words might be fulfilled that is written in the Torah (Ps. 35:19), 'THEY HATED ME WITHOUT A CAUSE.'

26 But when the Comforter is come, that I will send to you from the Father, even the Spirit of Truth, which proceeds from the Father, it shall testify of Me:
27 and you also shall bear witness, because you have been with Me from the beginning.
John 16
1 These things have I spoken to you, so that you should not be offended.

John 16

2 They shall put you out of the synagogues: yes, the time comes, that whoever kills you will think that they do God a service.

3 And these things will they do to you, because they have not known the Father, nor Me.

4 But these things have I told you, that when the time shall come, you may remember that I told you of them. And I didn't tell you these things from the beginning, because I was with you."

THE PURPOSE OF THE SPIRIT

With Jesus and the disciples, having moved from their original spot on the Mt. Olives when first leaving the upper room, we saw they subsequently moved once again (Luke 22:39; John 14:31). There Jesus related to the disciples the analogy surrounding the *Parable of the Vine and the Branches* (John 15:1-17), and further went onto comfort them in coming to terms with the knowledge that those not understanding the psyche of Jesus and the disciples, would in their ignorance, hate them (vv. 18-27; 16:1-4).

Continuing, Jesus exhorts them, comforting them with the news again, in sending the Holy Spirit, when He is no longer there (vv. 5-16), through which their sorrow will be turned to joy (vv. 17-33). Directly afterwards, Jesus prays for Himself (17:1-5), and for the disciples (vv. 6 19), and then for all other believers (vv. 20-26).

Thus, this brings us up to the point, when finally they move towards Gethsemane (18:1), to the place where Jesus would be subsequently arrested.

John 16

5 "But now I go My way to Him who sent Me; and none of you asks Me, 'Where are You going?'

6 But because I have said these things to you, sorrow has filled your heart.

7 Nevertheless I tell you the truth: it is expedient for you that I go away: for if I don't go away, the Comforter won't come to you; but if I depart, I will send the Spirit to you.

8 And when the Spirit is come, it will reprove the world of sin, and of righteousness, and of judgment:

9 about sin, because they don't believe in Me;

10 of righteousness, because I go to My Father, and you'll see Me no more;

11 of judgment, because the Prince of this world is judged.

12 I have yet many things to say to you, but you cannot bear them now.

13 Nevertheless when it, the Spirit of Truth, is come, it will guide you into all truth: for it shall not speak from itself; but whatever it shall hear, it'll speak that: and it will show you things to come.

14 It shall glorify Me; for it will receive from Me, and shall show it to you.

15 Everything that the Father has is Mine: therefore I said, '*For it will receive from Me, and shall show it to you*' (14:26; 15:26).

16 A little while, and you will not see Me: and again, a little while, and you shall see Me, because I go to the Father."

17 Then said some of his disciples among themselves,

"What is this that He says to us, '*A little while, and you won't see Me: and yet again, a little while, and you shall see Me'* (v.16): and, *'Because I go to the Father'?"* (v. 16; 14:28).

18 They said therefore, "What is this that He says, *'A little while?'* We cannot tell what He says."

THEIR SORROW TURNED TO JOY

19 Now Jesus knew that they were desirous to ask Him, and said to them, "Do you inquire among yourselves over what I said, *'A little while, and you will not see Me: and again, a little while, and you shall see Me'?*
20 Indeed, indeed, I say to you, that you shall weep and lament, but the world shall rejoice: and you shall be sorrowful, but your sorrow shall be turned to joy.
21 A woman when she is in labor has sorrow, because her hour is come: but as soon as she is delivered of the child, she remembers no more the anguish, for joy that a human being is born into the world.

22 And you now therefore have sorrow: but I will see you again, and your heart shall rejoice, and your joy no one shall take from you.
23 And in that day you will not question. Truly, truly, I say to you, whatever you shall ask the Father in My Name, He will give it you.
24 Up till now have you asked anything in My Name: ask, and you shall receive, that your joy may be full.

25 These thing have I spoken to you in analogies: but the time comes, when I shall no more speak to you in analogies, but I shall show you plainly through the Father.
26 In that day you shall ask in My Name: and I don't say to you, that I will pray to the Father for you:
27 for the Father Himself loves you, because you have loved Me, and believed that I came from the Father.
28 I came from the Father, and am come into the world, furthermore, I will leave the world, and return to the Father."

29 His disciples said to Him, "Look, now You speak plainly, and do not speak figuratively.
30 Now we are sure that you know all things, and don't need for anyone to question you: by this we believe that you came forth from God."
31 Jesus answered them, "Now do you believe?
32 Understand, the hour comes, yes, is now come, that you shall be scattered, every one to his own, and shall leave Me alone: and yet I am not alone, because the Father is with Me.
33 These things I have spoken to you, that through Me you might have peace. In the world you shall have tribulation: but be of good cheer; I have overcome the world."

THREE PRAYERS BEFORE GETHSEMANE

John 17

1 These words spoke Jesus, and lifted up His eyes to the heavens, and said, "Father, the hour is come; glorify Your Son, so Your Son also may glorify You:

2 as You have given Him power over all flesh, so that He should give life eternal to as many as You have given Him.

3 And this is life eternal, that they might know You the Only True God, and Jesus the Messiah, whom You have sent.

4 I have glorified You on the earth: I have finished the work that You gave Me to do.

5 And now, Oh Father, glorify You Me with Yourself with the glory that I had with You before the world was.

6 I have manifested Your Name to those who You gave Me out of this world: Yours they were, and You gave them to Me; and they have kept Your word.

7 Now they have known that all things whatever You have given Me are from You.

8 For I have given to them the words which You have given Me; and they have received them, and have known surely that I came out from You, and they have believed that You did send Me.

9 I pray for them: I pray not for the world, but for those whom you have given Me; for they are Yours.

10 And all Mine are Yours, and Yours are Mine; and I am glorified in them.

11 And afterwards I am no more in the world, but these are in the world, and I coming to You. Holy Father, keep through Your Own Name those whom You have given Me, so that they may be one, as We are.

12 While I was with them in the world, I kept them in Your Name: those whom You gave Me I have kept, and none of them are lost, but the son of perdition; so that the Scripture (Ps. 41:9) might be fulfilled.

13 And now I coming to You; and these things I speak in the world, that they might have My joy fulfilled in themselves.

14 I have given them Your word; and the world has hated them, because they are not of the world, even as I am not of the world.

15 I don't pray that You should take them out of the world, but that You should keep them from evil.

16 They are not of this world, even as I am not of the world.

17 Sanctify them through Your truth: Your word is truth.

18 As You have sent Me into the world, even so have I also sent them into the world.

19 And for their sakes I sanctify Myself, so that they also might be sanctified through the truth.

John 17

20 I neither pray for these alone, but for those who also shall believe on Me through their word;

21 that they may be one; as You, Father are in Me, and I in You, that they may also be one in Us: that the world may believe that You have sent Me.

22 And the glory, which You gave Me, I have given them; so that they may be one, even as We are One:

23 I in them, and You in Me, so they may be made perfect in unity; and so that the world may know that You have sent Me, and have loved them, as You have loved Me.

24 Father, I wish that they also, whom You have given Me, be with Me where I am; so that they may see My glory, which You have given Me: for You loved Me before the foundation of the world.

25 Oh righteous Father, the world has not known You: but I have known You, and these have known that You have sent Me.

26 And I have declared to them Your Name, and I will declare it: that the love with which You have loved Me may be in them, and I in them."

THEY MOVE TOWARDS GETHSEMANE

After Jesus' last prayer before entering the Garden of Gethsemane, John (vv. 20-26) indicates that it was at that particular point they moved once more, nearer to the garden, and subsequently entered (18:1).

However, before we continue with the next following incidents we must first take into consideration a couple of other factors.

We saw that it was Matthew (26:30) and Mark (14:26) who both paralleled again after relating to the betrayer, and *The Eucharist,* and that, having concluded with the singing of a psalm, they left the upper room for the Mt. Olives, giving us the point at which the next events took place on the Mt. Olives.

Luke and John had also given us additional detail of what transpired at the Supper, and afterwards had also paralleled with the other two Synoptics regarding *Peter's Denial,* which we saw would have taken place on the mount, where they had originally gone when leaving the upper room. In facilitating to this first spot on the mount, they would have had to cross the Kidron Valley.

No doubt they had stopped on the mount, at this emotional time, as they had done many times previously. This gave rise to the scenario relating to the mental turmoil of being offended over the Striking of the Shepherd, the foretelling of *Peter's Denial,* and the two swords, at which junction John's narration, where Jesus comforts them afterwards (14:1-30), concludes (v. 31), in synchronizing and dovetailing with Luke (22:39), through the aspect of moving to another spot.

It is obvious that the object of their next subsequent move was to position themselves nearer to arriving finally at Gethsemane. Thus, in moving again, from the spot on Olivet where they had stopped, meant, in facilitating nearer to Gethsemane, they would not have to cross the Kidron Valley again, as Gethsemane was at the foot of Olivet over against the Brook Kidron, from the particular vantage point of being below the west side of the mount.

Hence, John ch. 15 and 16 relate to the narrative taking place at this second place they stopped on the mount, with ch. 17 containing Jesus' last three prayers before moving once more towards the objective of arriving at Gethsemane. No doubt they had paused for a while at this other spot to listen to Jesus' last words. After that, they proceeded to Gethsemane, at which point all the Gospels align together and parallel at the actual arrival at Gethsemane (Mat. 26:36; Mark 14:32; Luke 22:40; John 18:1).

However, John 18:1 has been translated with the idea that Jesus and the disciples went '*over the Brook Kidron*', from the vantage of leaving the upper room originally, without having stopped to listen to Jesus twice on the mount. Furthermore, here in John's verse, the Greek word '*peran*' has been translated '*over*'.

Having already dealt with the Greek word '*peran*' previously, at p. 277, where it had been translated '*beyond*', we, saw moreover, that it can also refer to the aspect of '*over against*' or the nearside of.

Because Jesus would have already gone over the Brook Kidron, in leaving the upper room originally, to their first spot on the mount, consequently, when facilitating to another spot on their way to Gethsemane, would naturally not have required going over the Brook Kidron again, since the garden, as shown in all relevant atlases, is located across the other side of the Brook Kidron [Valley] from Jerusalem. Hence, we have translated the word '*peran*', '*over against*', leaving the upper room originally, to their first spot on the mount, consequently, when facilitating to another spot on their way to Gethsemane, would naturally not have required going over the Brook Kidron again, since the garden, as shown in all relevant atlases, is located across the other side of the Brook Kidron [Valley] from Jerusalem. Hence, we have translated the word '*peran*', '*over against*', as in any case Gethsemane was near to the Brook Kidron.

THREE PRAYER'S IN GETHSEMANE

Matthew 26:36 Mark 14:32 Luke 22:40 John 18:1
When Jesus had spoken these words, He went forward with His disciples
over against the Brook Kidron, where was a garden. And then comes Jesus with them.

And when He and they had come to the place that was called and named Gethsemane into which He entered, and His disciples, He spoke saying to His disciples, "You sit here, while I shall go and pray yonder. Pray that you don't enter into temptation."

Matthew 26:37 Mark 14:33
And He takes with Him Peter and the two sons of Zebedee, James and John, and began to be greatly overwhelmed, and to be very heavy;
Matthew 26:38 Mark 14:34
and then He says to them, "My soul is very sorrowful, even to death: you wait here, and watch with Me."
John 18
2 For Judas, also who betrayed Him, knew the place: for Jesus often resorted there with His disciples.

Matthew 26:39a Mark 14.35 Luke 22:41
And He went forward a little further, and He was withdrawn from them about a stone's cast, and kneeled down, and fell on His face on the ground, and prayed that, if it were possible, the hour might pass from Him.
Matthew 26:39b Mark 14:36 Luke 22:42
And He said, "Oh Abba, My Father, all things are possible to You; if it be possible, if You be willing to remove this cup - let this cup pass from Me: nevertheless not as My will - what I will, but as Yours - what You will, be done."

Luke 22
43 And there appeared an angel to Him from Heaven, strengthening Him.
44 And being in agony He prayed more earnestly: and His sweat was as it were great drops of blood falling down to the ground.

Matthew 26:40a Mark 14:37a Luke 22:45
And when He rose up from prayer, coming to His disciples, He finds them sleeping for sorrow, and says to Peter, "Simon"!
Matthew 26:40b-41 Mark 14:37b-38 Luke 22:46
And said to them, "Why do you sleep? What, couldn't you watch with Me one hour? Rise and watch, and pray that you don't enter into temptation, the spirit truly indeed is ready, and willing, but the flesh is weak."

Both Matthew and Mark mention that it was Peter, James and John [though Matthew relates James and John as '*the two sons of Zebedee*'], who Jesus asked to watch (Mat. 26:36-38; Mark 14:33 34), while He prayed some distance away (Mat. 26:39; Mark 14:35-36; Luke 22:41-42) from the rest of the disciples (Mat. 26:36; Mark 14:32).

Luke, however, refers only to the first prayer with the unique information that Jesus initially '*kneeled down*' (22:41), whereas Matthew (26:39) and Mark (14:35) indicate He also fell to the ground, directly afterwards. Luke alone further reveals that an angel strengthened Him during the first prayer (22:43-44).

Moreover, Luke (22:45) continues relating to and paralleling by means of the first prayer with Matthew (26:40), through the first question, where Jesus returns the first time to Peter, James and John, synchronizing and paralleling also with Mark (14:37) through the words, '*Why do you sleep?*' (22:46), at which point Matthew and Mark follow on together, both referring to the next question, '*could you not watch with Me one hour?*'

Furthermore, Luke (22:46) with his following phraseology of '*rise and pray, that you enter not into temptation*', synchronizes and directly parallels with Matthew (26:41) and Mark (14:38) through their phrase, '*watch and pray that you enter not into temptation*'.

Matthew, concluding after the first prayer, indicates there was a '*second time*' Jesus prayed (26:42), and also a '*third time*' (26:44), whereas, though Mark relates to the three prayers, he amazingly only mentions it through the phrase, '*He comes the third time*' when Jesus finally returns to all the disciples (Mark 14:41).

Matthew 26:42 Mark 14:39
And again He went away, the second time, and prayed, and spoke the same words saying, "Oh My Father, if this cup may not pass away from Me, except I drink it, Your will be done".

Matthew 26:43 Mark 14:40
And when He came returning, He found them asleep again, (for their eyes were heavy,) neither knew they what to answer Him.

Matthew 26
44 And He left them, and went away again, and prayed the third time, saying the same words.

Matthew 26:45 Mark 14:41
And then He comes the third time to His disciples, and says to them,
"Sleep on now, and take your rest: it is enough, understand, the hour is at hand and come; consider, the Son of Humanity is betrayed into the hands of sinners.
Matthew 26:46 Mark 14:42
Rise up, let us be going; look, he who betrays Me is at hand."
Matthew 26:47 Mark 14:43 Luke 22:47a John 18:3
And immediately, while He yet spoke, a crowd appeared, and he who was called Judas, one of the twelve, arrives. Judas then, having received a band of men and officers, went before them - approaching, and with him a great crowd with lanterns and torches and weapons (swords and staves), from the Chief Priests and the Scribes and Pharisees, and the Elders of the People.

Matthew 26:48 Mark 14:44
And now he who betrayed Him had given them a token sign, saying,
"Whoever I shall kiss, that same is He; take Him and hold Him fast, and lead
Him away safely."
John 18
4 Jesus therefore, knowing all things that should come upon Him, went
forward, and said to them, "Whom do you want?"
5 They answered Him, "Jesus of Nazareth."
Jesus says to them, "I AM He."

And Judas also, who betrayed Him, stood with them.

6 As soon then as He had said to them, '*I AM He*,' they went backward, and
fell to the ground.
7 Then He asked them again, "Whom do you want?"
And they said, "Jesus of Nazareth."
8 And Jesus answered, "I've told you that *I AM He*: if therefore you want Me,
let these go their way:"
9 that the saying might be fulfilled, which He spoke, '*Of those whom You gave
Me I have lost none* (17:12).'

THE FORTY-SECOND MIRACLE - MALCHUS' EAR

Matthew 26:49 Mark 14:45 Luke 22:47b
And as soon as Judas was come, he immediately went up toward Jesus to kiss
Him, and spoke saying, "Hail, Master, Master!" and kissed Him.
Matthew 26
50a And Jesus said to him, "Friend, why are you come?"
Luke 22
48 Then Jesus said to him, "Judas you betray the Son of Humanity with a kiss?"

49 When they who were about Him saw what would follow, they said to Him,
"Lord, shall we strike with the sword?"

Matthew 26:50b Mark 14:46
And then came they, and laid their hands on Jesus, and took Him.
Matthew 26:51 Mark 14:47 Luke 22:50 John 18:10
And, then, suddenly one of them, Simon Peter, who was with Jesus, who
stood by having a sword, stretched out his hand and drew his sword, and
struck the servant of the High Priest, and striking cut off his right ear.
The servant's name was Malchus.
Luke 22
51 And Jesus answered and said, "Grant you this far."
And He touched his ear, and healed him.

THE ARREST

With the healing of Malchus' ear, *The Forty-Second Miracle*, the only one recorded since the withering of the barren fig-tree, we find, moreover, it is the last miracle before Jesus' resurrection. All the Gospel writers converge and parallel, attesting to the fact that the servant of the High Priest's ear was cut off (Mat. 26:51; Mark 14:47; Luke 22:50; John 18:10). However, it is Luke alone who mentions that Jesus actually healed him (22:51)!

The Gospel of John exclusively reveals that it was Simon Peter who struck with the sword, along with naming the servant of the High Priest, though only both Luke and John indicate it to have been the right ear.

Also, without John (18:12) telling us that Jesus was bound, after facing those that had come to arrest Him, we would not have known this from any of the Synoptics.

Matthew 26:52 John 18:11a
Then said Jesus to Peter,
"Put up again your sword into the sheath - its place: for all those who take the sword shall perish with the sword.
Matthew 26
53 You think that I cannot now pray to My Father, and He shall presently give Me more than twelve legions of angels?
54 But how then shall the Scriptures be fulfilled, since so it must be?
John 18
11b The cup which My Father has given Me, shall I not drink it?"

Matthew 26:55 Mark 14:48-49a Luke 22:52-53
In that same hour, then Jesus answered and said to the Chief Priests, and Captains of the Temple, the Elders, and the crowd, who were come to Him,
"You are come out as against a thief with swords and staves for to take Me?
When I was sat with you daily teaching in the Temple, you didn't stretch out your hands against Me to seize hold of Me, and you didn't arrest Me: but this is your hour, and the power of darkness.
Matthew 26:56 Mark 14:49b-50
But all this was done, that the Scriptures of the Prophets might be fulfilled."

And then all the disciples forsook Him, and fled.
Mark 14
51 And there followed Him a certain young man, having a simple loose linen garment on; and the young men laid hold of him:
52 And leaving the fine linen garment, fled them without it.

John 18
12 Then the band and Captain and the officers of the Jews took Jesus and bound Him,
13 and led Him away to Annas first; for he was father-in-law to Caiaphas, who was High Priest that same year.

14 Now Caiaphas was he, who gave counsel to the Jews, *that it was expedient that one Man should die for the people* (11:50).
24 Now Annas sent Him Bound to Caiaphas the High Priest.

INTERROGATED AT CAIAPHAS'

John who [as tradition avers] was probably known by Caiaphas the High Priest (18:15), made a peculiar point in revealing that Jesus was led to Annas first, Caiaphas' father-in-law (v. 13). Directly afterwards, Annas sent Him bound to the Council (v. 24), where Jesus was being held at Caiaphas' residence, where Jesus was firstly interrogated (Mat. 26:57-59; Mark 14:53-55; Luke 22:54).

John would have been familiar with the details surrounding this night, by which both Matthew and mark had mentioned the first part of the interrogation. However, John further added the unique piece of information relating to the dialogue, which concluded the second part of the interrogation (18:19-24), and did not address the first part: neither did Luke.

Moreover, John does not refer to Jesus being led to the Courthouse from Caiaphas' Palace after the interrogation, though the Synoptics are in synchronized and paralleled agreement that Jesus was led there through the next successive occurrence (Mat. 27:1; Mark 15:1; Luke 22:66-71), with Luke relating the greater narrative which took place there. Furthermore, John after the interrogation at Caiaphas', and the recounting of Peter's subsequent denials (18:17-27), simply mentions Jesus being led to Pilate, by which he returns paralleling in sync with the Synoptics (Mat.27:2; Mark 15:1; Luke 23:1; John 18:28).

We have placed John 18:24 in its natural position to which it successively relates, as well as leaving it its original place, after the interrogation at Caiaphas'. Nevertheless, in the Greek original, the addition of the word '*had*' is wanting in this verse, and thus we have omitted it in the requisite previous main text, where we have placed it directly after v. 14 to which it specifically relates.

Luke, in a similar vein to John, had simply mentioned that Jesus was taken '*into the High Priest's house*', and did not record the details of the interrogation (22:54). Though, uniquely, Luke is the only writer to refer to the second cruel mocking taking place there (vv. 63-65), that consequently would have been after the first mocking of which Matthew (26:67-68) and Mark (14:65) mention.

Hence, after the second interrogation, including Peter's denials, the subsequent events at Caiaphas' house and Palace, all were concluded directly after the second cruel mocking. Jesus was then led to the Courthouse, through which the Synoptics all parallel once more (Mat. 27:1; Mark 15:1; Luke 22:66).

It is John who returns to the previous scenario before the first part of the interrogation begins, after Jesus was taken to Annas (18:12-14), by also indicating that Peter was specifically let into the confines of the Palace (vv. 15-16), agreeing with the Synoptics, that it took place at Caiaphas' (v. 24). Additionally, John relates that the second part of the interrogation subsequently transpired directly after Peter's first denial (Mat. 26:70; Mark 14:68; Luke 22:57; John 18:17).

All the Gospels align and parallel together over the relevant details surrounding Peter being in the Palace before his first denial (Mat. 26:58; Mark 14:54; Luke 22:54-55; John 18:15-16).

The criterion in remembering the successive order of events held at the Council meeting at Caiaphas', before they moved to the Courthouse, is through the specific order of the second repeatings that occurred after the first part of the interrogation. This included the first cruel mocking, Peter's first denial with the first cockcrow, Peter's second and third denial with the second and final cockcrow, and the second cruel mocking.

In simpler terms there were two separate parts of the interrogation, two cruel mockings, three denials, and two cockcrows at the residence of Caiaphas.

[1] Thus, the <u>first interrogation</u> (Mat 26:57-66; Mark14:5 3-54; Luke 22:54; John 18:24):
the <u>first cruel mocking</u> (Mat. 26:67-68; Mark 14:65), and
the <u>first denial</u> of Peter (Mat. 26:69-71; Mark 14:66-68; Luke 22:56-57; John 18:17-18), with
the <u>first cockcrow</u> (Mark 14:68):
[2] leads into the <u>second interrogation</u> at Caiaphas' (John 18:19-24), and the subsequent details of
Peter's <u>second denial</u> (Mat. 26:71-72; Mark 14:69-70; Luke 22:58; John 18:25):
and <u>third denial</u> (Mat. 26:73; Mark 14:70-71; Luke 22:59-60; John 18:26): before
the <u>second cockcrow</u> (Mat. 26:74-75; Mark 14:72; Luke 22:60-62; John 18:27),and
the <u>second cruel mocking</u> at Caiaphas' (Luke 22:63-65), after which point Jesus is then led to their Courthouse and
the <u>third interrogation</u> with Caiaphas (Mat. 27:1; Mark 15:1; Luke 22:66-71),
and directly afterwards is finally led to Pilate (Mat. 27:2; Mark 15:1; Luke 23:1; John 18:28).

Matthew 26:57 Mark 14:53 Luke 22:54a

And then those who laid hold on Jesus took Him. And they led Jesus away, and brought Him into Caiaphas', the High Priest's house: where were assembled with

him all the Chief Priests and the Elders and the Scribes.
Matthew 26:58a Mark 14:54a Luke 22:54b John 18:15
And nevertheless, Simon Peter followed Jesus afar off, and so did another
disciple: that disciple was known to the High Priest, and went in with Jesus
even into the Palace of the High Priest:
John 18
16 but Peter stood at the door outside.

Then went out that other disciple, who was known to the High priest, and spoke
to her who kept the door, and brought in Peter.

Matthew 26:58b Mark 14:54b Luke 22:55
And when they had kindled a fire in the midst of the hall, and were sat down
together, Peter sat down among them: and he sat down with the servants, to see
the end, and warmed himself at the fire.

Matthew 26:59-60a Mark 14:55
And now the Chief Priests, and the Elders, and all the Council sought for false
witnesses against Jesus to put Him to death; and nonetheless found none.
Matthew 26:60b Mark 14:56
For many bore false testimony against Him, but their testimony didn't agree
with each other: yes, though many false witnesses came, yet found they none.

Matthew 26:60c-61a Mark 14:57
And at the last there came certain two false witnesses, and rose bearing false
witness against Him, and declared, saying,
"This fellow said -
Matthew 26:61b Mark 14:58
we heard Him say, '*I am able to destroy the Temple of God, that is made with
hands, and I will rebuild another made without hands to rebuild it within
three days*' (John 2:19)."
Mark 14
59 Even so, their testimony did not agree.

Matthew 26:62 Mark 14:60
And the High Priest rose, standing up in the midst, and asked Jesus,
exclaiming to Him, saying,
"You answer nothing? What is it that these testify against You?"
Matthew 26:63 Mark 14:61
But Jesus held His peace, and answered nothing.

And again the High Priest answered and said to Him, asking,
"I adjure You by the Living God, that You tell us whether You are the Messiah,

the Son of God the Blessed?"
Matthew 26:64 Mark 14:62
And Jesus spoke saying to him,
"You have said: I am: and nevertheless, I say to you: hereafter you shall SEE
THE SON OF HUMANITY SITTING ON THE RIGHT HAND OF POWER (Ps. 110:1), and COMING
IN THE CLOUDS OF THE HEAVENS (Dan. 7:13)."

Matthew 26:65 Mark 14:63-64a
Then the High Priest tore at his clothes, and exclaimed,
"He has spoken blasphemy; what need have we of any further witnesses?

See, now you have heard His blasphemy.
Matthew 26:66 Mark 14:64b
What do you think?" They answered and said, "He is guilty of death."
And they all condemned Him to be guilty of death.

Matthew 26:67 Mark 14:65
And then did some of them begin to spit in His face, and on Him, and to cover
His face, and to buffet Him, and to say to Him, "Prophesy:" and the servants
did strike Him with the palms of their hands: and others struck Him with rods
in their hands,
Matthew 26
68 saying, "Prophesy to us, You Messiah, who is it that hit You?"

The first cruel mocking, in the above preceding main text closes the first interrogation by Caiaphas.

After that point all the Gospel writers correlate together, either paralleling or dovetailing again, regarding the first denial of Peter, since the last time they completely paralleled and converged together with the following of Peter and John [as tradition relates] to Caiaphas' Palace.

The conclusion of the first cruel mocking above, and directly afterwards Peter's first denial sets the scene for the second part of the continuing interrogation

PETER'S FIRST DENIAL

Both Mark (14:54) and Luke (22:55) were the first to relate Peter being by the fire, during the first part of the interrogation, though Mark alone mentions Peter warming himself. Moreover, both Mark (14:67) and Luke (22:56) continue, a little later, to repeat again the same scenario at the fire, directly before Peter's first denial, which subsequently leads up to the second part of the interrogation.

However, Matthew (26:57-58) at no point reveals a fire or Peter warming only that he was present at Caiaphas' residence and sat with the servants awaiting the result during the first part of the interrogation.

John, nevertheless, relates to the servants and officers, who had previously made the fire and continued warming themselves, with Peter now standing with them, after his first denial (18:17), as they all continue to await the outcome during the second part of the interrogation (v. 18).

Furthermore, it is Mark who exclusively mentions the first cockcrow (14:68b), thus, clearly further cementing the synchronization of the subsequent conclusion of the first part of the interrogation, whereby we are led into the second part, of which John alone recorded the details surrounding this continuing episode (18:19-24). Consequently, this brings us into the second denial of Peter (Mat. 26:71b-72; Mark 14:69-70a; Luke 22:58; John18:25), and lastly the third denial, with the second and final cockcrow (Mat. 26:73-74; Mark 14:70b-72a; Luke 22:59-60; John 18:26-27).

Matthew 26:69a Mark 14:66 John 18:17a
And now as Peter sat outside beneath in the Palace, there comes approaching to him a young woman who kept the door, one of the maids of the High Priest:
Matthew 26:69b Mark 14:67 Luke 22:56 John 18:17b
and notwithstanding when that certain maid saw Peter, observing him, as he sat by the fire warming himself, she earnestly looked upon him, and said,
"This man was also with Him" - saying, "You too were with Jesus of Nazareth from Galilee. Aren't you also one of this Man's disciples?
Matthew 26:70 Mark 14:68a Luke 22:57 John 18:17c
But he denied Him before them all, saying, "I am not. Woman, I don't know Him. I don't know - neither do I understand what you say."
John 18
18 And the servants and officers stood there, who had made a fire of coals; for it was cold: and they warmed themselves: and Peter stood with them, and warmed himself.

Matthew 26:71a Mark 14:68b
And when he was gone out into the porch the rooster crowed.

John 18
19 The High Priest then asked Jesus about His disciples, and about His doctrine.
20 Jesus answered him,
"I spoke openly to the world; I always taught in the synagogues and in the Temple, where Jews always resort; and in secret I said nothing.
21 Why do you ask Me? Ask those who heard Me, what I have said to them: look, they know what I said."
22 And when He had thus spoken, one of the officers who stood by struck Jesus

with a rod in his hand, saying, "You answer the High Priest so?"
23 Jesus answered him, "If I have spoken evil, bear witness of the evil: but if well, why do you strike Me?"
24 Now Annas had sent Him bound to Caiaphas the High Priest.

John, exclusively, twice mentions Peter warming himself after Peter's first denial (18:18), which directly leads into Peter's second denial (v. 25). Thus, altogether, there were four separate, though related, scenarios, which depict Peter warming himself, with three before the second interrogation.

Also, all the Gospel writers correlate together and parallel in synchronized agreement, through Peter's subsequent three denials, with the conclusion of the second and last cockcrow. Though, however, it is Mark alone who actually mentioned the first cockcrow (14:68b).

PETER'S SECOND AND THIRD DENIAL

Matthew 26:71b Mark 14:69 Luke 22:58a John 18:25a
And Simon Peter stood and warmed himself.

And after a little while another maid saw him again, and began to say to those who were there, standing by,
"This fellow is also one of them, and was with Jesus of Nazareth,"
and they said therefore to him, "Are you not also one of them, His disciples?"
Matthew 26:72 Mark 14:70a Luke 22:58b John 18:25b
And Peter spoke denying it again with an oath, and said, "Man, I am not. I do not know the Man."

And after some while, about the space of one hour after, they came to him who stood by, and another, one of the servants of the High Priest, being his kinsman whose ear Peter cut off, confidently affirmed, saying,
"With certainty this fellow was with Him: for he is a Galilean."
And said again to Peter,
"Surely you are also one of them; didn't I see you in the garden with Him? For you are a Galilean, for your speech corresponds exposing you."

Matthew 26:74 Mark 14:71-72a Luke 22:60 John 18:27
But Peter then began to curse and swear, denying again, saying,
"Man I don't know what you're saying. I don't know the Man of whom you speak."

And immediately, the second time, while he yet spoke, the rooster crowed.
Matthew 26:75a Mark 14:72b Luke 22:61
And the Lord turned, and looked upon Peter.

And Peter called to mind, how He had said to him, remembering the word of the Lord that which Jesus had said (Mat. 26:34; Luke 22:34; Mark 14:30; John 13:38), *'Before the rooster crows twice, you shall deny Me three times.'*

Matthew 26:75b Mark 14:72b Luke 22:62
And when Peter thought on it, he went out, and wept bitterly.

Luke 22
63 And the men who held Jesus mocked Him, and beat Him.
64 And when they had blindfolded Him, they struck Him on the face, and asked Him, saying, "Prophesy, who is it that hit You?"
65 And many other things they blasphemously spoke against Him.

So, with the second cruel mocking at the conclusion of the *Interrogation At Caiaphas' Palace*, as Luke exclusively recorded (26:22-65), Jesus is subsequently led to the Courthouse in the first light of the morning (Mat. 27:1; Mark 15:la; Luke 22:66).

AT THEIR COURT

With the concluding of the second part of the *Interrogation At Caiaphas' Palace* , and the second cockcrow, Jesus looked knowingly across to Peter, after which we saw Luke's exclusive dialogue on the second cruel mocking followed (22:63-65).

Moreover, we shall see that altogether, there were four mockings which occurred prior to the crucifixion. We have seen that two transpired at Caiaphas'. The third takes place in front of Herod, with the fourth directly after Pilate's initial sentence.

However, with the events at Caiaphas' over and the morning light approaching, it is Luke who once more continues, filling in this time revealing detail especially unique to his Gospel. Luke revealed that it was after Jesus had been at Caiaphas' Palace during the early morning night, that they led Jesus to their Court for the trial (22:66). Though the Synoptics synchronize and parallel with each other at that particular junction, nevertheless, both Matthew (27:1) and Mark (15:1a) only indicate that they took consultation, or counsel, although both Matthew and Mark had not actually stated where it specifically took place. It is Luke who further resumes the dialogue, relating again to the scenario, with his indigenous information of the narration at the trail (22:67-71), obviously at their Courthouse, before Jesus is finally led to Pilate.

John, also, did not feel it necessary to mention the trial at the Court, though obviously Caiaphas continued to officiate, after the second part of the interrogation of which John alone had specially highlighted. John simply writes, '*then they led Jesus from Caiaphas... and it was early*' (18:28), further agreeing that it was not until the morning light, and after the trial, that they led Jesus finally to Pilate (v. 29).

Moreover, Matthew alone referred to the narration surrounding Judas' guilt, where he is depicted at that particular point of knowing that Jesus was condemned, through returning the money to the Chief Priests and Elders (27:3-10). Matthew would have known where the trial took place, and knew it would be where the Sanhedrin [their Court] was held, even though he did not actually mention Jesus being led from Caiaphas' to the Court, as Luke had. In any case, Matthew positioned his narration regarding Judas next to where the Court would have made their decision on Jesus' fate (27:1-2).

Matthew, nonetheless, further indicated that Judas came to where the Sanhedrin was being held, with him subsequently knowing that Jesus had been officially condemned by the Chief Priests and Elders, before they converged with Jesus to Pilate.

Because Jesus is brought to Pilate after the details that Luke wrote on the trial (22:67-71), and that the Synoptics nevertheless parallel together once more, at the point when, first thing in the morning, the trial began and concluded (Mat. 27:1; Mark 15:1a; Luke 22:66), we have naturally positioned Mat. 27:2, which relates to Jesus being taken to Pilate, directly after the narrative regarding Judas (Mat. 27:1; Mark 15:1a; Luke 22:66), we have naturally positioned Mat. 27:2, which relates to Jesus being taken to Pilate, directly after the narrative regarding Judas (Mat 27:3-10), as the four Gospels parallel together at the precise junction (Mat. 27:2; Mark 15:1b; Luke 23:1; John 18:28).

Matthew 27:1 Mark 15:1a Luke 22:66
And immediately in the morning [14th Nissan], as soon as it was day - when the morning was come, all the Elders of the People and the Chief Priests and the Scribes came together, and led Him into their Council, holding a consultation with the Elders of the People and the Scribes and the whole Council, taking counsel against Jesus to put Him to death, saying,
Luke 22
67 "Are You the Messiah? Tell us."
And He said to them, "If I tell you, you will not believe:
68 and if I also ask you, you will not answer Me, nor let Me go.
69 Afterwards shall the Son of Humanity sit on the right-hand of the Power of God."

70 Then they all said, "Are You the Son of God?"
And He said to them, "You say that I am."
71 And they said, "What need we any further witness? For we ourselves have heard from His own mouth."

Matthew 27
3 Then Judas, who had betrayed Him, when he saw that He was condemned, repented himself, and brought again the thirty pieces of silver to the Chief Priests and Elders,
4 saying, "I have sinned in that I have betrayed innocent blood."
And they said, "What is that to us? You see to that."

Matthew 27:5 Acts 1:18
And he cast down the pieces of silver in the Temple, and departed. Now this man purchased a field with the reward of iniquity, and went and hanged himself, and falling headlong, his abdomen burst open, and all his intestines gushed out.

Matthew 27
6 And the Chief Priests took the silver pieces, and said,
"It is not lawful for to put them into the Treasury, because it is the price of blood."
7 And they took counsel, and bought with them the Potter's Field, to bury strangers in.

Matthew 27:8 Acts 1:19

And it was known to all the inhabitants at Jerusalem; insomuch as therefore that field was called in their proper tongue, *Hakeldama*, that is to say, the *Field of Blood*, to this day.

Acts 1

20 For it is written in the book of Psalms,

"LET HIS HABITATION BE DESOLATE, AND LET NO MAN DWELL THEREIN (69:25): AND HIS OFFICE LET ANOTHER TAKE (109:8)."

Matthew 27

9 Then was fulfilled that which was spoken by Jeremiah the prophet, saying (Zech. 11:12-13),

"AND THEY TOOK THE THIRTY PIECES OF SILVER, THE PRICE OF HIM THAT WAS VALUED, WHOM THEY OF THE CHILDREN OF ISRAEL DID VALUE;

10 AND GAVE THEM FOR THE POTTER'S FIELD, AS THE LORD HAD APPOINTED ME."

Because Luke in Acts 1:18-20 reveals additional detail of Judas' suicide attempt, we have included it in Matthew's record, as it would have transpired.

The phrase, '*now this man purchased a field*' (Acts 1:18), is rhetorical, referring to the ratification of the betrayal, when Judas earlier received the thirty pieces silver, and to which subsequently the money was ultimately used after his death (Mat. 27:7).

Matthew had revealed that Judas went to hang himself (v. 5), whereas Luke indicated that the hanging went wrong, consequently resulting in Judas falling headlong from some height, and splitting open his abdomen in the fall (Acts 1:18).

PILOT'S FIRST EXAMINATION

Matthew 27:2 Mark 15:lb Luke 23:1 John 18:28

And the whole crowd of them rose, and when they had bound Jesus, then they led Jesus away, bringing Him from Caiaphas, to the Hall of Judgment, and delivered Him to Pontius Pilate the Governor: and it was early [14th Nissan]; and they themselves went not into the Judgment Hall, lest they should be defiled, so that they might eat their Passover [15th Nissan].

John 18

29 Pilate then went out to them, and said,

"What accusation do you bring against this Man?"

30 They answered and said to him,

"If He were not a malefactor, we would not have delivered Him up to you."

Luke 23

2 And they began to accuse Him, saying, "We found this Fellow perverting the nation, and forbidding to give tribute to Caesar, saying that He Himself is the

Messiah a King."
3 And Pilate asked Him, saying, "You are the King of the Jews?"
And He answered him and said, "You said it."

4 Then Pilate said to the Chief Priests and to the people, "I find no fault in this Man."
John 18
31 Then Pilate said to them, "You take Him, and judge Him according to your Law."
The Jews therefore said to him, "It is not lawful for us to put anyone to death:"
32 that the saying of Jesus might be fulfilled, which He spoke, signifying what death He should die (Mat. 20:19; 26:2; Mark 10:33; Luke18:32-33).
Luke 23
5 And they were more the fiercer, saying, "He stirs up the people, teaching throughout all Jewry, beginning from Galilee to this place."

6 When Pilate heard of Galilee, he asked whether the Man were a Galilean.
7 And as soon as he knew that He belonged to Herod's jurisdiction, he sent Him to Herod, who himself was also at Jerusalem at that time.

Having already mentioned that all the Gospel writers aligned again and paralleled together at the very beginning of Pilate's examination of Jesus: it is after Jesus is returned from Herod, which Luke alone mentions (23:7-12), that both Matthew (27:11) and Mark (15:2) parallel once more with John (18:34), though also dovetailing with Luke (23:13) and John (18:33) preceding.

Similarly, like John who did not refer to the first part of the interrogation at Caiaphas', or Herod, both Matthew and Mark do not mention Herod either, but only narrate with further detail regarding the second examination by Pilate, after Jesus had returned from Herod, after the incident of the cruel ridiculing and mocking there (Luke 23:11).

Also, it was Luke alone who recorded the previous mocking at the conclusion of Caiaphas' second interrogation at his Palace (22:63-65). Whereas Matthew (26:67-68) and Mark (14:65), both referred to the first cruel mocking at the end of the first part of the interrogation at Caiaphas'.

Luke 23
8 And when Herod saw Jesus, he was extremely glad: for since a long while he was desirous to see Him, because he had heard many things about Him; and he hoped to have seen some miracle done by Him.
9 Then he questioned Him with many words; but He answered him nothing.

10 And the Chief Priests and Scribes stood and vehemently accused Him.

11 And Herod with his men of war treated Him in contempt, and mocked Him, and arrayed Him in a gorgeous robe, and sent Him again to Pilate.

12 And the same day Pilate and Herod were made friends together: for before they were at enmity between themselves.

PILOT'S SECOND EXAMINATION

Luke 23:13 John 18:33

And then Pilate, when he had called together the Chief Priests and the Rulers and the People, entered into the Judgment Hall again, and called Jesus.

Matthew 27:11 Mark 15:2 John 18:34

And Jesus stood before Pilate the Governor: and the Governor asked, saying to Him, "You are the King of the Jews?"

And Jesus answering said to him, "You said it. Do you say this thing of yourself, or did others tell it you about Me?"

John 18

35 Pilate answered,

"Am I a Jew? Your own nation and the Chief Priests have delivered You to me: what have You done?"

36 Jesus answered,

"My Kingdom is not of this world: if My Kingdom were of this world, then would My servants fight that I should not be delivered to the Jews: but now My Kingdom is not through this situation."

37 Pilate therefore said to Him, "You are a King then?"

Jesus answered,

"You rightly say that I am a King. To this end was I born, and for this cause came I into the world, that I should bear witness to the truth. Everyone who is of the truth hears My voice."

38 Pilate said to Him, "What is truth?"

And when he had said this, he went out again to the Jews, and spoke to them, "I find no fault in Him at all."

Luke 23

14 And said to them,

"You have brought this Man to me, as one who perverts the people: and, understand, I, having examined Him before you, have found no fault in this Man touching those things whereof you accuse Him:

15 no, nor yet Herod: for I sent you to him; and, consider, nothing worthy of death is done by Him.

16 I will therefore chastise Him, and release Him."

17 (For of necessity he must release one to them at the Festival.)

Jesus remained silent at various stages when being questioned. Altogether, there were four times Jesus remained silent throughout the subsequent examinations leading up to His crucifixion. The first occurred during the first *Interrogation At Caiaphas'*, which is found in both Matthew (26:62-63) and Mark (14:60-61). The second took place in front of Herod, which Luke alone recorded (23:7-10), and the third was during the second examination by Pilate, to which only Matthew (27:12-14) and Mark (15:3-5) relate to in the following Scriptural text.

Furthermore, there were five times Pilate wanted to release Jesus. The first was prior to Pilate sending Him to Herod, at the first examination, at which point Luke (23:3-6) and John (18:31-32) both dovetail and converge together over. The second time, was after Jesus had returned from Herod, with Luke (23:14-17) and John (18:38) once more continuing to coincide and dovetail with their dialogue of the second examination by Pilate.

With Pilate having wanted to release Jesus already twice, in the following scenario, it leads us into the third time Jesus had remained silent, and now the first time in front of Pilate (Mat. 27:12-14; Mark 15:3-5).

The fourth time Jesus remained silent, though actually the second and last in front of Pilate (John 19:9-10), is just before the final, and fifth time, Pilate wishes Jesus released, which John alone recorded (19:11-12).

Matthew 27:12 Mark 15:3
And when He was accused of the Chief Priests and Elders, of many things, He answered nothing.
Matthew 27
13 Then said Pilate to Him, "Don't you hear how many things they witness against You?"
Mark 15
4 And Pilate asked Him again, saying, "Have you no answer? Consider how many things they witness against You."
Matthew 27:14 Mark 15:5
And nonetheless, yet Jesus gave him no answer, no, not a word; inasmuch, so that Pilate the Governor marveled greatly.

THEY WANT BARABBAS

Matthew 27:15 Mark 15:6
Now at that Festival, he the Governor was accustomed to release to the people one prisoner, whomever they would desire.
Matthew 27:16 Mark 15:7
And they were then holding a notorious prisoner, called Barabbas, who lay bound with them who had made insurrection with him, who had committed murder in the insurrection.

Mark 15

8 And the crowd crying aloud began to desire him to do as he had always done to them.

Matthew 27:17 Mark 15:9 John 18:39

Therefore when they were gathered together, nevertheless Pilate answering said to them, "However you have a custom that I should release to you one at the Passover: whom do you want me therefore to release to you? Barabbas, or do you want Jesus who is called the Messiah the King of the Jews?"

Matthew 27:18 Mark 15:10

For he knew that the Chief Priests for envy they had delivered Him.

Luke 23:18 John 18:40

And then they cried out all again at once, saying,

"Not this Man - away with this Man, but release to us Barabbas!"

Now Barabbas was a robber:

Luke 23

19 who for a certain sedition made in the city, and for murder, was cast into prison.

The third time Pilate wanted to let Jesus go, was directly after the first cry for the release of Barabbas, which both Luke (23:18) and John (18:40) relate and parallel together over.

Continuing, at that specific junction Luke (23:20) dovetails and further parallels with Matthew (27:21) at the point where Pilate is willing the third time to release Jesus, after his wife's advice on having nothing to do with the situation he found himself in (Mat. 27:19). This subsequently culminates in Pilate asking whom they would prefer, though Luke alone records the specific part where Pilate *'said to them the third time'* (27:22), through which he synchronizes again and parallels with Matthew (27:23a) and Mark (15:14a).

Matthew 27

19 When he was sat down in the judgment seat, his wife sent to him, saying, "You have nothing to do with that just Man: for I have suffered many things this day in a dream because of Him."

Matthew 27:20 Mark 15:11

But the Chief Priests and Elders stirred up the people, persuading that they should ask for Barabbas - rather releasing Barabbas to them, and destroy Jesus.

Matthew 27:21 Luke 23:20
Pilate the Governor therefore, willing to release Jesus, answering again
exclaimed and said to them,
"Whether of the two do you want that I release to you?"
They said, "Barabbas."

Matthew 27:22a Mark 15:12
And Pilate answered and requested again saying to them,
"What do you then want that I should do with Jesus who is called the
Messiah, whom you call the King of the Jews?"
Matthew 27:22b Mark 15:13 Luke 23:21
And nevertheless they all said, crying out again to him,
"Crucify Him, crucify Him, let Him be crucified."

Matthew 27:23a Mark 15:14a Luke 23:22
And then Pilate the Governor said to them the third time,
"Why, what evil has He done? I have found no cause of death in Him: I will
therefore chastise Him, and let Him go."

Matthew 27:23b Mark 15:14b Luke 23:23
And nonetheless they were instant with loud voices, crying out much more,
requiring that He might be crucified, saying,
"Crucify Him, let Him be crucified."
And the voices of them and of the Chief Priests prevailed.

Matthew 27
24 When Pilate saw that he could prevail nothing, but rather a tumult was
made, he took water, and washed his hands before the crowd, saying,
"I am innocent of the blood of this just Man: you see to it."
25 Then answered all the people, and said,
"His blood be on us, and on our children."

Mark 15:15a Luke 23:24
And so Pilate, willing to satisfy the people gave sentence that it should be as
they required.

THE FOURTH MOCKING

The second cry (Mat. 27:23; Mark 15:14; Luke 23:23) came after '*the third time*' Pilate wanted Jesus' release, which Luke (23:22) had specifically pointed out.

Moreover, there were four separate cruel mockings before Jesus' crucifixion. The first ended the first interrogation by Caiaphas, with the second concluding the second part of the interrogation. The third mocking occurred when Jesus was in front of Herod.

The Fourth Mocking (John 19:2-3), was subsequently after the preliminary sentencing of Pilate (Mat. 27:26; Mark 15:15; Luke 23:24-25), and before the fifth time Pilate sought for Jesus' release (John 19:11-12).

Matthew 27:26a Mark 15:15b Luke 23:25
And then he released to them Barabbas, him who for sedition and murder was cast into prison, whom they had desired; and regardless he delivered Jesus to their will.

Matthew 27:26b Mark 15:15c John 19:1
Then Pilate took Jesus, and scourged Him: and when he had scourged Jesus, he delivered Him to be crucified.

Matthew 27:27 Mark 15:16
And then the soldiers of the Governor led Him away into the Common Hall, called the Praetorium; and they called together, gathering to Him the whole cohort.
Matthew 27:28 Mark 15:17a John 19:2a
And the soldiers platted a crown of thorns, and they stripped Him, and they dressed Him, clothing Him with a scarlet-purple robe.
Matthew 27:29 Mark 15:17b-18 John 19:2b-3
And when they had platted a crown of thorns, they put it on His head and twisted it about His head, and put a reed in His right hand: and mocked Him, and began to salute Him, and they bowed their knees exclaiming,
"Hail, King of the Jews!"
And they hit Him with their hands.
Matthew 27:30 Mark 15:19
And they spat upon Him, and took the reed, and they hit Him on the head with the read, and continued to spit upon Him, and bowing their knees worshiped Him.
John 19
4 Pilate therefore went out again and says to them,
"Look, I bring Him out to you, that you may know I find no fault in Him."

John 19

5 Then came Jesus out, wearing the crown of thorns, and the purple robe. And Pilate says to them, "See, the Man!"
6 When the Chief Priests therefore and officers saw Him, they cried out, saying, "Crucify Him, crucify Him."
Pilate says to them, "You take Him, and crucify Him: for I find no fault in Him."
7 The Jews answered him, "We have a Law, and by our Law He ought to die, because He made Himself the Son of God (Lev. 24:16)."

At this junction, after Pilate had already desired to release Jesus four times (19:4-5), the third shout follows for Jesus' crucifixion, which John alone recorded (v. 6).

John (19:1-3) nonetheless agrees and aligns with the Synoptics in synchronizing, dovetailing, and paralleling with both Matthew and Mark at Pilate's preliminary sentencing of Jesus, and the subsequent specific detail of the scourging with the fourth mocking, which took place directly after (Mat. 27:26-30; Mark 15:15-19).

Luke (23:24-25), however, referred to the sentencing, but chose not to record the detail of the scourging, or the fourth mocking.

Though the Synoptics do not portray Jesus returning from the Common Hall to Pilate after the scourging and fourth mocking, John nevertheless was clear that the final sentencing took place, after, the scourging and fourth mocking, as Jesus returned to Pilate still wearing the crown of thorns and the purple robe. Furthermore, even Matthew (27:29), Mark (15:18), and John (19:3) all have the same phrase, '*Hail, King of the Jews*', during the mocking. Thus, John's (19:4-15) unique narrative dovetails after the fourth mocking, before once again paralleling with Matthew (27:31) and Mark (15:20) where Jesus is delivered to be crucified, and subsequently parallels once more with all the Synoptics, at the precise point where Jesus was finally taken away (Mat. 27:32; Mark 15:21; Luke 23:36).

FOURTH CRY FOR CRUCIFIXION

In the meanwhile, returning to the trial, which John alone continues with, we come to the fourth time Jesus successively remained silent, though now at this juncture the second and last time in front of Pilate (John 19:9-10). Jesus thus remained silent, after the third shout for His crucifixion (v. 6), including the statement whereby He is accused of making '*Himself the Son of God*' (v. 7), and where Pilate had become increasingly afraid of the whole situation (v. 8).

Hence, the fifth, and final time Pilate sought for Jesus' release (v. 12), came after Jesus referred to God's Power from above (v. 11), and obviously before the fourth, and last cry for Jesus' crucifixion (v. 15).

With the trial at the Judgment Hall officiated by Pilate concluding, before the crucifixion, John (19:16) returns in sync with Matthew (27:31) and Mark (15:20), who all continue with their dialogue once more, until, all four Gospels correlate and parallel together in relating the specific information on the crucifixion itself (Mat. 27:32; Mark 15:21; Luke 23:26; John 19:17).

John 19

8 When Pilate therefore heard that saying (v. 7), he was the more afraid,
9 and went again into the Judgment Hall, and says to Jesus, "Where are You from?"
But Jesus gave him no answer.
10 Then says Pilate to Him, "You don't speak to me? Don't You know that I have power to crucify You, and have power to release You?"
11 Jesus answered, "You could have no power at all against Me, except it were given you from Above: therefore those who delivered Me to you have the greater sin."
12 And from then Pilate sought to release Him: but the Jews cried out, saying, "If you let this Man go, you are not Caesar's friend: whoever makes himself a King speaks against Caesar."
13 When Pilate therefore heard that saying, he brought Jesus out, and sat down in the judgment seat in a place that is called the Pavement, but in the Hebrew, Gabbatha.
14 (And it was the preparation of the Passover [14th Nissan], at about noon.) And he says to the Jews, "Look, your King!"

15 But they cried out, "Away with Him, away with Him, crucify Him."
Pilate says to them, "Shall I crucify your King?"
The Chief Priests answered, "We have no King but Caesar."

Matthew 27:31 Mark 15:20 John 19:16
Then after that he delivered Him therefore to them to be crucified. And they having mocked Him, they took the purple robe from off Him, and put His own clothes on Him, and they took Jesus, and led Him out to crucify Him.

THE ULITMATE PASSOVER LAMB

At John's reference to '*the preparation of the Passover, at about noon*' (19:14), we have omitted the '*and*', as it is wanting in the original Greek, and have replaced it with the better rendering, of '*at*', along with the modern equivalent of '*the sixth hour*'. Jesus was crucified at '*the third hour*', i.e. 9 a.m, as Mark alone pointed out (15:25), and remained on the cross six hours, as he further indicates by stating that it was over at '*the ninth hour*', i.e. 3 p.m. (vv. 34-37).

Subsequently, it went dark at '*the sixth hour*', i.e. noon, until 3 p.m. (v. 33). Moreover, the Temple sacrifices, because of the volume involved started being slain, from about noon up until 3 p.m. on the 14th Nissan, so as to be ready before the eve of the 15th Nissan, the first Sabbath High Day of the Passover period.

John was pointing out, by interrupting the flow of the dialogue, with reference to '*the preparation of the Passover* [lambs] *at about noon*', of the urgency of the situation over the problem Pilate had in appeasing the Chief Priests, in making sure the bodies did not remain on the crosses before the annual Sabbath High Day arrived (19:31), and in not allowing a situation whereby a riot could develop (Mat. 27:24).

Owing to the fact of the amount of sacrifices brought to the Temple at the Passover, the Priests started sacrificing their lambs at noon on the 14th Nissan, so as to have them ready for the beginning of the 15th Nissan, wherein they ate their Passover meal. The first evening of the 15th Nissan was an Annual High Day Sabbath, and thus the 14th Nissan was their last preparation day before their Passover, as John (19:14, 31, 42) had especially made a point of indicating. Also the Synoptics confirm the same (Mat. 27:62; Mark 15:42; Luke 23:54). The 15th Nissan commemorated the symbolism of the original Exodus from Egypt (Num. 33:3), which the Jews still observe to this day.

Nonetheless, Jesus and the disciples ate their first Passover Supper in the first evening of the 14th Nissan, commemorating a different symbolism of the original Passover when it was eaten indoors, as Jesus had already been crucified by the time the first Annual Sabbath High Day had arrived.

However, the Synoptics also show the 13th Nissan was also a day of preparation, as '*then came the First Day of Unleavened Bread*' (Mat. 26:17; Mark 14:12; Luke 22:7), symbolically connected to the arrangements with the unleavened bread (Ex. 12:18), and also the rest of the factors in preparation for the disciple's first Passover Supper.

Hence, the Synoptics indicate the disciples and Jesus had prepared for their Passover Supper, just before the first evening of the 14th Nissan arrived, indicating the 13th Nissan being a preparation day for Jesus and the disciples, with the 14th Nissan being the last preparation day for the Jewish Passover, which was eaten in the first evening of the 15th Nissan. Nevertheless, Jesus the ultimate Passover Lamb, was crucified in the day time of the 14th Nissan, and slowly gave His life as the lambs were being slain in the Temple, wherein the Priests were preparing for their Passover, ready for partaking of when the 15th Nissan came, which commemorated the original Exodus from Egypt, a symbolism of freedom from slavery, and of freedom from sin, too.

Thus, the disciples and the Jews, both had the correct day for the commencement of the Passover week, just that different symbolisms were observed by both at varying points in the same day in the 14th Nissan and in its waning.

JESUS IS LED AWAY

Matthew 27:32 Mark 15:21 Luke 23:26 John 19:17a
And as they came out, He bearing His cross went forward. And as they led Him away, they found a man, who passed by, Simon by name, a Cyrenian, the father of Alexander and Rufus, coming out of the country, upon him they compelled to bear His cross, and on him they laid the cross, so he might bear it after Jesus.
Luke 23
27 And there followed Him a great company of people, and of women, who also cried and mourned for Him.

28 But Jesus turning to them said,
"Daughters of Jerusalem, don't cry for Me, but cry for yourselves, and for your children.
29 For understand, the days are coming, in which they shall say, 'Blessed are the barren, and the wombs that never bore, and the breasts that never nursed.'
30 'Then shall they begin TO SAY TO THE MOUNTAINS, "FALL ON US;" AND TO THE HILLS, "COVER US" (Hos. 10:8).'
31 For if they do these things in a green tree, what shall be done in the dry?"

32 And there were also two other, malefactors, led with Him to be put to death.

All the Gospel writers converge and parallel together once again over the information of Jesus being led away (Mat. 27:32; Mark 15:21; Luke 23:26; John 19:17). It is John alone who specifically tells us Jesus started to carry the cross, though it is the Synoptics who together mention Simon the Cyrenian, by name, who carried the cross afterwards.

Luke with his unique dialogue of Jesus addressing the *'Daughters of Jerusalem'*, and the two malefactors, continues with his narrative (23:27-32), and once more parallels and unites with all the Gospels in the arrival at Golgotha (Mat. 27:33; Mark 15:22; Luke 23:33a; John 19:17b).

Furthermore, all the Gospels continue to parallel dovetail and relate together with the subsequent details surrounding the crucifixion (Mat. 27:34-35; Mark 15:23; Luke 23:33b; John 19:18). John alone revealed that the Chief Priests were annoyed with the way Pilate had phrased the title over the cross (19:19-22). John also used the words on the cross the way he did by indicating through antithesis, emphasizing specifically where Jesus was brought up, by referring to *'JESUS OF*

NAZARETH, as normal, rather than Divine as he had throughout his Gospel. See *The Four Faces of God*, by John Bickersteth and Timothy Pain, Kingsway Publications, how each Gospel revealed Jesus.

Subsequently, with the wording on the cross, each of the Gospel writers chose the words that were poignant to what they were trying to individually reveal. However, when combining all the subsequent words on the cross from the four Gospels, the heading would have actually read, '*THIS IS JESUS OF NAZARETH THE KING OF THE JEWS*'.

THE CRUCIFIXION

As Jesus is crucified, Luke exclusively recorded the words, '*Father, forgive them; for they don't know what they are doing*' (23:34), at which juncture, Luke and the other three Gospels correlate and parallel together again over the parting of Jesus' clothes (Mat. 27:35b; Mark 15:24; John 19:23).

In relationship to the drink Jesus was offered immediately before the soldiers first hammered the nails, seven times the Greek word '*oxos*', has been translated '*vinegar*', each time surrounding the scenario at the cross. Although vinegar is a derivative of wine, nevertheless, it does not fit the complete evidence of the setting relating to the soldiers, whereby they had a vessel of this near the cross, as John (19:29) pointed out. The drink rather fits the description of the common drink that the Roman soldiers used to drink in those days, through which a vessel was at hand in the soldiers' possession. Jesus was offered this drink, obviously by the soldiers, on three separate occasions while He was on the cross. The first, was directly before the soldiers placed Jesus on the cross (Mat. 27:34; Mark 15:23), the second, was while Jesus hung on the cross (Luke 23:36), and thirdly, just before His death (Mat. 27:48; Mark 15:36; John 19:29). We have thus replaced the word '*vinegar*', for the more logical, though obsolete word '*posca*' [see *The New Shorter Oxford Dictionary*], which the soldiers had for their own benefit.

Matthew 27:33 Mark 15:22 Luke 23:33a John 19:17b
And they bringing Him, when they were come into the place which is called *Calvary*, in the Hebrew, *Golgotha*, that is to say being translated, the *Place of the Skull*,
Matthew 27:34 Mark 15:23
there THEY GAVE HIM TO DRINK WINE-POSCA MINGLED WITH myrrh and GALL (Ps. 69:21): and when He had tasted it, would not drink, or take it.
Matthew 27:35a Luke 23:33b John 19:18
And there they crucified Him, and two others with Him, the malefactors, on either side, one on the right hand, and the other on the left, and Jesus in the middle.

John 19

19 And Pilate wrote a title, and put it on the cross. And the writing was, "JESUS OF NAZARETH THE KING OF THE JEWS."

20 This title then read many of the Jews: for the place where Jesus was crucified was near to the city: and it was written in Hebrew, and Greek, and Latin.

21 Then said the Chief Priests of the Jews to Pilate, "Don't write, '*The King of the Jews*;' but that 'He said I am the King of the Jews.'"

22 Pilate answered, "What I have written I have written."

Matthew 27:35b Mark 15:24 Luke 23:34 John 19:23

And then when the soldiers had crucified Jesus, then said Jesus, "Father, forgive them; for they don't know what they are doing."

And THEY took and PARTED HIS GARMENTS, making four parts, to each soldier a part, AND CAST LOTS UPON THEM (Ps. 22:18), what each man should take, and also His coat: now the coat was without seam, woven from the top throughout.

Matthew 27:35c John 19:24

They said therefore among themselves, "Let us not cut it, but cast lots for it, whose it will be:" that the Scripture might be fulfilled, which was spoken by the prophet, which says, "THEY PARTED MY GARMENTS AMONG THEM, AND UPON MY CLOTHES THEY DID CAST LOTS FOR THEM (Ps. 22:18)."

These things therefore the soldiers did.

Mark 15

25 And it was 9 a.m. when they crucified Him.

Matthew 27

36 And sitting down they watched Him there;

Matthew 27:37 Mark 15:26

and set up over His head was the superscription of His accusation inscribed, "THIS IS JESUS THE KING OF THE JEWS."

Matthew 27:38 Mark 15:27

And now there were with Him the two crucified thieves; the one on the right hand, and the other on His left.

Mark 15

28 And the Scripture (Luke 22:37) was fulfilled, which says, "AND HE WAS NUMBERED WITH THE TRANSGRESSORS (Is. 53:12)."

Luke 23

35 And the people stood watching. And the Rulers also with them ridiculed Him, saying, "He saved others; let Him save Himself, if He be the Messiah, the Chosen of God."

Luke 23

36 And the soldiers also mocked Him, coming to Him, and offering Him posca,
37 also exclaimed, "If You be the King of the Jews, save yourself."

38 And a superscription was also written over Him in letters of Greek, and Latin,
and Hebrew, "THIS IS THE KING OF THE JEWS."

All the Gospels emphasized the words on the cross peculiar to them through
antithesis. Matthew had all the way through his Gospel depicted Jesus as King. At
the scenario of the crucifixion, he now chose words from the cross depicting how
this humble innocent Man was crucified, by highlighting, '*THIS IS JESUS*'. And
before that exclusively quoted the Psalms in portraying the ordinary soldiers sharing
Jesus' clothes.

Though Mark throughout his Gospel had shown Jesus as a Servant, and even
uniquely quoted Scripture from the chapter on the Righteous Servant (Is. 53),
which depicted Jesus on the cross as being counted amongst the lowliest of the
low (v. 12). However, with his choice of words from the cross, emphasized the
aspect through antithesis, that Jesus was actually '*THE KING*'. By not including
the word '*JESUS*', he stressed Jesus' special Kingship.

Luke's emphasis throughout his Gospel was that Jesus was the ideal Man -
the Man. With his choosing of the words from the cross he included both the
words of Matthew and Mark, though also deliberately leaving out His human
name, '*JESUS*'.

Furthermore, in his subsequent dialogue he positioned his version of the words
on the cross, to typify Jesus, as the Messiah. This is seen by his two references to
'*the Messiah*' (23:35, 39), which he alone recorded, and is besides the Greek
equivalent to the Hebrew meaning '*the Anointed*', which also related to kings
being anointed. Of course, Jesus was the Messiah-King, and Luke further
addressed the Kingship aspect, by exclusively at that juncture portraying the
soldiers mockingly saying to Jesus, '*if You be the King of the Jews*' (v. 36-37),
directly before referring to the title on the cross (v. 38).

THE CONCLUDING RIDICULE

Subsequently, there were five different groups of people who ridiculed Jesus while hanging on the cross: firstly there were some of the Rulers of the People [Sanhedrin]; secondly, some of the soldiers at the cross; thirdly those that passed by (Mat. 27:39-40; Mark 15:29-30); fourthly the Chief Priests, Scribes, and Elders (Mat. 27:41-43; Mark 15:31-32a); lastly the thieves on the cross (Mat. 27:44; Mark 15:32b).

Matthew (27:44) and Mark 15:32) had both revealed those crucified next to Jesus, followed the taunts of those at the cross.

Moreover, Luke's exclusive information had one of the malefactors continue with the abuse (23:39), while the other, after having repented, admitted that they had received their due reward, and asked Jesus to remember him, when He returned and had started His Kingdom (vv. 40-43).

The context of the question, of the repentant malefactor (v. 42), and Jesus' subsequent answer (v. 43), along with the factor that Jesus was resurrected three days afterwards, warranted moving the comma in v. 43 to its logical and natural place, as to convey its intrinsic meaning. However, in the original Greek no comma is found, and without it, the verse would still have the same meaning, as it would where we have positioned it.

Matthew 27:39 Mark 15:29
And those who passed by raved at Him, WAGGING THEIR HEADS (Ps. 22:7; 109:25; Lam. 2:15), and said,
"Ah, You who destroys the Temple, and builds it in three days.
Matthew 27:40 Mark 15:30
Save Yourself, if You be the Son of God, and come down from the cross."
Matthew 27:41 Mark 15:31
Likewise also the Chief Priests mocking said amongst themselves with the Scribes and Elders, saying, "He saved others; Himself He cannot save.
Matthew 27:42 Mark 15:32a
Let Messiah if He be the King of Israel, let Him descend now from the cross, that we may see and we will believe Him.
Matthew 27
43 HE TRUSTED IN GOD; LET HIM DELIVER Him now, IF HE WILL SAVE HIM (Ps. 22:8): for He said, '*I am the Son of God.*'

Matthew 27:44 Mark 15:32b
And the thieves also who were crucified with Him insulted Him, and hurled the same words at Him.
Luke 23
39 And one of the malefactors who hung ranted at Him, saying,

"If You be the Messiah, save Yourself and us!"
40 But the other answering rebuked him, saying,
"Don't you fear God, seeing you are in the same condemnation?
41 And we indeed justly; for we receive the due reward of our deeds: but this Man has done nothing amiss."

42 And he said to Jesus, "Lord, remember me when You come into Your Kingdom."
43 And Jesus said to him, "Truly I say to you today, you shall be with Me in Paradise."

John had recorded two incidents, which occurred during the beginning half of the crucifixion period, after 9 a.m. and before noon: the dividing of Jesus' clothes (19:23-24), and the committing of Jesus' mother into his care (vv. 25-27). John returns to the scenario three hours later, with further detail about the end of the crucifixion.

John Wenham in his book *The Easter Enigma* [Paternoster Press], pp. 60-63, suggests John took Mary to his house during the second period of the crucifixion, i.e. noon till 3 p.m., along with Salome [Mary's sister and John's mother], to comfort and spare her the last hours of the crucifixion. He further relates that John returned later to witness the last minutes (vv. 28-30).

John 19
25 Now there stood by the cross His mother, and His mother's sister, Mary the wife of Cleopas, and Mary Magdalene.

26 When Jesus therefore saw His mother, and the disciple standing by, whom He loved, He says to His mother, "Woman, welcome your son!"
27 Then He said to the disciple, "Welcome your mother!"
And from that hour that disciple took her to his own home.
Matthew 27:45 Mark 15:33 Luke 23:44
And it was about noon. Now when it was come, from noon there as darkness over all the whole land until 3 p.m.

THE STROKE OF THE SPEAR

Matthew 27:46 Mark 15:34
And at about 3 p.m. Jesus cried with a loud voice, saying,
"ELOI, ELOI, LAMA SABACHTHANI?"
Which is, that is to say, being translated,
"MY GOD, MY GOD, WHY HAVE YOU FORSAKEN ME (Ps. 22:1)?

Matthew 27:47 Mark 15:35
And some of them who stood nearby, when they heard it, said,
"Listen, this Man, He calls for Elijah."
John 19
28 After this, Jesus knowing that all things were now accomplished, that the
Scriptures (Ps. 69:21) might be fulfilled, says, "I am thirsty."

Matthew 27:48 Mark 15:36 John 19:29
Now there was set a vessel full of posca: and immediately one of them ran and
took a sponge, and they filled the sponge full of posca, and put it upon a
hyssop-reed, and he putting it to His mouth, gave Him to drink, saying,
"Leave alone: let us see whether Elijah will come down to take Him down."
Matthew 27
49a The rest agreeing, said,
"Let us see whether Elijah will come to save Him."
John 19
30a When Jesus therefore had received the posca, He said, "It is finished."
Matthew 27
49b And another took a spear and pierced His side, and there came out water
and blood.
Luke 23
45 And the sun was darkened, and the veil of the Temple was torn in the
middle.
Matthew 27:50 Mark 15:37 Luke 23:46 John 19:30b
And when Jesus had cried again with a loud voice, He exclaimed,
"Father, INTO YOUR HANDS I COMMIT MY SPIRIT!" (Psalms 31:5).
And having said this, He bowed His head, and He yielded giving up the spirit.

It is clear through the all the Synoptics, during Jesus' concluding words, the veil
of the Temple was torn (Mat. 27:51; Mark 15:38). Though Luke had referred to
the start of the tearing (23:45), both Matthew and Mark had recorded the aspect
of the tearing having been completed.

John had indicated that Jesus received the posca, and then said immediately
afterwards, '*It is finished*' (19:30), directly before one of the soldiers threw a
spear (v. 34).

Jesus was dead when the other soldiers came to break His legs (v. 33),
though John mentions the spearing after the breaking of the legs. Nevertheless,
John in retrospect wished us naturally to understand that the spearing would
have caused Jesus' death. At which point Jesus cried out in pain, prior to
exclaiming, 'Father, INTO YOUR HANDS I COMMIT MY SPIRIT!' He then bowed His
head in death, before the soldiers could break His legs. John laid great stress in

the next verse after mentioning the spearing, by testifying what he wrote was true, so we might believe (v. 35). Hence, John further related the two incidents, of not having His legs broken and the spearing, to the fulfilling of two Scriptures (vv. 36-37), related to Num. 9:12 and Zech. 12:10.

Furthermore, earlier manuscripts contain, *'And another took a spear and pierced His side, and there came out water and blood'*, directly after, *'Let us see whether Elijah will come to save Him'* (Mat. 27:49). While this verse is unique to Matthew, the AV does not have this part of the sentence included in its verse, referring to the spearing. Nonetheless, we have included it, as it is an additional witness and conveys precisely how Jesus died.

Moreover, with both the prophecies of Zech. 12:10 and Rev. 1:7, referring to this piercing, and the prophecy of the Servant in Is. 53, which is symbolic of the ultimate Jew - Jesus, in v. 8 there is also reference to what actually finalized Jesus' death. Using the alternative margin translation, it reads and avers:

"HE WAS TAKEN AWAY BY DISTRESS FROM RESTRAINT AND JUDGMENT; AND WHO SHALL DECLARE HIS GENERATION? FOR HE WAS CUT OFF OUT OF THE LAND OF THE LIVING: FOR THE TRANSGRESSION OF MY PEOPLE WAS THE STROKE UPON HIM."

Finally, and now upon the cross, one of the soldiers of the group in charge of guarding the cross, put a sponge on a reed full of posca to Jesus' mouth (Mat. 27:48; Mark 15:36). John added that the filling of the sponge and the giving Jesus a drink involved this group (19:29), as one of the soldiers put the hyssop reed to Jesus' mouth with the sponge on the end.

With the conversation between the soldier who placed the reed to Jesus' mouth to leave Jesus alone (Mark 15:36), and the other soldiers, in seeing if Elijah would come to help Jesus, an agreement followed with the rest of the soldiers to leave Jesus alone (Mat. 27:49). Likely, it was the Centurion in charge, overseeing the situation who accepted this agreement. At that precise instance, in the heat of the moment, no doubt the Centurion, who had started to believe that Jesus was the Son of God, while the rest of the soldiers had agreed to wait, threw the spear in mercy, resulting in Jesus' death, before the time came for the other soldiers to carry out the instructions of the next undignified spectacle of breaking the legs, as the Sabbath High Day was drawing near.

Because the eve of the Sabbath High Day was approaching, wherein the Priests did not want any of the bodies remaining on the cross, they had requested Pilate that the legs should be broken so as to bring on a quicker death (John 19:31), as then the bodies could not hold themselves up any longer in adequately breathing. Without the spearing or the breaking of the legs, the crucifixion would normally have lasted much longer.

The soldiers who broke the legs of the two malefactors (v. 32), when they came to Jesus they found Him dead already (v. 33), as one of the soldiers had brought about Jesus' death a little earlier by throwing the spear into His side, at which point Jesus cried out, and the residue of blood and fluids spilled themselves out (Mat. 27:49; John 19:34), resulting in Him expiring.

John had also placed his narration to show the reason why they broke the legs, as it was the Sabbath shortly, with mentioning Jesus' spearing after the legs were broken. But the fact that Jesus was dead already meant that His legs did not need breaking, and that He certainly did not need spearing if He were dead anyhow. Hence, John was referring to what had already transpired (19:34), that He had been speared shortly before. Thus, we have included the verb '*had*' in the main text, so as to confer more clarity to the complete scenario, as the verb '*had*' was also included by the translators of the AV in John 18:24 [when wanting in the Greek], in the setting where Jesus was first taken to Caiaphas' Palace (v. 13). However, all the Gospels parallel together again over Jesus expiring (Mat. 27:50; Mark 15:37; Luke 23:46; John 19:30).

We considered at the beginning of this section that Luke had explained that the veil in the Temple started to tear in the middle. This would have occurred just before the very moment when Jesus cried out after being speared, and then exclaimed His last words, and breathed His last breath (23:45), transpiring directly after He had said '*It is finished*', as the earthquake continued to exert its tension on the structure of the Temple and veil. Both Matthew (27:51) and Mark (15:38) indicate the completion of the tearing, just after Jesus expired, when the full effects of the earthquake had been felt, even though Luke and Mark do not in word, actually mention the earthquake, only its effect.

Matthew 27:51 Mark 15:38
And, immediately, the veil of the Temple was torn in two from the top to the bottom; and the earth did quake, and the rocks split;
Matthew 27
52 and the graves were opened; and many bodies of the saints who slept rose,
53 and came out of the graves after His resurrection, and went into the holy city and appeared to many.
Matthew 27:54 Mark 15:39 Luke 23:47
And now when the Centurion, who stood over against Him, saw that He cried out, and gave up the spirit, and they who were with him, watching Jesus, saw the earthquake, and those things that were done, he glorified God, and said affirming, "Certainly this was a righteous Man - truly this Man was the Son of God!"

Luke 23
48 And all the people who came together to that sight, watching the things that were done, beat their chests, and returned.
John 19
31 The Jews therefore, because it was the preparation, that the bodies should not remain upon the cross on the Sabbath Day, (for that Sabbath Day [15th Nissan] was a High Day,) asked Pilate that their legs might be broken, and that they might be taken away.

32 Then came the soldiers, and broke the legs of the first, and of the other that was crucified with Him.
33 But when they came to Jesus, and saw that He was dead already, they didn't break His legs.
34 But one of the soldiers with a spear had pierced His side, and immediately blood and water came out.
35 And he who saw it bore record, and his record is true: and he knows what he says is true, that you might believe.
36 For these things were done, so that the Scripture should be fulfilled (Num. 9:12), "A BONE OF HIM SHALL NOT BE BROKEN."
37 And again another Scripture (Zech. 12:10) says, "THEY SHALL LOOK ON HIM WHOM THEY PIERCED."

Matthew 27:55 Mark 15:40a Luke 23:49
And there were all His acquaintances, also many women who followed Jesus from Galilee, who ministered to Him, who stood looking afar off, watching these things:
Matthew 27:56 Mark 15:40b
among whom was Mary Magdalene, and Mary the mother of James the Less and of Joses, and Salome the mother of Zebedee's children.
Mark 15
41 (Who also, when He was in Galilee, followed Him, and ministered to Him;) and many other women who came up with Him to Jerusalem.

JOSEPH OF ARIMATHEA

With the two Scriptures fulfilled, mentioned by John, concluding the death of Jesus, and Jesus' acquaintances and the women having witnessed the events at the cross, all the Gospels correlate again, paralleling and dovetailing together, with the information surrounding the subsequent burial arrangements organized by Joseph of Arimathea (Mat. 27:57-58; Mark 15:42-45; Luke 23:50-52; John 19:38).

All the Gospels mention Joseph by name, with Matthew indicating him to be '*a rich man*' (27:57), and John agreeing with Matthew that he was a disciple of Jesus (19:38). Whereas, both Mark (15:43a) and Luke (15:50) revealed he was a member of the Sanhedrin, with Luke (v. 51) showing he had nothing to do with the Court's decision over Jesus.

Matthew 27:57 Mark 15:42-43a Luke 23:50 John 19:38a
And now after this, consider, when the evening was approaching, because it was the preparation, that is the day [14th Nissan] before the Sabbath [15th Nissan], there came a rich man named Joseph of Arimathea, an honorable Counselor; and he was a good and just man, who also himself was a disciple of Jesus, but secretly for fear of the Jews.
Mark 15:43b Luke 23:51 John 19:38b
The same had not consented to their Council and deed; he was of Arimathea, a city of the Jews: whom also was himself waiting for the Kingdom of God.
Matthew 27:58a Mark 15:43c Luke 23:52 John 19:38c
This man, he came and went in boldly to ask Pilate, and earnestly begged that he might take away the body of Jesus:
Mark 15
44 and Pilate marveled if He were already dead: and calling to him the Centurion, he asked him whether He had been dead a while.
Matthew 27:58b Mark 15:45 John 19:38d
And when he knew it of the Centurion, then Pilate gave him permission, commanding the body to be delivered, he granting the body to Joseph. He came therefore, and took the body of Jesus.

Mark exclusively reveals Pilate's amazement in Jesus being dead already (15:44).

Now, because the crucifixion took place on the preparation day before the first annual Sabbath High Day at the start of the Passover week, Pilate had agreed with the Chief Priests not to allow the bodies to remain on the crosses before the eve of that Sabbath. This agreement would have been a standing order, as any crucifixions transpiring before the eve of any of the previous Sabbaths, the Priests would have expected the same ruling, as not to have the Sabbaths tainted by the spectacle of dying men, as was in accordance with the Law, which actually applied to any day (Deut. 21:22-23).

Pilate's amazement on hearing that Jesus was dead, after 3 p.m. meant that there was a specific time agreed, in calculating when to break the legs and the bodies being taken down, so as to have them clear of the crosses before the Sabbath. The Priests would have agreed with Pilate as to the time.

With Pilate's surprised reaction to Jesus' early death, indicated that, when Joseph arrived to see him, the time for the breaking of their legs had not transpired, otherwise Pilate would not have shown any amazement, neither would he have had to confirm Jesus' death, knowing the deaths on the crosses would have been complete shortly after the breaking of the legs.

THE CENTURION

Joseph made sure he saw Pilate before they would start taking the bodies down. After Pilate had summoned the Centurion in charge of the crucifixions, permission was given for Joseph to take Jesus' body (Mark 15:44-45).

Jesus, having been spared from having His legs broken, with His death quickened through the stroke of the thrown spear into His side, meant the time agreed for the breaking of the legs must have been obviously some time shortly after 3 p.m.

Thus, a conjecture develops over the Centurion who was in charge of the crucifixion in not allowing anything to develop which would mar his position in overseeing that the crucifixion was carried out accordingly.

No doubt it seems that this Centurion was the one who threw the spear in mercy (Mat. 27:49; John 19:34), so as to save Jesus the further indignity in having His legs broken, which moreover fulfilled the two Scriptures John had referred to. The Centurion would also have been privy to the scene over putting the posca to Jesus' mouth this third time, when there was a dispute over leaving Jesus alone regarding whether Elijah would come and save Him (Mat 27:48-49; Mark 15:36).

Surely, before that, the Centurion would have witnessed the other soldiers having mocked Jesus earlier, the second time they had offered Him posca (Luke 23:36). Furthermore, he obviously had the greater authority over the ordinary soldiers, who would have been disciplined through such an action as throwing a spear. And since they all, subsequently, a little later, came to see that Jesus was the Son of God, they would have kept the matter to themselves, anyhow. Hence, prior to the soldiers who were to go around and break the legs, the Centurion threw the spear in the presence of the other soldiers at the cross who were waiting if Elijah would come and save Jesus. At which moment the earthquake began to exert its pull on the veil in the Temple, through which it started to tear (Luke 23:45). Directly afterwards Jesus exclaimed '*Father, INTO YOUR HANDS I COMMIT MY SPIRIT!*' (v. 46).

It was through this subsequent scenario, and especially the earthquake occurring precisely when it did, with it once again returning to the light of the day, that the Centurion and the soldiers at the cross affirmed their belief, that '*Truly this was the Son of God!*' (Mat. 27:54). Hence, the combined testimonies of the parallel accounts also confirm the Centurion glorifying God, through the all-inclusive words in declaring, '*Certainly this was a righteous Man - truly this Man was the Son of God!*' (Mat. 27:54; Mark 15:39; Luke 23:47).

After having heard Jesus cry, '*ELOI, ELOI, LAMA SABACHTHANI*' (Mat. 27:46; Mark 15:34), and then directly afterwards, '*I thirst*' (John 19:28), was the point at which Jesus was given the posca on the reed. Moreover, this whole incident at the cross transpired in relationship to '*the rest*' of the soldier's comments, who agree to wait and see whether Elijah would save Jesus at this late hour (Mat. 27:48-49), before they knew the order for the breaking of the legs would be carried out.

Thus, while they waited to see if Elijah would come to save Him, meant at some point this Centurion and the soldiers around the cross just before Jesus died, were beginning to have some apprehension, with an inkling realization that maybe this was the very Son of God, in their misunderstanding in thinking Jesus cried for Elijah. However, having been familiar with the the outcome of Jesus' cry. Having also witnessed the manner in which Jesus conducted Himself in death, when comparing it to the many crucifixions they no doubt had witnessed. Combined with the earthquake occurring precisely just before Jesus' death, and having been dark since noon, with it returning to light again, confirmed to this Centurion, and '*the rest*' of the soldiers with him (Mat. 27:49), that '*Truly this was the Son of God*' (v. 54)!

Furthermore, these soldiers, though they would have been familiar with some of the Jewish beliefs - as living in that country, and would have had some knowledge of Aramaic, nevertheless, when Jesus cried, '*ELOI, ELOI, LAMA SABACHTHANI*', had confused '*Eloi*' with '*Elijahu*' - '*Elijah*'. Any Jew would have understood the difference between these two words, and certainl the rest of the sentence, which in any case was loudly exclaimed by Jesus.

THE BURIAL

John 19

39 And there also came Nicodemus, who at the first came to Jesus by night, and brought a mixture of myrrh and aloes, about a hundred pound weight.

Mathew 27:59 Mark 15:46a Luke 23:53a John 19:40

And Joseph bought fine linen, and he took Him down, and wrapped Him in a clean linen sheet.

And then when Joseph and they had taken the body of Jesus, he wound it in linen strips with the spices, as the manner of the Jews is to bury.

Luke 23:53b John 19:41

Now in the place where He was crucified there was a garden; and in the garden a new tomb that was cut in stone wherein was never yet anyone laid before.

Matthew 27:60 Mark 15:46b Luke 23:53c John 19:42

There they laid Jesus therefore in the tomb - Joseph's own new tomb which was cut out in the rock, because of the Jews' preparation day; for the tomb was near at hand: and he rolled a great stone to the door of the tomb, and departed.

Luke 23

54 And that day [14th Nissan] was the preparation, and the Sabbath [15th Nissan] drew on.

Matthew 27:61 Mark 15:47 Luke 23:55

And the women also, who came with Him from Galilee, had followed after, and there was Mary Magdalene and the other Mary the mother of Joses, sitting over against the tomb and saw the tomb where He was laid, and how His body was laid.

Luke 23

56 And they returned, and prepared spices and ointments; and rested the [Annual] Sabbath Day [15th Nissan] according to the Commandment (Ex. 12:16; Lev. 23:6-7; Num. 28:17-18; 1 Cor. 5:7-8).

Matthew 27

62 Now in the morning [15th Nissan] that followed the day of preparation [14th Nissan], the Chief Priests and the Pharisees came together to Pilate,

63 saying, "Sir, we remember what that deceiver said, while He was yet alive, '*After three days I will rise again* (John 2:20).'

64 Command therefore that the tomb be made sure until the third day, lest His disciples come by night, and steal Him away, and say to the people, 'He is risen from the dead:' so the last error shall be worse than the first."

65 Pilate said to them, "You have a guard: go your way, make it as sure as you can."

66 So they went with the guard and made the tomb secure, sealing the stone.

Mark 16

1 And when the [Annual] Sabbath [15th Nissan] was past [16th Nissan], Mary Magdalene, and Mary the mother of James, and Salome, had bought sweet spices that they might come and anoint Him.

THE TWO ANGELS

All the Gospels parallel together once again, with the women coming early to the tomb. John, who was familiar with the events of what the others had written, however, concentrates on Mary Magdalene alone, choosing not to mention the rest of the women, but highlights the points he felt ought to be stressed, though, complementing the other versions of the Synoptics.

Matthew 28:1 Mark 16:2 Luke 24:1 John 20:1a

Now after the [weekly] Sabbath [17th Nissan], upon the first day of the week [18th Nissan] while it was yet dark, as it began to dawn towards day, Mary Magdalene and the other Mary came very early in the morning. They came to see the tomb at the rising of the sun, bringing the spices that they had prepared, and certain others with them.

Mark 16

3 And they said among themselves, "Who shall roll us away the stone from the door of the tomb?"

Mark 16:4 Luke 24:2 John 20:1b

And when they looked, noticing they saw and found the stone was rolled away, and moved from the tomb: for it was very great.

Matthew 28

2 And, understand, there had been a great earthquake: for an angel of the Lord descended from Heaven, and came and rolled back the stone from the door, and sat upon it.

3 His countenance was like lightning, and his clothing white as snow:

4 and for fear of him, the guards shook, and became like dead men.

Matthew 27

52a And the graves were opened; and many bodies of the saints who slept arose,

53a and came out of the graves after His resurrection, and went into the holy city, and appeared to many.

Mark 16:5a Luke 24:3

And [the women] they entered into the tomb, and didn't find the body of the Lord Jesus.

John 20

2 Then Mary Magdalene runs, and comes to Simon Peter, and to the other disciple, whom Jesus loved, and says to them,

"They have taken away the Lord out of the tomb, and we don't know where they have laid Him."

Obviously, through the combined information contained in the accounts, the women all entered the tomb together. Though Mary left immediately, she was fully aware that the body was no longer in the tomb, and runs to tell Peter and John (20:2), thus leaving the other women in the tomb, as both Mark (16:5a) and Luke (24:3) reveal.

While the other women were perplexed over the disappearance of the body (Luke 24:4a; Mark 16:5b), they notice the angel that Matthew had exclusively mentioned first, who had rolled the stone away and sat atop of it (28:2), subsequently, now sitting inside the tomb, as Mark uniquely pointed out.

Luke in his version of the same event pictured two angels, though he describes the setting after the one angel had spoken first.

Moreover, John had not specifically mentioned the other women also coming early to the tomb, with Mary Magdalene, though nevertheless, he alluded to it where Mary is quoted as saying '*we*', through the aspect of the women having entered the tomb together (20:2). Likewise both Matthew and Mark decided only to refer to one angel in their dialogue. Nonetheless, there was actually more than one, in either case.

Both Matthew (28:5) and Mark (16:6a) concentrated their narrative by focusing on the one angel with the wonderful news of the outstanding and important message about Jesus having been resurrected (Mat. 28:6; Mar. 16:6b). They both were clear that only one angel spoke initially. So the angel appearing in the reposed position, thus looking up to them, no doubt, not unnecessarily wanting to frighten the women in their perturbed state, but rather wanted to appease the women in their shock in having noticed him (Luke 24:4a; Mark 16:5b). Consequently, before standing up, he assures them that he was aware that they sought Jesus. Hence, both Matthew and Mark's phraseology of the message of the angel, is in the idiom of the first person.

However, Luke complemented the scenario by pointing out that subsequently there were actually two angels (24:4b), with the other obviously having materialized while they were being assured by the first angel's news, who had been sitting previously while he spoke. Therefore, the women were shocked once again (v. 5) after the first angel stood up and fully revealed himself, with the other naturally materializing in joining him. Both the angels were now standing together, as the women, afraid again, bowed their heads, as the other angel now became a twofold witness to the good news that Jesus had risen.

Furthermore, Luke (24:6) at that particular point parallels both with Matthew (28:6) and Mark (16:6b) recounting virtually word for word with the angels' message, '*He is not here, for nonetheless He is risen*'.

Obviously, both angels now spoke in unison over witnessing the resurrection of Jesus the Messiah. So John (20:11-13), also depicts the two angels later addressing Mary, too.

Luke (24:7) further indicated that the angels continued reassuring them, through refreshing their memories, by referring to what Jesus had previously said about His resurrection, when they were last in Galilee. Thus, they now recalled the words Jesus had spoken there (v. 8).

Following, after dovetailing with Luke, Matthew (28:7), and Mark (16:7) parallel together, though Mark exclusively mentions the women were to tell Peter the message, and also confirm the news to the disciples, and further inform them about seeing Jesus afterwards when returning to Galilee after the Passover week.

Moreover, with Luke's (24:4-7) part of the dialogue of the two angels, preceding Matthew (28:7) and Mark's (16:7) extended narration, there is no specific directive from the angels to inform anyone about any particular message, though the women are shown later to be so doing by Luke (24:9b-10). It is as if Luke curtailed the incident, although having given other additional detail. However, with the concluding part in Matthew and Mark, the scenario returns once more to the idiolect of the first person, depicting one angel again, now delivering the specific message.

Mark 16:5b Luke 24:4a

And it came to pass, as they were much perplexed, they saw a young man sitting clothed in a long white garment; and they were afraid.

Matthew 28:5 Mark 16:6a

And the angel answered and declared saying to the women,

"Don't you fear - don't be afraid: for I know who you seek Jesus of Nazareth, who was crucified."

Luke 24

4b Then, suddenly in his company another stood by him in shinning garments:
5 and as they were afraid, and bowed down their faces to the ground, they said to them, "Why do you seek the living among the dead?

Matthew 28:6 Mark 16:6b Luke 24:6

He is not here, for nonetheless He has risen, as He said. Come, see the place where the Lord lay, where they laid Him: remember how He spoke to you when He was in Galilee,

Luke 24

7 saying, '*The Son of Humanity must be delivered into the hands of sinful men, and be crucified, and the third day rise again* (Mat.17:22-23; Mark 9:31; Luke 9:44)'".

8 And they remembered His words.

Matthew 28:7 Mark 16:7

"And notwithstanding go quickly your way, and tell His disciples and Peter that He is risen from the dead; and, understand, that He goes before you into Galilee; there shall you see Him as He said to you (Mat. 26:32; Mark 14:28): mind, we have told you."

Matthew 28:8 Mark 16:8 Luke 24:9a

And they went out and departed quickly, and fled returning from the tomb; for they trembled with fear and great joy and were amazed: neither said they anything to anyone; for they were afraid; and did run to bring His disciples word.

With the women running to bring word to Peter and the disciples, the Synoptics parallel again and converge, correlating together (Mat. 28:8; Mark 16:8; Luke 24:9a). Part of the sentence in Luke (24:9b) though, where he alone specifically refers to '*the eleven, and to all the rest*' of the other disciples being told of the resurrection, subsequently occurred after Peter, John and Mary had returned from the tomb. Hence, we cover this part of Luke's verse in its appropriate setting, a little later.

In the meantime, Peter and John after, having heard Mary's discovery, arrive at the tomb (Luke 24:12a; John 20:3). After Peter and John had examined the tomb, they return again to the place they were staying at while in Jerusalem, during this Passover week (Luke24:12c; John 20:10), while Mary lingers in the garden.

Mary, having decided to stay longer started to weep and ponder over the events, and as she looks inside the tomb she now sees the previous two angels that the other women had seen earlier (John 20:11-12). At that point the angels ask Mary why she is weeping, and directly after she tells them, Jesus appears. Thus, Mary, after having recognized Jesus, had witnessed the **forty-third miracle,** and *The First Appearance* of Jesus since His resurrection (John 20:13-16).

Luke 24:12a John 20:3
Then Peter rose therefore and went out, and that other disciple, and came to the tomb.
John 20
4 So they both ran together: and the other disciple did outrun Peter, and came first to the tomb.
5 And he stooping down, and looking in, saw the linen strips lying; yet he didn't enter.

Luke 24:12b John 20:6
Then comes Simon Peter following him, and went into the tomb, and stooping down, he sees the linen strips lying by themselves,
John 20
7 and the head linen, that was around His head, not lying with the linen strips, yet wrapped together by itself separately.
8 Then went in also that other disciple, who came first to the tomb, and he saw and believed.
9 For as yet they knew not the Scriptures (Mat. 20:19; Mark 10:34; Luke 18:33; John 2:20-22), that He must rise again from the dead.
10 Then the disciples departed and went away again to their own companions,
Luke 24
12c Peter wondering in himself at that which was come to pass.

THE FIRST APPEARANCE - TO MARY

John 20
11 But Mary stood outside at the tomb weeping: and as she wept, she stooped down, and looked into the tomb,
12 and sees two angels in white sitting, the one at the head, and the other at the feet, where the body of Jesus had lain.
13 And they say to her, "Woman, why do you weep?"
She says to them, "Because they have taken away my Lord, and I don't know where they have laid Him."
14 And when she had said this, she turned herself back, and saw Jesus standing, and knew not that it was Jesus.

Mark 16

9 Now when Jesus had risen, early the first day of the week, He appeared first to Mary Magdalene, out of whom he had cast seven devils.

John 20

15 Jesus says to her, "Woman, why are you weeping? Whom do you seek?" She, supposing Him to be the gardener, says to Him, "Sir, if you have taken Him from here, tell me where you have laid Him, and I will take Him away."

16 Jesus says to her, "Mary." She turned herself, and says to Him, "Rabboni;" which is to say, 'Master.'

17 Jesus says to her, "Don't touch Me; for I haven't yet ascended to My Father: but go to My brothers and sisters, and say to them, 'I am ascending to My Father, and your Father; and to My God, and your God.'"

The angels had appeared to the women first, and additionally Jesus had appeared to Mary first, rather than any of the men.

Mary was no doubt symbolic of 'the New Woman', whereas contrariwise throughout the ages, women were looked upon as being secondary to man. Moreover, '*the woman*' was depicted as the Church, of who the Messiah was 'spiritually' to marry (2 Cor. 11:2; Eph. 5:23; Rev. 19:7). Hence, though the first woman came out from a man, conversely, they were to become one through the union of marriage.

Furthermore, Jesus having been associated with many women throughout His ministry, revealed them equal to men in their own right, and as being one through the Messiah (Gal. 3:28). Nonetheless, God had from the very beginning, always stressed the spiritual attributes, as being more important than the physical. Though, of course because of their physical differences, in the main women held different work roles; and as time progressed even these different orientations through the bounty of science, and technology started to erode.

The miraculousness of the first appearance is validated by the particular factor that Mary witnessed Jesus with His new resurrected body - which no human had seen since His death, rather than seeing Him appear from out of nowhere so to speak, as two other appearances relate, and where conversely another one has Jesus vanishing. Now, because the specific moment of Jesus' resurrection did not involve any other person and that every one of the other miracles related primarily to the individuals themselves [though we can count Jesus' resurrection as the **forty-third miracle**], it must also be considered in a completely different light, in an aspect distinct and that transcends all the others, as it was the greatest miracle of all, and in that sense cannot be classified in the same category as the others.

Whats more, since the first appearance of Jesus is intrinsically connected to understanding the importance between the next miracle - *The Second Appearance* - naturally we will consider this in the following sections, and primarily after the next two, *All the Women Tell the Apostles* [pp. 406-410] and *The Messiah the Firstfruit* [pp. 410-413].

ALL THE WOMEN TELL THE APOSTLES

Mark 16:10 John 20:18

And Mary Magdalene went and came and told the disciples who had been with Him, as they mourned and wept that she had seen the Lord, and that He had spoken these things to her [to not touch Him, since He was about to ascend to His Father].

Mark 16

11 And they, when they had heard that He was alive, and had been seen of her, they disbelieved.

Luke 24

9b Also the other women told all these things to the eleven, and to all the rest.

10 It was Mary Magdalene, and Joanna, and Mary the mother of James, and the other women who were with them, who told all these things to the apostles.

11 And their words seemed to them as idle tales, and they didn't believe them.

Mark (16:9), who confirms that Jesus appeared to Mary first, along with John's explicit narration of the event (20:11-17), both continue with Mary going to tell the apostles the good news (Mark 16:10; John 20:18). Though, Matthew and Luke are silent as to *The First Appearance.*

Previously the Synoptics had synchronized and paralleled together over the women at the tomb running to tell the apostles first the outstanding news of Jesus' resurrection (Mat. 28:8; Mark 15:8; Luke 24:9a), before telling '*all the rest*' of the disciples (Luke 24:9b). Naturally, the informing of '*all the rest*' transpired after the women had told the apostles.

Some see Matthew 28:9-10 applying to the women running to tell the apostles the good news of Jesus' resurrection, when, at that point, Jesus appeared. However, we will see that with the proceeding of the women in v. 9, relates to when they were going to tell '*all the rest*' of the disciples the news of Jesus' resurrection, after they had already told the apostles. The angel at the tomb had first spoken to the women about informing the eleven regarding seeing Jesus in Galilee later. The message at that time did not include telling '*all the rest*' about the meeting in Galilee. We shall further see in v.10, Jesus refers to the aspect of wanting '*all the rest*' of '*My brothers*' - these other disciples, also, to hear of a meeting with Him in Galilee. It would bestrange if the women did not do what the angel originally told them, in telling the apostles first that He was resurrected. Moreover, if Jesus had appeared at that juncture, there would have been no need for the angel's message, as they would have been able to see, that He was resurrected.

Nevertheless, these women were the first to believe in the angel's message, and Jesus made sure that He appeared to them personally, after they had told the apostles, and had set out on the considerable task of informing the five hundred. He specifically and directly, made sure that they not only tell tell '*all the rest'* about

His resurrection, but, that they were to give '*all the rest*' the message about meeting in Galilee, too.

Furthermore, all of the apostles at that point still did not believe, except John when he and Peter, saw the empty tomb and John was the first apostle to believe (John 20:8).

The fact of telling '*all the rest*' of the disciples, obviously would have transpired after the women had first tried to convince the majority of disbelieving apostles of the miraculous event of Jesus' resurrection, which would have taken some time before the women set out again.

Though the AV has, '*And as they went to tell the disciples*' (Mat. 28:9), nonetheless it should be read as relating to all of the rest of the disciples, those other than the apostles. Moreover, many translations do not include this section of the verse, and the NU-Text omits this first clause. Hence, it is easy to confuse Jesus Jesus appearing to the women directly after they started running to tell the eleven, rather than appearing to them as they went in a normal fashion to them as they went in a normal fashion to tell all the rest of the disciples later in that same day.

So, Mat. 28:8, where the women were running, should be read in the past tense, with them having arrived earlier, and having already given the apostles the angel's message, when, '*neither said they anything to anyone*' (Mark 16:8).

However, the AV appropriately indicates a new paragraph at Mat. 28:9, and when we consider the aspect of Jesus' personal message to the women being directed expressly to '*all the rest*', and the fact in v. 11 where it is stated, '*Now when they were going*', it would certainly add credence to the aspect that they were now going to tell '*all the rest*' of the disciples.

They had already told the apostles as Mat. 28:8, Mark 16:8, and Luke 24:9a should indicate. They were still going in Mat. 28:9, and even still yet '*going*' in v. 11. Also, there is antithesis between the factor of running in the first instance, and later just normally '*going*' to tell the rest of the other disciples, which would have taken some time.

Thus, Matthew's unique verses on the subject (28:9-11), should relate to after the women had told the apostles, as the Synoptics preceding verses (Mat. 28:7-8; Mark 16:7-8; Luke 24:9a), should also correlate and parallel together and confirm that the women had already told them.

Of course the seventy, and no doubt the five hundred, had come to the Festival for the Passover week, and the angels had made sure that the news of Jesus' resurrection, and the aspect of meeting afterwards in Galilee, went firstly to the apostles. Later, the additional message from Jesus to '*all the rest*' about meeting in Galilee was given when He appeared and spoke directly to the women, encouraging them, as they set off, to also inform all '*My brothers*', about the meeting in Galilee. These other disciples would in any case return to their subsequent homes, after the week long Festival. Jesus made sure not only were the apostles to meet in Galilee, but all of His disciples (Mat. 28:9-10).

Earlier that morning, Jesus had originally used the all-embracing expression '*My brothers*', when addressing Mary Magdalene in relating the message of His resurrection, though in that instance it referred to giving the news to the apostles first (John 20:17). Nevertheless, the expression would naturally include all of Jesus' followers, as when He used it again when He appeared to the women.

John was the only apostle at this particular point, directly after the women had first believed the angels, who also believed. Because the other apostles had hardly believed the women's report, it would take various repeated recounts during the rest of the Festival by all of those that had witnessed Jesus' resurrected body, in alleviating the doubts and confirming the news to *The Seventy* and *The Five Hundred* too.

After the women had given the angel's message to the apostles, and later that day had witnessed the resurrected Jesus, the apostles would shortly after Jesus had appeared to them, confirm that their words were true. Though it would take Jesus speaking directly to Thomas, with Thomas handling Jesus, and Jesus afterwards meeting with '*all the rest*' in Galilee, to dispel eventually all of the of the final doubts.

But now at this juncture, the women having related the message of the angels about Jesus' resurrection and the meeting in Galilee with the apostles leave once more to bring the news of Jesus' resurrection '*to all the rest*' of the disciples, namely *The Seventy*, and no doubt *The Five Hundred*, before Jesus appears to them, informing them to tell all the rest of His brothers also, regarding meeting Him after the Festival week, at the mount in Galilee (Mat. 28:16).

These other disciples would receive this message through the women first, with the apostles confirming it too, after they had also witnessed Jesus' resurrected body. Thus, it transpired when the women were leaving to give the good news of Jesus' resurrection, that Jesus subsequently met them, and at that particular point allowed them to hold Him, whereas earlier He had asked Mary not to do so. Now, with the fact that these women had actually held Jesus, they continued in their task of going to tell these brother-disciples staying around Jerusalem, about Jesus' resurrection, and the additional message where Jesus confirmed that they were also to go to Galilee, after the Festival had concluded, where He would meet with them and they would all see Him (v. 10).

Hence, where Jesus appears to these women was not when they were running to tell the apostles, whom they would have already told earlier, but when they were now on their way to tell '*all the rest*' of '*My brothers*'. Jesus appeared to them to make sure they did not only tell '*all the rest*' about the resurrection, but about meeting in Galilee too.

However, before Jesus actually appears to these women in the successive order of events within our Biblical text, there is yet another appearance we must consider, which we earlier pointed out was intrinsically linked to *The First Appearance - To Mary*, and was in fact *The Second Appearance* by Jesus, before He appeared to the women.

The appearance to these women would subsequently be *The Third Appearance* since Jesus' resurrection, and we will cover it somewhat further, after having discussed *The Second Appearance*.

By the time Mary had returned to tell the apostles that Jesus had appeared to her, also the other women had already arrived too, and told them of the message of the angel. But the apostles were incredibly dubious over the whole thing (Mark 16:11; Luke 24:9b-11). John nevertheless, being the first apostles to believe, no doubt, because of his close loving relationship with Jesus, there was no necessity for a personnel miraculous appearance for him.

However, Peter had also started to wonder at the tomb whether Jesus was resurrected (Luke 24:12), and while the nine did in their despondency blind their own eyes to the women's revelations, Peter must have started to wonder further, in what he had heard the women all confirm, and that Jesus had appeared to Mary first!

Luke in his version calls the apostles, the eleven (24:9b), to alleviate any confusion when Mary Magdalene, Joanna, and Mary the mother of James, inform them of the news of Jesus' resurrection (v. 10). Luke, as was his particular specialty in various places in his Gospel, points out the difference in distinguishing between the two groups of disciples. At this particular junction, he does it by addressing the seventy disciples and the five hundred as '*all the rest*'.

Though the four Gospels all agree together over the women informing the apostles about the news of Jesus' resurrection, with Luke having indicated those other than the apostles as '*all the rest*', it is Matthew who exclusively mentions the women holding Jesus' feet, and the actual message '*to all the rest*' about the coming meeting in Galilee.

To keep these various movements at the tomb clear in our minds, in simple terms, there are three basic factors to remember:

Firstly: the angels who appeared to the women, one told the women to first tell Peter and the apostles about the resurrection, and the subsequent meeting in Galilee:

Secondly: Mary whom Jesus appeared to first, after the women had left the tomb, told her to tell the apostles He was to ascend to Heaven. In Mary informing the apostles, inherent in her message would be the fact that He was already resurrected:

Thirdly: all the women would give the good news of Jesus' to them about the meeting in Galilee '*to all the rest*' of the disciple-brothers, who would be in Jerusalem with the other pilgrims, after having first given their message to the apostles.

While the eleven had received the news from the women who were told by the angels that Jesus had been resurrected, and the news of Mary having actually seen Jesus first, nevertheless, the ten were however still despondent in disbelief.

John, had perceived that Jesus was resurrected, without having actually seen Him. John had also stated before that point, that they had not yet believed the Scripture that Jesus must rise again from the dead (20:8-9). Nonetheless, John, directly after seeing the empty tomb and the way the burial linen was found, started believing, with Peter wondering about all the events and the women's witness began wondering if it were all true after all.

Some place the appearing of Jesus to the women, whom the two angels had just spoken to, directly after *The First Appearance - To Mary*, suggesting Jesus told Mary not to cling to Him, to show Jesus was inferring His relationship with His followers, from that point, for the next forty days would be different. Though, in actuality, Jesus was to continue as before in His relationship with His disciples, for the next forty days, in which they would eat with Him and even touch His new body which transcended the material!

The women had all reached the apostles well before Jesus appeared to them later, as they left to tell '*all the rest*' of the disciples who would have been spread out in the environs around Jerusalem. It was then Jesus met them, before they had had chance to give '*all the rest*' the news of His resurrection; miraculously appearing to them, He encouraged them to continue with their mission of informing '*all the rest*'. And because of the particular importance in the five hundred also believing, and being ready for the meeting in Galilee, Jesus added the instruction to tell all these other disciples the details about the meeting of the final great commission (Mat. 28:9-10).

THE MESSIAH THE FIRSTFRUIT

John had purposely emphasized, and placed his record of *The First Appearance* of Jesus where Mary is not allowed to hold Him (20:11-17), and in Mary informing the apostles that Jesus was about to ascend to '*your Father; and to My God, and your God*' (v. 18), next to *The Fifth Appearance - To The Ten* later that same day in Jerusalem when Thomas was not present. Through positioning these selected appearances, John contrasted Jesus showing them the wounds of His body (vv. 19-25), along with eight days later with Jesus' sixth appearance, when Thomas was now present in allowing him to handle His body (vv. 26-29)! John highlighted the difference between the two narratives where Jesus is deliberately emphasizing the aspect of touching His body if they wished, and *The First Appearance - To Mary* where He cautions her natural inclination to hold Him. Furthermore, John further connects connects the incident of Thomas finally believing - being the last apostle to believe - with *The First Appearance - To Mary*, in respect of what Jesus told her when not permitting her to hold Him, at which point Jesus specially related He was to ascend to '*My God, and your God*'. After Thomas had touched Jesus' body he believed and affirmed '*My Lord and My God*', echoing the final part of Jesus' first words since His resurrection!

Moreover, John wrote his Gospel involving and interspersing references to various days within the parameters of the Jewish Festivals, in which Jesus spoke and fulfilled certain aspects of their symbolism relating to what these days represented.

Jesus had told Mary, to whom He especially appeared to first, not to hold Him. Yet when appearing to the rest of the women later in the same day, after the women had believed the two angels, He then allows them to hold Him by the feet (Mat. 28:9).

Jesus fulfilled every part of the Scriptures it was possible to fulfill in regards to symbolism and meaning. Furthermore, the disciples, in fulfilling the promise of being ready for the Holy Spirit, had to await fifty days from Jesus' resurrection, for the Day of Pentecost, wherein the Holy Spirit would further inspire the apostles in their commissioning work on preaching the resurrection (Acts 2:1-4, 30-33).

However, Jesus was nevertheless the Firstfruit of the Resurrection (1 Cor. 15:20), and symbolic of the firstfruit sheaf of the early harvest sheaves, which was presented before the Lord on the day after the weekly Sabbath (Lev. 23:9-11), which fell in the Days of Unleavened Bread (vv. 5-8). In v. 11, the AV has the sheaf '*waved*' before the Lord, whereas *The Jewish Publication Society* translation of the *Tanakh* [Old Testament] in the same verse has chosen the more relevant description, of '*elevate*' before the Lord.

In the early evening at the closing of the weekly Sabbath, in a solemn ceremony that was carried out by the Levitical Priesthood, the first sheaf was cut. It prefigured in picturing the resurrected Messiah, the Firstfruit of the First Harvest of souls, for it was then in the very same morning the waved sheaf was offered, that the Messiah was accepted by His Father as the spiritual '*Elevated Sheaf*' offering in Heaven.

Thus, Jesus was clearly informing Mary early in the morning when He first appeared to her, to wait until He had returned from presenting Himself to the Father, '*My God, and your God*', before she could hold Him. And that she was first to go and tell the apostles where He was about to go, in presenting Himself to their Father and God. Of course, Mary would have joined the other women in trying to confirm His resurrection to the apostles. However, the ten still at that point could not believe in all these outstanding miraculous claims.

When the women left to tell '*all the rest*', subsequently much later, Jesus appeared as we shall see, in the afternoon, though still in '*the first day of the week*', after He had returned from the Father, as He later appeared to Cleopas and Mary (Luke 24:18; (Luke 24:18; John 19:25), his companion and wife on the road to Emmaus, directly after He had just spoken with the women.

Cleopas and Mary also confirmed, while they were in Jerusalem, where they would have heard the recounting of the angel's message from the women (Luke 24:23), that Jesus had not appeared to the women earlier (v. 24)! Jesus pointed out to Cleopas and Mary that they were slow in understanding the Scriptures He had to fulfill (v. 25), as they had already heard the angel's message and had not believed He had already been resurrected earlier (v. 22). No doubt He also alluded to the time lapse since actually meeting up with them as He had just returned from the Father, through admonishing them over their lack of perception in not comprehending the particular reason of not having met with them earlier, by stating, '*Ought not the Messiah to have suffered these things, and to enter His glory*' (v. 26).

He went on to expound to them, no doubt the symbolism relating to what had just transpired, found in Leviticus, the third book of Moses, of what we previously suggested about Jesus being the Firstfruit of the Resurrection, and various other Scriptures prefiguring aspects in the Prophets surrounding the Messiah at this particular time (v. 27).

In warning Mary not to touch Him is also reminiscent of previous places in the OT wherein it was forbidden to come near or touch in certain circumstances. Hence Jesus was relating to the special relationship - the specific Holiness He had with His Father, and Mary's Father; and with His God, and Mary's God, directly before, He was to '*ascend to the Father, and your Father: and to My God, and your God*'. Through the priority and special significance of that intrinsic moment, Mary was to concern herself with informing the apostles of the reason He would not appear to them until later on (John 20:17-18), when she could then hold Him. Of course, Jesus revealed a respect for His Father, which He expected His followers also to perceive and embrace in, with the Father being their God too, through the Holy Spirit, even before His ultimate Ascension, which was forty days away.

After forty days, Jesus, with His new body that transcended the material, had no need to continue His life on earth as previous, as the Holy Spirit would maintain the relationship of His and the Father's would be the same as before, in which He allowed them to touch Him, and, eat with them.

But afterwards, when Jesus finally ascended to Heaven and sat on the right hand of His Father, His relationship with His disciples, though as close as before, would be very different.

Thus, when Jesus returned later that same day, after having presented Himself to the Father during the morning, directly afterwards, Luke revealed Jesus had already appeared to Peter (24:34), before appearing to Cleopas and Mary his wife, as they were walking to Emmaus from Jerusalem. He also concluded that Jesus spent some time with them, and later pointed out it was now '*toward evening*' (29).

We will continue with *The Second Appearance*, which was to Peter with the next chapter.

THE SECOND APPEARANCE - TO PETER

Just before Jesus appeared to Cleopas and Mary his wife later that afternoon, earlier He would have already appeared to the women, when they were now allowed to handle Him.

Subsequently, afterwards, He ate with Cleopas and Mary his wife, and later even allowed the disciples to touch His body. Consequently, directly before appearing to the women, and Cleopas and Mary have appeared to Peter. Cleopas and Mary related to the apostles that Jesus had already appeared to Peter, when they had returned to Jerusalem late in the same day, after Jesus had miraculously vanished from in front of them (Luke 24:34).

John and Peter were the first of the apostles to believe that Jesus had been resurrected, even though Peter was slow to believe at first, nevertheless, both believed without any miraculous appearance to confirm it. Because John had a deeper perception at that time and was the disciple *'whom Jesus loved'*, nevertheless, he didn't need any miraculous affirmation to verify his belief. While John had first believed at the sepulcher, from that particular moment, Peter had started to wonder (Luke 24:12), and subsequently with all the women's testaments no doubt must have begun believing later that morning. When Peter had returned from leaving the empty tomb, the women would declare the angels message that Jesus had been resurrected, along with Mary's confirmation too, that Jesus had actually appeared to her, and had given her a different message, that He was to ascend to the Father first, before appearing again (John 20:17-18).

After the rest of that morning was over, and Cleopas and his wife had left Jerusalem for Emmaus, now the afternoon, with Jesus having returned from the Father, He would have appeared to Peter at the next earliest opportunity, before appearing to the other women, whom in any case believed the angel's message that He had already been resurrected.

Jesus obviously told Cleopas and Mary his wife of His appearance to Peter, directly after the third appearance to the women, who had also left to tell *'all the rest'* of the disciples gathered in and around Jerusalem, even though the nine apostles were still in a state of disbelief, before He appeared late that same day to the apostles. Thus, Peter in his turn after Mary Magdalene, saw Jesus.

However, at this particular point, the disciples, except John and Peter, were still in a state of confusion and disbelief, with their egos being doubly wounded, after hearing the message given to the women from the angel, and, who did not appear to the apostles first, but - to women; moreover, that Mary had also related that Jesus had specially appeared to her - again, a woman - before that of any of the apostles! Furthermore, they would have expected Jesus to have at least appeared to John, *'the disciple whom Jesus loved'*, as well as Peter before Mary. But, no, Jesus had something for them all to learn.

Nevertheless, Peter was the disciple to whom the angels message, regarding the news of the meeting in Galilee was specifically addressed (Mark 16:7). Who also was chosen as the prime servant, with Jesus asking him three times to make sure His sheep were cared for (John 21:15-17), who would thus be responsible for feeding the sheep, and initially responsible in spearheading the disciples' first directives in their mission of the gospel going to all the world.

Jesus could have appeared to Peter first, and Mary second, or appeared to the apostles altogether first, or even appeared to Peter, directly after He appeared to Mary before ascending to the Father. But, no, the sequences of the appearances were specially chosen so as to mark various profound symbolic aspects, and to teach the apostles and us important lessons.

In the first three paragraphs in the section entitled *The First Disciples* [p. 36], we had considered certain criteria relating to the factor of order, and the specific coincidences of numbers associated at the beginning of Jesus' ministry. We suggested Jesus originally chose Peter as a disciple, and gave him that particular name on the forty-fifth day after His baptism, or on the very point in the narrative of the Gospel of John where there are three disciples first mentioned (1:40-41), with Peter, moreover, being the third disciple Jesus actually called.

Amazingly, when we accept Jesus' resurrection to be the forty-third miracle, naturally, Jesus' first appearance, would be the forty-fourth, when He appeared to Mary. Subsequently, the factor of forty-five would figure again in respect to Jesus' next appearance to Peter, in that it would consequently be the **forty-fifth miracle**. Furthermore, when including Jesus' resurrection as the first miracle after the *Forty-Second Miracle* of the healing of *Malchus' Ear,* the appearance to Peter would be the third miracle. Moreover, John alone, successively and collectively mentions three appearances to the apostles after the resurrection.

Nonetheless, the incident where Jesus specially appeared to Peter is only briefly highlighted, and uniquely so by Luke, and none of the other Gospels, and specifically through Cleopas and Mary returning to the apostles in Jerusalem later in the afternoon after they had just seen Jesus. Because of the concise record of the appearance to Peter, obviously there was not to be any unwarranted importance attached to it.

However, Peter, nevertheless, was commissioned three times, and moreover, during the third and last miraculous recorded event involving the apostles, to *'feed My sheep'* (John 21:14-15): and no doubt because of the primacy relating to Peter in that case, Jesus wanted to highlight the principle of the *'chief, as they who do serve'* foremost in the apostles and Peter's mind, as furthermore, Jesus had especially made a point, at the conclusion of the Last Supper and just prior to Peter's promise of not denying Him three times, in stressing the particular aspect of the chief serving (Luke 22:26)!

Notwithstanding, Peter was *'the first'* disciple as worded in Matthew's list of apostles (10:2), and as headed in the lists of the other two Synoptics. Moreover, in Paul's list of Jesus' appearances directly relating to Jesus' disciples [and not the appearances to the women], he mentions Peter first, indicating Peter was the first apostle that Jesus appeared to. Furthermore, he also addresses him as Cephas, reminding us when Peter was originally called, he was firstly named Cephas by Jesus, as recorded exclusively in the Gospel of John (1:42), part of which aspect we have just considered regarding the factor relating to forty-five and originally in pp. 36-42.

Additionally, with Peter being the first person to have seen Jesus after He returned from the Father, there is further significance in Jesus returning from the wilderness, where He also spent time talking with the Father, and then shortly afterwards calling Peter, and giving him a new name. Thus, as Jesus originally called Peter first after returning from being with the Father in the wilderness, similarly He appeared to Peter first now, giving him new responsibilities, after returning from having ascended and having been with the Father in Heaven.

We mentioned earlier, that when the women had arrived from the tomb to where the apostles were gathered together, the majority of the apostles didn't believe (Mark 16:11; Luke 24:11), though John had already believed at the tomb, with Peter beginning to believe later that morning. With the angel having instructed the women to expressly inform Peter, there is a hint in the angels' message, of his coming priority as the prime servant, and that his coming priority as the prime servant, and that he would be the one Jesus would appear to after Mary, who nevertheless, as the Woman, was representative of the Church, and Peter its leader.

Because of the symbolism attached to the woman representing the church, as we mentioned in the section where Jesus appeared to Mary first [pp. 403-404], and that Peter represented the leader of the church, also considering the aspect where Jesus had presented Himself to the Father, typifying the *Firstfruit Elevated-Sheaf* of the Resurrection after appearing to Mary [pp. 410-412], then, the second appearance when Jesus had returned from the Father, would intrinsically have been to Peter, as moreover, the next appearance [the third] would have been to the women, who were collectively figurative of all the individuals in the church in that they were going to inform all the rest of the other disciples [the church] the good news of the resurrection. Subsequently, from that particular point they could all hold Jesus, with His new resurrected body, after respectfully presenting Himself to the Father, as now from that instance, He was to embrace all the church in a more spiritual way, in the next phase of the gospel.

As Paul is the only other writer to mention the second appearance, or the **forty-fifth miracle**, in his resurrection chapter, whereas Luke relates Cleopas and Mary his wife informing the disciples, "saying, '*The Lord is risen indeed, and has appeared to Simon*'" (24:34), we have combined Paul's reference to Simon's surname, Peter, in Hebrew, '*Cephas*' (1 Cor. 15:5a), and the word, "*how*" [Gr. '*hoti*'], along with Luke's, so as to be read in its entirety, including both of their similar statements, applying and rephrasing the two references, as if Cleopas and Mary along with Paul are addressing their audiences with the complete detail given on this appearance, so the information relates to the whole sense and in the successive order in which it subsequently occurred.

Luke 24:34 1 Corinthians 15:5a
"The Lord is risen indeed, and how He has appeared to Simon Cephas".

THE THIRD APPEARANCE - TO THE WOMEN

If we accept the appearance to Peter was the second time Jesus had shown Himself since His resurrection, and that the next appearance was to the women as they left the apostles to inform '*all the rest*' of the disciples of the angels message that Jesus was resurrected, obviously it would make the appearance to the women the third, or the forty-sixth miracle, with the following appearance [the fourth] being to Cleopas and Mary his wife on the road to Emmaus.

We have already covered considerably the criteria surrounding the third appearance in the sections, *All the Women Tell The Apostles* [pp. 406-410], and *The Messiah The Firstfruit* [pp. 410-412], where we also considered the first and second appearances. Our premise, as we suggested, was that Mat. 28:9 referred to when the women went to tell '*all the rest*' (Luke 24:9) of the disciples, and not the apostles. Hence, the main text referring to the third appearance, where Jesus appeared to the women, would naturally follow below, after the previous main Scriptural text of the second appearance.

Matthew 28:9 Luke 24:9c
And as they went to tell all the rest of the disciples, suddenly, Jesus met them saying, "Hello all."
And they came and held Him by the feet and worshiped Him.
Matthew 28
10 Then said Jesus to them,
"Don't be afraid: go tell My brothers that when they leave for Galilee, there they shall see Me."

11 Now when they were gone, consider, some of the guards came to the city, and showed to the Chief Priests all things that were done.

12 And when they were assembled with the Elders, and had taken counsel, they gave substantial money to the soldiers,
13 saying, "You say, 'His disciples came by night, and stole Him away while we slept'.

Matthew 28
14 And if this come to the Governor's ears, we will persuade him, and shield you."
15 So they took the money, and did as they were instructed: and this saying is commonly reported among the Jews until this day.

The statement in Mat. 28:11, is referring to *'when they were gone'* to tell all the rest, of the disciples, that some of the soldiers who had been guarding the tomb eventually had a meeting with the Chief Priests. Naturally, the meeting took place after the comings and goings at the tomb. Subsequently, after the great earthquake, the guards knew the angel had been instrumental in removing the stone from the mouth of the tomb (Mat. 28:2-4), and when they ascertained for certain Jesus' body was no longer there, went to tell the Chief Priests, who when they had made enquiries in the apprehensive situation after having an assembly over the matter, could back up their guise to the guards in informing Pilate that the disciples had stolen the body.

THE FOURTH APPEARANCE - TO CLEOPAS AND WIFE

So the next appearance of Jesus, the fourth, was to Cleopas and Mary his wife and companion, as they had decided to leave Jerusalem earlier that morning for Emmaus, after Mary had witnessed the empty tomb with the other women and heard the angels' message of the resurrection. (Luke 24:22-24).

But, like the ten apostles, Cleopas and Mary accepted the news of Jesus resurrection as confusing since they had not seen Jesus' body: they believed in the death of Jesus, but did not perceive He had been resurrected, and only accepted that His body was no longer in the tomb.

Cleopas and Mary would have thus left Jerusalem sometime before "*all the rest*" of the women left to tell the apostles earlier that morning, and became disillusioned with the fact Jesus' had not appeared to them.

By the time they had traveled to Emmaus it would be the afternoon before they had entered the house and prepared a meal, to which Jesus had been invited and had also been asked to stay overnight (vv. 29-30).

However, the other women who had also originally witnessed the two angels, having also left, though they believed Jesus was resurrected, and were not perturbed by the lack of belief of the others, but went to give the good news of the angels' message about the resurrection, *'to all the rest'* of the other disciples around Jerusalem.

Furthermore, as mentioned previously, when they returned very early from the tomb to tell the apostles, they ran to bring the good news, whereas, now later in the morning, when going to tell *'all the rest'* of the other disciples, as the initial astonishment and excitement had now settled somewhat at this point, they left in the normal manner as they had to be careful in not drawing attention to themselves.

John, as we also mentioned earlier had believed, in what the women confirmed, and before Jesus appeared Peter had at some stage left the house where they had all been together, to mull things over in his mind, privately away from the previous excitement of the women, and the despondency of the others. Therefore, with Jesus appearing to Mary first, and the special message He had given her about ascending to the Father, also added to Peter's reason in leaving the room where they had been together, so he could be left alone and think things through. Moreover, he would be praying that he too could see Jesus!

So Jesus, having returned from the Father, first appeared to Peter, who just before that precise instance no doubt was still wondering about all the aspects surrounding Jesus' message to Mary, and the angels' message to the women. Thus, as the women were now going to tell '*all the rest*' of the other disciples, shortly after having appeared to Peter, Jesus appeared to the women as they were on their way. With this appearance to the women, Jesus told them also to tell '*all the rest*' of the other disciples about the meeting in Galilee, where they would all see Him. Directly afterwards, He was about to appear to Cleopas and Mary his wife as they were nearing the village of Emmaus.

There is no mention of Jesus' mother at the tomb, and John, who had also believed, and who was comforting Jesus' mother, no doubt had, in comforting her, revealed his belief to her, that her Son had been resurrected, having understood and explained the meaning of the Scriptures, after seeing the empty tomb (John 20:8-9).

No doubt the factor of Jesus appearing to Mary Magdalene first, and not His mother, would indicate that His mother had also believed through John, as well as accepting the stories of all the women, and in that sense, did not need an appearance to confirm her belief, though obviously, at some point she did see and embrace her Son once again.

The delay of many hours, in Jesus appearing to any of the other disciples, after first having appeared to Mary Magdalene, naturally added to the exasperation in the minds of those who had not perceived He was already resurrected, and who could not understand the Scriptures He was fulfilling.

Nonetheless, Jesus had revealed in His conversation to Cleopas and his wife about the appearance to Peter. Since when they returned to Jerusalem late that same afternoon, and now when arriving, much nearer the evening, they declared that He had appeared to them and Peter earlier (Luke 24:34-35). Furthermore, with Jesus having discussed and expounded the Scriptures to Cleopas and Mary his wife (v. 27), through which He referred to certain prophetical criteria surrounding the events of His Passion (v. 25), and the following of the next sentence referring to the antithesis between the sequel of what He had just suffered, and the glorification in ascending to His Father, it states (v. 26), '*ought not the Messiah to have suffered these things, and to enter into His glory*', no doubt fulfilling the requirement of the Firstfruit sheaf of the Resurrection, in presenting Himself as the '*Elevated-Sheaf*', and as the *Ultimate Lamb*, now renewed and in acknowledgment in offering Himself to the Father (Lev. 23:10-12). Additionally, there is a further hint, where Jesus is praying to the Father directly before His Passion in John 17:1, regarding '*the hour has come*', being the hour when shortly He was to be glorified in ascending to the Father, and where it says '*and now I come to You*' (v. 13), besides having a more immediate fulfillment also when He would finally ascend to Heaven.

Mark 16:12a Luke 24:13
And afterwards, consider, two of them went the same day to the village called Emmaus, which was from Jerusalem, about seven miles.
Luke 24
14 And they talked together of all these things which had happened.

Mark 16:12b Luke 24:15
And it came to pass, that, while they conversed together and reasoned, Jesus Himself drew near forming, and appeared differently as they walked, and went with them.
Luke 24
16 But their eyes kept from recognizing Him.
17 And He said to them, "What manner of conversation is this that you have one with another, as you walk, and are sad?"

18 And one of them, whose name was Cleopas, answering said to Him, "Are You only a stranger in Jerusalem, and have not known the things which are come to pass there in these days?"
19 And He said to them, "What things?"

And they said to Him,
"Concerning Jesus of Nazareth, who was a Prophet mighty in deed and word before God and all the people:
20 and how the Chief Priests and our Rulers delivered Him to be condemned to death, and have crucified Him.
21 But we trusted that it had been He who would have redeemed Israel: and besides all this, today is the third day since these things occurred.
22 Yes, and certain women of our company made us astonished, who were early at the tomb;
23 and when they didn't find His body, they came, saying, that they had also seen a vision of angels, who said He was alive.
24 And certain of them who were with us went to the tomb, and found it even so as the women had said: but they didn't see Him."

Luke 24

25 Then He said to them,

"Oh fools, and slow of heart to believe all that the Prophets have spoken:
26 ought not the Messiah to have suffered these things, and to enter into His glory?"

27 And beginning at Moses and all the Prophets, He expounded to them in all the Scriptures the things concerning Himself.

28 And they drew near to the village, where they went: and He made as though He would have gone further.
29 But they constrained Him, saying, "Stay with us: for it is towards evening, and the day is far spent."

And He went in to stay with them.
30 And it came to pass, as He sat at dinner with them, He took bread, and blessed it, and breaking it, gave it to them.
31 And their eyes were opened, and they knew Him; and He vanished out of their sight.
32 And they said one to another,

"Weren't our hearts burning within us, while He talked with us along the way, and while He opened to us the Scriptures?"

Mark 16:13a Luke 24:33

And they rose up and they went the same hour, and returned to Jerusalem, and found the eleven gathered together, and told it to the residue who were with them,

Luke 24

34 saying, "The Lord is risen indeed, and has appeared to Simon!"

Mark 16:13b Luke 24:35

And they explained what had happened on the road, and how He was known by them before breaking the bread in pieces: neither did they believe them.

THE FIFTH APPEARANCE - TO THE TEN

After Jesus partook of the meal with Cleopas and Mary his wife, He vanishes out of sight, at which point they excitedly return to Jerusalem to find the eleven and others gathered together. It is both Mark (16:13) and Luke (24:33-35) who conclude this event of the fourth appearance. When Jesus had disappeared that same afternoon, they also returned in '*the same hour*', and arrived back at Jerusalem, now nearing the evening, where they confirmed their news, which further endorsed the news of women, that they had seen the resurrected Messiah, too.

Of course Peter had seen Jesus earlier, and we can only speculate whether he told the others, or if he remained silent about it until Cleopas and Mary his wife had mentioned it to the eleven and the others, when they arrived back at Jerusalem, subsequently confirming the good news further still. Peter may well have told John, or John, alternatively, with his perception may have noticed Peter's body language, and thus knew it to be the case. Besides Peter must have known at some point that Jesus would shortly appear to the other apostles, as Jesus no doubt had also related certain information to him regarding the next stage of events.

When Cleopas and Mary his wife recounted to the apostles and certain others that Jesus had appeared to them and to Peter earlier, with John and Peter being the only two apostles who believed so far, no doubt Thomas decided at that particular instance that he had had enough for one day, and must have left, as shortly afterwards, Jesus suddenly appears to the rest of the doubters, materializing in their very midst, even though the doors were locked. It is both Luke (24:33-49) and John (20:19-25), who inform us of this next appearance to the ten apostles, *The Fifth Appearance* of Jesus, or the **forty-eighth miracle**, as Thomas was not present obviously having left the room before Jesus appeared. John also relates this appearance, as the first appearance to the apostles, as he confirms that Jesus appeared subsequently three times altogether, when the apostles were together at various occasions after His resurrection (21:14).

Additionally, John specifically pointed out as the Greek avers, it was still '*the same day late afternoon, being the first day of the week*' since Jesus had been resurrected (20:19). Though it was now transpiring further into the evening, and nearing the change between computing one day and another, as remember, Jews count their days from evening to evening.

Luke 24:36 John 20:19
Then the same day late afternoon, being the first day of the week [18th Nissan], when the doors were shut, where the disciples were assembled for the fear of the Jews, as they thus spoke, Jesus Himself came and stood in the midst of them, and says to them, "Peace be to you."

Luke 24

37 But they were terrified and frightened, and supposed that they had seen a spirit.

38 And He said to them,

"Why are you troubled? And why do thoughts arise in your hearts?

39 See My wrists and My feet, that it is I Myself: handle Me, and see; for a spirit doesn't have flesh and bones, as you see Me have."

Luke 24:40 John 20:20

And when He had thus spoken, He showed them His wrists and His feet, and His side. Then were the disciples glad, when they saw the Lord.

Luke 24

41 And while they yet believed not, for joy, and wondered, He said to them, "Have you got any food?"

42 And they gave Him a piece of broiled fish, and some honeycomb.

43 And He took them, and ate in front of them.

44 And He said to them,

"These are the words which I spoke to you, while I was yet with you, that all things must be fulfilled, which are written in the Law of Moses, and in the Prophets, and in the Psalms concerning Me."

45 Then He opened their understanding, that they might understand the Scriptures,

46 and said to them,

"Thus it is written, and so it behooved the Messiah to suffer, and to rise from the dead the third day (Mat 20:19; Mark 10:34; Luke 18:33):

47 and that repentance and remission of sins should be preached in His Name among all nations, beginning at Jerusalem.

48 and you are witnesses of these things.

49 and, understand, I send the promise of My Father among you: but you wait in the city of Jerusalem, until you be endued with Power from on High."

John 20

21 Then said Jesus to them again,

"Peace be to you: as My Father has sent Me, even so I send you."

22 And when He had said this, He exhaled, and says to them,

"Receive of the Holy Spirit:

23 whosoever's sins you remit, they are remitted to them; and any whosoever's sins you retain, they are retained."

24 But Thomas, one of the twelve, called Didymus, was not with them when Jesus came.

25 The other disciples therefore said to him, "We have seen the Lord."

But he said to them, "Except I shall see in His wrists the prints of the nails, and put my finger into the print of the nails, and press my hand into His side, I will not believe."

In Luke's dialogue, which follows the incident where Jesus appeared to Cleopas and Mary his wife near to Emmaus (24:36-49), though there were eleven disciples and others gathered together, when they returned to Jerusalem informing them that Jesus had appeared to them (v. 33), nevertheless, Thomas was not present when Jesus suddenly appeared shortly after. Luke had not indicated there were only ten disciples present at the particular instance when Jesus appeared. However, John was quite clear about that specific point (20:24). Also it is clear when comparing Luke's parallel account with John's, the similarities between the two is further reflected by the aspect where Jesus shows them His body (Luke 24:40); John 20:20), and afterwards, talks about the *"remission of sins"* (Luke 24:47); John 20:23). Even though both accounts have different detail, the actual context of each dialogue is the same. Besides, Luke does not refer to any other appearance afterwards, and concludes his Gospel with reference to the Ascension (24:50-53).

Now Jesus appeared again eight days later, when the eleven were gathered together once more, which is then substantiated through Thomas being present this time. John (20:26) parallels with Mark (16:14) over this event, as Mark is quite clear that Jesus appeared to eleven disciples, by specifically using the word '*eleven*' to designate the number of apostles in the upper room at the particular instance.

John actually records it the second appearance, as represented through the structure of his narrative in his Gospel, of the three successive appearances to the apostles after Jesus' resurrection.

Though, both Luke and John mention the first appearance to the apostles when Thomas was absent, including, referring to the time of day, Luke had indicated this in his narrative by showing Cleopas and Mary his wife having returned to Jerusalem by the late afternoon, near the evening, with John relating the same time, but giving a more specific indication, when Jesus appeared at the end of that first day of the week. Nonetheless, in both cases it was still in the same day that Mary Magdalene, Peter, the women, Cleopas and Mary his wife, had all seen Jesus earlier.

Furthermore, it is John, who once again, gives us the time of eight days later, when the next appearance to the eleven occurred, where he parallels with Mark (16:14). We will discuss this subsequent appearance as we continue.

However, when counting the successive appearances of Jesus, the first appearance to the ten apostles, would make it the fifth appearance. Obviously the next one would be the sixth appearance, through which again two of the Gospels parallel and correlate together relating to this same particular incident (Mark 16:14; John 20:26-29). Both Luke and John recounted the fifth appearance to the ten, or the first appearance to the apostles. The factor that though the eight [not including Peter and John], were still doubting what had been reported to them, nonetheless, not until Jesus had shown them His body, eaten in front of them, and opened up their understanding to the Scriptures relating to His Passion, did they now readily at that instance accept Him.

Luke had referred to Jesus explaining the Scriptures that typified His Passion (24:44-46), through which Jesus also mentioned the *'remission of sins'* (v. 47). John, as well as Luke, had also referred to the aspect of remitting sins, directly after Jesus had exhaled and suggested they, there and then, also to continue receiving some measure of the Spirit (20:21-23). The whole incident, after witnessing directly afterwards where Jesus opened up their minds to the Scriptures, and following, where He exhaled indicating they would shortly be able to remit sins, is predominantly one of a positive nature, even though Thomas was not present when all the apostles now believed.

The apostles, after returning to Galilee, were to return again to Jerusalem and await the Day of Pentecost, upon which day the Holy Spirit would give them even more Power for the next phase of the Gospel, when it was to reach into all the world, beginning from Jerusalem (vv. 48-49).

THE SIXTH APPEARANCE - TO THE ELEVEN

However, the main difference between the narrative of the appearance to the ten, and the eleven when Thomas was present, is through the greater emphasis placed on the aspect of doubting, through which Thomas became the epitome of all doubters. This is further brought out and emphasized by Mark (16:14), when Jesus, after having spoken to Thomas about believing (John 20:29), no doubt at that point, admonishes the eleven, though not discriminating between them, for not believing the report of the others who believed in various stages after seeing Him. Undoubtedly, Jesus mentioned this when the eleven were all present, to vindicate Thomas, and as a lesson for us all, in realizing that Thomas was really no different to any of the others, because it had been just a matter of the circumstances and time in any case before any of them believed.

Moreover, the other specific difference between the appearance to the ten and the eleven is that eight days later, the eleven were actually having a meal (Mark 16:14), whereas, at the appearance eight days previous, Jesus asked them if they had any food (Luke 24:41). Obviously, had they been partaking of a meal, in that case, Jesus would naturally have been invited to join them, and would not have had to ask if they had any food at hand.

Also, John closes his account on the appearance to the eleven, in reference to the specific miracle signs that had occurred throughout Jesus' ministry, including the appearances, which he relates were all written that we might believe (20:30-31), and conversely, that we should not be doubters, as depicted by Thomas [and all the disciples at various stages]. Besides, Jesus informs Thomas, at the point where he now believes, after handling Jesus' body, *'blessed are they that have not seen, and yet believed'* (20:29)! Whereas, when the ten [actually eight, John and Peter having already believed], were asked to handle Jesus' body, they first witnessed His wrists, His feet, and His side, just like Thomas did, but, additionally, saw Jesus eat in front of them, with Jesus further dispelling any doubts they still had in also opening up their minds to understand certain Scriptures, before they finally believed.

Besides, John could have placed his comments on the miraculous signs at the conclusion of his Gospel. But, no, he positioned them so as to show antithesis, contrasting between the appearance to the ten, and the next appearance to the eleven, where Thomas is epitomized as representing all doubters, but, in believing, perceived Jesus, as *'My Lord and My God'*!

Also, Thomas typified any other disciples who had not yet seen Jesus, and of course, Jesus in returning to Galilee, with the purpose of meeting *The Five Hundred* shortly, as we shall see, there was still to be doubt amongst that group.

Though John had indicated that Jesus had appeared eight days later (20:26), after having first appeared to the ten (vv. 19-25), he did not reveal if additional disciples were present, as Luke had done with his version of the first appearance to the ten apostles (24:33). Because John had not mentioned these others, even as when Jesus appeared to the eleven apostles, it did not mean that others were not present. It is clear from the reference to the hundred and twenty gathered in the upper room directly after the Ascension (Acts 1:13-15), that the room could hold a considerable number.

Thus, as Luke had revealed several other times throughout his Gospel, there were other disciples present at various occasions, when the other Gospels had not included that fact in their parallel accounts.

These other disciples naturally included Joseph Barsabbas-Justus, and Matthias [who was to make up the number of the twelve], and who, were also witnesses to Jesus' ministry and the resurrection (Acts 1:21-25).

The Gospel of Mark concludes with the Ascension (16:19-20), after the appearance to the eleven apostles (v. 14), and the narrative relating to them preaching the gospel to the entire world and the *'signs'* inherent with that mission (vv. 15-18). Furthermore, Mark is the only Gospel that mentions these miracle *'signs'* in the conclusion of his final words. Of course, we have placed these verses addressed to the eleven, in the main text, where Jesus refers to these *'signs'*, directly after the Gospel of John, as the context preceding and following indicates, that John had also recounted the aspect of these *'signs'* (20:30-31)! Hence, both the narratives of Mark and John regarding the appearance to the eleven contain reference to miracle *'signs'*.

At the particular instance where Jesus appeared to the ten, eight days previously, He spoke about preaching the gospel to all the world, mentioning the Holy Spirit and the remission of sins: at the appearance to the eleven He reiterated the words of preaching the gospel again and mentioned the miracle *'signs'* while

Thomas was present (Mark 16:15-18), and no doubt, elaborated further, though undoubtedly, not every deed and word of Jesus was recorded.

Moreover, when Jesus met with *The Five Hundred* later in Galilee, He would have spoken similar words as highlighted by the other Gospel, according to John.

Because Paul in his list of appearances referred to, twelve apostles (1 Cor. 15:5b), we have included the word '*twelve*' in the main text below. Though, Paul would have accounted for, in his reference on the appearing '*to the twelve*', the three times Jesus appeared to the apostles, as John specifically pointed out, combining together the three appearances, of the ten (20:19-25), the eleven or twelve (vv. 26-31), and shortly after the seven (21:1-13), together, as they subsequently all occurred successively and directly one after another (v. 14). Nevertheless, it would have been this sixth appearance, when all of the apostles were present, that Paul had referred to in his list, knowing that Matthias must have also been present, and in due course '*was numbered with the eleven apostles*' (Acts 1:26), making twelve, having also been one of these other disciples who followed Jesus.

Mark 16:14a John 20:26 1 Corinthians 15:5b
And subsequently, after eight days [26th Nissan] again His disciples were within, and Thomas with them: then came Jesus appearing to the eleven (now twelve), the doors being shut, and stood in the midst of them as they sat together eating, and said, "Peace be to you."
John 20
27 Then He says to Thomas, "Reach here your finger, and see My wrists; and reach here your hand, and press it into My side: and don't be faithless, but believe."
28 And Thomas answered and said to Him, "My Lord and My God."

29 Jesus says to Him, "Thomas, because you have seen Me, you have believed: blessed are those who have not seen, and yet have believed."
Mark 16
14b And he admonished them for their unbelief and hardness of heart, because they didn't believe them who had seen Him after He was risen.
John 20
30 And many other signs truly did Jesus in the presence of His disciples, which are not written in this book:
31 but these are written, that you might believe that Jesus is the Messiah, the Son of God; and that believing you might have life through His Name.
Mark 16
15 And He said to them, "Go into all the world, and preach the gospel everywhere.
16 Those who believe and are baptized shall be saved; but they who disbelieve shall be condemned.

Mark 16

17 And these signs shall follow those who believe; in My Name shall they cast out devils; they shall speak with new languages;

18 if they arouse snakes; or even if they drink any deadly thing, it shall not hurt them; they shall lay their hands on the sick, and they shall recover."

Matthew 28

16a Then the eleven disciples went away into Galilee.

THE SEVENTH APPEARANCE - TO THE SEVEN

After the sixth appearance of Jesus in Jerusalem, the apostles leave for Galilee. They would have known about the meeting to be held at the '*mount where Jesus had appointed them*' (Mat. 28:16b). This subsequently included all of the rest of the disciples too, as Jesus had related, at His third appearance - *To The Women* (v. 10), and as the angel had originally told the women to tell the apostles (v. 7). No doubt arrangements were made to make sure of the day and time it was to take place before *The Five Hundred* left the environs of Jerusalem. Matthew's reference, to the disciples leaving Jerusalem, contains two time factors: a) when the disciples actually left; and b) including the meeting at the mount, which evidently was much later.

Thus, we have placed the latter occurrence, relating to when they were gathered together, found in the other half of the verse, in its appropriate position, after the seventh appearance, or in other words, the third one to the apostles. Furthermore, because the whole of Matthew's verse corresponds to the apostle Paul's reference to the meeting of *The Five Hundred* (1 Cor. 15:6), we have used the first part again (Mat. 28:16a), as the context also applies, in any case, to when the eleven had returned to Galilee, and, when eventually setting off for the meeting at the mount to meet up with *The Five Hundred*. They naturally would have had to leave the places where they resided once more to go '*away into Galilee, to the mount where Jesus had appointed them*'.

Undoubtedly after the sixth appearance, when all the twelve were present, which Paul highlighted in his list (1 Cor. 15:5b), and directly afterwards, the importance of Paul specifically mentioning the meeting of *The Five Hundred* (v. 6), arrangements of the date of that meeting had already been confirmed.

Consequently, the meeting with *The Five Hundred* would not take place until after the seventh appearance, which was to the apostles once more, when they had returned to Galilee. John had clearly stated the order in which Jesus appeared three times (21:14): the first in Jerusalem, to the ten, on the Sunday that Jesus showed Himself after His resurrection (20:19-24); the second, eight days later to the eleven or twelve, still in Jerusalem (vv. 26-29); and the third, to the seven in Galilee (21:13). Additionally, the context of where Jesus commissions Peter to feed His Sheep directly after they had eaten breakfast (vv. 15-17), and the following narrative (vv. 18-24), relates to the same setting, indicating that the meeting at the mount would have taken place after Peter had been appointed by Jesus to '*feed My Sheep*', as that specific request pertains to the very establishment of continuing to feed *The Five Hundred* brothers, too.

John 21

1 After these things Jesus showed Himself again to the disciples at the Sea of Tiberias; and in this manner He showed Himself.

2 There were together Simon Peter, and Thomas called Didymus, and Nathanael of Cana of Galilee, and the sons of Zebedee, and two other disciples.

3 Simon Peter says to them, "I'm going fishing."

They say to him, "We'll also go with you."

They went along, and entered into a boat immediately; and that night they caught nothing.

4 But when the morning was come, Jesus stood on the shore: but the disciples didn't know that it was Jesus.

5 Then Jesus says to them, "Children, have you any fish?"

They answered Him, "No."

6 And He said to them, "Cast the net on the right side of the boat, and you shall find."

They cast therefore, and now they were not able to draw it for the mass of fishes.

7 Therefore that disciple whom Jesus loved says to Peter, "It is the Lord." Now when Simon Peter heard that it was the Lord, he wrapped his outer garment around him, (for he had removed it,) and threw himself into the sea.

8 And the other disciples came in the small boat; (for they were not far from land, but as it were one hundred yards,) dragging the net with the fishes.

9 As soon then as they were come to land, they saw a fire of coals there, and fish laid upon it, and bread.

10 Jesus says to them, "Bring some of the fish which you have now caught."

11 Simon Peter went up, and drew the net to land full of large fishes, a hundred and fifty three: and for all there were so many, yet the net was not broken.

12 Jesus says to them, "Come and have breakfast."

And none of the other disciples ventured to ask Him, "Who are you?" knowing that it was the Lord.

John 21

13 Jesus then comes, and takes the bread, and gives it them, and the fish likewise.

With the seventh appearance of Jesus, though there is no hint in the text that Jesus miraculously appeared at the seashore, nonetheless, the miraculousness is associated with the catch of the fishes (John 21:6), and that Jesus already had fish (v. 9). John is careful to explain '*in this manner He showed Himself*', with Jesus appearing in an ordinary fashion (v. 1), as the scenario depicts Him already standing on the seashore at dawn, with them not recognizing Him (v. 4), until John perceived it, and related it to Peter (v. 7).

Previously, in the first year of Jesus' ministry, the disciples in a break from traveling with Jesus, had also decided to go fishing, while awaiting for the next phase of the ministry (Luke 5:1-11); now in like manner three years later, and again in a respite from the stupendous incidents which had occurred since Jesus was first resurrected, did the same once more. With the overwhelming events surrounding the miraculous six appearances, and the excitement of the new phase of the gospel shortly to begin on the Day of Pentecost, these disciples for a night of change, had returned to their old profession, for a break, in contrast to the previous momentous events.

Moreover, the same thing had occurred in the first year of Jesus' ministry, and, as relating to the number of the miracle, of the catch of fishes being the seventh miracle. Once again, this second catch of fishes became the seventh miracle since the resurrection, and the fiftieth altogether, and the last miracle of Jesus' ministry, before the conclusion of His mission on the earth with the Ascension.

We have now addressed the last recorded miracle before the Ascension. Though the factor of this seventh appearance and the **fiftieth miracle** did not involve the appearance as the actual miracle itself, nonetheless, the catch of fishes was.

However, after this seventh miracle, there are two more special meetings, as the apostle Paul successively recorded in his list. As these next two special meetings - the meeting with the five hundred, and afterwards James - moreover, do not have any indication in the requisite texts of any inherent miraculous detail associated with them seeing Jesus, we cannot count them in the same way as the preceding miracles. Nonetheless, in one sense we can still count them, as the eighth and the ninth, but it is clear they are not to be included in the number of the fifty miracles before the Ascension, as each of those particular miracles had a specific aspect included in the text by the Holy Spirit that rendered them miracles!

PETER COMMISSIONED

John 21

14 This is now the third time that Jesus showed Himself to His disciples, after that He was raised from the dead.

15 So when they had eaten, Jesus says to Simon Peter,
"Simon, son of Jonas, do you love Me more than these?"

He says to Him, "Yes, Lord; You know that I love You."
He says to him, "Feed My Lambs."

16 He says to him again the second time,
"Simon, son of Jonas, do you love Me?"

He says to Him, "Yes, Lord; You know that I love You."
He says to him, "Tend to My Sheep."

17 He says to him the third time, "Simon, son of Jonas, do you love Me?"
Peter was grieved because He said to him the third time, "*Do you love Me?*"
And he said to Him, "Lord, You know all things; You know that I love You."

Jesus says to him, "Feed My Sheep.
18 Truly, truly, I say to you, when you were young, you dressed yourself, and walked where you wanted: but when you are grown, you shall stretch out your hands, and another shall dress you, and carry you where you wouldn't wish to go."

19 This He spoke, signifying by what death he should glorify God.
And when He had spoken, He says to him, "Follow Me."

20 Then Peter, turning about, sees the disciple whom Jesus loved following; who also leaned on His chest at supper, and said, "Lord, who is he who betrays You?"

21 Peter seeing him says to Jesus, "Lord, and what about him?"
22 Jesus says to him,
"If I wish he remain until I come, what is that to you? You follow Me."

23 Then went this saying abroad among the brothers and sisters, that this disciple wouldn't die; yet Jesus didn't say to him, he wouldn't die; but, *"If I wish that he remain till I come, what is that to you?"*

24 This is the disciple who testifies of these things, and who wrote these things: and we know that testimony is true.

Jesus now, after breakfast, confirmed Peter's role as the leading disciple in being responsible for administering the feeding of the sheep (John 21:15-17). Thus, this preempted the next scene, of Jesus meeting with all the rest of the disciples - the five hundred.

With Jesus having confirmed Peter's role, and Peter having wondered about John's position in all this (vv. 20-22), John with Peter, the first apostles to have believed in the resurrection, John now brings his Gospel to a close, in relating to Peter and himself, the two foremost disciples (vv. 20-24), who would be instrumental from the Day of Pentecost in spearheading the gospel of the resurrection, first to Jerusalem and then spreading out from there.

However, before that, the meeting with the five hundred would take place at the mount that Matthew had referred to, which no doubt was the same mount near Capernaum where Jesus had first ordained the twelve (Luke 6:12-16), as we suggested in that section, and where some of these other disciples had originally become Jesus' disciples too (v. 17).

No doubt, the commissioning of the five hundred occurred nearer the end of the forty days, before they returned to Jerusalem for the final stage of events, culminating with the gospel of the resurrection being preached on the very Day of Pentecost, first at Jerusalem (Acts 2), and then progressively outwards to the rest of the world.

Furthermore, John, in closing his Gospel, distinguishes between Jesus' last appearance '*to the disciples*' in Galilee (21:1), having just met the them at breakfast, in now using the Greek word '*adelphoi*' - '*brothers*' (v. 23), as if alluding that the next appearance would be to the five hundred brothers. Jesus used the same expression before being represented as the *Firstfruit Elevated Wave-Sheaf* to the Father, when speaking to Mary (20:17), and in returning from Heaven, in giving the message of that meeting to take place in Galilee to the women (Mat. 28:10).

As mentioned earlier though there is no miraculous criteria recorded in the actual text connected with the meeting with the five hundred, we may still count it as the eighth; nevertheless, as the Holy Spirit deemed the text so, it cannot be included in the number associated with the factor relating to any of the miraculous incidents. However, if we were to count it along with the other miracles, it would be the fifty-first.

Because all the disciples, including the five hundred from wherever they lived, '*went away into Galilee*' at some prearranged date, '*to the mount where Jesus had appointed them*', we have thus placed the words of Paul, '*after that*' (1 Cor. 15:6a), following Mat. 28:16, which begins with '*Then*', as it would relate to the rest of Paul's verse (6b), regarding the meeting with the five hundred, the greater part of whom were still alive twenty years later when Paul wrote, and who were all witnesses to the resurrection, after they had all seen the resurrected Messiah.

Matthew 28:16b 1 Corinthians 15:6a
Then after that the eleven disciples went away into Galilee, to the mount where Jesus had appointed them.
Matthew 28:17 1 Corinthians 15:6b
And He was seen of above five hundred brothers at once.
When they saw Him, they worshiped Him: but some doubted; of who the greater part remain to this time, but some are fallen asleep.

Matthew 28
18 And Jesus came and spoke to them, saying,
"All Power is given to Me in Heaven and in the earth.
19 Go therefore, and teach all nations baptizing them in the Name of the Father, and of the Son, and of the Holy Spirit:
20 teaching them all things, whatever I have commanded you: and, understand, I am with you always, even to the end of the world. Amen."

Matthew (28:18-20) closes his Gospel with the commission to all disciples,which Luke affirmed would shortly begin when they had received the extra Power of the Holy Spirit on the Day of Pentecost (Acts 2:1-2), ten days after the Ascension (1:3-4, 8). Matthew limited his record of the appearances of Jesus exclusively to the women as they went to inform '*the brothers*' [the five hundred] of the angel's message that Jesus was resurrected, at which point Jesus confirmed that the brothers were to meet in Galilee too (28:9-10), as well as to the eleven [or twelve].

Where Matthew has '*but some doubted*' (v. 17), he is obviously referring to the five hundred brothers, who like the eleven before, had not believed until their doubts had been dispelled. It is clear that after the subsequent appearances to the ten, and eight days later to the eleven [or twelve], in each particular case, the disciples believed. Hence, Matthew is directing our attention to the doubt of some of the five hundred, at the instance of first seeing Jesus, and not the eleven, who by that time were confirmed believers. After the meeting in Galilee had concluded, naturally the five hundred believed too, as shortly afterwards they were all to be witnesses to fact that Jesus had been resurrected.

Mark, in closing his Gospel, as we recalled earlier at *The Sixth Appearance - To The Eleven* or twelve, referred exclusively to the miraculous aspects relating to the new beginning of the commission of the disciples (16:17-18), which as mentioned, would not transpire until ten days after the Ascension. He accentuated the importance of *The Sixth Appearance*, by not mentioning any other appearances afterwards, making this the penultimate meeting, before finally concluding his Gospel with his account of the meeting before the Ascension (v. 19), and the manifestation of the miraculous signs he had earlier alluded to at *The Sixth Appearance* (v. 20).

However, Luke concludes his Gospel with details of where Jesus ascended to Heaven from, and that the disciples continued with great joy thanking God in the Temple for the amazing good news they had been privy to (24:50-53), nonetheless, he continues in Acts, furnishing further detail, elaborating additional information relating to the disciples returning to Jerusalem from Galilee, where they were to await until Pentecost for the unique occurrence of the outpouring of the Holy Spirit en bloc.

John ends his unique account with *The Seventh Appearance*, where Peter has been confirmed as the leading apostle with the responsibility of feeding the sheep (21:17-20). John also refers to '*the brothers*' [the five hundred], who thought that John would not die before Jesus returned, as Jesus had told Peter not to worry what John's role would be, by stating, '*If I wish that he remains until I come, what is that to you?*' (vv. 21-23). He further concludes, by referring, no doubt to all the disciples, whom he referred to as '*we*', in that they knew John's testimony of Jesus in his Gospel was true (v. 24), and relates in conclusion that Jesus did many other things which had not been written down (v. 25).

Though Paul's list follows on successively, it does not include all the appearances, but he limits his list specifically to apostles who were sent out, or who were involved in having witnessed the resurrected Messiah.

After the meeting with the five hundred subsequently he indicates the next special meeting to be with James (1 Cor. 15:7).

THE MEETING WITH JAMES

1 Corinthians 15
7a After that, He was seen of James

After the meeting of the five hundred brother-disciples (v. 6), it is revealed, '*after that*', Jesus '*was seen by James*', recorded by the last of all the apostles, Paul, who was born-again, as it were, out of due time (v. 8).

This James was not the brother of John, of the sons of Zebedee, neither James the Less, one of the twelve, but was '*the Lord's Brother*' (Gal. 1:19), who became the leader of the Jerusalem Church (Gal. 2:9, 12; Acts 12:17; 15:13), and who is around and mentioned during ten chapters of Acts, up until ch. 21:18 [c. AD 60], until the last seven chapters.

Jesus' family still lived in Galilee, and would have returned home, though Jesus had entrusted His mother into John's care while still in Jerusalem, helping her in enduring the tribulation of Jesus' crucifixion.

Nevertheless, the disciples had all returned to Galilee, where Jesus had told them He would see them, including the five hundred.

Luke who had compiled book of *The Acts Of The Apostles*, highlighted various events, and mentioned James as being leader of the Jerusalem Church in amongst over a third of his narration, though he does not actually name James in the first eleven chapters, or indicate Jesus' meeting with him, as he did with Jesus' appearances to Peter and Paul.

The first seven chapters of *The Acts* relate exclusively to the area of Jerusalem. The first chapter indicating that James, with his brothers, Jesus' mother, and the disciples (Acts 1:13-14), returned there for the Ascension and Pentecost.

Moreover, as we shall see, Luke alluded to a further two meetings there. The first one, where they were instructed not to leave Jerusalem (vv. 4-5), and the last farewell meeting (vv. 6-8), concluding with the Ascension (vv. 9-11).

Jesus no doubt met with James in Galilee, before they returned to Jerusalem, revealing to him that while the other apostles were to be busy with preaching the gospel of the resurrection to the environs of Jerusalem, and subsequently progressively further afield, he was to assume charge of the fast growing and large Jerusalem church (2:41; 4:4; 6:1, 7).

Though Luke did not mention the meeting with James, nonetheless, he exclusively recorded for us the other details relating to James, and the additional information as to what occurred after the disciples returned from Galilee to Jerusalem. Had Jesus met with James in Jerusalem, he could have briefly referred to it, when outlining the meeting with the apostles, where they were not to depart from Jerusalem, and the farewell meeting, directly before the Ascension, as he did when briefly relating that Jesus had appeared to Peter.

After John's last recorded miracle, the seventh since Jesus' resurrection, the meeting with the five hundred followed, and subsequently the one after that, with James. Nevertheless, as mentioned there is no evidence to suggest Jesus appeared at the previous two meetings in a miraculous manner in the text, although with Peter and the apostles there is. Notwithstanding, we are concerned mainly with what the text actually clearly reveals to us, through what the Holy Spirit guided to be recorded.

All the seven appearances had some miraculous aspect associated with them, plainly within the text, as did all the forty-three previous miracles from the start of Jesus' ministry.

Because Paul's list deals exclusively with the '*apostles*' [Gr. *ones sent out*], and does not concern itself with the other miraculous appearances, such as to the women, and Cleopas and his wife, it should be recognized as such. As it rather confines itself specifically with Jesus having special meetings with those primarily associated with the actual dissemination of the good news of Jesus' resurrection.

Consequently, the number of miracles associated with Jesus' ministry prior to the Ascension is paramount in showing that the attesting signs of the miracles, fifty in all, prefigured in also witnessing to the sublime Power of the Holy Spirit. The awaiting of the Holy Spirit at Pentecost [Gr. *fiftieth*], also related to the fifty days that were to be counted after the weekly Sabbath in the Passover Week (Lev. 23:15-16), when Pentecost would be '*fully come*' (Acts 2:1).

It also has profound symbolism associated within that factor, as it had when we suggested previously in the sections, *The Two Growing Boys* [p. 21], *Jesus' Baptism* [pp. 29-30], the calling of *The First Disciples* [p. 36], the ordinations [pp. 108-109; 188-191], or new beginnings, and especially the narrative relating to the penultimate Pentecost [see section *The Last Summer* pp. 275-278, before the Pentecost directly after Jesus' Ascension.

Now, because we only have very brief references to the meeting with *The Five Hundred*, and likewise with the next meeting with James, of which both Paul alone specifically refers to, and who does not stipulate expressively that they were of a miraculous nature, even though to Peter and the apostles they were, we cannot count them in the same category as the fifty miracles.

As also mentioned at *The First Appearance - To Mary* [pp. 403-405], because Jesus had already been resurrected, that miraculous element alone would intrinsically be wound up in His presence each time He first met with anyone. However, since Jesus allowed Himself to be touched, and that He ate, walked, and moved with those He spoke to as before, and appeared to be virtually the same when conducting Himself with them, only the obvious miracles can be counted. Yet, as the texts show, He did materialize, and conversely disappear, except for *The Seventh Appearance* where the catch of fishes became the miracle.

In comparison with the meetings with *The Five Hundred* and James, there is no detailed record of any other miraculousness specially mentioned in the text, and thus, they should be counted separately. Clearly the Holy Spirit, which guided what would be written in the text of the Bible, decreed that these two last meetings were to be classed differently, and related to a different aspect.

Evidentially, as James became the head of the Jerusalem Church, which warranted the importance of being included in Paul's list, and moreover, that he was the brother of Jesus, in overseeing the Jerusalem Church while the apostles were away on their gospel missions, he was crucial to the early developing stages of the church, in the unifying process of the truth, as various schisms shortly started evolving afterwards.

Thus, with this special meeting with James, and as we have already stressed, because there is no specific suggestion of any miraculous detail in the text itself, while it was important enough to be mentioned, we cannot count it, in the same light as the other clearly defined miracles.

After Jesus' meeting with James, who was also His brother, when returning to Jerusalem, Mary is united again with her other sons for the next events (Acts 1:14). Although James, and indeed all the apostles left their respective home towns for the gospel's sake, it would seem that Mary was united with the rest of her family, as James became more prominent in the Jerusalem Church, while all the apostles, for the first two years concentrated their efforts with preaching the gospel to the environs of Jerusalem (8:1), with John being associated alongside Peter (3:1; 4:13, 19).

Following that, the gospel went to Samaria through Philip (8:5), to where Peter and John went, being still together (v. 14), while James was the presiding head of the Jerusalem Church as Peter was increasingly away from Jerusalem along with John.

In the meantime, it is Luke who continues with our story (1:1-3), and who reveals further detail in confirming that Jesus, '*being seen forty days*' after His resurrection, was preparing the apostles as leaders of the next and new phase of the gospel, with 'things pertaining to the Kingdom of God'. Luke additionally refers to the 'many infallible proofs' associated also with regards to the **seven miraculous appearances**.

Acts 1

1 The former treatise have I made, oh Theophilus, of all that Jesus began both to do and teach.

2 Until the day in which He was taken up, after that He through the Holy Spirit had given instructions to the apostles whom He had chosen:

3 to whom also He showed Himself alive after His Passion by many infallible proofs, being seen of them forty days, and speaking things pertaining to the Kingdom of God.

Acts 13

31 And He was seen many days of those who came up with Him from Galilee to Jerusalem, who are His witnesses to the people.

LAST TWO MEETINGS IN JERUSALEM

Moreover, Luke in quoting Paul later on again (Acts 13:31), refers to the fact that Jesus '*was seen many days*', not just on the days that were recorded in the Gospels. Subsequently, Jesus did not miraculously appear every time. Nonetheless, for the most part Jesus conducted Himself as before when meeting with His followers.

We had suggested in the last intersection how the meeting with *The five Hundred* brothers, and James, afterwards in Galilee, would no doubt have been towards the end of the forty days, as the fortieth day after the resurrection, the apostles would witness the Ascension, and were already in Jerusalem, where they were to have two more meetings with Jesus.

Additionally, they had to wait after the Ascension (1:4-5), a further ten days until Pentecost had fully come (2:1). Surely the seventy disciples would have also come up to Jerusalem in preparation for Pentecost, arriving there well before, the fortieth day.

However *The Five Hundred* were not in the company of the hundred and twenty (1:15) in the upper room, who undoubtedly would have lodged in and around Jerusalem, so as to be present at the Temple on Pentecost, where they and the great crowds from every nation, would witness the apostles preaching (2:4-13) and hear Peter's powerful inspirational address (vv. 14-36), on this historical day which would trigger the new phase of the gospel story.

But before that, Luke indicates another two meetings, the penultimate meeting with the disciples in Jerusalem (1:4-5), which occurred before the following meeting when the apostles have their last meeting (v. 6), and where Jesus leads them to the Mt. Olives overlooking Bethany (Luke 24:50; Acts 1:12), and from where He returns to the Father.

Acts 1

4 And, being assembled together with them [Jesus] instructed them that they should not depart from Jerusalem but wait for the promise of the Father, "Which, you have heard from Me (John 14:16, 26; 15:26).
5 For John truly baptized with water; but you shall be baptized with the Holy Spirit not many days from now."

At v. 4 we have the first indication of the next meeting Jesus had with His disciples in Jerusalem. Jesus was already '*assembled together with them*', and instructed them not to depart from Jerusalem but wait ten days until Pentecost. This meeting was the penultimate meeting, at which Jesus reaffirmed the purpose for coming to Jerusalem, and awaiting Pentecost.

The difference between the penultimate meeting where Jesus reaffirmed they were to await in Jerusalem until Pentecost and the final meeting, was that Jesus would repeat the words of their commissioning again, in conclusion, before ascending to the Father. He had already told the ten at the fifth appearance (Luke 24:49), that they were to wait in Jerusalem, for the promise of the Father in sending the extra Power of the Holy Spirit.

Though Matthew concluded his Gospel with the commission of all disciples (28:18-20), and did not mention the Ascension, neither did John. Nevertheless, the last words of Jesus in Matthew, as related in his closing three verses, mirror some of the essence of what Jesus also repeated at the last meeting directly before leading the apostles to the Mt. Olives for the Ascension (Acts 1:7-8). No doubt, Matthew in closing his Gospel wished to portray the importance of the words relating to the commission of all disciples, and in so doing reflected what was both repeated at his last recorded meeting and the final meeting of disciples.

Because of this, we have included Jesus' words again in the main Scriptural text of the final meeting before the Ascension (Mat. 28:18a-20a), ending the meeting, doubtlessly, with Jesus' last recorded comforting promise, '*understand, I am with you always, even to the end of the world*' (v. 20b).

However, at this final meeting, the apostles were still wondering whether Jesus would '*at this time restore again the Kingdom of Israel?*' (Acts 1:6), even though, during the last forty days He had spoken '*of the things pertaining to the Kingdom of God*' (v. 3).

Jesus went on to explain that the time factor was in the hands of the Father, and that they were to concern themselves with the continuance of preaching the gospel; as from Pentecost, the Holy Spirit would give them further perception in understanding the issues relating to the gospel of the Kingdom of God, which gospel would go forth from Jerusalem first, then Judea, Samaria, and the rest of the world. It was not just limited to Israel (vv. 7-8).

V. 6 relates, '*When they were come together*' thus, differing from the previous meeting (vv. 4-5), where they were already '*assembled together*', denoting it as a separate meeting, and the final one with Jesus.

Luke did not have to mention the phrase, '*when they were come together*', since in the first instance they were already '*assembled together*'; he could have continued with the dialogue relating to the Ascension, if he had not intended to indicate two separate meetings. Additionally, this was the last meeting that Paul also referred to (1 Cor. 15:7b).

FINAL MEETING ON MT. OLIVES

Matthew 28:18a Acts 1:6a 1 Corinthians 15:7b
And when all the apostles therefore were then come together [25th Iyar], Jesus came to them and spoke to them, saying,
"All Power is given to Me in Heaven and in the earth.
Matthew 28
19a Go therefore, and teach all nations, baptizing them in the Name of the Father, and of the Son, and of the Holy Spirit:
20a teaching them too observe all things, whatever I have commanded you."

Acts 1
6b They asked of Him, saying,
"Lord, will You at this time restore again the Kingdom of Israel?"
7 And He said to them, "It is not for you to know the times or seasons, which the Father has put in His own Power.
8 But you shall receive Power, after that the Holy Spirit is come among you: and you shall be witnesses to Me both in Jerusalem, and in all Judea, and in Samaria, and to the uttermost part of the earth.
Matthew 28
20b And, understand, I am with you always, even to the end of the world. Amen."

Luke exclusively reveals after the last meeting with the apostles at Jerusalem (Acts 1:6-8), they went from there to Bethany on the east slope of the Mt. Olives (Luke 24:50), and to the Mt. Olives from where Jesus ascended (Acts 1:11-12).

In Luke's first reference in his Gospel where the apostles leave Jerusalem for the Mt. Olives, the AV translates the Greek word '*heos*', '*as far as*', and the following word '*eis*' - '*to*' (24:50). Nevertheless, the Greek word '*eis*', can mean '*towards*', as it has been translated on numerous other occasions, and thus, the actual intended meaning becomes clearer when considering Luke's second reference to the event in Acts 1:12, where it is evident that Jesus ascended from the Mt. Olives. Bethany was nearly two miles from Jerusalem. Thus, we have retranslated Luke 24:50 in our main text accordingly.

Luke was informing us that after the last meeting with the apostles in Jerusalem, Jesus led '*them out* [of Jerusalem] *towards Bethany*', across the Kidron Valley to the Mt. Olives (Acts 1:12), which would mean when taking all the facts, and topography into consideration, that Jesus led them to the plateau of the mount, whereby one could overlook Bethany, towards the east, and Jerusalem, to the west.

Additionally, in the prophecy of Zechariah (14:4), the Lord returns to the Mt. Olives, as further indicated by the two angels directly after the Ascension (Acts 1:11-12).

Luke 24
50 And He led them out towards Bethany, and He lifted up His hands, and blessed them.

Mark 16:19a Luke 24:51 Acts 1:9
And so then, it came to pass, while He blessed them, when after the Lord had spoken to them these things, while they watched, He was parted from them, and He was carried and taken up into the heavens; a cloud receiving Him out of their sight.

Mark 16:19b Acts 1:10
And while they looked steadfastly toward the heavens as He went up and sat on the right hand of God, suddenly, two men stood by them in white apparel;
Acts 1
11 who also said, "You men of Galilee, why do you stand gazing up into the heavens? This same Jesus, who is taken up from you into the heavens, shall so come in like manner as you have seen Him go into the heavens."

Luke 24:52 Acts 1:12
And they worshiped Him, and then they returned with great joy to Jerusalem from the Mount (called) Olivet, which is from Jerusalem a Sabbath Day's journey:
Luke 24
53 and were continually in the Temple, praising and blessing God.

Mark 16

20 And they went out, and preached everywhere, the Lord working with them, and confirming the word with signs following.

John 21

25 And there are also many other things that Jesus did, which, if they should be written every one, I suppose that even the world itself could not contain the books that should be written.

John, who had begun the story of the Gospels before that of any of the Synoptics with informing us of aspects even before prehistory, now closes the record of the four Gospels by stating not every incident had been transcribed. And if one was to keep writing about the things pertaining to Jesus, '*that even the world itself could not contain the books that should be written*' (21:25).

Moreover, John earlier, in the last two verses of his penultimate chapter, indicated that there were other attesting miracle signs, not written in his book, but those that he had recorded, were for the purpose that one might believe that Jesus was the Messiah (20:30-31). These two verses were placed directly before **The Seventh Appearance** (21:1-14), his last miracle, and the **fiftieth miracle**!

THE CONCLUSION

Furthermore, T*he Seventh Miracle - The Catch Of Fishes*, in the first year of Jesus' ministry (Luke 5:11), has analogical parallelism with the seventh miracle of the second catch of fishes, after the resurrection, by which it is also the last miracle before the Ascension. Both were symbolic, relating also to the aspect of catching people, in respect to preaching the gospel. Additionally, this last miracle was a prelude to Jesus appointing Peter as a leader, with the overall responsibility in feeding the catch of people - the church.

We had previously considered that the firstfruit wave-sheaf was presented to the Lord the day after the Sabbath, which fell in the Days of Unleavened Bread, and was symbolic of Jesus being the Firstfruit Elevated-Sheaf, in presenting Himself to the Father on the Sunday morning after the Sabbath, in which the women had come to the tomb. It was fifty days after that particular Sabbath in the Passover week, on which the Day of Pentecost [Gr. *fiftieth*] fell.

The original Biblical instructions were to count seven weeks (Lev. 23:15), which equals forty-nine days, and then the fiftieth day, would be Pentecost (v. 16).

Hence *The Seventh Appearance - To The Seven* apostles, the final catch of fishes, including originally *The Seventh Miracle - The Catch Of Fishes*, both symbolic of catching people (Mat. 4:19; Mark 1:17), and now actually concluding as the fiftieth miracle, typifies belief, through the acceptance of the Holy Spirit, and is also the last miracle, before the Ascension which concluded Jesus' earthly ministry!

Yet, when counting the miracles without the miracle of Jesus' resurrection there are forty-nine.

Besides, *The Reappearances*, seven, must be classed differently, unique, and complete in themselves, since their miraculousness related to Jesus again, and seven is the number of perfect completeness as in Biblical Numerology and as outlined in E. W. Bullinger's amazing book, *NUMBER IN SCRIPTURE* (pp. 167-168).

We should thus also notice as mentioned before that though there are fifty miracles when counting Jesus' resurrection, because the specific moment of Jesus' resurrection did not involve any other person, and that every one of the other miracles related primarily to the individuals themselves [though we can count Jesus' resurrection as the forty-third miracle], it must also be considered in a completely different light, in an aspect distinct and that transcends all the others, as it was the greatest miracle of all, and in that sense cannot be classified in the same category as the others.

Similarly, the same with the Ascension, the final and closing miracle was exclusive to Jesus Himself.

So in the conclusion with the Ascension, when counting Jesus' resurrection as the forty-third miracle, and thus the fifty-first in including the seven others of *The Reappearances*, we see that fifty-one in Biblical Numerology is the Divine number as outlined in E. W. Bullinger's amazing book, *NUMBER IN SCRIPTURE* (p. 269):

Fifty-One

This is the number of Divine revelation, for
there are 24 books of the Old Testament, and
<u>27</u> books in the New Testament,
making <u>51</u> in all.*

---

*"This is, of course, reckoning the Divine separation of the books, as exhibited in the Hebrew MSS, which form our only authority, and not reckoning according to human manipulation of them; for both Jewish and Gentile fancies and reasonings make quite a different and conflicting number.

In other words, the number and order of the books of the Bible come to us on precisely the same authority as its facts and doctrines.

In the Hebrew MSS Ezra and Nehemiah are always reckoned as one book, with the one name, Ezra. Each of the double books is reckoned as one book (e.g. 1 and 2 Samuel, 1 and 2 Kings, and 1 and 2 Chronicles), and all the Minor Prophets are also reckoned as one book. This makes 24 books in all. This is 8 x 3, both factors stamping the number with the seal of Divine perfection." – E.W. Bullinger

AMEN

THE MIRACLES OF JESUS

	Matthew	Mark	Luke	John
1 Water to Wine				2:1-11
2 The Demoniac		1-21-27	4:31-36	
3 [Simon] the Leper	8:1-4			
4 Nobleman's Son				4:46-54
5 Centurion	8:5-13			
6 Peter's Mother-in-Law	8:14-15	1:29-31	4:38-49	
7 Catch of Fishes			5:1-11	
8 The Tempest	8:24-27	1:40-45	5:12-15	
9 Second Leper				
10 Two Demoniacs	8:28-34			
11 Paralytic Man	9:1-8	2:1-12	5:17-26	
12 Withered Hand	12:9-13	3:1-5	6:1-11	
13 Centurion's Servant			7:2-10	
14 Man in Coffin			7:11-17	
15 Blind Dumb Man	**12:22-24**	3:22		
16 The Storm		4:37-41	8:22-25	
17 Legion of Devils		5:1-20	8:26-39	
18 Woman's Issue	9:18-22	5:25-34	8:43-48	
19 Jairus' Daughter	9:23-26	5:22-43	8:40-56	
20 Two Blind Men	9:27-31			
21 Dumb Man	9:32-34			
22 Crippled Man				5:2-16
23 Feeding of the 5000	14:16-21	6:36-44	9:12-17	6:5-14
24 Walks on Water	14:24-33	6:47-52		
25 Woman's Daughter	15:21-29	7:24-30		
26 Deaf Mute Man	15:30-31	**7:31-37**		
27 Feeding of the 4000	15:32-39	8:1-9		
28 Blind Man		8:22-36		
29 Transfiguration	17:2-13	9:2-13	9:28-36	

	Matthew	Mark	Luke	John
30 Deaf Mute Child	17:14-18	9:14-27	9:37-47	
31 Paying Tribute	**17:24-27**	9:33		
32 Casts Out Devil			11:14	
33 Bowed Woman			13:10-17	
34 Man with Oedema			14:1-6	
35 Blind Man				9:1-12
36 Ten Lepers			17:12-19	
37 First Blind Man			18:35-43	
38 Blind Bartimeus		**10:46-42**		
39 Two Blind Men	20:30-34			
40 Lazarus Raised				11:34-46
41 Fig Tree Dead	21:19-20	11:20-21		
42 Malchus' Ear	26:51-54	14:47	**22:50-51**	18:10-11
1 Appearance to Mary		16:9		20:12-15
2 Appearance to Peter			24:34 [1 Cor. 15:5]	
3 Appearance to Women	28:9-10			
4 Cleopas and Wife		16:12	24:15-27	
5 Appearance to the 10			24:36-49	20:19-23
6 Appearance to the 12		16:14 [1 Cor. 15:5]		20:26
7 Appearance to the 7				21:1-14

Both the references **highlighted** of Matthew and Mark indicate the mentioning of the actual miracle itself, whereas their other two references just mention the setting.

Though at the forty-second miracle all the references mention the incident, it is only Luke who mentions the healing.

THE PARABLES IN THE GOSPELS

The list of parables covers them in their successive order as outlined in this book.

There are two basic sets of parables, those directed at the disciples, and those that were not. The distinction obviously is in the context to whom they were addressed. Therefore for easier reference those spoken to the disciples are in plain type, and those to others are in *italics*.

There are 86 altogether in our list, 48 given to the disciples, and *38 in italics to others*. Also some parables were given twice, like the *Parable of Salt,* and the *Parable of Not Hiding the Light,* yet actually mentioned three times in separate scenarios. These two were the first parables spoken to the disciples. The parables given more than once comprise of 42. We have underlined these when that is the case.

Also when some parables are related twice, sometimes Jesus uses the original parable later on in a different scenario, and adds another part of a parable mentioned earlier to bring out an alternate meaning. When this occurs in our list, the nuance of the adapted parable is used alongside the original title of the parable.

1 *1 Being Born-Again* John 3:1-8

2 1 Salt Mat. 5:13

3 2 Not Hiding the Light Mat. 5:14-16

4 3 Cutting it Out Mat. 5:29-30

5 4 The Light of the Body Mat. 6:22-23

6 5 The Speck and Beam (Judgment) Mat. 7:1-5

7 6 Pearls of Wisdom Mat.7:6

8 7 The Narrow Gate Mat. 7:13-14

9 8 House on Rock Mat. 7:24-27

10 *2 Living Water* John 4:10-15

11 9 The Sower and the Reaper John 4:35-37

12 *3 Children of the Bride Chamber* Mark 2:18-20; Luke 5:33-35

13 10 New Cloth on an Old Garment Mark 2:21; Luke 5:36

14 *4 New Wine in Old Wineskins* Mark 2:22; Luke 5:37-39

15 11 Blind Leading Blind (Speck and Beam) Luke 6:39-42

16 12 Fruits of the Heart and Mouth Luke 6:43-45

17 13 House on the Rock Luke 6:47-49

18 *5 Hypocritical Judgment* Mat. 11:16-19; Luke 7:31-35

19 *6 Satan Casting Out Satan* Mat. 12:25-30; Mark 3:23-27

20 *7 Fruits of the Heart and Mouth* Mat. 12:33-37

21 *8 Unsuccessful Cleansing of the Mind* Mat. 12:43-45

22 14 The Sower Mat. 13:3-8, 18-23; Mark 4:2-9; 14-20; Luke 8:4-8, 11-15

23 15 Not Hiding the Light Mark 4:21-23; Luke 8:16-17

24 *9 The Growing Seeds* Mark 4:26-29

25 *10 Wheat and Tares* Mat. 13:24-30; 36-43

26 *11 The Mustard Seed* Mat. 13:31-32; Mark 4:30-32
27 12 Leaven Mat.13:33
28 16 Treasure in a Field Mat. 13:44
29 17 Fine Pearls Mat. 13:45-46
30 18 The Great Net Mat. 13:47-50
31 19 Treasure Old and New Mat. 13:52
32 20 Children of the Bride Chamber Mat. 9:14-15
33 21 New Cloth on an Old Garment Mat. 9:16
34 22 New Wine in Old Wineskins Mat. 9:17
35 *13 The Bread From Heaven* John 6:32-58
36 23 Defilement Mat.15:10-11, 15-20; Mark 7:14-16, 17-23
37 24 The Father Plants (Blind Leading Blind) Mat. 15:13-14
38 25 The Leaven of Hypocrisy Mat. 16:5-12; Mark 8:14-21
39 26 Faith as a Grain of Mustard Seed Mat. 17:19-21; Mark 9:28-29
40 27 Cutting it Out Mat. 18:8-9 Mark 9:43-48
41 28 Salt Mark 9:49-50
42 29 The Lost Sheep Mat. 18:12-14
43 30 The Unmerciful Servant Mat. 18:23-35
44 *14 The Good Samaritan* Luke 10:25-37
45 31 The Friend at Midnight Luke 11:2-13
46 *15 Satan Casting Out Satan* Luke 11:17-23
47 *16 Unsuccessful Cleansing of the Mind* Luke 11:24-26
48 32 Not Hiding the Light Luke 11:33
49 33 The Light of the Body Luke 11:34-36
50 34 The Leaven of Hypocrisy Luke 12:1-3
51 *17 The Rich Fool* Luke 12:16-21
52 35 The Watchful Servants Luke 12:35-40
53 36 The Thief Luke 12:39-40
54 37 The Faithful Steward Luke 12:42-48
55 *18 The Barren Fig-Tree* Luke 13:6-9
56 *19 The Mustard Seed* Luke 13:18:19
57 *20 Leaven* Luke 13:20-21
58 *21 The Narrow Gate* Luke 13:23-30
59 *22 Places of Honor* Luke 14:7-14
60 *23 The Great Banquet* Luke 14:16-24
61 *24 Building a Tower* Luke 14:28-30
62 *25 The Warring King* Luke 14:31-33
63 *26 Salt* Luke 14:34-35
64 *27 The Lost Sheep* Luke 15:3-10
65 *28 The Prodigal Son* Luke 15:11-32
66 *29 The Unjust Manager* Luke 16:1-13
67 *30 The Rich Man and Lazarus* Luke 16:19-31

68 38 <u>Faith as a Grain of Mustard Seed</u> Luke 17:5-6

69 39 Unworthy Servants Luke 17:7-10

70 *31 The Door* John 10:1-10

71 *32 The Good Shepherd* John 11:11-18

72 33 The Persistent Widow Luke 18:1-8

73 *34 The Pharisee and the Tax Collector* Luke 18:9-14

74 40 The Workers in the Vineyard Mat. 20:1-16

75 *35 The Ten Pounds* Luke 19:11-27

76 *36 The Two Sons* Mat. 21:28-32

77 *37 The Wicked Tenants* Mat. 21:33-41; Mark 12:1; Luke 20:9

78 *38 The Wedding Banquet* Mat. 22:1-15

79 41 The Fig-Tree Mat. 24:32-36; Mark 13:28-33; Luke 21:29-33

80 42 <u>The Watchful Servants</u> Mark 13:34-37

81 43 <u>The Thief</u> Mat. 24:43-44

82 44 <u>The Faithful Steward</u> Mat. 24:45-51

83 45 The Ten Virgins Mat. 25:1-13

84 46 The Talents Mat. 25:14-30

85 47 Sheep and Goats Mat. 25:31-46

86 48 The Vine and Branches John 15:1-8

It is John who both opens with the first parable and closes with last parable, and was also the first Gospel writer to begin and end scenario of the gospel story.

SCRIPTURE GRAPH DATES

Notice, at the following page [449], in the first *Scripture Graph 1,* the subheadings, '*Time*', '*Place*', along with the '*Event*', '*The Beginnings*' is left blank, as Jesus, "*the Word, was with God*" (John 1:1-3) before, the creation of the physical world and time.

Following that, we have used the date c. 4000BC, estimated through the calculation of the genealogies from the creation, not the world, but of Adam onwards. It is based on the date of 4004BC, determined by archbishop, scholar and historian James Ussher (1581-1658), in his work '*Annales Veteris et Novi Testamenti*' where he added four years to the span of 4000 years, from when Jesus was born in 4BC. His work resulted in many editions of the KJ or AV Bibles being printed with this date proceeding throughout the margins of these Bibles. Though it is not particularly important to the basic findings of this book, which dating system we may each prefer, nevertheless, the general consensus amongst most Biblical scholars is that, there has been 4000 years since the creation of Adam, up until the birth of Jesus.

Moreover, we use the date 4BC for the birth of Christ, as the Gospel of Matthew (2:1, 15) indicates that Jesus was born prior to the death of Herod, who according to the vast majority of modern references also died in that particular year. The Jewish historian, Josephus in the '*Antiquities of the Jews*' (17.6.4), speaks of a lunar eclipse in Herod's last year. In the book by Kudlek and Mickler, '*Solar and Lunar Eclipses of the Ancient Near East*', they confirm that the eclipse took place on March 13, 4BC. Josephus recorded that after the eclipse, Herod suffering with a grievously horrible disease, went to bathe in the hot sulfur springs beyond the River Jordan. His condition did not get any better, but worsened, and he returned to Jericho, where the paranoid king, in a fierce frenzy planned the death of various members of his family, many prominent Jews, and, the death of the infants in the environs of Bethlehem (Mat. 2:16). All this would have taken some months.

Josephus additionally relates that Herod's death transpired before a spring Passover (*Antiquities* 17.9.3). The Passover in April 3BC occurred 13 months after the lunar eclipse and according to Jewish tradition, a few months after Herod's death.

When relating these factors together it confirms the 4BC date for the birth of Jesus.

Scripture Graph I

Time / The Beginnings	Event	Place	Matthew 1:1	Mark 1:1	Luke 1:1-4	John 1:1-3
c. 4000BC	The Lineages	Middle East	1:2-17		3:21-38	1:4-5, 9-13
5BC Month 1	Gabriel Sent to Zacharias	Jerusalem			1:5-23	
" " 1-5	Conception of John	Judah			1:24-25	
" " 6	Conception of the Messiah	Nazareth	1:18		1:26-38	
" " "	Two Pregnant Women	Judah			1:39-57	
" " 9	John's Birth & Circumcision	"			1:56-65	
4 " 3	Mary Returns	Nazareth	1:19-24		1:56	
" " 9	Joseph & Mary Leave	"			2:1-4	
" " "	The Arrival	Bethlehem			2:5	
" " "	Christ's Birth	"	1:25, 2:1		2:6-20	1:14
" " "	The Magi & Herod	Jerusalem	2:2-7			
" " "	The Magi Leave	Bethlehem	2:8-12			
" " "	Jesus Circumcised	"			2:21	
" " 10	Jesus Presented	Jerusalem			2:22-38	
" " "	Back to Nazareth	Nazareth	2:13		2:39	
" " "	Flight to Egypt	Egypt	2:13-15			
" " "	Herod's Fury	Jerusalem	2:16-18			
" " "	Herod's Death	Egypt	2:19		2:39-40	
AD9	Jesus Returns *'Out of Egypt'*	Nazareth	2:20-23		2:40-41	
" Passover	Jesus 12 Years Old	Jerusalem			2:41-52	
" "	The Prophecy of Zacharias	Judah			1:66-79	
" 24	John Grows Too	"			1:80	
" 27	Starts His Mission	Israel		1:2	3:1-3	1:6-8
" "	Voice in the Wilderness	Bethabara	3:1-3	1:3-4	3:4-6	
" "	Crowds, His Dress and Diet	"	3:4-6	1:5-6		
" "	The Vipers	"	3:7		3:7	
" "	Fruits Worthy of Repentance	"	3:8		3:8	

449

Scripture Graph II

Time	Place	Event	Matthew	Mark	Luke	John
AD27	Bethabara	Abraham as Father	3:9		3:8	
"	"	The Axe	3:10		3:9	
"	"	What To Do			3:10-15	
"	"	Unworthy of Undoing Sandals	3:11	1:7	3:16	
"	"	Baptism of Holy Spirit & Fire	3:11	1:8	3:16	
"	"	The Chaff	3:12		3:17	
"	"	Exhortation of Other Things			3:18	1:15-18
[Pentecost]	"	Baptism of Jesus	3:13-17	1:9-11	3:21-23	
1st day	Judea	Jesus Goes to Wilderness	4:1	1:12	4:1	
"	"	40 Days & 40 Nights	4:2	1:13	4:2	
40 days	"	Stones into Bread	4:3-4		4:3-4	
"	"	Devil on the Mountain	4:5-7		4:5-8	
"	"	Pinnacle of the Temple	4:8-10		4:9-12	
"	"	Second Time in Mountain				
"	"	Angels Minister to Him	4:11	1:13	4:13	
43rd day	Bethabara	Jesus Returns to John				
44th day	"	Stands Amongst Pharisees				
"	"	John Testifies to the Baptism of Jesus Previously				1:19-28
45th day	Nr.	John Introduces Two Disciples				1:29-34
"	" "	Two Disciples Stay With Jesus				1:35-37
"	Bethabara	Andrew Finds Peter				1:38-40
"	Nr.	John is Taken Prisoner				1:41-42
46th day	" "	Jesus Hears John's in Prison	4:12	1:14	3:19-20	
"	Galilee	They Leave For Galilee				1:43-51
50th day	" "	They Arrive		1:14	4:14	
"	Cana	1st Miracle Water Into Wine				2:1-11
[Autumn]	Capernaum	Jesus Leaves Nazareth	4:13			2:12
"	Bethsaida	Fulfills Prophecy	4:14-17	1:14-15		
"	"	Disciples Join Him	4:18-22	1:16-20		
"	Galilee	Fame of Him Disperses			4:14-15	
Sabbath	Nazareth	Returns To Nazareth			4:16	

Scripture Graph III

Time	Place	Event	Matthew	Mark	Luke	John
AD27 Sabbath	Nazareth in Synagogue	Fulfills Prophecy			4:17-28	
" "		They Try to Kill Him			4:29-30	
" "	Capernaum	**2nd Miracle** The Demoniac		1:21-27	4:31-36	
	Galilee	**1st Circuit of Galilee**	**4:23-25**	1:28	4:37	
AD28 Passover	Temple	Purges Temple First Time				2:13-17
" "	"	Three Days New Temple				2:18-22
" " 1st Day	Jerusalem	Nicodemus - Born Again				2:23-25-3:1-21
" [2nd] "	Mt. Olives	The Beatitudes/11 Disciples	5:1-12			
" "	"	Salt, Light and Attitude to Law	5:13-48			
" "	"	Charity and the Lord's Prayer	6:1-15			
" "	"	Fasting True Treasure	6:16-21			
" "	"	Illumination and What One Serves	6:22-24			
" "	"	Attitude to God's Provisions	6:25-34			
" "	"	Judging Others Giving, Asking,	7:1-6			
" "	"	Seeking and Knocking	7:7-12			
" "	"	The Golden Rule Two Ways	7:13-14			
" "	"	False Prophets and The Doer	7:15-23			
" "	"	Two Foundations Ends Sayings	7:24-28			
" "	down	**3rd Miracle** [Simon the Leper]	8:1-4			
" April	Judea	Jesus and Disciples Baptize				3:22
" "	Aenon	John Out of Prison & Baptizing				3:23-36
" "May	Judea	Jesus and Disciples Leave Judea				4:1-5
" "	Sychar	The Woman of Samaria				4:6-34
" "	"	The Two Harvests				4:35-38
" "	"	Two Days Later Leaves				4:39-45
" "	Cana	**4th Miracle** Nobleman's Son 2nd				4:46-54
" "	"	Miracle in Cana				
" "	Capernaum	**5th Miracle** Centurion's Servant				
" "	"	Centurion Came	8:5-13			
" Sabbath	Bethsaida	**6th Miracle** Peter's Mother-In-Law	8:14-15	1:29-31	4:38-39	
" "	"	City Gathers to be Healed	8:16	1:32-34	4:40-41	

451

Scripture Graph IV

Time	Place	Event	Matthew	Mark	Luke	John
AD28 Evening	Bethsaida	Fulfills Prophecy	8:17			
" " a.m. Dark	Nr. "	Jesus Goes to a Solitary Place		1:35		
" " "	" "	Disciples Follow		1:36		
" " Daylight	" "	Disciples & People Find Him		1:37	4:42	
" " "	Galilee	**Leaves for 2nd Tour**		1:38-39	4:43-44	
" " "	Bethsaida	**7th Miracle** Catch of Fishes			5:1-11	
" " "	" "	Discipleship/Sails To Gergesa	8:18-23			
" " "	Sea of Galilee	**8th Miracle** The Tempest	8:24-27			
" " "	Gergesa	They Arrive	8:28			
" " "	" "	**9th Miracle** Second Leper		1:40-45	5:12-15	
" " [Sabbath]	Nr. "	Jesus Withdraws to Wilderness			5:16	
" " "	" "	**10th Miracle** Two Demoniacs	8:28-34			
" " [Sunday]	Capernaum	**11th Miracle** Paralytic healed	9:1-8	2:1-12	5:17-26	
" "	" "	Jesus Teaches by Seaside		2:13		
" "	in house	Matthew Levi Called	9:9	2:14	5:27-28	
" "	" "	Jesus Dines at Matthew's With	9:10-12	2:15-17	5:29-32	
	" "	Sinners/Question on Company				
	" "	They Question on Fasting too		2:18-20	5:33-35	
		New Cloth on an Old Garment	9:13	2:21	5:36	
		New Wine in Old Wineskins		2:22	5:37-39	
		Jesus Finally Reiterates				
" " 2nd Sabbath	Capernaum	Sabbath Questions	12:1-8	2:23-28	6:1-5	
" " Sabbath	in Synagogue	**12th Miracle** Man with	12:9-13	3:1-5	6:6-11	
		Withered Hand				
" "	Jerusalem	1st Council of Pharisee	12:14	3:6		
" "	Capernaum	Jesus Heals By Seaside	12:15-16	3:7-12		
" "	" "	Fulfills Prophecy	12:17-21			
" " Night	up mount	Goes On Mount to Pray		3:13	6:12	
" " Day	" "	Ordination of Twelve	10:1-42	3:14:19	6:13-16	
" " "	down mount	Starts To Teach & Heal	11:1		6:17-19	
" " "	" "	Sermon Down the Mount			6:20-38	
" " "	" "	Blind Leading Blind Commingled			6:39	
" " "	" "	With Teaching of Sermon On Mt.			6:40-49	

452

Scripture Graph v

Time	Place	Event	Matthew	Mark	Luke	John
AD28	Capernaum	Jesus & Disciples Leave Mount		3:19-21	7:1	
"	"	**13th Miracle** Centurion's				
" "Next Day	"	Servant [Elders Sent Now]			7:2-10	
" "	Nain	**14th Miracle** Man in Coffin			7:11-17	
" "	[Machaerus]	John's Disciples Inform John			7:18	
" "	Capernaum	**John's Disciples Come to Jesus**	**11:2-6**		**7:19-23**	
" "	"	John the Baptist Extolled	11:7-15		7:24-30	
" "	"	Jesus Compares Generations	11:16-19		7:31-35	
" "	At Pharisees'	Woman Anoints/Two Debtors			7:36-50	
" "	Galilee	**Third Tour**			**8:1-3**	
" "One Day	Capernaum	The Unrepentant Cities	11:20-30			
" "	"	**15th Miracle** Blind Dumb Man	**12:22-24**	3:22		
" "	in house	Parable - Satan Cast Out Satan	12:25-30	3:23-27		
" "	"	Blasphemy of the Holy Spirit	12:31-32	3:28-30		
" "	"	John Rebukes Pharisees	12:33-37			
" "	"	Jonah and the Resurrection	12:38-42			
" "	"	Unclean Spirits	12:43-45			
" "	"	Jesus' Mother & Siblings Come	12:46-50	3:31-35		
" "	"	Jesus Leaves House for Shore	13:1	4:1	8:4	
" "	in boat	Parable of the Sower	13:2-9	4:1-9	8:4-8	
" "	on land	Explains Parable to Disciples	13:10-23	4:10-20	8:9-15	
" "	"	Reason for Light & Hearing		4:21-25	8:16-18	
" "	"	Crowds Return Jesus' Mother and Siblings Try To Get Nearer			8:19-21	
" "	"	The Growing Seed		4:26-29		
" "	"	Wheat and Tares Mustard Seed	13:24-32	4:30-32		
" "	"	Leaven Finishes Teaching	13:33-35	4:33-34		
" "	in house	Jesus Explains To Disciples	13:36-52			
" "Evening	Capernaum	They Leave For Gadara	13:53	4:35-36	8:22	
" "Night	Lake	**16th Miracle** The Storm		4:37-41	8:23-25	

453

Scripture Graph VI

Time	Place	Event	Matthew	Mark	Luke	John
AD28 Day	Nr. Gadara	17th Miracle Legion of Devils		5:1-20	8:26-39	
" "	Capernaum	Back Again		5:21	8:40	
" "	"	John's Disciples Come Again	9:14-17			
" "	in house	18th Miracle Women's Issue	9:18-22	5:22-34	8:41-48	
" "	to house	19th Miracle Jairus' Daughter	9:23-26	5:35-43	8:49-56	
" "	left house	20th Miracle Two Blind Men	9:27-31			
" "		21st Miracle Mute Man	9:32-34			
" Sabbath	Nazareth	They Leave Capernaum	9:35, 13:54	6:1		
" "	in Synagogue	Jesus Marvels at Unbelief	13:35-58	6:2-6		
" "	Galilee	Fourth and Final Tour	9:35-38	6:6		
" [Tabernacles]	Judea	Second Judean Ministry		6:7-13	9:1-6	5:1
" "	[Machaerus]	John the Baptist Beheaded	14:1-11	6:14-28	9:7-9	
" "		His disciples Tell Jesus	14:12	6:29		[5:1]
" "		Apostles Meet Up With Jesus	14:13	6:30-31	9:10	
" Sabbath	Jerusalem	22nd Miracle Crippled Man				5:2-16
" "	"	The Father Works & the Son				5:17-23
" "	"	The Resurrection				5:24-30
" "	"	Witness of John the Baptist				5:31-36
" "	"	The Greater Witness				5:36-47

Time	Place	Event	Matthew	Mark	Luke	John
AD29 Spring	Tiberias	They Return To Galilee	14:13	6:32	9:10	6:1
" "	Bethsaida	Jesus Teaches & Heals Crowds	14:14	6:33-34	9:11	6:2
" Passover	on mount	Jesus & Disciples Retire				6:3-4
" "	"	People Come To Jesus Again	14:15	6:35	9:12	6:5
" "	"	23rd Miracle Feeding of 5000	14:16-21	6:36-44	9:12-17	6:5-14
" "		Sends Disciples & People Away	14:22-23	6:45-46		6:15
" "		Jesus Remains Alone To Pray	14:23	6:46		6:15-16
" 3-6 a.m.	Lake	24th Miracle Treads Water Sick	14:24-33	6:47-52		6:17-21
" Day	Gennesaret	Touch His Garment	14:34-36	6:53-56		
" Next Day	Bethsaida	People Seek Jesus				6:22-24

Scripture Graph VII

Time	Place	Event	Matthew	Mark	Luke	John
AD29 Unleavened Bread	Capernaum	in People Find Him				6:25
" "	Synagogue	The Bread of Life				6:26-59
" "	Capernaum	Many Desert Him				6:60-71
" "	"	Defilement and Parable	15:1-14	7:1-16		[7:1]
" "	in house	Explains Parable To Disciples	15:15-20	7:17-23		
" "	Phoenicia	25th Miracle Woman's Daughter	15:21-29	7:24-30		
" "	Decapolis	26th Miracle Deaf Mute Man	15:30-31	7:31-37		
" 3rd Day	"	27th Miracle Feeding Of 4000	15:32-39	8:1-9		
" "	Magdala	Signs Prophet Jonah Again	16:1-4	8:10-13		
" "	[Capernaum]	The Leaven of Hypocrisy	16:5-12	8:14-21		
" "	Bethsaida	28th Miracle Blind Man		8:22-26		
" "	Ituraea	Acknowledges His Discipleship	16:13-20	8:27-30	9:18-21	
" "	"	His Passion Peter Rebukes Him	16:21-23	8:31-33	9:22	
" "	"	Calls People Discipleship Takes	16:24-28	8:34-9:1	9:23-27	
" 6th Day	Mountain	Peter, James and John	17:1	9:2		
" 8th "	"	29th Miracle Transfiguration	17:2-13	9:2-13	9:28-36	
" Next Day	down	30th Miracle Deaf Mute Child	17:14-18	9:14-27	9:37-42	
" "	in house	As a Grain of Mustard Seed	17:19-21	9:28-29		
" "	Ituraea	They Leave		9:30		
" "	Galilee	Jesus Mentions His Fate Again	17:22-23	9:31-32	9:43-45	
" "	Capernaum	31st Miracle Paying Tribute	17:24-27	9:33		
" "	in house	Debate about Rank	18:1-5	9:33-37	9:46-48	
" "	"	Others Doing Good Works		9:38-41	9:49-50	
" "	"	Offending Little Children	18:6-11	9:42-48		
" "	"	Lost Sheep Settling Fault	18:12-20			
" "	"	Forgiveness Unmerciful Servant	18:21-35			
" Autumn	[Capernaum]	Jesus Delays Going to Festival				7:2-9
" "	"	Leaves Secretly	19:1		9:51	7:10
" "	Samaria/Judea	Sends Messengers Before Him			9:52-56	

Scripture Graph VIII

Time	Place	Event	Matthew	Mark	Luke	John
AD29 Autumn	Samaria/Judea	Heals Discipleship Again	19:2		9:57-62	
"	"	The Seventy Ordained			10:1-16	
"	"	They Return He Thanks Father			10:17-22	
"	"	Disciples Blessed The Lawyer			10:23-29	
"	"	Parable of Good Samaritan			10:30-37	
"	Bethany	Martha & Mary's Duties			10:38-42	
"	[Mt. Olives]	Lord's Prayer Again Friend at			11:1-13	
"	" "	Midnight and Commingling Again			11:14	
"	down	**32nd Miracle** Casts Out Devil				
"	"	Satan Cast Out Again			11:15-26	
"	"	Woman Blesses Sign of Jonah,			11:27-36	
"	in house	Resurrection and Light Again			11:37-38	
"	"	Dines with a Pharisee Again			11:39-54	
"	[Jerusalem]	Reproves Pharisees			12:1-12	
"	"	Leaven Again, Commingled With				
"	"	Points Taught Before				
"	"	Coveting Parable of Rich Man			12:13-21	
"	"	God's Provision and Charity Again			12:22-35	
"	"	Parable of Watchful Servant			12:36-41	
"	"	Parable of Faithful Manager			12:42-48	
"	"	Fire Already and Jesus' Baptism			12:49-50	
"	"	Concerning Divisions Again			12:51-53	
"	"	Discernment & Attitude Again			12:54-59	
"	"	Call to a Change of Attitude			13:1-5	
"	"	Parable of Barren Fig-Tree			13:6-9	
Sabbath	Synagogue in	**33rd Miracle** Bowed Woman			13:10-17	
"	Judea "	Mustard Seed & Leaven Again			13:18-21	
"	Judea	Teaches in Towns Journeying				
"	[1st Tabernacles] Jerusalem	Towards Jerusalem Narrow Door			13:22-30	
"	"	The Jews Seek Jesus at Festival			13:31	7:11-13
"	"	Pharisees & Herod			13:31-33	

456

Scripture Graph IX

Time	Place	Event	Matthew	Mark	Luke	John
AD29 [1st Tabernacles]	Jerusalem	Lament Over Jerusalem			13:34-35	
"	Nr. house	34th Miracle Man with Odema			14:1-6	
"	house	Dines Parable of Humility			14:7-14	
"	"	Parable of Slighted Invitation			14:15-24	
Next Day	Jerusalem	Teaches Crowds Discipleship			14:25-27	
"	"	Counting the Cost Salt Again			14:28-35	
"	"	Lost Sheep Again Lost Coin			15:1-10	
"	"	Parable of Prodigal Son			15:11-32	
"	"	Unjust Manager Attitude			16:1-15	
"	"	Perseverance - Purpose of Law			16:16:18	
"	"	Parable of Rich Man & Lazarus			16:19-31	
"	"	Offending & Forgiveness Again			17:1-5	
"	"	Faith Again Master & Servant			17:6-10	
4th Tabernacles	Temple	Jesus' Doctrine The Plotting				7:14-20
"	"	Jesus Mentions 34th Miracle				7:21-24
"	"	Differing Opinions about Him				7:25-32
"	"	Pharisees Puzzled as to Where				7:33-36
Last Great Day	"	Holy Spirit Officers Amazed				7:37-52
"	Mt. Olives	Festival Concludes/Jesus Leaves				7:53-8:1
Morning	Temple	Woman Taken in Adultery				8:2-11
Sabbath	Treasury	The Light The Two Witnesses				8:12-20
"	"	The Witness of the Father				8:21-32
"	"	Abraham's Seed Father of Lies				8:51-59
"	"	Eternal Light Jesus Leaves				8:33-50
"	Nr. Temple	35th Miracle The Blind Man				9:1-12
"	Temple	Blind Man Interrogated				9:13-34
"	Nr. Temple	Jesus Finds Him Outcast				9:35-41
"	"	Parable of the Messiah the Door				10:1-10
"	"	Parable of The Good Shepherd				10:11-21
Hanukkah	Temple	The Sheep Hear/Works Witness				10:22-38
"	"	They Try to Take Him/Escapes				10:39
AD30 Winter	Aenon Salim	Leaves Jerusalem and Judea		10:1	17:11	10:40

457

Scripture Graph X

Time	Place	Event	Matthew	Mark	Luke	John
AD30 Winter	Aenon Salim	Teaches & Many Believe in Him		10:1		10:41-42
" " [Spring]	" "	Pharisees Divorce and Marriage	19:3-9	10:2-9		
" "	in house	Clarifies to the Disciples	19:10-12	10:10-12		
" "	Aenon Salim	**36th Miracle** The Ten Lepers			17:12-19	
" "	" "	Pharisees & The Coming Kingdom			17:20-21	
" "	" "	Clarifies to the Disciples			17:22-37	
" "	" "	Parable of Persistent Widow &			18:1-8	
" "	" "	The Pharisee & Tax Collector			18:9-14	
" "	" "	Children Brought Leaves	19:13-15	10:13-17	18:15-17	
" "	Nr. Aenon Salim	The Young Lawyer and Riches	19:16-30	10:18-31	18:18-30	
" " Autumn	" "	Parable of Workers in Vineyard	20:1-16			
" " 3rd Day	Aenon Salim	Mary & Martha Send Message				11:1-6
" "	" "	Jesus & Disciples Prepare to Leave				11:7
" "	Nr. Aenon Salim	Leaving Mentions Passion Again	20:17	10:32	18:31	11:8-16
" "	" "	Further on Reiterates Passion	20:17-19	10:32-34	18:31-34	
" "	" "	Requests of Rank & Ministering	20:20-28	10:35-45		
" " 4th Day	Nr. Jericho	**37th Miracle** 1st Blind Man			18:35-43	
" "	Jericho -	**38th Miracle** Blind Bartimeus		**10:46-52**		
" "	Nr. house	Jesus Guest of Zaccheus			19:1	
" "	" "	Parable of the Money			19:2-10	
" " Morning	Nr. Jericho	Leaves Zaccheus' Home	20:29		19:11-27	
" "	" "	**39th Miracle** Two Blind Men	20:30-34		19:28	
" " afternoon	Mt. Olives	Sends Two Disciples	21:1-6	11:1-4	19:29-32	
" "	Nr. Bethany	Martha Meets Jesus & Returns				11:17-28
" "	" "	They all Return Back to Jesus				11:29-33
" "	Graveyard	**40th Miracle** Lazarus Raised				11:34-46
" "	[Bethpage]	Two Disciples Collect Animals	21:7-9	11:4-6	19:32-34	
" "	Mt. Olives	**Jesus Rides Into Jerusalem**		11:7-10	19:35-40	
" "	Jerusalem	Laments Again Over Jerusalem			19:41-44	
" " [Tabernacles]	Temple	Jesus Takes Note of Situation &		11:11		
" " - evening	Jerusalem	Leaves To Return to Bethany	21:10-11	11:11		

458

Scripture Graph XI

Time	Place	Event	Matthew	Mark	Luke	John
AD30 [Next Morning]	Jerusalem	Returns & Curses Fig-Tree	21:18-19	11:12-14		
" " "	Temple	**Final Purging of Temple**	21:12-13	11:15-18	19:45-46	
" " - afternoon	"	Heals Children Praise Him	21:14-16			
" " Evening	"	Lodges Again in Bethany	21:17	11:19		
" " morning	Jerusalem	**41st Miracle Fig-Tree Dead**	21:18-20	11:20-21		
" " "	"	Faith & Forgiveness Again	21:21-22	11:22-26		
" " "	Temple	Teaches Daily Plotting Again			19:47-48	11:47-53
" " [Tabernacles]	Ephraim	Jesus Escapes With Disciples				11:54
AD31 Nr. Passover	Temple	People Expect Jesus				11:55-57
" " 8th Nissan	Bethany in	The Anointing at Simon's	26:6-7	14:3		12:1-3
" " "	house	Some Disciples Murmur	26:8-9	14:4-5		
" " "	"	Judas Mentions the Cost				12:4-6
" " "	"	Jesus Reproves Him	26:10-13	14:6-9		12:7-8
" " "	"	People Know Jesus Returned				12:9-11
" " "	"	Judas Leaves to Betray	26:14-16	14:10-11		
" " 9th Nissan	Jerusalem	**The Final Ride Into Jerusalem**				12:12-18
" " "	Temple	'World Is Gone After Him'				12:19-22
" " "	"	Glorifying Voice From Heaven				12:23-30
" " "	"	Jesus' Death The Light				12:31-36
" " "	"	Jesus Hides Two Prophecies				12:36-43
" " 10th Nissan	"	The Lamb Presents Himself	21:23	11:27	20:1	12:44-50
" " "		They Question His Authority	21:23-27	11:28-33	20:2-8	
" " "		Parable of the Two Sons the	21:28-32	12:1		
" " "		Wicked Tenant Farmers and	21:33-41	12:1-9	20:9-16	
" " "		the Stone the Builders Rejected	21:41-46	12:10-12	20:17-18	
" " "		Parable of the Royal Wedding	22:1-14	12:12	20:19	
" " "		Try and Trap Him By Questions	22:15-16	12:13	20:20	
" " "		Tribute to Caesar	22:17-22	12:14-17	20:21-26	
" " "		Sadducees on the Resurrection	21:23-33	12:18-27	20:27-40	
" " "		Sadducees and Pharisees Friends	22:34			

Scripture Graph XII

Time	Place	Event	Matthew	Mark	Luke	John
AD31 10th Nissan	Temple	Lawyer & the Law	22:35-40	12:28-34		
" " " " "	"	Jesus Asks About Messiah	22:41-45	12:35-37	20:41-44	
" " " " "	"	They No Longer Question	22:46			
" " " " "	"	The Last Admonition	23:1	12:38	20:45	
" " " " "	"	Scribes & Pharisees an Act	23:2-5			
" " " " "	"	Clothes Greetings Seats	23:6-7	12:38-39	20:46	
" " " " "	"	Rooms Attitude To Rank &	23:6-12	12:39		
" " " " "	"	Kingdom Widow's Houses	23:13-14	12:40	20:47	
" " " " "	"	Proselytizing What is Greater	23:15-22			
" " " " "	"	Counting & Equity Clean Mind	23:23-26			
" " " " "	"	Dead Minds Resurrected Mind	23:27-39			
" " " " "	Treasury	The Widow's Last Money		12:41-44	21:1-4	
" " " " "	Mt. Olives	They Leave Temple's Fate	24:1-2	13:1-2	21:5-6	
" " " " "	"	The Signs Many Deceived	24:3-5	13:3-6	21:7-8	
" " " " "	"	Wars Earthquakes Famines	24:6-7	13:7-8	21:9-11	
" " " " "	"	Pestilences before Hostility	24:8	13:9	21:12-13	
" " " " "	"	Gospel Precedes Signs		13:10		
" " " " "	"	Think What Not To Say		13:11	21:14-15	
" " " " "	"	Betrayed By Family – to Death	24:9-12	13:12	21:16-17	
" " " " "	"	Overcoming is Gospel's Purpose	24:13-14	13:13	21:18-19	
" " " " "	"	Abomination of Desolation	24:15-22	13:14-20	21:20-24	
" " " " "	"	False Messiahs How He Comes	24:23-28	13:21-23	21:25-26	
" " " " "	"	Signs Above and Below	24:29	13:24-25		
" " " " "	"	The Last Sign	24:30-31	13:26-27	21:27-28	
" " " " "	"	Parable of the Fig Tree	24:32-36	13:28-33	21:29-33	
" " " " "	"	Parable of the Household Watching		13:34-37		
" " " " "	"	Luke's Last Words of Prophecy			21:34-36	
" " " " "	"	Of Noah, Taken or Left Again	24:37-42			
" " " " "	"	Parable of the Thief	24:43-44			
" " " " "	"	Parable of the Watchful Servant	24:45-51			
" " " " "	"	Parable of the Ten Virgins	25:1-13			

Scripture Graph XIII

Time	Place	Event	Matthew	Mark	Luke	John
AD31 10th Nissan	Mt. Olives	Parable of the Talents	25:14-30			
" "	" "	Parable of the Sheep and Goats	25:31-46			
" 11th Evening	" "	After Two Days the Passover	26:1-2	14:1	21:37	13:1
" - morning	Temple	People Return to Hear Him			21:38	
" "	"	The Ratification of Betrayal	26:3-5	14:1-2	22:1-6	
" 13th Nissan	Bethany	Disciples Ask About Passover	26::17-18	14:12-15	22:7-12	
" "	Jerusalem	They Make Ready the Passover	26:19	14:16	22:13	
" 14th Nissan	upper room	Jesus Prophesies Last Supper	26:20	14:17	22:14-16	13:2-3
" "	" "	and Washes Disciples Feet				13:4-19
" "	" "	1st Toast and 2nd Prophecy			22:17-18	
" "	" "	Speculation as to Betrayer	26:21-25	14:18-21		13:20-22
" "	" "	The Bread of Life	26:26	14:22	22:19	[1 Cor. 11:24]
" "	" "	2nd Toast - the Drink of Life	26:27-28	14:23-24	22:20	[1 Cor. 11:25]
" "	" "	3rd Prophecy 2nd Speculation	26:29	14:25	22:21-23	
" "	" "	Jesus Indicates to the Two				13:23-26
" "	" "	Judas Leaves Jesus Glorified				13:27-32
" "	" "	Attitude on Elevation			22:24-30	13:33-35
" "	" "	They Leave Upper Room	26:30	14:26		13:36-37
" "	Mt. Olives	On Being Offended	26:31-33	14:27-29		13:38
" "	" "	Peter's Denial Foretold	26:34-35	14:30-31	22:31-34	
" "	" "	The Buying of Swords			22:35-38	
" "	" "	The Way/The Truth/The Life				14:1-6
" "	" "	Seeing the Father/The Works				14:7-12
" "	" "	Asking The Holy Spirit				14:13-20
" "	" "	Commandments/Manifestation				14:21-31
" "	Nr. Gethsemane	They Facilitate Another Spot			22:39	14:31
" "	" "	The Vine and The Branches				15:1-11
" "	" "	No Greater Love Friends				15:12-15
" "	" "	Love Should Remain/Hostility				15:16-25
" "	" "	The Spirit's Work Testifies				15:26-27

461

Scripture Graph XIV

Time		Place	Event	Matthew	Mark	Luke	John
AD31 14th Nissan		Nr. Gethsemane	Executions/Comforter/Guide				16:1-15
"	"	"	Seeing By The Spirit Joy				16:16-25
"	"	"	Asking Belief Peace				16:26-33
"	"	"	Last Prayer Before Gethsemane				17:1-26
"	"	Gethsemane	Arrival at Garden	26:36	14:32	22:40	18:1
"	"	"	Peter, James, & John to Watch	26:37-38	14:33-34		
"	"	"	Judas knows the Place				18:2
"	10 p.m.	"	1st Prayer	26:39	14:35-36	22:41-42	
"	"	"	Angel Strengthens Jesus			22:43-44	
"	"	"	Peter, James, & John Asleep	26:40-41	14:37-38	22:45-46	
"	11 p.m.	"	2nd Prayer Asleep Again	26:42-43	14:39-40		
"	midnight	"	3rd Prayer Asleep Again	26:44-45	14:41		
"	"	"	The Arresting Party Arrive	26:46-48	14:42-44	22:47	18:3
"	"	"	Jesus Meets Questions Them				18:4-9
"	"	"	Judas Betrays With a Kiss	26:49-50	14:45-46	22:48-49	
"	"	"	**42nd Miracle** Malchus' Ear	26:51-54	14:47	**22:50-51**	18:10-11
"	"	"	Questions Mob Disciples Flee	26:55-56	14:48-50	22:52-53	
"	"	"	Young Man Nearly Caught		14:51-52		
"	"	Jerusalem	Jesus Taken to Annas First				18:12-14
"	"	Caiaphas'	Annas Sends Jesus Away Bound	26:57	14:53	22:54	18:24
"	"	"	Peter & John Follow	26:58	14:54	22:54-55	18:15-16
"	"	"	Finding Agreeing Witnesses	26:59-61	14:55-59		
"	"	"	Jesus Silent	26:62-63	14:60-61		
"	"	"	They Condemn Him to Death	26:64-66	14:62-64		
"	"	"	1st Cruel Mocking	26:67-68	14:65		
"	"	Palace Hall	Peter's 1st Denial & 1st Crow	26:69-71	14:66-68	22:56-57	18:17-18
"	"	Caiaphas'	2nd Interrogation				18:19-24
"	5 a.m.	Palace Hall	Peter's 2nd Denial	26:71-72	14:69-70	22:58	18:25
"	"	"	Peter's 3rd Denial & 2nd Crow	26:73-75	14:70-72	22:59-62	18:26-27
"	"	"	2nd Cruel Mocking			22:63-65	

Scripture Graph XV

Time	Place	Event	Matthew	Mark	Luke / Acts	John
AD31 Morning	Sanhedrin	Jesus Now Led to their Court	27:1	15:1	22:66-71	
"	Jerusalem	Judas Commits Suicide	27:3-10		Acts 1:18-20	
"	Praetorium	Jesus Led to Pilate	27:2	15:1	23:1	18:28
"	"	Pilate Comes Out to Them				18:29
"	"	1st Examination by Pilate			23:2	18:30
"	"	1st Time Pilate Wants Release			23:3-6	18:31-32
"	Herod's	Jesus Silent and is Mocked			23:7-11	
"	Praetorium	Herod Sends Him Back			23:11-12	
"	"	2nd Examination by Pilate	27:11	15:2	23:13	18:33-37
"	"	2nd Time Pilate Wants Release			23:14-17	18:38
"	"	Jesus Silent	27:12-14	15:3-5		
"	"	Cry For Release of Prisoner	27:15-16	15:6-8		
"	"	Cry For Barabbas	27:17-18	15:9-10	23:18-19	18:39-40
"	"	Cry For Barabbas Again	27:19-21	15:11	23:20	
"	"	1st Shout for Crucifixion	27:22	15:12-13	23:21	
"	"	3rd Time Pilate Wants Release	27:23	15:14	23:22	
"	"	2nd Shout for Crucifixion	27:23-25	15:14	23:23	
"	"	Pilate's Sentence - Barabbas	27:26	15:15	23:24-25	19:1
"	Common Hall	Scourging and Cruel Mocking	27:26-30	15:15-19		19:2-3
"	Praetorium	4th Time Pilate Seeks Release				19:4-5
"	"	3rd Shout for Crucifixion				19:6
"	"	Pilate Increasingly Afraid				19:7-8
"	"	Jesus Silent Once More				19:9-10
"	"	5th Time Pilate Wants Release				19:11-12
"	"	4th Shout For Crucifixion Jesus				19:13-15
"	"	Led Out for Crucifixion	27:31	15:20		19:16
"	Jerusalem	Simon of Cyrene Bears Cross	27:32	15:21	23:26	19:17
"		Talks To Company/Two Others			23:27-32	
"	Golgotha	They Arrive He/Refuses Drink	27:33-34	15:22-23	23:33	19:18
9 a.m.	"	Crucified With the Two	27:35	15:24-25	23:33	19:18

463

Scripture Graph XVI

Time	Place	Event	Matthew	Mark	Luke	John
AD31 9 a.m	Golgotha	Chief Priest Irate at Title				19:19-22
"	"	Jesus Forgives/Gamble Attire	27:35	15:24	23:34	19:23-24
"	"	Sitting Down They Watched	27:36			
"	"	The Accusation & Two Thieves	27:37-38	15:26-28	23:35	
"	"	People, Rulers, Soldiers Mock			23:35-38	
"	"	Passers & Chief Priests Mock	27:39-41	15:29-31		
"	"	Elders & Thieves Mock	27:41-44	15:32		
"	"	Rebuke of Thief & Prays Jesus			23:39-43	
"	"	The Women & John Near Cross				19:25-26
12 dark	"	John Looks After Mary				19:26-27
3 p.m.	"	Jesus Calls out to God	27:45-47	15:33-35	23:44	
"	"	Says, 'I Thirst'				19:28
"	"	Soldier Gives Him Drink They	27:48	15:36		19:29
"	"	Watch to See Elijah Come	27:49			
"	"	Veil in Temple Ripped			23:45	
"	"	Jesus Says, 'It's Finished'				19:30
"	"	Calls Out Again & Bows Head	27:50	15:37	23:46	19:30
"	"	Veil In Two Resurrection	27:51-53	15:38		
"	"	Centurion & Group Glorify God	27:54	15:39	23:47	
"	"	Crowds Start Returning Move			23:48	
"	"	The Breaking of the Legs				19:31-33
"	"	Two Scriptures Fulfilled				19:34-37
"	"	Those That Followed Witnessed	27:55-56	15:40-41	23:49	
"	Praetorium	Joseph Begs Pilate for Body	27:57-58	15:42-45	23:50-52	19:38
"	Golgotha	They Embalm & Entomb Body	27:59-60	15:46	23:53	19:38-42
"	"	The Women Witness Entombing	27:61	15:47	23:54-56	
15th Sabbath	Praetorium	Pilate Permits Guard on Tomb	27:62-66			
17th Sabbath	Golgotha	Mary & Salome Come to Tomb	28:1	16:1	24:1	20:1
18th Sunday	"	They Return With Others		16:2		

464

Scripture Graph XVII

Time	Place	Event	Matthew	Mark	Luke	John
AD31 18th Sunday	Golgotha	Wonder About Guard		16:3		
"	"	See Great Stone Moved		16:4	24:2	
"	"	Matthew Explains the Reasons	28:2-4			
"	"	The Body is Missing		16:5	24:3	
"	"	Mary Runs to Peter & John				20:2
"	"	The Others See Two Angels	28:5	16:5-6	24:4	
"	"	They Continued to be Afraid			24:5	
"	"	Angels Announce Good News	28:6-7	16:6-7	24:6-8	
"	"	They Run to Tell 11 and Rest	28:8	16:8	24:9	
"	"	Peter & John Arrive at Tomb			24:12	20:3-5
"	"	Peter Goes Into Tomb First			24:12	20:6-9
"	"	Peter & John Leave			24:12	20:10
"	"	Mary Weeps & Sees the Angels				20:11-13
"	"	1st Appearance - to Mary		16:9		20:14-15
"	"	Reveals Himself to Mary				20:16
"	Heaven	Presents Himself To Father				20:17
"	Jerusalem	Mary Tells/They Don't Believe		16:10-11		20:18
"	"	The Other Women also Tell			24:9-10	
"	"	They Still Don't Believe			24:11	
"	"	2nd Appearance - to Peter			24:34 [1 Cor. 15:5]	
" Afternoon	"	3rd Appearance - to Women	28:9-10		24:9	
"	"	Guards Tell the Priests	28:11-15			
"	To Emmaus	Cleopas & Wife Reminisce		16:12	24:13-14	
"	Nr. Emmaus	4th Appearance Cleopas & Wife		16:12	24:15-27	
"	Emmaus	Jesus Eats With Them			24:28-32	
"	Upper Room	Cleopas & Wife Return		16:13	24:33-35	
" Evening	"	5th Appearance to the 10			24:36-49	20:19-23
"	"	They Tell Thomas				20:24-25

Scripture Graph XVIII

Time	Place	Event	Matthew	Mark	Luke	John
AD31 Sunday	Jerusalem	**6th Appearance** to the 12		16:14	[1 Cor. 15:5]	20:26
"	"	Asks Thomas to Handle Him				20:27-28
"	"	Thomas Believes				20:29
"	"	John Reveals Why he Wrote				20:30-31
"		Commission of all Disciples		16:15-18		
"	Galilee	Disciples Return to Galilee	28:16			
"	Bethsaida	**7th Appearance** to the 7				21:15-19
"	"	Peter Commissioned to Feed				21:1-14
"		Peter Asks about John's Role				21:20-23
"	Mt. Bethsaida	Great Commission of the 500	28:16-20		[1 Cor. 15:6]	
"		Seen of Jesus [1 Cor. 15:7]				
"		Luke Testifies to the Events			Acts 1:1-3; 13:31	
25th Iyar	Jerusalem	They Must Wait for Pentecost			Acts 1:4-5	
"	"	Last Meeting With Jesus	28:18		Acts 1:6 [1 Cor. 15:7]	
"	"	Not Sure When Kingdom			Acts 1:6	
"		Reiterates Commission	28:19-20		Acts 1:7-8	
"	Mt. Olives	He Leads Them To Mount			24:50	
"	"	**The Ascension**		16:19	24:51; Acts 1:9	
"	"	The Promise of the Angels			Acts 1:10-11	
"		They Return to Jerusalem			24:52-53; Acts 1:12	
Pentecost	Jerusalem	The Commission Proceeds		16:20		
"	"	John Concludes the Canon				21:24-25

BIBLIOGRAPHY

Books considered but not necessarily agreed with, or directly quoted from. The ones quoted from, are mentioned in the main text.

Adam Clarke Commentary - (Vol. 5), New York Ed.

Aid to Bible Understanding - International Bible Students Association Brooklyn, 1971.

Analytical Concordance to the Bible - Young, Lutterworth, 1966.

Annales Veteris et Novi Testamenti - Ussher, 1650-54.

Antiquities of the Jews - Josephus, 93.

Banisters Survey of the Holy Land - Binns & Goodwin.

Easter Enigma - Wenham, Paternoster, 1992.

Exegetical Fallacies - Carson, Paternoster, 1996.

Good News Study Bible- Harper Collins, 1997.

Introduction to Judaism - Fishman, Jewish Chronicle Publications, 1978.

Matthew Henry Commentary - Marshall Pickering 1960.

New International Bible Commentaries - Matthew - Mounce, Mark - Hurtado, Luke - Evans, John - Michaels. Paternoster, 1995. *New Revised Standard Version* - Oxford, 1995.

New Testament - Arendzen, Sheed & Ward, 1947.

New World Translation of the Holy Scriptures - International Bible Students Association, Brooklyn, 1970. *Number in Scripture* - Bullinger, Kregel, 1992.

Pentateuch & Haftorahs - Hertz, Sonico. 1980. *Philip's New Scripture Atlas Redating Matthew, Mark & Luke* - Wenham, Hodder & Stoughton, 1991.

Solar and Lunar Eclipses of the Ancient Near East - Kudlek & Michler.

SwordSearcher – Version 4. Brandon Staggs, 1996-2001, bstaggs@ swordsearcher.com

The Bible Reader's Encyclopedia and Concordance - Collins.

The Contemporary Parallel New Testament (KJV, NCV, NIV, NKJV, NASB, CEV, NTL, The Message) - Oxford 1997.

The Emphatic Diaglott - containing the Original Greek Text of the Vatican Manuscript, No. 1209, Griesbach, International Bible Students Association Brooklyn, 1942.

The Four Faces of God - Bickersteth & Pain, Kingsway, 1993.

The Holy Bible (RSV) - Collins, 1952.

The Kingdom Interlinear Translation of the Greek Scriptures - based on the Text of Westcott & Hort, 1881. International Bible Students Association Brooklyn, 1969.

The Life of Christ - Farrar, Cassell & Company.

The Lion Handbook to the Bible - 1983.

The Moffatt Translation of the Bible - Hodder and Stoughton, 1972.

The New English Bible - Oxford & Cambridge. 1970.

The New Lion Encyclopedia of the Bible - 1984.

The New Shorter Oxford English Dictionary - 1993.

The New Testament - Lattimore, Dent, 1998.

The Oxford Companion to the Bible, 1993.

The Revised English Bible - Oxford, 1997.

The Revised Standard Bible - Collins, 1952.

The Tanakh - The Jewish Publication Society, 1992.

The Times Concise Atlas of the Bible, 1991.

The Truth Behind the Bible Code - Satinover, Sidgwick, & Jackson, 1997.